# THE ROUTLEDGE HAND_ _ PHILOSOPHY OF IMAGINATION

Imagination occupies a central place in philosophy, going back to Aristotle. However, following a period of relative neglect there has been an explosion of interest in imagination in the past two decades as philosophers examine the role of imagination in debates about the mind, cognition, ethics, and aesthetics, as well as epistemology, science, and mathematics.

This outstanding *Handbook* contains over thirty specially commissioned chapters by leading philosophers organized into six clear sections examining the most important aspects of the philosophy of imagination, including:

- Imagination in historical context: Aristotle, Descartes, Hume, Kant, Husserl, and Sartre
- What is imagination? The relation between imagination and mental imagery; imagination contrasted with perception, memory, and dreaming
- Imagination in aesthetics: imagination and our engagement with music, art, and fiction; and the problems of fictional emotions
- Imagination in philosophy of mind and cognitive science: "imaginative resistance," imagination and creativity, the self, action, child development, and animal cognition
- Imagination in ethics and political philosophy, including the concept of "moral imagination" and empathy
- Imagination in epistemology and philosophy of science, including learning, thought experiments, scientific modeling, and mathematics.

*The Routledge Handbook of Philosophy of Imagination* is essential reading for students and researchers in philosophy of mind and psychology, aesthetics, and ethics. It will also be a valuable resource for those in related disciplines such as psychology and art.

**Amy Kind** is Professor of Philosophy at Claremont McKenna College, USA. She is editor of *Philosophy of Mind in the Twentieth and Twenty-First Centuries*, volume 6 of *The History of the Philosophy of Mind* (Routledge, forthcoming), and with Peter Kung she is editor of the forthcoming collection *Knowledge Through Imagination*.

# ROUTLEDGE HANDBOOKS IN PHILOSOPHY

*Routledge Handbooks in Philosophy* are state-of-the-art surveys of emerging, newly refreshed, and important fields in philosophy, providing accessible yet thorough assessments of key problems, themes, thinkers, and recent developments in research.

All chapters for each volume are specially commissioned, and written by leading scholars in the field. Carefully edited and organized, *Routledge Handbooks in Philosophy* provide indispensable reference tools for students and researchers seeking a comprehensive overview of new and exciting topics in philosophy. They are also valuable teaching resources as accompaniments to textbooks, anthologies, and research-orientated publications.

Available:

THE ROUTLEDGE HANDBOOK OF EMBODIED COGNITION
*Edited by Lawrence Shapiro*

THE ROUTLEDGE HANDBOOK OF NEOPLATONISM
*Edited by Pauliina Remes and Svetla Slaveva-Griffin*

THE ROUTLEDGE HANDBOOK OF CONTEMPORARY PHILOSOPHY OF RELIGION
*Edited by Graham Oppy*

THE ROUTLEDGE HANDBOOK OF PHILOSOPHY OF WELL-BEING
*Edited by Guy Fletcher*

Forthcoming:

THE ROUTLEDGE HANDBOOK OF THE STOIC TRADITION
*Edited by John Sellars*

THE ROUTLEDGE HANDBOOK OF PHILOSOPHY OF COLOUR
*Edited by Derek Brown and Fiona Macpherson*

THE ROUTLEDGE HANDBOOK OF THE PHILOSOPHY OF BIODIVERSITY
*Edited by Justin Garson, Anya Plutynski, and Sahotra Sarkar*

THE ROUTLEDGE HANDBOOK OF PHILOSOPHY OF THE SOCIAL MIND
*Edited by Julian Kiverstein*

THE ROUTLEDGE HANDBOOK OF COLLECTIVE INTENTIONALITY
*Edited by Marija Jankovic and Kirk Ludwig*

THE ROUTLEDGE HANDBOOK OF BRENTANO AND THE BRENTANO SCHOOL
*Edited by Uriah Kriegel*

THE ROUTLEDGE HANDBOOK OF EPISTEMIC CONTEXTUALISM
*Edited by Jonathan Jenkins Ichikawa*

THE ROUTLEDGE HANDBOOK OF EVOLUTION AND PHILOSOPHY
*Edited by Richard Joyce*

THE ROUTLEDGE HANDBOOK OF MODALITY
*Edited by Otávio Bueno and Scott Shalkowski*

THE ROUTLEDGE HANDBOOK OF THE PHILOSOPHY OF ECONOMICS
*Edited by Julian Reiss and Conrad Heilmann*

THE ROUTLEDGE HANDBOOK OF LIBERTARIANISM
*Edited by Jason Brennan, Bas van der Vossen, and David Schmidtz*

THE ROUTLEDGE HANDBOOK OF METAETHICS
*Edited by Tristram McPherson and David Plunkett*

THE ROUTLEDGE HANDBOOK OF PHILOSOPHY OF INFORMATION
*Edited by Luciano Floridi*

THE ROUTLEDGE HANDBOOK OF PHILOSOPHY OF PAIN
*Edited by Jennifer Corns*

THE ROUTLEDGE HANDBOOK OF PHILOSOPHY OF EMPATHY
*Edited by Heidi Maibom*

THE ROUTLEDGE HANDBOOK OF PHILOSOPHY OF ANIMAL MINDS
*Edited by Kristin Andrews and Jacob Beck*

THE ROUTLEDGE HANDBOOK OF EPISTEMIC INJUSTICE
*Edited by Ian James Kidd, José Medina, and Gaile Pohlhaus*

THE ROUTLEDGE HANDBOOK OF PHILOSOPHY OF MECHANISMS
*Edited by Stuart Glennan and Phyllis Illari*

THE ROUTLEDGE HANDBOOK OF MORAL EPISTEMOLOGY
*Edited by Karen Jones, Mark Timmons, and Aaron Zimmerman*

THE ROUTLEDGE HANDBOOK OF PANPSYCHISM
*Edited by William Seager*

THE ROUTLEDGE HANDBOOK OF PHILOSOPHY OF TEMPORAL EXPERIENCE
*Edited by Ian Philips*

THE ROUTLEDGE HANDBOOK OF SCIENTIFIC REALISM
*Edited by Juha Saatsi*

THE ROUTLEDGE HANDBOOK OF PHILOSOPHY OF MEMORY
*Edited by Sven Bernecker and Kourken Michaelian*

THE ROUTLEDGE HANDBOOK OF PHILOSOPHY AND SCIENCE OF ADDICTION
*Edited by Hanna Pickard and Serge Ahmed*

THE ROUTLEDGE HANDBOOK OF PHILOSOPHY OF EMERGENCE
*Edited by Robin Hendry, Sophie Gibb, and Tom Lancaster*

THE ROUTLEDGE HANDBOOK OF PHILOSOPHY OF EUROPE
*Edited by Darian Meacham and Nicolas de Warren*

THE ROUTLEDGE HANDBOOK OF THE PHILOSOPHY OF CHILDHOOD AND CHILDREN
*Edited by Jurgen De Wispelaere, Gideon Calder, and Anca Gheaus*

THE ROUTLEDGE HANDBOOK OF APPLIED EPISTEMOLOGY
*Edited by James Chase and David Coady*

THE ROUTLEDGE HANDBOOK OF THE PHILOSOPHY OF EVIL
*Edited by Thomas Nys and Stephen de Wijze*

THE ROUTLEDGE HANDBOOK OF THE PHILOSOPHY OF THE CITY
*Edited by Sharon Meagher*

THE ROUTLEDGE HANDBOOK OF THE PHILOSOPHY OF DISCRIMINATION AND EQUALITY
*Edited by Kasper Lippert-Rasmussen*

THE ROUTLEDGE HANDBOOK OF THE PHILOSOPHY OF EVIDENCE
*Edited by Trent Dougherty and Maria Lasonen-Aarnio*

THE ROUTLEDGE HANDBOOK OF THE PHILOSOPHY OF PUBLIC HEALTH
*Edited by Alex Broadbent and Sridhar Venkatapuram*

THE ROUTLEDGE HANDBOOK OF THE PHILOSOPHY OF PATERNALISM
*Edited by Kalle Grill and Jason Hanna*

THE ROUTLEDGE HANDBOOK OF END-OF-LIFE ETHICS
*Edited by John Davis*

THE ROUTLEDGE HANDBOOK OF NEUROETHICS
*Edited by Syd Johnson and Karen S. Rommelfanger*

THE ROUTLEDGE HANDBOOK OF SOCIAL EPISTEMOLOGY
*Edited by Miranda Fricker, Peter J. Graham, David Henderson, Nikolaj Pedersen, and Jeremy Wyatt*

THE ROUTLEDGE HANDBOOK OF VIRTUE EPISTEMOLOGY
*Edited by Heather D. Battaly*

# THE ROUTLEDGE HANDBOOK OF PHILOSOPHY OF IMAGINATION

*Edited by Amy Kind*

Routledge
Taylor & Francis Group
LONDON AND NEW YORK

First published 2016 by Routledge

2 Park Square, Milton Park, Abingdon, Oxfordshire OX14 4RN
711 Third Avenue, New York, NY 10017

*Routledge is an imprint of the Taylor & Francis Group, an informa business*

First issued in paperback 2017



*British Library Cataloguing in Publication Data*
A catalogue record for this book is available from the British Library

*Library of Congress Cataloging in Publication Data*
The Routledge handbook of philosophy of imagination / edited by Amy Kind. -- 1 [edition].
pages cm. -- (Routledge handbooks in philosophy)
Includes bibliographical references and index.
ISBN 978-0-415-73948-1 (hardback : alk. paper) -- ISBN 978-1-315-65790-5 (e-book)
1. Imagination (Philosophy) I. Kind, Amy, editor.
B105.I49R68 2016
128'.3--dc23
2015024465

ISBN: 978-0-415-73948-1 (hbk)
ISBN: 978-1-138-57407-6 (pbk)

Typeset in Bembo
by Taylor & Francis Books

# CONTENTS

# ILLUSTRATIONS

## Figures

# CONTRIBUTORS

**Andrew Arana** is a logician and philosopher of mathematics. He is maître de conférences (associate professor) of philosophy at the University of Paris 1 Panthéon-Sorbonne, and a member of the Institute for History and Philosophy of Science and Technology (IHPST). He has previously been on the philosophy faculty at Stanford University, Kansas State University, and the University of Illinois at Urbana-Champaign.

**Ruth M.J. Byrne** is Professor of Cognitive Science in the School of Psychology and the Institute of Neuroscience at Trinity College Dublin, University of Dublin, Ireland. Her research expertise is in the cognitive science of human thinking, including experimental and computational investigations of reasoning and imaginative thought. Her books include *The Rational Imagination: How People Create Alternatives to Reality* (2005, MIT press), and *Deduction*, co-authored with Phil Johnson-Laird (1991, Erlbaum).

**Peter Carruthers** is Professor of Philosophy at the University of Maryland. His most recent books are *The Opacity of Mind: An Integrative Theory of Self-Knowledge* (Oxford, 2011) and *The Centered Mind: What the Science of Working Memory Shows Us about the Nature of Human Thought* (Oxford, 2015).

**Greg Currie** teaches philosophy at the University of York, UK, where he is currently Head of Department. He is a Fellow of the Australian Academy of the Humanities and a Past Fellow of St. John's College, Oxford. In 2014 he was Visiting Professor, École des hautes études en sciences sociales, Paris. His most recent book is *Narratives and Narrators* (Oxford, 2010). He is writing a book on getting knowledge (and ignorance) from fiction.

**Dorothea Debus** teaches Philosophy at the University of York, UK. Her main research interests lie in the philosophy of mind and moral psychology, and her published work considers philosophical questions relating to memory, imagination, attention, and the emotions.

**Fabian Dorsch** is SNSF (Swiss National Science Foundation) Research Professor at the University of Fribourg, Switzerland. His research addresses various issues in the philosophy of mind, epistemology, metaethics, metaphysics, and aesthetics. In addition to many articles on the imagination, he has published a monograph on the topic with De Gruyter, while another one is forthcoming with Routledge.

**Natalie M. Fletcher** is a philosophical practitioner and research consultant from Montreal, Canada, where she teaches in the philosophy department at John Abbott College and works on large-scale government initiatives, including projects with the United Nations. She is the founding director of Brila Youth Projects, a registered educational charity that fosters critical thinking and imagination in young people through philosophical dialogue and digital magazine production.

**Stacie Friend** lectures in philosophy at Birkbeck College, University of London, and is Vice-president of the British Society of Aesthetics. She received her PhD from Stanford University and has held Fellowships from the Mellon Foundation and the British Academy/ Leverhulme Trust. Her research focuses on aesthetics, language, and mind, especially our engagement with fiction.

**Dominic Gregory** works in the Department of Philosophy at the University of Sheffield, UK. He has published papers on aesthetics, formal and philosophical logic, metaphysics, modal epistemology, and the philosophy of mind; he also published a book (*Showing, Sensing, and Seeming: Distinctively Sensory Representations and Their Contents*) with Oxford University Press in 2013.

**Robert Hopkins** is in the Philosophy Department at New York University. He works on various issues at the intersection of philosophy of mind and aesthetics, including perception, memory, imagination, and our experience of distinctively visual representations, such as pictures and sculpture.

**Jonathan Jenkins Ichikawa** is an Associate Professor of Philosophy at the University of British Columbia, Canada. He has published in epistemology, philosophical methodology, and philosophy of mind. He is the co-author (with Benjamin Jarvis) of *The Rules of Thought* (Oxford University Press) and editor of the forthcoming *Routledge Handbook of Epistemic Contextualism*.

**Julia Jansen** is Professor of Philosophy at the Husserl Archive, Institute of Philosophy at KU Leuven. She specializes in Husserl and Kant, and has published extensively in both fields, especially on questions concerning the imagination. She is also co-editor of two books on related issues in aesthetics: *Critical Communities and Aesthetic Practices* (Springer, 2011) and *Rediscovering Aesthetics* (Stanford University Press, 2009).

**Mark Johnson** is the Philip H. Knight Professor of Liberal Arts and Sciences in the Department of Philosophy at the University of Oregon. His research has focused on the philosophical implications of the role of human embodiment in meaning, conceptualization, reasoning, and values. He is co-author, with George Lakoff, of *Metaphors We Live By* (1980) and *Philosophy in the Flesh* (1999) and author of several books including *Moral Imagination: Implications of Cognitive Science for Ethics* (1993) and *Morality for Humans: Ethical Understanding from the Perspective of Cognitive Science* (2014).

**Amy Kind** is Professor of Philosophy at Claremont McKenna College. Her research concerns a variety of topics in philosophy of mind with a particular emphasis on issues concerning imagination and phenomenal consciousness. With Peter Kung she has edited the forthcoming collection *Knowledge through Imagination* (Oxford University Press).

**Peter Kung** is Associate Professor of Philosophy at Pomona. He has held visiting or teaching appointments at New York University, Stanford University, Claremont Graduate University, and the National University of Singapore. His research centers on two areas: the philosophy of mind, in particular thought experiments; and epistemology, where he focuses on the limits of skeptical challenges and the proper treatment of probabilistic reasons.

**Shen-yi Liao** is Assistant Professor of Philosophy at the University of Puget Sound and Marie Curie Fellow at the University of Leeds. His research projects span cognitive science, philosophy of mind, aesthetics, and moral psychology.

**Samantha Matherne** is Assistant Professor of Philosophy at the University of California, Santa Cruz. Her research focuses on issues in perception and aesthetics in Kant and post-Kantian traditions, including phenomenology and Neo-Kantianism. She is currently writing *Cassirer* for the Routledge Philosophers series.

**Aaron Meskin** is Associate Professor of Philosophy at the University of Leeds, UK. He is the author of numerous journal articles and book chapters on aesthetics and other philosophical subjects. His current work primarily focuses on experimental approaches to philosophical aesthetics.

**Robert W. Mitchell** is Foundation Professor in the Department of Psychology at Eastern Kentucky University. He is the coordinator for both the interdisciplinary Animal Studies program (which he founded with the support of other faculty) and the General Psychology Masters program. He has edited and co-edited books examining a range of psychological topics about animals and children, produced a monograph on the history of psychological studies of great apes, and published numerous articles and book chapters on the psychology of animals and on human–animal interaction.

**Kengo Miyazono** is a JSPS (Japan Society for the Promotion of Science) Postdoctoral Research Fellow at Keio University, UK. His primary area of research is philosophy of mind, especially the intersections of philosophy of mind with psychiatry and cognitive science.

**Deborah K.W. Modrak** is Professor of Philosophy at the University of Rochester. She has written numerous articles on Ancient Greek theories of mind and perception and philosophy of language and epistemology. She is the author of *Aristotle: The Power of Perception* (Chicago, 1987) and *Aristotle's Theory of Language and Meaning* (Cambridge, 2001).

**Bence Nanay** is Professor of Philosophy and BOF Research Professor at the University of Antwerp, Belgium, and Senior Research Associate at Peterhouse, Cambridge University. He is the author of *Between Perception and Action* (Oxford University Press, 2013) and *Aesthetics as Philosophy of Perception* (Oxford University Press, 2015) and of more than 90 articles on philosophy of mind, aesthetics, and philosophy of biology.

**Dilip Ninan** is Assistant Professor of Philosophy at Tufts University. His main areas of philosophical interest are the philosophy of language, metaphysics, and the philosophy of mind. His work has appeared in *The Philosophical Review*, *Semantics and Pragmatics*, and *Philosophy and Phenomenological Research*.

**Elizabeth Picciuto** works on issues involving stimulus-independent thought, imagination and supposition, creativity, pretense, fiction, and the emotions. She is an instructor at University of Maryland, Baltimore County.

**Dennis L. Sepper** is Professor in the Department of Philosophy and the Institute of Philosophical Studies at the University of Dallas, Irving, and chair of the Department of Human Sciences in the Contemporary World. He is the author of several books, including *Descartes's Imagination: Proportion, Images, and the Activity of Thinking* (University of California Press, 1996).

**Neil Sinhababu** is Associate Professor of Philosophy at the National University of Singapore. His work on desire and decision-making has appeared in *The Philosophical Review* and *Noûs*. He also has published on Nietzsche, ethics, imagination, and metaphysically interesting romantic relationships. His PhD is from the University of Texas.

**Aaron Smuts** is Assistant Professor of Philosophy at Rhode Island College. His interests range across a wide variety of topics in ethics and the philosophy of art. Currently he is working on two projects. The first is on the nature and value of well-being. The other project concerns the normative assessment of emotions.

**Roy Sorensen** was conceived in a thought experiment on his father's birthday. This made *Thought Experiments* possible thirty-five years later. Indeed, it made six other books actual: *Blindspots, Pseudo-Problems, Vagueness and Contradiction, A Brief History of the Paradox, Seeing Dark Things*, and *A Cabinet of Philosophical Curiosities*. Professor Sorensen teaches at Washington University in St. Louis where he dreams of completing two other books: *A Brief History of Nothing and Lying without Deception*.

**Shannon Spaulding** is Assistant Professor of Philosophy at Oklahoma State University. Her general philosophical interests are in philosophy of mind, philosophical psychology, and philosophy of science. The principal goal of her research is to construct a philosophically and empirically plausible account of social cognition.

**Kathleen Stock** is a Reader in Philosophy at the University of Sussex, UK, and has written a number of articles on imagination, fiction, and the relations between them.

**Dustin Stokes** is an Assistant Professor in the Department of Philosophy at the University of Utah. He works primarily in philosophy of mind and cognitive science, focusing on perception, imagination, creativity, and also on these phenomena as they occur in the context of appreciating and creating art.

**Karsten R. Stueber** is Professor of Philosophy at the College of the Holy Cross. He publishes in the area of philosophy of language, philosophy of mind, and the philosophy of the social sciences. He is the author of *Rediscovering Empathy: Agency, Folk Psychology, and the Human Sciences* (MIT Press 2006, 2nd edition 2010) and *Donald Davidson's Theorie sprachlichen Verstehens* (Anton Hain, 1993). In addition he has co-edited several anthologies, including *Empathy and Agency: The Problem of Understanding in the Human Sciences* (Westview, 2000) and the forthcoming *Moral Sentimentalism* (Cambridge University Press).

**Adam Toon** is a Marie Curie Research Fellow in the Department of Sociology, Philosophy, and Anthropology at the University of Exeter, UK. He is the author of *Models as Make-Believe: Imagination, Fiction and Scientific Representation* (Palgrave Macmillan, 2012).

**Neil Van Leeuwen** currently teaches at Georgia State University, where he holds appointments in the Department of Philosophy and the Neuroscience Institute. He is a Senior Fellow at University of Johannesburg and has held postdoctoral fellowships at Rutgers University and Tufts University. His work on belief, imagination, self-deception, and self-knowledge has appeared in such journals as *Journal of Philosophy*, *Philosophical Studies*, *Philosophical Psychology*, *Philosophical Papers*, *Philosophy Compass*, and *Erkenntnis*.

**Deena Skolnick Weisberg** is a Senior Fellow in the Department of Psychology at the University of Pennsylvania. She received her PhD from Yale University and subsequently trained as a postdoctoral researcher at Rutgers University and at Temple University. Dr. Weisberg's primary research interests are the development of imaginative cognition, the role that the imagination plays in learning, and scientific thinking and reasoning in children and adults.

**Nick Wiltsher** is a postdoctoral fellow at the Federal University of Rio Grande do Sul in Porto Alegre, Brazil. He works on imagination, aesthetics, phenomenology, and philosophy of mind.

**James O. Young** is Professor of Philosophy at the University of Victoria. He is the author of *Global Anti-realism* (1995), *Art and Knowledge* (2001), *Cultural Appropriation and the Arts* (2008), *Critique of Pure Music* (2014), and over 50 articles. He has translated, annotated, and introduced Batteux's *The Fine Arts Reduced to a Single Principle* (2015).

# ACKNOWLEDGMENT

Thanks to the terrific team at Routledge for their vision and guidance throughout the process of shepherding this volume to publication. I appreciate the helpful feedback provided by three anonymous referees who read the original proposal. Many of my colleagues throughout the Claremont Colleges – including Chuck Young, Patricia Easton, and especially Peter Kung – provided crucial help at various stages of this project. I am also grateful to my student research assistant, Jared Goldberg, for his invaluable assistance in compiling the index.

As always, my deepest gratitude is reserved for my husband, Frank Menetrez.

# INTRODUCTION

## Exploring imagination

*Amy Kind*

These early years of the twenty-first century have witnessed a groundswell of philosophical interest in imagination. Much of the philosophical research sits at the intersection of philosophy of mind, aesthetics, and moral psychology, though interest in imagination extends even more broadly from ethics to epistemology, from philosophy of science to philosophy of mathematics. The 34 chapters in this book address a host of issues concerning imagination, ranging from its treatment in the history of philosophy to its invocation in a diverse set of contemporary philosophical contexts. But one question may be left surprisingly unanswered – or at least insufficiently answered – by those discussions, namely, the question of what imagination is. Interestingly, this question has proved remarkably difficult to answer – so much so, in fact, that many authors, including many of the authors in this collection, explicitly refrain from even trying to do so. Rather, they rely instead on our intuitive understanding of the phenomenon under discussion. To give one particularly noteworthy example, when spelling out his influential theory of make-believe, Kendall Walton surveys several dimensions along which imaginings vary from one another and then asks:

> [S]houldn't we now spell out what they have in common? Yes, if we can. But I can't. Fortunately an intuitive understanding of what it is to imagine, sharpened somewhat by the observations of this chapter, is sufficient for us to proceed with our investigation.
>
> *(Walton 1990, 19)*

In light of this practice, one might worry that there is no single conception of imagination in play in philosophical discussions and that philosophers have relied on importantly different conceptions in putting imagination to work in different philosophical contexts. (For a development of this worry, see Kind 2013.) This worry has recently been given colorful expression by Noël Carroll, who notes that imagination has become "the junkyard of the mind" – a place where everything gets thrown in.[1] If that is right, then perhaps it's not surprising after all that the chapters in this collection do not provide a clear and univocal sense of what imagination is.

That said, however, there are some points about which there is widespread agreement, and there are some other basic taxonomic considerations that – even though they are not universally accepted – can be helpful starting points when engaging with philosophical work on imagination. Thus, in the first part of this introduction, I attempt to lay out some points of general consensus as well as tracing some of the fault lines. Then, in the second part of this introduction I discuss some of the uses to which imagination is often put, both in everyday life and in philosophical theorizing. Throughout this introduction, I direct readers to chapters in this volume where they can find more extensive treatment of the issues I mention.

## 1 The nature of imagination

### *Situating imagination*

I begin with four basic claims about imagination that enjoy near universal agreement and that help us to situate imagination within our cognitive architecture. Interestingly, however, even these claims proceed largely by distinguishing imagination from other aspects of our mental life rather than by giving us a positive characterization of it. As we will see, there is considerably more consensus on the issue of what imagination is *not* than there is on the issue of what imagination is.

First, almost everyone agrees that

1 Not every use of the word "imagine" or its cognates in ordinary language corresponds to an exercise of imagination.

Sometimes, for example, the word "imagine" is used simply to pick out instances of mistaken belief. Jackie, who is ignorant of her spouse's extramarital activities, might naturally be described as imagining that her spouse is working late – or if Jackie is less ignorant, her spouse might naturally be described as imagining having pulled one over on Jackie. Of course, there might be times that Jackie vividly pictures her spouse hard at work in the office, papers strewn across the desk and computer screen glowing, while a moonlit sky is visible through the window. We might naturally describe this case using the very same words as before – "Jackie imagines that her spouse is working late" – but unlike in the previous example we would now be picking out an exercise of Jackie's imagination. Context typically enables us to tell the difference between these kinds of cases. Given the widespread (though not universal) agreement about claim (1), there is also widespread (though not universal) agreement that a philosophical theory of imagination need not account for these cases of what we might call "belief gone wrong" (see Currie and Ravenscroft 2002, 9), and more generally, that it need not account for every use of the term "imagine" or its cognates in ordinary language.[2]

Though the examples just considered suggest that we have some intuitive grasp of which sorts of mental activities count as exercises of imagination, we have not yet said anything about what those exercises are. Starting to answer this question brings us to the second point of widespread agreement about imagination:

2 Imagination is a primitive mental state type (or group of types), irreducible to other mental state types.

(I here use "state" in a broad sense so as to include mental events, activities, and processes within the class of mental states.) In particular, imagination is different from both perception (Chapter 9) and belief (Chapter 8) and cannot be reduced to either of them. Situating imagination as distinct from perception plays an important role in many historical treatments of imagination – from Aristotle (Chapter 1) to Husserl (Chapter 5) to Sartre (Chapter 6). Imagination also seems importantly different from memory (Chapter 10). Philosophers of mind and cognitive scientists often attempt to map out the cognitive architecture of the mind using what's referred to as *boxology* – a diagram of boxes and arrows, with each box picking out a discrete cognitive capacity or process and the arrows showing the functional interactions between them.[3] We can cast claim (2) in boxological terms as the claim that imagination deserves its own box.

As we will see, however, although imagination is thought to deserve its own box, there may still be various ways in which it is like both perception and belief. One important similarity arises from the fact that imagination is a representational state. Representational states have what philosophers call *intentionality*, that is, they are *about* or *directed at* some object or state of affairs. My belief that my dog is snoozing on the couch is about my dog; when I turn around and see him sleeping there, my perception is about him too. My dog actually exists, but mental states can also be directed at or about objects that don't. For example, if Ponce de Leon believes that the Fountain of Youth is in Florida, his belief is an intentional mental state even though there is no such thing as the Fountain of Youth. This discussion of intentionality gives us our third claim:

3 Imagination is intentional, i.e., imaginings have intentional content.

Some philosophers think that all mentality has intentional content, and, in fact, that intentionality is constitutive of mental states. But even if this is wrong and some mental states, say itches or tickles, are not intentional, it seems clear that imagining is.

Though imagining resembles perception and belief in being representational, we should here note one important way in which it differs from them. Both perception and belief are constitutively connected to truth. In perceiving something, we are connected with truths about the actual world. Likewise, though we can have false beliefs, in believing something we at least aim to be connected with truth. In contrast, imagination does not have this same inherent connection to truth. As German philosopher Edmund Husserl put it, imagining should be understood as an experience of something in the mode of "nonactuality" or "irreality" (see Chapter 5). We can deliberately imagine what we know to be false; in fact, this often seems to be the very point of imagination. The difference between belief and perception on the one hand and imagination on the other is often put in slogan form: "Perception is to the actual as imagination is to the possible" or "Imagining aims at the fictional as belief aims at the true."[4] Seventeenth-century Scottish philosopher David Hume captured this general point by noting that "nothing is more free" than human imagination (Hume 1777/1975, 47; see also Chapter 3). We thus have our fourth claim:

4 Imagination is not constitutively constrained by truth.

Given claim (4), imagination is often classified as a *speculative* mental state. As such, imagining is grouped with other speculative mental states such as supposing and conceiving. But now, having laid out these four points of agreement about imagination, we hit our first significant fault line in theorizing about imagination. Philosophers have staked out vastly different positions on how exactly these three speculative mental states relate to one another. Some philosophers take there to be no difference between imagining and conceiving (e.g., Hume 1777/1975). Other philosophers take imagining to be a subclass of conceiving; in particular, they treat imagining as an imagistic form of conceiving (e.g., Chalmers 2002). And yet other philosophers take there to be a sharp distinction between imagining and conceiving (e.g., Balcerak Jackson forthcoming; Peacocke 1985). Oftentimes, the matter seems to hinge on the role that these mental activities play in justifying modal beliefs (see Chapter 32). There is similar disagreement about the relationship between imagining and supposing. Many philosophers take there to be a sharp distinction between imagining and supposing. They argue, for example, that imagining and supposing have very different affective consequences (Gendler 2000; Weinberg and Meskin 2006, 195) and different connections to action (Chapter 21). But other philosophers take supposing to be a subclass of imaginings; typically, such philosophers take supposings to be belief-like imaginings (Currie and Ravenscroft 2002; Ichikawa and Jarvis 2012; see also Arcangeli [2014] who argues that supposition is a type of imagination, but who treats it as *sui generis*, importantly unlike belief).

In many ways, this disagreement about the relationship between imagination and other speculative mental states signals a deep fault line concerning philosophers' views of the nature of imagination. How imagining relates to supposing and conceiving depends crucially on what imagination is. Historically, philosophers have given very different accounts of the imagination (six of which are addressed in Part I), and these differences have carried over to contemporary discussions of imagination (addressed in Part II).[5] Disagreement about the nature of imagination can perhaps most usefully be understood in the context of a taxonomy of imaginative states. It's to this I now turn.

## *Carving up imagination*

In developing a taxonomy of imagination, it will be useful to have some examples of imaginings before us. Consider Max and Sammy, who are playing a game of make-believe. "Let's imagine that a scary monster is chasing us," Max might say. "What does it look like?" Sammy asks. Max scrunches up his face, picturing the monster, before answering: "It's 20 feet tall, green with orange spots; it has huge claws, spikes on its tail, and big crooked teeth." Sammy shudders as he imagines seeing such a monster. "I'd be really scared if I ever ran into that monster in real life," he tells his brother. "Let's hide behind that mountain," he adds, pointing to the living room sofa. Later that night, while lying in bed, Sammy finds himself worrying that the monster has snuck into the closet and is waiting to attack the boys as they sleep. No matter what he tries, he can't stop himself from imagining it.

These examples illustrate at least five important dimensions along which imaginings vary:

- Prompts: While Max's initial imagining doesn't seem prompted by anything in particular, the later imaginings are prompted by (and indeed guided by) his initial suggestion.
- Voluntariness: All of Sammy's imaginings have been prompted by Max, but not all of them are taken on voluntarily. When Sammy imagines the monster secreted away inside the closet, he does so involuntarily. The other imaginings seem to have been taken on by choice.
- Props: Some of the boys' imaginings involve props, as when they imagine the sofa to be a mountain, while others don't.[6]
- Collaboration: Some of the boys' imaginings are pursued jointly, as when they both imagine that the sofa is a mountain. Others are not: consider again Sammy's bedtime imagining of the monster in the closet.
- Form: Max's initial imagining takes the form of an *imagining-that*. He imagines *that a monster is chasing them*. In later imaginings, the boys simply imagine *the monster itself*.

While all of these dimensions along which imaginings can vary are discussed in the literature on imagination, this last dimension has come in for particular attention. Acts of imagination that take the form of imagining-that are what philosophers typically call *propositional* or *attitudinal imagining*, and this is typically contrasted with *sensory* or *imagistic* imagination.[7] Let's discuss each of these forms in turn.

First, consider attitudinal imagining. There are many different attitudes that one can take toward a certain propositional content. Instead of (or in addition to) imagining that a scary monster is in pursuit, one might believe, or desire, or hope that it is. Moreover, each of these attitudes is different from the others. Philosophers tend to divide them up into two classes: the cognitive and the conative. Cognitive attitudes have what's called *mind-to-world* direction of fit – they're successful (true) when the content of the attitude matches the world. In contrast, conative attitudes have what's called *world-to-mind* direction of fit – they're successful (satisfied) when the world matches the content of the attitude. As should thus be clear, belief is a paradigmatic cognitive attitude, while desire is a paradigmatic conative attitude. Attitudinal imagining looks like it falls on the cognitive side of the divide. In this case, however, the relevant world in its mind-to-world direction of fit is best understood to be a make-believe or fictional world rather than the actual world.[8]

Interestingly, some philosophers have recently argued that attitudinal imagining comes in a conative variety in addition to its cognitive variety. For example, in addition to imagining that there is a monster chasing them, Max and Sammy might also imaginatively desire that it fails to catch up to them. (For discussion, see Chapter 12.) In thinking about this purported form of attitudinal imagination, the natural questions concern how it is or is not like desire. Likewise, in considering the more familiar cognitive form of attitudinal imagining, the natural questions concern how it is or is not like belief. Current philosophical literature contains a lively discussion of these issues. (For an overview, see Chapter 8.) Though we do not have the space to take them up here, it's worth noting that the similarities between attitudinal imagination and belief are not taken to threaten claim (2) above, i.e., imagination is still generally seen to be a primitive mental state. These dual points about cognitive attitudinal imagining – that it resembles belief and yet is not reducible to it – are often encapsulated by referring to attitudinal imagining as a *distinct cognitive attitude* (DCA).[9]

Next, consider sensory imagining. Max and Sammy engage in this form of imagining when they imagine the scary monster itself, when they picture it in what is often metaphorically (if misleadingly) referred to as the "mind's eye." Though the word "image" has a visual connotation, philosophers in this context typically extend the notion of imagery to apply to the products of other sensory modalities as well, so that there is also auditory imagery and olfactory imagery, and so on, along with visual imagery. Were the boys to imagine the monster's roar, such an imagining could also be referred to as imagistic in nature. Imagining the monster itself – either its horrific appearance or its deafening roar – is thought to be importantly different from imagining just that there is a monster with such-and-such appearance or such-and-such a roar. (For further discussion of sensory imagination, see Chapter 7.)

What about when Sammy imagines seeing the monster and when he imagines feeling scared? Here he's engaged in what philosophers tend to call *experiential imagining*. When we're engaged in experiential imagining, we project ourselves into an imagined situation and imagine the experiences – visual, auditory, emotional, and so on – that we would have. It's for this reason that experiential imagining is also often referred to as *imagining from the inside*. Whereas attitudinal imagining tends to be expressed using a that-clause (Sammy imagines that a monster was chasing him), sensory imagining (Sammy imagines the monster) and experiential imagining (Sammy imagines seeing the monster) tend to be expressed using a direct object construction. Only in experiential imagining, however, does the direct object tend to be expressed using a gerund phrase.

Finally, we might want to refer to the boys' overall imaginative endeavor, a temporally extended process that arises from many different specific imaginings of the sorts we have just distinguished. This imaginative process has been called the *constructive imagination* (Van Leeuwen 2013). When we engage with a work of fiction or play a game of make-believe, when we consider a philosophical thought experiment or fantasize about an upcoming vacation – all of which are activities that tend to involve a multifaceted and multistage imaginative project – we exercise this constructive capacity.

Other philosophers offer taxonomies that might initially seem to carve up imagination in different ways. For example, in their influential book *Recreative Minds*, Gregory Currie and Ian Ravenscroft distinguish *creative imagination* from *recreative imagination*. Someone exercises the capacity for creative imagination when she "puts together ideas in a way that defies expectation or convention: the kind of imaginative 'leap' that leads to the creation of something valuable in art, science, or practical life" (Currie and Ravenscroft 2002, 9; for an extended discussion of creative imagination, see Chapter 18). In contrast, recreative imagination is a capacity for perspective-shifting, i.e., it is "the capacity to put ourselves in the place of our own future, past, or counterfactual self: seeing, thinking about, and responding to the world as the other sees, thinks about, and responds to it" (Currie and Ravenscroft 2002, 8–9). It turns out, however, that recreative imagining comprises the various different sorts of imaginings distinguished by the taxonomy above. For Currie and Ravenscroft, recreative imagining involves the production of states that are not perceptions or beliefs or experiences but are in various ways like those states – so there are a bunch of different kinds of *X*-like imaginings, where *X* can stand for perception, belief, and so on. It seems likely, however, that their perception-like imagining is essentially our imagistic imagining (plus, perhaps, the perceptual modes that we've called *experiential imagining*), while their belief-like imagining is our attitudinal imagining.

So it's probably fair to say that most philosophers would accept the above taxonomy or something very much like it. But even with such a taxonomy in hand, there are many further questions that remain unaddressed. One important disagreement centers around whether one of the above types of imagining is primary, and if so, which one. Some philosophers, for example, think that all imagining is fundamentally experiential in nature. As Christopher Peacocke claims, "to imagine something is always at least to imagine, from the inside, being in some conscious state" (Peacocke 1985, 21). To imagine a monster is really to imagine seeing a monster (or perhaps hearing a monster, or smelling a monster, and so on) while imagining that a monster is chasing you is really to imagine seeing a monster chasing you. This might be imagined from your ordinary perspective, as when you look over your shoulder, or it might be imagined from an external perspective, analogous to how the scene would be depicted by security camera footage of the incident. In criticizing this experiential analysis of imagination, other philosophers note that it implausibly requires all imagining to have a nested structure that assumes too much conceptual sophistication on the part of the imaginer. Young children may imagine monsters even without the concepts of *seeing* and *hearing*. The experiential analysis may also be criticized for getting the object of imagining wrong, for it seems to make all imaginings egoistically directed. When Sammy imagines a monster, we want to be able to say that his imagining is about a monster, but if the experiential analysis is right, then what he's really doing is imagining himself seeing a monster, i.e., his imagining is really about himself.

In contrast, other philosophers claim that imagining is fundamentally imagistic in nature. This view seems to be found in Descartes:

> if I want to think of a chiliagon, although I understand that it is a figure consisting of a thousand sides just as well as I understand the triangle to be a three-sided figure, I do not in the same way imagine the thousand sides or see them as if they were present before me … . But suppose I am dealing with a pentagon: I can of course understand the figure of a pentagon, just as I can the figure of a chiliagon, without the help of the imagination; but I can also imagine a pentagon, by applying the mind's eye to its five sides and the area contained within them. And in doing this I notice quite clearly that imagination requires a peculiar effort of mind which is not required for understanding.
>
> *(Descartes 1641/1986, 50–51)*

It seems plausible that this "peculiar effort of mind" should be understood in terms of mental imagery. (See Chapter 2 for a detailed discussion of Descartes' theory of imagination; for a more recent defense of an imagery-based account of imagination, see Kind 2001.) But accounts of imagining that claim that imagination necessarily involves imagery face numerous alleged counterexamples, because there seem to be many situations that cannot be imaged. White notes that we can imagine an objection or a difficulty as we can imagine a school bus. Or, to take an example from Neil Van Leeuwen: "When I imagine, on reading *Lord of the Rings*, that elves can live forever, I'm fictionally imagining a proposition that I couldn't imagine using mental imagery. It would take too long!" (Van Leeuwen 2013, 222).

## 2 The uses of imagination

Having reflected on the nature of imagination and some of its key characteristics, I now turn to discuss some of the many ways in which imagination is employed. In fact, imagination plays a role in a wide swath of everyday activities – from pretense to engagement with fiction, from the creation and appreciation of art and music to empathizing, strategizing about the future, and learning about the world. As we will see, imagination also plays a role in several fundamental philosophical activities, from moral theorizing to modal epistemology. Though the following discussion provides only a very brief sketch of these uses, they are discussed in considerably more detail in the chapters constituting Parts III–VI of this volume.

First, as our above example of Max and Sammy suggests, imagination occupies a prominent place in the lives of children as they immerse themselves in games of make-believe (see Chapters 22 and 23). But even once we've outgrown such games, imagination continues to play an important role in allowing us to escape from the monotony of everyday life. Whether we're stuck in a boring meeting or on a long train ride, we frequently aim to imaginatively transport ourselves somewhere else more exotic and enjoyable. (While these imaginative exercises can generally be viewed as harmless fun, there may be instances in which the content of someone's imaginative fantasies gives one reason for moral worry – see Chapter 28.) We also escape from reality via our dreams at night, and it seems plausible to think that dreams should be understood as a species of imagination (Chapter 11).

Another kind of imaginative escapism comes from our interactions with works of art, be they visual or musical or literary. Artistic engagement and appreciation seem to require us to become imaginatively involved with the work in question (Chapters 13 and 14). Let's consider in particular our engagement with works of fiction (Chapter 15). When we watch Luke

Skywalker battle Darth Vader, or when we read about Bilbo Baggins' face-off with the dragon Smaug, it seems plausible to suppose that we imagine the unfolding events. Certainly I don't believe that an actual battle is taking place when I'm watching *Return of the Jedi*, and I don't take *The Hobbit* to be a work of nonfiction. I know that neither Jedi Knights nor hobbits actually exist. So it doesn't seem that we can explain my engagement with fiction in terms of beliefs. Granted, I may well believe that a battle is taking place *on screen*, and I may well believe that Bilbo encounters Smaug *in the book*, but it doesn't seem that this fully captures what's going on with me, at least in most cases. Such an explanation keeps me at too much of a distance from the fictional worlds in which I am often deeply immersed and to which I am often having intensely emotional reactions (Chapter 16). A further role for imagination in our engagement with fiction arises when we consider that literary works typically leave many important details unspecified, and it is up to the reader to exercise her imagination to fill these in.

Interestingly, however, there seem to be limits on what we are willing or able to imagine when engaging with fiction. In particular, we often balk with respect to certain kinds of morally deviant claims, as when readers of *The Turner Diaries* resist imagining the truth of the book's racist and anti-Semitic proclamations. In light of our willingness to imaginatively engage with all sorts of non-morally deviant claims, this phenomenon – what has become known as *imaginative resistance* – has struck many as puzzling, and it has consequently been the subject of considerable recent discussion (Chapter 17).

Turning now from our imaginative engagement with works of art, music, and fiction to the creation of such works, we are led to another important role that imagination plays, namely, as a driver of creativity. It not only takes imagination for the readers to flesh out the details of the fictional worlds with which they engage, but it also requires imaginative creativity on the part of authors who construct those worlds. Creativity (Chapter 18) underlies a vast array of human activities ranging from art to music to science. Historically, the role of imagination in creativity was discussed in detail by both Kant (Chapter 4) and Sartre (Chapter 6). More recently, work by Michael Polanyi (1966/2009) focuses on scientific creativity; on his view, the interplay of imagination and intuition is crucial to scientific discovery.

Some authors adduce evolutionary considerations to underscore the connection between imagination and creativity (e.g., Carruthers 2002). Other contemporary authors such as Berys Gaut (2003, 2010) and Dustin Stokes (2014) have argued that certain features of imagination – and in particular its freedom, its playfulness, and its disconnection from action – make it especially well suited for creative pursuits. Via imagination, we are able to safely explore new hypotheses, or try out new strategies, without the commitments that come along with actual implementation. As this suggests, imagination also seems implicated in enabling us to achieve new understanding of the world around us, i.e., imagination facilitates learning (Chapter 30).

The uses of imagination that we've started with – pretending; dreaming; engagement with art, music, and fiction; creativity – are all what we might call *transcendent* uses. In each case, imagination is employed to allow us to escape from, or transcend, the everyday world in which we live. As we begin to talk about learning, however, we switch from transcendent uses of imagination to *instructive* ones. In these uses, imagination is not called upon to take us out of the world in which we live but rather to teach us something about it. The importance of imagination in enabling us not only to escape from the world around us but also to learn from it might seem somewhat surprising. These two roles may even seem in tension with one another. As we noted above, imagination is not constitutively connected to the truth. What we imagine, and how we imagine it, are entirely up to us. It's these features of imagination that enable us to imaginatively project ourselves into all kinds of fantastical scenarios.

But how can the capacity that enables us to fly completely free from reality also enable us to learn something about it? This question is what Amy Kind and Peter Kung (Kind and Kung forthcoming) have recently called *the puzzle of imaginative use*. Ultimately, however, Kind and Kung believe that the apparent tension between imagination's transcendent and instructive uses can be dissipated. In their view, the key to solving the puzzle involves recognizing various ways in which imagination is subject to constraints. Some of these constraints are architectural in nature, while others may be voluntarily imposed. (See also Kind forthcoming.)

One important context in which the imagination plays a significant instructive role is in the pursuit of scientific understanding. For example, in order adequately to explain the practice of scientific modeling – where, e.g., clay balls stand in for planets – it seems likely that we will need to rely on imagination (Chapter 33). A related context concerns the pursuit of mathematical understanding. Imagination plausibly can be said to underlie a wide swath of geometric reasoning (Chapter 34). And unsurprisingly, perhaps, imagination also plays an instructive role in the activity of philosophy. As we saw above, though there is no constitutive connection between imagination and truth, there does seem to be an important connection between imagination and possibility, i.e., it's often thought that imagination can in some way serve as an epistemological guide to possibility and impossibility (Chapter 32; see also Chapter 20 for a puzzle this raises for imaginings involving the self). At least since Plato proposed the Ring of Gyges, philosophers have been relying on thought experiments both to object to their opponents' views and to further their own (Chapter 31). If the imaginability of a given thought experiment shows that the scenario is possible, then we have a formidable objection to any philosophical theory that cannot countenance such a possibility.

But the instructive use of imagination extends well beyond these academic domains. When I am trying to decide whether the green or the brown curtains will look better in my living room, or when I am trying to determine whether I will have to disassemble the desk I just bought to get it through the narrow hallway and into my home office, I might naturally use imagination to help me. Likewise, imagination might be helpful when I need to figure out whether I can climb from one branch of a tree to the next or when I want to predict how I will react were a particular chain of events to occur. More generally, it seems crucial for our abilities to plan for the future and to make rational decisions (Chapter 25). And humans are not the only animals to learn from imagination. There is evidence that nonhuman animals ranging from ravens to chimpanzees utilize imagination in various problem-solving endeavors (Chapter 24).

A crucial aspect of our capacity for learning via imagination is our ability to predict and explain the behavior of others, what philosophers and cognitive scientists often call *mindreading*. As we make our way in the world, we are constantly having to interpret those around us – whether it's to understand that a colleague's grin actually signals anger and not amusement, or to predict that she will vote against the proposal that's before us, or to decide what might best persuade her to change her position on the issue. According to one influential view, imaginative projection underlies our mindreading abilities (Chapter 19). I imaginatively put myself in my colleague's shoes to determine what she's thinking and feeling and what she's likely to do next. This same capacity for imaginative projection seems to be central to our ability to empathize with one another (Chapter 27), which in turn allows imagination to play a significant role in our moral decision-making (Chapter 26).

Finally, given the vast array of uses to which imagination is put in our daily lives – in both transcendent and instructive ways – it's perhaps not surprising that it receives mention as one of a group of capabilities that makes human life meaningful and worthwhile. In developing her Capabilities Account, Martha Nussbaum notes that "being able to use the senses, to imagine, think, and reason – and to do these things in a 'truly human' way" is central for human flourishing (Nussbaum 2011, 33–34; see Chapter 29). In this way, imagining has not only the aesthetic and epistemic dimensions discussed above, but a political dimension as well.

## Notes

1 Carroll's remark came during his commentary on Derek Matravers' *Fiction and Narrative* at the 2015 Pacific Division meeting of the American Philosophical Association.
2 For one notable exception, see White (1990), who claims that a theory of imagination must account for all common uses of the term "imagine."
3 For one notable example of the use of boxology in the literature on imagination, see Nichols and Stich 2003.
4 Something like the first slogan can be found in Hart 1988; the second comes from Walton 1990, 41.
5 Though Part I focuses only on six historical treatments of imagination, it is worth noting that imagination features prominently in the work of many other philosophical figures – from Wittgenstein to Coleridge to Merleau-Ponty. For helpful discussions of the treatment of imagination throughout the history of philosophy, see Warnock 1976, White 1990, and Brann 1991.
6 The *locus classicus* for discussion of props in imagination comes in Walton 1990, 35–43.
7 Sometimes the contrast is drawn not between propositional/attitudinal imagining and sensory/imagistic imagining but between propositional/attitudinal imagining and *objectual* imagining, i.e., between imaginings directed at propositional contents and imaginings directed at objects. Insofar as there can be nonimagistic objectual imaginings – e.g., imagining the number 5, or imagining an invisible spirit – these two ways of drawing the distinction might be thought importantly different. (But see Kind 2001 for arguments that all imagining is imagistic.)
8 See Gendler 2011 for a discussion of imagining's direction of fit.
9 Although there is widespread agreement that attitudinal imagining is a DCA, that agreement is not universal. For a minority view, see Langland-Hassan 2012.

## References

Arcangeli, M. (2014) "Against Cognitivism about Supposition," *Philosophia* 42: 607–624.
Balcerak Jackson, M. (Forthcoming) "Imagining, Conceiving, Supposing," in A. Kind and P. Kung (eds.) *Knowledge through Imagination*, Oxford: Oxford University Press.
Brann, E. (1991) *The World of the Imagination*, Lanham, MD: Rowman & Littlefield.
Carruthers, P. (2002) "Human Creativity: Its Cognitive Basis, Its Evolution, and Its Connections with Childhood Pretence," *British Journal for the Philosophy of Science* 53: 225–249.
Chalmers, D.J. (2002) "Does Conceivability Entail Possibility?" in T.S. Gendler and J. Hawthorne (eds.) *Conceivability and Possibility*, Oxford: Oxford University Press, 145–200.
Currie, G., and I. Ravenscroft (2002) *Recreative Minds: Imagination in Philosophy and Psychology*, Oxford: Oxford University Press.
Descartes, R. (1641/1986) *Meditations on First Philosophy: With Selections from the Objections and Replies*, trans. J. Cottingham, Cambridge: Cambridge University Press.
Gaut, B. (2003) "Creativity and Imagination," in B. Gaut and P. Livingston (eds.) *The Creation of Art*, Cambridge: Cambridge University Press.
Gendler, T.S. (2000) "The Puzzle of Imaginative Resistance," *Journal of Philosophy* 97(2): 55–81.
Gendler, T.S. (2011) "Imagination," in E.N. Zalta (ed.) *Stanford Encyclopedia of Philosophy* (Fall 2013 edition), <http://plato.stanford.edu/archives/fall2013/entries/imagination/>.
Hart, W.D. (1988) *The Engines of the Soul*, Cambridge: Cambridge University Press.
Hume, D. (1777/1975) *Enquiries Concerning Human Understanding and Concerning the Principle of Morals*, eds. L.A. Selby-Bigge and P.H. Nidditch, Oxford: Oxford University Press.
Ichikawa, J., and B. Jarvis (2012) "Rational Imagination and Modal Knowledge," *Noûs* 46: 127–158.
Kind, A. (2001) "Putting the Image Back in Imagination," *Philosophy and Phenomenological Research* 62(1): 85–110.
Kind, A. (2013) "The Heterogeneity of the Imagination," *Erkenntnis* 78(1): 141–159.

Kind, A. (Forthcoming) "Imagining under Constraints," in A. Kind and P. Kung (eds.) *Knowledge through Imagination*, Oxford: Oxford University Press.
Kind, A., and P. Kung (eds.) (Forthcoming) *Knowledge through Imagination*, Oxford: Oxford University Press.
Langland-Hassan, P. (2012) "Pretense, Imagination, and Belief: The Single Attitude Theory," *Philosophical Studies* 159(2): 155–179.
Nichols, S., and S. Stich (2003) *Mindreading: An Integrated Account of Pretence, Self-Awareness, and Understanding Other Minds*, Oxford: Oxford University Press.
Nussbaum, M. (2011) *Creating Capabilities: The Human Development Approach*, Cambridge, MA: Harvard University Press.
Peacocke, C. (1985) "Imagination, Experience, and Possibility," in J. Foster and H. Robinson (eds.) *Essays on Berkeley: A Tercentennial Celebration*, Oxford: Oxford University Press.
Polanyi, M. (1966/2009) "Creative Imagination," repr. in K. Bardsley, D. Dutton, and M. Krausz (eds.) *The Idea of Creativity*, Leiden: Brill Press, 147–163.
Stokes, D. (2014) "The Role of Imagination in Creativity," in E.S. Paul and S.B. Kaufman (eds.) *The Philosophy of Creativity*, Oxford: Oxford University Press.
Van Leeuwen, N. (2013) "The Meanings of 'Imagine' Part I: Constructive Imagination," *Philosophy Compass* 8(3): 220–230.
Walton, K.L. (1990) *Mimesis as Make-Believe: On the Foundations of the Representational Arts*, Cambridge: Harvard University Press.
Warnock, M. (1976) *Imagination*, Berkeley: University of California Press.
Weinberg, J.M., and A. Meskin (2006) "Puzzling over the Imagination: Philosophical Problems, Architectural Solutions," in S. Nichols (ed.) *The Architecture of the Imagination: New Essays on Pretence, Possibility, and Fiction*, Oxford: Oxford University Press, 175–202.
White, A.R. (1990) *The Language of Imagination*, Oxford: Blackwell.

# PART I

# Historical treatments of imagination

# 1

# ARISTOTLE ON *PHANTASIA*

*Deborah K.W. Modrak*

The breadth of Aristotle's conception of imagination (*phantasia*) is extraordinary and sets the stage for the discussion of imagination in subsequent literature.[1] Aristotle appeals to *phantasia* to explain behavior of all sorts, especially to explain behavior that seems to be guided by reason, but is not, in cases where the agent (a child, a drunken adult or a nonrational animal) lacks the capacity for rational judgment. He also appeals to *phantasia* to explain the human mind's ability to transition seamlessly between perception and thought. In this capacity, *phantasia* is required for thinking. In addition, he assigns nonveridical perceptual experiences to *phantasia*, including cases of illusion, delusion and dreaming.

The wide scope of Aristotle's vision of *phantasia* is – if a unified analysis underwrites it – a great strength. If it should turn out that Aristotle has made a number of only minimally connected claims about *phantasia* in different contexts, the breadth of his account would become a weakness. The goal then is to attempt to bring the various functions of *phantasia* together in a way that displays the comprehensiveness of his account while maintaining its unity. The approach to be followed here will be to begin with Aristotle's account of *phantasia* in *De Anima* III.3 and to offer an interpretation of *phantasia* based on this chapter, which emphasizes the sensory character of *phantasia*. Taking this to be Aristotle's core concept of *phantasia*, we will turn to the roles Aristotle assigns *phantasia* in his analyses of memory, dreaming, thought and voluntary motion in the *De Anima, Parva Naturalia* and elsewhere. The core concept is, it will be argued, at work in all these contexts.

## *De Anima* III.3: What *phantasia* is

After defining the functions of the soul and discussing the basic perceptual functions at length in *De Anima* II, Aristotle turns in *De Anima* III.3 to the nature of *phantasia*. *Phantasia* is "that in virtue of which we say an image [*phantasma*] arises in us" (428a1–2).[2] To fill out this preliminary account, Aristotle begins by establishing the similarities between perceiving and thinking and then he argues that they are activities of distinct psychic faculties. He also argues against assigning *phantasia* either to the perceptual faculty of the soul or the rational faculty. Neither sensing nor thinking *simpliciter* has all the same characteristics as *phantasia*. Sensing cannot occur in the absence of an appropriate object. For instance, I cannot see red, if there is nothing red in my visual field, but I can imagine red. Thinking sometimes contradicts *phantasia*, for instance, as when one sees a small golden disk in the sky but thinks that the sun is larger than the earth (428b2–4). *Phantasia* has one foot in each camp; it is in some respects like perception and in others like intellection and so Aristotle briefly considers making it a function of the two combined, but this option is quickly ruled out as well.

> It is clear, therefore, that *phantasia* will be neither belief together with perception, nor belief through perception, nor a blend of belief and perception.
>
> *(428a24–26)*

Having ruled out a quick and unqualified identification of *phantasia* with perception or thought or the two combined, Aristotle sets out to build an account of *phantasia* which is sensitive to the common features shared by both types of cognitive faculties. *Phantasia* has an important role to play in the explanation of both the similarities of perceptual and intellectual cognition and their differences. First, however, the distinctive characteristics of *phantasia* must be determined. One such feature is *phantasia*'s vulnerability to error, unlike perception; another is *phantasia*'s widespread occurrence, nearly all animals possess it, unlike intellection; yet another is its dependence upon perception for its origin and its objects.

> Since *phantasia* is thought to be a kind of movement … this movement cannot exist apart from perception or in things, which do not perceive and in respect of it, it is possible for its possessor to do and be affected by many things, and it may be both true and false.
>
> *(428b11–17)*

*Phantasia* is described as a movement because it is an active awareness of certain objects. These objects are the same as those realized in acts of perceptual awareness, namely colors-as-seen, sounds-as-heard, etc. *Phantasia* plays a central role in our cognitive life, both as active awareness and as a source of retained sensory information. All these features, taken together, support the identification of *phantasia* with a kind of sensory experience that is distinguishable from perception. Aristotle's grounds for distinguishing between them are several.

For Aristotle, cognitive activities just are the realization of cognitive objects in acts of awareness. The objects of *phantasia* are the same as the objects of perception; the only difference is the requirement that the objects of perception must be actualizations of perceptible qualities (colors, sounds, etc.) of external objects, which are the immediate causes of the perceptual experience. *Phantasia* is different; it may, but need not, occur in the absence of an external sensory stimulus. It cannot occur in cognizers lacking sensory capacities or in the absence of past or concurrent sensory experience. Because its objects are sensory objects, *phantasia* is able to bridge the divide between perception and thought. Perception proper is constrained, not only by the requirement that its immediate cause be present in the external environment, but also by the requirement of verisimilitude. Perception of proper objects (sensible qualities such as color or sound) is always correct (427b12); and while other types of perception admit error, for the most part perception provides accurate information about perceptible, external objects. Because its connection with the external world is more attenuated, *phantasia* is much more liable to error. In short, the picture of *phantasia* that emerges from a careful reading of *De Anima* III.3 is one of a very versatile cognitive capacity; *phantasia* is a distinct way of apprehending sensory objects and *phantasia* may represent its intentional objects accurately or not, because unlike perception it is not constrained by a requirement of verisimilitude. To summarize the conception of *phantasia* that underlies Aristotle's findings in

III.3: *phantasia* is the awareness of a sensory content under conditions that are not conducive to veridical perception.[3]

Taking *De Anima* III.3 to be the canonical account of *phantasia*, some commentators have also been led to identify *phantasia* with nonveridical appearance.[4] This interpretation is problematic, however, because it limits the role of *phantasia* in ways that would be detrimental to Aristotle's account of voluntary motion and action and his account of thinking. He needs a concept of *phantasia* that is indeterminate with respect to the reliability of the sensory content it presents. In the case of visual illusion, such as the case of the size of the sun mentioned by Aristotle, *phantasia* is the awareness of a colored shape that is misleading as to the actual size of the sun. In other instances, such as the triangle contemplated by the geometer, *phantasia* presents sensorially useful and reliable images. To remember is an exercise of *phantasia* and in this case it is important to have a content that is often reliable but sometimes not. One of the advantages of the conception of *phantasia* developed in III.3 is that as the awareness of a sensory content under conditions that are not conducive to veridical perception, *phantasia* may be invoked in explanations both of illusory appearance and of accurate recall.[5]

The sensory character of *phantasia* is emphasized by Aristotle as he wraps up his analysis in III.3.[6] However, it is worth noting that the characteristics of *phantasia* that make it thought-like play an important part in his arriving at this conclusion. The form of thinking that is at issue is belief (*doxa*) because it may be either true or false. He considers, only to reject, the possibility that *phantasia* is belief combined with perception (428a24–27). Moreover, the chapter ends with a discussion of the conditions under which *phantasia* is true or more liable to error.

> The movement that comes about as a result of the activity of perception will differ in so far as it comes from these three kinds of perception. The first is true as long as perception is present, while the others may be false whether it is present or absent.
> *(428b25–29)*

As the awareness of a sensory content under conditions that are not conducive to veridical perception, *phantasia* has the breadth Aristotle desires; any object that can be the content of a perception can also be presented in a *phantasma* (object of *phantasia*) and the content so presented may be an accurate representation of an actual object or it may fall short of accuracy due to the conditions under which it is realized. For instance, a visual experience occurring during a fog is much more likely to meet the conditions for *phantasia* than to meet the conditions for having a veridical perception. A memory of an object seen many years before will rely on *phantasia* for the presentation of the object; it may or may not be an accurate representation of the object as originally perceived.

## *Phantasia*: remembering and dreaming

Memory (*mneme*) is the subject of a short, psychological treatise, *De Memoria*. Aristotle asks and ultimately answers the question, "What is memory?" It is "a disposition of a *phantasma* [an image], as a likeness to that of which it is a *phantasma*" (451a15–18).[7] A *phantasma* is a complex of sensory characters that are perceptible through any or all senses. Aristotle's account is intended to cover auditory, olfactory, gustatory and tactile images as well as visual ones and thus a *phantasma* (image) is made the vehicle for memory. Memory also requires a concomitant awareness of the passage of time. It is not a memory, Aristotle believes, unless we are aware of the remembered object as an object of a past perception.

> Sometimes we are in doubt whether it is a memory or not. But sometimes it happens that we reflect or recollect that we heard or saw it before.
>
> *(451a5–7)*

This account of memory involves a dual-level exercise of *phantasia*. The image or images, the sensory content(s), which are the vehicle for remembering a past event, are presented to the cognizer by *phantasia* as standing in a relationship to the experience in which they originated. Aristotle describes the memory image as a likeness (*eikon*) to capture the referential character of a memory. It is, not only the awareness of a past experience, it is the awareness of that experience as past. This is a complex representation including as it does a reference to the past. Aristotle says that memory belongs to the same psychic faculty as the recognition of time. Later he assigns both to the perceptual faculty of the soul. In explaining how this kind of awareness is possible, he looks to two cases. One is the experience of an object that leaves us in doubt about whether we are having a memory. The other is a case of the mind's using a sensory content presented in *phantasia* for a different purpose than merely apprehending the object. In the former, the sensory content is realized as an object of awareness but it fails to refer to the past experience that caused it. This failure is partially due to the representation, which lacks markers of the past, and partially due to the way the cognizer employs the image. In the second case, the mode of awareness involved is emphasized. The geometer, according to Aristotle, apprehends the geometrical object in thought by using a specific image, e.g., a triangle, and then taking it to represent the abstract triangle about which she reasons. The image has a particular size but not so the abstraction, which it represents (450a1–6). Just as a viewer may look at a painting of an animal as an array of colors and shapes or may take it as a representation of an actual animal, the cognizer may take the *phantasma* as an array of sensible characters or as a likeness of something perceived in the past.

Aristotle appeals to the deliberate use of mnemonic devices to elucidate further his notion of using an image to refer to something outside itself.[8] For instance, one might envisage a series of houses and then associate each image with an item in a series of things in order to remember the series. In this instance, there is a deliberate use of an image to represent something else. Often, however, in the case of deliberate recall, something beyond memory (*mneme*) is involved. This is recollection, *anamnesis*. It is a psychic capacity peculiar to humans and not shared with other animals. To recollect is to set about trying to bring a memory to mind. It requires the capacity to reason. It is by deliberately moving from one thought to another that we are able to prompt memories. Otherwise memories are (like other perceptual activities) responses to environmental sensory stimulation. But in the case of recollection, we set out to try to retrieve a memory. Recollection is a joint function of the perceptual and rational capacities of the human psyche. Recollection is not the only complex, cognitive activity which requires the collaboration of the perceptual and rational faculties. Whenever such collaboration is involved, Aristotle turns to *phantasia* to facilitate the collaboration, as shall be seen when we turn to deliberate action and abstract thought.

Memory is an exercise of *phantasia* where verisimilitude is a requirement. Dreaming by contrast is not but it, too, is the topic of a short psychological treatise and it is also addressed in a second work on divination.[9]

> A dream seems to be a kind of imagery [*phantasma*] … and it is apparent that dreaming belongs to the perceptual faculty but belongs to it qua *phantastikon* [capacity for *phantasia*].
>
> (De Ins. *459a18–22)*

Dreaming occurs during sleep and is not to be confused with perceiving something in sleep, e.g., hearing a cock crow (462a24–25). It is only a dream insofar as what is presented is not an accurate representation of the immediate environment. That said, dreaming as an exercise of *phantasia* has its origin in previous perceptions. The sensory contents making up a dream are new arrangements of sensory materials that are present in the psyche. Aristotle turns to physiology to explain how the images (*phantasmata*) that are representational in dreams exist as dispositional objects. The bodily organs of perception including the heart, which is the central organ of perception, undergo many changes when we are awake and the peripheral organs of perception are bombarded with stimuli. The stronger of these movements are realized as perceptions; but not all these changes become immediate objects of perceptual awareness; many of them remain in the heart as latent objects of awareness (*Div. Somn.* 463a8–10). During sleep, when the peripheral organs of perception (eyes, ears, etc.) are inactive, some of the physiological changes in the perceptual organs become objects of awareness. Because dreams are realized pieces of perceptions, they can be, Aristotle suggests, causes of subsequent behavior by the dreamer as well as being effects of earlier experience (*Div. Somn.* 463a23–30).

Dreams are often elaborate representations of events that are (insofar as the dreamer is aware at the time) indistinguishable from perceptions. Aristotle recognizes this feature of dreams and believes that *phantasia* on his analysis has the right characteristics to be the active faculty during dreaming. On the one hand, the physiological characteristics of *phantasia*, originating in the stimulation of peripheral sense organs and lasting indefinitely as changes in the internal perceptual system, are such that *phantasia* is well positioned to explain the origin of dream imagery during sleep. On the other hand, the sensory character of *phantasia* explains how the physiological changes involved can provide objects of awareness that are sensory objects. Dreaming is a species of sensory experience that occurs under conditions such that they would not be conducive to veridical perception. This, however, does not undermine the representational aspect of *phantasia*; dream images also refer, just not to the objects which in the context of the dream are their apparent referents. The dreamer may envision a monster which is in actuality a composite of sensible characteristics found in a variety of previous perceptions. The image refers in the context of the dream to a monster but there is no monster in the world to serve as its actual referent. Aristotle likens this aspect of dreams to deluded appearances; for instance, when a feverish person looks at a crack on a wall and sees a terrifying creature (*De Ins.* 460b12–13). The representational content of dream imagery is only loosely connected to the world. It is, however, crucial for Aristotle's story that the origin of the sensory content be one or more past perceptions. If not, the *De Anima*'s analysis of *phantasia* would be violated and the assignment of dreaming to the perceptual faculty functioning as the capacity for *phantasia* (the *phantastikon*) would be undermined.

## Thought and *phantasia*

From the *De Anima* to the short psychological treatises, Aristotle consistently distinguishes between perceptual capacities in general (including *phantasia*) and rationality. The former are widespread in nature as perception is common to all animals; the latter belongs only to humans. That said, Aristotle is inclined to make the gulf between the two as narrow as possible. He frequently points out similarities between exercises of the perceptual faculty and those of the rational faculty and he envisages areas of cognitive activity involving both. Recollection is one such case but even more striking is his insistence upon the dependence of abstract thought on *phantasia*. This is a constant theme from the first book of the *De Anima*, where he suggests that such dependence would link thought to the body, even if thinking has no physical organ (403a8–10). The idea that all psychological activities are dependent upon the body is consistent with Aristotle's conception of the psyche as the form of the body and it also fits his model of explanation of cognitive activities. He has, in addition, concerns that are specific to his conception of the cognitive powers of human beings.

In *De Interpretatione* I.1, Aristotle gives an account of meaning that makes reference to a meaning-bearing psychological state. He indicates that the nature of this state will be further explored in his psychology. The sole reference to meaning in the *De Anima* occurs in II.8.

> Consequently speech is the impact of the inbreathed air against that which is called the windpipe by the soul in these parts ... what produces the impact must have soul in it and must be accompanied by an act of *phantasia* for speech is a sound with a meaning and not merely inbreathed air as a cough is.
>
> *(420b27–33)*

Speech is peculiar to humans. Although Aristotle does not explicitly limit rationality to creatures with language, his account of rationality presupposes the capacity for having meaning-bearing thoughts and expressing thoughts in spoken language. Meaning in the *De Interpretatione* depends upon the existence of states of mind that are likenesses of external objects (16a3–8).[10] As the occurrence of a sensory content under conditions that are not conducive to veridical perception, *phantasia* is well suited to play the role of a meaning-bearing psychological state. In the case where the word is the name of a natural kind, the meaning of the term would be conveyed by an image of one or more exemplifications of the kind. In this case, at least in rough outline, Aristotle's explanation of how the name bears the signification it does seems plausible. His account seems weaker when the term in question is the name of an abstract concept, for instance, the name of a very large number. Nevertheless, Aristotle has better reasons for extending his account of *phantasia* to include signification than to assign this role to any other cognitive activity; the other leading candidate would be a state of the rational soul, but thought lacks the connection with the world that *phantasia* has. Without the ability to grasp meanings, the ability to think would be undermined. Nor does solipsism appeal to Aristotle; the psychological state that links word and object must be such that it is conditioned by the external world's impact on the psyche. Meanings connect the cognizer's thoughts to the world and this connection is mediated by *phantasia*.

Not surprisingly, when Aristotle turns to thinking in *De Anima* III.4, he begins by pointing out all the ways in which it is similar to perception; he even considers the possibility that the cognition of an essence (a universal) and the cognition of the object to which the essence belongs (a sensible particular) belong to the same cognitive faculty differently disposed (429b10–18). Despite stopping short of identifying thought with perception, Aristotle goes on to develop an account of thinking that makes it dependent upon *phantasia* and that emphasizes the similarities between the rational and perceptual faculties in general. The capacity for discrimination (*kriptikon*) is exercised through two faculties, perception and thought (432a15–16; cf. 427a17–22). Moreover, thinking is about an object, not directly present in the external world; its objects are universals. Nevertheless, thought requires the presentation of particular exemplifications of a universal in order for the intellect to apprehend the universal. Universals that are actual natures must exist in their exemplifications. Aristotle argues for this claim in a variety of works for a variety of epistemological and ontological reasons.[11] While these arguments are not made in the psychological treatises, the ontology of real universals manifested in sensible particulars is presupposed there. Because the universal is found in the world, grasping the universal in thought requires a representation of an exemplification of the universal (cf. *An. Post.* I.18, 81a38–b6).

> Since there is no subject that exists separately, so it seems, apart from magnitudes which are objects of perception, objects of thought [*noeta*] exist in perceptible forms, both the objects that are called abstract and those that are states and dispositions of perceptible objects.
>
> *(*De An. *432a3–6)*

Aristotle conceives the relation between perceptible and intelligible objects as one in which the intelligible object exists in the perceptible particular and is grasped in thought in a cognitive state that mirrors the relation between the universal and a particular that exemplifies it in the world. In *De Memoria*, Aristotle points out that the same sensory content can be cognized in different ways; it can be cognized at face value so to speak, as happens in perception; a drawing remains a drawing; the geometer cognizes the actual magnitude of the triangle he is envisaging. Or, the viewer focuses on what the drawn figure represents; the geometer thinks about the imagined triangle as having a magnitude but not a particular magnitude (450a1–5). The second way of taking the sensory content is the analogue to grasping the universal in one of its exemplifications. The exemplification is not cognized as a particular but as an exemplification of the universal. As an exemplification of a human being, Socrates' individuating features, such as being snub-nosed, are ignored and only the nature he shares with other humans is apprehended by the intellect. Typically, the intellect's apprehension of the universal is not through an occurrent perception of a particular exemplifying the universal – although it may be – but rather it is through an image (a sensory content) originating in a perception of (one of) the exemplifications of the universal. For this reason, Aristotle says that thinking requires images (*phantasmata*) (*De An.* 432a12–14; *De Mem.* 450a13).

*Phantasia* is essential to the cognition of universals because the mind needs to have immediate access to sensible particulars exemplifying universals in order to realize the universal as an object of thought. Thinking proper is about universals not particulars. Perception proper is about particulars. *Phantasia* enables the thinker to bring materials from perception to bear on the apprehension of universals that are exemplified by sensible particulars. In order to explain complex behaviors without appealing to rationality, Aristotle develops a notion of representation through sensory contents. This allows him to invoke either *phantasia* or perception as the vehicle for the complex cognitive activities that are required for seemingly intelligent behavior or are required to ground abstract cognitive activities in the world of concrete objects. In the latter case, objects represented sensorially are conceptualized by the mind in a way that enables it to employ symbolic representations as well as sensory ones. Only rational animals are capable of so conceptualizing sensory contents.

Another mark of rationality is the ability to draw inferences. In *De Anima* III, Aristotle invokes *phantasia* to explain this rational capacity as well.

> Perceptive *phantasia* then, as has been said, belongs also to the other animals, but deliberative *phantasia* belongs only to rational animals for whether to do this or that, is already the work of the rational faculty; and it is necessary to measure by one; for a person pursues the greater and so must be able to make one out of many images [*phantasmata*].
>
> *(434a7–19; cf. 431b6–8)*

"Deliberative [*bouleutike*] *phantasia*" is Aristotle's name for the employment of *phantasia* to present sensory contents in a way that enables a rational agent to arrive at a conclusion to do something. It seems to be the same kind of cognitive activity as the cognitive exercise employed in order to recollect a memory in *De Memoria*. In both cases, the mind manipulates a series of images in order to reach a particular result. In both cases, the final cognition is one involving a presentation of a particular. The decision to act is a choice of a particular option from among a range of possibilities; recollection ends in remembering a particular perceived in the past. Aristotle's examples of deliberation, nevertheless, cast light on how he envisages the relation between thought (even if its object is a universal) and *phantasia*. Sensory contents (images) are used as representational devices. The intellect is able to focus on a particular past event or a particular course of action because it has available, through *phantasia*, a sensory representation of the event or the course of action. It may be instructive to compare Aristotle's conception of deliberative *phantasia* to the modern notion of propositional or cognitive imagination. His conception is similar to ours in assigning a representational function to *phantasia*. It differs in one important respect in making sensory contents the vehicle for the representation. Recent philosophical accounts of imagination draw a sharp distinction between cognitive imagination and sensory or imagistic imagination.[12]

In short, *phantasia* provides thought with images that are put to specific uses by the mind. This is accomplished by the way in which the images are conceptualized in the act of thinking. The same image, for instance an image of Socrates, might serve as a way to conceptualize an indefinite number of universals, for instance, human, one, short, snub-nosed, etc. The conceptualizations would be distinct thoughts, each individuated by the universal realized as its object. Thinking just is a way of conceptualizing a sensory content. This explains why Aristotle invokes similarities between the exercise of the perceptual faculty of the soul and the exercise of the rational faculty and at the same time insists upon the distinctness of their objects. Because they have distinct objects, they are distinct cognitive faculties. In contrast to thought, *phantasia*'s object is the same as the object of perception and thus Aristotle says that the capacity for *phantasia* (the *phantastikon*) is the same faculty as the capacity for perception (the *aisthetikon*) (*De Ins.* 459a21–22). The same faculty is sometimes exercised in a way that issues in *phantasia* (imagination) and sometimes exercised in a way that issues in *aisthesis* (perception).

## *Phantasia* and action

Whenever Aristotle talks about the psychological causes of the voluntary movements of animals in general or more specifically about acting deliberately (which only rational animals do), he assigns *phantasia* an important role. Broadly speaking, Aristotle's analysis of voluntary, self-originated movement is in terms of two factors, a cognitive component and an affective one. The bird will not eat the seed from the feeder unless it first perceives the presence and availability of seeds. In addition to this cognitive factor, the bird must also have an active desire for food. If it is satiated and no longer hungry, merely seeing or smelling the seed would be insufficient to prompt movement toward the feeder. Although in the case of human action, the picture may be more complicated and may involve an elaborate chain of reasoning, the two causal factors are the same, namely a cognitive factor and an affective one.

> It is at any rate clear that these two produce movement, either desire or intellect, if one sets down *phantasia* as a kind of thought [*noesis*]; for many follow their

> imaginings [*phantasiai*] against their knowledge, and in the other animals thought and reasoning do not exist, although *phantasia* does.
>
> (De An. *III.10, 433a9–12)*

*Phantasia* is much more likely to provide the crucial cognitive content for movement than either perception proper or thought. This is due to its critical ability to bring forward sensory contents in the absence of an appropriate sensory stimulus in the environment. Not only does the bird go to the feeder when a feeder pops up in its visual or olfactory environment, but it also travels some distance to a feeder where it has found food in the past. When a human agent does something analogous, Aristotle would appeal both to memory and to deliberation (a rational capacity) to explain the action. In the bird's case, he would also appeal to memory but in addition to a further exercise of *phantasia* that enables the bird to arrive at a location where sense perception can take over. The transition between memory and perception is seamless because the sensory content (*phantasma*) that is actualized when remembering the feeder originated in a perception of the feeder and will be replaced as an object of awareness by another perception of the feeder.

The affective and cognitive factors do not operate independently, according to Aristotle. The object as presented in the cognition must be such that it elicits the desire that prompts the animal to act. This requires *phantasia*.

> At the same time, so to speak, that one thinks one ought to go, one also goes, unless something else hinders him. For the affections fittingly prepare the organic parts, and desire prepares the affections, and *phantasia* prepares desire; and *phantasia* arises through thought or through perception.
>
> (De Motu An. *702a16–19)*

Aristotle reasons that something besides the mere perception of food to eat or the mere conclusion that one ought to eat healthy food is required to prompt desire, which in turn moves the agent to consume the cognized food. The something else is the presentation of the object of perception or thought as desirable. *Phantasia* is the vehicle for the required association with pleasure to be integrated with the other sensory features of the object as presented. When the response is one of avoidance rather than desire, *phantasia* has presented the object in a way that included the association of pain with it.[13]

A similar conception of the role *phantasia* plays in triggering pleasures or pains that lead to a decision to act is found in Aristotle's account of anger and feelings of fear and confidence in the *Rhetoric*.

> Since pleasure is the perception of an emotion, and *phantasia* is a weak perception, there will be in the person, remembering something or expecting something, a *phantasia* of that which is remembered or expected.
>
> *(1370a27–30)*

Aristotle goes on to make use of this picture to explain why revenge and the expectation of revenge are pleasant even when the agent is experiencing anger which is in itself a pain at a slight (1378a30–b10). The person who believes that he has been insulted is angry just so long as the pain caused by the insult is present to his consciousness. What keeps it present is the remembered perception of the occasion of the insult and this requires *phantasia*. Also insofar as there is a positive feeling associated with making plans for revenge, *phantasia* is involved in envisioning the anticipated revenge. *Phantasia* can have this dual role as vehicle for memory and expectation because it is a form of sensory representation, which does not require an external object of perception to be present in the immediate environment (cf. 1370a33–35).

Aristotle identifies three types of oratory in the *Rhetoric* – epideictic, forensic and political. He analyzes the structure of emotions in order to help the orator learn how to influence the audience. The goal of the forensic or political orator is to persuade the audience to do something and thus the orator needs to understand what motivates people to act. To this end, Aristotle examines the wellsprings of action – emotions. By emphasizing the role of imagery, Aristotle keeps the orator focused on particular examples that will invoke the desired emotion and insure that a specific course of action is adopted.

A voluntary movement is a singular occurrence; its object, whether pursued or fled from, is always a particular object. The desire to have a house may be general but the house that is built is a particular object. Particulars are objects of perception or *phantasia*. While drawing inferences (about how to proceed in order to build a house) is an exercise of rationality, bringing such reasoning to bear on particular cases always requires *phantasia* or perception. This explains the importance Aristotle attaches to *phantasia* in the cognitive life of human and other animals.

In the interest of brevity, *phantasia*'s role in moral reasoning will not be covered here in detail. However, it is worth noting that Jessica Moss (2012) has argued for the dependence of practical reason on an evaluative cognition of the desired object as good. She identifies the evaluative cognition with a kind of *phantasia*. This would be another case where *phantasia* presents a particular object as desirable by associating the object with pleasure.

In sum, the capability to move voluntarily requires *phantasia*; many rational animals as well as all nonrational ones use *phantasia* to guide their movements. Rational animals can use reason to shape their decisions to act but without *phantasia* they would be unable to engage in this type of reasoning. In addition, the association of pleasure or pain with an object presented to a prospective agent through perception or thought is typically mediated by *phantasia*.[14]

## Conclusion

To return to the question with which this chapter began: does Aristotle have a comprehensive and unified account of *phantasia*? Aristotle appeals to *phantasia* in a wide variety of contexts. He consistently identifies roles for it in sensory experience, in memory and dreaming, in thinking and in acting. In light of this, one might suspect that he is using the same term for very different cognitive activities. Up to a point, this suspicion is justified. What keeps it from being fully justified is the consistency of Aristotle's core concept of *phantasia*. *Phantasia* is exercised under a variety different conditions that result in distinguishable cognitive states; but at its core *phantasia* is always the same. The core conception is the one articulated in *De Anima* III.3. There, after a detailed discussion, the conception of *phantasia* that emerges is that of awareness of a sensory content under conditions which are not conducive to veridical perception. *Phantasia* may occur in the presence of a sensory stimulus under conditions that are unlikely to lead to a veridical perception. If a straight stick, for example, is partially submerged in water, the sensory content is that of a bent stick. Or, the content occurs in the absence of the stimulus as in a memory or in a dream. Or, the content carries with it associations of affective characteristics that go beyond the immediate perceptual situation. Seeing a snake does not require *phantasia*; experiencing the snake as dangerous does.

Were it possible, according to Aristotle, to think about an abstract universal in isolation from all its instances, *phantasia* would not be required for thinking; it is not possible, and so to serve as the source of an instantiation of the universal, *phantasia* is always required for thought. The notion of *phantasia* that Aristotle invokes in all these cases is at core the notion of an active state of awareness of a sensory content that represents a particular object. The context under which a particular occurrence of *phantasia* takes place determines its other, distinguishing features; these mark the occurrence as a dream, a memory, an association of pleasure or pain, or an instantiation of a universal. Aristotle has, it is reasonable to conclude, met the challenge of providing a very versatile and comprehensive account of *phantasia*.

One final question remains: how closely related is the modern notion of imagination to Aristotelian *phantasia*? In several respects, they are similar. Aristotle builds his account around the recognition that *phantasia* is the awareness of an image; it is that in virtue of which images arise in us. His conception of the *phantasma* (image) as a complex of sensible characteristics fits our notion of images having sensory qualities; visual images, for instance, are conceived as having the sensible qualities that are typical of visible objects. Another similarity is the modern association of imagination with creativity. While Aristotle emphasizes this aspect less, his conception of *phantasia* as occurring in the absence of an external stimulus and occurring on occasion as the result of a cognitive agent's efforts provides a basis for the freedom manifested in creative thought.[15] This freedom is also relevant to the modern emphasis on cognitive imagination's role in entertaining propositions, even though the mechanisms are different.[16]

The chief differences between modern accounts and Aristotle's are the consequence of his model of the psyche as consisting of distinct faculties, including in the case of human beings, two cognitive faculties, and the essential role of sensory contents in his account of imagination. His conception of the psyche leaves him with the challenge of explaining the interaction between the perceptual and rational faculties. Aristotle appeals to *phantasia* to explain a variety of cognitive functions, for which the modern notion of imagination (either sensory or propositional) would not be invoked to explain. These include explanations of how the intellect grasps abstract objects and how rational deliberation can issue in action. In short, *phantasia* on Aristotle's account has a larger role to play in the cognitive life of human beings than does imagination; nevertheless, the core conception is remarkably similar. Moreover, recent work in cognitive science has provided some evidence challenging a narrow construal of imagination's cognitive and affective roles. T. Gendler (2010) has argued from empirical findings about imaginative resistance (unwillingness to even imagine morally objectionable scenarios) and imaginative contagion (imagination having similar effects to those of belief and perception) to the conclusion that imagination plays a much greater role in our cognitive and practical lives than has been recognized.[17]

In sum, there are some striking similarities between Aristotle's conception of *phantasia* and recent work on imagination, several notable differences notwithstanding.

## Notes

1 In the remainder of this paper, I will use Aristotle's term, *phantasia*, rather than the English term, imagination. This will allow the reader to appreciate how broad Aristotle's conception of *phantasia* is and to concentrate on the parameters of *phantasia* without trying to fit it into modern notions of imagination. The abbreviations of the cited works of Aristotle are as follows: *An. Post.*, *Analytica Posteriora* ("Posterior Analytics"); *De An.*, *De Anima* ("On the Soul"); *De Ins.*, *De Insommiis* ("On Dreams"); *De Mem.*, *De Memoria* ("On Memory"); *De Motu An.*, *De Motu Animalium* ("On the Movement of Animals"); *Div. Somn.*, *De Divinatione per Somnia* ("Divination in Sleep").

2 Aristotle also mentions the metaphorical use of *phantasia* only to set it aside in III.3. There is no evidence that when Aristotle appeals to *phantasia* in other places that he is using the term metaphorically.

3 For a detailed defense of the Sensory Content Analysis of *phantasia*, see Modrak 1986 and 1987.

4 See, e.g., Nussbaum 1978, 223–321. Conceiving *phantasia* as appearances has prompted other commentators to downplay the role of imagery in it. See, e.g., Schofield 1978, 102.
5 See, for a different interpretation of the canonical account, Wedin 1988, ch. 2, which argues for the functional incompleteness of *phantasia*.
6 Cf. Schofield 1978, which characterizes Aristotle's conception of imagination in III.3 as nonparadigmatic sensory experience.
7 Below *phantasma* will be translated as "image."
8 Aristotle refers to mnemonic devices at *De Ins.* 458b20–24 and elsewhere. There is a detailed discussion of ancient Greek mnemonic techniques in Sorabji 1972, 22–34.
9 Aristotle, *De Insomniis* and *De Divinatione per Somnum*.
10 For a detailed discussion of the grounds for identifying *phantasia* with the cognitive activity required for the use of language, see Modrak 2001, ch. 7.
11 It is beyond the scope of this paper to review Aristotle's arguments for his conception of universals. For an extended and detailed argument for the claims made here, see Modrak 2001.
12 See McGinn (2009), "Imagination," in the *Oxford Handbook of Philosophy of Mind;* see also Nichols' (2006) introduction to *The Architecture of the Imagination*, which argues for the centrality of propositional imagination in many cognitive activities, including hypothetical reasoning.
13 Aristotle appeals to pleasure and pain to explain action; in both cases, he uses the terms in a generic sense; the feelings of pleasure might be mild and those of pain, mere discomfort, or they might be quite intense.
14 Aristotle is interested in giving a general account of voluntary movement and to this end he insists upon a role for *phantasia* in contrast to perception or thought. He does not insist that every cognition triggering a voluntary motion involves *phantasia*, although many do.
15 See Dustin Stokes, Chapter 18, on imagination and creativity.
16 Nichols, "Imaginative Blocks and Impossibility: An Essay in Modal Psychology," in Nichols 2006.
17 Gendler 2010, esp. chs. 7, 9, and 12.

## References

Gendler, T.S. (2010) *Intuition, Imagination, and Philosophical Inquiry*, Oxford: Oxford University Press.

Modrak, D.K. (1986) "Phantasia Reconsidered," in *Archiv für Geschichte der Philosophie* 68: 47–69.

Modrak, D.K. (1987) *Aristotle: The Power of Perception*, Chicago: University of Chicago Press.

Modrak, D.K. (2001) *Aristotle's Theory of Language and Meaning*, Cambridge: Cambridge University Press.

Moss, J. (2012) *Aristotle on the Apparent Good: Perception, Phantasia, Thought and Desire*, Oxford: Oxford University Press.

Nichols, S. (ed.) (2006) *The Architecture of the Imagination: New Essays on Pretence, Possibility, and Fiction*, Oxford: Oxford University Press.

Nussbaum, M. (1978) *Aristotle's De Motu Animalium*, Princeton: Princeton University Press.

Schofield, M. (1978) "Aristotle on Imagination," in G.E.R. Lloyd and G.E.L. Owen (eds.) *Aristotle on Mind and the Senses: Proceedings of the Seventh Symposium Aristotelicum*, Cambridge: Cambridge University Press.

Sorabji, R. (trans. and commentary) (1972) *Aristotle on Memory*, Providence, RI: Brown University Press.

Wedin, M. (1988) *Mind and Imagination in Aristotle*, New Haven: Yale University Press.

# 2
# DESCARTES

*Dennis L. Sepper*

René Descartes (1596–1650) has rarely been regarded as a major philosopher of imagination. One reason is that the writings in which imagination featured most centrally were published either just before his death or posthumously; they had little effect on how Descartes was interpreted. Other reasons have more to do with us than with him: it seems improbable to us that imagination can figure large in modern rationalism, and the now century-old tradition of antipsychologism in professional philosophy and psychology makes it seem unlikely we can learn much from old-fashioned philosophical psychology.

It is one thing to claim we should reassess Descartes's conception of imagination; it is quite another to argue (as this essay does) that he transformed the theory and the function of imagination in Western culture. This transformation happened because of his *practice* of imagining in mathematics and science. Descartes's imagination was revolutionary despite its being neglected *ad litteram*, because it was intrinsic to the physicomathematical theorizing he initiated and that following centuries emulated with passion. Descartes thus stands, with figures like Aristotle and Kant, as one of a handful of Western thinkers who have philosophized about imagination in a way that profoundly shaped the future, and very nearly unique in combining such philosophizing with a new imaginative practice.

## The problematics of imagination before Descartes

At the Jesuit Collège Henri IV in La Flèche, France, which Descartes attended for eight and a half years (probably 1607–15), he was schooled in the Aristotelian tradition of late medieval Latin scholasticism.[1] This tradition – in psychology drawing above all from Aristotle's *On the Soul* (*De Anima*) and associated philosophical and medical developments in late ancient and medieval Islamic and Jewish thought – regarded the human soul as an embodied activity of interacting powers (see also Deborah K.W. Modrak, "Aristotle on *Phantasia*," Chapter 1 of this volume). There were (1) intellectual powers plus (2) *internal senses* possessed by at least some animals (memory, imagination/phantasy, and common sense), and (3) *external senses* possessed by most or all animals (touch, taste, smell, hearing, and vision). Soul, in the first instance, was understood as form to the matter of the living body (whether the life was vegetal, animal, or animal-human); more particularly, soul and its powers were the *activity of the organized body potentiated with life.* [2]

External sensation was an activity in the sense organ. Sensible qualities, say an apple's *being red*, were conceived as an activity in the thing giving rise to a motion. The motion was physically conveyed through a medium from object to organ, and in the latter it set off new activity. The activity in the sense organ was said to be the same as in the object, though without the original matter. Furthermore, Aristotle understood differences of sense quality (e.g., between red and blue) as differences in the ratios of the qualitative activity in the sense organ. Differences in sensation thus corresponded to mathematically proportional differences in both object and organ.

Internal sensation commenced when and where the five external senses came together in the body so as to produce a common *field* of sense experience. This was called common sense. The forms of the experience of the individual senses and of common sense – forms called *species* or *phantasms*, eventually known as *ideas* and *images* – could be physiologically preserved, for future psychological reactivation, by being passed to other parts of the body. Memory and imagination, along with common sense, were the universally acknowledged internal senses, though further refinements and subdivisions were common in medieval authors. Often added was another internal sense, called *estimativa* in animals and *cogitativa* in human animals, which attached valuations (like instinctive liking or fear) to the phantasms. In human beings, it further served to attach concepts to phantasms: this thing before me thus can be called "apple" and "red." All these internal sense activities were regarded as localized in the hollows between the two brain hemispheres known as *ventricles*.[3]

Aristotle defined sensation in general as a motion (*kinêsis*) and imagination as a follow-on motion originating in the activity of sensation (*On the Soul* III.3). When the activity of sensation starts its follow-on motion, that motion goes elsewhere in the body; when it reaches its destination it completes itself by reactivating the phantasm-appearance presented originally in the sense organ's activity. From there other new motions can follow: for example, a common sensation can be moved to a memory location and preserved there for future reactivation. In human beings, the goal of the imagination-motion is to reactivate phantasm-appearances so that intellect can discover, grasp, and thus think the forms of intelligibility implicit in them. This principle was formalized in the Aristotelian dictum that *there is no thinking without phantasms*. For strict Aristotelians, there can be no such thing as purely intellectual thinking. All thinking – all theoretical, practical, artistic-technical, probabilistic, and scientific reasoning – requires phantasms or images, thus imagination or other internal senses.

Platonism more easily accepted the possibility of pure thinking, one without the assistance of images. Nevertheless, a close reading of Platonist traditions shows that they had more than a little difficulty in suppressing images. One reason was the ancient neo-Platonic attempt to reconcile Aristotle and Plato. In psychology, Aristotle was usually considered the greater master. Another was Plato's dialogues, in which the ascent to the Platonic forms always commences with images in and of the material world; moreover, the forms always retain the unfortunate penchant (from the perspective of pure rationalism) for producing material forms and images. The tradition of Platonism through Proclus even gave rise to a conviction that the realm of mathematics required the existence of an *intelligible matter* in which mathematical entities were realized. This implied that there was another kind of imagination besides sensory imagination: a *higher, more rational* kind that allowed human beings to think and produce mathematical things (Nikulin 2002).

With this Aristotelian and Platonic background it is easier to see the significance of Descartes's own distinctive and revolutionary conception of imagination.

## Descartes, thinking through the tradition

The earliest extant writings of Descartes, from 1618 to the early 1620s (but published posthumously), contain relatively little *theory* of imagining, but they provide abundant evidence of how he *used* it and of how thoroughly it pervaded his thought-practices. The small amount of theory is nevertheless pregnant with consequences.

In the short, early treatise *Compendium of Music* (1618) Descartes used abundant figures and images to represent musical relations. (There was, of course, already a long tradition of using figures in discussions of musical theory.) The basic premises, stipulated at the outset as postulates, reflect a quasi-Aristotelian psychological understanding of music based on the physical and physiological embodiment of mathematical proportions in sound. The one passage in which the term "imagination" is used presents it as a dynamic power of grasping, projecting, and synthesizing the proportional relations in musical rhythm.

> When we hear the first two parts [*or* notes, in a musical phrase], we conceive them as one; when [we hear] the third part, we now conjoin that with the first ones, so that the proportion is triple; thereafter, when we hear the fourth, we join that with the third so that we conceive [them] as one; thereupon we again conjoin the two first with the latter two so that we conceive these four simultaneously as one. And thus our imagination [*imaginatio*] proceeds all the way to the end, where finally it conceives the entire song as one thing fused out of many equal parts.
>
> *(AT 10: 94)*

This process is conjectural and self-correcting; a song's meter is fully determined only after hearing several beats, but it continues, both retrospectively and projectively, until the entire piece has been heard. This first Cartesian presentation of the imaginative power is all the more remarkable in that it anticipates the complex dynamism and psychophysiological interactivity that imagination displayed in his later scientific and philosophical thought.

Notebooks that Descartes was keeping around this time show a very early interest in topics that feature in later work: (1) the psychological power called *ingenium*, (2) the roles of imagination and memory in cognition, and (3) active mathematical and scientific imagining as such.

(1) *Ingenium* is a common term in early modern thought, especially in rhetoric. It indicates wit, spirit, and inventiveness; more generally, personal character (a person's native spirit). The French term corresponding to both is *esprit*.[4] Descartes's notes consider many examples of how differences in *ingenium* lead to different kinds of responsiveness to situations and stimuli.

(2) Rhetorical manuals taught the *art of memory*, which contrived images both for the sake of recalling speeches and for retaining acquired knowledge. One of the typical practices of this memory art involved, first, committing to memory a familiar place, like the interior of a basilica, and then populating its various parts with vivid images devised for representing the successive topics, sections, and even individual sentences of a speech. They could then be recovered by taking an imaginary walk through the place. Each image was designed to be maximally memorable, and even if there were certain conventions and rules of thumb, the important thing was that it was memorable for the speaker-rememberer, not for anyone else.

In a note from the early 1620s Descartes criticizes a fairly typical version of memory art, then proposes an alternative as the "true art of memory" (AT 10: 230). Although the details are somewhat obscure, Descartes uses images of projectiles hurled up and down a staircase to express ratios existing between different elements or components of a problem. His rationale makes abundantly clear the aim: a way of proceeding that allows each new image to evolve in a regulated way from the images that precede. That is, Descartes's suggested technique abandons arbitrary single images in favor of multiple images interconnected by proportions. The proportional, thus mathematically expressible, relations could be actively generated from one another according to a rule-governed physical model. The proportions, or ratios, provide a governing principle of *rationality*.

Other more "poetic" notes also have programmatic significance. One concludes with a reflection that poets manage to express more "weighty judgments" than philosophers because they work "through enthusiasm and the force of imagination." Philosophers try to extract, as though from flintstone, "seeds of knowledge" with reason, whereas "by poets they are driven out through imagination and shine out all the more." The preceding paragraph remarks that "as imagination uses figures to conceive bodies, so intellect uses certain sensible bodies to figure spiritual things, like wind and light: from which, philosophizing, we can by cognition raise the mind higher into the sublime" (AT 10: 217). On the one hand, this sounds more like Renaissance musings than early modern rationalism. Understanding occurs by analogy (recalling that *analogia* for the Greeks meant extended proportion: *a* is to *b* as *c* is to *d*, or, more arithmetically, $a/b = c/d$). On the other hand, it suggests the biplanar, or multiplanar, projective character of Descartes's later imagination. In the realm, or plane, of sensation one experiences bodies, projects them by geometrical figuration into a mathematically imaginative plane, and then by arithmetic formulation into a more abstractly imaginative plane. One can also start with bodies and project them analogically to figure the spiritual realm.

(3) From these origins emerged the first flowering of Descartes's imagination in many mathematical and scientific notes. He situates points, lines, or two-dimensional figures in space, then sets them moving, sliding, and rotating with respect to one another. Imagined points get subjected to multiple straight-line impulses compelling them to move in straight or curved lines. Lines and figures rotate in two or three dimensions, with other points and lines providing the frame of reference (the first anticipation of coordinates). The lines and figures are made proportionate to problem elements, so that the relations that evolve through the motions, rotations, and translations express new proportions and generate new figures with lengths and areas that solve the original problem. Thus Descartes was taking very seriously what he had proposed as an improvement to the memory art: to use simple images representing the elements of a problem and then to generate from them new images according to exacting rules and principles of proportioned relations. This was his way of thinking through phantasms. He adapted these speculations to propose new types of calculating instruments (called "compasses") based on such carefully regulated and interrelated (in fact, interlocking) motions.

These early practices led almost seamlessly to the work that many scholars consider to be the first philosophically serious, though unfinished, work of Descartes, *Regulae ad directionem ingenii* (*Rules for the Direction of the Spirit*).[5] It was planned in three parts of twelve rules each. The use of geometric and other kinds of representative figures for solving problems is mentioned at the end of the first part (in Rule 12) and partially developed in the next (Descartes stopped in the middle of this part). Rule 14 argues that the technique can and should be applied to arrive at knowledge about *everything* capable of being imagined. Moreover, an underlying principle of the *Regulae* is that anything that can in some respect be ordered or measured is capable of being represented to the imagination. For example, although the relation of father to children is not accessible to the senses or directly picturable, it can be represented/imaged in a genealogy chart (a simple example of which Descartes gives in Rule 14).

The *Regulae* as a whole is Descartes's execution of the "noblest example" of problems, as he calls it in Rule 8 (AT 10: 395). The problem requires determining how intellect arrives at knowledge by cooperating with its adjutant's sensation, memory, and imagination. Rule 12 explains the underlying rationale. The sense organs receive from things in the world an impression, essentially a two-dimensional pattern, on their receptive parts. This image-impression is transmitted by the nerves to the organ of common sense, and from there the image-impression travels on to the *phantasia*-organ (the organ of imagination), which can send the result to be preserved in memory locations in the brain (and receive them back when needed) or can convey them to the knowing power (*vis cognoscens*). The knowing power in turn can form new images in the *phantasia*, and it can extend its operation into other parts of the body, always by means of the *phantasia*: to common sense and the individual senses, to the places of memory, or to the nerves and the motor functions of the body. This is Descartes's modernized version of Aristotelian physiological psychology.

In a crucial passage of Rule 12, Descartes discusses the knowing power as "purely spiritual." He says that it is "one and the same power" in all its operations:

> if it applies itself with imagination to the common sense it is called seeing, touching, etc.; if to the imagination alone, insofar as that is outfitted with diverse figures, it is called remembering; if to the same [imagination] as shaping new ones, it is called imagining or conceiving; if finally it acts alone, it is called understanding … . And also for that reason this same power joined to these diverse functions is called either pure intellect, or imagination, or memory, or sense; it is properly declared *ingenium* when it sometimes forms new ideas in the *phantasia*-organ, sometimes bears down on those already made.
>
> *(AT 10: 415–416)*

In this passage Descartes says four important things for our purposes. He declares that every perceptive or cognitive act is an act of the spiritual knowing power; that except when the knowing power acts on its own it acts in or through the imagination; that imagining and conceiving are the same action; and that *ingenium* in its most proper sense is the power of forming and attending to images in the organ of imagination. If the knowing power or intellect is king of the cognitive life of human beings, imagination is viceroy, and nothing that has to do with the world or the body bypasses it. The second part of the *Regulae* then goes on to explore how one can use images to address any problem involving order and measure.

Imagination makes two remarkable cameo appearances earlier in the first part. The first occurs in Rule 3, in the definition of the most basic cognitive act of the mind, *intuitus*/intuition. Descartes begins to define it negatively, as *not* "the fluctuating confidence of the senses, nor the fallacious judgment of a badly composing imagination" (AT 10: 368). That is not an indictment of imagination; it is a criticism of its bad use. The *Regulae* intends to forestall bad usage by teaching the right use of *ingenium*, the power of forming and attending to images. When imagination is used properly it can take indubitable, "easy and distinct concepts of a pure and attentive mind" – the positive definition of what results from *intuitus* – and combine them in acts of step-by-step deduction. In Rule 7 he accordingly refers to "a continuous and in no way interrupted motion of thought." A few lines later comes the second cameo appearance: this motion of thought is a "continuous motion of imagination" (AT 10: 387–388).[6]

In any case, "the whole secret of the art" of the *Regulae*, as Descartes calls it in Rule 6, takes all things we encounter and promptly orders and measures them for their proportional participation in different natures, the most fundamental of which are called *simple natures*.

What can count as a nature is extraordinarily flexible. The leading example of Rule 6 takes the number 3 as a nature which is participated in differently by 12 and 48 (namely, the former contains the nature four times, the latter sixteen times).[7] It is these proportionalized measures of participation that form the evidentiary basis for the geometric and algebraic representation that is taught in the second part of the book, the use of which enables the mind to continuously and uninterruptedly move from problem to solution by means of imagination. It is too simplistic and too rationalistic to call this a "mathematization of thought," even if Descartes refers to *mathêsis universalis* as the inspiration for the *Regulae*. That universal *mathêsis* is grounded by the participation of things in proportionally representable order and measure. This type of "mathematization" is a byproduct of imagination's regulated use. Descartes does not mathematize thought so much as make it rigorously imaginative.

## The transition to the canonical works

As Jean-Luc Marion has argued, the *Regulae* develops an imperfect, chiefly implicit ontology of simple natures (call it quasi-Platonist) that is at odds with the dualistic division of everything into thinking thing and extended thing Descartes arrived at soon thereafter (Marion 2015). The dualism – which Descartes, always very careful with terms, called the "real distinction between thinking and extension" – appears at latest by the time of *The World*, which Descartes composed in the period 1630–33 but did not publish after Galileo was convicted of heresy for teaching heliocentrism (which *The World* supported).

If the earlier philosophy used imagination both strictly and analogously, the later uses it in a more rigorous way. Descartes effectively announces this in a letter of April 15, 1630, where he introduces the notion of the *mathematical truths*, which his correspondent insisted on calling "(created) eternal truths" (AT 1: 144–145). This notion was a consequence of the metaphysical thinking he undertook during a nine-month stay in Holland (1628–29), the central focus of which, he says, was to know God and himself – perhaps an extension of the noblest problem of Rule 8 – but which also led him to discover the foundations of physics, laid out in the opening chapters of *The World*. The basic reasoning behind the mathematical truths is simple: God could have created the world in any way that pleased him. He chose to create it in a way that observed simple mathematical regularities, in particular the tendency to straight-line motion. God also endowed human beings with the ability to grasp these regularities and to represent and conceive the universe accordingly in imagination. Imagination can be random and willful – it can imagine, for instance, that the natural tendency of all things is circular, or erratically swerving – but when it is directed by the intellect's apprehension of simple principles, it can produce a virtually perfect model of the actual universe. The universe conceived in the imagination under the direction of intellect is an image of the actual universe as a whole. In such a world and for such a mind, the imagination no longer works by conceptual analogy – the proportional interparticipation of natures – but literally. It produces an imaginary realm that is three-dimensionally spatial, divisible, and mobile in perfect proportion to real space.

In this light, there is no unbridgeable gap between the imagination of Descartes's early philosophizing and the mature mathematical and physical works. The figurate representation of the early phase is retained, as is the guidance of the imaginative *ingenium*/spirit by the highest knowing power. Imagination has, as always, a physical location and a specific psychical character. It continues to be biplanar: it has presented to it forms of things that it then reconfigures into more abstracted forms (like geometric figures) and yet again into the symbolic yet still at least minimally concrete and materially referential sign-images of algebra. This abstractive imagining can be reversed, in the direction of concretion, with the possibility of making it so concrete that it becomes a direct image of a real-world problem. This method does not aim to settle issues of the natures of things but of their interrelationships. The new version of imagining, however, stipulates a single, real simple nature underlying all these possibilities: extension, the extension of space-matter. This means, for example, that there is no longer need to talk of colors in things or colors impressed on the retina (which the *Regulae* does; AT 10: 412–413): one can deal only and entirely in terms of extension, its motions, and its tendencies to motion. Only in consciousness does one need to change to the language of colors. Thus the new imagining gains a coherence, consistency, and exactitude that makes it sovereign in understanding by producing and reproducing the motions exhibited in the created world. A question left unresolved in Rule 12 – whether the way of understanding according to natures corresponds to the way things are (AT 10: 418) – is answered positively by reducing all corporeal natures to extension.

*The World* and the 1637 *Geometry* (the third of three scientific essays, to which the *Discourse on the Method* was preface) thus carry out more perfectly and completely the project of the 1620s by virtue of the real distinction between thinking and extension established through Descartes's metaphysical philosophizing in Holland. It is no accident that in *The World* Descartes begins constructing an exact model of the real universe by resorting to "imaginary spaces" (AT 11: 31). The *Geometry* then executes a thoroughgoing and comprehensive isomorphism between the things and motions in space, the geometric representation of the lines and figures these trace, and the formulaic symbolization in algebra of the parts and the proportions exhibited by the geometrical entities – in two words, the *analytic geometry* that Descartes invented. These mental gymnastics are the rigorous work of the biplanar projective imagination that Descartes had begun conceiving in his earliest writings. That is not to minimize the originality of the *Geometry* but rather to understand it as bringing rigorous imagining to completion. To those who think there is a substantial difference between the early and the later method, it should be sufficient to point out what Leslie Beck demonstrated half a century ago: the paragraphs immediately following the enunciation of the four rules of method in part 2 of the *Discourse* unmistakably describe Descartes's continuing commitment to the imaginative processes he had begun formally articulating in the rules of the *Regulae* (Beck 1952).

Thus Descartes established a way of imagination that became the field of play for future science and mathematics. Even as researchers opened further realms of rigorous imagining untouched by Descartes, they followed the same strategy of intellectually guided, biplanar imaginative projection that he had presented as the most basic way to human knowledge – a way predicated on the right use of intellect and all its adjutants. Frequently enough, however, those who cultivated it conceived it as nonimaginative, as the work of pure intellect. And that leads us to the problem of imagination in Descartes's later canonical works.

## Imagination after the *Discourse*

Descartes's revolutionary theory of imagination appears to go into eclipse in the *Meditations*. Although imagination is a kind of thinking, it may not belong to the essence of a thinking thing taken precisely as such (AT 7: 28). The phantasms/ideas of sensation often conflict. Hallucinations and dreams are deceptive. The greatest genius in geometry cannot clearly and distinctly imagine a thousand-sided figure, whereas the intellect has no problem conceiving it. Imagination appears as a minor, negligible, and defective power.

Yet imagination keeps slipping back in even after being dismissed. In Meditation 1, after discussing madmen and dreamers, the meditator turns to mathematics, which, as we have seen, is a preeminently imaginative activity for Descartes. Only the doubtful notion that God created us to err about even the simplest mathematical things casts any doubt on mathematical truth. At this point the meditator, growing fatigued and finding old prejudices rooted in memory returning, resolves to treat *everything* that appears to him as "false and imaginary." He reinforces the decision by supposing there is a "malign genius, supremely powerful and cunning" (AT 7: 22), who devotes all his efforts to deceiving the meditator. The genius is a willed device of rigorous (though not mathematical) imagining. In Meditation 2, having proved his existence strictly as a thinking thing, the meditator exercises imagination to try to conceive all possible appearances of a piece of wax. They are limitless, so he concludes that it is thinking proper, not imagination, that conceives the wax as a single substance. To prove the existence of God in Meditation 3, the meditator first rehearses once again all imaginable things that appear to consciousness (as he does also at the very beginning of Meditation 2 in recapitulating Meditation 1), now with the emphasis on their classification and on what causes them all. Just as at the end of Meditation 2, in Meditation 3 he discovers that a new limitlessness – real, positive infinity – escapes imagination's power, but not that of intellectual perception.

The strategy of the *Meditations* is, put very generally, to exercise the lower powers of the meditator – most of all and most properly the power of imagination – until the meditator reaches a point where they have to be, and are, transcended. Nevertheless, there are very few things we know through this transcending power of intellect acting alone (self's existence in Meditation 2, God's existence in Meditation 3). The return to the realm of extension and embodied powers (starting at the very end of Meditation 5[8] and proceeding through Meditation 6) finally shows that imagination and the other lower powers exist less for the sake of science than for the sake of survival, of maintaining the union between soul and body. These powers are not of the meditator's most precise essence as thinking thing, but they are part of his whole being or nature (which is called "the intercombination [*complexionem*] of all those things bestowed on me by God," AT 7: 80).

In the *Regulae* Descartes had invoked a medieval method (*remotio*) in his careful differentiation of how we must use images to understand the truth of similar statements such as "extension occupies place," "the extended occupies place," "body has extension," and "extension is not body" (see AT 10: 443–446). Of these four, the first three, to be true, require forming and holding certain appropriate images in mind, although even they severally require different kinds of "taking-in" of the image. However, understanding the fourth, a negation, does not intrinsically involve viewing an image. Instead, it works by conceiving the universalized meaning of "extension" and recognizing that any viewed image of body falls short of the totalizing universality of that subject term. This is remotion, a moving away from imagination to intellection.[9] First one imagines, then one moves away from imagining as inadequate for the intended purpose. The method of the *Meditations* is, similarly, to imagine as extensively and rigorously as possible – though not necessarily in mathematical form – and then for a few brief moments of essential insight to stop imagining, because any image is misleading. Then one immediately resumes imagining.

When we take the *Meditations* as the endpoint and goal of Cartesian philosophy, we implicitly make the same mistake as the Princess Elisabeth of the Palatinate (1618–80; also called Elisabeth of Bohemia). In the first letter she ever sent to Descartes (May 6, 1643, AT 3: 660) she asked him to expand the account of how matter and soul interact in his metaphysical system, the soul "being only a thinking substance." Descartes makes a subtle correction in his response. Her question appears to him most reasonable in light of his published writings, he says, "because, there being two things in the human soul on which depends all the knowledge we can have of its nature, one is that it thinks, the other is that, being united to the body, it can act and suffer with it." In those writings, he says, there is almost nothing about the second point, since his main aim was "to prove the distinction between soul and body" (May 21, 1643, AT 3: 664–665). Thus begins Descartes's genuine treatment of how the soul acts and suffers with the body, much of it in the continuing correspondence with Elisabeth. It culminated in his last canonical work, published just five months before his death, *The Passions of the Soul* (1649). Many interpret the *Passions* according to a superficial impression they find reinforced by Descartes's claim that he wrote it *en physicien*: as an application of Cartesian mechanical science to human physiology. But in Descartes's day the meaning of *en physicien* was less "as physicist" than "as physician," in the sense of a medical doctor who can address soul as well as body, with the goal of helping the patient live well.

The *Passions* presents the doctrine of passions as not foundationally a matter of rhetoric or ethics, as it had been traditionally presented, but as a question of psychophysiology. In particular, the body and the mind interact in noncognitive consciousness as much as in cognitive ways. The key to working out the problem follows the lead of Descartes's physiological physics and psychology. In earlier writings he had presented the "operating" system of the body as the network of nerves and brain filled with animal spirits, with the organ of imagination the key point of relay between body and intellect. The physiological system, it turns out in the *Passions*, has a character that leads not just to sensation, images, and thought but also to affect and feeling.

Book 1 of the *Passions* presents the basic phenomena of the psychophysiology his earlier work had established; then books 2 and 3 develop in detail the role passions and affects play therein. Nerves convey to the brain the impulses impinging on nerve endings in the sense organs. In the brain the impulses reach the other end of the nerves, which open into the central hollows that are filled with animal spirits and in which the pineal gland is suspended. The motions that the nerve impulses transfer to the animal spirits affect/move the surface of the gland and trace image pressure-patterns there. Associated with these, by God's fundamental institution of the soul–body connection as modified by experience, are conscious mind-events. In animals and in automatic human behavior a counteraction can commence at this point, without any higher mental activity, because the gland can impress a new motion, radiating outward through the spirits back toward the periphery of the brain chamber. Sometimes this radiating motion activates places in the brain where images are stored, sometimes it leads to outwardly directed nerve impulses that produce muscle contractions, etc.

There is also in human beings the power not just to attend to images produced by pineal-gland motions but also to vary and change those images and to form new ones. In the *Regulae* this was the function of *ingenium*. What guides this power, according to the *Passions*, is will. The images actively formed by imagination are the product of *voluntatês*, of acts of will.

The *Passions* argues that, like everything else that changes, the thinking thing can be looked at under a passive aspect and an active aspect. The passive aspect of thinking is perception, whether intellectual or sensitive. Most readers of Descartes wrongly take this aspect as the most noble and proper in the thinking thing. But even perceived intellectual ideas, like positive infinity, God, or the self as thinking, are passivities. What is active and at work in these events is will.[10] And what is most surprising for the philosopher of imagination is that active imagination is will's direct action in the body. If intellection is understood as the perception of truth, and imagination as an activity of will, then imagination is more characteristic and representative of the active nature of the thinking thing than is intellect!

That is a deliberatively provocative way of putting a basic Cartesian truth. From the time of the *Regulae* Descartes's cognitive questioning was not just about a search for truth and its criterion (what made an intuition true) but also the question of where the mind should go and what it should do at every single step in its search for truth (a practical and ethical question of method and order). The will to truth is at least as basic to the thinking thing as is the recognition of truth; truths are sought not for their own sake but because they help guide human action, whether that is cognitive action or intelligent bodily action. In this sense imagination is a more appropriate medium for conceiving human things and actions than pure intellection. There would be no productive imagination of this type if there were no intellectual perception, it is true, but even the highest intellectual perception is the passive side of an act of will. The descent of human being from the highest "rationalist" moments (of God and self as thinking thing) back into the imaginative mathematical and personal world is always swift and foreordained by human finitude and human nature.

There is one last lesson to be learned from the *Passions*' psychophysiology. In the pineal-gland chamber the image-impressions move through the animal spirits from nerve ends to gland (and perception) and from (will and) gland to memory locations and muscles. This human physiology sustains the worldly effectiveness of will, intellect, and imagination. Animal spirits, as a fluid in the nerves and the pineal-gland chamber, are subject to roilings, eddies, and turbulence. This is where passions enter into the system. Because of the way the body's organs work, there are many essential but also incidental stimuli of animal spirit motions that can produce as byproduct conscious but not directly cognitive effects – feelings, affects, and passions. The second and third parts of the *Passions* are devoted to these phenomena, and they provide not only a detailed accounting of mind–body interaction far beyond anything Descartes had written before but also give substance to an understanding of precisely what Descartes meant when he justified sensation in Meditation 6 as oriented to the maintenance of the mind-body union, thus not primarily to truth. What the system of passions does is provide a preferential orientation of the body-mind union through physiology and attendant feeling to certain types of objects and certain typical responses to them. These can also be shaped by will and its regulated imagination into virtues (or vices), although the will cannot in fact directly affect the passions (one cannot stop being afraid by simply willing not to be, for example); it can do this only through reasoning implemented by imagining. Thus the *Passions* is a kind of prolegomenon to an unwritten Cartesian ethics of the willing-understanding-imagining being that is *Homo sapiens*. It establishes not merely ways to manage and control the passions but also to exercise them for the benefit of the human being as a whole. In the last analysis, in the words of the last paragraph of the *Passions*, those whom the passions "can move the most are capable of tasting the greatest sweetness in this life" (AT 11: 488) and able to benefit from accompanying evils.[11] Imagination, for Descartes the principal way thought – never as pure intellect – works in and through body, turns out to be the principal instrument of living well.

## Legacy

Many of Descartes's contemporaries and immediate followers recognized how essential imagination was to his conception of mathematics and science, but some were wary of its broader use. For example, Blaise Pascal, in the *Pensées*, showed a typical ambivalence about imagination. On the one hand, like Descartes he sees it as necessary for understanding the physics of the world and for representing the best knowledge human beings have of it, in mathematical form. On the other hand, it degrades human beings by immersing them in trivialities and vanities that subject them to the blandishments of the corporeal and social worlds and thus distract them from the spiritual path to God. A more historically effective seventeenth-century expression of a similarly ambivalent Christian view is found in Malebranche, whose intellectual career was transformed by his early discovery of Descartes's posthumously published treatise *On Man*. In his classic *Search for Truth* he elaborated the Cartesian psychophysiology of imagination in light of human fallenness in order to demonstrate its corporeal and social pathologies – a strong-willed personality, for example, can exert malign influence on weaker souls through the physical effects of his powerful imagination. Malebranche nevertheless still acknowledged and affirmed, as Pascal and others had, the importantly and essentially imaginative character of mathematics and the sciences.

Nevertheless, because the reception of Descartes's philosophy as rationalist and mechanist had hardened by the mid-1640s and because nothing of the early notes and speculations entered the public domain until decades, even centuries, later, scarcely anyone noticed the larger significance and tonality of the *Passions*' account. A faulty assumption – that the metaphysics of Cartesian consciousness implies the priority of intellect over imagination and will – led most readers to the conclusion that, for Descartes, the imagination was inessential and even unimportant.

In the course of the later seventeenth and the early eighteenth centuries there was an increasing tendency in European thought to take mathematics, especially in its algebraic and analytic forms, as essentially an exercise of pure intellect.[12] Descartes's insights into its fundamentally imaginative character were lost from view. Imagination came to be ever more closely associated with mere aesthetics, arbitrariness, and deception. A living sense for the relation between imagination and intellect that in Aristotle had been expressed as intellect's power to think the intelligibilities in images and in Descartes as biplanar, projective imagination – not to mention in imagination's ethical significance – disappeared from Western experience. The split between rationality and imagination that eventually produced the Romantic rebellion was thus prefigured by the failure to recognize how deeply reason is rooted in the anthropology and psychology of imagination.

## Acknowledgments

I owe a special thank-you to Amy Kind and an anonymous reviewer for their very helpful remarks and corrections.

## Notes

1 For biographical matters see Rodis-Lewis 1998. Descartes's works will be cited by volume and page in the great eleven-volume French and Latin edition edited by Charles Adam and Paul Tannery (universally referred to as "AT"). Readers of Descartes in English should be forewarned that translations of psychological terms are often misleading or inconsistent. For example, the currently most-cited translation of the *Regulae ad directionem ingenii* renders *ingenium* in four different ways. All translations in this essay are my own; they are usually very literal.

2 For a brief account of the history of imagination before Descartes, see Harvey 1975 and Hatfield 1998.

3 Aristotle himself had preferred locating them near the heart. The pineal gland of Cartesian fame is located in these hollows. See Smith et al. 2012.

4 In Descartes's French writings it is typical to find *esprit* where the Latin has, or would be expected to have, *ingenium*.

5 I shall refer to the work as a whole as *Regulae*; individual rules will be identified in the format "Rule *n*." In the 1960s some scholars started to contend that Descartes began the *Regulae* as early as 1619, but the older notion that it dates entirely from the mid- to late 1620s seems more probable again in light of

the discovery of a copy of an early manuscript version at the University of Cambridge library by Richard Serjeantson. Although Descartes himself apparently did not give any title to the work, *ingenium* is central to the argument and one of the most frequently occurring terms. In English it has long been customary to translate it as "mind," but recent work has suggested better alternatives, like "native intelligence."

6 This latter phrase is sometimes emended, replacing *imaginatio* with *cogitatio*, but that contradicts both the published Latin version, known as "A," and the copy, likely commissioned by Leibniz and called "H," of another manuscript version.

7 Color (whiteness), sharpness (of tone), and anything at all that can be measured according to the more and the less are treated as natures in Rule 14 (AT 10: 441).

8 See Nolan 2005. The last sentence of Meditation 5 says that certainty about God's existence allows the meditator to know plainly and certainly countless matters, "both about God and other intellectual things, and also about that whole corporeal nature that is the object of pure Mathesis" (AT 7: 71). The term *mathêsis*, encountered in the *Regulae*, marks a continuity with his earliest writings, which understood it as the most basic discipline of rigorous mathematical imagining.

9 "All these and similar propositions are to be removed [*removendae*, the verb from which *remotio* is derived] entirely from imagination to be true" (AT 10: 445). The propositions mentioned are "figure is not body; number is not the thing numbered; a surface is the boundary of a body, a line of a surface, a point of a line; unity is not a quantity, etc." In all these cases, to understand the proposition one must conceive the terms by imagination, then recognize that the truth is about a negation or delimitation of the terms and images that cannot be directly shown by them but only grasped by mind. See Sepper 2000 for more about the sophisticated use of imagination in techniques of meditation, including the spiritual exercises that Descartes practiced at the Jesuit college of La Flèche.

10 For a fuller explanation of how this direction of intellectual perception by will works, see Sepper 2013, ch. 7.2.

11 I do not discount the importance of §147's development of "the interior emotions of the soul" (AT 11: 440–441), but because they are truly emotions and often joined with human psychophysiology they are hardly support for restoring "Cartesian rationalism."

12 See Sepper 2013 for an account and critique of these developments.

## Further reading

The scholarly rehabilitation of the role of imagination in Descartes's mathematics began with P. Boutroux, *L'Imagination et les mathématiques selon Descartes* (Paris: Alcan, 1900), and is continued in L. Nolan (2005); and Cartesian imagination more generally was first treated in depth by J.H. Roy, *L'Imagination selon Descartes* (Paris: Gallimard, 1944). For further development of arguments in the main essay, see D.L. Sepper, *Descartes's Imagination: Proportion, Images, and the Activity of Thinking* (Berkeley and Los Angeles: University of California Press, 1996). V. Fóti, "The Cartesian Imagination," *Philosophy and Phenomenological Research* 46 (1986): 631–642, is an excellent brief introduction to the major philosophical questions. On the long tradition of psychophysiology, see Smith et al. (2012).

## References

Beck, L.J. (1952) *The Method of Descartes: A Study of the Regulae*, Oxford: Clarendon Press.

Descartes, R. (1974–86) *Oeuvres de Descartes*, 11 vols., eds. C. Adam and P. Tannery, 2nd edn, Paris: Vrin.

Harvey, E.R. (1975) *The Inward Wits*, London: Warburg Institute.

Hatfield, G. (1998) "The Cognitive Faculties," in D. Garber and M. Ayers (ed.) *The Cambridge History of Seventeenth-Century Philosophy*, vol. 2, Cambridge: Cambridge University Press, 953–1002.

Marion, J.-L. (2015) *Descartes's Grey Ontology: Cartesian Science and Aristotelian Thought in the Regulae*, trans. S. Donahue, South Bend: St. Augustine's Press.

Nikulin, D. (2002) *Matter, Imagination and Geometry: Ontology, Natural Philosophy and Mathematics in Plotinus, Proclus and Descartes*, Burlington, VT: Ashgate.

Nolan, L. (2005) "The Role of the Imagination in Rationalist Philosophies of Mathematics," in A. Nelson (ed.) *A Companion to Rationalism*, Oxford: Blackwell, 224–249.

Rodis-Lewis, G. (1998) *Descartes: His Life and Thought*, trans. J.M. Todd, Ithaca and London: Cornell University Press.

Sepper, D.L. (2000) "The Texture of Thought: Why Descartes' *Meditations* Is Meditational, and Why It Matters," in S. Gaukroger, J. Schuster, and J. Sutton (eds.) *Descartes' Natural Philosophy*, London: Routledge, 736–750.

Sepper, D.L. (2013) *Understanding Imagination: The Reason of Images*, Dordrecht: Springer.

Smith, C.U.M., E. Frixione, S. Finger, and W. Clower (2012) *The Animal Spirit Doctrine and the Origins of Neurophysiology*, Oxford: Oxford University Press.

# 3
# HUME

*Fabian Dorsch*

## 1 Introduction

This chapter overviews Hume's thoughts on the nature and the role of imagining and how the two are linked to the relevant contemporary discussions, with an almost exclusive focus on the first book of the *Treatise of Human Nature.*[1]

Over the course of this text, Hume draws and discusses three important distinctions among our conscious mental episodes (or what he calls "perceptions").[2] First, he divides them into "impressions" and "ideas" – or, as he also says, into "feelings" and "thoughts" (1.1.1). The former comprise "sensations, passions and emotions, as they make their first appearance in the soul" (1.1.1.1) – that is, perceptual experiences, bodily sensations, and basic feelings of desire and emotion. By contrast, the latter include "the faint images of [impressions] in thinking and reasoning" (ibid.) – such as memories, occurrent beliefs and, indeed, imaginings.

Hume then distinguishes two types of ideas, namely "ideas of the memory" and "ideas of the imagination" (1.1.3 and 1.3.5). Finally, the ideas of the imagination are again separated into "ideas of the judgment" (or "beliefs" or "opinions") and "ideas of the fancy" (or "mere fictions"; 1.3.7ff. and the Appendix). Ideas of the fancy comprise what we call today instances or episodes of imagining – such as visualizing or auditorily imagining something, imagining or supposing that something is the case, or imagining feeling or doing something. By contrast, ideas of the judgment include occurrent beliefs and judgmental thoughts, while ideas of the memory are identical with episodes of remembering or recalling. All of these ideas are contrasted by Hume with perceptual experiences and other types of impressions.

From the point of view of philosophy of imagination, all three of Hume's distinctions are of particular significance. The difference between impressions and ideas is central to the issue of how to tell apart sensory forms of the imagination (e.g., visualizing) from their perceptual counterparts (e.g., seeing) (see Bence Nanay, "Imagination and Perception," Chapter 9 of this volume). The contrast between memory and imagination as distinct sources of ideas is relevant for the differentiation of episodic memory from imaginative experience (see Dorothea Debus, "Imagination and Memory," Chapter 10 of this volume). And the distinction between occurrent beliefs and mere fictions is Hume's attempt at distinguishing what we would nowadays treat as distinct types of thought or propositional attitude (see Neil Sinhababu, "Imagination and Belief," Chapter 8 this volume).

I shall discuss each distinction in turn (Sections 2–3). In addition, I consider Hume's views on the imagination as a faculty aimed at the production of ideas (Section 3), as well as on the role that imagining plays in the wider context of our mental lives, notably in the acquisition of modal knowledge and in the comprehension of stories and opinions that we take to be false or fictional (Section 4). I close with some remarks about why Hume's views on the imagination are still important from a contemporary perspective (Section 5).

## 2 Seeing, visualizing and the Copy Principle

Hume's contribution to the debate about the nature of visualizing and other forms of sensory imagining and their distinction from the corresponding perceptual experiences is encapsulated in his conception of the relationship between impressions and ideas. When describing this relationship, Hume follows his empiricist predecessors Locke (1690/2008) and Berkeley (1710/2009) in claiming that all knowledge or belief has to start with perception. In particular, the concepts involved in our thoughts cannot be innate but have to be acquired empirically. We cannot recall, imagine or think about something blue (or salty, musky, etc.) unless we have experienced something blue (or salty, musky, etc.).

This empiricist doctrine is embodied in Hume's famous "Copy Principle," according to which "*all our simple ideas in their first appearance are deriv'd from simple impressions, which are correspondent to them, and which they exactly represent*" (1.1.1.7). The two types of mental episode are therefore distinguished by Hume in terms of their origin: while simple ideas are "nothing but copies and representations" of simple impressions (1.1.7.5), simple impressions are not copies of any preceding perceptions (Hume 1748/2007, II.17; Cohon and Owen 1997, §2; Landy 2006, 124f.). The restriction of the Copy Principle to *simple* ideas and impressions is meant to take into account that we can recall, imagine or think about more complex things like a blue circle even if we have never seen one. All that is required is that we have seen a blue object, as well as a (possibly different) round object.

Hume highlights several aspects of the copying relation. First, it is a relation of asymmetric dependence: every simple idea depends, in one way or another, on the simple impression that it is a copy of. Second, the relation of copying is also a relation of correspondence: "all simple ideas and impressions resemble each other" (1.1.1.6). More specifically, they resemble each other in what they make us aware of. If a simple impression makes us aware of something round, then its copy, in the shape of some simple idea, also makes us aware of something round. Third, these two aspects of the copying relation are closely related. For simple ideas depend on simple impressions in such a way that the two end up resembling each other. Fourth, the kind of dependence in question is causal: "our impressions are the causes of our ideas" (1.1.1.8). This means that every simple idea has to be causally preceded by a corresponding simple impression – which is why we cannot have an idea of something round, say, without the prior existence of an impression of something round.

These four aspects of the copying relation may be summarized by the slogan that copies are causal reproductions. That is, simple ideas are derived from simple impressions in roughly the same way in which photocopies are derived from the original sheets of paper. In both cases, the copies causally depend on the originals and, as result, also resemble them in relevant aspects (ibid., 125ff.). Now, understanding simple ideas as causal reproductions of simple impressions has two important consequences, both of which apply to impressions and ideas independently of whether they are simple or complex.

First, because impressions make us exclusively aware of concrete objects and their features, ideas do so, too (1.1.7; Laurence and Margolis 2012, §2). Whenever we are recalling, imagining or thinking about a triangle, we always have an individual and relatively specific triangle in mind (e.g., an equilateral one of a certain size). So there are no genuinely general or abstract ideas: we cannot think about triangles or triangularity in abstraction from particular instances. Our ideas of triangles always make us aware of individual triangles with determinate angles, sides and so on. One way of understanding this conclusion – though not necessarily the only one – is that not only experience, but also thought is always imagistic in nature (Prinz 2002, ch. 5; Martin 2006, 76).

Second, impressions and ideas "differ only in degree, not in nature" (1.1.1.5). That only ideas, but not impressions, are copies does not constitute a difference in nature, because causal origin is not an essential feature of mental episodes. Similarly, the two types of mental episode are not distinguished by what they make us aware of. Nor do they differ in how they make us aware of things. Hume is a relationalist and indirect realist about impressions, meaning that he takes them to acquaint us with internal, mind-dependent objects (1.2.6; 1.4.2) or "images" (Hume 1748/2007, XII.1). And the same has to be true of ideas, given that they are nothing but causal reproductions of impressions. In particular, Hume does not share our contemporary conception of thoughts as nonrelational (or intentional) representations.

Hume describes the quantitative difference between impressions and ideas as a difference "only in their strength and vivacity" (1.1.7.5) and makes clear that he takes the difference to be open to introspection.[3] Moreover, the introspectible and quantitative character of the difference really only leaves two options (Govier 1972, 48; Martin 2001, 270).[4] On the one hand, impressions may differ from ideas in being more detailed or more determinate in their presentation of their concrete objects. On the other hand, impressions may differ from ideas in the intensity or specificity of their qualitative (and possibly nonpresentational) aspects (1.3.7.5). Moreover, both differences in degree can be explained by reference to the notion of causal reproduction. Just as photocopying leads to a loss of clarity and saturation of the ink marks on the paper, recalling, imagining or thinking about something previously seen leads to a loss of detail and determinacy in awareness.

However, Hume acknowledges that this impact of the copying relation on vivacity does not prevent impressions from being very faint, and ideas from being very lively, with the consequence that we cannot always correctly identify them as what they are (1.1.1.1). As a result, there is not always a recognizable threshold of vivacity which strictly separates impressions from ideas (Landy 2006, 121). Indeed, even though it is unclear whether Hume would go that far, it seems plausible to assume that there can be certain ideas (e.g., very vivid memories, or a very detailed visualizations) that are more lively than certain impressions (e.g., visual perceptions during the night, or in foggy weather; Allison 2008, 16f., and Budd 1991, 104). Perhaps all that can be argued is that a given idea can never be more vivid than the particular impression that it is a copy of. Correspondingly, although photocopying may be unable to improve the print quality of the text on the original sheet, say, it is surely possible that some original documents are almost unreadable because of smear and indistinct characters, while some photocopies show very clear and sharp print.

As a consequence, the recognizable difference in vivacity between impressions and ideas is merely typical, meaning that it obtains often, but not all the time. That a mental episode is very lively is thus not always an indication that the episode is an impression rather than an idea. Given that, for Hume, there are no other features that might reveal to us in introspection which causal origin mental episodes possess, we cannot always introspectively tell whether a given episode is an impression or an idea (Garrett 2008, 42f.).

Hume's resulting empiricist theory of the conscious mind faces several well-known objections, two of which I will mention here. The first is the famous example of the missing shade of blue, which Hume acknowledged himself as a counterexample to his Copy Principle (1.1.1.10). His claim is that it is possible for us to visualize a particular shade of blue without ever having seen it, just on the basis of seeing an arrangement of all other shades of blue, especially those that are very close in hue to the missing shade. But if Hume is right about this possibility (and it seems difficult to deny this), we have a simple idea that is not preceded by a corresponding simple impression. Hume's own assessment of the significance of this counterexample to the Copy Principle is that "the instance is so particular and singular, that it is scarce worth our observing, and does not merit that for it alone we should alter our general maxim" (1.1.1.10).

However, it is doubtful that Hume can really be so nonchalant about the case (Stroud 1999, 34; Broadie 2009, 155). First of all, there are probably many more examples like this (e.g., concerning sounds, smells, tastes; ibid., 154; Garrett 1997, 50). But the main problem is that, if the Copy Principle is indeed just a "general maxim," "empirical rule" or "empirical generalization" (Morris and Brown 2013, §5; Garrett 1997, 50) that allows for exceptions or "near misses" (ibid., 52; Garrett 2008, 51), the distinction between impressions and ideas collapses. For instance, we may visualize the missing shade in a very vivid manner. In this case, our imaginative experience may be as lively as the experience of someone who sees the same shade of blue. Moreover, both experiences are originals, rather than copies. Hence, it remains unclear how Hume could still distinguish our idea from the other person's impression, given that they differ neither in their vivacity, nor in their causal origin.

The second major objection to Hume's treatment of the distinction between impressions and ideas – and, hence, between seeing and visualizing – is simply that there are many good reasons to conclude that the two types of mental episode differ qualitatively in their nature, i.e., that visualizing is not just a weak or faint form of seeing.

First, visualizing lacks the immediacy of seeing (Hopkins 1998, ch. 7; Martin 2002). When we see an object, it seems to us to be directly before us, as part of our actual environment. But the same is not true of visualizing. If you sit in your living room, close your eyes and simply visualize a car, you do not visualize it as being in your actual surroundings (e.g., next to the sofa). Taken by themselves, episodes of visualizing are neutral about which objects are located where in our actual environment, while episodes of seeing are not (ibid.; Dorsch 2010). But this phenomenological difference – which Malebranche (1674/1997, 79 and 87f.), Husserl (1901/1970, A413), Sartre (1940/2004, 12f.) and others have tried to capture by saying that objects seen appear to be "present," while objects visualized seem to be "absent" – is one of kind, not of degree.

Another important qualitative difference between the two kinds of episode concerns their functional and rational role. Seeing something has an impact on belief and action that visualizing does not have. For example, if we see a glass of water before us on the table and are unaware of any defeaters, we are normally inclined and entitled to believe that there is a glass of water before us, and to try to grab it if this would further our ends (e.g., if we are thirsty). But if we are merely visualizing a glass of water while looking at the table, we are usually neither moved, nor justified, to believe in the presence of the glass, or to try to seize it. Again, the difference at issue is not a quantitative one.

Finally, seeing and visualizing differ in how they relate to voluntary agency (Dorsch 2012, chs. 13f.). Although seeing may involve, or be intimately connected to, deliberate action concerning aspects like the focus and duration of attention, or the direction of gaze (O'Shaughnessy 2003, pt. 2; Crowther 2010), it is never up to us which objects we end up seeing, and how we end up seeing them as being, once we have decided to look with open eyes in a certain direction. For instance, if there is a red apple before me,

I cannot decide to see a green pear in its stead. Visualizing, on the other hand, involves at least the general possibility to exert this kind of control. Although we may sometimes fail to produce or banish a certain image, we typically are able to visualize a green pear, say, if we want to. But, anew, whether something is open to voluntary influence is not a matter of degree.

Because of objections like these, it is probably better to reject Hume's account of ideas. The question is only how much of it we should give up. As some neo-Humean views illustrate, it is possible to largely hold on to the Copy Principle, and to modify only one of the four aspects of Hume's original conception of copies. More specifically, the suggestion is to continue to understand ideas as resembling impressions because of their asymmetric dependence on the latter, but to deny that the dependence in question is causal. Rather, the constitutive relation between the two types of episode should be taken to be representational: ideas are inherently representations of impressions, in roughly the same sense in which paintings are inherently representations of what they depict (Munoz-Dardé 2002, 2; see Cohon and Owen 1997, §2, and Garrett 2006 for different interpretations of the "representationality" of ideas).

Copies that are inherently representational differ from causal reproductions in that they do not require the existence of what is copied. One can paint a man without painting any particular man that existed prior to or during the act of painting. Good examples are Dutch genre images from the seventeenth century, which depict only certain types of people (e.g., the drunkard or the love interest). Instead, paintings depend on what they depict in a different sense: they are partly constituted and individuated by what they represent. No representation could exist without something being represented. And a representation would cease to be the same if what it represents were to change. It is in this sense that neo-Humeans assume imaginative experiences to be nonrelational representations or "imaginations" of perceptual experiences, as captured by the so-called Dependency Thesis that "to imagine sensorily φ is to imagine experiencing φ" (Martin 2002, 404; see also Peacocke 1985 and O'Shaughnessy 2003, ch. 12).

If we understand ideas as copies in the sense of representations, both objections against the Copy Principle lose their force. The missing shade of blue is not a counterexample anymore, because imagining seeing something with a particular hue does not presuppose having seen that hue before – just as we can depict a man with a certain appearance without ever having seen someone who looked like the depicted.

In addition, the difference between impressions and ideas turns out to be qualitative. If impressions are assumed to relationally *acquaint* us with objects (whether internal or external), impressions and ideas differ in kind because the latter are taken to be non-relational representations (Dauer 1999, 85f.). If, on the other hand, impressions are conceived of as inherently *representing* their objects, the two kinds of mental episode differ qualitatively because they represent different entities (i.e., mental episodes vs. their objects). It is thus possible to account for the various differences in kind between seeing and visualizing. Notably, the latter's lack of immediacy may be due to the fact that what we directly imagine is just a perceptual experience of an object, and not the object itself (Dorsch 2010).

Of course, the endorsement of something like the Dependency Thesis is not without its own problems – not the least with respect to whether it can be extended to more thought-like ideas, such as judgments (Dorsch 2012, ch. 9). But, at least, it offers a way of holding on to empiricism and the Copy Principle in the face of some of the main objections to Hume's original account of ideas.

## 3 Recalling, believing and imagining

Hume's distinction between perceptions and imaginative episodes in terms of impressions and ideas does not yet tell us anything about the latter's difference from other nonperceptual experiences or thoughts, notably episodic memories and occurrent beliefs. Hume addresses this further issue by contrasting the three types of idea already mentioned: (i) ideas of the memory; (ii) ideas of the judgment; and (iii) ideas of the fancy (Garrett 2008, 45). That impressions and ideas vary merely in degree has the consequence that the same also holds for the three types of idea. For if there were differences in kind among them, not all of them could be of the same kind as impressions. Hence, there can only be quantitative, but no qualitative variances in nature between ideas – which explains why Hume usually maintains that the three types of idea differ just in their "force" or "vivacity" (1.3.5.3; 1.3.7.7; 1.3.8.15f.; Cottrell 2015, §2).

However, Hume is not completely happy with this description of the difference in degree between ideas (1.3.7.7; 1.3.8.15f.). He writes that "there are other differences among ideas, which cannot be properly comprehended under these terms" and suggests that speaking of a difference in "feeling … shou'd have been nearer the truth" (Appendix, 22). In accordance with this thought, Hume identifies the vivacity of ideas (and, incidentally, also of impressions) with the feeling of "assent," which "alone distinguishes [memory and the senses] from the imagination" (1.3.6.7), and also "the ideas of the judgment from the fictions of the imagination" (1.3.7.7).

We can identify at least five different features of assent. First, it is an aspect of mental episodes which is accessible to introspection (i.e., "felt by the mind"; 1.3.7.7). Second, it pertains both to impressions and to certain ideas, namely memories and occurrent beliefs (ibid.; 1.3.6.7). Third, it has an impact on the causal or functional role of the episodes concerned (1.3.7.7 and 1.3.10.3; Govier 1972, 47; Everson 1988). In particular, it increases their influence on our agency, on our emotions and on our imagination-based formation of beliefs. When we see, remember or believe that someone is in danger, we have a much stronger tendency to help him, to fear for him or to reason to the belief that he might really die, than when we merely imagine that he is in danger. In this way, Hume can explain, for instance, why we do not respond in the same ways to real-life cases and to fictional stories (Walton 1990). Fourth, the feeling of assent renders the episodes concerned more persistent (i.e., "infixes them in the mind"; 1.3.7.7), possibly in the form of dispositional mental states (Govier 1972, 48; Loeb 2002, ch. 3.2; Marusiç 2010). We are more inclined to acquire dispositional beliefs on the basis of perceptions, memories and judgments than on the basis of mere imaginings. Fifth, assent – like any other feeling – comes in degrees. It thus comes close to what we would call the subjective confidence or degree of belief pertaining to our judgmental thoughts (Govier 1972, 52; Loeb 2002, ch. 4).

The resulting difference is again, however, at best a typical difference, given that ideas of the fancy can be very lively and have a strong impact on belief and agency, while ideas of the memory or the judgment may be very weak and without much influence on other mental phenomena (1.3.5.6). As in the case of the contrast between impressions and ideas, this means that we cannot always tell by introspection whether a given idea is a recollection, an occurrent belief or an episode of imagining (1.3.5.3ff.; Traiger 2008, 64, 66f.).

Moreover, any differentiation of these three types of idea has to make reference to their distinct and nonessential origins, namely to the different ways in which they are produced by the mind. As their name suggests, ideas of the memory originate in the faculty of memory. The other two types of idea are, for Hume, the product of the imagination (ibid., 60). Even beliefs formed on the basis of reasoning are said to be outputs of the imagination, in stark opposition to the more traditional view that beliefs are the product of reason.

But Hume is not always consistent in his terminology, as he himself acknowledges in a footnote added after the first publication of the *Treatise* (1.3.9.19; Furlong 1961, 65; Winkler 1999; Wright 2013). When he speaks of "the imagination," what he usually has in mind is the "faculty, by which we form our fainter ideas" (1.3.9.19, n. 22). This faculty is responsible for the production of all ideas, except the more vivid ideas of the memory. Hume's notion of the imagination is thus – like Kant's (1781/1999) – wider than our contemporary one in encompassing not only imagining, but also thinking and occurrently believing. However, sometimes, Hume also uses the term "imagination" in a narrower sense that does not refer to the faculty of the imagination as a whole, but only to those of its exercises that occur outside of reasoning-based belief formation (1.3.9.19, n. 22; Cottrell 2015, §2). The narrower notion concerns solely what Hume on occasion calls "mere fictions" or "ideas of the fancy" (1.3.13.9) and comes close to what we today would take to be imagining proper. The subsequent discussion focuses on Hume's primary, wider notion of the imagination, according to which it is the faculty of producing nonmnemonic ideas.

Both memory and imagination operate with simple ideas that are copied from simple impressions. But they differ, according to Hume, in that "the imagination is not restrain'd to the same order and form with the original impressions; while the memory is in a manner ty'd down in that respect, without any power of variation" (1.1.3.2). What matters for the difference is whether the relations between the simple ideas concerned are causally determined by, and thus mirror, the relations between the relevant simple impressions (1.1.3.3; Traiger 2008, 62f.).

However, we cannot come to know introspectively whether the order and form of the simple ideas indeed correspond to, and are causally determined by, the order and form of previous simple impressions. For this would require that we could compare the two – which we cannot do anymore, given that the impressions concerned have already ceased to exist. And, of course, trying to recall these impressions would not help, since what is at issue is precisely how to determine when a given idea is a recollection, and not an imagining, of a previous impression (1.3.5.3). So, our best hope to distinguish the two types of idea in introspection is to focus on their degree of vivacity – which, as already mentioned, does not always help us to successfully tell them apart.

Turning our attention to ideas of the imagination, two questions are particularly pressing. First, why does Hume think that one and the same faculty is responsible for both judging and imagining? And, second, how do the two types of idea still differ in origin?

With respect to the first question, the orthodox view – not only among traditional rationalists like Descartes (1637–41/1980) or Kant (1781/1999), but also among contemporary philosophers with strong empiricist tendencies (Williams 1980; Railton 2003; Dretske 1988; Owens 2000) – is that the faculty producing judgments or beliefs is reason, and not imagination. The underlying thought is that beliefs are in need of justification, and that we can ensure that our beliefs are justified only if we form them in response to reasons. But Hume spends much time arguing that we are unable to justify our (contingent and empirical) beliefs in this way, neither on the basis of perception (1.4.2), nor on that of inductive reasoning (1.3.6). In other words, he is skeptical about the role of reason in our mental life and does not think that we acquire our beliefs (or other attitudes: 2.3.3) in response to reasons (see Garrett 1997; Millican 1998; Owen 1999; Allison 2008; Cottrell 2015, §7; and Schmitt 2014, div. 4, for further debate).

Instead, we are said to form them due to habit, in the shape of causal mechanisms of association that determine our imagination: "[w]hen the mind, therefore, passes from the idea or impression of one object to the idea or belief of another, it is not determin'd by reason, but by certain principles, which associate together the ideas of these objects, and unite them in the imagination" (1.3.6.12). For example, if it happens that, whenever a subject has an impression of smoke, she also has an impression of fire, her mind will come to associate smoke with fire. As a result, she will be prompted to judge that there is a fire if she sees some smoke, and to judge that smoke always comes with fire if she reflects on the nature of smoke. Furthermore, this associative link will be weakened or undermined, once she encounters smoke that derives from a different source than fire (e.g., from a chemical reaction). By contrast, when the person imagines smoke, she is free to imagine it to be due to, or connected with, anything that she wants (1.1.3.4). So, while both ideas of the judgment and ideas of the fancy are produced by the associative imagination, their origins differ because there are very distinct constraints on their production in play (Cottrell 2015, §§2f.). Hume's response to the first question thus also provides his answer to the second.

It remains unclear, however, why we should follow Hume in assuming that episodes of believing and episodes of imagining are the result of one and the same faculty. Though they both combine ideas without recreating the form and order of the relevant impressions, they do not have much else in common. Indeed, they differ, for instance, in whether they allow for the voluntary determination of what we end up experiencing or thinking – that is, in whether we can make use of the "liberty of the imagination to transpose and change its ideas" (1.1.3.4). While we enjoy at least some control over what we are imagining, it is not up to us which proposition we end up endorsing in judgment or belief (Williams 1973; Owens 2000). Indeed, since episodic memories share this aspect of involuntariness with occurrent beliefs (i.e., we also cannot influence how we remember things as being), it is not easy to understand why these two types of episode should pertain to different faculties, but not involuntary beliefs and voluntary imaginings. After all, reasoning seems to be much closer to memory than to voluntary imagination in how it brings about, and determines the content of, mental episodes (Dorsch 2009).

In any case, the differences in origin between ideas of the memory, ideas of the judgment and ideas of the fancy promise to explain why the first two generally involve a stronger feeling of assent than the last ones. As said earlier, ideas receive their vivacity from the – normally stronger – vivacity of the impressions that they are copies of. And the same should apply to assent, given that Hume identifies it with (part of) vivacity. However, since all ideas are copied from impressions, the copying relation alone is unable to account for every difference in assent among the various types of idea. Not surprisingly, Hume stresses that it also matters how the ideas are combined with each other, or with impressions (e.g., when we judge that some seen smoke is due to an unseen fire).

According to him, the two ways of preventing a partial or even complete loss of the original strength of assent are recollection and association (1.3.8f.). In both cases, the ideas in question are said to acquire a high degree of assent not merely because they are copies of vivid impressions (for this is true of all ideas), but primarily because they preserve some of the relations between those impressions. Either the ideas repeat the connections between several particular impressions – for instance, when we remember that a certain instance of smoke was related to a certain instance of fire. Or the ideas reflect the constant conjunction of two types of impression individuated by what they make us aware of – which happens, say, when seeing smoke prompts us to think of fire as its cause, because each time that we perceive smoke, we also perceive fire. By contrast, the combination of the idea of wings and the idea of a horse, say, is not backed up by experience in the same way, which is why imagining a winged horse lacks the vivacity characteristic of memory and belief.

One immediate problem with this picture of ideas is that it does not easily apply to simple ideas. While Hume does not really address this issue, he is clear that simple ideas can involve assent or vivacity to different degrees (see 1.3.7.6; 1.3.10.3). This raises the question of why some simple ideas are livelier than others, and whether these lively simple ideas are ideas of the memory, of the judgment, or of a third, yet unnamed type.[5] The two criteria just discussed cannot provide us with an answer, because both concern exclusively ways in which ideas might be combined with other ideas (or impressions), which is not what happens during the production of a simple idea.

The other main difficulty for Hume's account of ideas is, again, that it fails to capture important qualitative differences among recollections, occurrent beliefs and imaginings. To start with, there are good reasons to assume that the contents of thought differ in kind from the contents of experience. For example, thought contents are subject to propositional logic, but sensory contents are not (Crane 2009). If we are able to think that *p* or that *q*, then we are also able to think their negation, conjunction, disjunction, implication, and so on. But we cannot see the negation of a green tree (which is not the same as not seeing a green tree, or as seeing a red tree).[6] The same is true of qualitative differences in functional and rational role.

In order to handle these objections, while staying as close to Hume's initial account of ideas as possible, two adjustments should probably be made. First, the difference in kind between sensory and thought contents should be acknowledged. This might actually require giving up the Copy Principle for thoughts and limiting it to imaginative and mnemonic experiences, both of which differ from perceptual ones in their lack of sensory immediacy (Martin 2001). Second, assent should not be understood as a feeling, but rather as an aspect of functional or rational role (Loeb 2002). This move preserves Hume's observation that there are respects in which occurrent beliefs are closer to perceptual and mnemonic experiences than to imaginative experiences or thoughts, namely concerning their links to belief and agency. Moreover, both modifications should be compatible with Hume's broadly naturalistic and empiricist outlook on mind and world.

## 4 Modal knowledge and imaginative resistance

Let us now turn to the issue of which role Hume supposes the imagination to play in our mental life. We already noted that he takes this faculty to be responsible for the production of both occurrent beliefs and episodes of imagining. But, according to Hume, the imagination also has a particular epistemic function: to discover modal truths. Hume first claims that conceivability implies metaphysical possibility (i.e., possibility of existence): "[w]e can form the idea of a golden mountain, and from thence conclude that such a mountain may actually exist" (1.2.2.8). He also claims that inconceivability – at least if due to contradiction (Garrett 2008, 54) – implies metaphysical impossibility: "[w]e can form no idea of a mountain without a valley, and therefore regard it as impossible" (1.2.2.8). Given these two claims, we can come to know whether something is possible by reflecting on whether it is conceivable.

It is clear from Hume's remarks on the issue that he identifies conceivability with imaginability (1.2.2.8; Lightner 1997, 115; Cottrell 2015, §6). Accordingly, what is indicative of whether something could exist is primarily whether we can have an idea of it. Furthermore, because of his endorsement of empiricism, Hume takes conception always to be specific and imagistic (see Section 2 above) – in sharp contrast to Descartes (1637–41/1980) who assumes that modal knowledge is instead grounded in abstract, intellectual understanding (Gendler and Hawthorne 2002b; Cottrell 2015, §6).

Hume's conclusion that the imagination provides us with access to modal truths is jointly motivated by three central elements of his theory of the mind: (i) his empiricist doctrine that all concepts are ultimately derived from perception; (ii) his relationalism about perception; and (iii) his indirect realism about perception (see Section 2 above). Since all simple ideas are copies of simple impressions, and since ideas can be combined only in exactly the same ways as impressions because both types of episode involve the same kind of awareness of concrete objects and their features, it follows that, for each possible idea, there is a corresponding possible impression. In short, if something is conceivable, then it is also perceivable. That we can think of a golden mountain or a winged horse, say, indicates that we could also see one (if one were to exist). Similarly, that we cannot perceive a round square (because there could not exist any) means that we cannot conceive of one, either.

Now, for Hume, perception is genuinely relational: whenever we have a perceptual experience, there really exists a concrete object that we are thereby acquainted with. But if the perception of an object implies its actual existence, then perceivability implies possible existence. Taken together, empiricism and relationalism entail Hume's first claim that conceivability entails possibility. Of course, these considerations show that perception, too, is a guide to possibility. But imagination has the advantage that it is not constrained by the actual world and, hence, allows for the freedom necessary to explore the full range of unrealized possibilities.

The modal truths in question concern the objects of perceptual experience. According to Hume's indirect realism, these objects are identical with internal (i.e., experience-dependent) objects, rather than with external (i.e., experience-independent) ones (Hume 1748/2007, XII.9). Moreover, he is – contrary to Locke (1690/2008) – skeptical about there being any (knowable) resemblances between the two kinds of object and, hence, any justified inference from features of internal objects to features of external objects (1.4.2; Hume 1748/2007, XII.11f.; Strawson 1989, 45 n. 19). As a result, the imagination does not provide us with access to modal truths about external reality. At best, it may serve as the origin of an unjustified projection of modal truths about internal objects onto external ones – which is why Hume is standardly classified as an anti- or quasi-realist about modality (Kail 2003; Coventry 2006). In addition, since internal objects are dependent on the respective mental episodes, modal truths about the first (e.g., that a red circle is possible) are inseparable from corresponding modal truths about the second (e.g., that an experience or a thought of a red circle is possible). So, in learning something about experience-dependent objects, we simultaneously learn something about experience and thought.

Empiricists who reject Hume's assumption that we perceive internal objects may still hold on to the idea that conceivability gives us access to modal truths about external reality. But dropping indirect realism deprives their account of an important resource needed to establish Hume's second claim that inconceivability implies impossibility. External objects can exist not only without being perceived, but also without being perceivable. Hence, that something is unperceivable – and thus also inconceivable due to the Copy Principle – does not mean that it is impossible. By contrast, internal objects cannot exist without being perceived. Their unperceivability therefore implies their impossibility. So, Hume can validate his second claim about the imagination's epistemological role only because he endorses indirect realism, in addition to empiricism and relationalism.

Hume's take on modal epistemology may be attacked in various ways. In addition to rejecting one of the three elements of his theory of mind just highlighted, it is possible to object that Hume can at best establish his first claim, that imaginability is a guide to possibility. We discover whether something is conceivable by actually trying to conceive of it and introspectively noting whether we are successful in this attempt. We normally have no difficulties noticing whether and what we are imagining. But, in situations where we fail to imagine something, introspection may tell us only that this is *actually* the case, and not that we could not *possibly* imagine it. In addition, noting our inability to imagine something seems to require recognizing the *modal* truth that we could not imagine it, thus threatening to lead to a vicious regress (Yablo 1993, §5f.). Both observations speak against Hume's second claim that unimaginability is a guide to impossibility.

Furthermore, philosophers have objected against Hume's first claim by arguing that at least some impossibilities are conceivable – for example, that "any two sides of a triangle are together equal to the third" (Reid 1785/2002, ch. 4.3), that "Goldbach's conjecture is wrong," or that "water is not $H_2O$" (Gendler and Hawthorne 2002b, 10; see also Gendler 2000, 57). But it is not obvious that cases like these really speak against Hume's claims (Casullo 1979; Woudenberg 2006; Powell 2013). While we have no problems understanding the sentences describing these alleged counterexamples, it is doubtful that we can really conceive of a concrete situation in which it is true that two sides of a triangle are not longer than the third, or that the stuff that we refer to as "water" is not identical with the stuff that we refer to as "$H_2O$" – especially if conceptions are understood as copies of perceptions and thus as being concerned exclusively with concrete objects.

Finally, Hume appears to challenge his own view. In a famous passage, he acknowledges moral limitations to what we can imagine, given that "where vicious manners are described, without being marked with the proper characters of blame and disapprobation … [we] cannot, nor is it proper [we] should, enter into such sentiments" (Hume 1757/2008, §32f.). When we encounter the views of others (notably in fictional works), we normally can imagine those views to be true, even if we take them to be false. For instance, in response to hearing Prometheus describing Earth as surrounded by the river Okeanos, we can easily imagine our planet as a flat disk (Aeschylus 2011, ll. 206ff.). But the situation is very different if we are concerned with normative opinions contrary to our own. In particular, Hume believes that we are both psychologically unable to and normatively forbidden from imagining the adequacy of moral views that differ from our own (Gendler 2006, 54). We may resist, for example, imagining the moral permissiveness of randomly killing innocent children.

But such imaginative resistance threatens to undermine the claim that unconceivability entails impossibility. For it is arguably possible that, in some very remote world, arbitrarily bringing about the death of innocent children is morally allowed or even required (Kölbel and Zeman 2012; MacFarlane 2014), even though we might be bound to fail in our attempts to imagine such a world. Perhaps the most promising Humean response maintains that the type of imagining resisted is different from the type of imagining relevant for modal epistemology. While we have no problem dispassionately or hypothetically imagining that random killings of innocent children are moral, we are unable or unwilling to get more involved with this imaginative project (Moran 1994; Gendler 2006). In particular, since "a very violent effort is requisite to change our judgment of manners, and excite sentiments of approbation or blame, love or hatred" (Hume 1757/2008, §33), what we may resist is the cognitive and emotional identification with the moral view that we imagine to be true, and not the mere imaginative assumption of its truth (Walton 1994, §4).

## 5 Conclusion

The preceding considerations reveal that Hume's views on the imagination continue to have a significant influence on contemporary philosophy. First, his thoughts still serve as the starting point for discussions about modal knowledge and imaginative resistance (Gendler and Hawthorne 2002a; Nichols 2006). Indeed, Hume's famous remarks on both topics have not merely shaped, but in fact initiated the respective debates (Yablo 1993; Moran 1994).

Additionally, the neo-Humean views suggested at the end of Sections 2 and 3 figure prominently in the current disputes about the nature of perception, episodic memory and imaginative experience. In particular, it is much discussed whether perceptions are relations (albeit to external objects), and whether episodic memories and imaginative experiences are representations of such relational perceptions (Peacocke 1985; Hopkins 1998, ch. 7; Martin 2002). Similarly, there have been various recent attempts to define imaginative episodes in terms of their difference in functional or cognitive role from their perceptual and judgmental counterparts (Van Leeuwen 2014; Neil Sinhababu, "Imagination and Belief," Chapter 8 of this volume).

Finally, Hume's outlook is also methodologically very close to certain contemporary ones. Not only does he aim to establish a naturalistic "science of human nature" which is based on the "experimental method" of empirical observation (Introduction; 1.1.1.12). But he also pays much attention to, and engages in reflection on, introspective evidence – notably with respect to vivacity and assent. Hume even endorses the Cartesian idea that, "since all actions and sensations of the mind are known to us by consciousness, they must necessarily appear in every particular what they are, and be what they appear" (1.4.2.7; see also 1.4.2.5 and Schmitt 2014, 71ff.). His approach to the mind thus combines empiricism and naturalism with what we nowadays call the phenomenological method (see Julia Jansen, "Husserl," and Robert Hopkins, "Sartre," Chapters 5 and 6 of this volume) – a combination which also appeals to many contemporary philosophers of mind and imagination (such as Martin 2001, 2002).

## Acknowledgments

I am very grateful to Amy Kind, Jonathan Cottrell and an anonymous referee for detailed comments on a previous draft and to Veronique Munoz-Dardé and Mike Martin for extensive discussions on Hume's philosophy. My research on this chapter was generously funded by the Swiss National Science Foundation (PP00P1_139004) and the Fundación Séneca (18958/JLI/13).

## Notes

1 A longer version of this chapter is available at <http://doc.rero.ch/record/256025>. All references are to Hume 1739/2007, unless stated otherwise. The numbering system employed names, in this ordering, the book, part, section and, if applicable, paragraph of the passage referred to; or, in the case of the Appendix, just the paragraph.

2 Hume is not always consistent in his conception of what he calls "perceptions." While he typically takes them to be mental episodes or events (e.g., 3.1.1.2), he also sometimes describes them as the internal objects that such episodes directly present us with (1.4.5.15f.). A closely related ambiguity pertains to Hume's talk of "objects" (e.g., 1.1.7.4). Grene (1994) identifies three different uses which denote, respectively: (i) the direct objects of mental episodes; (ii) the objects of introspection, that is, the mental episodes themselves; (iii) the external referents of mental episodes. Hume clearly thinks that (iii) are entities distinct from the other two (1.2.6.7). By contrast, he tends to switch seamlessly between (i) and (ii), not the least because he takes the two to be inseparably linked to each other: (i) are internal objects that depend for their existence on (ii) and can be seen as constituents of (ii). In what follows, I assume that "perceptions" are mental episodes (ii), while "objects" are their mind-dependent objects (i).

3 See, e.g., 1.1.3.1, 1.3.5.5, 1.3.7.7 and 1.4.2.7, as well as Garrett 2008, 42. Dauer (1999, 83f., esp. n. 1) compares this phenomenological reading of vivacity with Everson's (1988) functionalist understanding,

while Govier (1972) argues that there is a place for each interpretation. See also the discussion of Hume's notion of assent in Section 3 below.

4 Note that Hume is likely to reject the idea that impressions and ideas can differ in determinacy (1.1.7.5). But this still leaves the possibility of differences in detail or intensity.

5 Which is what Traiger (2008, 59) seems to think. See also Russow 1980, 343, for discussion.

6 Other important differences are that only thought contents involve propositional prediction (Burge 2010, 537ff.), and that only thought contents are composed of elements that are subject to what Evans (1982) has called the "Generality Constraint."

## Further reading

A comprehensive overview of Hume's views on the nature and role of the imagination, as well as of their historical context, is provided by Cottrell (2015). Garrett (2008) and Traiger (2008) survey Hume's thoughts on ideas, and on memory and imagination, respectively. Most other interesting works concerned with Hume's treatment of the imagination are already a bit older, such as J. Wilbank's book *Hume's Theory of the Imagination* (The Hague: Martinus Nijhoff, 1968) and G. Streminger's article of the same title (*Hume Studies* 6 [1980]: 91–118). Some more recent good discussions of Hume's view on the imagination and especially its epistemological role can be found in Garrett (1997, ch. 1) and Allison (2008). Martin (2001, 2002) is one of the foremost proponents of a neo-Humean theory of perception and episodic memory. Moran (1994) has introduced Hume's observations about imaginative resistance into contemporary discussion, while Yablo (1993) and the introduction in Gendler and Hawthorne (2002a) explore the relevance of Hume's thoughts for present-day modal epistemology. Both issues are further discussed in the introduction and parts 3 and 4 of Nichols (2006).

## References


Aeschylus (2011) *The Complete Aeschylus*, eds. P. Burian and A. Shapiro, Oxford: Oxford University Press.

Allison, H.E. (2008) *Custom and Reason in Hume: A Kantian Reading of the First Book of the Treatise*, Oxford: Clarendon Press.

Berkeley, G. (1710/2009) *Principles of Human Knowledge and Three Dialogues*, ed. H. Robinson, Oxford: Oxford University Press.

Broadie, A. (2009) *A History of Scottish Philosophy*, Edinburgh: Edinburgh University Press.

Budd, M. (1991) *Wittgenstein's Philosophy of Psychology*, London: Routledge.

Burge, T. (2010) *Origins of Objectivity*, Oxford: Oxford University Press.

Casullo, A. (1979) "Reid and Mill on Hume's Maxim of Conceivability," *Analysis* 39(4): 212–219.

Cohon, R., and D. Owen (1997) "Hume on Representation, Reason and Motivation," *Manuscrito* 20: 47–76.

Cottrell, J. (2015) "David Hume: Imagination," in J. Fieser and B. Dowden (eds.) *Internet Encyclopedia of Philosophy*, <http://www.iep.utm.edu/hume-ima/>.

Coventry, A.M. (2006) *Hume's Theory of Causation: A Quasi-Realist Interpretation*, London: Continuum.

Crane, T. (2009) "Is Perception a Propositional Attitude?" *Philosophical Quarterly* 59(236): 452–469.

Crowther, T. (2010) "The Agential Profile of Perceptual Experience," *Proceedings of the Aristotelian Society* 110: 219–242.

Dauer, F.W. (1999) "Force and Vivacity in the Treatise and the Enquiry," *Hume Studies* 25(1): 83–99.

Descartes, R. (1637–41/1980) *Discourse on Method and Meditations on First Philosophy*, Indianapolis: Hackett.

Dorsch, F. (2009) "Judging and the Scope of Mental Agency," in L. O'Brien and M. Soteriou (eds.) *Mental Actions*, Oxford: Oxford University Press, 38–71.

Dorsch, F. (2010) "Transparency and Imagining Seeing," *Philosophical Explorations* 13(3): 173–200.

Dorsch, F. (2012) *The Unity of Imagining*, Berlin: De Gruyter.

Dretske, F. (1988) *Explaining Behaviour*, Cambridge, MA: MIT Press.

Evans, G. (1982) *The Varieties of Reference*, Oxford: Oxford University Press.

Everson, S. (1988) "The Difference between Thinking and Feeling," *Mind* 97: 401–413.

Furlong, E.J. (1961) "Imagination in Hume's *Treatise* and *Enquiry concerning the Human Understanding*," *Philosophy* 36(136): 62–70.

Garrett, D. (1997) *Cognition and Commitment in Hume's Philosophy*, Oxford: Oxford University Press.

Garrett, D. (2006) "Hume's Naturalistic Theory of Representation," *Synthese* 152(3): 301–319.
Garrett, D. (2008) "Hume's Theory of Ideas," in E.S. Radcliffe (ed.) *A Companion to Hume*, Oxford: Wiley-Blackwell, 41–57.
Gendler, T. (2000) "The Puzzle of Imaginative Resistance," *Journal of Philosophy* 97(2): 55–81.
Gendler, T. (2006) "Imaginative Resistance Revisited," in S. Nichols (ed.) *The Architecture of the Imagination: New Essays on Pretence, Possibility, and Fiction*, Oxford: Oxford University Press, 149–174.
Gendler, T.S., and J. Hawthorne (eds.) (2002a) *Conceivability and Possibility*, Oxford: Clarendon Press.
Gendler, T.S., and J. Hawthorne (2002b). "Introduction: Conceivability and Possibility," in T.S. Gendler and J. Hawthorne (eds.) *Conceivability and Possibility*, Oxford: Oxford University Press.
Govier, T. (1972) "Variations on Force and Vivacity in Hume," *Philosophical Quarterly* 22(86): 44–52.
Grene, M. (1994) "The Objects of Hume's Treatise," *Hume Studies* 20(2): 163–177.
Hopkins, R. (1998) *Picture, Image and Experience*, Cambridge: Cambridge University Press.
Hume, D. (1739/2007) *A Treatise of Human Nature: A Critical Edition*, eds. D. Fate Norton and M.J. Norton, Clarendon Edition of the Works of David Hume, Oxford: Clarendon Press.
Hume, D. (1748/2007) *An Enquiry concerning the Principles of Morals*, Oxford: Oxford University Press.
Hume, D. (1757/2008) "Of the Standard of Taste," in *Selected Essays*, ed. S. Copley, Oxford: Oxford University Press.
Husserl, E. (1901/1970) *Logical Investigations*, vol. 2, London: Routledge.
Kail, P. (2003) "Conceivability and Modality in Hume: A Lemma in an Argument in Defense of Skeptical Realism," *Hume Studies* 29(1): 43–61.
Kant, I. (1781/1999) *Critique of Pure Reason*, Cambridge: Cambridge University Press.
Kölbel, M., and D. Zeman (eds.) (2012) *Relativism about Value*, special issue, *Southern Journal of Philosophy* 50(4).
Landy, D. (2006) "Hume's Impression/Idea Distinction," *Hume Studies* 32(1): 119–139.
Laurence, S., and E. Margolis (2012) "Abstraction and the Origin of General Ideas," *Philosophers' Imprint* 12(19): 1–22.
Lightner, D.T. (1997) "Hume on Conceivability and Inconceivability," *Hume Studies* 23(1): 113–132.
Locke, J. (1690/2008) *An Essay concerning Human Understanding*, ed. P. Phemister, Oxford: Oxford University Press.
Loeb, L.E. (2002) *Stability and Justification in Hume's Treatise*, Oxford: Oxford University Press.
MacFarlane, J. (2014) *Assessment Sensitivity: Relative Truth and Its Applications*, Oxford: Oxford University Press.
Malebranche, N. (1674/1997) *The Search after Truth*, eds. T.M. Lennon and P.J. Olscamp, Cambridge: Cambridge University Press.
Martin, M.G.F. (2001) "Out of the Past: Episodic Recall as Retained Acquaintance," in C. Hoerl and T. McCormack (eds.) *Time and Memory*, Oxford: Oxford University Press, 257–284.
Martin, M.G.F. (2002) "The Transparency of Experience," *Mind & Language* 17(4): 376–425.
Martin, M.G.F. (2006) "In Praise of Self: Hume's Love of Fame," *European Journal of Analytic Philosophy* 2(1): 69–100.
Marusiç, J.S. (2010) "Does Hume Hold a Dispositional Account of Belief?" *Canadian Journal of Philosophy* 40(2): 155–183.
Millican, P. (1998) "Hume on Reason and Induction," *Hume Studies* 24(1): 141–159.
Moran, R. (1994) "The Expression of Feeling in Imagination," *Philosophical Review* 103: 75–106.
Morris, W.E., and C. Brown (2013) "David Hume," in E.N. Zalta (ed.) *Stanford Encyclopedia of Philosophy* (Spring 2013 edition), <http://plato.stanford.edu/entries/hume/>.
Munoz-Dardé, V. (2002) "Seminar on David Hume's Treatise on Human Nature," handout, University College London.
Nichols, S. (2006) *The Architecture of the Imagination: New Essays on Pretence, Possibility, and Fiction*, Oxford: Clarendon Press.
O'Shaughnessy, B. (2003) *Consciousness and the World*, Oxford: Oxford University Press.
Owen, D. (1999) *Hume's Reason*, Oxford: Oxford University Press.
Owens, D. (2000) *Reason without Freedom: The Problem of Epistemic Normativity*, London: Routledge.
Peacocke, C. (1985) "Imagination, Experience and Possibility," in H. Robinson and J. Foster (eds.) *Essays on Berkeley*, Oxford: Clarendon Press.
Powell, L. (2013) "How to Avoid Mis-Reiding Hume's Maxim of Conceivability," *Philosophical Quarterly* 63(250): 105–119.
Prinz, J. (2002) *Furnishing the Mind: Concepts and Their Perceptual Basis*, Cambridge, MA: MIT Press.

Railton, P. (2003) *Facts, Values, and Norms: Essays toward a Morality of Consequence*, Cambridge: Cambridge University Press.
Reid, T. (1785/2002) *Essays on the Intellectual Powers of Man*, University Park: Pennsylvania State University Press.
Russow, L.-M. (1980) "Simple Ideas and Resemblance," *Philosophical Quarterly* 30(121): 342–350.
Sartre, J.-P. (1940/2004) *The Imaginary: A Phenomenological Psychology of the Imagination*, London: Routledge.
Schmitt, F.F. (2014) *Hume's Epistemology in the Treatise: A Veritistic Interpretation*, Oxford: Oxford University Press.
Strawson, G. (1989) *The Secret Connexion: Causation, Realism, and David Hume*, Oxford: Clarendon Press.
Stroud, B. (1999) *Hume*, London: Routledge.
Traiger, S. (2008) "Hume on Memory and Imagination," in E.S. Radcliffe (ed.) *A Companion to Hume*, Oxford: Wiley-Blackwell, 58–71.
Van Leeuwen, N. (2014) "The Meanings of 'Imagine' Part II: Attitude and Action," *Philosophy Compass* 9(11): 791–802.
Walton, K. (1990) *Mimesis as Make-Believe: On the Foundations of the Representational Arts*, Cambridge, MA: Harvard University Press.
Walton, K. (1994) "Morals in Fiction and Fictional Morality," *Proceedings of the Aristotelian Society, Supplementary Volume* 68: 27–50.
Williams, B. (1973) "Deciding to Believe," in *Problems of the Self: Philosophical Papers 1956–1972*, Cambridge: Cambridge University Press, 136–151.
Williams, B. (1980) "Internal and External Reasons," in *Moral Luck*, Cambridge: Cambridge University Press, 101–113.
Winkler, K. (1999) "Hume's Inductive Skepticism," in M. Atherton (ed.) *The Empiricists: Critical Essays on Locke, Berkeley, and Hume*, Lanham, MD: Rowman & Littlefield, 183–212.
Woudenberg, R. (2006) "Conceivability and Modal Knowledge," *Metaphilosophy* 37(2): 210–221.
Wright, J. (2013) "The Understanding," in J.A. Harris (ed.) *The Oxford Handbook of British Philosophy in the Eighteenth Century*, Oxford: Oxford University Press, 149–170.
Yablo, S. (1993) "Is Conceivability a Guide to Possibility?" *Philosophy and Phenomenological Research* 53(1): 1–42.

# 4

# KANT'S THEORY OF THE IMAGINATION

*Samantha Matherne*

## 1 Kant and the power of the imagination

Immanuel Kant's theory of the imagination is one of the most enduring aspects of his philosophy, inspiring philosophers ranging from Hegel to Sellars, Heidegger to Strawson. The lasting legacy of Kant's account is due, in part, to his *broad* conception of the imagination. In contrast to philosophers who construe the imagination as something that operates in fairly narrow confines, e.g., just in acts of make-believe or visualization, Kant conceives of the imagination as a more pervasive mental capacity that contributes to the cognitive, aesthetic, and moral aspects of our lives. Though compelling, the breadth of Kant's account also poses a certain challenge to readers: in what sense are the wide range of activities that Kant ascribes to the imagination to be understood as exercises of a *single* capacity? Moreover, given that he explicitly distinguishes between different levels of imaginative activity, e.g., empirical and transcendental, and different types of imaginative activity, e.g., productive and reproductive, how are we to understand the underlying unity of the imagination as Kant characterizes it?

In light of these questions, before we can proceed to an analysis of the contribution Kant takes the imagination to make in cognition, aesthetics, and morality, respectively, we need to begin with a discussion of his *basic* conception of the imagination. To this end, it will be helpful to consider two passages in which Kant offers a more general definition of the imagination. In the first passage, which appears in the so-called "B edition" of the *Critique of Pure Reason* (1787), Kant claims, "*Imagination* [Einbildungskraft] is a faculty for representing an object even *without its presence* in intuition" (B151).[1] As this definition suggests, Kant conceives of the imagination as a faculty of representation, more specifically, a faculty that is responsible for *intuitive*, i.e., sensible representations of objects that are not immediately present to us. This often happens when we imagine a physical object or property of an object that is no longer present to us, e.g., when I imagine a Frank Stella painting I saw two months ago or I see a house as having a back side even though I am only looking at its front side. However, as we shall see, on Kant's view, the imagination is not confined to representing objects in only this narrow physical sense; rather he takes the imagination to also be able to produce sensible representations of objects that are not present in virtue of being intellectual objects, e.g., concepts and ideas. This happens, for example, in make-believe when a child sees a stick as a wand, in fiction when I picture what Natasha from *War and Peace* looks like, or in mental imagery when I imagine the paragon of moral virtue. On a Kantian analysis, in each of these cases, the imagination plays a pivotal role because it brings something nonsensible, e.g., the absent Stella painting, the unseen back side of the house, the wand, Natasha, or moral virtue, to bear on our sensible representations. What this line of thought ultimately points to is Kant's idea that the imagination is fundamentally a capacity for producing representations that bridge the gap between what is sensible, on the one hand, and what is nonsensible or intellectual, on the other, and this mediating activity is one Kant takes to be crucial for our cognitive, aesthetic, and moral experience.

In the second passage, which is from the *Anthropology from a Pragmatic Point of View* (1798), Kant states,

> The power of imagination (*facultas imaginandi*), as a faculty of intuition without the presence of the object, is either *productive*, that is, a faculty of the original presentation [*Darstellung*] of the object (*exhibitio originaria*), which thus precedes experience; or *reproductive*, a faculty of the derivative presentation of the object (*exhibitio derivativa*), which brings back to mind an empirical intuition that it had previously.
>
> *(Kant 2006, 7:167)*

As we see in this passage, after reiterating the definition of the imagination from the first *Critique*, Kant claims that the imagination can produce a "presentation," i.e., a sensible representation of an object that is not directly present, in one of two ways. The imagination can act in a *productive* way when it functions as the original source of a presentation. For example, when Tolstoy develops the character Natasha in *War and Peace*, he produces an imaginative presentation of her that, in effect, brings her to life. Furthermore, rather than relying on past experience, in its productive exercise, the imagination makes experience possible. Although this can happen at the empirical level, e.g., Tolstoy's creation of Natasha makes the reader's particular experience of her possible, on Kant's view, this can also happen at the transcendental level, namely, when the imagination produces original representations that make experience *in general* possible. Meanwhile, in its *reproductive* exercise, the imagination acts in a wholly empirical way, producing presentations that are derived from past experience. For example, when I form an imaginative presentation of the Frank Stella painting I saw two months ago, I am reliving a past experience, rather than bringing something to life. What we learn from the *Anthropology*, then, is that the imagination can mediate between what is sensible and nonsensible in either a productive fashion, in which case it makes particular experiences or experience in general possible, or in a reproductive fashion, in which case it is constrained by past experience.

Taking these two passages together, we find that, for Kant, the imagination in general is a capacity for sensibly representing what is not present in either a productive or reproductive way and in so doing it mediates between the sensible and nonsensible aspects of our lives. With this overall framework for the imagination in place, we are now in a position to examine the distinctive contribution Kant takes the imagination to make to cognition and perception (Section 2), aesthetic judgment and artistic creation (Section 3), and morality (Section 4).

## 2 The imagination in cognition and perception

In the first *Critique*, Kant's account of cognition turns on his analysis of the various representational capacities and representations that make cognition possible. In addition to the imagination, he highlights two other capacities, namely, sensibility and understanding. Kant describes sensibility and understanding in dichotomous terms: whereas sensibility is a receptive and passive capacity, by means of which we are affected by the world, understanding is an active and spontaneous capacity, by means of which we think about the world. This dichotomous theme is carried over into Kant's description of the type of representation each capacity is responsible for. While sensibility provides intuitions, which are representations that are "immediately related to the object" and are "singular," understanding provides concepts, which are representations that relate "mediately" to objects "by means of a mark, which can be common to several things" (A320/B377). In spite of these differences, however, Kant insists that it is only through the combination of intuitions and concepts that cognition can arise:

> Intuition and concepts therefore constitute the elements of all our cognition, so that neither concepts without intuition corresponding to them in some way nor intuition without concepts can yield a cognition.
>
> *(A50/B74)*

Yet given the contrasts between sensibility and intuition, on the one hand, and understanding and concepts, on the other, how could they ever be brought together in cognition?

In order to answer this question, Kant appeals to the imagination: "Both extremes, namely sensibility and understanding, must necessarily be connected by means of this transcendental function of the imagination" (A124).[2] Kant claims that the imagination is able to play this intermediary role because it shares features with both sensibility and understanding. As we saw above, in §24 of the B Deduction, he claims that insofar as the imagination produces intuitive, sensible representations, it is aligned with sensibility (B151). However, he maintains that unlike the intuitions of sensibility that arise through passive affection, the intuitive representations for which the imagination is responsible are produced through the spontaneous activity of *synthesis*. On Kant's view, synthesis is an activity that involves different ways in which the manifold of intuition is "gone through, taken up, and combined," and he claims that both the imagination and understanding are capable of engaging in it (A77/B103). For this reason, he suggests that the imagination is similar to the understanding. Thus, given its dual nature as a capacity for producing sensible representations through synthetic activity, Kant thinks the imagination is able to mediate between sensibility and understanding in the way that is required for cognition.

According to Kant, this imaginative synthesis occurs in different ways in the cognitive context: it proceeds in both an *empirical* and *reproductive* way in perception and in a *transcendental* and *productive* way that lays the ground for the possibility of experience in general. Let's begin with Kant's account of the imagination's empirical contribution to perception. In a rather striking passage, Kant indicates that imaginative synthesis is a "necessary ingredient" of perception:

> No psychologist has yet thought that the imagination is a *necessary ingredient* of perception itself. This is so partly because … it has been believed that the senses do not merely afford us impressions but also *put them together*, and *produce images* of objects, for which without doubt something more than the receptivity of impressions is required, namely a function of the synthesis of them.
>
> *(A120 n., my emphasis)*

In this passage, Kant articulates one of the differences between his view and the "psychological," i.e., empiricist view of perception: whereas the empiricists treat perception as a passive process that depends on affection through sensibility alone, Kant insists that perception requires the imaginative activity of synthesis. More specifically, he thinks we need the imagination to put together intuitive representations in order to form a distinctive type of perceptual representation that he calls an "image" (*Bild*). This, indeed, is one of the important themes he pursues in his account of perception in both the Transcendental Deduction and in the so-called Schematism chapter.

However, before we consider the types of synthesis required for image formation, a few words are in order about the nature of images themselves. One of Kant's most helpful descriptions of images is found in his *Metaphysics $L_1$ Lectures* from the mid-1770s:

> My mind is always busy with forming the image of the manifold ... . The mind must undertake many observations in order to illustrate an object differently from each side ... . There are thus many appearances of a matter according to the various sides and points of view. The mind must make an illustration from all these appearances by taking them all together.
>
> *(Kant 1997, 28:235–6)*

As we see in this passage, Kant uses the term 'image' in what might seem like an unorthodox way: while we often think of an image as a representation of a single instant, e.g., a snapshot, he conceives of an image as a sensible representation of an object we perceive from multiple sides and points of view over time, e.g., a three-dimensional image. In other words, for Kant, an image is a single, complex sensible representation that illustrates the various perspectival appearances (or what Husserl might call "adumbrations") of an object. For example, when I perceive the pineapple on my table, depending on the position of my body, the lighting conditions, which side of it is facing me, etc., it will appear to me in different ways and, on Kant's view, an image of it unifies the representations of those appearances together in a single, more complex representation of the pineapple from those different sides and points of view.[3]

Kant offers his most extended analysis of the empirical synthesis required for image formation in the A Deduction, specifically in his analysis of the so-called "threefold synthesis" of apprehension, reproduction, and recognition (A97). Of these three syntheses, he attributes apprehension and reproduction to the imagination (reserving recognition for the understanding) and he claims that apprehension and reproduction are distinct, but "inseparably combined" forms of empirical imaginative synthesis that are aimed at image formation (A102, 120).[4] Kant characterizes apprehension as the act through which the imagination "run[s] through and then take[s] together" the manifold of intuition (A99). It successively gathers together the perceptual representations of an object that unfold across space and over time, e.g., the representation of the pineapple in front of me in the morning and the representation of it across the room from me at night. However, Kant says that,

> apprehension of the manifold alone would bring forth no image ... were there not a subjective ground for calling back a perception, from which the mind has passed to another ... i.e., a reproductive faculty of the imagination.
>
> *(A121)*

As this passage indicates, on Kant's view, the synthesis of reproduction is what allows us to "call back" representations in the manifold that are past and combine them with what we are representing here and now, e.g., now that it is evening, calling back the representation of the back side of the pineapple I formed in the morning. Kant aligns the synthesis of reproduction with what the empiricists call "association" and suggests that the laws that govern association are "merely empirical," based on the representations we have often associated with each other in the past (what Hume calls "custom" and "habit") (A100). On Kant's view, once apprehension successively takes up representations in the manifold and reproduction calls forth representations from the past, we are able to form the sorts of images that are required for perception.

However, this is not the whole story of imaginative synthesis in the Deduction, for Kant argues that the empirical syntheses of apprehension and reproduction are, in turn, made possible by the *transcendental* synthesis of the *productive* imagination. It is in this context that he clarifies how the imagination makes experience in general possible, highlighting its contribution on two counts, namely, to establishing the affinity of appearances and the objective reality of the categories. Beginning with affinity, according to Kant, in order for our imaginations to be able to empirically synthesize the manifold, there must be something about the appearances represented in the manifold that allows us to do so. To illustrate this point, Kant uses the example of cinnabar, the ore of mercury: "If cinnabar were now red, now black, now light, now heavy ... then my empirical imagination would never even get the opportunity to think of heavy cinnabar on the occasion of the representation of the color red" (A101). Yet the empirical rules governing apprehension and reproduction cannot be responsible for this associability because they presuppose it. Therefore, Kant claims there must be transcendental activities that account for the associability or "affinity" of appearances and he attributes some of these activities to the imagination (A122).

In particular, Kant argues that the imagination contributes to the possibility of affinity through a special act of transcendental synthesis in which it synthesizes together the a priori forms of intuition, i.e., space and time, and the a priori concepts of the understanding, i.e., the twelve categories, like *cause, substance, reality*, etc. Insofar as space and time are the a priori conditions of all appearances, when the imagination applies the categories to space and time, the categories will come to determine all possible appearances and this will make them associable. In the A Deduction, Kant calls this the "transcendental function" of the imagination (A123). Meanwhile in §24 of the B Deduction, he labels this the "figurative synthesis" (*synthesis speciosa*) of the imagination, which he describes as follows.

> the imagination is ... a faculty for determining the sensibility *a priori*, and its synthesis of intuitions, *in accordance with the categories*, must be the transcendental synthesis of the *imagination*.
>
> *(B152)*

Not only does this ground the affinity of appearances, but also in §24 Kant argues that through this imaginative act the categories acquire "objective reality, i.e., application to objects that can be given to us in intuition" (B150–1).[5] This is no small feat given Kant's aim in the Deduction to prove that the categories are objectively valid with respect to objects of the senses.

Although in the Deduction Kant establishes *that* the productive imagination engages in this transcendental synthesis that mediates between sensibility and understanding, he has not yet told us *how* this takes place: the latter is the task of the brief (and notoriously dense) chapter called "On the Schematism of the Pure Concepts of the Understanding."[6] The Schematism is the first chapter of Kant's "Transcendental Doctrine of the Power of Judgment" and he suggests that there is a puzzle about how those judgments are possible in which we subsume intuitions under the categories:

> Now pure concepts of the understanding, however, in comparison with empirical (indeed in general sensible intuitions), are entirely unhomogeneous and can never be encountered in any intuition. Now how is the *subsumption* of the latter under the former, thus the *application* of the category to appearances possible?
>
> *(A137–138/B176–177)*

In order for this subsumption to take place, Kant argues that there must be some "third thing" that is capable of mediating between the two, something that is sensible, on the one hand, and intellectual, on the other (A138/B177). He identifies this third thing as a special type of "mediating representation" produced by the imagination, which he labels a 'schema,' and he claims that it involves a "rule" or "procedure" by means of which the imagination brings the relevant concepts and intuitions together (A138/B177, A140–1/B180).

More specifically, Kant claims that in order to mediate between the categories and intuition, the imagination produces a particular type of transcendental schema, which he describes as a "time-determination," i.e., a determination of the a priori manifold of time in accordance with the categories (A138/B178). Insofar as these schemata are determinations of time *in general* they attain a level of universality that makes them homogeneous with the categories, and insofar as they are *temporal*, they are homogeneous with intuition (A138–139/B177–178). To cite a few examples, Kant claims that the schema for *substance* is "the persistence of the real in time" and that the schema for *causality* involves a particular "succession" in the manifold, such that "whenever [one thing] is posited, something else always follows" (A144/B183). Another interesting example with respect to Kant's theory of mathematics is the schema of *magnitude*, under which heading falls the concepts of *unity, plurality*, and *totality*: "The pure *schema of magnitude* (*quantitas*), however, as a concept of the understanding, is *number*, which is a representation that summarizes the successive addition of one (homogeneous) unit to another" (A142/B182). After discussing the schemata that are connected to each category, Kant concludes his discussion by reiterating the idea that the productive imagination, here in its schematizing activities, contributes to the objective significance of the categories: "the schemata of the concepts of pure understanding are the true and sole conditions for providing them with a relation to objects, thus with *significance* [*Bedeutung*]" (A145–6/B185).

Although this analysis of transcendental schematism takes place at a high level of abstraction, Kant also discusses two more sensible forms of schematism: the schematism of "pure sensible" (mathematical) concepts, e.g., the concept *triangle*, and of empirical concepts, e.g., the concept *dog* (A141/B180). This discussion returns him to a different theme in the Deduction, namely, that of image formation; Kant claims that these sensible schemata are that "through which and in accordance with which the images first become possible" (A142/B181). According to Kant in the Schematism, an image is a sensible representation that "must be connected with the concept," and it is once again a schema that mediates this connection between the sensible and conceptual (A142/B181). More specifically Kant suggests that we should think of these more sensible schemata as "monograms," i.e., basic outlines or gestalts we have in our minds that represent the relevant concept in sensible form, e.g., the schema for the concept *triangle* is a vague outline of an enclosed three-sided figure and the schema for the concept *dog* is a basic gestalt of the generic features of dogs, e.g., being four-legged, furry, slobbery, etc. (A141/B181). However, Kant insists that these schemata are not to be confused with images: whereas images are *particular* representations of an object we currently perceive, a schema is a *generic* representation that is supposed to apply to multiple instances of a concept, e.g., my schema for triangles must apply to equilateral and right alike (A141/B180). On his view, schemata make images possible because the monograms that they involve serve as rules or procedures we follow in synthesizing various manifolds of intuition in accordance with one and the same concept. So understood, the schema serves as something like a stencil we follow when we engage in the sorts of empirical synthesis required for image formation. My schema for the concept *dog*, for example, serves as a guide for me to follow in synthesizing the different manifolds of intuition I have in such a way that in each case, I can produce an image that is connected to the concept *dog*. Thus Kant's analysis of the schematizing activities of the imagination not only explains how the categories can apply to intuition at an a priori level, but also completes his account of how synthesis and image formation are possible at an empirical level.

In the end, whether we consider Kant's analysis of the reproductive synthesis of the imagination and image formation or its productive exercise in figurative synthesis and schematism in the first *Critique*, the imagination emerges as a capacity that makes perception and cognition possible by mediating between intuitions and concepts at both the empirical and transcendental levels.

## 3 The imagination in aesthetics

In the next two sections, we will shift our attention toward Kant's account of the imagination in the *Critique of the Power of Judgment* (1790), addressing how it contributes to both the aesthetic and moral aspects of our lives. To appreciate this contribution, however, it is important to situate Kant's analysis of the imagination within his larger project in the third *Critique*. While in the first *Critique*, Kant explicates the domain of nature and in the second *Critique*, he explores the domain of freedom, the task he sets for himself in the third *Critique* is to explain how to bridge the "great chasm" between these two domains (KU 5:195). Though Kant's full explanation of how this happens by means of the power of judgment is quite complicated, for our purposes it will suffice to examine the ways in which the specifically productive activities of our imagination help reach across this divide. Let's consider how this works in the case of aesthetic judgment and artistic creation.

In §1 of the third *Critique*, Kant begins his analysis of aesthetic judgments, in which we judge an object to be beautiful, by distinguishing them from the sorts of cognitive judgments he was concerned with in the first *Critique*: "The judgment of taste is therefore not a cognitive judgment … but rather aesthetic, by which is understood one whose determining ground *cannot* be *other than subjective*" (KU 5:203). He identifies this subjective determining ground as a special type of pleasure we take in the beautiful: a pleasure that is intersubjectively shareable or communicable (*mittheilbar*) and produced through the free play of our imagination and understanding.

With regard to the shareability of pleasure, Kant claims that when we judge an object to be beautiful, we believe that we "have grounds for expecting a similar pleasure of everyone" (KU 5:211). In Kant's technical language, the beautiful is an object of "universal" and "necessary" satisfaction. However, given that not every felt pleasure is one we can expect all other human beings to share with us, e.g., though I find the taste of pineapple pleasurable you may not, the question becomes how to account for the distinctive type of shareable pleasure we feel in the beautiful.

In §9, Kant answers this question by appealing to the notion of the free play of the imagination and understanding. In this section he takes up the question of whether in a judgment of taste the feeling of pleasure precedes the judging of the object or whether the judging of the object precedes the pleasure. He rules out the first option because he argues that if the pleasure came first, then the judgment would be grounded on what is agreeable to our senses, something that is of "only private validity" (KU 5:217). By contrast, he claims that if pleasure in the beautiful is grounded in the judging of the object, insofar as this judging involves something that is communicable, then the pleasure will be communicable as well.

More specifically, Kant argues that, "[n]othing ... can be universally communicated except cognition" and even though an aesthetic judgment does not involve a cognitive judgment in which we apply a concept to an object, nevertheless Kant claims that it still has a cognitive dimension insofar as it involves the interaction between our cognitive capacities, specifically the imagination and understanding. As he tends to make this point, aesthetic judgments involve a "state of mind" that is at work in "cognition in general" (KU 5:217). This being said, Kant argues that in aesthetic judgment the imagination and understanding are proportioned to each other in a special way, namely, in a state he describes as free play:

> The powers of cognition that are set into play by this representation [of the beautiful] are hereby in a free play, since no determinate concept restricts them to a particular rule of cognition.
>
> *(KU 5:217)*[7]

In this state of free play, Kant suggests that there is a particular "harmony" that arises between the capacities: they are "enlivened through mutual agreement" and the "inner relationship [between the capacities] is optimal for the animation of both powers of the mind (the one through the other)" (KU 5:218, 219, 238). Now, according to Kant, being in a state of free play while judging the object gives rise to pleasure and insofar as the state itself is shareable, the subsequent pleasure can be shareable as well: "this merely subjective (aesthetic) judging of the object ... precedes the pleasure in it, and is the ground of this pleasure in the harmony of the faculties of cognition" (KU 5:218).

Though this account of pleasure plays a pivotal role in Kant's analysis of judgments of taste, the idea that the imagination here engages in a state of *free* play is important for his overall goal in the third *Critique*. On his view, unlike in its reproductive exercise, where the imagination is "subjected to the laws of association," in aesthetic judgment, the imagination acts in a way that is "productive and self-active" (KU 5:240). The imagination no longer has to synthesize a manifold in light of a particular concept, but is rather free to explore or play with putting the manifold together in a multitude of different ways. For example, when we look at Caravaggio's *The Calling of Saint Matthew*, we do not have to see it simply as instancing one concept, say, *chiaroscuro*; though we can see it through this lens, we are free to also see it in terms of, say, the foreground-background structure, the use of color, how the painting conveys the feeling of responsibility, etc. This being said, although the imagination plays in a *free* way in aesthetic judgment, on Kant's view it must nevertheless be in free play *with* the understanding. For this reason, Kant characterizes the imagination's state as one of "free lawfulness" (KU 5:240).[8] On his view, the imagination's state is lawful because even without a specific concept guiding it, our imaginative activity must still accord with the understanding's demand that there be "unity" in what the imagination synthesizes (KU 5:287). When looking at the Caravaggio painting, my imagination must still help me see it in ways that are unified and ordered; were I to detect only chaos, this would not be a state of free play. Setting the details aside, what is ultimately significant about free play for Kant's overarching purposes is that it is a state in which although we encounter spatial and/or temporal objects, i.e., objects that belong to the sensible world, we are exercising our imaginative capacities in a way that is free with respect to these objects.

A second way in which the imagination's aesthetic activities contribute to the mediation between nature and freedom emerges in Kant's analysis of artistic activity, especially of genius. Kant defines genius as "the exemplary originality of the natural endowment of a subject for the *free* use of his cognitive faculties" (KU 5:318). In §49, he identifies the relevant cognitive faculties as the imagination and understanding and (echoing his account of aesthetic judgment) he argues that unlike in cognition, in genius, the imagination relates to the understanding in a free way:

> in the use of the imagination for cognition, the imagination is under the constraint of the understanding and is subject to being adequate to its concept; in an aesthetic respect, however, the imagination is free to provide, beyond that concord with the concept, unsought extensive undeveloped material for the understanding.
>
> *(KU 5:316–7)*

On Kant's view, when the artist's imagination relates to the understanding in this free way, it reveals itself as a "productive" capacity that can act creatively:

> The imagination (as a productive cognitive faculty) is, namely very powerful in creating, as it were another nature, out of the material the real one gives us … in this we feel our freedom from the law of association.
>
> *(KU 5:314)*

According to Kant, when the artist's imagination acts in this productive and creative way, it produces a special type of imaginative representation that he labels an 'aesthetic idea,' i.e., the idea that is expressed through her work of art.

Kant defines an aesthetic idea as follows:

> In a word, the aesthetic idea is a representation of the imagination, associated with a given concept, which is combined with such a manifold of partial representations in the free use of the imagination that no expression designating a determinate concept can be found for it.
>
> *(KU 5:316)*

Notice that Kant claims an aesthetic idea is a representation of the imagination that is connected to a given concept. On his view, in order for an activity to count as art, the artist must be guided by some intention she sets through her understanding, i.e., some "determinate concept of the product, as an end," however vague or changeable this concept may be (KU 5:317). Once the artist has a concept, Kant claims that her imagination sets to work in producing an aesthetic idea that simultaneously "presents" and "expands" that original concept (KU 5:317, 315). He maintains that the artist does this by adding "aesthetic attributes" to the concept, i.e., imaginative representations that are connected to, though not logically contained in, the concept (KU 5:315). Consider, for example, Yeats's poem "Sailing to Byzantium," the guiding concept of which is something like the state of one's soul at the end of one's life (Yeats 1996, 193–194).[9] On a Kantian analysis, by means of powerful images ("aesthetic attributes") like an old man sailing away to Byzantium, seas teeming with salmon and mackerel, tattered coats on sticks, gold mosaics, dying animals, etc., Yeats produces an aesthetic idea which articulates and expands his original concept in a rich way. As Kant might make this point, Yeats,

> add[s] to a concept a representation of the imagination that belongs to its presentation, but which by itself stimulates so much thinking that it can never be grasped in a determinate concept, hence which aesthetically enlarges the concept itself in an unbounded way.
>
> *(KU 5:315)*

The imaginative world of this poem is so expansive that we can find no determinate concept or single interpretation that would adequately capture the wealth of meaning that it contains. From a Kantian perspective, then, Yeats's genius consists in his natural talent for exercising his imagination in a free, productive, and creative way in order to extend concepts beyond their ordinary limits.

This, in turn, points toward the way genius mediates between nature and freedom. To begin, insofar as genius is a *natural* talent for *free* activity, there is something about the artist herself that unifies nature and freedom. Moreover, insofar as the production of an aesthetic idea involves an artist freely transforming nature in light of her concepts and ends, genius signals a way in which if we act "in accordance with principles that lie higher in reason … nature can be transformed by us into something entirely different, namely into that which steps beyond nature" (KU 5:314).

## 4 The moral imagination

The final dimension of Kant's account of the imagination that we shall consider pertains to morality and his claim that the imagination can help bridge the gap between nature and freedom in virtue of the role it plays in aesthetic contexts that have a specifically *moral* dimension. In particular in his analysis of aesthetic ideas, beauty as a symbol of morality, and the sublime, he argues that the imagination helps us see how we as moral agents can have influence on the sensible world.

Beginning with the moral significance of aesthetic ideas, Kant says that some aesthetic ideas "make sensible rational ideas" (KU 5:314). On his view, rational ideas are a special class of ideas that involve concepts that lie "beyond experience" in the sense that an object that corresponds to them can never be given in intuition, e.g., ideas like freedom and the highest good (KU 5:342). Kant claims that oftentimes artists will develop aesthetic ideas that strive to sensibly present these rational ideas and this process can be morally valuable insofar as it offers us moral encouragement. On his view, these aesthetic ideas give rational ideas the "appearance of an objective reality," i.e., they make it seem as if rational ideas can, in fact, be realized in sensible ways (KU 5:314). Consider, for example, Kant's description of the "ideal of beauty" in §17. According to Kant, the ideal of beauty is an aesthetic idea that represents a human being as both a sensible and moral exemplar: not only is this person correctly proportioned physically, but also she embodies moral virtues. Describing the ideal of beauty, Kant says,

> The visible expression of moral ideas, which inwardly govern human beings … make visible in bodily manifestation (as the effect of what is inward) their combination with everything that our understanding connects with the morally good in the idea of the highest purposiveness – goodness of soul, or purity, or strength, or repose, etc.
>
> *(KU 5:235)*

Insofar as this aesthetic idea and others like it present us with a picture of how our moral ideas can be realized by an embodied human being, they encourage us in our attempts to do the same.

According to Kant, another way in which the imagination can bring together nature and freedom is by leading us to engage in acts of reflection that are conducive to morality. This emerges in §59: "On Beauty as the Symbol of Morality."[10] He begins this section by distinguishing two ways in which the imagination can present a concept in sensible form: through "schematic" or "symbolic" presentation (KU 5:351). According to Kant, while a schema is a "direct" presentation of a concept, e.g., the schema of the category *cause*, a symbol is an "indirect" presentation of a concept that induces a "form of reflection ... which corresponds to the concept" (KU 5:351). To borrow Kant's example, a hand mill is a symbol of a despotic state because the way we reflect on the mechanical nature of a hand mill parallels how we reflect on the mechanical nature of a despotic state (KU 5:352). For Kant, then, symbols are imaginative presentations that invite a pattern of reflection in us that is similar to the pattern of reflection the relevant concept calls for.

Kant goes on to assert that "the beautiful is the symbol of the morally good" (KU 5:353). He suggests that the symbolic relation between the two is grounded in the fact that reflection on both beauty and the morally good involves two things: first, "a certain ennoblement and elevation above the mere receptivity" (KU 5:353). Unlike cases in which we are merely passive with respect to the world, in our aesthetic and moral reflection, we regard ourselves as free and active. Second, Kant claims that our judgments about the beautiful and the morally good require us to "esteem the value of others": whether we think of the intersubjectivity built into the feeling of pleasure we take in the beautiful or the moral demand to respect others, in both judgments we must take others into account, instead of just focusing on ourselves (KU 5:353). For these reasons, Kant thinks the imagination's presentation of beauty as the symbol of morality "makes possible the transition from sensible charm to the habitual moral interest without too violent a leap" because it helps us develop the reflective capacities required for morality (KU 5:354).

On Kant's view, however, there is a further way in which the imagination can play a role in alerting us to our moral vocation and this occurs in judgments of the sublime (§§23–29). Kant distinguishes between two types of the sublime: the mathematically sublime, which involves objects that are very large, e.g., the Grand Canyon, and the dynamically sublime, which involves objects that are very powerful, e.g., a hurricane. Whereas in judgments of beauty the imagination relates to the understanding, Kant claims that in judgments of the sublime the imagination relates to reason (KU 5:247). Moreover, he claims that unlike the purely pleasurable experience involved in the free play of our faculties in judgments of the beautiful, judgments of the sublime involve two moments: an initial feeling of displeasure when we realize our sensible limits and a subsequent feeling of pleasure when we recognize the superiority of reason in us over nature.

In teasing out the imagination's contribution to judgments of the sublime, it may be tempting to think that given its connection to sensibility, the imagination is solely responsible for the displeasure we feel, while reason alone is the source of pleasure. Kant does indeed indicate that the displeasure we feel is connected to the limits of the imagination. For example, he claims that in the case of the mathematically sublime, we feel displeasure because the object is so large that although the imagination can "apprehend" it, the imagination fails when it tries to "comprehend" it, i.e., combine the manifold of intuition together into a single image (KU 5:252). However, although the imagination's inadequacies give rise to the displeasure we feel in the sublime, Kant also maintains that the imagination makes a positive contribution to the pleasure we feel.

In more detail, Kant argues that when we initially perceive the object we judge to be sublime, the imagination acts in a reproductive way, i.e., "in accordance with the law of association [and] makes our statement of contentment physically dependent" (KU 5:270). Given the large or powerful nature of the physical objects we perceive, this gives rise to displeasure. Yet Kant argues that there is a second moment in the sublime, a moment in which the imagination discovers that it has a higher "vocation," namely, serving as an instrument of reason (KU 5:257):

> the very same imagination, in accordance with principles of the schematism of the power of judgment (consequently to the extent that it is subordinate to freedom) is an instrument of reason and its ideas …, a power to assert our independence in the face of influences of nature, to diminish the value of what is great according to these, and so to place what is absolutely great only in its (the subject's) own vocation.
>
> *(KU 5:269)*

Part of our feeling of pleasure in the sublime, then, stems from the imagination finding that it is not just bound by nature, but has a higher calling to act in accordance with reason and freedom. This is yet another expression of how the imagination spans across the domains of nature and freedom insofar as its interaction with a natural object reveals our ability as free agents to rise above natural constraint.

In the end, whether we consider aesthetic ideas, beauty as a symbol of morality, or the sublime, we find Kant highlighting the significant moral function of the imagination as it mediates between nature and freedom, encouraging us to see the former as something that can be transformed in light of the latter and making us aware of the latter within us. This, however, is but another way in which the imagination plays its fundamental role in Kant's system, bridging the gaps in human life, enabling us to see beyond what is here and now to the rich layers of meaning that give our human world its texture.

## Acknowledgments

I would like to thank Dai Heide, Amy Kind, Colin Marshall, James Messina, and Dennis Sepper for helpful feedback on this entry.

## Notes

1 References to Kant's (1998) *Critique of Pure Reason* are to the A and B pagination of the first (1781) and second (1787) editions (A/B). All other references are to the volume and page of *Kants gesammelte Schriften*. KU, *Critique of the Power of Judgment* (Kant 2002).

2 For the argument that the imagination is, in fact, the "common root" of sensibility and understanding (A15/B29), see Heidegger 1990, 1997. For criticism of Heidegger's view, see Henrich 1994.

3 Insofar as Kant's images involve the perceptual representation of features of an object that are no longer present to us, e.g., when I represent the pineapple as having a back side even though only its front side is currently present to me, Kant's account bears on what Noë (e.g., 2004) calls the "problem of perceptual presence." For a discussion of how Kant's account of the imagination bears on this problem, see Sellars 1978, Thomas 2009, and Kind forthcoming.

4 There is a debate as to whether this imaginative synthesis occurs preconceptually or must be guided by the conceptual synthesis of recognition, see, e.g., Strawson 1974, Young 1988, and Ginsborg 2008. This issue is further complicated by the fact that in the B edition, Kant seems to attribute all synthesis to the understanding (see, e.g., B130, B162 n.).

5 For a further argument that our representation of space and time (discussed at B160–1 n.) depends on the transcendental synthesis of the imagination, see Waxman 1991, pt. 1, Longuenesse 1998, pt. 3.

6 For a discussion of the Schematism and relevant debates in the secondary literature, e.g., about whether Kant needed to write this chapter at all, why he identifies transcendental schemata as temporal and not spatial, the relationship between empirical and transcendental schemata, and whether empirical schemata collapse to empirical concepts, see Allison 2004, ch. 8.
7 See Guyer 2005 for a discussion of the debate whether free play occurs without any concepts or whether it involves some concepts, perhaps a multiplicity of them.
8 See Ginsborg 1997 for a discussion of how free lawfulness plays a role in Kant's account of aesthetic and cognitive judgment.
9 Describing his intentions in a draft for a BBC broadcast, Yeats says, "I am trying to write about the state of my soul, for it is right for an old man to make his soul, and some of my thoughts about that subject I have put into a poem called 'Sailing to Byzantium'" (in Jeffares 1968, 253).
10 For a discussion of the relevant secondary literature and how §59 bears on the connection between works of genius and moral motivation, see Ostaric 2010.

## Further reading

G. Banham, *Kant's Transcendental Imagination* (London: Palgrave Macmillan, 2006) examines Kant's analysis of the imagination in the first *Critique*, with a thorough discussion of secondary literature. J. Bates, *Hegel's Theory of Imagination* (New York: SUNY Press, 2004), ch. 1, discusses the relationship between Kant's theory of the imagination and that of Fichte, Schelling, and Hegel. A systematic treatment of how the imagination bridges the gaps in cognitive, aesthetic, and moral experience is found in S. Gibbons, *Kant's Theory of Imagination* (Oxford: Oxford University Press, 1994). J. Kneller, *Kant and the Power of Imagination* (Cambridge: Cambridge University Press, 2007) analyzes Kant's account of the freedom of the imagination and his relationship to the early Romantics. R. Makkreel, *Imagination and Interpretation in Kant* (Chicago: University of Chicago Press, 1990) offers a systematic treatment of the hermeneutic themes in Kant's account of the imagination in the first and third *Critiques*. M.L. Thompson (ed.) *Imagination in Kant's Critical Philosophy* (Berlin: de Gruyter, 2013) is a recent collection of essays on the role the imagination plays in Kant's metaphysics, epistemology, aesthetics, and moral theory. And M. Zinkin, "Film and the Transcendental Imagination: Kant and Hitchcock's *The Lady Vanishes*," in D. Lopes and M. Kieran (eds.) *Imagination, Philosophy, and the Arts* (London: Routledge, 2003), 245–258, is a defense of a Kantian theory of film that is based on his account of the transcendental imagination and meant to contrast with more contemporary psychological and psychoanalytic theories.

## References

Allison, H. (2004) *Kant's Transcendental Idealism*, New Haven: Yale University Press.
Ginsborg, H. (1997) "Lawfulness without a Law: Kant on the Free Play of Imagination and Understanding," *Philosophical Topics* 25(1): 37–81.
Ginsborg, H. (2008) "Was Kant a Nonconceptualist?" *Philosophical Studies* 137: 65–77.
Guyer, P. (2005) "The Harmony of the Faculties Revisited," in *Values of Beauty: Historical Essays in Aesthetics*, Cambridge: Cambridge University Press, 77–109.
Heidegger, M. (1990) *Kant and the Problem of Metaphysics*, 5th edn., trans. R. Taft, Bloomington: Indiana University Press.
Heidegger, M. (1997) *Phenomenological Interpretation of Kant's Critique of Pure Reason*, trans. P. Emad and K. Maly, Bloomington: Indiana University Press.
Henrich, D. (1994) "On the Unity of Subjectivity," in *The Unity of Reason*, trans. G. Zöller, Cambridge: Harvard University Press, 17–54.
Jeffares, A. (1968) *Commentary on the Collected Poems of W.B. Yeats*, Stanford: Stanford University Press.
Kant, I. (1997) *Lectures on Metaphysics*, trans. K. Ameriks and S. Naragon, Cambridge: Cambridge University Press.
Kant, I. (1998) *Critique of Pure Reason*, trans. P. Guyer and A. Wood, Cambridge: Cambridge University Press.
Kant, I. (2002) *Critique of the Power of Judgment*, trans. P. Guyer and E. Matthews, Cambridge: Cambridge University Press.
Kant, I. (2006) *Anthropology from a Pragmatic Point of View*, trans. R. Louden, Cambridge: Cambridge University Press.

Kind, A. (Forthcoming) "Phenomenal Presence," in F. Dorsch, F. Macpherson, and M. Nide-Rumelin (eds.) *Perceptual Presence*, Oxford: Oxford University Press.

Longuenesse, B. (1998) *Kant and the Capacity to Judge*, trans. C. Wolfe, Princeton: Princeton University Press.

Noë, A. (2004) *Action in Perception*, Cambridge: MIT Press.

Ostaric, L. (2010) "Works of Genius as Sensible Exhibitions of the Idea of the Highest Good," *Kant-Studien* 101(1): 22–39.

Sellars, W. (1978) "The Role of the Imagination in Kant's Theory of Experience," in H. Johnstone Jr. (ed.) *Categories: A Colloquium*, University Park: Pennsylvania State University, 231–245.

Strawson, P.F. (1974) "Imagination and Perception," repr. in *Freedom and Resentment and Other Essays*, New York: Harper & Row, 50–72.

Thomas, A. (2009) "Perceptual Presence and the Productive Imagination," *Philosophical Topics* 37(1): 153–174.

Waxman, W. (1991) *Kant's Model of the Mind*, Oxford: Oxford University Press.

Yeats, W.B. (1996) "Sailing to Byzantium," in *The Collected Poems of W.B. Yeats*, ed. R. Finneran, New York: Scribner, 193–194.

Young, J.M. (1988) "Kant's View of Imagination," *Kant Studien* 79: 140–164.

# 5
# HUSSERL

*Julia Jansen*

Hardly any other philosopher in the history of philosophy has paid as much detailed attention to the nature of imagining and to the distinct characteristics of imagined objects as Husserl. Yet, Husserl's lectures on imagination have been translated into English only relatively recently (Husserl 2005), and even in the German original they have been available in print only since 1980 (Husserl 1980). Scattered discussions of imagination can be found throughout Husserl's *oeuvre*, from the *Logical Investigations* (1900–1) to the posthumously published *Experience and Judgment* (1939) – evidence of the significance it had for him. This is not surprising, given that Husserl himself stresses the central importance of imagination, famously referring to it as a "vital element" of phenomenology (Husserl 1983, 160)[1]. In particular, Husserl exploits our ability to "vary" examples of experiential types (e.g., examples of perception, examples of judging, etc.) for the purpose of identifying their "essential" features. Thus, imagination is indispensable for the phenomenological method Husserl calls "eidetic analysis" (Husserl 1973, §§86–88; Mohanty 1997; Sokolowski 1974). Far from being a marginal topic of "special interest" for fiction, pretense, or "mind reading," for example imagination is, for Husserl, a crucial key to answering fundamental questions concerning consciousness. The picture that emerges from his in-depth investigations differs significantly from classical philosophical accounts of imagination: Imagination is neither reducible to waning after-images, derivative of perception – a view dominating modern philosophy at least from Hobbes to Hume; nor is it a basic mental capacity for synthesis – another dominant idea, finding its most systematic formulation in Kant's account of imagination (see "Kant" and "Hume," Chapters 4 and 3 in this volume).

Rather than inferring the nature of imagination from certain functions ascribed to it in an overall theory of mind and cognition, Husserl's phenomenological method delivers descriptions of concrete acts of imagining in an attempt to identify its essential characteristics. In these descriptions, Husserl distances his account clearly from available philosophical "constructions" of imagination and connects it more obviously to how imagining is actually experienced "in real life." He thus avoids the standard philosophical term for imagination, *Einbildungskraft*, and instead speaks of *Phantasie*, which is the more widely used and less technical term for imagination in German. Moreover, *Phantasie* has the advantage of lacking any suggestion that imagination operates by means of mental images (*Bilder*) – an inevitable connotation of *Einbildungskraft*. According to Husserl, imagining is a distinct and nonderivative act of consciousness that constitutes a direct sensory awareness of objects, i.e., an awareness that is unmediated by images. Imagining thereby resembles perception and differs from another distinct act of consciousness that Husserl identifies: "image consciousness [*Bildbewusstsein*]," the awareness of an image qua image. However, imagining also differs from perception insofar as its objects are not experienced as real, or actually perceived, and insofar as the activity of imagining is itself experienced as a simulation of a possible perception, or as a "quasi perception."

Husserl's views have influenced several generations of philosophical treatments of the imagination. However, these influences remain largely unacknowledged, most likely due to prevalent preconceptions about Husserl's general philosophical position, which tend to motivate a certain skepticism concerning the value and significance of his account of imagination for current debate. In particular, Husserl's reputation in some circles (Føllesdal's 1969, 1990; Smith and McIntyre 1984) as an idealist representationalist, who is stuck in a post-Cartesian-subject philosophy, tends to obstruct the view on his profound and original systematic work on the imagination. This representationalist interpretation considers Husserl's notion of intentionality to rely on separate intensional entities (representations) that mediate the relation of the mental event or state to the world. The very fact that Husserl attributes such importance to the imagination may then be taken only to corroborate this interpretation, especially if one assumes that cases of imagination are paradigmatic cases of such representational mediation. This leads one to expect a rather conventional story from Husserl, which may be safely ignored. What's more, the imagination's declared "vital" methodological function for phenomenology only ties Husserl's account of imagination to one of the most contested notions in his work overall, namely, the notion of "eidetic analysis" understood as a search for "essences" of experience. Suspicions regarding the latter easily slide into suspicions regarding the former.

However, the standard picture of Husserlian idealism is now slowly being replaced by a new interpretation – one that is based on a far more comprehensive view of his *oeuvre* and that takes the ways in which Husserl radically reappropriates idealist, as well as empiricist, currents of philosophy within his original phenomenological framework far more seriously. This development has enabled a fresh and open look at Husserl's original account of imagination, which, upon close examination, lends further support to the view that Husserl's *transcendental* idealism is inextricably linked to a strong antirepresentationalist realism – a view that is increasingly gaining currency in the scholarship (Drummond 2012; Zahavi 2003). This puts Husserl in much closer proximity to Heidegger and Merleau-Ponty than to Descartes and Hume and renders questionable any quick dismissal of his idea of "essence" (or *eidos*) as indicative of a laughable neo-Platonic antirealism.

Insofar as Husserl's investigations into imagination span over thirty years of work and are found mainly either in the form of lectures and research manuscripts, or scattered throughout his published books in the midst of discussions concerning other topics, he never supplied one explicit and definitive treatise on the matter. Moreover, he significantly and fundamentally changed his views in the course of his investigations, which begin in seriousness around 1904 and stabilize around ten years later with what we might call his "mature" account. In what follows, I attempt a careful reconstruction of his mature view with some references, for the sake of contrast, to positions Husserl held during earlier phases of his work on imagination.

## Imagining: a Husserlian description

Husserl describes imagining as an experience of something in the mode of "nonactuality" or "irreality" (*Unwirklichkeit*). Genuine cases of imagining (as opposed to, for example, cases of "mere supposing," or of "imagining that") are cases of sensory imagination. Imagining is, in the language of German philosophy, "intuitive [*anschaulich*]," that is, we do not simply imagine something, we imagine *seeing, hearing, smelling, tasting and/or touching* something. An imagined object or scene is imagined as *being seen, heard, smelled, tasted and/or touched*. An object that (*de jure*, not *de facto*) *cannot* be experienced in at least one of these modes is "unimaginable" in the relevant sense. Hence, the distinction between imagining and perceiving does not depend on the absence or presence of such sensory contents, nor, as Hume would have it, does it depend on their comparative vivacity. Instead, it depends on the distinct mode in which they are experienced: namely, in the mode of "nonactuality" [*Unwirklichkeit*] or "actuality" [*Wirklichkeit*] respectively.

To say that an imagined object is experienced as "nonactual" or "irreal," rather than as "unreal," is meant to avoid the impression that only a particular set of objects are imaginable, namely, those that are unreal, or nonexistent. We may, but need not, imagine unreal, nonexistent objects, such as unicorns and golden mountains. We may just as well imagine objects that in fact exist, such as a gorgeous beach, or a cold beer; or we may imagine being at that beach, or having that cold beer. Imagining does not involve a relation to objects of a special ontological category, e.g., nonexistent or fictional objects, but rather involves a particular mode of relating to objects. Referring to imagined objects as "nonactual" suggests that they are experienced as objects that *could* be actual (because they are, to speak with Kant, "possible objects of experience"); they *are* not, or at least not in the present environment of the person imagining. Referring to imagined objects as "irreal" suggests that the person imagining is indifferent toward their ontological status, real or not; the usual positionality – which, according to Husserl, accompanies other acts (in perception, objects are posited as actual; in memory, objects are posited as having been actual, etc.) – is *neutralized*. The senses of both "nonactual," which points toward imagining as awareness of *possibilities*, and "irreal," which points toward its ontological *neutrality*, are combined in the sense of the German *unwirklich*.

In Husserl's terminology, imagining is "quasi-perceptual"; a *Phantasie* is a "quasi-perception [*Quasi-Wahrnehmung*]." Whereas in perception "the object appears to us, so to speak, 'in person,' as itself present"; the imagined object appears as merely represented or as only possible (but not actual): "it is as though it were there, but only as though" (Husserl 2005, 18). But how is this sense of *Unwirklichkeit*, this "as if," generated? Husserl gives further descriptions that contrast imagined (nonactual) objects with perceived (actual) ones, and imagining (which gives us a sense of irreality) with perceiving (which gives us a sense of reality). Imagined objects appear differently from perceived objects, or at least they do not consistently behave like perceived ones. Imagined objects may transgress the spatiotemporal and causal rules that perceived objects are subject to. They may change color, shape, location, size, etc., in an instant and for no apparent reason. They may appear and disappear without further ado. They may defy the laws of gravity and of nature more generally, and hence they can do what their perceived counterparts cannot (e.g., float in the air, although they are far too heavy; speak, although they are inanimate objects, etc.). In short, imagined objects are independent from, or even inconsistent with, the laws that we take to govern the real (perceptual) world, and they do not causally interrelate with objects of the real (perceptual) world. Thus to imagine, especially when it involves not just single objects but entire scenes, is also to imagine an imaginary world, i.e., a nexus of interrelated objects and meanings that are distinct and independent from the actual perceptual world.

These features are aspects of what Husserl calls the *noematic* dimension of imagining, that is, the dimension of imagined *objects*. However, phenomenologists like Husserl consider the noematic dimension a correlate of what they call the *noetic* dimension, that is, in this case, the dimension of the *experienced activity of imagining*. The correlation between the noetic and the noematic dimensions of imagination is not an arbitrary assumption, but it is borne out in the actual structure of consciousness. Just as perception consists in a dynamic unfolding of the correlation between objects perceived by someone and that someone perceiving them, imagination too consists in a dynamic unfolding of the correlation between imagined objects and imagining subject. For example, what is visible of a visual object is what is visible to someone, the side facing the seeing subject. Changes in the position or perceptual ability of the subject will necessarily correlate with changing visual profiles of the object. Husserl finds the same in imagination: we imagine objects in relation to possible perceptions we could have of them. Visualizing an object is always at the same time imagining *seeing* it. Imagining an acoustic object, such as a melody, is always at the same time imagining *hearing* it.

*Noetic* analysis reveals that the experience of imagining is significantly different from the experience of perceiving. Perceiving involves a presentation [*Gegenwärtigung*], "in which the object itself appears to us in its own person, as it were, as present itself." Imagining, by contrast, involves a presentification [*Vergegenwärtigung*[2]], "in which the object appears …, but it does not appear as present. It is only presentified [*vergegenwärtigt*]; it is as though it were there, but only as though" (Husserl 2005, 16). There is therefore a phenomenal difference between perceiving and imagining: in the first case, we simply apprehend what is itself present; in the latter case, we are (tacitly) aware that we are "making" something present that is not itself present – we are "presentifying" it. What's more, at least in cases of voluntary imagining – for this is not always the case: think, for example, of being lost in daydreams, or of compulsively fantasizing a scenario – we are (tacitly) aware of the control we have over our imagination. We may decide to have the imagined object change color, shape or size; we may imagine ourselves in front of it, or behind it, under it, etc. We may imagine one thing now and quite another a moment later. In fact, we can both begin to imagine and cease imagining as we please. These are liberties we simply do not have with regards to perceiving, which inescapably exposes us to our (real and present) environment.

For all these reasons we are able, under normal circumstances, to distinguish whether we are perceiving or imagining, just as we are able, under normal circumstances, to distinguish imagined objects from perceived ones – although it is certainly also possible to err in this regard (such as in cases of hallucination). In fact, awareness of the contrast between perceiving and imagining is required for a genuine experience of imagining itself as it is a constitutive moment of its "irreality." While imagining, we are also (tacitly) aware of our actual surroundings; we are (tacitly) aware that whatever we are imagining is in conflict with our actual, perceived surroundings. Of course, we can become so immersed in our imagining that this environmental awareness is minimized. Yet, if we were to become unanchored from the actual situation completely, we would then enter into a different experience altogether, such as hallucinating or dreaming, which requires a phenomenological analysis in its own right, and no longer under the name "imagination." It is noteworthy, however, that even in cases of hallucinating and dreaming, we do not necessarily lose our "real" bearings completely. People who suffer from Charles Bonnet Syndrome are usually aware that they are hallucinating, because they recognize the incongruence between their hallucinations on the one hand and their perceptions and assumptions about what counts as real on the other (Sacks 2012, 11). In the case of dreaming, we know that actual perceptions may be incorporated into a dream, e.g., a ringing doorbell may be incorporated into a dream as a ringing school bell, or as an ambulance siren. However, no matter how vivid our imaginings, sooner or later something (such as a phone call, or the feeling of being hungry) will draw our attention again to our actual perceptual environment, of which we never completely ceased to be aware.

While it is important to distinguish imagining from perceiving, it is equally important for Husserl that we recognize essential commonalities between the two. Here the systematic importance of a thorough investigation of imagining begins to become apparent: Husserl's description contradicts one of the most basic tenets of modern representationalist philosophies, whose classical formulation is provided by John Locke's claim that "since the things the mind contemplates are none of them, besides itself, present to the understanding, it is necessary that something else, as a … representation of the thing it considers, should be present to it: and these are ideas" (Locke 1975, IV.xxi.4). Against this "way of ideas," Husserl points out that the most important feature imagining shares with perceiving is that both constitute an *immediate* intuitive awareness of objects. Neither of them, according to Husserl, involves awareness of representations or ideas (from which an object may at best be inferred). Both of them constitute an unmediated object consciousness in which "the intention aims … at an object in a direct way" (Husserl 2005, 161). This also means that imagination does not, as is often thought (Thompson 2008), lack an object, or replace it with its "representative," e.g., a mental image "inside" the head.

Consequently, Husserl vehemently rejects the "erroneous *image-theory*" which assumes "that: 'Outside the thing itself is there (or is at times there); in consciousness there is an image which does duty for it'" (Husserl 2001a, 125, 5th Log. Inv., app. to §11 and §20). It is not the viewing of mental images that characterizes imagining, but the *simulation* of possible experiences. Imagining something is simulating a possible experience of it (Thompson 2008; Currie and Ravenscroft 2002; see "Simulation theory," Chapter 19 in this volume). This does not mean that imagining is derivative of perceiving, as would be the case if it simulated actual (e.g., past) perceptions. Instead, imagining makes us aware of perceptual possibilities, regardless of whether they were, or ever will be actualized. This modal capacity of imagining depends on and makes evident a "parallelism" between perception and phantasy, which remains a leading systematic idea throughout Husserl's work (cf. Husserl 2001a, 285 f., 6th Log. Inv., §47; Husserl 1969, 183; Husserl 1973, 28, §6) and bears great methodological significance.

## The immediacy of imagination: Husserl's transcendental antirepresentationalism

During the time between the publication of the *Logical Investigations* (1900–1) and *Ideas I* (1913), Husserl worked intensively on "phantasmata," understood as intuitive contents, analogous to sensations, which he initially believed provided the "content" of imagining upon being "animated" by a specific mode of apprehension. However, as the result of his studies, Husserl comes to discard the idea. Phantasmata are integral moments of the experience of imagining. They can be singled out in abstract thought for purposes of analysis, but they are not "bits of things [*Sächelchen*]" (Husserl 1983, 227), *present* "in" consciousness while representing *absent*, merely imagined, objects (Husserl 2005, 161). In a text already written in 1909, Husserl rejects his earlier representationalist model, which construed sensory or phantasmatic "contents" as representing "entities," in favor of an account that does justice to the dynamic intentional nature of consciousness:

> in the case of perception understood as a concrete experience, we do not first of all have a color as content of apprehension and then the characteristic of apprehension that produces the appearance. And likewise in the case of phantasy we do not again have a color as content of apprehension and then a changed apprehension,

> the apprehension that produces the phantasy appearance. *On the contrary*: "Consciousness" consists of consciousness through and through, and the sensation as well as phantasm is already "consciousness."
>
> (Husserl 2005, 265)

His investigations into imagining thus helped Husserl discover his new "transcendental" approach, which describes intentionality in terms of noetic-noematic correlations. "Noesis," i.e., the mode of intending, and "noema," i.e., the object as it is intended, are now understood by Husserl as two inextricably linked dimensions of consciousness. This also enables a new account of imagining: Noematically speaking, the imagined object is taken as not "really" present, that is, as "presentified." Noetically, however, imagining is presently lived through in inner consciousness and "reproduces" an experience. Husserl's technical term "reproduction" is somewhat misleading here as he does not intend to say that in imagining we are confined literally to "reproducing" a former *actual* experience. What the term is meant to signify instead is that imagining always implies a *possible* perception by simulating it.

Husserl's revised "transcendental" account of imagining lacks commitment to any particular "natural" causal explanation. The existence of sensuous contents understood as physical "dead" matter is neither denied nor affirmed. It is a matter not of the "sense" of imagining, but of a possible causal explanation, which is the business of a natural science (e.g., empirical psychology, cognitive science, etc.). According to Husserl, it is the business of phenomenology to attempt a careful description of the explanandum and to guard it from preconceptions or misconstruals any assumed explanation might introduce "through the backdoor." The phenomenological account thus becomes "transcendental" in Husserl's sense, which differs substantially from Kant's insofar as it does not limit itself to an identification of purely formal conditions of possibility for a priori cognition. By contrast, Husserl's account of imagination becomes "transcendental" in his sense *both* by restricting (or, "reducing") it to a description of the noetic-noematic correlations between imagining and the imagined *and* by restricting (or, "reducing") this description to the essential invariants (the "essence") of imagining in general. The results of Husserl's analysis of imagination thus reaffirm his general method as it is stated, for example, in *Ideas I*:

> On its own peculiar basis phenomenology must come to consider mental processes not as any sort of dead fact such as "content-complexes" which merely exist without signifying anything, without meaning anything; … transcendental phenomenology should instead make itself master of the *essentially unique set of problems* which mental processes offer, and offer *purely by their eidetic essence*, as *intentive* mental processes, as "*consciousness-of*."
>
> (Husserl 1983, 178)

This reaffirmation is an important one. For the case of imagination is routinely cited as evidence supporting a general representationalist account of consciousness. The very fact that we can imagine absent or nonexisting objects, counts, in the representationalist framework, as evidence that we relate to objects by means of representations (ideas, images, etc.), which do not even depend on those objects, as the case of imagination is taken to prove. According to representationalism, then, we never relate to objects directly, and in the case of imagination, we do not relate to objects at all, but only to our "mental images" of them (Thomas 2014). Husserl's descriptions of imagining contradict this view. To imagine something is to relate to *it*, albeit in the mode of nonactuality or irreality; to imagine something is *not* to relate to a mental image that represents the object in its absence. Not only in cases of veridical perception, but *in all cases*, consciousness of an object amounts to a relation *to an object*, and *not* to a mental representation.

However, Husserl's account of imagining also challenges at least one alternative to representationalism commonly referred to as "disjunctivism" (Haddock and MacPherson 2008). Disjunctivists reject the assumption that a veridical perception and a hallucination may share the same "content" (i.e., the same mental representation) and only differ with regards to whether the object thus represented is actually present or not. Instead disjunctivists believe that veridical perception is constituted by a direct relation to an actual object, whereas hallucination either does not constitute any such relation, or constitutes a relation to a different kind of "object," e.g., to a "mere appearance" or to a "mental image." Husserl's account of imagining challenges both representationalism and disjunctivism by maintaining that imagining neither lacks object relation, nor is it satisfied with a relation to something other than its object, e.g., a "mere appearance," or a "mental image." Imagining is relational, as is hallucinating. In cases of genuine imagining, we relate to imagined objects and are aware that they are nonactual or irreal. In cases of hallucinating, we relate to objects and may be under the erroneous impression that they are actual or real; or we may know intellectually that they are not, and still, uncannily, experience them as not "merely" imagined. Whatever the case may be, it is not a matter of an existing or missing match between a mental representation and an external object (present or absent). In fact, in first-person experience, it is not known "in advance," as it were, whether the relevant object is "really" there or not. It is rather the other way around: From the first-person perspective, we know of an object's "reality" only through ongoing and coherent perceptions; that is, the experience of actuality is itself generated in ongoing perceptual syntheses in which perceptual expectations are continuously fulfilled. For example, we expect to get closer to an object when we move toward it. In veridical perception, this expectation, along with numerous others, is continuously fulfilled, which motivates the perceptual belief in the actuality of the perceived object. Veridical perceptual consciousness is thus confirmed continuously, but never "once and for all," owing to the fact that further perceptions could always conflict with and thus invalidate earlier ones. When such "frustrations" and "disappointments" occur, we become aware that what we took to be a perception was really an illusion or a hallucination (Husserl 2001b, 3–78). When I walk for hours toward an oasis in the desert, for example, without ever getting any closer to it, I will, under normal circumstances, come to the conclusion that it is not an oasis after all, but only a mirage. In genuine cases of imagining – in which we are, at least tacitly, aware that we are imagining and in which we therefore "neutralize" our ontological commitments – such "disappointments" do not arise in the same way. In fact, different types of imagining may involve different expectations. For example, when I am daydreaming, my standards for coherence may be very low; when I am visualizing something in order to simulate how it would look from a certain perspective (let's say, I am a designer and I am doing this professionally), my standards are bound to be much higher. This also means that the "parallelism" Husserl observes between perceiving and imagining is more obvious in more "controlled" episodes of imagining, and it also depends in part on the nature of the imaginative project in pursuit of which control is exercised. The parallelism is the most obvious when we imagine an object or an experience with the express intention of simulating such an object or such an experience. It is far less obvious in other cases: for example, when we imagine objects and experiences playfully without purpose, or when we do so obsessively and against our will.

## Imagining possibilities: imagination as indispensable element of the phenomenological method

The notion of imagination as "quasi-perception," or as simulation of actual experiences, indicates its function as consciousness of possibilities. When we imagine something, be it something that exists (like that beautiful beach in the Caribbean) or that does not (like a pink elephant, or a golden mountain), we simulate possible experiences of (seeing, hearing, touching, etc.) it, which *could* become actual under different circumstances. The *as if*-appearance of an *actual* object is also an *actual* appearance of a *possible* object (Husserl 2005, 507, 529, 547 f.; 1975, 66, 94). By imagining, we may presentify an actuality or present a possibility (Husserl 1959, 116–19). Thus, although imagining, with its "voluntary refrain from any position," belongs to "the realm of purposelessness, of play" (Husserl 2005, 577; 2001b, 10–14) and thus seems incapable of constitutive accomplishment (Husserl 2005, 558), it also frees us from the constraints of our actual perceptual environment and places us into the realm of possibility. Instead of being restricted to considering actual empirical objects, we are also able to consider possible objects and hence different possible ways for the same kind ("essence") of object to be what it is. We are able, for example, to turn away from the particular actual visual object in our environment and to consider instead different possible visual objects, which, in turn, enables us to identify the essential features of any visual object whatsoever, or, which amounts to the same thing, the essence "visual object as such." Imagining, then, is indeed the "vital element" of phenomenology understood as an "eidetic" science, i.e., as a science *not* concerned with empirical objects and their actual causal connections, but with kinds of objects (i.e., essences) and with the a priori "eidetic" laws that regulate the possibilities of their various empirical instantiations. All of this depends not only on imagination's constitution of possibilities, but also on the "parallelism" between imagined and actual experience as well:

> There is a necessary parallelism between perception and imagination, which guarantees that a possible imagination (or more precisely a whole series of imaginations) having the same essence, corresponds to each possible percept …
>
> *(Husserl 2001a, 285, 6th Log. Inv., §47)*

Husserl believes that it belongs to the sense of contingency that it is correlated with a sense of necessity. To say that each individually existing thing is "contingent" is to say that it could be different *and still be the same kind of thing*. "It is thus; *in respect to its essence* it could be otherwise" (Husserl 1983, 9; my italics). This is why, according to Husserl, each thing, by virtue of being contingent, has *its* essence, i.e., "*its* stock of *essential* predicables which must belong to it" (ibid) if it is to be a thing of this kind. Those invariant features make up the *eidos* or "essence" of that thing, where 'thing' may refer not only to any object in the widest sense (a physical object, for example, or even a law, or a social institution), but also to any act of consciousness, such as perceiving and imagining. The account Husserl gives of imagining, then, is meant to be an account of the essence of imagining, that is, of the essential invariants of any act of imagining as such. Husserl is neither attempting to describe actual occurrences of imagining in particular psychological subjects, nor is he interested in the causal processes required for an actual instantiation of imagining. When he investigates the relation between imagining and, for example, perceiving, he is not interested in the *de facto* relations between this or that act of imagining and this or that act of perceiving; he is interested in the *de jure* relations between imagining as such and perceiving as such. In fact, strictly speaking, the essence of imagining is quite independent from any actual imagining. The different ways in which imagining *can* be what it is, are thus not known "after the fact" (a posteriori), but are valid for all possible actual instantiations of imagining, and are valid with generality and necessity (a priori) (Husserl 1973, 339 f., §86).

> When we take into consideration that, for each kind of actual experience ... there is a corresponding pure phantasy, an "as-if" experience ..., we surmise that there is also an a priori science, which confines itself to the realm of pure possibility (pure imaginableness) and, instead of judging about actualities of transcendental being, judges about its a priori possibilities and thus at the same time prescribes rules a priori for actualities.
>
> *(Husserl 1975, 66)*

There is only one claim of Husserl's that has caused more skepticism, and even ridicule, than his claim that there are such things as "essences," namely, his claim that it is somehow possible to "intuit" them. According to Husserl, essences can be "made evident" by an act that is *not* a simple act of perception (essences cannot be literally "seen"), but that nonetheless is "intuitive [*anschaulich*]": it surpasses a mere conception of such an essence and "fulfills" it. In an "intuition of essence" or "eidetic seeing" [*Wesensschau*], an essence becomes evident not as constructed by thought, but as given in, and in fact governing the various possibilities of a thing to be what it is. In *Experience and Judgment*, we find Husserl's most explicit and detailed attempt to explain this complex act. Husserl describes it as a process in terms of three methodological phases. The first one is the phase of "free variation." One takes some instantiation of the essence one wishes to investigate as an "arbitrary example" and uses it as "guiding 'model'" for a subsequent "act of volition" in which one arbitrarily produces "free variants" of the given example. The imagination is free here in at least two important respects: it is free of all commitment to actualities, exploring strictly pure possibilities; and it produces arbitrary variations that are ultimately experienced as an "infinitely open" multiplicity. The *eidos* emerges from a multiplicity for which it is a matter of indifference whether I continue to produce further variations. "I could continue in this way," but I need not; when it becomes evident that all further variations would only confirm what is already evident, I may stop and leave it at "and so on, at my pleasure" (Husserl 1973, 342, §87b).

> In this transition from image to image, from the similar to the similar, all the arbitrary particulars attain overlapping coincidence in the order of their appearance and enter in a purely passive way, into a synthetic unity in which they all appear as modifications of one another and then as arbitrary sequences of particulars in which the same universal is isolated as an *eidos*.
>
> *(Husserl 1973, 343, §87c)*

This passively emerging "coincidence" – the second phase of the process – makes possible the third: the active identification of "the same universal ... as an *eidos*" as it is exemplified in the arbitrary multiplicity of entertained variations. The normativity of the *eidos* is disclosed by the fact that the "free variation" does not permit just any variation to enter the "overlapping coincidence." The *eidos* is grasped as "that without which an object of a particular kind cannot be thought, i.e., without which the object cannot be intuitively imagined as such" (Husserl 1973, 341, §87a).

The free variation of possible instances – which, according to Husserl, enables us to grasp a priori essences – is an act of pure imagination. Thus, for Husserl, it is by means of the imagination that from "every concrete actuality, and every individual trait actually experienced in it or capable of being experienced, a path stands open to the realm of ideal or pure possibility and consequently to that of a priori thinking" (Husserl 1973, 353 f., §90). Imagining, or, as Husserl puts it more provocatively, "fiction," is thus indeed "the source from which the cognition of 'eternal truths' is fed" (Husserl 1983, 132). It enables phenomenology as "an a priori science, which confines itself to the realm of pure possibility (pure imaginableness) and, instead of judging about actualities of being [*Seinswirklichkeiten*], judges about its a priori possibilities and thus at the same time prescribes rules a priori for actualities" (Husserl 1975, 66).

## Imagining and picture consciousness: wider implications

One of the most important aspects of Husserl's account of imagination is his fierce rejection of any "image-theory" or "picture theory" of imagining.[3] Part of the justification for this rejection are his detailed descriptions of imagining, which show no evidence of any awareness of images – as we know it from experiences of seeing something in, for example, paintings or photographs – in the experience of imagining or of imagined objects. Even though this leaves open the possibility that some notion of "image" (e.g., a neurological one) might still be instrumental for *explaining* how imagining works, it would be wrong, according to Husserl, to start with the assumption that the image is therefore part of the experience that such an explanation is meant to explain. These considerations also prompt Husserl to deliver a detailed description of picture consciousness [*Bildbewusstsein*], i.e., of the experience of something as a picture, which may also involve the experience of depiction. While picture consciousness is of interest to Husserl mainly as a contrast to imagining, he still provides us with one of the most insightful analyses on the topic to date.

The experience of imagining shares important aspects with the experience of seeing something as a picture. When I imagine something, or when I see it in a picture, I do not experience the imagined or depicted object as present or as real. I "understand" (even though I typically do not think about it) that which appears to me in a picture as nonactual or absent. Husserl thus speaks of the "nonpositing" character that imagination and picture consciousness have in common. This similarity explains why imagining is often understood by analogy with "seeing something in an image," and why we speak of "imagination" in the first place. Husserl himself, especially in his earlier works, uses the generic term "imagination [*Imagination*]," and distinguishes "perceptual phantasy," i.e., image consciousness, from "pure phantasy."

Against such conflations, Husserl points out a fundamental structural difference. Picture consciousness involves an awareness of a perceptual image (for example a photograph, canvas or computer screen), which mediates the experience of the object that it depicts or lets us "see." In fact, when I look at a picture and see something "in it," my experience involves, according to Husserl, three distinct moments: (1) the *physical picture*, such as the patches of color distributed on the canvas, or the pixels on the screen; (2) the *picture object*, the image, or figure, which appears through a certain distribution of colors and shapes; and (3) the *picture subject*, the object, person or scene depicted or represented by the picture (Husserl 2005, 19 f.). We have to perceive the physical picture in order to be able to apprehend the actual picture object and in order to "see" the picture subject depicted in it (or, indeed, "hear" it if we are listening to a musical "picture"). This last part is, as we know from abstract art, not essential. It is possible to apprehend something as a picture without also experiencing it as depicting something. Conversely, in imagining, we do not have such tripartite (or even dual) structure. Imagining, like perceiving, *directly* engages with its objects. Imagining is thus not simply "not quite" like seeing something in a picture, it is *fundamentally and structurally different*.

In many ways, Husserl's account of picture consciousness has been at least as influential as his account of imagining. It has certainly drawn more attention in recent discourse. One possible reason is the fact that Husserl pays so much attention to the imagination and that he makes it integral to his controversial method of "eidetic seeing," which actually causes some embarrassment for scholars who have worked hard over the last two decades or so to distance Husserlian phenomenology from charges of idealism and subjectivism. Another reason might be that in the French reception in particular, Husserl's account is often read as part of a more general debate on the nature of the image (think, for example, of Henri Bergson, Jean-Paul Sartre, Gaston Bachelard, Gilles Deleuze and Jean Baudrillard). Finally, while the imagination is often associated with the idealisms and romanticisms of the nineteenth century, our age is more commonly seen as the age of imagery and virtuality, which has brought about its own kind of science: the "science of pictures [*Bildwissenschaft*]." In a way, this development is consistent with Husserl's departure from the philosophical tradition, which used to turn imagination into a fundamental and generic faculty. Freed from the ballast of that tradition, it is now possible to examine the specificities of imagining and of picture consciousness in a new, less romantically charged light, which is in many ways more compatible with contemporary research on the imagination coming out of analytic circles than with the all-encompassing accounts typical of classical philosophies of imagination. It is also consistent with Husserl's insistence on the distinction between imagining and picture consciousness, which first of all establishes image consciousness and the nature of images as a worthwhile and independent philosophical topic in its own right, where Husserl's account applies not only to pictures narrowly conceived, such as paintings and photographs, but also to images considered more broadly, as they appear in music, poetry, sculpture, theatre, cinema, the social media and in many other venues of the public sphere.

However, Husserl's analyses provide us with more than just technical details and systematic investigations into specific modes of consciousness. Read with more existentialist eyes, Husserl's writings on imagining also remind us of the awesome human power to *neutralize* ontological or explanatory commitments, to suspend the demands of the actual, and to move imaginatively beyond the immediate, the familiar and the expected in search of alternatives and *possibilities*. This enables us to consider two truly life-changing distinctions: the distinction between the inessential and the essential, and the difference between what is and what could be. Both of these distinctions open us up to the realization that the world is not a monolithic reality of actual matters-of-fact, but a complex dynamic structure with *modal* as well as *normative* dimensions, and that we are *free* to make a difference in it.

## Notes

1 Page references are to the Husserliana series German edition (e.g., 25 = Husserl 2001b/Hua vol. 11, p. 25), except for Husserl 1975 and 2001a. This is because the latter works contain no original German pagination in the margins. For those, section numbers are added to enable easy access to the original text.

2 I translate *Vergegenwärtigung* not as "re-presentation" (as Brough does in Husserl 2005), but as "presentification" in order to emphasize the sense of "making" present what is not "by itself" present, and in order to deemphasize the sense that this necessarily involves a re-petition, or re-collection of an earlier experience, as is the case in memory.

3 Here I translate *Bild* as "picture" (not as "image"), and *Bildbewusstsein* as "picture consciousness" (not as "image consciousness," as Brough does in Husserl 2005), in order to avoid the confusion of Husserl's relevant notion of *Bild*, which requires a perceptual basis, with the notion of "mental images." According to Husserl, representationalist accounts of imagining are often based on precisely this confusion.

## Further reading

The most comprehensive Husserlian account of image consciousness available to date is J. Brough, "Something That Is Nothing But Can Be Anything: The Image and Our Consciousness of It," in D. Zahavi (ed.) *The Oxford Handbook of Contemporary Phenomenology* (Oxford: Oxford University Press, 2012), 545–563. The most recent work on some of the details of Husserl's notion of imagination and its impact on a theory of fiction is J.E. Carreño Cobos, "The Many Senses of Imagination and the Manifestation of Fiction: A View from Husserl's Phenomenology of Phantasy," *Husserl Studies* 29(2) (2013): 143–162. E. Casey, *Imagining: A Phenomenological Study*, 2nd edn. (Bloomington: Indiana University Press, 2000) is the classic study on phenomenological and existentialist accounts of imagination, starting from Husserlian insights. B. Elliot, *Phenomenology and Imagination in Husserl and Heidegger* (London: Routledge, 2005) is the only available in-depth study of Husserl's account of imagination in the English language to date, which is, however, heavily influenced by Heidegger. A detailed discussion of the various potential applications of Husserl's account of imagination to contemporary interdisciplinary discourses in philosophy and cognitive science can be found in J. Jansen, "Phenomenology, Imagination and Interdisciplinary Research," in S. Gallagher and D. Schmicking (eds.) *Handbook of Phenomenology and Cognitive Science* (Dordrecht: Springer, 2010), 141–158. The same author's "Husserl's First Philosophy of Phantasy: A Transcendental Phenomenology of Imagination," *Phenomenology and the Cognitive Sciences* 4 (2): 121–132 gives a detailed presentation of the shift between Husserl's early account of imagination and his later transcendental account. E. Marbach, "Phantasy, Pictorial Consciousness, Memory," in R. Bernet, I. Kern and E. Marbach (eds.) *An Introduction to Husserlian Phenomenology* (Evanston: Northwestern University Press, 1993), 141–153 is the most comprehensive summary of the contents of Husserliana 23 to date, which combines Husserl's lectures on imagination, picture consciousness and memory.

## References


Currie, G., and I. Ravenscroft (2002) *Recreative Minds: Imagination in Philosophy and Psychology*, Oxford: Oxford University Press.

Drummond, J. (2012) "Intentionality without Representationalism," in D. Zahavi (ed.) *The Oxford Handbook of Contemporary Phenomenology*, Oxford: Oxford University Press, 115–133.

Føllesdal, D. (1969) "Husserl's Notion of Noema," *Journal of Philosophy* 66: 680–687.

Føllesdal, D. (1990) "Noema and Meaning in Husserl," *Philosophy and Phenomenological Research* 50(suppl.): 263–271.

Haddock, A., and F. MacPherson (eds.) (2008) *Disjunctivism: Perception, Action, Knowledge*, Oxford: Oxford University Press.

Husserl, E. (1959) *Erste Philosophie (1923/4)*, vol. 2: *Theorie der phänomenologischen Reduktion*, Husserliana VIII, The Hague: Martinus Nijhoff.

Husserl, E. (1969) *Formal and Transcendental Logic*, trans. D. Cairns, The Hague: Martinus Nijhoff.

Husserl, E. (1973) *Experience and Judgment*, trans. J. Churchill and K. Ameriks, Evanston: Northwestern.

Husserl, E. (1975) *Cartesian Meditations*, trans. by D. Cairns, Dordrecht: Kluwer.

Husserl, E. (1980) *Phantasie, Bildbewusstsein, Erinnerung (1898–1925)*, ed. E. Marbach, Husserliana XXIII, The Hague: Martinus Nijhoff.

Husserl, E. (1983) *Ideas Pertaining to a Pure Phenomenology and to a Phenomenological Philosophy*, First Book, trans. F. Kersten, The Hague: Martinus Nijhoff.

Husserl, E. (2001a) *Logical Investigations*, vols. 1 and 2, trans. J.N. Findlay, ed. D. Moran, London: Routledge.

Husserl, E. (2001b) *Analyses concerning Passive and Active Synthesis*, trans. A. Steinbock, Dordrecht: Kluwer.

Husserl, E. (2005) *Phantasy, Image Consciousness, and Memory (1898–1925)*, trans. J. Brough, Dordrecht: Springer.

Locke, J. (1975) *An Essay concerning Human Understanding*, ed. P. Nidditch, Oxford: Oxford University Press.

Mohanty, J.N. (1997) *Phenomenology: Between Essentialism and Transcendental Philosophy*, Evanston: Northwestern University Press.
Sacks, O. (2012) *Hallucinations*, New York: Picador.
Smith, D.W., and R. McIntyre (1984) *Husserl and Intentionality: A Study of Mind, Meaning, and Language*, Dordrecht: Reidel.
Sokolowski, R. (1974) *Husserlian Meditations*, Evanston: Northwestern University Press.
Thomas, N.J.T. (2014) "Mental Imagery," in E.N. Zalta (ed.) *The Stanford Encyclopedia of Philosophy* (Fall 2014 edition), <http://plato.stanford.edu/archives/fall2014/entries/mental-imagery/>.
Thompson, E. (2008) "Representationalism and the Phenomenology of Mental Imagery," *Synthese* 160: 397–415.
Zahavi, D. (2003) *Husserl's Phenomenology*, Stanford: Stanford University Press.

# 6
# SARTRE

*Robert Hopkins*

For Sartre, imagining is central to mental life. Along with perceiving, it is one of the two main forms that consciousness takes. Imagining and perceiving are fundamentally different, both in phenomenology and in their deeper nature. Neither can be reduced to the other, and they cannot combine in a single mental state. The range of imagining includes not merely visualizing and the purely mental states that provide its equivalents in other sense modalities, but also our engagement with a range of external objects and events, such as "seeing" faces in the flames of a fire or reading a novel. Indeed, imagining is the basis of our engagement with all art. More than this, however, it is essential to consciousness, in the form in which we enjoy it, and to the freedom that consciousness essentially involves. Few other thinkers have given the imagination such significance in human life, and few have explored so thoroughly what marks it apart from other mental states.

In elaborating Sartre's position, I draw mostly on *L'Imaginaire* (Sartre 1940): all unattributed page numbers below refer to the most recent English translation of this work (Webber trans., Sartre 1940/2005).[1] This book represents the height of Sartre's engagement with Phenomenology, the tradition in philosophy that centers on the study of the structure of conscious states, as experienced by their subjects. At its core is thus a description of the phenomenology (with a small 'p') that distinguishes imagining from perceiving: the features of each that characterize what it's like to undergo them. I begin with those features (Section 1), before turning to the range of phenomena Sartre takes to exhibit them (Section 2). However, Sartre steps beyond both phenomenology and Phenomenology in offering an account of the deep nature of the state that has those features, in his doctrine of the "analogon" (Section 3). I close by briefly sketching his views on the significance of imagining (Section 4).

## 1 Phenomenology: the four characteristics

Sartre cites four "characteristics" of imagining that are intended to capture its "intentional structure," and thus its phenomenology. While the later three distinguish imagining from perceiving, the first describes a feature common to the two.

*First*, as Sartre puts it "the image is a consciousness" (5). Reflection on the phenomenology of imagining shows it to be a way of being related to things in the world. Despite the readiness with which common sense resorts to talk of mental images, and despite various theories that have sought to describe what these images are, and how they differ from "percepts," the experience of imagining itself gives us no reason to believe in them. If I visualize the chair in my office, the only object of which I am aware is the chair. No "image" figures in my experience, if that means something like an inner picture of the chair; or a Humean "idea," a percept in less vivid form. Indeed, no mental thing of *any* kind forms the immediate object of my imagining. When I imagine the chair, just as much as when I see it, my mental state presents me as directly related to something in the world. The relations are very different, in ways to be described by the remaining three characteristics, but the basic structure is the same.

Since phenomenology suggests there are no mental particulars mediating our relation to what we imagine, and if (as Sartre assumes) phenomenology does not mislead us here, it might seem we should drop talk of mental images altogether. However, like others who have traded particulars for states and activities in the ontology of the mental (e.g., Smart 1959), Sartre sees no harm in allowing himself talk that suggests otherwise. The trick is to remember that it has content only as paraphrasing claims about the relevant states and processes or, as Sartre prefers, "consciousnesses." It is true that there are mental images of chairs, provided we mean by that no more than that people sometimes have "imaging consciousness" of chairs – i.e., they are related to chairs in the way distinctive of imagining.

What, though, of cases in which what we imagine does not exist? How can that be construed as a distinctive relation to some object in the world? Sartre has remarkably little to say about this problem. Various solutions might be offered him, but the simplest is perhaps the following. When imagining does relate me to worldly objects, it has the distinctive features described below. Perhaps those features can also characterize a nonrelational form of consciousness, when what is imagined is merely imaginary. Imagining is sometimes relational, sometimes not, but is never mediated by mental objects. It does, however, always exhibit the remaining three characteristics.

*Second*, the image admits only of "quasi-observation." The contrast here is with genuine observation, the provision of which is essential to perception. In perceiving, we grasp a world which extends beyond our reach, and which is given as doing so. To use Sartre's example, when we see a cube, certain of its faces will be hidden from view. Perception is not confined to what is explicitly given. We see the thing as a cube, not a mere facade. In going beyond what is explicitly given in this way, perception involves an "hypothesis" about the nature of its object. So there is always the possibility of confirming, or disconfirming, that hypothesis, by moving around the thing, scrutinizing it more closely, or attending differently (e.g., by focusing on the reflection of the object's rear in the mirror behind). These various ways of testing what perception suggests without guaranteeing are all forms of observation.

Observing is integral to perceiving, because all perception presents us with a world that outstrips our purchase on it. But this last depends on the fact that perception is perspectival, that it presents the world from a limited position within it, a position from which certain features of the world are immediately accessible, and others are not. (This point is most familiar for vision, but it transfers, albeit sometimes with a little strain, to perception in the other traditional sense modalities, and beyond.) But perspective is not a feature of every way in which the mind engages the world. Consider, for instance, conceiving. Thinking of a cube, Sartre says, is not perspectival: I conceive of all its sides, faces and angles at once, and there is no perspective, within the world conceived, from which the cube is presented. In consequence, there is no room for hypotheses here, no room for uncertainty about whether what I conceive really is a cube, and no role for observation in confirming that fact.

Imagining is an intermediate case. Like perception, it is perspectival. To visualize a cube is to picture how it looks from some point, or perhaps points, in its surroundings; to imagine a cube in a tactual way is to imagine it in contact with some part of one's body. However, like conceiving, imagining presents its object in its entirety. Despite the fact that my visual image of the cube presents only some sides as facing me, that it is a cube is given not as mere "hypothesis," but with certainty (cf. Wittgenstein 1965, 39; Peacocke 1985, 20). It would be idle to rotate the cube in imagination, since its nature is already secure. If, in rotating it, I picture more cube faces, I merely stay true to the thing as initially imagined. And if I don't, I cease to imagine a cube, and start imagining something else. Thus imagining has the perspectival character that normally makes room for observation, without involving the uncertainty that it is observation's role to resolve. There is an invitation to observe here, but no possibility of taking it up. Hence "quasi-observation."

Is Sartre right to make these claims? The next section discusses cases that pose particular challenges to the idea that all imagining is perspectival. Here let us consider Sartre's claim about the epistemology of imagining. He sometimes expresses this by saying we learn nothing from our images. That is certainly false. I can learn whether I'm capable of imagining a fugue in three parts by attempting to do so. And can't we find out about the aesthetic and spatial realms by consulting our imaginings, for instance by imagining this tie with that shirt, or this peg going into that hole? However, we should distinguish between the world imagined (the real things, if any, that provide the objects of our imagining) and the world as imagined (how we imagine things, including any real things our imaginings concern, to be). Sartre's key thought is not that imagining can't teach us about the former, but that it doesn't allow us to learn about the latter. (Indeed, strictly speaking, he need claim only that there is no room to learn about the world as imagined *through observation*.) That thought is rather harder to evaluate. If the only way for imagining to teach us about the world imagined involved our learning about the world as imagined, refining Sartre's claim in this way would be pointless. However, it is not true that these forms of learning are tied in that way. It's at least possible that the real story involves learning that the shirt clashes with the tie, not by imagining the two together and observing the effect, but by finding that I cannot imagine the two going well together (Hopkins 2011, 111–113). Moreover, while there is a small psychological literature that seeks to test issues closely related to those raised by Sartre's claim, the results are inconclusive (Peterson et al. 1992; Reisberg 1996).

The *third* characteristic is that while perception presents things as real, imagining does not. As Sartre puts it, imagining "posits its object as nothingness." Sartre sometimes refers to this positing as an "act of belief" (12). Certainly perceiving something tends to engender the belief that such a thing exists, whereas imagining it does not. But Sartre's claim is not about the different relations in which these states stand to belief, but about features of the states themselves that are responsible for those differences. It is integral to perception to present itself as revealing how the world is, and integral to imagining not to do so. Any consequences for belief are downwind of that more fundamental contrast.

In fact, imagination's positing takes one of four more specific forms. It can present its object as not existing, as absent, as existing elsewhere, or it can merely not present the object as existing. Sartre does not give examples of all four forms, and one can expend considerable energy trying to work out if there really is room for this many subspecies. However, what is central to the four is that they all, explicitly or implicitly, involve negation (12). In this they contrast, not only with perception, but with conception too. For conceiving also presents things as real, only the things so presented are "universal essences." That is, Sartre apparently thinks of conceiving as a matter of grasping the features essential to the concept's referent, without concern as to whether there is in fact anything corresponding to that concept. Conceiving shows us how things are, only not with the world in itself, but with our concepts. From this point of view, conceiving and perceiving are of a piece, positing as real, and imagining is the only consciousness that has negation ("nothingness") at its core.

It is this feature of imagining that will prove the source of its deepest significance (below, Section 4). It is also perhaps the least controversial of the three ways in which imagining is supposed to differ from perceiving. True, we might fruitfully investigate how best to construe Sartre's claim: here, as with all the other characteristics, my discussion is far briefer than the richness of the material deserves. (For more, see Casey 1981.) True too, some have taken positions squarely opposed to Sartre's, preferring to treat both imaginings and perceptions as failing to lay claim to show how things are, their connections to belief having to wait upon our judgment about which fit into a series sufficiently coherent to suggest they reflect reality. (Collingwood 1938, ch. 9 offers a particularly well-developed version of such a view.) But any such view ignores finer grained differences that Sartre details elsewhere, such as the way the identity and nature of imagined objects is fluid as those of perception are not (II:V) and the gappy and elastic nature of the spatial and temporal structures within which imagined objects are presented (IV:I). If only some of these claims are true of only some images, that is enough to show that at least some imaginings come clearly marked as such, and so need not wait on assignment to a series before they can be identified for what they are.

It is, of course, another question whether every imagining has this feature. The most serious challenge to Sartre's claims about positing lies in cases in which imagining and perceiving are apparently mistaken for one another. The possible counter examples here include hallucinations and dreams, in which prima facie imagining is mistaken for perceiving; and the famous Perky experiments (Perky 1910), in which observers apparently confuse seeing a faint projection of an object for imagining that thing. For if perceiving always presents its objects as real, and imagining never does so, how could we ever confuse the two?

The challenge here is of course more general. It confronts any attempt to distinguish imagining from perceiving by their phenomenology, and thus faces each of the three characteristics Sartre casts in that role. He sees clearly the threat from hallucination and dreams, offering sophisticated treatments of each (IV:III and IV:IV). For example, he treats dreaming as analogous to the state of being absorbed in a story. The fascinated dreamer is so wrapped up in her dream that she loses her sense of the reality with which the dream world contrasts. Her dream does not present its world as real, but she has no sense of the real against which to locate the unreality it conjures for her. As for the challenge from experimental work, here Sartre is inappropriately (and unusually) dismissive (52). Fortunately, there are other, more serious, doubts one might have about what Perky's experiments prove (Segal 1971; Hopkins 2012).

*Fourth*, and last, imagining exhibits spontaneity. "A perceptual consciousness appears to itself as being passive. An imaginative consciousness, on the contrary, presents itself to itself as an imaging consciousness, that is, as a spontaneity that produces and conserves the object as imaged" (14).

In perception, one experiences oneself as responding to how things are in the world, as being receptive to the nature of those things. In contrast, imagining involves the generation of objects from within one's own mental resources, and that this is so is integral to its phenomenology. Of course, since at least Kant the idea has been familiar that perception cannot be entirely passive. Organization must be imposed on the input the senses provide if mere sensation is to be transformed into cognition. And, of course, sometimes what we imagine is driven by external forces, as when I cannot get a catchy tune out of my head. But perception must be passive at its core, if it is to inform us about the world. And imagining can have external causes without that fact being intimated by the phenomenology of imagining itself. What is so frustrating about the recurring tune is precisely that in imagining it I myself bring it back to life. If instead it plagues me because you won't stop singing it, my annoyance has a quite different character.

Is the idea of spontaneity that imagining is an exercise of agency, or merely that its immediate causes lie within the conscious subject? In describing imagining, Sartre makes very little use of the notion of agency. He does say something about the related notion of the will. He explicitly distinguishes willing and spontaneity (18; 134). (He is thus not flummoxed by cases, such as the "ear worm," in which imagining is clearly not governed by the will.) Of the two, spontaneity is more basic. Indeed, Sartre seems to think that imagining is never perfectly determined by the will, and that the will cannot govern how a given imaginative project develops (135). Perhaps he thinks the notion of agency unhelpful, there being various cases intermediate between minimal spontaneity and full-blown willing, and little reason to draw a line that classifies only some as genuine actions.

While positing as nothing is the source of imagining's significance, spontaneity is in some respects the most fundamental of the characteristics. It explains quasi-observation, and necessarily accompanies positing as nothingness (14). Indeed, Sartre seems to say that it is spontaneity that above all identifies imagining for what it is. It is because it presents itself as spontaneous that imagining is given to us as imagining.

## 2 The scope of Sartre's account: the image family

So much for the phenomenology of imagining. Across what range of activities does it extend? It is easy to assume that Sartre intends his description only to apply to cases of visualizing and its analogues in other sense modalities, such as "hearing" sounds in one's head. In fact, Sartre devotes considerable space to discussing a far wider range of cases. In addition to what we might think of as internal sensory imaginings, he also includes sensory imaginings that involve an essential role for external objects; and internal imaginings that do not have a clear sensory character. Let's take these in turn.

While visualizing is one – perhaps the – paradigm of imagining, Sartre sees it as part of a wider range that includes our experience of realistic paintings and photographs, appreciating impersonations, caricatures and other schematic pictures, seeing things in the flames of a fire, and having hypnagogic imagery – the very vivid images that some people experience while drifting off to sleep. To count as imagining, these cases need only exhibit the characteristics above. Do they?

The easiest characteristic to apply across the entire range is positing as nothingness. In every case we are directed to something other than what is really before us: the scene we see in the picture, the face we see in the fire, the person who is being impersonated, the arrangement of colors and 3D shapes the hypnagogic image presents us with. And in no case does being presented with those things tempt us to form the belief that they are really before us. This is at least evidence that in every case the relevant object is "posited as nothingness."

What, though, of spontaneity and quasi-observation? Sartre himself arranges his cases on a spectrum. At one end lies pure visualizing, at the other seeing things in realistic pictures. Everything else lies between, so we pass from visualizing, through hypnagogic imagery, to seeing faces in the fire, on through our experience of relatively schematic representations (caricatures and impersonations), until we reach the least schematic, namely realistic paintings and photographs. The further we retreat from this last pole, the more obvious it is both that we ourselves create what we use the marks, sounds or flames to present, and that there is nothing more to be found in them than we ourselves currently find there. (It would be bizarre to scrutinize the fire to find out more about the face in it, or to insist that seeing it there is mere openness to the nature of the flame, rather than a creative act wrought upon it.) But at the least schematic end, we might wonder whether either characteristic holds. If I look at a detailed oil portrait in realist style, is seeing the sitter really down to me? And, rather than excluding observation, doesn't the painting present me with that person in a way that invites me to look harder, to find out more?

As far as spontaneity goes, it is important to remember that it is not equivalent to will. We clearly cannot will what we see in detailed pictures to the degree we can what we see in "droodles" or the flames. Even so, the former might still involve some manifest input from us. Seeing the scene in the photograph is a creative act on our part in which we "animate" the marks, as seeing things in the flesh is not (25). Perhaps the threat to quasi-observation can also be finessed. Of course we can observe the painting or photograph itself: after all, that is there to be perceived, and where there is perception there is observation. What Sartre has to deny is that we are ever in a position to observe *the depicted scene*. If we're tempted to think otherwise, that is because we confuse observing the canvas with observing the scene it enables us to envision. Observing the marks no doubt can cause us to imagine the scene in more detail, thus encouraging the confusion. Even so, that confusion should be avoided. Or so, at least, Sartre can claim.

At this point, however, we run into another important theme. Sartre thinks consciousness always forms a synthetic unity. It is thus not possible to be in a single state of mind that involves features that are fundamentally in tension with one another. Since the features of imagining and perceiving are, as described above, radically opposed, imagining and perceiving cannot be combined: it is not possible both to perceive and to imagine at one and the same time. This is perhaps the claim of Sartre's that is hardest to swallow. However, his commitment to it cannot be gainsaid – he repeats it at several points. Taking it seriously has two consequences that are of immediate relevance. First, Sartre cannot treat our consciousness of any picture, highly realistic ones included, as a simultaneous mix of perceiving the canvas and imagining the object. Instead he must say that at most we alternate rapidly between the two. This complicates his explanation of why we are tempted to think we can observe depicted objects, at some cost to its plausibility.

The second consequence is to limit the range of cases Sartre can take as falling under imagining. Many have been tempted to treat cases of so-called "aspect perception" as precisely involving an imaginative enrichment of materials that perception provides (e.g., Scruton 1974; White 1990). We see the dark wire frame of a (3D) Necker cube, but reversing its apparent orientation is a matter of imagining first one face closer than its opposite number, then vice versa. Others again have sought to treat imagination as a component in all perception. The tradition exploring this idea is long and distinguished (see Strawson 1970), but a recent manifestation is to apply the idea to what is now called "amodal completion," i.e., the perceptual phenomenon of seeing things as cubes, or complete patterns in carpets, even though not every face of the object, nor every part of the rug, is visible (e.g., Nanay 2010). Given the doctrine of incompatibility, Sartre must reject both these ideas. If aspect perception is by definition a matter of imagination infiltrating perception, then there is no such thing; and, while, as we saw above, he certainly recognizes the phenomenon of amodal completion, the proposed analysis of it is one he repeatedly rejects (e.g., 180–181).

However, while Sartre thus excludes some sensory phenomena from being genuine cases of imagining, he also expands the category so as to include imaginings the sensory character of which is at least highly dilute, and perhaps even absent altogether, except *in potentia*. These states form a kind of half-way house between pure grasp of meaning and full-blown imagining. Like the former, they involve the mind's directedness toward things without capturing any of those things' definite sensible character; but like the latter, they do present those things as belonging to the sensible world. Sartre cites experiments in which subjects report themselves as "seeing" (in the mind's eye) two objects that are different, though not in any particular way (59). A more familiar example might be having a word on the tip of one's tongue: one is aware of the very approximate form of the target, but not of any of the "matter" (the marks or sounds) that fills out that form. Such states attribute no determinate sensory character to the things they concern, and may indeed not even clearly belong to one sense modality rather than another. Nonetheless, Sartre says, they aim at their targets *as objects*, at things that might populate a sensory world, and not at mere conceptions of those things. That is why they count as imaginings. These are the states that dominate our engagement with literature. The words in a novel generally do not prompt detailed sensory imaginings, but nor are they mere vehicles for pure meaning. Instead, they "represent the surface of contact" between us and a world, a world that has a structure, however indeterminate the character of the nodes within it. The scene described at one point in a story is experienced as related in certain vague but ever present ways to the characters and events described elsewhere (64–68).[2]

## 3 Imagining's psychological substrate: the analogon

The various activities and mental states described in the last section all count as imagining in virtue of exhibiting its characteristic phenomenology. However, Sartre thinks they are also alike in another respect: they share a deep structure. In each, we are presented with something absent or nonexistent *through* something else, something real that consciousness engages and animates in order to produce the imagined thing. Sartre calls this the "analogon."

The idea is easiest to grasp in the context of imaginings involving external objects. When I see Charles VIII in a portrait of him, the analogon is the painted canvas. I am conscious of Charles in the way distinctive of imagining only because the canvas is before me. Its role is not merely causal: the imagining consciousness itself incorporates the marked surface. Charles is presented to me *in* those marks. I organize them with thoughts of the king, with the result that he is presented to me – though not, of course, as really here.

Similarly, says, Sartre, with every other case on the spectrum above. The flames in the fire and the body and speech of the impersonator equally act as analogon for what they enable me to become conscious of. In every case, something real acts as an "object for consciousness" (53), where it is clear this is distinct from consciousness's intentional object, the thing imagined. The analogon need not be external to the body: in the case of hypnagogic images, the role is filled by entoptic lights (40–49). However, external or not, something must play this role: even in the case of such purely interior phenomena as visualizing or rehearsing a tune in one's head. Otherwise, imagining would not differ from perceiving or conceiving. In perception, the mind "faces" the very thing of which we are conscious; in conceiving its direction toward the thing conceived is "empty," unaided by any real thing being before the mind. As a result, perception presents things as really here; and conceiving fails to present them at all. If imagining is to present things, but as not really here, something must really be before the mind, but not the intentional object itself. The analogon provides that substitute (52–53).

There is, however, one important difference between the cases. In almost all, from hypnagogic imagery to seeing portraits, it is possible to study the analogon directly. We cannot observe it while using it to imagine, since, as discussed above, perceiving and imagining are incompatible. What we can do, however, is to stop imagining and then observe the very thing that acted as analogon for that imagining. In the case of purely mental imagery, Sartre acknowledges, this is not possible. Whatever acts as analogon in these cases is destroyed, or fundamentally changed, when our consciousness alters. Shifting from the imaginative to the perceptual attitude transforms or annihilates the material that sustained the former. Thus, if we are to know the nature of these "psychic contents," we must change tack. We must abandon phenomenological description, and the certainty its results enjoy, and turn instead to empirical investigation. Only psychology can reveal the nature of the analogon in purely mental imagining, and any conclusions we draw, as with any other inference to unobservable entities, will be no more than probable (53).

Drawing on a range of the psychological literature then available, as well as some more homely observations of his own, Sartre speculates that in internal imagining the role of analogon is played by bodily movements; by emotions, broadly conceived; or by a mixture of the two. He finds that when he visualizes a tennis match and places his fingers on his eyelids, he can feel the eyeballs turning as if following the ball back and forth across the net. His idea is that the subject is subliminally conscious of the rotation even when not touching his eyes. The movement is not an effect of his visualizing the game, but rather the material out of which the imaginative act constitutes the visualized scene. In other cases, this work is done by affect – by feelings that may, but need not, be directed towards the imagined object. As my mind turns to a colleague and rival, perhaps I dimly feel pangs of the jealousy she provokes. If I then find myself picturing her downfall, I do so by using those feelings as the peg onto which to hang my imaginative consciousness of the scene.

Of course, there must be more to imagining these things than the mere presence of such "objects for consciousness." The other essential ingredient in imagining is what Sartre calls "knowledge" (II.I). Just as I need knowledge of how something looks if I am to see it in a picture, similarly it is my knowledge of how my colleague looks, talks and acts, or what a tennis match looks and sounds like, that enables me to animate the jealous feeling or movements of the eye so as to visualize those things. Like others before and after him (e.g., Wittgenstein 1965; Peacocke 1985), Sartre thus sees imagining as "a synthetic act that links a concrete, not imaged, knowledge to elements which are more properly representative" (9).

Now, some would say the same about perception. If perceiving involves more than having sensory impressions, because those impressions must also be organized by concepts, isn't this last reasonably described as exercising "knowledge"? However, even so, a strong contrast with imagining, as Sartre construes it, remains. Whereas in perceiving the sensory input tightly constrains the nature of the object of which we are conscious, in imagining almost all the work is done by knowledge. The analogon, while essential, is in many cases almost infinitely malleable, in terms of the things we might use it to imagine. The structure of imagining is thus consistent with quasi-observation and spontaneity – indeed, Sartre can even explain them, by appeal to the dominant role of knowledge in determining what is imagined. (Compare Peacocke 1985, 26–27.)

Given this, it would clearly be a mistake to construe the analogon as a form of inner picture. True, Sartre himself treats movements and affect in visualizing as playing the same role that the canvas plays in the case of the painted portrait. But the parallel is purely structural: in each, something real must be before the mind through which it makes the imagined object present. In the case of realistic pictures, what plays that role meets certain conditions – e.g., it must resemble the depicted object, or have similar effects on our visual system (22). But those cases are the exception. The order Sartre finds in his various cases of imagining precisely reflects the retreat from cases in which the analogon meets strict conditions and constrains tightly what is imagined, to ones in which ever more work is done by the "knowledge" the subject brings to bear. The more schematic the picture, the wider the range of things we can see in it. We might see almost anything in flames in the fire, or have hypnagogic imagery of almost anything, given the entoptic lights that provide the material for such imaginings. So much the more so, then, for visualizing and other cases of inner imagining: there are even fewer restrictions on the range of things we might envision when using knowledge to animate particular sensations of movement or feelings. To appeal to the analogon in visualizing and other internal imagining is thus emphatically not to appeal to some inner model of the thing imagined. To suppose otherwise, Sartre says, is to succumb to the "illusion of immanence," transferring features of the object imagined to features of the vehicle by which we imagine it (53; cf. 5).

The theory of the analogon is thoroughly distinctive. Applying it to imagining in both inner and outer forms enables Sartre to offer highly original accounts both of visualizing and of pictorial experience. But is the theory well motivated? Is it even coherent? And, if it is, are its psychological speculations borne out by subsequent research?

We can usefully separate Sartre's reasons for thinking that there must be an analogon in every case of imagining from his speculations about the precise nature of that thing, in cases where observing it is not possible. While the latter involve inferences on the basis of psychological evidence, the justification for the former claim is philosophical. Treating perception as involving the presence before the mind of the perceived, and imagining as involving the presence before the mind of something else, through which, using knowledge, we present ourselves with the imagined object, allows us to explain the phenomenology of the two. Quasi-observation, positing as nothingness and spontaneity can all be derived from this metaphysics of imagining, without too much ingenuity.

Only, however, if the theory is coherent. Anxiety on this score centers on the idea that the analogon is "an object for consciousness." Sartre can hardly claim less – if the analogon were merely a cause of imagining, it would not be an element within it, and would thus be incapable of explaining its phenomenology. But is the stronger claim really available to him? He accepts that, at least in cases of inner imagining, the subject is aware of none of the analogon's features. She is not aware of them while imagining, since then consciousness is wholly directed at the imagined scene. Indeed, if this were not so, imagining would not have the phenomenology described in the first characteristic, that of relating us to the imagined, unmediated by any mental particular. But nor is she aware of the analogon once imagining is over – else it would be something she could then observe. But if she is never aware of any of its features, in what sense is the analogon an "object for" her consciousness? What can this phrase mean?

Before addressing this problem, let us add a second, from the other end of the imagining spectrum. Consider our experience of pictures. When we see Charles VIII in his portrait, the phenomenology is surely not the same as when we visualize him. Even setting aside differences of how detailed and stable our imagining is likely to be, isn't there some more fundamental difference between the two? But what can this be, if the canvas plays the role of analogon? Sartre is adamant that, when it is so used, it is not *perceived*. And if, while seeing Charles in it, we are not aware of its features in any other way, the nature of the painted marks seems to make no difference to our consciousness. But then, whence the difference between this case and pure visualizing? Assuming that in each case we imagine Charles as bearing all the same features, the two experiences should be precisely alike.

To solve both these problems, I think we must treat the relation of being an object for consciousness as basic. This is a genuine relation: only what really exists can act as such an object. And it is fundamental to both perceiving and imagining. However, the relation fits into a very different structure in each case. In perception, the object for consciousness is the thing we perceive; in imagining it provides the material we animate in order to imagine something else. In the former, we are directly aware of its properties. In the latter, those properties are never perceived. However, it is not true, as assumed above, that we are not aware of them in any way. What is true is that we are only aware of them insofar as they contribute to the character of the imagined object. We cannot extract their contribution to that character from the whole. So we can't derive from our experience a description of the analogon's nature – not if that experience is imagining consciousness of Charles gained through his portrait, nor if it is visualizing him aided by sensations of movement or feelings. Nor are we aware of any thing distinct from Charles, the presence of which would prevent imagining being consciousness that directly aims at Charles himself. Nonetheless, in each case the Charles we imagine is "inflected" by the means through which he is imagined, by the material out of the properties of which he is formed. Since the nature of the analogon does contribute to our experience in this way, we are in some sense aware of its properties, albeit not *as properties of the analogon*, and thus the idea that it is an object for consciousness makes sense. And since the analogons of which we are thus obliquely aware differ across our two cases (in one, a canvas with paint on it; in the other, inner sensations and feelings), we can accommodate the difference in phenomenology between them.

Thus there is at least hope for saving Sartre's theory from the philosophical challenges it faces, while preserving his justification for it. What of the psychological evidence? Here I will confine myself to three observations. First, Sartre was fully aware that his speculations about the precise form taken by analogons for inner imagining were hostage to future scientific work. Second, at least some of that work supports his idea that sensations of movement play some role in imagining. (Consider here, for instance, the evidence that imagining words is often accompanied by subvocalization, and that if one prevents the latter from occurring, subjects find it much harder to undertake the imaginings requested [Smith et al. 1992].) Third, Sartre's view is quite consistent with the growing body of work, in both psychology and neurophysiology, supporting the idea that visual imagining exploits some of the same neural processing as visual perception. Of course, Sartre is adamantly opposed to the idea that imagining is, except in certain very broad respects (e.g., in involving perspective), phenomenologically akin to perceiving. But in the current state of our knowledge of the brain, it is unclear that overlap in processing establishes any closer kinship; and the use of the visual system in visual imagining does not clearly preclude a role in it for other "psychic" elements, of the kind Sartre's speculations concern.

## 4 The significance of imagining

Only half of *L'Imaginaire* is devoted to the exposition and direct defense of Sartre's claims about the phenomenology and deep structure of imagining. In the rest, he launches a series of investigations into its place in the wider mental economy: its relation to feeling and to symbolic thinking, its role in dreaming, in hallucination and in thought, and its central place in art. Those investigations, often brilliant, sometimes frustratingly suggestive, have often been ignored by those who've engaged with the book. In many ways, however, they complete his position, by drawing consequences from the claims at its core, or offering subtle defenses of them. There is no space here to enter into any of these topics in sufficient detail to make discussion worthwhile. The interested reader is encouraged to explore for herself.

What cannot be omitted, however, is at least a brief outline of Sartre's views on the deepest significance of imagining. Imagining is not merely one of the basic forms of consciousness, it holds the key to the most important feature of consciousness in general: freedom. To be free is to be able to step out of the stream of reality, to resist responding immediately to what reality puts before us, and to consider how we should act. If consciousness only presented us with the real, it would not be possible to step back in this way. For that, we need a sense of what is not, but which might be; we need the ability to grasp "nothingness." Nothingness cannot be intuited: there is no consciousness that presents us with pure nothingness. Yet there is, of course, one form of consciousness that has the idea of negation written into its intentional structure. That form of consciousness is imagining, and the ability to imagine thus underpins our freedom. Indeed, it underpins anything recognizable as human consciousness at all. Since nothing can be presented as real unless the contrast with what is not real is available, perceptual and imaginative consciousness are in fact interdependent. Neither can exist without the other, but it is the imaginative form, through positing as nothingness, that is the immediate source of human freedom (184–188; cf. Sartre 1943, 25–26).

Thus *L'Imaginaire* is the springboard to *Being and Nothingness* and the wider ambitions of that influential work. Even without that famous successor, however, the earlier book has a great deal to offer. It remains the most systematic and insightful expression of resistance to Humeanism about imagining, i.e., the attempt to treat it as perception in some degraded or weakened form. Despite the powerful attack on that view offered by various major thinkers in earlier part of the twentieth century, Humeanism has proved very resilient. Indeed, it remains the largely unquestioned assumption behind a good deal of philosophical and psychological work on imagining, at least in its sensory forms. To my mind, Sartre's view provides a powerful and in many ways plausible alternative. Even those who disagree should value his thought for offering the stimulus to future thinking that only a radical challenge to orthodoxy can bring.

## Notes

1 While *The Imaginary* comes in the middle of a sequence of publications exploring the themes above, it is the work in which Sartre develops his theory of imagining in far greater depth than elsewhere. A preceding book, *L'Imagination* ("The Imagination": Sartre 1936), is largely a review of existing psychological literature on the topic. And the *magnum opus* to follow, *L'Être et le Néant* ("Being and Nothingness": Sartre 1943), concentrates on working through the account of consciousness and freedom sketched briefly at the close of *The Imaginary*, leaving imagining itself aside.

2 Nowadays, it is common to suggest that imagining has both sensory and propositional forms. The latter is treated as involving a distinctive attitude, taken toward a given proposition. It should be clear from the above that Sartre would have no truck with such a view. All imagining is directed at objects, at elements in a world. The states sometimes now described as propositional imaginings, he would consider not to be imaginings at all, but forms of supposition, or some such.

## Further reading

W.L. McBride, "Sartre and Phenomenology," in L. Lawlor (ed.) *Phenomenology: Responses and Developments* (Durham: Acumen, 2010) is a useful guide to how Sartre's engagement with Phenomenology fits into the broader development of his thought. Chapter 8 of Gilbert Ryle's *Concept of Mind* (1949) in some ways pushes the anti-Humean position even further than Sartre does. C. McGinn's *Mindsight: Image, Dream, Meaning* (Cambridge, MA: Harvard University Press, 2006) offers a plain-speaking contemporary account of imagining that takes inspiration from Sartre's view at many points.

## References


Casey, E. (1981) "Sartre on Imagination," in P.A. Schilpp (ed.) *The Philosophy of Jean-Paul Sartre*, La Salle: Open Court.

Collingwood, R.G. (1938) *Principles of Art*, Oxford: Clarendon Press.

Hopkins, R. (2011) "Imagination and Affective Response," in J. Webber (ed.) *Reading Sartre: On Phenomenology and Existentialism*, Abingdon: Routledge.

Hopkins, R. (2012) "What Perky Did Not Show," *Analysis* 72(3): 1–9.

Nanay, B. (2010) "Perception and Imagination: Amodal Perception as Mental Imagery," *Philosophical Studies* 150(2): 239–254.

Peacocke, C. (1985) "Imagination, Experience and Possibility: A Berkleian View Defended," in J. Foster and H. Robinson (eds.) *Essays on Berkeley*, Oxford: Oxford University Press.

Perky, C.W. (1910) "An Experimental Study of Imagination," *American Journal of Psychology* 21(3): 432–452.

Peterson, M.A., P.M. Kihlstrom, P.M. Rose, and M.L. Glisky (1992) "Mental Images Can Be Ambiguous: Reconstruals and Frame Reversals," *Memory & Cognition* 20: 102–123.

Reisberg, D. (1996) "The Nonambiguity of Mental Images," in C. Cornoldi, R. Logie, M. Brandimonte, G. Kaufmann, and D. Reisberg (eds.) *Stretching the Imagination: Representation and Transformation in Mental Imagery*, New York: Oxford University Press.

Sartre, J.-P. (1936/1962) [originally *L'Imagination*, 1936] *The Imagination: A Psychological Critique*, trans. F. Williams, Ann Arbor, MI: University of Michigan Press.

Sartre, J.-P. (1940/2005) [originally *L'Imaginaire*, 1940] *The Imaginary: A Phenomenological Psychology of the Imagination*, trans. J. Webber, London: Routledge.

Sartre, J.-P. (1943/1969) [originally *L'Être et le néant*, 1943] *Being and Nothingness: An Essay on Phenomenological Ontology*, trans. H. Barnes, London: Routledge.

Scruton, R. (1974) *Art and Imagination*, London: Methuen.

Segal, S.J. (1971) "Processing of the Stimulus in Imagery and Perception," in S.J. Segal (ed.) *Imagery: Current Cognitive Approaches*, New York: Academic Press.

Smart, J.J.C. (1959) "Sensations and Brain Processes," *Philosophical Review* 68: 141–156.

Smith, J.D., D. Reisberg, and M. Wilson (1992) "Subvocalization and Auditory Imagery: Interactions between Inner Ear and Inner Voice," in D. Reisberg (ed.) *Auditory Imagery*, Hillsdale, NJ: Lawrence Erlbaum Assoc.

Strawson, P.F. (1970) "Imagination and Perception," in L. Foster and J.W. Swanson (eds.) *Experience and Theory*, London: Duckworth.

White, A. (1990) *The Language of Imagination*, Oxford: Blackwell.

Wittgenstein, L. (1965) *The Blue and Brown Books*, New York: Harper.

# PART II

# Contemporary discussions of imagination

# 7
# IMAGINATION AND MENTAL IMAGERY

*Dominic Gregory*

## 1 Introduction

Our imaginative activities often exploit our ability to produce sensory mental images. Indeed, putative links between mental imagery and the imagination are enshrined within the definitions issued by respected lexicographers: the *OED* states that, on one usage, 'imagination' is "the faculty or action of forming ideas or mental images." Philosophical attempts to identify the imagination's nature have also often traded upon its supposed links to mental imagery, as we will see below.

Very many of us would respond to, say, the instruction to "imagine an explosion" by entertaining visual and auditory mental imagery that presents the sights and sounds created by something exploding. Similarly, the imaginings in which many of us engage while reading fiction revolve around mental images that illustrate the scenes being described. One important way in which mental imagery and the imagination seem to be connected is thus as follows: *what we imagine* – the "content" of our imaginings – is often significantly shaped by what is shown in mental images.

Suppose that an imaginative episode features some mental imagery that plays a part in determining what is being imagined. Then the imagining is *imagistic*. So, suppose that I imagine a wooden table by visualizing a wooden table. My imagining of a wooden table is imagistic, as the imagining's content derives partly from the details of the visual image that I produced. As we will see in the next section, though, what is shown by the mental images featuring in imagistic imaginings can relate more or less straightforwardly to the contents of those imaginings. This fact raises interesting questions about the precise nature of the ways in which the mental images that occur within imagistic imaginings may affect the contents of the latter.

Another fundamental question about the relationship between the imagination and mental imagery is whether there can be *nonimagistic* imaginings. Are there imaginings, that is, whose contents do not derive in any way from the contents of mental images? Indeed, can there be imaginings that do not feature mental images at all?

Here is the plan for what follows. The next section sets things up for later parts of the chapter by distinguishing some of the different ways in which mental images may contribute to the contents of imaginative episodes. Sections 3–5 consider some interesting philosophical questions concerning imagistic imaginings, questions that are raised by the especially sensory nature of mental images. Sections 6–8 then broaden the discussion, by examining whether mental images are essential to our imaginative abilities.

Before proceeding, a caveat. The following sections often focus upon questions about the nature of the relationships obtaining between the contents of mental images and the contents of imaginings. A fuller survey of the imaginative consequences of the contents of mental images would need to reckon, though, with the additional question of just what sorts of contents mental images may possess.

Can our visual images literally show cats as such, for instance – that is, as falling under the concept *cat* – or are they rather limited to portraying "colour, light and shade, shape, size, motion, and spatial relations"?[1] Can they display Bertrand Russell as such, say, rather than merely showing someone who is visually indiscernible from Russell himself? Can we conjure auditory images of "Three Blind Mice" as played on a trombone, rather than merely a series of imaged sounds that share certain audible properties with a trombone's rendition of "Three Blind Mice"?

Those questions about the potential contents of mental images parallel related questions about the potential contents of sensory experiences themselves: do we literally seem to see cats as such, for instance?[2] And one might suspect that the previous correspondence is no accident, for the potential contents of mental images seem to be closely related to the potential contents of suitable experiences.[3] The previous questions thus lead rather inevitably to tricky questions in the philosophy of perception. Thankfully, however, the following pages will be able to avoid becoming embroiled in the latter debates.

So, produce a visual mental image "of a cat." It is a good question whether the visual mental image that you have just produced really displays a cat or rather just displays some item that looks the way that a cat might look. But it is, for communicative purposes, helpful to waive that question and simply to indulge one's inclination to speak of the image's being "of a cat"; the resulting description is, after all, acceptable enough by ordinary standards. By contrast, there probably isn't any similar license for the claim that your image characterizes the cat that it displays as once owned by Bertrand Russell.

For the purposes of what follows, then, I will talk of mental images that display things like cats and people, without meaning to incur a commitment to the view that mental images are genuinely capable of explicitly presenting such items as such; instead, I will just be exploiting some handy ways of talking. I will also rely upon some hopefully appealing claims about what particular mental images *do not* display; but if the reader is not convinced by the claims thereby made about the examples being discussed, he or she should feel free to substitute more convincing ones of his or her own devising.

## 2 Varieties of imagistic imaginings

Imagine a cat, just by producing a visual mental image of a cat. The nature of what you have imagined – whether the cat is a thin black one or a fat tabby, whether it was face-on or in profile – depends entirely upon what was displayed by the visual image that you produced. Or imagine a trombone playing a tune, simply by producing some auditory mental imagery of a tune being played on a trombone. Again, what you have imagined – the tune's dynamics, the trombone's timbre – depends entirely upon how things "sounded in your inner ear."

Both of the imaginings that you just produced were alike in being *purely imagistic*: their contents were entirely fixed by what was presented in the mental imagery featuring in the imaginings. Purely imagistic imaginings are, in terms of the role played by sensory mental imagery within them, the simplest variety of imagistic imaginings.

Now use some visual mental imagery just like that which you recently produced, to imagine a cat of exactly the same visible kind as the cat that you just imagined; but imagine in addition that the cat is one whose owners have recently jetted off to Paris. In this case, the visual mental imagery that you produced settles some but not all of the content of your imagining. The imagery fixes the cat's visible features, but there is nothing in the image itself that determines that the cat's owners have lately departed for France. This last imagining is thus imagistic but not *purely* imagistic.

The visual mental imagery in the previous imagining settled some but not all of the imagining's content. What else played a part in determining what it was that you then imagined?

A natural thought is that you did something roughly like this: you made various suppositions concerning what was displayed within the visual image, where those supposition-like elements served to extend the content of what you imagined beyond what the image strictly showed.[4] Thus Christopher Peacocke says, in a well-known paper discussed further below, that the differences between distinct imaginings that nonetheless feature the same mental imagery arise through "differences in which conditions are *S-imagined* to hold," where the initial 'S' in his term is for "suppose."[5] He distinguishes S-imagining from supposing in general; but he remarks that "it shares with supposition the property that what is S-imagined is not determined by the subject's images."

While the imagining that we just considered was not purely imagistic, each of the details of its accompanying mental imagery was nonetheless directly reflected by a corresponding feature of what was imagined: the various ways that your visual mental imagery showed the imaged cat as looking corresponded to features that the cat was imagined to have. But imagistic imaginings do not seem always even to work like that.

Suppose, for instance, that you were asked to imagine a regular heptagon. If you are like me, you would be unable to generate a visual mental image that simply displays a regular heptagon, as you cannot quite visualize the precise array of sides and angles needed for the job. Yet you could surely obey the request "to imagine" a regular heptagon, by combining visual mental imagery with suitable supposition-like elements. So, you might produce a visual mental image of a regular hexagon and then "S-imagine" that there is some shape of the same general kind as the one that you have visualized but which has seven sides rather than six.

In this last case, the six-sidedness of the visualized shape would not be directly reflected by an imagining of a hexagon; the imaginative task on which you had embarked would lead you instead to leave six-sidedness out from among the properties belonging to what was ultimately imagined. As Bernard Williams puts in, in another well-known paper discussed below, your "imaginative project" would have led you to perform an imagining that illustrates how "when we imagine by way of visualising" – that is, when we perform imagistic imaginings employing visual mental imagery – "we can properly be said to imagine something lacking an element which is present in what we visualise."[6]

The three examples of imagistic imaginings considered above illustrate just some of the ways in which mental imagery may help to fix the contents of imagistic imaginings. In particular, the final two cases illustrate how supposition-like elements can interact with mental imagery to yield imagistic imaginings whose contents derive in potentially rather complicated ways from the images' contents. These potential complexities will be relevant at numerous points in what follows.

## 3 Mental images and experiences

The previous section briefly cited a well-known paper by Williams. The paper's primary aim is to shed light upon the extent to which the imagination might reasonably be hoped "to provide a reliable road to the comprehension of what is logically possible" "with regard to the self."[7] But it starts with an extensive investigation of some questions concerning the relationship between mental images and the contents of imagistic imaginings.

Williams starts by considering a famous argument of Bishop Berkeley's for the conclusion that one cannot "conceive it possible for any mixture or combination of qualities, or any sensible object whatever, to exist without the mind."[8] The details of Berkeley's argument need not concern us here, but Williams suggests that the argument gains some superficial attractiveness from the fact that "it is plausible to say that if I visualise something, then I think of myself seeing it."[9]

Suppose it is true that "if I visualize something, then I think of myself seeing it." Then it may seem that one who, say, imagines a cat by visualizing a cat must "think of himself" seeing the cat; and hence that he must have imagined the cat as being seen by someone. More generally, it may seem that whenever we imagine a scene of some sort on account of producing mental images showing a scene of the relevant kind, we must thereby be imagining the relevant scene as witnessed by someone.

That line of thought goes too fast, though. To bring out the crucial point here, let's assume that mental images are "subjective," in that they meet the following condition:

(A) Consider a mental image that shows things as looking or sounding or smelling or tasting or … a certain way. Then the image shows things as looking or sounding or smelling or … that way *in the course of a sensory episode.*

Now suppose that somebody imagines a cat, in the course of an imaginative episode that features a visual mental image which shows a cat. Given (A), the relevant visual image shows things as looking a certain way in the course of a sensory episode: the visual image captures a visual encounter with cat. But that does not immediately imply that the *imagining* is an imagining of a cat that is being seen. For the imagining's overall content might have been affected by additional supposition-like elements, as noted in the previous section.

So, for instance, the person doing the imagining might have produced the visual mental image and then, on top of that, S-imagined a cat looking just like the one shown in the image but which is located in a situation in which there are no observers.[10] The fact that the contents of imagistic imaginings may be affected by supposition-like elements thus means that assumption (A) does not in itself imply that imagistic imaginings are always imaginings of scenes that are witnessed by someone. But what about those imagistic imaginings that don't feature supposition-like elements? That is, what about purely imagistic imaginings?

Suppose that somebody performs a purely imagistic imagining; suppose, for example, that the person imagines a cat merely by producing a visual mental image of a cat. Then, by (A), the visual image shows things as looking a certain way in the course of a visual episode. The image thus characterizes the cat that it presents as being seen. But the person's imagining of a cat is purely imagistic; so the imagining's content is just inherited from the content of the visual mental image by means of which the person performed the imagining. In this case, the person therefore has imagined a cat as seen.

More generally, the truth of (A) would ensure the following:

(B) Any purely imagistic imagining of an *F* is an imagining of an *F* as witnessed by someone.[11]

Is (B) to be accepted? Must we accept that anyone who imagistically imagines some scene, without imagining it as being witnessed, must be engaged in the sort of relatively complicated imagistic imagining that we considered two paragraphs back? Or are there reasonable grounds for rejecting both (A) and (B)?

## 4 Purely imagistic imaginings and imagined experiences

One concern that one might have with (A) is that it threatens to overgeneralize. Sensory mental images are just one family of representations that show things as looking or sounding or otherwise standing sensorily certain ways. Many pictures show things as looking certain ways, for instance, and playbacks of audio recordings can show things as sounding certain ways. The idea that, say, visual mental images must always show things as looking certain ways to an observer accordingly seems at first glance to be on a par with the thesis that ordinary pictures have to be subjective in the same manner. Yet that last claim is somewhat implausible: we do not automatically assume that the ways that things are shown to us as looking in pictures are meant to reflect the ways that things look to a viewer.

Williams seeks to block the derivation of (B) from (A) by exploiting the sorts of analogies just indicated. He suggests that "I as perceiver do not necessarily belong inside the world that I visualise, any more than … the painter in the scene that he paints; or the audience in the world of the stage."[12] He claims that, for instance in cinematic and theatrical contexts, we are shown things from certain perspectives although "[w]e cannot say, at least without great care, that it is *our* point of view. … In the standard case, it is not anyone's point of view. Yet we see the characters and action from that point of view."[13] Correspondingly, Williams holds that there is "no reason at all for insisting that the point of view" involved in a visualization is "of one *within* the world of what is visualised."[14]

Martin argues, in response to Williams, that "the point of view in [imagistic] imagining must be part of the imagined scene."[15] He holds that visualizing inherits a crucial feature of visual experience itself, as it presents "objects as oriented within egocentric space: they are presented as above one, below, to the left or to the right." Martin points out that, for example, "[o]ne can visualise a red light to the left and a green light to the right. If you now visualise the reverse – a green light to the left and a red one to the right – how you are visualising is different from the first case."

How best to explain why it is that the contents of the two imagistic imaginings just cited are distinct? Martin observes that we can account for the differences between the two cases only if "there is a point of view [within the imagined scene] relative to which the one object is to the left and the other to the right, or *vice versa*." Williams must therefore be wrong, he claims, in holding that the perspectives involved in what we are shown by visual mental images need not be present within the scenes that are being visualized. Yet, Martin claims, "if one does have to imagine a point of view within [a visualized scene], one thereby must be imagining an experience within the scene."[16]

Why so? Well consider the status of the perspective from which things are shown within a certain visual mental image. That perspective is not generally among the items that are explicitly shown by the visual mental image that one has produced. Rather, its inevitable presence within the visualization results from the fact that the items shown in the visual mental image are oriented in relation to it: "if one can fix the location of those objects, one thereby determine[s] the location of" the perspective. So, Martin urges, the items that are explicitly shown by the visual mental images are "being imagined as presented to a point of view within [the imagined] situation, and hence as being experienced" from that perspective.[17] Is this correct?

## 5 Perspectives and experiences

Martin is right to hold, I think, that the perspectives that he is discussing are present within the scenes that are being imagistically imagined. But it is less clear that their presence within the relevant scenes requires that the scenes are being imagined *as witnessed*.

To take an analogous case, pictures commonly show things as looking certain ways from certain perspectives; that is, they capture the ways that things look from oriented positions in space. And part of what one appreciates when one looks comprehendingly at such pictures is that the relevant perspectives are being characterized as bearing certain relationships to the explicitly pictured items. The relevant perspectives are, in that sense, in the world that is pictured. But it does not seem to follow that the perspectives are inevitably characterized as occupied: pictured scenes are not always represented as viewed by someone.

It thus seems that representations such as pictures and mental images can show things as, say, looking certain ways *from perspectives* without thereby showing things as looking the relevant ways *in the course of experiences*.[18]

Unless we assume that visual mental images do characterize visual experiences, though, how are we to explain Martin's observation that there is a definite difference between, first, visualizing a red light to the left and a green light to the right and, second, visualizing a pair of such lights in the opposite orientation? Well, we need merely assume that the relevant visual mental images show things as looking certain ways from suitable perspectives. Any perspective from which things look the way that the first visual image shows things as looking must be distinct from a perspective from which things look the way that the second visual image shows things as looking.

But what exactly is the difference between, say, a visual image that shows things as looking a certain way "from a perspective" and one that shows things as looking some way "in the course of a visual episode"? Indeed, and more fundamentally, what is it for things to look some way "from a perspective"?

Consider the way that things look to you right now. Given that your current visual sensation is a genuine seeing, the way that things look to you really is a way that things look from your current perspective. For things look to you to be *thus*; and, relative to the perspective that you actually occupy, things are indeed *thus*. More generally, then, a way for things to look is a way that things look "from a perspective" just in case the visual appearances involved in that way for things to look accurately reflect what things are like relative to the relevant perspective. By contrast, a way for things to look is a way that things look "in the course of a visual episode" just in case the relevant visual episode is of a suitable type. And parallel distinctions are available for nonvisual modes of sensing.

Now, consider a purely imagistic imagining that features a visual mental image that shows things as looking a certain way in the course of a visual episode. The visual image's content characterizes a visual episode as being one in which things look the relevant way. But the imagining is purely imagistic; hence its content is fixed entirely by the content of the visual image that it involves. In this case, then, the purely imagistic imagining is indeed an imagining of a visual episode in which things look some way. Some purely imagistic imaginings are thus indeed imaginings of experiences.

By contrast, though, consider a purely imagistic imagining that features a visual mental image that merely shows things as looking a certain way from a perspective. This time, the visual image's content characterizes a perspective as being one whose surroundings are correctly reflected by the visual appearances involved in the relevant way for things to look. In doing that, however, the image's content merely characterizes the nature of some portion of the world; it does not characterize the relevant situation as being seen. Some purely imagistic imaginings therefore are not imaginings of experiences.[19]

The distinction just exploited – between showing things as, say, looking some way "from a perspective" rather than "in the course of an experience" – is one whose importance isn't restricted to the imagination.[20] For there are many additional forms of representation that are analogous to visual mental images in certain ways and to which the distinction seems to be applicable. (While many pictures just represent portions of the world, for instance, others are used to capture what things once looked like to subjects.) Our initial and relatively narrow question concerning the contents of purely imagistic imaginings – whether purely imagistic imaginings must always be imaginings of experiences – thus has wider ramifications than one might expect. But just how extensive is the category of imagistic imaginings; and how does it relate to the totality of imaginings as a whole? The next few sections focus on those questions.

## 6 Are images essential to the imagination?

Just how important are mental images to our imaginative capacities? More specifically, do they always play some part in fixing the contents of our imaginings? Or can there be non-imagistic imaginings – that is, ones whose contents are not even partly determined by what is shown in accompanying sensory mental imagery? Can there even be imaginings which do not have *any* accompanying mental images?

Many philosophers, of very different persuasions, have regarded it as fairly clear that imaginings need not feature accompanying mental imagery: Ryle dismisses the view that imaginings require imagery fairly quickly, for instance, as does Walton.[21] But some rather venerable philosophers presumed that mental images must feature in imaginings. So, in the second *Meditation* Descartes states that "to imagine is nothing more than to contemplate the figure or image of a corporeal thing,"[22] while Hume identified the imagination as that faculty by means of which we conjure the most "faint and languid" "images" of our "impressions" – under which last term Hume "comprehend[s] all our sensations, passions and emotions, as they make their first appearance in the soul."[23]

Descartes and Hume were thus *simple imagery essentialists*[24] – they subscribed to the following principle:

(C) Necessarily, a mental episode is an imagining only if it includes some mental imagery.

Note that while simple imagery essentialism entails that imaginings must always feature mental images, the view says nothing about what those images *do* within imaginative episodes.

Other accounts of the relationship between imagery and the imagination go further. One possible reading of the earlier quotation from Descartes, for instance, would take him as having meant to communicate something like this: "to imagine [an *F*] is nothing more than to contemplate the figure or image of [an *F*]." But given that, first, any imagining must be an imagining *of* something[25] and, second, the content of any imagining is determined by what it is an imagining *of*, it would then follow that Descartes is committed to the following – which implies (C) but it not implied by it:

(D) Every possible imagining is such that, first, it features some accompanying sensory mental images and, second, its content is determined entirely by the contents of its accompanying mental images.

Now, the view that (D) captures – the view that imagery is the sole source of all imaginative content, so that imaginings must always be *purely* imagistic – is implausible. For it ignores the evident possibility of some of the kinds of cases discussed in Section 2 above. In particular, it overlooks the way in which supposition-like elements often put the contents of our imaginings at some distance from what is explicitly shown in the mental images that accompany them. (Recall the discussion of an imaginary cat whose owners are holidaying in Paris.)

A weaker relative of (D) is less immediately problematic, however:

(E) Every possible imagining is such that first, it features some accompanying mental images and, second, its content is at least partly determined by the contents of its accompanying mental images.

The view that (E) holds – the view that every possible imagining is imagistic, but not necessarily *purely* imagistic – is consistent with all of the examples of imaginings that were presented in Section 2. For, in each of those cases, the imagining featured mental imagery which played some role in fixing the imagining's content.

There are other interesting principles besides (C)–(E) concerning the relationships between mental imagery and imaginings in general.[26] But two of the principles just introduced – namely, (C) and (E) – will suffice for what follows. The next section will discuss whether simple imagery essentialism should be endorsed; the question whether there can be nonimagistic imaginings will join simple imagery essentialism as the focus of Section 8.

## 7 Challenging cases

It is clear that mental images often figure in our imaginings. But why would one assert or deny simple imagery essentialism? What reasons might one have, that is, for taking a stand on whether, necessarily, a mental episode is an imagining only if it includes some mental imagery?

Some of the most compelling reasons for *denying* simple imagery essentialism flow from putative examples of imaginings that do not essentially feature mental imagery. Ryle considers the example of a child "playing bears," for instance. The child "roars, he pads around the floor, he gnashes his teeth, and he pretends to sleep in what he pretends is a cave." Now assume that simple imagery essentialism holds. Ryle notes that, "according to this view, only if [the child] sees pictures in his mind's eye of his furry paws, his snowbound den, and so on, is he imagining anything." But, Ryle suggests, this is "patently absurd."[27]

Upholders of simple imagery essentialism might reasonably respond to this case by insisting that what Ryle finds to be "patently absurd" is in fact true. While we would tend naturally to assume that a child playing bears is engaged in all sorts of vivid imaginings, those imaginings are not themselves constituted by the child's overt behavior – by his roars, his teeth-gnashings, and so on. The mere bodily actions involved in the child's pretense at being a bear thus do not themselves seem to necessitate any accompanying imaginings; just, of course, as they also do not necessitate any accompanying mental images. While there might not be any mental imagery present in Ryle's example, then, there might not be any imaginings present either. But, simple imagery essentialists might now fairly ask, what is absurd about the suggestion that, for imaginings certainly to be present in the case Ryle envisages, some mental imagery would need also to be found?

But additional examples can be used to put further pressure on simple imagery essentialism. Kind suggests that "[t]he most plausible counterexamples" to her own view that mental images play an essential role in imaginings are provided by "predicative object-directed imaginings in which what [one] predicates of the imagined object seems to be something that cannot be imaged."[28] So, to take one of Kind's own examples, one cannot produce a mental image that shows "Bill Clinton having a secret desire to be a rock and roll star": no image will explicitly portray Clinton as having that secret desire. Yet one can surely imagine Clinton as having that secret desire.

As Kind notes, though, the fact that one can imagine Bill Clinton's secret desires yet one cannot produce mental images that actually display them does not establish the falsity of simple imagery essentialism; nor does it even establish the falsity of the view that imaginings must be imagistic. For defenders of those positions may claim that imaginings of Clinton's covert wants must at least involve mental images that feature *Bill Clinton*, even if what is shown by the images does not completely settle the contents of the relevant imaginings. They may claim, that is, that the envisaged cases merely establish the falsity – yet again! – of the view that imaginings are always purely imagistic.[29]

It is worth noting that the response just suggested derives whatever plausibility it possesses from the specific nature of the mental imagery – as at least featuring Bill Clinton – that it cites. So, suppose that some defender of simple imagery essentialism just stubbornly insists that imaginings of Clinton's secret desires must feature some mental imagery; but suppose that the person is also happy to allow that what the imagery shows may have nothing whatsoever to do with Clinton. Then that person would surely be mounting a wholly unsatisfying defense of simple imagery essentialism. If an imagining's accompanying mental imagery may have nothing at all to do with the imagining's content, why couldn't the imagining occur without the imagery?

This all suggests the following: if sensory mental images must indeed always accompany imaginings, that is because they must always play some part in determining what the imaginings are about. It suggests, that is, that simple imagery essentialism (as given by [D]) holds only if (to summarize [E]) imaginings must always be imagistic.[30] The next section therefore focuses directly upon the question whether there can be nonimagistic imaginings.

## 8 More challenging cases

Kind's response to the sorts of examples considered toward the end of the previous section – "predicative object-directed imaginings in which what [one] predicates of the imagined object seems to be something that cannot be imaged" – trades on an important role which sensory mental images often play in relation to the contents of imaginings relating to specific objects: the images often serve to single out the particular things that are being imagined. Many of our other imaginings do not relate to individual items so directly, however; and it is less clear that mental images play an essential role in fixing the contents of those imaginings.

Thus consider imaginings involving negative claims featuring properties that cannot be displayed using mental images: imagine that, say, nothing at all has any secret desires. There is no particular thing – no particular individual like Bill Clinton – that must be displayed by some mental imagery that accompanies an imagining that everything lacks secret desires. And, as remarked by Kind, facts concerning the presence or absence of secret desires are not the sort of thing that can be displayed by mental images. But nor are facts to the effect that nothing has a certain property: while an image may not display anything that is square, for instance, the image does not thereby show that *nothing at all* is square.

Any mental image which occurs alongside an imagining that everything lacks secret desires will therefore bear a notably indirect relationship to the imagining's content. One might produce a mental image of a person and then make the additional supposition that the person shown in the image, along with everything else, lacks secret desires. But why would one insist that an imagining of a total absence of secret desires *must* work in that baroque manner, unless one is already convinced that imaginings necessarily feature mental imagery?

One might respond to the case just discussed by mobilizing an observation commonly made in the literature on the imagination: namely, that mere "supposition" is to be distinguished from imagining proper.[31] (So, I can *suppose* for the sake of argument that it is raining and it is not raining; my supposition licenses both the conclusion that it is raining and the conclusion that it is not, for instance. But I cannot *imagine* that it is raining and it is not raining.) It might thus be claimed that, while we can suppose that nothing has secret desires, we cannot literally imagine that nothing has secret desires.

The distinction between supposing and imagining is a helpful one. But this does not seem to be a case in which it applies. Just intuitively, putative imaginings that nothing at all has any secret desires do not seem to be problematic in the way that, for example, ostensible imaginings that nothing has secret desires but something has secret desires seem to be. More generally, there are no apparent grounds for always insisting on the inevitably suppositional status of putative imaginings of negative claims featuring properties that cannot be displayed using mental images. (It is worth noting that counterparts of all the points just made in relation to suitable apparently imaginable *negative* claims also apply to apparently imaginable *universal* claims featuring properties that cannot be displayed using mental images, such as the claim that everything has secret desires.)

To summarize, then, numerous philosophers have held that imaginings can occur without accompanying mental images. They have often argued for this view by supplying ostensible examples of imaginings that need not be accompanied by sensory mental images. Many of those examples do not prove the required point, however: the relevant cases merely refute the view that imaginings must be purely imagistic. Yet further examples suggest that the weaker thesis that imaginings must be imagistic is in fact problematic, as also is the simple imagery essentialist view that imaginings must be accompanied by mental imagery.

## 9 Conclusion

This chapter has just focused upon one broad strand of the pressing philosophical questions concerning the relationships between sensory mental imagery and the imagination: it has been dominated by questions concerning the roles played by mental images in relation to the *contents* of imaginative episodes. But there are other important questions that might also have been discussed.

In particular, a huge amount of work by psychologists and philosophers has examined the neurological bases for sensory mental imagery; its main focus has been the question whether the forms of mental representation underlying visual mental imagery are "pictorial" in some sense.[32] Given that mental images play important roles in imaginative episodes, this work also has consequences for thought about the imagination. More specifically, it has consequences for questions about the nature of the cognitive processes that underlie many of our imaginings.

While those issues are important ones, though, their precise bearing upon our understanding of the imagination depends upon the nature of the relationships between sensory mental imagery in general and the imagination. The topics broached in this chapter are thus in a sense more elementary than the ones just described.

To conclude, sensory mental images play important roles within many of our imaginative activities. But one must be wary of oversimplifying those roles. In particular, interactions between mental images and supposition-like elements mean that the contents of even those imaginings to which sensory mental images are essential cannot simply be read off what is shown within the sensory mental images that accompany the relevant imaginings. And there are, too, reasons for thinking that sensory mental imagery is not essential to the imagination, even though some of the cases that have been held to support that view do not really do so. The relationships between sensory mental imagery and the imagination are thus notably complex and – like so many of the philosophical areas to which the imagination is central – ripe for further investigation.

## Acknowledgments

I owe many thanks to Amy Kind and an anonymous referee, who provided very helpful comments on an earlier draft of this chapter.

## Notes

1 Armstrong 1962, 5.
2 See Macpherson 2011 for a helpful survey of the issues in this area of the philosophy of perception.
3 See, for example, Gregory 2013, ch. 3, and Nanay 2015 for discussions of the relationships holding between the contents of mental images and of experiences.
4 The precise nature of these additional content-fixing elements – and, in particular, their precise relationship to suppositions proper – is a matter that deserves more attention than it can receive here; I will fudge the issue by talking of "supposition-like" elements of imaginings.
5 Peacocke 1985, 25. Something like the same idea is appealed to by Anscombe, in her discussion of what it is to imagine "a rabbit coming into being without a cause"; although she puts the point in terms of one's ability to "form an image and give [one's] picture that *title*" (Anscombe 1974, 150 – italics added). Kung (2010) appeals to both labels and stipulations in presenting a nicely refined picture of the manner in which the contents of our imaginings may be based upon, while yet extending, what is shown within the mental images featured in the imaginings.
6 Williams 1973, 33: the case in the text is based on Williams's example of a man whose imaginative powers have been skewed by his recent exposure to Bonnard's paintings of his wife in the bath.
7 Williams 1973, 45.
8 Berkeley 1734/2008, 182.
9 Williams 1973, 27. As we will see, Williams himself thinks that the previous claim's plausibility is misleading.
10 Williams recognizes this sort of possibility: he writes that "on this account [the view formulated as (A) above] a man can imagine an unseen tree, and by way of visualising a tree; but he does not, and cannot, visualise an unseen tree, and the reason why what he visualises is different from what he imagines is that he is allowed to discard elements from his visualisation incompatible with the essentials of his imaginative project" (Williams 1973, 34). See also Martin 2002, 417 for a related treatment of imagined visual hallucinations.
11 Principle (B) corresponds to an "Experiential Hypothesis" discussed by Peacocke, which states that for "imaginings describable pre-theoretically as visualisations, hearings in one's head, or their analogues in

other modalities ... to imagine being φ in these cases is always at least to imagine from the inside an experience as of being φ" (Peacocke 1985, 22) and that "for such forms as 'imagining a valley,' we can say that to imagine an F is always at least to imagine from the inside an experience as of an F" (23); see also the "Dependency Thesis" discussed by Martin ("to imagine sensorily a φ is to imagine experiencing a φ"; Martin 2002, 404).

12 Williams 1973, 35.

13 Williams 1973, 36–37.

14 Williams 1973, 36.

15 All the quotations in this paragraph are from Martin 2002, 408.

16 This quotation and the one in the previous paragraph are from Martin 2002, 409. The view that the perspectival nature of imagistic imaginings implies that imagistic imaginings are always imaginings of experiences has commonly surfaced in discussions of the imagination: it seems to underlie aspects of the discussion in Peacocke 1985, for instance, while Currie cites Walton as arguing in conversation that the perspectival nature of "perceptual imagining" means that perceptual imaginings are imaginings of sensory episodes (Currie 1995, 188).

17 All quotations in this paragraph from Martin 2002, 410.

18 As also noted by Wollheim (1987, 103).

19 See Gregory 2010 and forthcoming for more detailed discussion of these ideas, in relation to the imagination and forms of sensory memory.

20 Gregory (2013) uses the above distinction in articulating an account of the special nature of the contents of a very broad family of "distinctively sensory" representations that includes mental images, pictures, and many further cases.

21 See Ryle 1949, 243–244, and Walton 1990, 13. Other writers who have explicitly denied that imaginings must include imagery include Scruton (1982), Thomas (1997), White (1990); also, the approach to the imagination developed by Nichols and Stich (see, for instance, Nichols 2006) doesn't accord an essential role to mental imagery.

22 See Descartes 1641/1993, 53; see Chapter 2 on Descartes in the current volume for further discussion of his views.

23 See Hume 1739, 8–9, plus 1; see Chapter 3 on Hume in the current volume for further discussion of his views.

24 Kind (2001) also defends imagery essentialism; see below for more discussion.

25 See, for instance, Kind 2001, 90.

26 Kind (2001) proposes that imagery is essentially involved in the imagination because it has "the role of capturing the object of the imagination," for instance, just as the role that paint plays in a painting is that of "captur[ing] the object of [the] painting" (108). One potential way of developing this analogy would lead to an identification of Kind's view with that expressed by (E) above; but there may be other interpretations available which would put her position at a distance from (E).

27 All the quotations in this paragraph are from Ryle 1949, 243.

28 Kind 2001, 103.

29 See Kind 2001, 103–105. On p. 101 of her article, Kind quotes a series of examples owed to White (1990): each of them only really speaks to whether imaginings are always purely imagistic. But I think that some other cases that White mentions – in particular, he briefly notes that we can imagine that "no men or all men have red hair" – are closer to being genuinely problematic; see below.

30 Kind (2001) presents a positive argument for holding that imagery always plays an essential role in the imagination: she argues that, by assuming that to be true, we can explain certain crucial features of the imagination identified in §3 of her paper. In particular, Kind holds that the representational character of mental imagery explains why imaginings are also representational. In line with the suggestion made in the text, this explanatory argument for imagery's essential role appears to assume that the contents of imaginings are partly determined by the contents of accompanying mental images; that is, it apparently assumes that imaginings must be imagistic. For why otherwise would the representational character of mental imagery be relevant to the imagination's representational character?

31 See, for instance, Gendler 2000, 81; Gregory 2004, 329; and White 1990, 139; see Meskin and Weinberg 2006 for a relatively detailed exploration of the relationship between supposing and imagining, which leads them to claim (108) that "imagination and supposition are simply different ways in which one representational system may be used."

32 See the "Further reading" section below for some introductory references.

## Further reading

The notes to the current chapter contain numerous possibilities for further reading relating to the main topics discussed above. There is a vast philosophical and psychological literature on the issues concerning the neurophysiology of mental imagery mentioned briefly in the conclusion: N. Block (ed.) *Imagery* (Cambridge, MA: MIT Press, 1981) contains some classic papers on the topic, while Z.W. Pylyshyn, *Seeing and Visualizing* (Cambridge, MA: MIT Press, 2006) is a recent contribution from one of the major protagonists in the debate; for primarily philosophical discussion, see also, e.g., M. Tye, *The Imagery Debate* (Cambridge, MA: MIT Press, 1991), and D. Gregory, "Visual Imagery: Visual Format or Visual Content?," *Mind & Language* 25 (2010): 394–417. One response to the diversity of examples of imaginings discussed in this chapter would be to hold that there is no single unified mental process that counts as "imagining," and Amy Kind has recently endorsed this idea – see her paper on "The Heterogeneity of the Imagination," *Erkenntnis* 78 (2013): 141–159. The discussion in the text of the view that purely imagistic imaginings are always imaginings of experiences exploits certain relationships between mental images and representations like pictures: see D. Gregory, *Showing, Sensing, and Seeming: Distinctively Sensory Representations and Their Contents* (Oxford: Oxford University Press, 2014) for a detailed account of the nature of these relationships.

## References


Anscombe, G.E.M. (1974) "'Whatever Has a Beginning of Existence Must Have a Cause': Hume's Argument Exposed," *Analysis* 34: 145–151.

Armstrong, D.M. (1962) *Bodily Sensations*, London: Routledge & Kegan Paul.

Berkeley, G. (1734/2008) *Three Dialogues between Hylas and Philonous*, in D.M. Clarke (ed.) *Berkeley: Philosophical Writings*, Cambridge: Cambridge University Press.

Currie, G. (1995) *Image and Mind: Film, Philosophy, and Cognitive Science*, Cambridge: Cambridge University Press.

Descartes, R. (1641/1993) *Meditations on First Philosophy*, in S. Tweyman (ed.) *René Descartes: Meditations on First Philosophy in Focus*, London and New York: Routledge.

Gendler, T.S. (2000) "The Puzzle of Imaginative Resistance," *Journal of Philosophy* 97: 55–81.

Gregory, D. (2004) "Imagining Possibilities," *Philosophy and Phenomenological Research* 69: 327–348.

Gregory, D. (2010) "Imagery, the Imagination and Experience," *Philosophical Quarterly* 60: 735–753.

Gregory, D. (2013) *Showing, Sensing, and Seeming: Distinctively Sensory Representations and Their Contents*, Oxford: Oxford University Press.

Gregory, D. (Forthcoming) "Sensory Memories and Recollective Images," in F. Macpherson and F. Dorsch (eds.) *Perceptual Memory and Perceptual Imagination*, Oxford: Oxford University Press.

Hume, D. (1739–49/1978) *A Treatise of Human Nature*, eds. L.A. Selby-Bigge and P.H. Nidditch, 2nd edn., Oxford: Clarendon Press.

Kind, A. (2001) "Putting the Image Back in Imagination," *Philosophy and Phenomenological Research* 62: 81–110.

Kung, P. (2010) "Imagining as a Guide to Possibility," *Philosophy and Phenomenological Research* 81: 620–633.

Macpherson, F. (2011) Introduction to F. Macpherson and K. Hawley (eds.) *The Admissible Contents of Experience*, Hoboken: Wiley-Blackwell.

Martin, M.G.F. (2002) "The Transparency of Experience," *Mind & Language* 17: 376–425.

Meskin, A., and J. Weinberg (2006) "Puzzling over the Imagination: Philosophical Problems, Architectural Solutions," in S. Nichols (ed.) *The Architecture of the Imagination*, Oxford: Oxford University Press.

Nanay, B. (2015) "Perceptual Content and the Content of Mental Imagery," in *Philosophical Studies* 172(7): 1723–1736.

Nichols, S. (2006) "Just the Imagination: Why Imagining Doesn't Behave Like Believing," *Mind & Language* 21: 459–474.

Peacocke, C. (1985) "Imagination, Experience, and Possibility," in Foster J. and H. Robinson (eds.) *Essays on Berkeley*, Oxford: Clarendon Press.

Ryle, G. (1949) *The Concept of Mind*, New York: Barnes & Noble.

Scruton, R. (1982) *Art and Imagination*, London: Routledge & Kegan Paul.

Thomas, N.J.T. (1997) "Imagery and the Coherence of the Imagination: A Critique of White," *Journal of Philosophical Research* 22: 95–127.

Walton, K.L. (1990) *Mimesis as Make-Believe: On the Foundations of the Representational Arts*, Cambridge, MA: Harvard University Press.
White, A. (1990) *The Language of Imagination*, Cambridge: Blackwell.
Williams, B. (1973) "Imagination and the Self," in *Problems of the Self*, Cambridge: Cambridge University Press.
Wollheim, R. (1987) *Painting as an Art*, London: Thames & Hudson.

# 8
# IMAGINATION AND BELIEF

*Neil Sinhababu*

Belief and imagination are both states of mind that represent things as being a particular way. So one way of trying to understand the nature of imagination is by considering how it resembles belief and how it differs. If a concise statement of the similarities and differences between imagination and belief helps us understand how imagination works, and perhaps how the mind works in general, it'll provide a simple and illuminating theory of imagination. While some philosophers propose theories on which imagination and belief are fundamentally similar or on a continuum with each other, others see the differences between imagination and belief as too deep for unified approaches to explain, and argue that these mental states must be understood in fundamentally different ways.

This chapter surveys theories of imagination along both lines. I'll begin by considering the view that belief and imagination are fundamentally different, which is widely accepted by philosophers working on imagination (including myself). Then I'll consider more unified ones on which there are intermediate states between belief and imagination, or on which they're similar except that we apply the normative aim of truth only to belief and not to imagination. Throughout, I'll focus on propositional imagination, in which we imagine that some state of affairs obtains – for example, imagining that lava is flowing, as opposed to imagining lava. This may be the kind of imagination for which unified approaches are the most promising, since belief is a propositional attitude – one can believe that lava is flowing, but it doesn't make sense to talk about believing lava. There are many other philosophically important topics that a chapter on belief and imagination might explore, including the complex relations between belief and imagination in supposition (Arcangeli 2014), aesthetics (Walton 1990), make-believe games (Walton 1993), and philosophical methodology (Gendler 2010). But here I'll address such topics only insofar as they bear on general theories about what kind of mental state imagination is, and how much it's like and unlike belief.

First I'll consider functional properties of belief which imagination doesn't seem to share, and which suggest treating them as broadly different mental states. Second I'll consider functional properties of imagination which belief doesn't seem to share, which also support seeing the two states of mind as fundamentally different. Third will be the view of Shaun Nichols and Stephen Stich (Nichols and Stich 2000), which accounts for pretense by treating the cognitive mechanisms involved in imagination and belief as fundamentally different. Fourth will be Susanna Schellenberg's (2013) arguments that cases of imaginative immersion demonstrate imagination and belief to be on a continuum ranging from pure imagination to pure belief. Fifth will be Andy Egan's (2008) arguments that accounting for psychological delusions requires mental states intermediate between imagination and belief. Sixth will be theories from John Urmson (1967), Lloyd Humberstone (1992), and Nishi Shah and David Velleman (Shah and Velleman 2005), which explain the differences between belief and imagination not by appealing to the intrinsic properties of the representational states involved, but in terms of whether we apply a norm of truth to them.

## 1 Properties of belief that imagination lacks

While believing and imagining both involve representations, broad differences between them suggest that they're fundamentally different kinds of representational states that can't be understood in any especially unified way. This section considers some central properties of belief, and describes how imagination doesn't share them. The next section will consider some properties of imagination, and describe how belief doesn't share them.

Consider three properties that are attributed to belief on standard functionalist views, described by Eric Schwitzgebel (2006). First, beliefs create and eliminate other beliefs as the logical relations between their contents suggest. Believing that *p*, believing that if *p* then *q*, and attending to these propositions typically leads to forming the belief that *q*. We're strongly disposed to not believe contradictions when we attend to them. Second, perceptual states dispose us to believe that things are as we perceive them. When perceiving that *p* and attending to this feature of the perceived state of affairs, one typically forms the belief that *p*. Third, beliefs about what would raise the probability of desire-satisfaction interact with desires to motivate action. If one desires that *d* and believes that action *a* would make *d* more likely, this will give one some motivation to *a*.[1] As I'll describe, these properties of belief don't in general seem to be functional properties of imagination.

First, belief and imagination don't have the same logical relations with each other that each has with states of its own kind. One can easily imagine that *p* while believing that not-*p*. I can imagine that I'm Spider-Man while believing that I'm not Spider-Man. As with belief, there are strong psychological pressures against explicitly imagining contradictions – it's hard to simultaneously imagine that I'm Spider-Man and that I'm not Spider-Man, just as it's hard to believe both of these things. But if *p* is the content of belief and not-*p* is the content of imagination, or vice versa, we can easily hold onto both at once. It's easy to imagine that you're Spider-Man while believing that you're not Spider-Man. Our capacities for reasoning also lead us to imagine the logical consequences of what we imagine, when we attend properly to the premises and the conclusions. But even if beliefs interact with each other in the same way that imaginings interact with each other, belief and imagination don't in general interact with each other in these ways. If I imagine that I'm Spider-Man, and believe that Spider-Man doesn't exist, this won't lead me to believe or imagine that I don't exist. And if I imagine that I'm Spider-Man trying to shoot webs, and believe that if I try to shoot webs I'll fail, this won't lead me to imagine that I'll fail. While our beliefs about the world often influence what we imagine, we don't draw conclusions from a mix of believed and imagined propositions that we're attending to in the swift way that we believe the logical consequences of believed propositions that we're attending to, or in the swift way that we imagine the logical consequences of imagined propositions that we're attending to. When we fill in imagined scenarios with believed details, it's because the rules governing what we're supposed to imagine specifically allow us to do so, as Kendall Walton (1990, 1993) describes.

Second, imagining comes unmoored from one's immediate sensory experiences far more easily than belief does. Readers of novels imagine characters and their interactions instead of the pages they see. Daydreamers imagine pleasant or exciting situations instead of their boring surroundings. Players of make-believe games imagine that objects in their games have properties different from those sensation presents. Believing that things aren't as our sensory experiences suggest typically requires a reason to doubt our experiences, and can involve some cognitive strain. But we typically imagine things being different from how our senses present them.

Third, one doesn't usually act on imagined means to ends in the way one acts on believed means to ends. Daydreaming about being Spider-Man typically doesn't result in actually trying to shoot webs, and imagining that one is Harry Potter while reading of his adventures doesn't usually result in trying to cast spells. Sometimes in the context of make-believe games or Choose Your Own Adventure books, people do act on what they imagine. David Velleman (2000) claims that this demonstrates imagination to have motivational power, much as belief does. But even then, action on imagined means is highly restricted. When playing at making mud pies, children don't usually eat the mud. And in Choose Your Own Adventure books, one's real action isn't the imagined action of actually entering a time machine, but the believed action of turning to the page corresponding to the choice to enter the time machine. Even though action is involved in these cases, the behavioral roles of imagination and belief differ. Arguments along these lines from Paul Noordhof (2001), Lucy O'Brien (2005) and Neil Van Leeuwen (2009) that carefully consider the relation between imagination and motivation seem decisive against Velleman's claim.

## 2 Properties of imagination that belief lacks

While there's less agreement about the nature of imagination than about the nature of belief, imagination clearly seems to have some properties that belief lacks. These properties provide further reasons to regard the two states of mind as fundamentally different, and further obstacles for unified approaches.

One difference between belief and imagination is that it's easy to perform an intentional action of imagining something that isn't the case. It's hard or impossible to perform an intentional action of believing something that isn't the case. (While our desires can affect our beliefs in wishful thinking, that typically doesn't involve an intention to believe otherwise.) If I intend to imagine that someone is juggling pineapples in front of me, I can do so. But if I intend to believe that someone is juggling pineapples in front of me, I'll fail. My sensory experiences and other beliefs strongly dispose me to believe that there's no pineapple juggler in front of me. Any intentions to the contrary will be in vain, unless (for example) they move me to hire a pineapple juggler so that I'll form the belief by the standard sensory means. Imagination is free from such constraints. While we don't always imagine things intentionally – Amy Kind (2001) provides the example of unintentionally imagining gruesome scenes from horror movies that we'd rather get out of our heads (91) – we can do it if we want.

A second difference is that phenomenology is more closely tied to imagination than to belief. Kind provides an example and a strong statement of this view:

> Suppose that I were to imagine my friend's orange dress. My imagining clearly has a phenomenology. Moreover, the qualitative feel involved in my imagining is essential to it. Most importantly, however, there is nothing special about this particular imagining that provided it with its phenomenology. No matter what I imagine, my

> imagining will involve an experiential aspect. Without such an experiential aspect, a mental exercise is not an act of imagining.
>
> *(93–94)*

She notes an experiment by C.W. Perky (1910) in which subjects faced a blank screen, and were told to imagine objects on the screen. Faint images of these objects were projected onto the screen with increasing intensity until they'd be visible to anyone entering the room. Subjects asked to imagine a banana didn't report having genuine visual images of a banana when a banana was actually projected onto the screen. Instead, they said that the imagined banana had simply changed in size or spatial orientation. While Robert Hopkins (2012, 2013) argues that the banana images weren't literally perceived but were instead pictorially represented in a fashion that doesn't count as perception, Bence Nanay (2012) argues that standard views of pictorial representation preserve the conclusion that imagining and perceiving "are phenomenally very similar."

If Nanay's and Kind's interpretation of Perky's results is correct, imagining and perceiving have been experimentally demonstrated to be similar enough that it's hard to tell the difference between them. While these cases involve imagining a thing rather than a state of affairs, propositional imagination seems similar in its connection to phenomenology. Imagining that one's friend is wearing an orange dress and imagining that there's a banana on the screen seem to have similarly rich phenomenological effects. Examples like this can only show that imagination often has a rich phenomenology rather than demonstrating that this phenomenology is essential to it. But they still provide striking demonstrations of how phenomenologically rich imagining can be. Neuroscience provides further empirical evidence of similarities between perception and imagination. Research by O'Craven and Kanwisher (2000) demonstrates that imagining faces and places activates very similar regions of the brain to those involved in actually seeing those faces and places.

Belief doesn't have such a strong sensory phenomenology. If it did, evidence from sensation couldn't easily change our beliefs. Our beliefs could simply produce nonveridical sensations supporting them, even when we were in position to perceive otherwise. Falsely believing that my phone is on the bedside table won't create the visual experience of a phone when I look at the bare table. Belief and imagination differ in the direction of their strongest causal relation with experience. Imagination mainly causes us to experience things as being as we imagine them, while our experiences cause us to believe that the world is as we experience it.

This is not to deny that belief and imagination have intriguing common features. They both involve mentally representing the state of affairs that is their content in some way. And while I've distinguished their relations to desire and action, they both interact in desire in some way to cause pleasure. Humeans like Timothy Schroeder (2004) and myself (Sinhababu 2009, forthcoming) note that if you desire something strongly, you'll be pleased either when you discover that it's more likely to come about, or when you vividly imagine it in a daydream. Perhaps a unified way to describe this relationship with desire is that either believing or imagining something desired causes pleasure, in proportion to the degree to which the desired situation is represented. (See Amy Kind, "Desire-like imagination," Chapter 12 of this volume.)

I hope the list of differences in this section and the previous one explain why most theorists don't see belief and imagination as fundamentally similar. It would be impressive to tell a unified story about how the two mental states are basically similar except for some simple fact that explains all of their differences. And it's very hard to do, as impressive things often are.

## 3 Nichols and Stich on pretense

Shaun Nichols and Stephen Stich's influential paper, "A Cognitive Theory of Pretense," provides an account of how imagination works in cases of pretense. They argue that imaginative mental representations are stored in an "Imagination Box," separate from the mental compartment in which beliefs reside.[2] Their main reason for invoking a separate mental compartment for the imagination is to explain the phenomenon of "cognitive quarantine" – how we can believe that things are a certain way, while imagining that things aren't as we believe them to be. Since beliefs and imaginative representations are of different types, believing that not-*p* and imagining that *p* are compatible.[3] Philosophers who use 'cognitive' in areas like metaethics should note that in Nichols and Stich's title it doesn't mean "belief-based," but something more like "psychological." A strong psychological distinction between believing and imagining is at the core of their view, and allows them to explain cognitive quarantine.

Nichols and Stich, like many theorists addressing psychological questions, seek to describe the various types of human mental states and how they interact to cause the observed psychological phenomena. A useful metaphor for this purpose is that of several boxes in the mind, one for each type of mental state (belief and desire being two examples) in which the contents of the mental states are held. To have the content "I am Spider-Man" in the belief box is to believe that one is Spider-Man, to have it in the imagination box is to imagine that one is Spider-Man, and to have it in the desire box is to desire that one be Spider-Man. Nichols and Stich offer box-and-arrow diagrams displaying these mental state types and the causal relations between them that explain psychological phenomena. I can imagine that I'm Spider-Man while believing that I'm not Spider-Man, because these representations are in different boxes. Pairs of contradictory representations don't last long in either the belief or the imagination boxes. To put it in nonboxy terms, it's hard to believe contradictions or imagine contradictions. So splitting up the pairs to put "I'm not Spider-Man" in the belief box and "I am Spider-Man" in the imagination box explains how I can pretend I'm Spider-Man despite not believing that I am.

Nichols and Stich describe two psychological processes important to understanding how imagined scenarios develop. Since our representations of imagined scenarios can change rapidly and fluidly in response to new information, they invoke an "UpDater" that changes the contents of the Imagination Box. This explains how new events in the course of make-believe games can shift what's imagined, just as new evidence can rapidly change our beliefs. For example, if it's in the Imagination Box that a teddy bear at a tea party has started drinking vodka instead of tea, the UpDater may add the proposition that he'll soon become drunk. And since many new things that happen in pretense aren't simply entailed by representations of the pretended scenario and beliefs about how scenarios usually play out, they invoke a "Script Elaborator" that fills in additional details of the scenario, possibly in creative ways. The introduction of vodka to a properly innocent stuffed animal tea party would likely be the product of a mischievous imaginer's Script Elaborator. Nichols and Stich don't say much about the processes by which the Script Elaborator works, but one might expect that the agent's desires that the imagined scenario proceed in a particular way would play an important role.

Nichols (2006) clarifies further similarities and differences between belief and imagination. The emotional effects of imagining the destruction of the world in black comedies like Dr. Strangelove and in some philosophical thought experiments, as he notes, are very different from those of believing that the world has been destroyed. The difference is not only in degree, but in kind – one may be amused by the way Slim Pickens rides a nuclear bomb to his doom or be intrigued by the thought experiment, rather than being horrified by the deaths of billions. Nichols suggests that these differences concern the greater flexibility in how desire and imagination can interact to cause emotions. (See Stacie Friend, "Fiction and emotion," Chapter 16 of this volume.) If we were to focus on the deaths of billions, we'd be overwhelmed by horror, but our desires concerning philosophy and black comedy lead us to think about these topics in ways that don't involve imaginative engagement with horrific features of the situations. The resulting view treats belief and imagination as different mental state types which interact with desire in different ways, but are expressed in a "single code" that leads to similar affective responses.

Views along the lines Nichols and Stich suggest, on which belief and imagining involve fundamentally different types of mental states, are described as "the orthodoxy in contemporary debates about the imagination" by Sam Liao and Tyler Doggett (2014, 262), who note that they're shared by Currie and Ravenscroft (2002), Doggett and Egan (2007, 2011), Kind (2011), and Weinberg and Meskin (2005, 2006). While Nichols and Stich's distinctive terminology for the psychological components they describe hasn't caught on, most philosophers share their view that believing and imagining are deeply different states of mind.

An interesting objection to this orthodoxy comes from Peter Langland-Hassan (2012), who argues that pretense doesn't require a distinctive mental state of propositional imagination in addition to belief. To make the speech acts and perform the other actions involved in pretending that teddy bears are having a tea party, I merely need to have a variety of beliefs about how one should act in make-believe games, and a desire to act as I should. So instead of imagining that the teddy bears like tea and acting on desires to affect the imagined scenario in various ways, I believe that I should act as if the teddy bears like tea and act on desires to do as I should. On Langland-Hassan's picture, I need not believe or imagine simply that the teddy bears like tea – instead, I believe that the norms of the game require me to act as if they do. Since I don't have any attitudes strictly contradicting my belief that the teddy bears are inanimate objects who can't like tea, there's no problem of cognitive quarantine that would require the addition of a separate mental state type to house the otherwise contradictory belief.

While Langland-Hassan provides an elegant theory of the mental states driving our actions in cases of pretense, his picture doesn't seem to support a general account of other activities commonly explained in terms of imagination. While the behaviors performed in pretense can be understood in terms of believing that one should act as if things are different than they actually are, daydreaming and engaging with fiction involve less behavior and more phenomenologically rich representations. So they seem to require a different treatment that will invoke a distinct cognitive attitude of imagining. Imaginative immersion in pretense – the topic of the next section – may require a separate treatment as well. So while Langland-Hassan offers us a simpler explanation of one type of imaginative activity, it's hard to see how his arguments would lead us to reconceive the mental state of imagination in general.

## 4 Schellenberg on imaginative immersion and the belief-imagination continuum thesis

Now I'll turn to approaches that suggest a continuum between belief and imagination, with intermediate states that have some of the properties of each. Susanna Schellenberg (2013) uses cases of imaginative immersion to argue that belief and imagination are on a continuum that allows intermediate states. Imaginative immersion involves vivid imaginative representations that affect action and belief-formation with spontaneity like that of belief. A typical example involves children engrossed in make-believe games, acting spontaneously on what they imagine. If two young friends are trying to hit each other with sticks while immersed in imagining that they're dueling, they need not have explicit thoughts about how striking a friend in reality interacts with the rules of the game to constitute the make-believe action of killing the rival and winning the imagined duel. The imagined representation that striking would kill the rival interacts with their desire to win the imagined duel as spontaneously as beliefs interact with desires, motivating the act of striking. These representations are belief-like in how smoothly they seem to interact with desire in motivating action, and also imagination-like in representing the imagined scenarios themselves rather than anything genuinely believed. There are many similar examples of spontaneous action emerging from imaginative immersion in adults, involving method actors and participants in live-action roleplaying games. For an example of imaginative immersion in which beliefs interact with each other to produce further beliefs rather than interacting with desire to motivate action, consider scientists imagining future experiments and forming beliefs about the results. The experience of imagining what would happen in an experiment and the experience of coming to believe that these things will happen when the experiment will happen may be exactly the same. Schellenberg claims that "the phenomenon of imaginative immersion can be fully accounted for only if the functional roles of imaginings and beliefs are understood as being on a continuum" (508). Her view draws support from the seeming unity of imagining something and acting or forming a belief that follows from it in these cases.

If there are states of mind that are produced in the way imaginative representations are and not in the way beliefs are, but which also have the effects of belief and not of imagination, they would stand in the middle of a continuum between belief and imagination. Schellenberg accepts that we may have pure imaginings and pure beliefs at either end of the continuum. She argues that we should also countenance mid-continuum states, seeing imaginative immersion as involving a single state of mind with the content of imagination as well as the cognitive and motivational effects of belief: "The point is that accounting for imaginative immersion requires accounting for the possibility of moving seamlessly from mental states that could be called pure imaginings to mental states that are at least to some degree belief-like" (509). Invoking one state of mind intermediate between belief and imagination makes the transition from imagination like and belief like states seamless, as it simply involves having one state and doesn't involve extra transitions between states of two different kinds.

Liao and Doggett note some unappealing consequences of Schellenberg's view that being immersed in imagination involves a somewhat belief-like state of mind. They offer a case in which a mother is dragged into pretending she's a cop in a make-believe game with her daughter and becomes "gripped by the game and gets totally into being a cop" (Liao and Doggett 2014, 266). She goes from having occurrent beliefs about pretending to be a cop to full imaginative immersion into being a cop, where she doesn't have any experience of conscious thought about how she's playing a make-believe game. But as they note, "At no time did Mom imagine herself to be a mother who is pretending to be a cop in a game or believe herself to be a cop" (266). If imaginative immersion involved a mid-continuum mental state with the content "I'm a cop," Mom would need to believe this instead of imagining it, to whatever extent the mental state fell on the belief side of the continuum. Instead, it seems that Mom's imaginative immersion involves her coming to imagine more and more vividly that she is a cop. She need not enter into an even partially belief-like state with the content that she is a cop. Liao and Doggett point out that to whatever extent such a state was belief-like, it would be irrational. Furthermore, it predicts implausible actions. Mom is unlikely to note that she hasn't received a paycheck from the police department, and make a phone call inquiring about why it hasn't arrived.

Regarding imagination as perceptual rather than belief-like, along the lines suggested by Kind (2001), might account for the seamless transition between imaginings and belief-like mental states that Schellenberg discusses. If imagining an experiment involves seeing it in one's mind's eye, and imagining one's daughter as a robber in a make-believe game involves seeing her as a robber, the seamlessness that Schellenberg describes can be explained in terms of how experience causes belief. This need not simply be a belief that her daughter is a robber – all the beliefs can end with "in the make-believe game." So mom's experiences make her believe that her daughter is a robber in the make-believe game, that catching her daughter will be catching a robber in the make-believe game, and so on. Even though sensation and belief are distinct mental states, the transition between them is often phenomenologically seamless, just like the transition between imagining and belief in imaginative immersion. Perceptual representations of desired objects can seamlessly generate beliefs about how to satisfy our desires. When I'm hungry and I see tasty food on my plate, the perceptual representation quickly generates belief that it's there and that I can eat it by putting it in my mouth, just as imagination seamlessly generates beliefs that the imagined scenario is a particular way and performing a particular action will change it in a desired way. In neither case do we need to explicitly think about how the imagined or perceived state provides evidence for the means–end belief.

Understanding imagination as broadly perceptual in this way allows us to achieve the benefits of the continuum thesis without accepting it or its drawbacks. Just as the close causal connections between sensation and belief don't suggest that there are mental states intermediate between them, the close connections between imagination and belief don't suggest that there are mental states in between them. Close causal connections don't in general support continuum theses. That smoking causes cancer doesn't entail the existence of anything whose nature is on a continuum between smoking and cancer. In addition to providing a positive story about imaginative immersion, treating the imagined state of affairs as the content of a perception-like state avoids entailing that imaginatively immersed people actually believe to some extent that things are as they imagine. So a perceptual account of imaginative immersion could provide the benefits of Schellenberg's continuum thesis, without the costs that Liao and Doggett's arguments reveal.

## 5 Egan on delusions

Another argument for intermediate states between belief and imagination comes from Andy Egan, who considers psychological disorders involving delusions. Especially prominent in his discussion is Capgras delusion, in which patients claim that their friends, family or even pets (Wright et al. 1994) have been replaced by impostors. A typical example involves a fifty-nine-year-old man who believed that his wife was such an impostor:

> Fred's wife reported that about 15 months from onset he began to see her as a "double" (her words). The first episode occurred one day when, after coming home, Fred asked her where Wilma was. On her surprised answer that she was right there, he firmly denied that she was his wife Wilma, whom he "knew very well as his sons' mother," and went on plainly commenting that Wilma had probably gone out and would come back later.
>
> *(Lucchelli and Spinnler 2007, 189)*

Egan argues that people like Fred don't simply believe that their wives have been replaced by doubles, noting that delusions aren't supported by ordinary sensory evidence as beliefs are, and that they persist in the face of strong contrary evidence. Their effects on patients' wider belief system and behavior aren't as broad as those we might expect from ordinary beliefs. Currie (2002), Currie and Ravenscroft (2002) and Currie and Jureidini (2002) accommodate these differences between delusions and ordinary beliefs by regarding the content of delusions as imagined rather than believed. But as Egan notes, delusions still have some belief-like effects, leading patients to sincerely assert that they're dead or that their families have been replaced. Their behavioral effects are displayed in sad cases where Capgras patients attack the supposed impostors. To accommodate all the belief-like and imagination-like aspects of delusions, Egan suggests thinking of them as mental states intermediate between these types. He adds, "We shouldn't expect to see the peculiar hybrid roles all over the place because they're pretty maladaptive" (Egan 2008, 275). Delusions, then, display the existence and maladaptiveness of states in between belief and imagination.

The moral of Egan's story is that we should explore the possibility of mental states that mix and match the functional roles we see in familiar states of mind like belief and imagination. He aims at "undermining the all-or-nothing-roles view which, if we endorsed it, would rule out such intermediate roles, states, and representations" (270). He regards delusions as such intermediate representations.

While Egan is right that patients with delusions aren't just believing or imagining, psychologists seem to be converging on a different explanation that invokes no intermediate states of mind: Capgras' delusion involves an emotional impairment where one loses the feeling of familiarity in looking at a face, causing the delusional belief in an impostor (Bredart and Young 2004). Hadyn Ellis and collaborators (Ellis et al. 1997) describe two different psychological pathways involved in facial recognition. One pathway is impaired in Capgras' delusion and the other is impaired in a disorder called prosopagnosia that leaves patients unable to say whose a face is (Ellis and Young 1990, 2001). When I look at my friend Ben's face, I can identify the face as Ben's, and I also have a feeling of familiarity that I don't have when looking at a stranger's face. This feeling of familiarity has physiological effects. Normal subjects have higher skin conductance responses (a bodily indication of emotional arousal) when looking at familiar faces than when looking at strangers' faces. If I had prosopagnosia, I wouldn't be able to identify the face as Ben's, but I'd still feel the familiarity and have the accompanying higher skin conductance. Patients with prosopagnosia have elevated skin conductance responses like normal people seeing familiar faces, suggesting that they feel the familiarity despite being unable to say whose faces they are (Bauer 1984). And even though they're right about which of two faces they've seen before only 53 percent of the time (barely better than chance), they prefer faces they've seen before 70 percent of the time (Greve and Bauer 1990). This seems to be because these faces feel more pleasantly familiar. Capgras delusion is the reverse of prosopagnosia, with patients attaching a name to the face, but having neither the feeling of familiarity nor the elevated skin conductance (Ellis et al. 1997). Positing two separate aspects of facial recognition explains the two separate facial recognition disorders.

This emotional explanation leaves no need for mental states intermediate between belief and imagination. If I had Capgras delusion and I saw Ben's face, the eerie absence of the usual familiar feeling would make me believe that I was looking at an impostor with Ben's face. If I lacked any good theory about why this had happened, I might just believe that a stranger had Ben's face, with minimal changes to the rest of my belief system. This isn't because imagination is doing anything, but because the loss of that specific emotional response only affects a narrow range of beliefs. This can happen when we have vivid experiences that contradict a narrow range of beliefs but have little direct bearing on other beliefs. If I woke up one morning and it kept looking like my whole body was blue, I'd probably come to believe that I was blue but be unsure why. So it wouldn't significantly affect my other beliefs. And apart from behaviors directly involving my blue skin (trying to wash the blue off or going to a UNC basketball game) I might not act very differently. My confidence that my skin was blue might wane if I didn't see myself for a while – I might think that I was misremembering my past experiences or that I'd been in bad light, since my other beliefs generate inferential pressure against thinking I'm blue. But seeing myself again would reinforce the belief that I was blue. One could understand the epistemic phenomena associated with Capgras' delusion along these lines (Breen et al. 2000).

If the moral of Egan's story is that we should consider new mixes of functional roles, the moral of my story is that psychological mysteries are often solved by looking down into perception and emotion, not by looking up for fancy new cognitive states. This lets us keep the list of mental states tidy and simple – belief, desire, imagination, attention and a few others with clearly defined properties, as well as the rich assortment of emotional and perceptual states we need to explain the richness of experience. Learn about the varieties of perception and emotion, consider how these experiences affect belief-formation, and elegant explanations of psychological phenomena will build themselves from the bottom up.

## 6 The norm-application theory

Some philosophers argue that imagining that *p* is like believing that *p*, except that it doesn't involve applying a norm of truth to one's representation that *p*, which is necessary for a mental state to be a belief. This norm-application theory of how belief and imagination differ fits nicely with an intuitive normative distinction between the two states of mind. One ought to believe what is true, while it's not the case that one generally ought to imagine what is true. And most people in fact apply the norm of truth to their beliefs but not to their imaginative representations. Norm-application theorists don't draw the distinction by saying that believing that *p* involves believing that *p* is true. Imagining that *p* also involves imagining that *p* is true, so this wouldn't successfully distinguish belief from imagination. Instead, they hold that having a further mental state that applies a norm of truth to a representation that *p* is necessary for believing that *p*. If no such norm is applied, the mental state is one of imagining that *p*, or perhaps some similar state like assuming that *p* for purposes of argument.

Norm-application theorists differ about which mental state one has when one applies the norm. According to John Urmson (1967) and Lloyd Humberstone (1992), it's the mental state of intending that a representation be true. So we intend our beliefs to be true, while we have no such intention regarding our imaginings. According to Nishi Shah and David Velleman (Shah and Velleman 2005), it's a special mental state of accepting a norm of truth, which seems to operate along the lines suggested by Allan Gibbard (1990). (None of them takes applying the norm to be believing that a norm of truth applies. Invoking beliefs about norms to explain the nature of belief would be a circular explanation.) They all agree that applying a norm to one's representations is necessary for making them beliefs, at least in human psychology, and perhaps in all metaphysically possible believers. Representations where one doesn't apply the norm of truth, then, remain in the realm of imagination.

I've argued (Sinhababu 2013) that the necessity claim accepted by norm-application theorists faces decisive counterexamples. Ceasing to accept a norm of truth doesn't turn all of one's beliefs into imaginings. If Priscilla wholeheartedly embraces a pragmatist view of epistemic norms, and ceases to apply norms of truth to any of her mental representations, the necessity claim at the heart of the norm-application theory entails that she ceases to have any beliefs. With no norm of truth applied to her mental representations that *p*, they all cease to be beliefs that *p* and become imaginings that *p*. Whatever problems pragmatic or otherwise non-truth-oriented accounts of epistemic norms may have, it's bizarre to think that accepting them turns all of one's beliefs about the world into mere acts of imagining. Since one can retain one's beliefs without applying the norm of truth to any of one's mental representations, the distinction between belief and imagination can't be that we apply the norm of truth to the former and not to the latter.

It also seems possible to apply a norm of truth to one's imaginative representations without turning them into beliefs. If I accept a norm of imagining that someone loves me only if she actually loves me, perhaps because I feel that it's unjust to imagine people loving me when they actually don't, this doesn't transform my imaginative representations of her love into beliefs. This is especially clear in cases where I get carried away and violate my own norm, perhaps with the intensity of my desire for her love driving me to uncontrollably fantasize that she loves me. Such cases involve having a representation that she loves me and applying the norm of truth to it, so the norm-acceptance theory entails that I believe she loves me. But my runaway fantasy that she loves me doesn't become a belief that she loves me just because I apply a norm of truth to it. Accepting the norm might make me feel guilty even as I fantasized about her love. And if I believed that she loved me, as the norm-application theory predicts, why would I feel guilty? I wouldn't believe I was doing anything wrong. All this suggests that the norm-acceptance theory can't be reconstructed as providing sufficient conditions for turning imagination into belief.

Accepting and recognizing the consensus that beliefs ought to be true while no such norm applies to the imagination, then, shouldn't move one to accept a norm-application theory of the distinction between belief and imagination. One can withhold the norm of truth from one's beliefs and apply such a norm to one's imaginings without converting one mental state into another. Rather than taking belief and imagination to be intrinsically similar forms of representation that differ in virtue of whether we apply a further attitude to them, we should see them as differing broadly in their intrinsic properties.

## Acknowledgments

Thanks to Amy Kind, Neil Levy and an anonymous referee for helpful comments on this chapter.

## Notes

1 Schwitzgebel notes a fourth property: people are disposed to assert what they believe, under conditions favoring sincere assertion. But since assertion is an action, this seems to be a special case of the third functional property instead of a distinct fourth one.

2 Their original paper calls it the "Possible Worlds Box," and Nichols' later work (Nichols 2006) renames this compartment the "Pretense Box." 'Pretense Box' is a better name, as possible worlds are invoked in many contexts other than pretense. Doggett and Liao provide the best name, calling it the "Imagination Box," which I use here. Like belief, imagination is a type of mental state. Pretense is one among many activities employing the mental state of imagination.

3 See Gendler (2003) for further discussion of the phenomena.

## References


Arcangeli, M. (2014) "Against Cognitivism about Supposition," *Philosophia* 42(3): 607–624.

Bauer, R.M. (1984) "Autonomic Recognition of Names and Faces in Prosopagnosia: A Neuropsychological Application of the Guilty Knowledge Test," *Neuropsychologia* 22: 457–469.

Bredart, S., and A.W. Young (2004) "Self-Recognition in Everyday Life," *Cognitive Neuropsychiatry* 9(3): 183–197.

Breen, N., D. Caine, and M. Coltheart (2000) "Models of Face Recognition and Delusional Misidentification: A Critical Review," *Cognitive Neuropsychology* 17(1–3): 55–71.

Currie, G. (2002) "Imagination, Delusion, and Halucinations," *Mind & Language* 15(1): 168–183.

Currie, G., and J. Jureidini (2001) "Delusion, Rationality, Empathy: Commentary on Martin Davies et al.," *Philosophy, Psychiatry, & Psychology* 8: 159–162.

Currie, G., and I. Ravenscroft (2002) *Recreative Minds*, Oxford: Clarendon.

Doggett, T., and A. Egan (2007) "Wanting Things You Don't Want," *Philosophers' Imprint* 7: 1–17.

Doggett, T., and A. Egan (2011) "How We Feel about Terrible, Non-existent Mafiosi," *Philosophy and Phenomenological Research* 84: 277–306.

Egan, A. (2008) "Imagination, Delusion, and Self-Deception," in T. Bayne and J. Fernández (eds.) *Delusions, Self-Deception, and Affective Influences on Belief-Formation*, Hove: Psychology Press, 263–280.

Ellis, H.D., and A.W. Young (1990) "Accounting for Delusional Misidentifications," *British Journal of Psychiatry* 157: 239–248.

Ellis, H.D., and L. Lewis (2001) "Capgras Delusion: A Window on Face Recognition," *Trends in Cognitive Science* 5(4): 149–156.

Ellis, H.D., A.W. Young, A. Quayle, and K.W. de Pauw (1997) "Reduced Autonomic Responses to Faces in Capgras Delusion," *Proceedings of the Royal Society: Biological Sciences* 246(1384): 1085–1092.

Gendler, T.S. (2003) "On the Relation between Pretense and Belief," in M. Kieran and D.M. Lopes (eds.) *Imagination, Philosophy, and the Arts*, London: Routledge, 125–141.

Gendler, T.S. (2010) *Intuition, Imagination, and Philosophical Methodology*, Oxford: Oxford University Press.

Gibbard, A. (1990) *Wise Choices, Apt Feelings*, Cambridge, MA: Harvard University Press.

Greve, K.W., and R.M. Bauer (1990) "Implicit Learning of New Faces in Prosopagnosia: An Application of the Mere Exposure Paradigm," *Neuropsychologia* 28: 1035–1041.

Hopkins, R. (2012) "What Perky Did Not Show," *Analysis* 72(3): 431–439.

Hopkins, R. (2013) "Perky, Phenomenal Similarity and Photographs: Reply to Nanay," *Analysis* 73(1): 77–80.

Humberstone, I.L. (1992) "Direction of Fit," *Mind* 101(401): 59–83.

Kind, A. (2001) "Putting the Image Back in Imagination," *Philosophy and Phenomenological Research* 62(1): 85–109.

Kind, A. (2011) "The Puzzle of Imaginative Desire," *Australasian Journal of Philosophy* 89(3): 421–439.

Langland-Hassan, P. (2012) "Pretense, Imagination, and Belief: The Single Attitude Theory," *Philosophical Studies* 159: 155–179.

Liao, S., and T. Doggett (2014) "The Imagination Box," *Journal of Philosophy* 111(5): 259–275.

Lucchelli, F., and H. Spinnler (2007) "The Case of Lost Wilma: A Clinical Report of Capgras Delusion," *Neurological Sciences* 28(4): 188–195.

Nanay, B. (2012) "The Philosophical Implications of the Perky Experiments: Reply to Hopkins," *Analysis* 72(3): 439–443.

Nichols, S. (2006) "Just the Imagination: Why Imagining Doesn't Behave Like Believing," *Mind & Language* 21: 459–474.

Nichols, S., and S. Stich (2000) "A Cognitive Theory of Pretense," *Cognition* 74: 115–147.

Noordhof, P. (2001) "Believe What You Want," *Proceedings of the Aristotelian Society* 101: 247–265.

O'Brien, L., (2005) "Imagination and the Motivational View of Belief," *Analysis* 65(1): 55–62.

O'Craven, K.M., and N. Kanwisher (2000) "Mental Imagery of Faces and Places Activates Corresponding Stimulus-Specific Brain Regions," *Journal of Cognitive Neuroscience* 12(6): 1013–1023.

Perky, C.W. (1910) "An Experimental Study of Imagination," *American Journal of Psychology* 21: 422–452.

Schellenberg, S. (2013) "Belief and Desire in Imagination and Immersion," *Journal of Philosophy* 110: 497–517.

Schroeder, T. (2004) *Three Faces of Desire*, Oxford: Oxford University Press.

Schwitzgebel, E. (2006) "Belief," in E.N. Zalta (ed.) *Stanford Encyclopedia of Philosophy* (Summer 2015 edition), <http://plato.stanford.edu/archives/sum2015/entries/belief/>.

Shah, N., and D. Velleman (2005) "Doxastic Deliberation," *Philosophical Review* 114(4): 497–534.
Sinhababu, N. (2009) "The Humean Theory of Motivation Reformulated and Defended," *Philosophical Review* 118(4): 465–500.
Sinhababu, N. (2013) "Distinguishing Belief and Imagination," *Pacific Philosophical Quarterly* 94: 152–165.
Sinhababu, N. (Forthcoming) *Humean Nature*, Oxford: Oxford University Press.
Urmson, J.O. (1967) "Memory and Imagination," *Mind* 76(301): 83–91.
Van Leeuwen, D.S. (2009) "The Motivational Role of Belief," *Philosophical Papers* 38(2): 219–246.
Velleman, D. (2000) "On the Aim of Belief," in *The Possibility of Practical Reason*, Oxford: Oxford University Press.
Walton, K. (1990) *Mimesis as Make-Believe: On the Foundations of the Representational Arts*, Cambridge: Harvard University Press.
Walton, K. (1993) "Metaphor and Prop Oriented Make-Believe," *European Journal of Philosophy* 1(1): 39–57.
Weinberg, J., and A. Meskin (2005) "Imagine That!" in M. Kieran (ed.) *Contemporary Debates in Aesthetics and the Philosophy of Art*, Cambridge, MA: Blackwell.
Weinberg, J., and A. Meskin (2006) "Puzzling over the Imagination," in S. Nichols (ed.) *The Architecture of the Imagination*, New York: Oxford University Press, 175–202.
Wright, B. et al. (1994) "Canine Capgras," *Irish Journal of Psychological Medicine* 11: 31–33.

# 9

# IMAGINATION AND PERCEPTION

*Bence Nanay*

## 1 Introduction

Look at a red apple. Now close your eyes and visualize this apple. Your perceptual state and your imagery of the apple are very similar in some respects. They are also different in some respects. The aim of this chapter is to address three questions about the relation between perception and imagination:

a How similar are perception and imagination and what explains this similarity?
b How different are perception and imagination and what explains this difference?
c How do perception and imagination interact?

The plan is the following. In Section 2, I clarify what is meant by "imagination" in these questions. Sections 3 and 4 are about the similarities and differences between perception and imagination, respectively. Finally, in Section 5, I consider two important ways in which perception and imagination interact: mixed perception/imagination cases and the possibility that imagination is in some sense necessary for perception.

## 2 Mental imagery

There are many uses of the term "imagination" as, no doubt, other contributors to this volume argued (see, e.g., the Introduction and Chapters 5, 7, and 34). The sense of imagination I will focus on here is mental imagery. Having mental imagery of an apple should be differentiated from *imagining that* there is an apple in the kitchen, an imagining episode, which amounts to having a propositional attitude. The sense of imagination where there are interesting questions about the relation between perception and imagination is not propositional imagination, but mental imagery.[1] These are often even labeled as "quasi-perceptual" states (see, e.g., Richardson, 1969, 2). If they are in fact quasi-perceptual, then it is important to clarify how they are related to perceptual states.

The example I used by way of introducing mental imagery at the beginning of this chapter was closing your eyes and visualizing an apple. This is clearly one example of mental imagery, but in some ways a misleading, or at least unrepresentative one. First, mental imagery is not necessarily visual: I use the term "mental imagery" to cover visual, auditory, tactile, olfactory, etc., imagery.

Second and more importantly, closing one's eyes was an example of an active, intended, and voluntary act. But mental imagery can also be passive and neither intended nor voluntary. We can have mental imagery even if we are not trying to visualize anything – when, for example, we are having involuntary flashbacks to some scene that we have seen earlier. This is especially clear in the auditory sense modality, as demonstrated by the phenomenon of earworms: tunes that pop into our heads and that we keep on having auditory imagery of, even though we do not want to. Further, if mental imagery is a necessary feature of episodic memory (Byrne et al. 2007; see also Berryhill et al.'s 2007 overview), then it is also involuntary inasmuch as episodic memory can also be involuntary.[2]

Third, I will assume that mental imagery, like most mental states, can be conscious or unconscious. Closing one's eyes and visualizing an apple is clearly a conscious instance of mental imagery, but mental imagery can also be unconscious. Ian Phillips has argued that the reason why there is a significant variation in people's reports of their use of imagery is not that some of them use imagery and others don't but that the imagery of some people tends to be conscious and the imagery of some others tends to be unconscious (Phillips 2014a, 2014b). I myself have argued for the claim that unconscious mental imagery is very widespread because the mental imagery by virtue of which we represent occluded parts of perceived objects is normally unconscious (Nanay 2010b; see also Section 5.1, below). While Sections 3 and 4 will be about conscious mental imagery, the unconscious cases will play an important role in Section 5.

Finally, the example of closing one's eyes and visualizing an apple is somewhat atypical inasmuch as the apple I visualize with my eyes closed is likely to be in some abstract visualized space. But we can also visualize an apple in our egocentric space: I can visualize an apple to be right here on the keyboard of my laptop. Again, having mental imagery of something in our egocentric space is not something unusual – we use mental imagery this way very often. When you are looking at your empty living room, thinking about what kind of furniture to buy, you're likely to try to form mental imagery of, say, a sofa not in an abstract space "in the mind's eye," but in your living room. And when you're trying to figure out whether this sofa would fit through the main entrance, again, you are having mental imagery of the sofa in the very concrete space of the main entrance of your house.

These three distinctions are orthogonal to one another: we can have conscious egocentric voluntary mental imagery, unconscious egocentric voluntary mental imagery, conscious egocentric involuntary mental imagery, and so on. But all these different kinds of mental imagery attribute properties, in a quasi-perceptual way, to a scene or object that this scene or object is not perceived as having. At this point, I use the term "quasi-perceptual" as a mere placeholder because part of what is at stake in answering the question I am now turning to, the question about the similarity between perception and mental imagery, is exactly a way of explicating what is meant by the quasi-perceptual nature of mental imagery.

## 3 The similarity between perception and mental imagery

As we have seen, if I visualize a red apple and if I see one, the phenomenal character of my experience will be similar. But how similar are these experiences? And how can we explain this similarity?

The standard starting point for the discussion of the similarity between mental imagery and perception is the Perky experiment, where subjects looking at a white wall were asked to visualize objects while keeping their eyes open. Unbeknownst to them, barely visible images of the visualized objects were projected on the wall. The surprising finding is that the subjects took themselves to be visualizing the objects – while in fact they were perceiving them (Perky 1910; Segal 1972; Segal and Nathan 1964). The standard interpretation of this experiment is that if perceiving and visualizing could be confused under these circumstances, then they must be phenomenally very similar (but see Hopkins's 2012 criticism and Nanay's 2012 response).

So far, I have talked about the phenomenal similarity between perception and mental imagery, but it is important to note that there has been a lot of research on the similarity between these two processes that does not show up in our phenomenology. There is, for example, an almost complete overlap between the brain regions involved in perception and the brain regions involved in mental imagery, which suggests that the mental processes that make perception possible are the very same mental processes that make mental imagery possible (see, e.g., Kosslyn et al. 2006). Further, the patterns of cortical activation are also similar in perception and mental imagery (Page et al. 2011).

Another important set of experimental findings in this context is about our eye movements during visual imagery and visual perception (I will focus on the visual sense modality for ease of exposition, but we have very similar phenomena in the olfactory sense modality; see Bensafi et al. 2003): our eye movement during visual imagery reenacts that of the perception of the same visual scene. When we visualize a scene, our spontaneous eye movements reflect the content of the visual scene (Brandt and Stark 1997; Laeng and Teodorescu 2002; Mast and Kosslyn 2002; Spivey and Geng 2001; Johansson et al. 2006; Altmann 2004; see also Laeng et al. 2014 for a good summary). When we perceive a pattern in a grid, our eye movements are isomorphic to our eye movements when we visualize the same pattern.[3]

But if it is true that perception and mental imagery are similar in all these respects then we should ask what explains this similarity. An obvious answer to this question is that the phenomenology of these two mental states is similar because their content is similar (Ishiguro 1967; cf. Kind 2001; Currie 1995, 36–37; and Currie and Ravenscroft 2002, 27; Noordhof 2002; Nanay 2015). The relation between perceptual content and perceptual phenomenology has been an important issue in philosophy of perception and one influential view there is intentionalism, the view that perceptual phenomenology supervenes on perceptual content. If the phenomenology of mental imagery also supervenes on the content of mental imagery, then the similarity of the phenomenology of mental imagery and of perception can be explained in a straightforward manner by the similarity of the content of these two mental states. But one does not need to endorse intentionalism to hold this view: as long as there is some dependence relation (not necessarily supervenience) between content and phenomenology, similarity between content can explain similarity between phenomenology.

It is important to emphasize that this is not an explanation for why mental imagery and perception have similar phenomenal character. It is, rather, an explanatory scheme, which can be turned into an actual explanation only if we supply an account of perceptual content and an account of the content of mental imagery. And at this point some philosophers of perception will refuse to take this route because they deny that perceptual states have content. I will come back to what they could say about the phenomenal similarity between perception and mental imagery below. But a further problem is that there is no agreement about how we should think about the content of perceptual states (and about the content of mental imagery). One widespread way of thinking about perceptual content is in terms of propositional content: perceptual states, just like beliefs and desires, are attitudes toward a proposition. But if we think of perceptual content and the content of mental imagery this way (see, e.g., Currie 1995, 36–37; Currie and Ravenscroft 2002, 27), then it becomes less clear how the similarity of content would explain the similarity of phenomenology. There are many propositional attitudes (beliefs, hopes, desires, etc.) that could share the same propositional content with perception and they do not seem to share the same phenomenology – at least not in the strong(er) sense we are trying to explain here. A further, not too promising, candidate for perceptual content would be to talk about the object of the perceptual state. This will not lead very far as the object of my perceptual state when I see an apple is the apple. The object of my mental imagery, in contrast, may not exist at all. So these may not be similar.

I take the most promising way of cashing out the phenomenal similarity between perception and mental imagery in terms of content to be grounded in a way of thinking about content as the attribution of properties to objects (Burge 2010; Peacocke 1986, 1989; Nanay 2010a, 2013). Perceptual states attribute properties to the perceived object. Mental imagery attributes properties to the imagined object. While the objects these properties are attributed to are very different (one exists; the other may not), the properties attributed to them are similar. And this makes the content of the two mental states similar, which, in turn, makes their phenomenology also similar. This is not supposed to be a full explanation. More needs to be said about these attributed properties and the way they are attributed. For example, I argued that we need to make some further assumptions about the way these properties are attributed by perceptual states and by mental imagery (more specifically, how the determinacy of these properties changes) in order to explain how our attention is exercised in the two cases (Nanay 2015).

None of this explanatory strategy is available to those who deny that perceptual states have content (see, e.g., Campbell 2002; Brewer 2011; Martin 2004). So what can they say about the phenomenal similarity between perception and mental imagery? The two can't resemble each other in virtue of their content because one of them has no content. Further, those who deny that perception has content tend to argue that it is constituted by the relation to the actual token perceived object. They tend to take this to be an essential feature of perceptual states. This comes out nicely in the discussion of the "common denominator," or lack thereof, between perception and hallucination – the disjunctivism debate. Perception of an apple and the hallucination of an apple can have very similar phenomenal character – we can, after all, take our hallucination to be veridical perception. But those who deny that perception has content tend to insist that there is no substantial common denominator between these two cases: between perception and hallucination. While they seem similar, they are, "by their nature," or "essentially," very different (Martin 2004): one of them is a relation to an actual token object, whereas the other isn't. But if the "nature" or "essence" of these two mental states can't explain the phenomenal similarity, then what does? Note that we can raise this question not just about the relation between perception and hallucination, but also about the relation between perception and mental imagery (I will say more about whether and in what sense hallucination could be considered to be a form of mental imagery in Section 4).

Those who deny that perception has content do have an account of this similarity: it is the Dependency Thesis. According to the Dependency Thesis, having mental imagery of an object consists of representing the experience of this object. So it is not the similarity of content that explains why perception and mental imagery are phenomenally similar. Rather, by representing it, mental imagery inherits the phenomenal properties of the perceptual state (Martin 2002, 406; Smith 2006, 53–54). This is the so-called Dependency Thesis (Peacocke 1985; Martin 2002; see also Noordhof 2002 for analysis).

How does this work? An extra premise that is needed is what Martin calls the "transparency" of imagined experiences. He says:

> I assume at this stage that Dependency commits one to the claim that in imagining some scene one thereby imagines an experience of the scene – it is no part of Dependency to deny that one imagines the scene when one imagines an experience of the scene.
>
> *(Martin 2002, 404)*

Thus, by imagining an experience of an apple, we do imagine an apple. Thus, the content of our mental imagery is the experience of an apple but it is also the apple itself (see also Smith 2006, n. 18). Both the content of mental imagery and the content of perceiving include the apple itself.

This somewhat complicated explanatory scheme has been criticized for a number of reasons (Noordhof 2002; Currie and Ravenscroft 2002; Gregory 2010, 2014). And while it seems that because of the transparency assumption the Dependency Thesis can explain the phenomenal similarity between perception and mental imagery, it is much less clear that it can explain the physiological and behavioral similarities. Consider the findings about the similarity of eye movements in vision and visual imagery. According to the Dependency Thesis, the mental imagery of $x$ consists of *representing* the experience of $x$. And representing is not something that would involve specific eye movements. In fact, most often, it doesn't. It is the content of this representation, that is, the experience of $x$ that involves eye movements. Why is it, then, that the vehicle of this representation requires identical eye movements to the ones the content of this representation requires? The Dependency Thesis can, no doubt, be supplemented by some further theory that would explain this. But it is not clear how such an explanation would go. And, in any case, no such explanation is entailed by the Dependency Thesis alone. In contrast, the explanatory scheme of accounting for similarities in phenomenology in terms of similarities in content can explain this behavioral similarity neatly (see Gregory 2014; Nanay 2015).

## 4 The difference between perception and mental imagery

Of course, seeing an apple and closing one's eyes and visualizing an apple are, in spite of all the similarities discussed in the previous section, very different experiences. Seeing an apple can prompt me to reach out and grab it. Having mental imagery of the apple very rarely prompts us to reach out and grab the imagined apple. Further, seeing an apple seems to have a certain phenomenal oomph that is missing in the case of imagining the apple. This phenomenal oomph is often described as "feeling of presence." When we see an apple, we have this feeling of presence. When we have mental imagery of it, we don't have this feeling of presence.

Thinking about the difference between perception and mental imagery is as important and as old as thinking about the similarity between them. Hume, an influential advocate of the similarity between imagery and perception, was also very explicit about how they differ: imagery is a paler version of perception. Regardless of whether we explain the phenomenal similarity between mental imagery and perception in terms of content or with the help of the Dependency Thesis, this explanation needs to extend to how these experiences differ.

And here those who deny that perception has content may seem to have some explanatory advantage: if mental imagery and perception are very different kinds of mental states in that the latter, but not the former, is constituted by the relation to an actual token object, then the presence or lack of this actual relation to an actual object can explain nicely how the two experiences differ in terms of the presence or absence of this oomph. We get a feeling of presence in perception because the perceived object *is* present – in fact, perception is being related to this object that is present. And in the case of mental imagery, there is no feeling of presence because there is nothing present.

How about those who explain the similarity of mental imagery and perception in terms of the content of these two mental states? What can they say about the difference between these two experiences? There are at least two options. One option would be to follow Hume and argue that the difference is that of intensity. Another option, and one I myself defended, is to argue that the differences in the determinacy of the attributed properties comes in a bottom-up way in perception, whereas it comes in a top-down way in mental imagery. If you are looking at the apple and you are attending to the exact shade of red of the patch on its righthand side, the high determinacy of this attributed color property comes in a bottom-up manner from what you see. But if you close your eyes and visualize an apple, you can still attribute this very determinate property to the patch on the righthand side of the apple, but in this case, this determinacy comes in a top-down manner: from our memory or beliefs or expectations. It is important that this difference is not a difference in determinacy in general: not that mental imagery is less determinate than perception (this would be a version of Hume's view), but that the extra determinacy comes from different sources.

One may worry that these differences fail to explain the difference in the feeling of presence or oomph of these two experiences. And this may be right. But I don't see any reason to take the difference in the feeling of presence to be a mark of the difference between the phenomenology of perception and mental imagery. It sounds right that perception is, at least when conscious, accompanied by a feeling of presence. But I see no reason to think that mental imagery in general is not accompanied by a feeling of presence. (See Jonathan Jenkins Ichikawa, "Imagination, dreaming, and hallucination," Chapter 11 in this volume.)

Two examples: first, take mixed perception/imagery cases (see Section 5.2). Suppose that you are looking at your laptop and imagine it to be yellow. Or you imagine it to be twice as big as it is. These are genuine examples of mental imagery but they are still accompanied by the feeling of presence: I still "feel" the laptop as very much present. The oomph is still there. The second example is perhaps more controversial. Dreams and hallucinations are often taken to be special cases of mental imagery (Allen 2015; see Ichikawa, Chapter 11, this volume): they represent their object by attributing properties to them quasi-perceptually that we don't perceive these objects as having. And they are very often (in the case of hallucination maybe always) accompanied by a feeling of presence.

We have seen in Section 2 that mental imagery is sometimes conscious, but sometimes it is not and while it is sometimes voluntary, sometimes it's not. Similarly, mental imagery is sometimes, but not always, accompanied by the feeling of presence. In the case of hallucinations, dreams, and of imagining the laptop I am looking at to be yellow, it is. When I'm closing my eyes and visualizing an apple, it is not. This is yet another way in which closing one's eyes and visualizing an apple is not representative of mental imagery in general.[4]

But then what originally appeared to be an explanatory advantage for those who deny that perception has content now seems to be a disadvantage as they would now need to explain why there is a feeling of presence in those cases where there are blatantly no actual token objects to be related to (like in the case of dreams and hallucinations). And they also need to explain, and do so with the help of the conceptual apparatus of the Dependency Thesis, how some instances of representing an experience get us the feeling of presence, whereas other instances of representing an experience don't. I am not saying that those who deny that perception has content have nothing to say about these questions. But their explanation of the differences between the phenomenology of perception and mental imagery will not come for free, to say the least.

## 5 The interaction between perception and mental imagery

In the remainder of this essay, I discuss two important debates about the interaction between perception and mental imagery: one about whether imagery is necessary for perception and one about mixed cases.

### *5.1 Is mental imagery necessary for perception?*

When talking about the interaction between perception and mental imagery, the most obvious question we can ask is whether one is necessary for the other. While it is an important question whether perception is necessary for mental imagery (and some experiments about the mental imagery of congenitally blind people show that the answer is not at all obvious; see, e.g., Arditi et al. 1988), what I take to be the more interesting and more controversial idea is that mental imagery is necessary for perception.

An old and influential (Kantian) idea about the interaction between perception and mental imagery is that mental imagery is "a necessary ingredient of perception itself" (Strawson 1974, 54 – the metaphor and the quote are originally from Kant [*Critique of Pure Reason*, A120 n. a; see also Sellars 1978; Thomas 2009; and Samantha Matherne's Chapter 4, on Kant, in this volume]). One way in which this idea can be cashed out is that in order to perceive something as it is, we need to imagine what it would be (or how it would look) if things were a little different. An example of this approach is the view that in order to see objects as three dimensional, we need to, in some sense, imagine how they would look if we were to look at them from a different angle (Lewis 1929, 117–153, 1946; Noë 2004).

Another way of arguing for a much more modest version of the necessity claim is to say that mental imagery is necessary for some forms of perception. Here is an example. Amodal perception is the representation of occluded parts of perceived objects: those parts of the cat, for example, that are hidden behind the tree.

How are occluded parts of perceived objects represented? It seems that they are not represented by beliefs – they seem to have sensory phenomenology. They are not represented perceptually either in the strict sense of the term as we receive no sensory stimulation from occluded parts of perceived objects (because they are, well, occluded). I have argued on empirical and conceptual grounds that they are represented by means of mental imagery: we have mental imagery of the cat's tail, which is occluded by the tree (Nanay 2010b; see also Briscoe 2011).

But if this is true then mental imagery is a pervasive feature of the vast majority of our perceptual states. As we live in a nontransparent world, amodal perception is a necessary feature of virtually all of our perceptual states – it would be very difficult to imagine a natural scenario where we see something but no amodal perception is involved: if we see something, those things that are behind this thing are occluded from our vision. But then if amodal perception is a way of having mental imagery, this gives us a version of the original Kantian claim: in this limited and restricted sense it is true that mental imagery "is a necessary ingredient of perception itself."

A related, so far unexplored argument for the claim that mental imagery is in some sense necessary for perception concerns peripheral vision. Vision can only attribute very determinable properties in peripheral vision. This is especially true when it comes to color properties, which is what I will focus on – there are no color receptor cells that would correspond to the periphery of our visual field on our retina. But our experience of the periphery of the visual field is not black and white. Where does the color experience come from then? If mental imagery is the quasi-perceptual attribution of properties to objects that these objects are not perceived as having, then it is mental imagery that supplies color (and the extra degree of determinacy for other properties that are perceived as determinable). Vision doesn't (and can't) attribute color properties (or other determinate properties) in peripheral vision. But mental imagery provides this missing degree of determinacy, which would explain why our visual experience of the periphery of our visual field is not black and white.

### 5.2 Perception/mental imagery mixed cases

I defined mental imagery as the quasi-perceptual attribution of properties to objects that we don't perceive these objects as having. There are two ways this attribution can happen: we can attribute properties to an object we imagine (and don't see). Visualizing the apple with eyes closed is an example of this. Or we can attribute imagined properties to an object we see.

Both of these ways of having mental imagery are consistent with mixed perception/imagery cases. When I am at the furniture store and I am looking at a sofa, imagining how it would look in the living room, I am looking at an actual object and attributing imagined properties to it – properties it does not have, like being in my living room. And then I go home and look around in my living room imagining the sofa (which is not here, it's still in the furniture store) into my egocentric space in the living room. I am attributing properties ("real" properties in some sense, for example, spatial location properties) to an imagined object – to an object that is not there.

These mixed perception/mental imagery cases are widespread. Neil Van Leeuwen has argued for their importance in understanding pretense (Van Leeuwen 2011; see also Schellenberg 2013). Robert Briscoe calls them "make-perceive" and examined the role it can play in the guidance of our actions (Briscoe 2008). If it is true that amodal perception involves mental imagery, then (virtually) all of our perceptual states are in fact mixed perception/mental imagery states. Here is an example: you are looking at the landscape through your very dirty window; you represent those parts of the landscape that are occluded by specks of dirt by means of mental imagery and you represent those parts of the landscape that are not occluded by specks of dirt perceptually. The same goes for seeing a scene behind a wire fence: you have wire-fence-shaped mental imagery and many square-shaped bits in between represented perceptually.

Explaining the phenomenology of these examples will be an important data point for any explanation of the similarity between the phenomenal character of perception and mental imagery. If we explain this similarity in terms of content, then we have an easy time as the content will be very similar. Remember that the difference between the ways perception and mental imagery represent a scene is in where the extra determinacy is coming from: from top-down (in mental imagery) or from bottom-up (in perception). But as there are mixed top-down/bottom-up cases (and, if we can believe the vast cognitive penetrability literature, that is, the literature on how perception is influenced by higher cognitive processes [see Lupyan et al. 2010; Macpherson 2012], these are the rule, not the exception), there are also mixed perception/mental imagery cases.

Proponents of the Dependency Thesis may find it more difficult to make sense of these mixed perception/mental imagery cases. Take the dirty window example. It would follow from the Dependency Thesis that while we have perceptual experience of those parts that are not occluded by specks of dirt, we represent perceptual experiences of those parts that are occluded by specks of dirt. I don't think that this is an impossible view to defend, but it may be safe to say that this way of describing our experience through the dirty window is lacking in elegance compared with the simple picture according to which our bottom-up-driven perceptual state is, where specks of dirt are occluding the view, helped out by some top-down effects.

## 6 Conclusion

I hoped to show that the relation between mental imagery and perception is crucial both for philosophers of perception and for philosophers working on imagination. It is crucial for those who are interested in imagination as the comparison with perception highlights the importance of some distinctions between different kinds of mental imagery: voluntary versus involuntary, conscious versus unconscious, egocentric versus nonegocentric, accompanied by the feeling of presence or not.

And the relation between perception and mental imagery is equally important for philosophers of perception because mental imagery is an important test case for those theories that deny that perceptual states are representations. And focusing on the comparison with the content of mental imagery can help those theories that take perceptual states to be representations make it more explicit what kind of representations perceptual states are.

## Acknowledgments

This work was supported by the EU FP7 CIG grant PCIG09-GA-2011–293818 and the FWO Odysseus grant G.0020.12N. I am grateful for Amy Kind's, Dominic Gregory's, and Margot Strohminger's comments on an earlier draft.

## Notes

1 Propositional imagination can, of course, also involve the exercise of mental imagery, so these two categories are not meant to be exclusive.

2 What I mean by mental imagery should not be confused with what is sometimes referred to as "sensory imagination." Sensory imagination (e.g., imagining seeing something) is one way in which we can exercise our mental imagery, but not the only one.

3 It is important to keep apart the question about the similarity between mental imagery and perception from the grand "Imagery Debate" of the 1980s (see Tye 1991 for a summary). More specifically, admitting that there are important similarities between mental imagery and perception (in terms of physiology, of behavior or of phenomenology) does not commit one to denying that mental imagery is propositional (as long as one, like Pylyshyn [2007], also holds that perception is propositional as well).

4 This way of thinking about the feeling of presence is not at all outside the mainstream. In fact, it is a direct consequence of one of the most influential accounts of the feeling of presence as metacognitive feeling (endorsed also by some who deny that perception has content; see Martin and Dokic 2013).

## References

Allen, K. (2015) "Hallucination and Imagination," *Australasian Journal of Philosophy* 93(2): 287–302.

Altmann, G.T.M. (2004) "Language-Mediated Eye Movements in the Absence of a Visual World: The 'Blank Screen Paradigm,'" *Cognition* 93: 79–87.

Arditi, A., J.D. Holtzman, and S.M. Kosslyn (1988) "Mental Imagery and Sensory Experience in Congenital Blindness," *Neuropsychologia* 26: 1–12.

Bensafi, M., J. Porter, S. Pouliot, J. Mainland, B. Johnson, C. Zelano, N. Young, E. Bremner, D. Aframian, R. Khan, and N. Sobel (2003) "Olfactomotor Activity During Imagery Mimics That during Perception," *Nature Neuroscience* 6: 1142–1144.
Berryhill, M.E., L. Phuong, L. Picasso, R. Cabeza, and I.R. Olson (2007) "Parietal Lobe and Episodic Memory: Bilateral Damage Causes Impaired Free Recall of Autobiographical Memory," *Journal of Neuroscience* 27: 14415–14423.
Brandt, S.A., and L.W. Stark (1997) "Spontaneous Eye Movements during Visual Imagery Reflect the Content of the Visual Scene," *Journal of Cognitive Neuroscience* 9: 27–38.
Brewer, B. (2011) *Perception and Its Objects*, Oxford: Oxford University Press.
Briscoe, R. (2008) "Vision, Action, and Make-Perceive," *Mind & Language* 23: 457–497.
Briscoe, R. (2011) "Mental Imagery and the Varieties of Amodal Perception," *Pacific Philosophical Quarterly* 92: 153–173.
Burge, T. (2010) *The Origins of Objectivity*, Oxford: Clarendon.
Byrne, P., S. Becker, and N. Burgess (2007) "Remembering the Past and Imagining the Future: A Neural Model of Spatial Memory and Imagery," *Psychological Review* 114: 340–375.
Campbell, J. (2002) *Reference and Consciousness*, Oxford: Oxford University Press.
Currie, G. (1995) "Visual Imagery as the Simulation of Vision," *Mind & Language* 10: 25–44.
Currie, G., and I. Ravenscroft (2002) *Recreative Minds: Imagination in Philosophy and Psychology*, Oxford: Oxford University Press.
Gregory, D. (2010) "Imagery, the Imagination and Experience," *Philosophical Quarterly* 60: 735–753.
Gregory, D. (2014) *Showing, Sensing, and Seeming: Distinctively Sensory Representations and Their Contents*, Oxford: Oxford University Press.
Hopkins, R. (2012) "What Perky Did Not Show," *Analysis* 72: 431–439.
Ishiguro, H. (1967) "Imagination," *Proceedings of the Aristotelian Society, Supplementary Volume* 41: 37–56.
Johansson, R., J. Holsanova, and K. Holmqvist (2006) "Pictures and Spoken Descriptions Elicit Similar Eye Movements during Mental Imagery, Both in Light and in Complete Darkness," *Cognitive Science* 30: 1053–1079.
Kind, A. (2001) "Putting the Image Back in Imagination," *Philosophy and Phenomenological Research* 62: 85–109.
Kosslyn, S.M., W.L. Thompson, and G. Ganis (2006) *The Case for Mental Imagery*, Oxford: Oxford University Press.
Laeng, B., and D.-S. Teodorescu (2002) "Eye Scanpaths during Visual Imagery Re-enact Those of Perception of the Same Visual Scene," *Cognitive Science* 26: 207–231.
Laeng, B., I.M. Bloem, S. D'Ascenzo, and L. Tommasi (2014) "Scrutinizing Visual Images: The Role of Gaze in Mental Imagery and Memory," *Cognition* 131: 263–283.
Lewis, C.I. (1929) *Mind and the World-Order: Outline of a Theory of Knowledge*, New York: Charles Scribner's Sons.
Lewis, C.I. (1946) *An Analysis of Knowledge and Valuation*, La Salle, IL: Open Court.
Lupyan, G., S.L. Thompson-Schill, and D. Swingley (2010) "Conceptual Penetration of Visual Processing," *Psychological Science* 21(5): 682–691.
Macpherson, F. (2012) "Cognitive Penetration of Colour Experience," *Philosophy and Phenomenological Research* 84: 24–62.
Martin, M.G.F. (2002) "The Transparency of Experience," *Mind & Language* 17: 376–425.
Martin, M.G.F. (2004) "The Limits of Self-Awareness," *Philosophical Studies* 120: 37–89.
Martin, J.-R., and J. Dokic (2013) "Seeing Absence or Absence of Seeing," *Thought* 2: 117–125.
Mast, F.W., and S.M. Kosslyn (2002) "Eye Movements during Visual Mental Imagery," *Trends in Cognitive Science* 6: 271–272.
Nanay, B. (2009) "Imagining, Recognizing and Discriminating: Reconsidering the Ability Hypothesis," *Philosophy and Phenomenological Research* 79: 699–717.
Nanay, B. (2010a) "Attention and Perceptual Content," *Analysis* 70: 263–270.
Nanay, B. (2010b) "Perception and Imagination: Amodal Perception as Mental Imagery," *Philosophical Studies* 150: 239–254.
Nanay, B. (2012) "The Philosophical Implications of the Perky Experiments," *Analysis* 72: 439–443.
Nanay, B. (2013) *Between Perception and Action*, Oxford: Oxford University Press.
Nanay, B. (2015) "Perceptual Content and the Content of Mental Imagery," *Philosophical Studies* 172(7): 1723–1736.
Noë, A. (2004) *Action in Perception*, Cambridge, MA: MIT Press.

Noordhof, P. (2002) "Imagining Objects and Imagining Experiences," *Mind & Language* 17: 426–455.
Page, J.W., P. Duhamel, and M.A. Crognale (2011) "ERP Evidence of Visualization at Early Stages of Visual Processing," *Brain and Cognition* 75(2): 141–146.
Peacocke, C. (1985) "Imagination, Experience, and Possibility: A Berkeleyan View Defended," in J. Foster and H. Robinson (eds.) *Essays on Berkeley*, Oxford: Clarendon, 19–35.
Peacocke, C. (1986) "Analogue Content," *Proceedings of the Aristotelian Society*, Supplementary Volume 60: 1–17.
Peacocke, C. (1989) "Perceptual Content," in J. Almong, J. Perry, and H. Wettstein (eds.) *Themes from Kaplan*, Oxford: Oxford University Press, 297–329.
Perky, C.W. (1910) "An Experimental Study of Imagination," *American Journal of Psychology* 21: 422–452.
Phillips, I. (2014a) "Lack of Imagination: Individual Differences in Mental Imagery and the Significance of Consciousness," in J. Kallestrup and M. Sprevak (eds.) *New Waves in Philosophy of Mind*, Basingstoke: Palgrave Macmillan, 278–300.
Phillips, I. (2014b) "The Temporal Structure of Experience," in V. Arstila and D. Lloyd (eds.) *Subjective Time: The Philosophy, Psychology, and Neuroscience of Temporality*, Cambridge, MA: MIT Press, 139–158.
Pylyshyn, Z.W. (2007) *Things and Places: How the Mind Connects with the World*, Cambridge, MA: MIT Press.
Richardson, A. (1969) *Mental Imagery*, New York: Springer.
Schellenberg, S. (2013) "Belief and Desire in Imagination and Immersion," *Journal of Philosophy* 110: 497–517.
Segal, S.J. (1972) "Assimilation of a Stimulus in the Construction of an Image: The Perky Effect Revisited," in P.W. Sheehan (ed.) *The Function and Nature of Imagery*, New York: Academic Press, 203–230.
Segal, S.J., and S. Nathan (1964) "The Perky Effect: Incorporation of an External Stimulus into an Imagery Experience under Placebo and Control Conditions," *Perceptual and Motor Skills* 19:385–395.
Sellars, W. (1978) "The Role of Imagination in Kant's Theory of Experience," in H.W. Johnstone (ed.) *Categories: A Colloquium*, University Park: Pennsylvania State University Press.
Smith, J. (2006) "Bodily Awareness, Imagination and the Self," *European Journal of Philosophy* 14:49–68.
Spivey, M., and J. Geng (2001) "Oculomotor Mechanisms Activated by Imagery and Memory: Eye Movements to Absent Objects," *Psychological Research* 65: 235–241.
Strawson, P.F. (1974) "Imagination and Perception," in *Freedom and Resentment*, London: Methuen, 45–65.
Thomas, A. (2009) "Perceptual Presence and the Productive Imagination," *Philosophical Topics* 37: 153–174.
Tye, M. (1991) *The Imagery Debate*, Cambridge, MA: MIT Press.
Van Leeuwen, N. (2011) "Imagination Is Where the Action Is," *Journal of Philosophy* 108: 55–77.

# 10
# IMAGINATION AND MEMORY

*Dorothea Debus*

## Introduction

All healthy human beings are, from an early age onwards, able to imagine and to remember things. Imaginings and memories occur regularly and frequently, and they play important roles in our daily lives. Imaginings and memories also seem closely related to each other. Indeed, Hobbes claims that "imagination and memory are but one thing, which for diverse considerations has diverse names" (Hobbes 1991, 16). This seems a fairly radical position, and is not a position that will be defended here. However, the fact that Hobbes is prepared to make such a radical claim indicates that at the very least, there must be some strong and important similarities and links between imagination and memory.

This chapter will explore relevant similarities and links which obtain between the two phenomena, and it will also discuss some important differences between the two. In considering those differences and similarities, we will encounter both metaphysical questions (i.e., questions related to the nature of imagination and memory) as well as epistemological questions (i.e., questions about how a subject might be able to know whether she is imagining or remembering, that is, how she might be able to tell imaginations and memories apart). Consideration of relevant differences and similarities will give us reason to resist Hobbes' claim that imagination and memory "are but one thing," but having considered the various similarities and links which do obtain between memory and imagination we should, by the end of the present chapter, also be in a position better to understand why Hobbes might have been tempted to make his overly radical claim.[1]

## Propositional vs. experiential

At its most general, we might hold that "memory, like imagination, enables us to think about that which is not, or is no longer, the case, or which we are not or are no longer now experiencing" (Warnock 1994, 7).[2] This in turn might explain why, when philosophers talk about either imagination or memory, they draw rather similar distinctions to one another. Philosophers who think about imagination often distinguish between propositional imagination on the one hand, and experiential, or "sensory," imagination on the other. Quite analogously, philosophers who think about memory usually distinguish between propositional (or "factual") memory on the one hand, and experiential, or "recollective," memory on the other. In the terminology that will be used here, "sensory imaginings" (or "S-imaginings") and "recollective memories" (or "R-memories") are those cases of imagination and memory which do have experiential characteristics, whereas "propositional imaginings" and "factual memories" are those cases of imagination and memory which do not have any experiential characteristics, but rather have important similarities with beliefs and judgments. Thus, both in the case of imagination and in the case of memory, we can distinguish between a propositional kind on the one hand, and an experiential kind on the other.[3]

Traditionally, philosophers who have thought about the relation between imagination and memory have been particularly interested in the relation between those cases of imagination and those cases of memory which have experiential characteristics. In other words, they have traditionally focused their attention on what I here call "sensory imaginings" and "recollective memories," those cases of remembering and imagining which characteristically "correspond to our use of the distinct senses" (M. Martin 2002, 403).

Everyday (self-)observation shows that we can, and frequently do, recollectively remember objects and events, and that we can, and frequently do, sensorily imagine objects and events. For example, try to remember what you did last Sunday. Maybe you went to have lunch at a friend's house. When remembering the event, you might have a visual experience – for example, an experience as if seeing the host welcoming you at the door again – which in turn should count as a recollective memory of the relevant past event. Similarly, try to imagine what you are going to do this coming Sunday. Maybe you are planning to go on a good long bike ride. When imagining what you are going to do this coming Sunday, you might have a visual experience as of cycling along a familiar road in the nearby countryside, and of your friend on her bike in front of you, an experience which in turn should count as a sensory imagining of a future event.

Recollective memories and sensory imaginings are of particular interest, because compared with propositional imaginings and memories, sensory imaginings and recollective memories are, in virtue of their experiential characteristics, particularly vivid, and they are therefore bound to play an especially important role in our mental lives.[4]

Furthermore, R-memories and S-imaginings might also be of particular interest here because considered in isolation and from the experiencing subject's own point of view, R-memories and S-imaginings are very similar. Indeed, considered in isolation and from the subject's own point of view, they might be difficult to tell apart. For example, if you were to consider your R-memory of what you did last Sunday in complete isolation from the context in which it occurs, it would probably be rather difficult (and might be impossible) for you to tell whether the relevant experience was an R-memory or an S-imagining. Similarly, if you were to consider your S-imagining of what you are going to do this coming Sunday in complete isolation from the context in which it occurs, it would probably be rather difficult (and might be impossible) for you to tell whether the relevant experience was an S-imagining or an R-memory.

Thus, self-experiments of the present kind as well as everyday (self-)observation of relevant ordinary real-life cases suggest that S-imaginings and R-memories might, when considered in isolation, seem indistinguishable from the subject's own point of view. However, normal healthy subjects usually can, and do, successfully distinguish between their sensory imaginings and their recollective memories. We seem to rely on our ability to distinguish between S-imaginings and R-memories very frequently in everyday contexts, and we make very different use of S-imaginings and R-memories, both epistemologically and in more pragmatic respects.

Indeed, we usually (quite rightly) take it that R-memories of past events present us with how things were in the past, and we therefore take the relevant experiences into account when making judgments about how things were in the past. By contrast, we usually (quite rightly) take it that S-imaginings only present us with how things might be, and we therefore take the relevant experiences into account only when making judgments about how things might be. Thus, we usually make different epistemological use of S-imaginings and R-memories, and, intuitively, it does seem reasonable for us to make such different epistemological use of S-imaginings and R-memories.

We also make different pragmatic use of S-imaginings and R-memories. For we usually (quite rightly) use our recollective memories of past events when trying to understand (and maybe also come to terms with) our past and to understand how we got to the situation we are in at the time of remembering. By contrast, we usually (quite rightly) use our sensory imaginings when trying to entertain ourselves, or when trying to make plans and decisions – one might, for example, try to S-imagine one's old sofa in the new living room, and might on that basis make a decision about where to put the sofa in the new room. Thus, we do make different pragmatic use of our S-imaginings and R-memories, and intuitively, it does seem reasonable for us to make such different pragmatic use of the two kinds of experiences.[5]

More generally, then, we find that subjects make different epistemological as well as different pragmatic use of their S-imaginings and R-memories, and we also find that it seems reasonable for them to do so. However, in order for it to be reasonable for subjects to make different epistemological and pragmatic use of their S-imaginings and R-memories, it is necessary that they are able to tell whether a certain experience presents them with how things were in the past, or whether it only presents them with how things might have been or might be; that is, subjects need to be able to tell those experiences which present them with how things were in the past (i.e., R-memories) apart from those experiences which present them with how things might have been or might be (i.e., S-imaginings). And indeed, we all do this successfully on a daily basis. But how do we do this, given that S-imaginings and R-memories are, from the subject's own point of view, rather similar, maybe even indistinguishable, when considered in isolation?

## Distinguishing features?

How do subjects tell S-imaginings and R-memories apart? In an attempt to answer this question, philosophers usually try to show that although S-imaginings and R-memories are, considered in isolation, rather similar from the subject's own point of view, S-imaginings and R-memories nevertheless do have distinguishing features which subjects can, and do, successfully detect in everyday contexts.

Firstly, someone might hold with Hume that we can tell R-memories and S-imaginings apart because they differ with respect to their force and vivacity. R-memories, so Hume holds, are less forceful and vivacious than perceptual experiences, but R-memories are more forceful and vivacious than S-imaginings.[6] On the basis of this systematic difference in force and vivacity, so runs the present suggestion, a subject might learn to take experiences with one degree of force and vivacity as presenting her with how things were in the past, and to take experiences with another degree of force and vivacity as presenting her with how things might be.

However, the idea at the heart of the present suggestion is not borne out by the everyday phenomenology. Although some R-memories might be more vivacious and forceful than certain S-imaginings, there are S-imaginings which are much more forceful and vivacious than some R-memories. For example, you might have a very vague R-memory of your first day at school, while you might be able to S-imagine very vividly what you are going to do tonight. Hence, it seems just false to claim that S-imaginings and R-memories differ systematically with respect to their force and vivacity. The present suggestion therefore does not help us to answer the question how subjects might be able to tell R-memories and S-imaginings apart.[7]

Alternatively, one might follow Russell and hold that R-memories are accompanied by a feeling which indicates to the subject that a relevant experience presents her with how things were in the past.[8] R-memories are always conjoined with such a "feeling of pastness," while S-imaginings never are. The presence or absence of a feeling of pastness will thus enable the subject to tell S-imaginings and R-memories apart. A subject who has an experience which is conjoined with a feeling of pastness will take it, and has reason to take it, that the relevant experience presents things as they were in the past, whereas a subject who has a relevant experience which is not accompanied by a relevant feeling of pastness will not take it, and does not have any reason to take it, that the relevant experience presents things as they were in the past. Russell himself seems hesitant in putting this view forward,[9] but views of the present kind have recently found some renewed attention (see, e.g., Dokic 2014), so we should give Russell's original suggestion careful consideration.

Firstly, we should accordingly ask which actual mental events are referred to as "feelings of pastness" here, and it is difficult to answer this question. Indeed, it remains unclear which actual mental phenomena the term "feeling of pastness" might refer to, and on the basis of everyday (self-)observation one might plausibly suggest that there are at least some cases of R-memory which are not accompanied by relevant feelings, and one might well come to hold that subjects do not usually experience any relevant "feelings of pastness" when they R-remember past events at all.

However, for the sake of the argument let us grant that some way might be found to determine which mental phenomena are here referred to as "feelings of pastness," and let us also grant that all cases of R-memory are accompanied by such a "feeling of pastness," while S-imaginings usually are not accompanied by any such feeling. Next, a defender of the present suggestion will then be asked to explain how a "feeling of pastness" might play the reason-giving role which it is said to play: On the view under consideration, the occurrence of a feeling of pastness gives a subject a reason to take it that a relevant experience – namely, the experience which the feeling is conjoined with – presents her with how things were in the past. But then, how could a feeling possibly play this role?

Indeed, it seems that in ordinary everyday cases, we usually are not prepared to rely on our feelings to the extent that is suggested here. Sometimes a lot depends on whether a certain experience should be taken to present things as they were in the past. For example, court cases often rely on witness reports which in turn rely on experiences that witnesses take to be R-memories. If a witness is pressed to explain why they make a certain claim about a relevant past event, they might well say things like "I can see it again in front of my mind's eye," or "I vividly remember it happening." We take such responses to be legitimate – that is, we ordinarily do think that R-memories give us reason to make relevant judgments about the past. But now, assume our witness is pressed to explain what reason they have to take their relevant experience to present them with how things were in the past. According to Russell's suggestion under consideration here, the witness should be expected to reply "I take the experience to present me with how things were in the past because I have a relevant feeling [i.e., a "feeling of pastness"] when the experience occurs."

This response seems epistemologically unsatisfactory. Having a feeling, so we might well say in reply, is not enough, especially not in cases as weighty and serious as the present one; having a relevant feeling (or a hunch) might give us reason to explore a certain issue further; thus, if an experience was accompanied by a "feeling of pastness," this might well give you reason to try to find out by other means whether the relevant experience presents things as they were in the past. However, we ordinarily, and quite plausibly, assume that feelings can be a little fickle and might at times be unreliable, and accordingly, we also usually take it that a feeling on its own could not possibly provide a subject with a sufficient reason to endorse a belief about the external world without any further enquiry. This in turn indicates that a "feeling of pastness" could not, on its own, provide us with a means of distinguishing between R-memories and S-imaginings. Russell's suggestion of how a subject might be able to tell R-memories and S-imaginings apart is therefore unsuccessful.

Alternatively and thirdly, we might consider a suggestion developed by Urmson. On Urmson's view, "the answer to the question how we can tell recollecting … on the one hand from free imagination on the other is that we tell just by knowing what we are at, knowing whether we have or have not chosen to act so that resemblance to actuality is a criterion of the success of our activity" (Urmson 1967, 90). Thus, on the present view, a subject can tell whether a certain present experience does or does not present her with how things were in the past because she knows about the intentions which she had in bringing the relevant experience about (see Urmson 1967, 87f.). Indeed, knowledge about relevant intentions might sometimes help a subject in telling whether a present experience does or does not present her with how things were in the past. However, many R-memories and S-imaginings seem to occur to subjects unintentionally. For example, when Claire sits at her desk trying to focus on work, but then drifts off and finds herself with vivid S-imaginings of her next holiday in the mountains, or with vivid R-memories of her last trip to Venice, she does not seem to have any intentions to bring the relevant experiences about. Rather, the relevant experiences just occur. Nevertheless, Claire takes it that her experiences as of the mountains present her with what her environment during her next holiday might look like, and that the relevant experiences as of Venice present her with how things were during her last trip to Venice, which in turn indicates that Urmson's suggestion cannot account for at least some, and arguably many, relevant cases.

Nevertheless, it does seem reasonable for subjects to take it that some of their experiences (namely, R-memories) present them with how things were in the past, and it also does seem reasonable for subjects not to take it that other experiences (namely, S-imaginings) do so. And indeed, I think we can account for this feature of our mental lives once we give up on considering relevant experiences more or less in isolation, as we have done so far.

## Context matters

Instead, I suggest that we turn our attention to the fact that in our ordinary everyday mental lives, both R-memories and S-imaginings usually occur within a context of other mental events and states of affairs. These contextual features matter. More specifically, I think we can show that R-memories (at least usually) have a characteristic relational property – they occur in a specific context of relevant beliefs – which S-imaginings lack, and that the relevant relational property gives subjects reason to take it that relevant experiences present them with how things were in the past, while in the absence of the relevant relational property in the case of S-imaginings, subjects lack reason to do so.[10]

More precisely, R-memories usually occur in a context of beliefs (which might, but need not, be occurrent at the time at which the R-memory occurs) on the basis of which a subject would be able to tell a reasonably detailed, autobiographical story which makes reference to the content of the relevant experience; and the idea at the heart of the present suggestion is that a subject has a reason to take it that a certain experience presents her with how things were in the past if she has beliefs on the basis of which she would be able to tell a reasonably detailed, autobiographical story which makes reference to the content of the relevant experience.

For example, consider Anna. Anna remembers meeting her friend Lucy for lunch yesterday, and she has a vivid R-memory of Lucy sitting at the table opposite her in the cafe, wearing a bright blue scarf and smiling very broadly. Furthermore, on the basis of various beliefs which she has about the past, Anna is able to tell a story about her day yesterday in general and about her lunch in particular. For example, she might say that the weather was glorious when she was walking from her office to the cafe to meet Lucy, that she had a cheese sandwich for lunch, and that after saying goodbye to Lucy she walked over to the big lecture hall to give her afternoon lecture. Among other things, Anna's story might also contain a reference to the content of her R-memory – namely, Lucy sitting opposite her during lunch. For example, Anna might say that Lucy was wearing a bright blue scarf and seemed very happy when they met yesterday.

Indeed, Anna's autobiographical story about her day yesterday is likely to be reasonably detailed, and it will implicitly describe a spatiotemporal route, traced by herself, which is of such a kind that it is quite plausible that the subject who traced the relevant spatiotemporal route witnessed a scene like the one presented by Anna's R-memory. Furthermore, Anna tells an autobiographical story. When referring to the subject whose spatiotemporal path is implicitly described by the story, the story makes use of the first-person pronoun. Accordingly, the ability to tell such a story will give Anna reason to assume that she actually witnessed the situation which her present experience presents to her. This in turn gives her reason to assume that the relevant situation did obtain in the past.

Thus, the present example might give us reason to accept the following:

> **Context Claim:** a subject has a reason to take it that a certain experience presents her with how things were in the past if the experience occurs in a context of beliefs on the basis of which she would be able to tell a reasonably detailed, autobiographical story which does make reference to the content of the relevant experience.

More generally, this claim might be supported with the help of the following train of thought:

When a subject is able to tell a reasonably detailed autobiographical story which, among other things, refers to the content of a certain experience, the subject is able to describe a sequence of events and states of affairs which identify the subject's own former self as a protagonist, and she is able to describe those events and states of affairs as held together by causal relations and by agents' intentions. The relevant story will provide the subject with some understanding of the events recounted in general, and of the content of the relevant experience in particular. An autobiographical story describes objects and events and says in which spatiotemporal order they occurred, and it implies that they have been witnessed by one and the same subject, namely, the storytelling subject herself. An autobiographical story thus contains a description of the storytelling subject's movement through time and space during the time span under consideration, even if this is not made explicit in the story.

Furthermore, when a subject tells an autobiographical story that contains a reference to the content of an R-memory which she experiences, the resulting autobiographical story usually describes a spatiotemporal route of such a kind that it is plausible to assume that a subject who has moved along the relevant spatiotemporal route might also have been in a position in which it was possible to witness an event of the kind presented by the R-memory. This makes it likely that the subject was, at some earlier time, in a position to witness an event of the kind presented to her by the R-memory. But then, whatever the subject was able to witness in the past must have taken place in the past. Thus, being able to tell an autobiographical story which contains a reference to the content of a certain experience does give the subject a reason to take it that the relevant experience presents her with how things were in the past. For the autobiographical story which the subject could tell on the basis of the relevant beliefs gives the subject some reason to accept that she witnessed events and situations of the kind presented by the R-memories, which in turn gives her some reason to accept that things were in the past as they are now presented to her by the relevant experiences (namely, her R-memories).

Of course, in most cases in which subjects have R-memories and take it that relevant experiences present them with how things were in the past, subjects do not explicitly set out to tell any relevant autobiographical story at all. However, in most cases in which subjects have R-memories they do have beliefs on the basis of which they could tell a relevant autobiographical story, and this ability, or so I would like to suggest, provides the subject with a reason to take it that the relevant experience presents her with how things were in the past. For it seems plausible to accept that a subject who has an experience which occurs in a relevant context of beliefs is aware of the experience's "fitting in" with the rest of her beliefs which are related to the experience's content, and a subject who is aware of a certain experience's "fitting in" with a set of relevant beliefs is primitively aware that a relevant explanatory relation obtains between the relevant experience and the contextual beliefs. Being aware that an R memory "fits in" with a certain set of other beliefs in the appropriate way in turn gives the subject reason to take it that the relevant experience presents her with how things were in the past. Thus, the Context Claim helps to explain why subjects usually (rightly) take it that certain experiences (namely, R-memories) present them with how things were in the past.

What is more, the Context Claim might also point us toward an answer to the question why, although R-memories and S-imaginings are phenomenologically rather similar, subjects usually do not take it that S-imaginings present them with how things were in the past. While R-memories (at least usually) do occur in a context of relevant beliefs (and experiences), everyday (self-)observation suggests that S-imaginings usually do not occur in such a context of relevant beliefs (and experiences). A subject who S-imagines an event or a situation usually does not (and usually also should not) have any beliefs with the help of which she might be able to tell an autobiographical story which makes reference to the content of the relevant experience. Thus, compared with a subject who experiences an R-memory, a subject who S-imagines something (quite appropriately) lacks at least one reason to take it that the relevant experience presents her with how things were in the past – namely, the reason which might be provided by the context in which the experience occurs.[11]

## "False memories"

Another set of cases the Context Claim might help us to understand are cases in which subjects mistakenly assume that certain S-imaginings present them with how things were in the past. In the empirical literature, these cases are commonly referred to as cases of "false memory" (but, as we will see in a moment, this is a somewhat misleading label, because the relevant experiences probably should not count as memories at all). Hyman and colleagues, for example, conducted an experiment in which they invited their subjects to remember various childhood events. The experimenters had spoken to the subjects' parents and asked them to describe some events that had occurred during the subjects' childhood, so some of the events that subjects were prompted to remember had indeed occurred during their childhoods, but one event that subjects were invited to "remember" had never occurred in the subjects' lives at all, but was instead invented by the experimenters themselves. Thus, subjects were asked to remember "attending the wedding reception of a friend of the family and accidentally spilling a punch bowl" (Hyman et al. 1995, 188), an event that the experimenters had made up. Being questioned about the relevant alleged past event repeatedly, some subjects eventually came to report vivid experiences as of some such event and they also (mistakenly) took it that the relevant experiences presented them with actual events in their own childhood. Thus, some subjects eventually reported having R-memories of a relevant event, although no such event had ever occurred in their lives at all.

How can we account for such cases of "false memory"? It seems that what happens in relevant cases is this: subjects are given a description of an event, they S-imagine an event which matches that description, and they then mistake a relevant S-imagining of a relevant event for an R-memory. The fact that subjects make this mistake can in turn be explained with the help of the Context Claim. Usually, subjects who make the present kind of mistake also have various (false) beliefs on the basis of which they would be able to tell an apparently autobiographical (but in fact fictional) story which is related in the appropriate detail to the content of the relevant S-imagining. For example, in the experiment by Hyman and colleagues just sketched, subjects were told by the experimenter that their parents had authoritatively reported that the relevant event had occurred in the subjects' lives, and this presumably made subjects think in detail about their past and possible contexts in which a relevant event might have taken place, and thus made them form relevant (false) beliefs about events surrounding the alleged past event. The Context Claim plausibly suggests that subjects then wrongly took it that an experience (namely, an S-imagining) presented them with how things were in the past because the relevant experience seemed to be embedded in a context of relevant apparently autobiographical beliefs, which in turn seemed to provide subjects with a reason to take it that their present experience presented things how they had been in the past.

Thus, subjects falsely took it that the relevant experiences (namely, S-imaginings) presented them with how things had been in the past because subjects had been made to form relevant (false) contextual beliefs, and those contextual beliefs in turn seemed to give subjects reason to take it that the relevant experience did present things as they were in the past, because the relevant experience "fit" into the relevant context. As the relevant beliefs were false beliefs, these beliefs obviously did not provide subjects with any such reason at all, but because subjects had been given good reason to think of relevant beliefs as true, they wrongly took it that they had some such reason anyway.

Thus, we find that the Context Claim can help us to understand cases of so-called "false memory." Our consideration of those cases of "false memory" in turn also highlights an important metaphysical difference between R-memories and S-imaginings. For, as we just said, in order for a subject to be said to R-remember anything at all, it is necessary that a relevant event did occur in the past, and that the subject witnessed it. This is what makes us hold that cases of "false memory" are not cases of memory at all, but instead must be understood as cases of S-imagination; for it is characteristic of those cases that a subject now has an experience as of a particular event (such as her knocking over the punchbowl at a wedding) which never occurred in the subject's life at all.

More generally, it seems plausible to accept that in order for a subject to R-remember a certain event, it is necessary that

(1) the relevant event actually occurred, and that
(2) the subject witnessed the event when it occurred.

What is more, it has also been plausibly argued that in order for a subject to R-remember a certain event, it is necessary that

(3) the relevant event's past occurrence has played a causal role in bringing about the subject's present experience.[12]

None of these conditions needs to be met in order for a subject to S-imagine a certain event, and this in turn highlights an important metaphysical difference between R-memories and S-imaginings. In order for a subject to have an R-memory, the relevant experience needs to be "bound" to actual past occurrences in the ways spelled out by the three conditions just listed; S-imaginings, by contrast, do not need to be "bound" to the actual world in any of these ways at all.

## "Mental time travel"

Another important set of possible similiarities between memory and imagination has recently been explored in the empirical sciences, especially in experimental psychology and the neurosciences, under the new paradigm of "mental time travel." The term is used metaphorically here, and the phenomena which are subsumed under the label have nothing to do with "real" time travel. Rather, the core idea of the new paradigm of "mental time travel" is that human beings can be aware of, and can direct their attention toward, both the past and the future – in memory and in foresight respectively – and that there might be important similarities between those two ways of relating to events, processes and states of affairs which are not present, but lie either in the past or in the future at the time at which the subject is aware of them. Thus, Suddendorf and Corballis, who are prominent proponents of the new paradigm, sketch the central idea by suggesting that we human beings have a

> general faculty of mental time travel that allows us not only to go back in time [in memory], but also to foresee, plan, and shape virtually any specific future event [in imagination].[13]

This presents the core idea in a somewhat metaphorical way. The relevant research does not mean to imply, nor to show, that we have any literal abilities of "foresight" or "time travel." Rather, the core idea just is that we can relate to, and direct our attention toward, both the past and the future from our present temporal location, and there might be important similarities between both these abilities. In pursuing this suggestion, neuroscientists have recently started to explore the hypothesis that there might be a unified neurophysiological basis which grounds cases of "mental time travel" into the past as well as "mental time travel" into the future, and evidence which supports that hypothesis has meanwhile been collected. But then, what might this mean for our understanding of the relationship between memory and imagination?

At least at first sight, and given what we have said so far, it would seem plausible to accept that remembering the past and imagining the future are two different kinds of mental occurrences. However, so someone might argue, given that cases of remembering and cases of imagining ultimately are nothing but neurophysiological events, if it was to turn out that the neurophysiological events which underlie cases of remembering the past and cases of imagining the future are ultimately events of the same kind, we should then also conclude that cases in which a subject remembers a past event and cases in which a subject imagines a future event are ultimately mental occurrences of the same kind. Indeed, we might say that they are all cases of "mental time travel."

This is a radical conclusion, and it is one that I think we should resist. More specifically, I think we should deny one of the premises of the proposed argument, namely, the claim that cases of remembering and cases of imagining are ultimately nothing but neurophysiological events.

One might reject this claim for various reasons. Firstly, one might hold that there is "something it is like" to find oneself in experiential states, and more specifically, that there is "something it is like" to experience R-memories and S-imaginings, and that these "qualitative characteristics" of experiential states in general, and of R-memories and S-imaginings more specifically, could not possibly be fully accounted for in neurophysiological terms.[14] Alternatively, someone might hold that R-memories and S-imaginings often give us reason to endorse various beliefs, and that those reason-giving (or normative) characteristics of R-memories and S-imaginings could not possibly be fully accounted for in purely neurophysiological terms.[15] Thirdly, one might argue (as I have done in Debus 2008) that a subject who R-remembers a past event stands in a relation to the relevant past event, and that R-memories are in part constituted by the past events that are remembered. On such a view, relevant past events (which are not neurophysiological events) are a constitutive part of R-memories, which in turn entails that R-memories could not possibly be accounted for in purely neurophysiological terms.

Thus, a more careful consideration of cases of R-memories of past events and S-imaginings of future events gives us various good reasons to deny that all cases of remembering and all cases of imagining are ultimately nothing but neurophysiological events. This in turn means that the earlier argument does not show that we should hold that all cases in which a subject remembers a past event and all cases in which a subject imagines a future event are ultimately mental occurrences of the same kind if it was to turn out that the neurophysiological events which underlie cases of remembering the past and cases of imagining the future are ultimately events of the same kind.

Moreover, I think we can also develop an argument which shows that, even if it was to turn out that the neurophysiological events which underlie cases of remembering the past and cases of imagining the future are neurophysiological events of the same kind, R-memories of past events and S-imaginings of future events nevertheless differ in some very important respects and should therefore continue to count as mental occurrences of two different kinds. In outline, the argument which supports this claim might be sketched as follows:[16]

When a subject R-remembers a past event, the subject is experientially aware of a past particular event. For example, when you R-remember what you did last Sunday, you are experientially aware of that particular event. Maybe you went for lunch at a friend's house last Sunday, and you now R-remember the friend welcoming you on their doorstep. In this case, you R-remember that particular past event – that is, you are experientially aware of the friend's welcoming you on their doorstep last Sunday.

By contrast, when a subject S-imagines a future event, the subject could not possibly be experientially aware of a particular future event. For example, consider the case in which you S-imagine what you are going to do this coming Sunday. Assume you have planned to go on a good long bike ride with a friend, and so when S-imagining what you are going to do this coming Sunday, you have a vivid visual experience as of your friend on her road bike on one of the familiar local roads in the countryside in front of you. But then, this S-imagining could not possibly count as your being experientially aware of a particular future event. For in order for a subject to be experientially aware of a particular event, it is necessary that the relevant event be, from the subject's own spatiotemporal perspective at the time, an actual event (rather than just a merely possible event). Now, on some metaphysical views (such as four-dimensionalism) future events are actual even at a time at which they still lie in the future. However, as I have argued elsewhere (see Debus 2014), even if we were to accept some such view, we have reason to accept that from the imagining subject's own point of view at the time of imagining future events, future events are not actual, but merely possible. Thus, when a subject S-imagines a future event, the subject could not possibly be experientially aware of a particular future event.

But then, being in an experiential state in which one is experientially aware of a particular event (which is how cases of R-memory should be characterized) and being in an experiential state in which one could not possibly be experientially aware of a particular event (which is how cases of S-imagination should be characterized) are two different kinds of mental state. Thus, we have good reason to conclude that R-memories of past events and S-imaginings of future events are mental occurrences of two different kinds.

This does not mean that we should disregard recent empirical research on "mental time travel." Quite on the contrary, that research is of great interest in so far as it highlights various important links between our ability to remember the past and our ability to imagine the future – not only with respect to the neurophysiological processes which underlie those abilities, but also with respect to how relevant abilities might develop in children (see, e.g., Perner et al. 2010), and how impairments of the ability to remember past events might be related to impairments of the ability to imagine future events (see, e.g., Klein and Loftus 2002, and Williams et al. 1996), and there is also a very active debate surrounding the question whether the two abilities of remembering the past and of imagining the future are characteristically human abilities, or whether other nonhuman animals might have these abilities as well (see, e.g., Suddendorf and Corballis 1997 and 2007).[17]

All this work seems important if we want to understand better why and how memory and imagination are similar to each other. However, as I have now tried to show, we should resist the temptation to go further and conclude that cases in which subjects R-remember past events and cases in which subjects S-imagine future events are mental occurrences of the very same kind. Quite on the contrary, we have reason to insist that, while imagining the future and remembering the past are unquestionably very similar in some respects, memories of past events nevertheless also do differ in very important ways from imaginings of future events.

## Conclusion

In the introduction, I quoted Hobbes, who claims that "imagination and memory are but one thing, which for diverse considerations has diverse names" (Hobbes 1991, 16). We have meanwhile seen that there are some strong and important links and similarities between imagination and memory, but we have also seen that there are some important differences between them. If we want to understand memory and imagination better, we will do well to keep both the similarities as well as the differences between them in view. Thus, we should reject Hobbes' claim that "imagination and memory are but one thing," but it is at the same time also clear that we can learn a lot about each of the two phenomena by considering them both together. Indeed, this is precisely what recent empirical research on "mental time travel" has started to do. Traditionally, philosophers have mostly considered each of the two phenomena discussed here separately – some working on imagination, others working on memory. It is highly likely that during the next ten or fifteen years, some of the most exciting research both on memory as well as on imagination will be done in a context in which relevant differences between both phenomena are acknowledged, but in which researchers with research interests either in memory, or in imagination, work jointly on furthering our understanding of both phenomena together.

## Acknowledgments

My thanks go to an anonymous referee and to Amy Kind, the editor of the present volume, who both offered helpful comments on an earlier version of this chapter. I am also grateful to the editor of the *Review of Philosophy and Psychology* for permission to draw on some of the material first published in Debus (2014).

## Notes

1 I have developed some of the material presented in the following survey article in much greater detail elsewhere, especially in Debus 2014 and Debus forthcoming-a.

2 Indeed, Warnock takes this to imply that "memory should be regarded as a sub-class of imagination, not a wholly separate 'faculty'" (ibid). A similar view has recently also been offered by Hopkins forthcoming. While the quote from Warnock (in the main text above) is intended to highlight an important similarity between memory and imagination, it seems clear that there are other ways in which imagination might be employed: indeed, we can also imagine things "veridically," that is, we can imagine things as they presently are, or as they were in the past. (Thanks to an anonymous referee for prompting the present clarification.)

3 Various related but different terminologies and taxonomies have been offered, especially in the literature on the imagination; Gendler (2013, §1) offers a useful survey. In this article relevant terms will only be used in the way just outlined.

4 What is more, with respect to imagination one might argue that only those mental occurrences which have here been called "S-imaginings" should count as cases of imagination at all. One might follow Kind and hold that "imagining must be characterized in terms of … its phenomenological character" (Kind 2001, 95), and as those mental occurrences which here have so far been referred to as cases of "propositional imagining" do not have any relevant phenomenological character, one might conclude that they should not count as cases of imagination either.

5 Of course, we can also try to understand our present situation by S-imagining various things, just as we can use R-memories in an attempt to entertain ourselves, or make plans and decisions about the future; thus, neither of the pragmatic roles which S-imaginings and R-memories might usually play are exclusive to S-imaginings and R-memories, respectively; but it seems plausible to accept that we usually and more frequently use R-memories in the one way, and S-imaginings in the other. (Thanks to Amy Kind for prompting the present clarification.)

6 See Hume 1978, I.i.3, I.iii.5, and Appendix 627f.

7 See also Fodor 2003, 125: "Imaginings can be quite as forceful and vivacious as memories are. You can't determine the bona fides of an Idea by attending, however closely, to what it feels like to have it."

8 See Russell 1989, Lecture 9 ("Memory"), esp. 176–187.

9 Russell concludes his discussion of the present view saying that "this analysis of memory is probably extremely faulty, but I do not know how to improve it" (Russell 1989, 187).
10 I develop the view outlined in the following in much greater detail in Debus forthcoming-a.
11 However, a subject might tell herself a counterfactual story about, say, her day yesterday, and in that context she might then also S-imagine some (counterfactual) past events (which never occurred). Does the account offered in the main text imply that a subject in such a situation should take it that relevant S-imagined events occurred in the past? This would be an implausible position to take, and not one that is taken here. Rather, in response to the present query we should point out that in order for a story to count as autobiographical, it is necessary that things occurred in the subject's own life as the story describes them, and events described by counterfactual stories never occurred in the subject's own life at all, which means that counterfactual stories should not count as autobiographical stories. Furthermore, subjects can usually tell autobiographical stories apart from counterfactual stories about their own past, because autobiographical stories are phrased in the indicative, counterfactual stories are not. However, there are cases in which a subject's ability to distinguish between autobiographical and counterfactual stories about her own past breaks down, and those cases will be considered directly, in the next section. (Thanks to Amy Kind for prompting the present set of clarificatory comments.)
12 See C. Martin and Deutscher 1966 for a classic defense of this claim.
13 Suddendorf and Corballis 2007, 299. Schacter et al. (2007) offer another useful review of relevant empirical research.
14 Classic points of reference for this suggestion are Block 1980 and Shoemaker 1975.
15 This thought can, for example, be found in Davidson 1980; the suggestion that R-memories might play a normative role seems plausible, but the analogous suggestion that S-imaginings can play such a normative role might be more controversial; the latter suggestion is considered by Kind forthcoming, and various of the papers collected in Kind and Kung forthcoming; for a helpful overview of relevant recent work see also Greg Currie's Chapter 30, this volume.
16 I develop the following argument in greater detail in Debus 2014, and relevant additional material is presented in Debus forthcoming-b.
17 Suddendorf and Corballis (1997 and 2007) argue that "mental time travel" is unique to humans; however, Corballis 2013 now argues for the opposite view.

## Further reading

Not much philosophical work has been published on the specific topic of this chapter during the last fifty years or so, but some new, contemporary philosophical work on the very theme of the chapter is presented in F. Dorsch and F. Macpherson (eds.) *Memory and Imagination* (Oxford: Oxford University Press, forthcoming).

## References

Block, N. (1980) "Troubles with Functionalism," in N. Block (ed.) *Readings in Philosophy of Psychology*, vol. 1, Cambridge, MA: Harvard University Press, 268–305.

Corballis, M.C. (2013) "Mental Time Travel: A Case for Evolutionary Continuity," *Trends in Cognitive Sciences* 17: 5–6.

Davidson, D. (1980) "Mental Events," *Essays on Actions and Events*, Oxford: Clarendon Press, 207–227.

Debus, D. (2008) "Experiencing the Past: A Relational Account of Recollective Memory," *dialectica* 62(4): 405–432.

Debus, D. (2014) "Mental Time Travel: Remembering the Past, Imagining the Future, and the Particularity of Events," *Review of Philosophy and Psychology* 5: 333–350.

Debus, D. (Forthcoming-a) "Memory, Imagination and Narrative," in F. Dorsch and F. Macpherson (eds.) *Memory and Imagination*, Oxford: Oxford University Press.

Debus, D. (Forthcoming-b) "On the Nature and Value of Imagining the Future," in K. Michaelian, S. Klein, and K. Szpunar (eds.) *Seeing the Future: Theoretical Perspectives on Future-Oriented Mental Time Travel*, Oxford: Oxford University Press.

Dokic, J. (2014) "Feeling the Past: A Two-Tiered Account of Episodic Memory," *Review of Philosophy and Psychology* 5: 413–426.

Fodor, J. (2003) *Hume Variations*, Oxford: Oxford University Press.

Gendler, T. (2013) "Imagination," in E.N. Zalta (ed.) *Stanford Encyclopedia of Philosophy*, <http://plato.stanford.edu/archives/fall2013/entries/imagination/>.
Hobbes, T. (1991) *Leviathan*, ed. R. Tuck, Cambridge: Cambridge University Press.
Hopkins, R. (Forthcoming) "Imagining the Past: On the Nature of Episodic Memory," in F. Dorsch and F. Macpherson (eds.) *Memory and Imagination*, Oxford: Oxford University Press.
Hume, D. (1978) *A Treatise of Human Nature*, 2nd edn., with text revised and notes by P.H. Nidditch, Oxford: Clarendon Press.
Hyman, I.E., Jr., T.H. Husband, and F.J. Billings (1995) "False Memories of Childhood Experiences," *Applied Cognitive Psychology* 9: 181–197.
Kind, A. (2001) "Putting the Image Back in Imagination," *Philosophy and Phenomenological Research* 62: 85–109.
Kind, A. (Forthcoming) "How Imagination Gives Rise to Knowledge," in F. Dorsch and F. Macpherson (eds.) *Memory and Imagination*, Oxford: Oxford University Press.
Kind, A., and P. Kung (eds.) (Forthcoming) *Knowledge through Imagination*, Oxford: Oxford University Press.
Klein, S.B., and J. Loftus (2002) "Memory and Temporal Experience: The Effects of Episodic Memory Loss on an Amnesic Patient's Ability to Remember the Past and Imagine the Future," *Social Cognition* 20: 353–379.
Martin, C.B., and M. Deutscher (1966) "Remembering," *Philosophical Review* 75: 161–196.
Martin, M.G.F. (2002) "The Transparency of Experience," *Mind & Language* 17: 376–425.
Perner, J., D. Kloo, and M. Rohwer (2010) "Retro- and Prospection for Mental Time Travel: Emergence of Episodic Remembering and Mental Rotation in 5- to 8-Year Old Children," *Consciousness and Cognition* 19: 802–815.
Russell, B. (1989) *The Analysis of Mind*, London: Routledge.
Schacter, D.L., D.R. Addis, and R.L. Buckner (2007) "Remembering the Past to Imagine the Future: The Prospective Brain," *Nature Reviews Neuroscience* 8: 657–661.
Shoemaker, S. (1975) "Functionalism and Qualia," *Philosophical Studies* 27: 292–315.
Suddendorf, T., and M.C. Corballis (1997) "Mental Time Travel and the Evolution of the Human Mind," *Genetic, Social, and General Psychology Monographs* 123: 133–167.
Suddendorf, T., and M.C. Corballis (2007) "The Evolution of Foresight: What Is Mental Time Travel, and Is It Unique to Humans?" *Behavioral and Brain Sciences* 30: 299–351 (With Open Peer Commentary.)
Urmson, J.O. (1967) "Memory and Imagination," *Mind* 76: 83–91.
Warnock, M. (1994) *Imagination and Time*, Oxford: Blackwell.
Williams, M.G., N.C. Ellis, C. Tyres, H. Healy, G. Rose, and A.K. MacLeod (1996) "The Specificity of Autobiographical Memory and Imageability of the Future," *Memory & Cognition* 24: 116–125.

# 11
# IMAGINATION, DREAMING, AND HALLUCINATION

*Jonathan Jenkins Ichikawa*

Descartes famously wrote, in his First Meditation:

> Nevertheless, I must remember that I am a man, and that consequently I am accustomed to sleep and in my dreams to imagine the same things that lunatics imagine when awake, or sometimes things which are even less plausible. How many times has it occurred that the quiet of the night made me dream of my usual habits: that I was here, clothed in a dressing gown, and sitting by the fire, although I was in fact lying undressed in bed! It seems apparent to me now, that I am not looking at this paper with my eyes closed, that this head that I shake is not drugged with sleep, that it is with design and deliberate intent that I stretch out this hand and perceive it. What happens in sleep seems not at all as clear and distinct as all this. But I am speaking as though I never recall having been misled, while asleep, by similar illusions.[1]

Descartes here makes several natural but substantive assumptions about the nature of dreaming. Most fundamentally, he assumes that dreaming is or involves a kind of experience – there is something it is like to dream. Obvious though it seems, this assumption is at least substantive enough to have been denied by some influential twentieth-century philosophers, most notably Norman Malcolm (1962).[2] But let us follow Descartes and contemporary orthodoxy in this first assumption. Dreaming involves a kind of mental experience while asleep.

Descartes's second assumption is more contentious. Notice the move from the observation midway through the quote above – Descartes sometimes dreams that he is by the fire, when he is really in bed – to the characterization at the end, according to which he is *misled*. To be misled is to have a false belief; so Descartes is supposing that when one *dreams* that one is by the fire, one thereby *believes* that one is by the fire. Although this assumption continues to enjoy orthodoxy, it has been contested on various grounds, many of which I shall lay out below. One might think instead that although dreaming that one is by the fire involves some kind of representation that one is by the fire, the propositional attitude in question needn't be belief. Perhaps, for instance, dreaming that one is by the fire involves *imagining* that one is by the fire, and so no more constitutes being misled than would *desiring* that one is by the fire, when one isn't.

Dreaming doesn't merely involve propositional attitudes. When Descartes dreams that he is by the fire, he's not merely representing to himself (whether via belief or some other attitude) the content *that he is by the fire*; there are sensory modalities involved, too. For instance, he undergoes some sort of vision-like experience, similar in at least some respect to the experience of seeing a fire. Perhaps there is some auditory experience as of crackling, or tactile experience as of warmth, as well. Perceptual experiences have imaginative correlates, just as belief does – the experience of seeing a fire is a different experience from that of imagining what a fire looks like. So another important question one may ask about dreaming is whether the perception-like experiences are the same kinds of experiences that occur during waking perception, or instead whether they represent another kind of experience – perhaps that of visual imagery.

## Imagination vs. hallucination

We can set out two contrasting approaches to these questions that may be helpful in appreciating what the questions here are. Although in the end one may wish to pick and choose among elements of each, or opt for a different kind of alternative altogether, the relatively simple contrast will help clarify some of the issues.

According to the *hallucination model of dreaming*, which Descartes seems to be assuming, when subjects dream, they undergo perceptual experiences of the same kind that they do while waking, although they are divorced from their usual perceptual causal origins.[3] Since the dreamers do not typically realize the unusual providence of these experiences, they take them to reflect the external world, and form beliefs about what is happening on their basis. So, for instance, while dreaming, Descartes has (many of) the same experiences he would have, were he sitting before the fire, and responds to those experiences in the usual way, by forming the belief that he is sitting before the fire.

By contrast, according to the *imagination model of dreaming*, when subjects dream, the experiences they suffer are different in kind from those involved in perception; instead, they are exercises of the imagination, including sensory imagery and propositional imagination. While dreaming, Descartes *imagines* that he is sitting before a fire, calling forth the corresponding visual *imagery*, but he does not form the mistaken *belief* that he is sitting before a fire.

In this chapter, I shall canvass considerations in favor of and against each of these approaches to dreaming. I have defended the imagination model in my previous work on dreaming; below, I'll rehearse and expand on some of the reasons I find the imagination model compelling. I'll also highlight what seem to me to be the central motivations for the competing hallucination model. My intent in this chapter is more to provide an overview of the debate than to defend a particular view; but I won't pretend not to have my own stance. I shall try to represent considerations favoring the hallucination model as fairly as possible.

Before getting into the arguments, however, it is important to highlight several significant issues that might be somewhat obscured at this stage. Setting out the imagination/hallucination dichotomy as I have done represents a significant simplification, for at least three reasons.

First, as alluded to above, it is possible to hold intermediate views between the imagination model and the hallucination model, so defined. For example, Colin McGinn (2005) thinks that dreaming involves mental imagery, rather than perceptual experience – and so agrees with part of the imagination model – but also holds, with the hallucination model, that dreamers form false beliefs on the basis of such imagery, and so are deceived.

Second, there is no obvious reason why belief and imagination, or perceptual experience and imagery, represent the only options for the kinds of mental states that might be involved. One view in logical space would hold that dreams are *sui generis*; they involve states that are neither imaginings nor beliefs, and neither perceptual experiences nor mental images.[4]

Third, it is an assumption of this way of characterizing the hallucination model that hallucination does, or at least can, involve the same kind of experience as veridical perception does. But this is a controversial assumption. Certain *disjunctivists* will hold that hallucination is a radically different kind of experience from perception, unified with perception only by the fact that subjects are unable to discriminate perception from it from the inside. If this is right, then it is not obviously possible to distinguish the idea that dreams involve hallucinations from the view that they involve a different, albeit indistinguishable, kind of imagistic experience. The relationship between the question of how to characterize dreaming and the question of disjunctivism is complex; I will turn to some of the possible implications near the end of the chapter. For now, however, I will follow the bulk of the extant literature on dreaming thus far in setting disjunctivism aside.

The hallucination model of dreaming is arguably a tenet of common sense. It is often implicitly assumed, as in Descartes's passage above; one can also find more explicit statements of it in both philosophical and psychological literature on dreaming. This passage from J. Allan Hobson (1999), for instance, is not unusual:

> What is the difference between my dreams and madness? What is the difference between my dream experience and the waking experience of someone who is psychotic, demented, or just plain crazy? In terms of the nature of the experience, there is none. In my … dream I hallucinated: I saw and heard things that weren't in my bedroom. I was deluded: I believed that the dream actions were real despite gross internal inconsistencies. I was disoriented: I believed that I was in an old hotel in New Orleans when I was actually in a house in Ogunquit.
>
> *(5)*

This orthodoxy, however, is not universal. Indeed, some authors have rather casually committed to something more like the imagination model. Consider, for instance, this passage from A.D. Smith (2008):

> As Descartes famously pointed out, we cannot, when we are dreaming, and simply on the basis of the experience itself, tell that we are not awake and perceiving. Dreams are not, however, hallucinations that we have while asleep: they are non-sensory episodes that merely seem sensory to the subject. In their actual nature they are akin to the sort of mental imagery that is involved in daydreaming and visualizing. We get so caught up in the imaginary scene that we cannot tell it apart from reality; but the experiences themselves remain merely imagistic, not sensory, in character. They are not the sorts of experiences that we would have if our brains were stimulated in just the way that they are when we actually see things for the sort that we seem to see in dreams. Or so I think.
>
> *(185)*

Along similar lines, Ernest Sosa (2007) writes:

> Dreams seem more like imaginings, or stories, or even daydreams, all fictions of a sort, or quasi-fictions. Even when in a dream one makes a conscious choice, one need not do so in actuality. Nor does one necessarily affirm in reality whatever one consciously affirms in a dream.
>
> *(7)*

It is essential, when considering questions about the nature of dreaming, to keep clear the distinction between discussion of the *contents* of dreams, and the discussion of features *of the dreamer*. This is the distinction Sosa has in mind when he writes that "[f]rom the fact that *in my dream* something happens it does not follow that it happens *while I dream*."[5] The following are obviously consistent:

1 Last night, in my dream, I was in China.
2 Last night, when I was asleep dreaming, I was not in China.

In the same way, the defender of the imagination model of dreaming will hold that these are consistent too:

3 Last night, in my dream, I believed I was in China.
4 Last night, when I was asleep dreaming, I did not believe I was in China.

According to the imagination model, (1) and (3) imply the following:

(1′) Last night, when I was asleep dreaming, I imagined I was in China.
(3′) Last night, when I was asleep dreaming, I imagined that I believed I was in China.

And (3′) is consistent with (4) in just the same way that (1′) is consistent with (2). This is why the imagination model is one according to which dreams do not typically result in false beliefs.

Why might someone embrace the imagination model of dreaming? Following are four lines of thought that have been used in its favor. As will become clear, these thoughts overlap in significant ways; dividing them into these four considerations is a conventional choice for ease of presentation.

## Imagination model consideration 1: comparison between dreams and fictions

Fictions comprise our paradigmatic imaginative engagements. To embrace the imagination model, then, is to say that dreams are in certain respects like fictions. Kendall Walton (1990) emphasizes some such respects of similarity in an early defense of the imagination model, pointing out that dreams, like fictions, depend on interpretation for full specification of their contents. It is widely appreciated that the contents of fictions extend beyond what they explicitly present. For an illustration of this familiar point, consider for example this passage from P.G. Wodehouse's novel *Carry On, Jeeves*:

> "No. I'm going to Wembley. I just came back to change and get the car. Produce some fairly durable garments which can stand getting squashed by the many-headed, Jeeves, and then phone to the garage."
>
> "Very good, sir. The grey cheviot lounge will, I fancy, be suitable. Would it be too much if I asked you to give me a seat in the car, sir? I had thought of going to Wembley myself this afternoon."
>
> "Eh? Oh, all right."
>
> "Thank you very much, sir."
>
> I got dressed, and we drove round to Biffy's flat.
>
> *(Wodehouse 1956, 135)*

It is true in the fiction that Jeeves asked for a ride to Wembley; so much is explicitly stated here. But more things that aren't explicitly stated are also true in the fiction. For example, it is true in the fiction that Jeeves phoned for the car – not merely that he was asked to do so. It is also true in the fiction that the car was brought around, and that Jeeves and Wooster each got into it. In general, the content of a story goes beyond what is explicitly given and even what is explicitly imagined.[6] Walton (1990) draws a parallel between this feature of fictions and a similar phenomenon involving dreams. He gives this example of a dream:

> One morning Doris reports a dream as follows:
>
> In my dream I telephoned Jones in New York from Chicago. Later I had another conversation with him, this time in person in his New York office. … I must have traveled to New York in the meantime.
>
> … The implication is that Doris did not dream that she traveled to New York, she did not imagine doing so, but that nevertheless it is "true in her dream" – that is, fictional in it – that she did. I am inclined to accept this implication at face value.
>
> *(45)*

As Walton points out, it is typical and sensible to construct a content to the dreams that extends beyond the contents explicitly represented in dreams; this feature of dreaming is shared with fictions.

Of course this structural similarity between dreams and fictions is not at all definitive in favor of the imagination model – not even if we assume that it and the hallucination model are the only options. A defender of the hallucination model will accept that the explicit contents of dreams are genuinely believed by subjects while they are sleeping; she might make sense of Walton's observation in at least two ways. First, she might suppose that the various other dream contents are *tacitly*, rather than explicitly, believed by dreamers. While Doris was dreaming, she held the tacit belief that she had traveled to New York, even though it was never explicitly raised to her consciousness.[7] Second, she might construct a notion of "truth in a dream" that differs from standard approaches to truth in fiction in letting dream contents depend on beliefs. For example, at a first pass, one might hold that what is true in a dream is what is true in the nearest worlds in which the dreamer's beliefs are true. This approach would obviously require subtle development – the issues are parallel to those concerning similar approaches to truth in fiction – but it could at least make sense of the idea that the content of the dream outstrips what is actually believed.

But although it is far from definitive, I think Walton's observation does count as at least a mark in the favor of the imagination model. It does show an interesting point of analogy between dreaming and fiction, which might make the imagination model of the former seem more plausible. Since engagement with fiction is uncontroversially an imaginative phenomenon, and since dreams share structural similarities to fictions, maybe engagement with dreams is imaginative, too.

## Imagination model consideration 2: the normative status of dream states

Ernest Sosa (2007) has emphasized an argument in favor of the imagination model that turns on normative considerations. He writes:

> In a dream you may covet thy neighbor's wife, in the dream a sultry object of desire. Do you then violate the biblical injunction? If you go so far as to succumb, are you then subject to blame? Having sinned in your heart, not only in your dream, but in actuality, you could hardly escape discredit. Is one then blameworthy for choices made in a dream? That has near-zero plausibility, about as little as does blaming a storyteller for his misdeeds as protagonist in a story spun for a child.
>
> *(6)*

Sosa is making two key claims here. The first is that one can have a *dream* in which one intends to do something morally wrong – or even one in which one actually *does* something morally wrong – without incurring moral blame. The second is that it is always blameworthy to intend to do something morally wrong. From these claims it follows that one can have a dream in which one intends something without actually intending to do that thing. Insofar as it is plausible that believing is in relevant respects similar to intending, this also puts pressure against the idea that one really believes contents by virtue of dreaming that one does.

It is also possible to run a version of this argument more directly in terms of belief. (Note that this argument supports only the belief/propositional imagination component of the imagination model; it appears neutral on the question of perceptual experience/mental imagery.) Setting aside questions of morality, the contents of dreams are very often ones it would be *irrational* to accept. If we do believe everything we dream, then we are, from an epistemic point of view, performing very poorly while sleeping. This of course is precisely the view of many defenders of the hallucination model, e.g., Hobson (1999), who argues that dreaming is a kind of "delirium."[8] But as cognitive agents, we generally have epistemic reasons to avoid irrational states. It seems that the hallucination model would predict, then, that we have some reason – even some defeasible reason – to avoid dreaming, or to discipline ourselves to be careful to only dream truths. This seems very implausible.[9]

## Imagination model consideration 3: psychological data

In this section I'll briefly rehearse two considerations from cognitive and developmental psychology that may favor the imagistic elements of the imagination model.

First, the brain areas particularly implicated in dreaming seem to be the same as those involved in imagery, as opposed to those involved in perceptual experience. Considering patients with brain damage resulting in imaginative deficits is particularly illuminating: such subjects tend to exhibit precisely analogous deficits in dreaming. For instance, Mark Solms, summarizing some of his work, writes that "the most robust finding of the present study was the observation that cessation or restriction of visual dream-imagery is invariably associated with a precisely analogous deficit in waking imagery" (Solms 1997, 131).

Second, a series of studies by David Foulkes suggests that the connection between dreaming and imagining is confirmed by developmental data. The capacity to dream develops gradually over early childhood, and in a series of studies of children conducted from the 1960s into the 1980s, Foulkes found that it develops alongside, in a way predicted by, imaginative capacities. For example, those children who develop richer imaginative capacities at an earlier age are also the children who tend to dream more often and in richer ways. Foulkes concludes:

> From all my data, the suggestion is that dreaming best reflects the development of a specific cognitive competence, indexed by certain kinds of tests of visual-spatial

imagination, leading to the conclusion that such imagination must be a critical skill in dream-making.

(*Foulkes 1999, 90*)[10]

## Imagination model consideration 4: conceptual issues

Another set of considerations in favor of the imagination model over the hallucination model, also laid out in Ichikawa (2009), can be classified as broadly "conceptual."[11] According to the hallucination model, someone dreaming that he is by the fire thereby believes that he is by the fire. But arguably, attractive philosophical theories of belief will not deliver the result that such subjects have such beliefs. For example, functionalists about mental states will hold that it is constitutive of a given representation's status as a belief that it occupy certain functional roles in a subject's psychology, but many of the functional roles apparently characteristic of belief seem to be absent in dreams. For example, beliefs tend to interact with desires in a characteristic way to result in action; but dream states do not obviously pattern with beliefs in this way. If I believed that my bed was infested with bedbugs, that belief would interact with certain desires I have, producing particular behavior: avoiding my bed. In contrast, if I *dreamt* that my bed was infested with bedbugs, I would exhibit no such behavior; indeed, I might well do so while remaining calmly in my bed.

The considerations here are admittedly subtle. A defender of the hallucination model might retort that while dreaming, I *do* form the intention to avoid my bed, but that this intention is thwarted by the kind of paralysis characteristic of sleep. Whether this is an adequate response turns on questions about how exactly to specify the functional role of belief.

## Hallucination model consideration 1: emotional engagement

Although dreaming doesn't seem straightforwardly to connect with action in the way paradigmatic belief does, dreams do seem to engage affective systems in a way that has motivated some theorists to suppose they must involve genuine belief. For example, J.F.M. Hunter writes:

> The fact that we are sometimes terrified by a dream, and that it is not just the dream self that is terrified (we wake up in a panic, and with accelerated heartbeat, etc.) may seem to show that it is not just the dream self that takes the dream events to be really happening.
>
> (*Hunter 1983, 90*)

Colin McGinn, who defends a hybrid model on which dreams involve not only imagery, but genuine belief, is also impressed by this kind of consideration:

> The sure test that dreams are suffused with belief is their ability to generate emotions that are conditional on belief, such as fear and elation – with which dreams are full.
>
> (*McGinn 2005, 112*)

However, once the imagination model of dreaming is on the table, according to which one imagines the propositional contents of dreams, rather than believes them, these kinds of considerations do not seem to tell in favor of the hallucination model. After all, it is characteristic of our imaginative engagements with fictions that they produce certain kinds of emotional responses, even though we do not literally believe their contents. Therefore, it appears very plausible that imagination may bring about something much like the affective responses that parallel belief would. Philosophers of fiction disagree about whether we should demarcate a separate state of "imaginative emotion" to accompany the fictional contents we don't believe; some, like Derek Matravers (1997), will say that imagination can generate genuine emotions just as belief can; others, like Walton (1990), prefer to say that there are "quasi-emotions" that feel much like genuine emotions, but which do not require belief; in either case, we admit that imaginings can generate states that feel much like emotions, even absent the relevant beliefs. So the affective component of dreams does not seem probative with respect to the imagination or hallucination models. (See also Stacie Friend, "Fiction and emotion," Chapter 16 of this volume.)

## Hallucination model consideration 2: phenomenology

A related reason some theorists prefer the hallucination model is that it is thought to capture more fully the phenomenology of dreaming. According to this line of thought, dreaming just *doesn't feel like* imaginative experience.

See for example this passage from Fabian Dorsch:

> Although [dream representations] seem to be similar to imaginings (and memories, for that matter), we do not really know what they are, or whether they can be compared in their non-cognitive character to the relevant elements of our waking mental lives. In particular, since they occur in a state of consciousness which is substantially different from wakefulness, they lack two closely related features that all (central) instances of imagining have in common: the feature of being phenomenally conscious (in the sense of wakeful consciousness), and the feature of being introspectively accessible. … This difference in how we "experience" imaginings and dream representations is [sufficient] to distinguish them in nature.
>
> *(Dorsch 2012, 54)*

Otávio Bueno (2009) combines a worry about phenomenology with one about emotional engagement:

> It seems difficult to reconcile the claim that no assertion or beliefs are involved in a dream with the fact that dreams do seem to move us, bother us, and in some cases frighten us. We form these genuine mental states in response to dreams – as we dream. Without our believing (even though perhaps falsely) that we are experiencing these things in our dreams, it's hard to understand how we can form such response to dreams.
>
> *(199)*

In her book on dreaming, Jennifer Windt (2015) also argues against the imagination model on phenomenological grounds.[12]

A comprehensive evaluation of these phenomenological considerations is beyond my scope here. I make only three notes. First, there are potential worries about the reliance on introspective reports of phenomenology – maybe especially for those involving dreaming. For example, Eric Schwitzgebel (2011) argues that there is reason to think that people in general systematically misremember such central features of their dreams as whether they involve color experience (though see Windt 2013 for a rejoinder). Second, we needn't assume any immediate connection between phenomenology and the imagination or hallucination models; the latter are views about what kinds of mental states dreaming *consists in*, not about what dreaming *feels like*. It seems at least coherent to suppose, for instance, that dreaming involves imagination that *feels like* belief. Whether such a view is well-motivated, of course, will turn on a wide variety of considerations, both about dreaming in particular and philosophical reflections on the essence of belief itself.[13] (If it is incoherent to suppose that imagination can feel like belief, of course, this view is a nonstarter.) Third, it is debatable whether the hallucination model really does better capture the phenomenology of dreaming than the imagination model does; Evan Thompson (2014, 180–182) argues that phenomenological considerations having to do with agency in dreams and the role of attention are best explained by the imagination model. (Thompson also cites other considerations in favor of the imagination model, including some of those mentioned above.)

## Dreaming, imagination, and epistemology

In the remainder of this chapter, I will consider what implication the imagination model, if true, would have for skeptical arguments based on dreaming. This is interesting in its own right; it will also foreground some of the connections between dreaming and disjunctivism about perception alluded to above.

Recall Descartes's argument. Since one is often *deceived* by dreams, dreams are a rational source of doubt. Sosa (2007) suggests that the dream scenario is especially epistemically challenging, as it doesn't require far-fetched possibilities like Descartes's evil demon; dreaming, if a source of defeat, seems particularly threatening to the *safety* of our beliefs.[14] But if the imagination model is correct, then dreams are not in general a source of false belief. What bearing would this have on epistemological worries about dream skepticism?

According to a skeptical line of thought, things wouldn't be any better. Even though dreaming doesn't involve false belief, but rather the mere imagining of various events, the fact remains that in typical (nonlucid) cases, dreamers have no *awareness* of the fact that they're dreaming, and so merely imagining things. So instead of describing the skeptical threat from dreaming as the possibility that I falsely believe it's sunny today because I'm just dreaming it, we should describe it as the possibility that I am imagining that it is sunny, but not realizing that I'm merely imagining it instead of believing it. I have defended this kind of skeptical response in the past,[15] and I continue to find something cogent about it; however, the epistemological issues are subtle.

Suppose, as the proponent of the imagination model says, that often when one dreams that *p*, the following are all true:

- *p* is false
- one imagines that *p*
- one does not believe that *p*
- one does not realize that one does not believe that *p*.

Is this sufficient for a skeptical scenario with respect to the belief that *p*? Notice that it is clearly *not* sufficient that we have a possible scenario in which *p* is false, where one can't tell that *p* is false. This is too weak a criterion. For example, the possibility that I died and was cremated last year does not generate skeptical pressure against my belief that I have hands, even though (assuming a mainstream naturalist approach to death) it is a scenario in which I do not have hands and am not in a position to realize that I don't have hands.[16] It doesn't follow directly from the fact that dreamers can't tell they're not awake that waking subjects can't tell they're not dreaming. If there is a skeptical challenge from dreaming here, it can't be *merely* a matter of indistinguishability; it must have something to do with genuine similarities between the dream state and a waking belief.

One of the things the case of death illustrates rather clearly is that the discriminability of possible cases won't always be a symmetric matter. There can be possible cases A and B, where, if one is in case A, one won't be able to know whether one's in A or B, but if one is in case B, one will be able to know.[17] Should a proponent of the imagination model of dreaming think that's what's going on in this case?

Sosa (2007) argues that the imagination model allows a distinctive response to dream skepticism along these lines. We don't form false beliefs when we dream, so dreaming is not a source of deception. As he puts it, the proposition that one is awake enjoys the same privileged epistemic status as does the *cogito* – any time one believes it, it is true.

It is widely recognized that belief and propositional imagining are similar in various significant respects. Are they sufficiently similar so as to warrant the positing of a broad state that includes both, and is suitable for the focus of epistemic evaluation? Claudia Lorena García (2010) argues that they are – she suggests that we should consider questions about the epistemology of dreaming at the level of "thin thought," where one "thin thinks" that *p* if one believes that *p* or otherwise represents that *p*, as in the case of imagination.

> [I]f I believe (thin sense) that one of my thoughts (thin sense) is a belief (thick sense), I may be wrong. In Sosa's account, there is a nearby possible world where I think I am awake but I am not awake – because the thought I have is only a thin thought. And it appears I have no reason to think (thin) that this possible world is not the actual world – I have no sensory beliefs to which I can appeal for this purpose. How can *I* tell whether the thought I am now having is not merely a thin thought but a thick one? ... Can I be deceived by my dreams – i.e., can I be led by my dreams to falsely believe (thin) I am awake? Certainly. Can I be led by my dreams to falsely believe (thin) I am having some beliefs (thick sense)? Certainly. So, why does Sosa say I cannot be deceived by my dreams? I do not see the logic of this. *(12)*

García's line here does vindicate the intuition that there is still a skeptical challenge from dreaming. But it does so at a rather extreme cost. In supposing that whenever one has thin thoughts with false contents, one is thereby "deceived," her approach will have the implication that there are many more sources of deception than we might have thought. For example, even conscious engagement with fictions typically results in thin thoughts with false contents. When I watch *Peter Pan*, I thin-think (i.e., imagine) that there are fairies who perform magic. And I also thin-think that I thick-think (believe) that there are fairies – that's why I clap at the appointed time. But this is no deception. The fact that dreams involve representation of false contents doesn't distinguish them from fictions; since fictions don't in general deceive, these considerations don't show that dreams do. The García suggestion is too skeptical.[18]

But Sosa's antiskeptical line may be problematically strong too. Notice that it relies only on the fact of the imagination model; facts about the frequency and contents of dreams are irrelevant for the purpose of Sosa's antiskeptical argument. This may give us reason to pause;

perhaps some of these features *should* matter. Suppose we stipulate certain skeptic-friendly contingencies. Suppose that every night, I dream about doing epistemology. In my dreams, I think about dream skepticism, and consider Sosa's arguments, and conclude that I don't need to be worried about the possibility that I'm dreaming. So, in my dream, I conclude that I'm not dreaming, confident in the thought that there's no nearby risk of forming a false belief thereby. And of course, *in my dream*, I'm not forming a false belief, because it's *true* in my dream that I'm not dreaming. (And of course, in reality, I'm not forming a false belief either, because I'm imagining things, not believing them.)

But if this dream happens every night, and I am aware of this fact, doesn't it still feel like there is a sense in which, when awake, it is right to wonder about whether I'm having the dream again? I really do often have the dream. Shouldn't there be a sensible way to ask whether I'm having it now? Sosa seems clearly right that, assuming the imagination model, believing that one is awake carries with it no substantial risk of error. But maybe these considerations show that more is required for responsible belief than safety, or even known safety.[19] Perhaps, for instance, we need to consider a broader category along the lines of *attempting* to form a true belief; dreaming shows that there is a risk of failing to do so, not because we'll form a false belief, but because we'll fail to form a belief at all.

## The imagination model and disjunctivism

This treatment of dreaming bears an interesting structural similarity to an epistemic disjunctivist's treatment of skeptical worries.[20] Consider, for example, the view of Pritchard (2012), according to which ordinary cases of perception give a subject reflective access to factive reasons of the form *I see that p*. Suppose for instance that one sees that there is a zebra in the zoo. What is the epistemic significance of the possibility that one is seeing a cleverly disguised mule, supposing that, if one were presented with such, one would think it was a zebra? On the disjunctivist view, although that is an error possibility, it is one that is conclusively ruled out by the available reasons. Even though, if it did obtain, the subject wouldn't know it did, since it does not, the subject knows it doesn't. We can think of the case as another instance of the asymmetry of indiscriminability – in the same way that one can know one is alive rather than dead, even though if one were dead one wouldn't be able to know it, so too can one know that one sees a zebra rather than a disguised mule, even though if one saw the latter, one wouldn't be able to know it.[21]

Sosa's line on dreaming says about being awake what the disjunctivist says about seeing a zebra (and what all nonskeptics say about being alive). The imagination theorist who is not also a disjunctivist represents an intermediate view, suggesting that the case of dreaming is more like the case of death than like the case of a cleverly disguised mule. As we have seen, the plausibility of this claim turns on sensitive questions about the proper locus of epistemic evaluation. If it is the evaluation of belief itself that is essential, then the imagination model of dreaming implies that dreaming is importantly like death and unlike the disguised mule: it does not involve false belief. Alternatively, if there is a "highest common factor" between belief and the imaginative states we have while dreaming, suitable for the locus of epistemic evaluation – some kind of "thin thought," or "attempted belief," or "seeming to believe" – this would provide motivation for treating the case of dreaming as very unlike that of death.

So the imagination model of dreaming invites epistemological theorizing as to just where to draw the line demarcating skeptical scenarios. The central question becomes, what is required of skeptical scenario? It is clearly not enough that the belief in question is false; the subject must be *in some sense* similar to the subject's actual state. But whether belief is necessary, or sufficient, or neither is an outstanding question at this stage in inquiry.

Another point to note, however, is that the availability of this disjunctivist-style move against dream skepticism doesn't seem to turn in an obvious way on the question of the imagination model of dreaming. One could hold that dreams do involve beliefs, and so are a source of perception, but that being awake and thinking clearly about it gives one conclusive reason to suppose one isn't dreaming. Consider for example the approach of A.D. Smith:

> Dreamers, it is allowed, cannot tell that they are not perceiving real things. But that is, the suggestion goes, simply because they are unfavourably placed to effect the discrimination. Someone better placed would be able to effect it. What, however, is the local impediment to reflection's discriminative power in this case? It is simply the fact that the subjects are asleep. So the suggestion would seem to be that subjects who are dreaming could tell that they were dreaming *if they were awake*.
>
> *(Smith 2008, 187–188; Emphasis in original)*[22]

So although the imagination model invites certain central questions in epistemology in addition to those in the philosophy of psychology and the philosophy of mind, at least some of those questions are pressing, whether or not one subscribes to the imagination model.

## Acknowledgments

Thanks for helpful discussion and feedback on drafts of this chapter to Amy Kind, Kengo Miyazono, Ernest Sosa, and Jennifer Windt.

## Notes

1 Descartes 1968, 145–146.
2 It is now generally agreed that Malcolm's arguments depended on an implausibly strong form of verficationism. See also Daniel Dennett 1976 for a different defense of a view similar to Malcolm's. Jennifer Windt (2013) offers a helpful critical summary and discussion of Malcolm's and Dennett's views.
3 See Windt 2010, 298, for a description of this view as orthodoxy.
4 This kind of view might be motivated in a way similar to the view of Andy Egan (2008) about delusion. Windt (2015) makes suggestions along these lines.
5 Sosa 2007, 4; emphasis in original.
6 On fictionality or "truth in fiction," see Walton 1990, Lewis 1978, and Currie 1990.
7 This option might be thought unappealing for the same reason Walton gives against the view that such contents are tacitly imagined – see his p. 45. He points out that Doris seems surprised by the realization in a way that would not occur if she'd tacitly believed it all along.
8 McGinn's (2005) hybrid view of dreaming, whereby it involves not only mental imagery but genuine belief, also shares this commitment; see his p. 113.
9 A version of this point is developed in Ichikawa 2009, 112.
10 For further discussion of Foulkes's studies and conclusions, see Ichikawa 2009, 109–110, and Sutton 2009, 532–536.
11 The standard terminology here is less than ideal; I do not mean to assume that "conceptual" considerations ultimately have anything in particular to do with concepts – only that they have to do with the traditional philosophical project of (perhaps a priori) analysis. We consider, from a philosophical point of view, what kind of state "counts as" a belief; this might, but needn't, be a matter of investigation into the concept *belief*.
12 Neither Dorsch nor Windt need be read as arguing *in favor of* the hallucination model; most directly, they argue *against* the imagination model. As mentioned above, there is room for alternative views, such as the view that dreaming is *sui generis*.

13 The abstract of Ichikawa (2009) began with the question: "What is it like to dream?" I now regret this choice of language, as it is suggestive of a phenomenological focus. Then and now, the question I'm focused on is this one: what mental states are involved in dreaming? Thanks to Jennifer Windt for helpfully clarifying discussion here.
14 A belief is safe to the degree to which there is no immediate danger of error; if, in all or nearly all nearby worlds in which the belief is formed in the same way, the belief is true, then that belief is safe. Many epistemologists consider safety, so characterized, to be necessary for knowledge. See e.g., Sosa 1999, Williamson 2000, Pritchard 2005, and Lasonen-Aarnio 2008.
15 Ichikawa 2008. See also García 2010.
16 This point is made in roughly this context by Sosa (2007, 14), and Macpherson (2010, 245).
17 Alternatively, one could hold that indistinguishability is symmetric, but that the relevant states need to be considered under particular modes of presentation. See Farkas 2008, 101–120, for discussion. This kind of view will also allow the coherence of the possibility that dreamers can't know they're not awake, but waking subjects can know they're not dreaming.
18 Nathan Ballantyne and Ian Evans (2010) press a similar skeptical challenge against Sosa's line, pointing out that "[t]here is a critical difference between the status of Descartes's *cogito* and Sosa's dream-*cogito*. It isn't possible for it to *seem* to one that one exists unless one exists. But it is possible for it to *seem* to one that one has a belief even when one doesn't. That difference makes all the difference" (251). See also Ahlstrom 2011.
19 Ichikawa (2008) suggests that there is a kind of *epistemic responsibility* that is lacking in this quick response to the dream skeptic. See also Brown 2009, 400–401, for a similar thought.
20 There are many varieties of disjunctivism; see Haddock and Macpherson 2008 for an overview. I am discussing a distinctively epistemological brand, with Pritchard as my exemplar.
21 Pritchard himself doesn't put things this way; he commits (p. 53 n. 3) to the symmetry of indistinguishability. But he does hold that in the good case, one can know that one is in the good case, even though in the bad case, one can't know that one is in the bad case.
22 See also Williams 1978, app. 3. Windt (2010, 300) summarizes empirical support for the idea that dreaming characteristically involves cognitive deficiencies.

## Further reading

J. Windt, *Dreaming: A Conceptual Framework for Philosophy of Mind and Empirical Research* (Cambridge, MA: MIT Press, 2015) is an excellent and thorough treatment of dreaming and dream experience, emphasizing phenomenal character. E. Thompson, *Waking, Dreaming, Being* (New York: Columbia University Press, 2014) offers a defense of the imagination model based in significant part on phenomenological considerations. For considerations about disjunctivism, and the relationship between disjunctivism and the kind of epistemic questions engaged in the last section of this chapter, I recommend the essays in – and the introduction to – A. Haddock and F. Macpherson (eds.) *Disjunctivism: Perception, Action, and Knowledge* (Oxford: Oxford University Press, 2008).

## References

Ahlstrom, K. (2011) "Dream Skepticism and the Conditionality Problem," *Erkenntnis* 75(1): 45–60.
Ballantyne, N., and I. Evans (2010) "Sosa's Dream," *Philosophical Studies* 148(2): 249–252.
Brown, J. (2009) "Sosa on Scepticism," *Philosophical Studies* 143(3): 397–405.
Bueno, O. (2009) "Sosa on Skepticism," *Metaphilosophy* 40(2): 195–202.
Currie, G. (1990) *The Nature of Fiction*, Cambridge: Cambridge University Press.
Dennett, D.C. (1976) "Are Dreams Experiences?" *Philosophical Review* 73: 151–171.
Descartes, R. (1968) *Meditations on First Philosophy*, in *The Philosophical Works of Descartes*, eds. Elizabeth S. Haldane and G.R.T. Ross, vol. 1, Cambridge: Cambridge University Press.
Dorsch, F. (2012) *The Unity of Imagining*, Berlin and Boston: De Gruyter.
Egan, A. (2008) "Imagination, Delusion, and Self-Deception," in T. Bayne and J. Fernández (eds.) *Delusion and Self-Deception: Affective and Motivational Influences on Belief Formation*, Macquarie Monographs in Cognitive Science, Hove: Psychology Press.
Farkas, K. (2008) *The Subject's Point of View*, Oxford: Oxford University Press.

Foulkes, D. (1999) *Children's Dreaming and the Development of Consciousness*, Cambridge, MA: Harvard University Press.
García, C.L. (2010) "Sosa's Responses to Dreaming Skepticism," *Critica: Revista hispanoamericana de filosofía* 42(125): 3–25.
Haddock, A., and F. Macpherson (2008) "Introduction: Varieties of Disjunctivism," in A. Haddock and F. Macpherson (eds.) *Disjunctivism: Perception, Action, Knowledge*, Oxford: Oxford University Press.
Hobson, J.A. (1999) *Dreaming as Delirium: How the Brain Goes Out of Its Mind*, Cambridge, MA: MIT Press.
Hunter, J.F.M. (1983) "The Difference between Dreaming and Being Awake," *Mind* 92(365): 80–93.
Ichikawa, J. (2008) "Scepticism and the Imagination Model of Dreaming," *Philosophical Quarterly* 58(232): 519–527.
Ichikawa, J. (2009) "Dreaming and Imagination," *Mind & Language* 24(1): 103–121.
Lasonen-Aarnio, M. (2008) "Single Premise Deduction and Risk," *Philosophical Studies* 141(2): 157–173.
Lewis, D.K. (1978) "Truth in Fiction," *American Philosophical Quarterly* 15(1): 37–46.
Macpherson, F. (2010) "A Disjunctive Theory of Introspection: A Reflection on Zombies and Anton's Syndrome," *Philosophical Issues* 20(1): 226–265.
Malcolm, N. (1962) *Dreaming*, London: Routledge & Kegan Paul.
Matravers, D. (1997) "The Paradox of Fiction: The Report versus the Perceptual Model," in M. Hjort and S. Laver (eds.) *Emotion and the Arts*, New York: Oxford University Press.
McGinn, C. (2005) *Mindsight: Image, Dream, Meaning*, Cambridge, MA: Harvard University Press.
Pritchard, D. (2005) *Epistemic Luck*, Oxford: Clarendon Press.
Pritchard, D. (2012) *Epistemological Disjunctivism*, Oxford: Oxford University Press.
Schwitzgebel, E. (2011) *Perplexities of Consciousness*, Cambridge, MA, and London: MIT Press.
Smith, A.D. (2008) "Disjunctivism and Discriminability," in A. Haddock and F. Macpherson (eds.) *Disjunctivism: Perception, Action, Knowledge*, Oxford: Oxford University Press.
Solms, M. (1997) *The Neuropsychology of Dreams*, Mahwah, NJ: Lawrence Erlbaum Associates.
Sosa, E. (1999) "How to Defeat Opposition to Moore," *Philosophical Perspectives* 33(suppl. 13): 137–149.
Sosa, E. (2007) *A Virtue Epistemology: Apt Belief and Reflective Knowledge*, vol. 1, Oxford:Oxford University Press.
Sutton, J. (2009) "Dreaming," in J. Symons and P. Calvo (eds.) *Routledge Companion to the Philosophy of Psychology*, London: Routledge.
Thompson, E. (2014) *Waking, Dreaming, Being*, New York: Columbia University Press.
Walton, K.L. (1990) *Mimesis as Make-Believe: On the Foundations of the Representational Arts*, Cambridge, MA: Harvard University Press.
Williams, B. (1978) *Descartes: The Project of Pure Inquiry*, Harmondsworth: Penguin Press.
Williamson, T. (2000) *Knowledge and Its Limits*, Oxford: Oxford University Press.
Windt, J.M. (2010) "The Immersive Spatiotemporal Hallucination Model of Dreaming," *Phenomenology and the Cognitive Sciences* 9(2): 295–316.
Windt, J.M. (2013) "Reporting Dream Experience: Why (Not) to Be Skeptical about Dream Reports," *Frontiers in Human Neuroscience* 7, <http://dx.doi.org/10.3389/fnhum.2013.00708>.
Windt, J.M. (2015) *Dreaming: A Conceptual Framework for Philosophy of Mind and Empirical Research*, Cambridge, MA: MIT Press.
Wodehouse, P.G. (1956) *Carry On, Jeeves*, London: Penguin Books.

# 12
# DESIRE-LIKE IMAGINATION

*Amy Kind*

Imagining typically takes many forms. Consider Huali, an avid young gymnast, who is imagining competing at the 2020 Olympic Games. Some of her imaginings might be sensory or perceptual, as when she imagines her parents' smiling faces as they watch from the stands or when she imagines the roar of the crowd as she finishes her routine. Some of her imaginings might be experiential, as when she imagines performing her dismount from the beam or when she imagines how it would feel to land it perfectly. And some of her imaginings might be attitudinal, as when she imagines that she wins the gold medal for her floor exercise or when she imagines that the Americans take first place in the all-around competition.

Attitudinal mental states – also called *propositional attitudes* – consist in one's adopting a mental attitude towards some propositional content. We can take different attitudes toward the very same content: I can believe that *p*, hope that *p*, desire that *p*, intend that *p*, and so on. Attitudinal imagining is often considered to be similar to belief in important ways. Perhaps most significantly, attitudinal imagining mirrors the inference patterns of belief. (See, e.g., Leslie 1994.) If Huali believes that she will be competing in the 2020 Olympic Games then, given her belief that those games will be held in Tokyo, she will be inclined to believe that she'll be in Tokyo in 2020. Likewise for imagining: if Huali imagines that she's competing in the 2020 Olympic Games then, given her belief that those games will be held in Tokyo, she will be inclined all else being equal to imagine that she'll be in Tokyo in 2020. Attitudinal imagining also shares with belief a mind-to-world direction of fit – though in the case of imagining, the relevant world is not the actual world but a make-believe or pretend world. While belief aims at the true, imagination aims at the fictional (Walton 1990, 41).[1]

Recently, several philosophers have argued that attitudinal imagining can also take a desire-like form. According to these philosophers, just as beliefs interact with desires, so too do belief-like imaginings interact with desire-like imaginings. So, for example, when Huali imagines competing at the 2020 Olympics, not only might she imagine her closest competitor falling on a difficult dismount but she might also imaginatively want this to happen. Or consider Yangjie, who is playing a game of make-believe. When imagining that her bed is a spaceship and that her stuffed animals are her copilots, Yangjie might also imaginatively want to fire the rocket boosters and imaginatively want to travel to Mars.

The existence of such desire-like imaginings is a hotly contested issue among contemporary philosophers of imagination. Proponents argue that such states are needed in order to account for varied phenomena such as pretend behavior and our emotional engagement with fiction. Opponents offer alternative explanations for such phenomena and thereby undercut the case for desire-like imagining. In this essay, I survey the state of the current debate. In the first section, I discuss in more detail what desire-like imaginings are meant to be. In the second, I examine the case in favor of desire-like imaginings while in the third I examine the case against them. Finally, in the closing section, I offer a brief assessment of the strengths of these two cases and explore how future research might help to settle the debate.

## 1 What are desire-like imaginings?

Over the last several decades, philosophers have grown increasingly skeptical of our commonsense understanding of mental states. Eliminative materialists, who endorse a particularly extreme form of this skepticism, claim that our folk psychological theory is deeply flawed; once we achieve a more scientifically sophisticated theory of the mind, we will see that "certain common-sense mental states, such as beliefs and desires, do not exist" (Ramsey 2013; see also P.M. Churchland 1981 and P.S. Churchland 1986). A less extreme form of this skepticism is evidenced by other philosophers who claim not that our folk psychological theory is fundamentally misguided but rather that it is incomplete. Though such philosophers wouldn't want to deny the viability of mental state categories like "belief" and "desire," they argue that we also need to recognize various mental states that are not part of our pretheoretic understanding of the mind, e.g., *alief* (Gendler 2008a, 2008b) and *besire* (Altham 1986). Desire-like imagining would be another such state – one that is not recognized by our folk psychological theory of imagination but that is nonetheless needed for a scientifically sophisticated understanding of the mind.

To get a handle on what such states are meant to be, it is useful to reflect briefly on imagination more generally. In their influential book *Recreative Minds*, Gregory Currie and Ian Ravenscroft distinguish creative imagination from recreative imagination. Someone employs creative imagination when she "puts together ideas in a way that leads to the creation of something valuable in art, science, or practical life" (Currie and Ravenscroft 2002, 9). In contrast, someone employs recreative imagination when she engages in perspective-shifting, i.e., when she imaginatively projects herself into a situation different in some way from her actual current situation. As Currie and Ravenscroft argue, just as someone might shift her perspective with respect to her current beliefs and thereby imaginatively try out different beliefs, she might also shift her perspective with respect to her current desires and thereby imaginatively try out different desires.

Of course, imaginatively trying out different beliefs does not consist in the adoption of those beliefs. When Yangjie points to her stuffed penguin and says, "She's my copilot," she is not reporting a belief. Rather, she is reporting a state that imaginatively stands in for a belief to that effect – a state that we normally refer to simply as an imagining. Likewise, Currie and Ravenscroft suggest that imaginatively trying out different desires does not consist in the adoption of those desires. When Yangjie announces, "I want to be the one to fire the rocket boosters this time," she is not reporting a genuine desire. Rather, she is reporting a state that imaginatively stands in for a desire to that effect. Though English does not have a word for this state, Currie and Ravenscroft introduce the term *desire-like imagining* for it.[2] Alvin Goldman (2006, 48), referring to the same kind of state, calls it *make-desire* (on analogy with the term *make-believe*). Tyler Doggett and Andy Egan (Doggett and Egan 2007) use the term *imaginative desire*, or *i-desire* for short, and as their terminology has subsequently been widely adopted by others, I too will frequently use it here. In doing so, however, I want explicitly to guard against a possible misunderstanding, since the term "i-desire" may seem to suggest that the relevant state is a special kind of desire. This suggestion would be a mistake. An i-desire is not meant to be a special kind of desire but rather a special kind of imagining. Doggett and Egan themselves are explicit about this point. Having claimed that i-desire is "the imaginative analogue of desire," they state unequivocally that "it's only an analogue. The states aren't the same" (Doggett and Egan 2012, 288).

The claim that i-desires constitute a special kind of imagining is meant to be a strong claim, i.e., proponents of i-desires take themselves to be positing a novel kind of imagining that stands alongside the more familiar category of belief-like imagining. In particular, i-desires should not be understood simply as a special subclass of belief-like imagining. Yangjie's i-desire to fire the rocket boosters, for example, should not be understood in terms of a belief-like imagining that she has the desire to fire the rocket boosters – to make this identification would be, as Currie and Ravenscroft put it, to confuse the character of an imagining with its content (Currie and Ravenscroft 2002, 27; see also Currie 1997, 67). Just as there is a distinction between desiring an ice cream and believing that one desires an ice cream, there is also a distinction between i-desiring an ice cream and imagining that one desires an ice cream. This latter state is a belief-like imagining *about* a desire, not an imaginative counterpart of that desire.

Our discussion thus far tells us more about what i-desires are not than it tells us about what they are. In fact, i-desire proponents do not typically offer much by way of a positive characterization of i-desires. Currie and Ravenscroft note explicitly that this should not trouble us: "Definitions of belief, desire, and perception have been hard to come by; none of those on offer seem to us secure enough to provide a basis for defining the states that are parasitic on them. Still, unless we are very troubled philosophically, most of us understand well enough what beliefs, desires, and perceptions are. If we understand these things, it should not be too much to ask us to understand their imaginative counterparts" (Currie and Ravenscroft 2002, 19).

As this suggests, then, we are supposed to get a handle on the notion by way of an analogy with desire (see also Doggett and Egan 2012, 287–288). Just as belief-like imagination mirrors the inferential patterns of belief, desire-like imagination mirrors the inferential patterns of desire. When I desire something, I typically desire the means to it. Likewise, when I i-desire something, I typically i-desire the means to it. Moreover, just as belief-like imagination shares the mind-to-world direction of fit had by belief, desire-like imagination shares the world-to-mind direction of fit had by desire – though, as with belief-like imagining, the world relevant to desire-like imaginings is a make-believe or fictional world. When a reader of *The Hobbit* i-desires that Bilbo Baggins defeats Smaug, that i-desire will be satisfied if, in the fictional world depicted by the story, Bilbo emerges victorious.

I-desires are also often said to be similar to desires with respect to their causal roles. But here we must draw a distinction between an internal and an external causal role. There is widespread agreement among proponents of i-desires that they can play the same kind of internal causal role as desires. For example, just as desires produce emotional responses in conjunction with our beliefs, i-desires too are claimed to produce emotional responses in conjunction with our imaginings. Yangjie's excitement during her game of pretend arises from i-desiring that she reach Mars and imagining that she's gotten there. There is less agreement among proponents of i-desires as to whether they can play the same external causal role as desires. Some think of i-desires as in principle disconnected from our action-guiding systems; they are "blocked off from behavior" (Currie 1997, 68). Though a desire for ice cream might prompt me to go to the freezer, an i-desire for an ice cream won't. On this way of thinking, i-desires are often referred to as "offline" states. Others think of i-desires as capable of causing behavior in an analogous way to the way that desires are capable of causing behavior: just as desires produce actions in conjunction with beliefs, i-desires are thought to produce action in conjunction with imaginings. Such proponents suggest that we can explain why Yangjie gets onto her bed during her game of make-believe, for example, via the conjunction of her imagining that her bed is a spaceship and her i-desire to go to Mars. We will return to the issue of the causal role of i-desires in the subsequent sections as we consider the cases for and against their postulation.

## 2 The case in favor

According to proponents of i-desires, these novel states are needed in order to account for several puzzling phenomena related to the imagination. Such phenomena, they argue, cannot be adequately explained when we limit ourselves only to beliefs, desires, and (belief-like) imaginings. Once we invoke i-desires, however, we allegedly achieve a satisfying account of the phenomena in question and the apparent puzzles dissolve. Four different phenomena have featured prominently in the case for i-desires: (a) mindreading, (b) imaginative resistance, (c) emotional engagement with fiction, and (d) pretend behavior. In this section, we consider each of these in turn.

### *2.1 Mindreading*

Since the 1980s, imagination has frequently been invoked to account for how we come to explain and predict the behavior of other people: via an imaginative simulation, we can project ourselves into another person's situation and thereby come to see why she did what she did and what she will likely do in the future (see, e.g., Gordon 1986 and Heal 1986). This view, known as simulation theory, contrasts with theory theory, a view that explains our mindreading abilities in terms of the employment of a folk psychological theory (see, e.g., Gopnik and Meltzoff 1997). Given our purposes here, I will bracket off this debate (though see Shannon Spaulding, "Simulation theory," Chapter 19 of this volume) to concentrate on the role that i-desires play in the simulationists' account of mindreading.

As the simulationists characterize their view, for someone (the "attributor") to project herself into the situation of someone else (the "target"), the attributor must imaginatively recreate the target's initial states. Given these inputs, the attributor can then in imagination reach a decision and thereby predict that the target would make the same decision. (See, e.g., Goldman 2006, 19.) This means the attributor must recreate the target's desires. How does the attributor do this, especially in the case when she lacks the desire herself? I-desires are thought to offer a plausible explanation. Consider a context in which we frequently engage in mindreading, namely, while playing board games. When playing Settlers of Catan, Stefanie needs to predict where her opponent is going to place his next settlement. She might start by simulating his beliefs: the spot on the left will generate wheat and ore, while the spot on the right will generate wood and brick. But this alone will not enable her to figure out what she needs to know, because the spot he will choose depends on whether he wants wheat and ore or wood and brick. It is not enough for Stefanie to consult her own desires here. The fact that she herself desires wood and brick does not show that her opponent does too – after all, he is in a different strategic situation from her. Thus, for Stefanie to be able to make any sort of effective prediction, she will have to simulate her opponent's desires along with his beliefs.[3]

The simulationists often refer to these simulations as instances of pretense, and they refer to the states produced by the simulation as "pretend beliefs" or "pretend desires." But it should be clear that such pretend states are what we have been referring to as, respectively, belief-like and desire-like imaginings. Goldman, for example, is explicit about this very point. On his view, pretend states are produced by what we have been calling recreative imagination, or in his words, by *enactment imagination*: "A pretend desire is the product of enacting, or attempting to enact, desire" (Goldman 2006, 48).

Determining whether simulation theory offers us the correct account of mindreading is, as noted above, beyond our purview here. But it's worth noting that even theory theorists tend to admit that we engage in imaginative simulations of the sort postulated by simulation theorists – what's primarily at issue between the two sides in the mindreading debate is not whether we simulate but whether (and to what extent) such simulations are theory-laden. Thus, reflection on mindreading – even without a commitment to the correctness of simulation theory – provides a forceful argument for the existence of i-desires.[4]

### 2.2 Imaginative resistance

The puzzling phenomenon of imaginative resistance, which seems to have been first noticed by Hume, has recently been much discussed in the literature on imagination (see, e.g., Walton 1994 and Gendler 2000; for an overview of the issue, see Kengo Miyazono and Shen-yi Liao, "The cognitive architecture of imaginative resistance," Chapter 17 of this volume). When we engage with fiction, we readily imagine all sorts of claims that we know to be factually mistaken or even factually impossible. But when confronted with a claim that seems to us to be morally mistaken or impossible, we tend to resist. We have no trouble engaging with a story that asks us to imagine a foreign militia taking over the island of Nantucket after slaughtering all of its present residents. But now suppose the author were to add an additional claim: "Of course, the militia did the right thing; after all, Nantucket has long been an enclave for wealthy snobs." Confronted with this sort of deviant moral claim, the typical reader is likely to experience some bewilderment. More to the point, she's likely to have difficulty going along with the story. Instead she'll resist what she's supposed to be imagining.

Among the many explanations of imaginative resistance that have been offered is an account in terms of desire-like imagining. On this view, one that has been developed by Currie, both singly (Currie 2002a) and in conjunction with Ravenscroft (Currie and Ravenscroft 2002), engaging with fiction involves both belief-like and desire-like imaginings. But, says Currie, there is a striking asymmetry between our willingness to take on certain kinds of belief-like imaginings and our willingness to take on certain kinds of desire-like imaginings: "We tolerate astonishing amounts of cruelty and suffering being represented in fictions, and are very willing to imagine that innocent people like Desdemona are murdered for no good reason, as long as we are not asked to take on in imagination the desires of the characters who bring about and delight in that suffering" (Currie 2002a, 217). Though we have a very high threshold for what we're willing to imaginatively believe, we have a much lower threshold for what we're willing to imaginatively desire. Thus, deviant factual claims in fiction don't raise our hackles the way that deviant moral claims do because the latter cases pose special problems with respect to our desire-like imaginings.

As part of an attempt to explain this asymmetry, Currie invokes the notion of the ideal spectator: "someone who is sufficiently rational, well-informed about, and disinterested in the action she surveys for it to be the case that, were she to think a certain outcome to the action morally right, she would desire that outcome, and were she to think that outcome morally wrong, she would desire its non-occurrence" (Currie 2002a, 217). In our engagement with fiction, we frequently approximate the ideal observer, so the moral claims we encounter activate our desire-like imaginings in a way that factual claims do not. In cases where the moral claims are deviant, we either resist directly the desire-like imaginings or our desire-like imaginings come into tension with our belief-like imaginings. In these latter cases, this tension explains the resistance that we feel. In short, then, Currie argues that once we recognize the existence of desire-like imaginings, imaginative resistance no longer seems puzzling.

### 2.3 Emotional engagement with fiction

Our engagement with fiction often engenders strong emotional responses – we're heartbroken when Charlotte dies at the end of *Charlotte's Web*, we're terrified by the flying monkeys in *The Wizard of Oz*, and we're disgusted when watching a politician forced to have sexual intercourse with a pig in *Black Mirror*. But such emotional response is puzzling, given that we know that the characters and events depicted are merely fictional. Why do we have emotional responses to things that are only imagined to be true?

This question has several aspects. First, insofar as we're inclined to think that we can only be rational in having emotional responses to events if we believe in the reality of such events, we might worry that our emotional responses to fiction cannot be both genuine and rational. This issue – often referred to as the *paradox of fiction* – has been much discussed in the literature on aesthetics. (For an overview, see Stacie Friend, "Fiction and emotion," Chapter 16 of this volume). But second, there is a related issue lurking in the vicinity. Insofar as we're inclined to think that emotional responses are typically generated by beliefs and desires, we might wonder how our emotional responses to fiction can even get off the ground in the first place – after all, the reader doesn't believe that Charlotte exists. So what mental states bring about reader's sadness?

Here it seems natural to claim that imagining plays the role of belief. Though the reader doesn't believe that Charlotte is dying, she imagines it, and this imagining contributes to the production of her affective response. But some conative state is also needed, and there doesn't seem to be a relevant desire that would fit the bill. Three different reasons tend to be offered to support this claim: (1) any such conative state would violate the normative constraints governing desire. As Currie notes, "Desires can be shown to be unreasonable, or at least unjustified, if they fail to connect in various ways with the facts" (Currie 2002a, 211). But here the reasonableness of my conative state is not threatened by the fact that Charlotte doesn't exist. (2) Any such conative state would not motivate action in the way that desires normally do. After all, when engaging with fiction we don't intervene in the unfolding events and try to take matters into our own hands. (See Currie 2002a, 211.) (3) There is no adequate way to understand the content of the conative state if it is a genuine desire. You can't have a desire about Charlotte herself – no such spider exists. (See Doggett and Egan 2007, 13–14.) Thus, philosophers such as Currie and Ravenscroft (2002) and Doggett and Egan (2007) have argued that the conative state in question must be an i-desire. A reader's sadness at the end of *Charlotte's Web*, for example, can be explained in terms of imagining Charlotte's death and i-desiring that Charlotte survive.

Here it might be worth taking a slightly closer look at (3), since there are a couple of obvious ways we might try to specify the content of a desire that the reader might have. Perhaps the most plausible candidate desire would be the desire that *in the fiction* Charlotte not die. Currie (2010) calls this the change-of-content solution, since it changes the content of the reader's desire from a desire about a fictional spider to a desire about a piece of fiction. The problem with the change-of-content solution is that the reader need not have a desire with that content. In fact, she might very well recognize that Charlotte's death is an important part of the story, that it's necessary to teach Wilbur (and young readers) about the cycle of life, death, and renewal. She might not want the story to have a saccharine ending. Or she might simply trust that E.B. White knows better than she does how the story should end. It seems just as unlikely that we explain the reader's emotional response by relying on her desires about real-life spiders. Even absent the desire that real-life spiders have extended lifespans, a reader will still experience sadness at Charlotte's death. Thus, as Doggett and Egan conclude, the only way to account for our emotional responses to fiction is to "expand our mental architecture beyond beliefs and desires" (Doggett and Egan 2012, 282), that is, to postulate the existence not only of imaginings but also of i-desires.

Before moving on, it's also worth noting that while Doggett and Egan take our engagement with fiction to support the introduction of i-desires because of the need to explain our affective responses, a related source of support arises directly from consideration of our conative responses. To redeploy one of their examples, consider a viewer's responses to the characters and events depicted in *The Sopranos*, an American television series that aired on HBO from 1999 to 2007 and centered around Tony Soprano, the head of a New Jersey mafia family. At the end of Season 5 when Tony is forced to flee from police on foot after he's caught up in a raid of a fellow mob member's home, a viewer will undoubtedly be rooting for Tony to escape capture – this is something toward which she has a conative attitude. But, as we saw above, the relevant conative attitude doesn't seem to be desire – she knows Tony Soprano is a fictional character, and so to have real desires about what does or doesn't happen to him would seem to require irrationality. Moreover, we can't understand her conative attitude in terms of general desires about mob bosses, because the typical viewer probably doesn't have any sort of general desire that mob bosses evade capture by the police. So this is a case where the viewer seems to want something that she doesn't want.[5] Proponents of i-desires have a nice explanation of this puzzling situation, since they take the conative attitude in question to be an i-desire rather than a desire.

### 2.4 Pretend behavior

When children play games of pretend, they engage in all sorts of unusual behavior. Aadhya, who is pretending to be a puppy dog, might say "woof woof" while crawling on all fours and licking her left hand. Imani, who is pretending to be a witch-in-training at Hogwarts, might wave around a tree branch while saying "Wingardium Leviosa." And Mirabel, who is pretending to be a mother, might rock a doll in her arms while making soothing sounds.

But what explains these pretend actions? Even as preschoolers, children do not actually believe themselves to be the characters they have adopted, nor do they take the props they employ to be the actual things they are pretending them to be. (See Deena Skolnick Weisberg, "Imagination and child development," Chapter 22 of this volume.) Imani, for example, knows that what's in her hand is a tree branch, not a wand, and she's not under any sort of delusion that she's really a witch. This means that an explanation of her actions in terms of beliefs and desires alone seems unlikely to be sufficient. In order to make sense of what pretenders are doing, it's generally accepted that we have to invoke belief-like imaginings: Imani imagines that she's a witch-in-training, and she imagines that the tree branch is a magic wand.[6] Even having posited these belief-like imaginings, however, it seems that we still lack the resources to achieve an adequate explanation of her actions. Rather, we are forced to offer an explanation that – as David Velleman has complained – casts the pretenders as "depressingly unchildlike." We'd have to say something like: Imani imagines herself to be a witch-in-training, she believes that a witch-in-training would wave around a wand, she is imagining the tree branch to be a wand, and she wants to behave like a witch-in-training would behave. This kind of explanation puts Imani at a considerable remove from her game of pretend. In Velleman's terms, if Imani were motivated in this way then she "would remain securely outside the fiction, thinking about it as such" (Velleman 2000, 257). Moreover, in some cases of pretending, this sort of explanation seems to go even more fundamentally awry. For example, dogs don't really say "woof woof," so if Aadhya wants to behave like a dog behaves, why would this be what she says? Perhaps we can explain her utterance by saying she wants to behave as one behaves when one is pretending to be a dog. But this builds the concept of pretense into her desire in a way that makes her mental states highly conceptualized – perhaps even over conceptualized – especially when we remember how young a pretender might be.[7]

According to the proponent of i-desires, an adequate explanation of pretense actions thus demands the postulation of i-desires. Just as regular behavior is generated by belief in conjunction with desire, there are a variety of cases in which pretense behavior is generated by belief-like imagining in conjunction with desire-like imagining. But, as we noted above, imagination and belief come apart in various ways. In particular, belief aims at the true while imagining aims at the fictional. Thus, as Doggett and Egan summarize their account: "People who believe that *P* are disposed to act in ways that would, if *P* were true, be likely to make the propositions that they desire true … . People who imagine that *P* are disposed to act in ways that would, if *P* were fictional, be likely to make the propositions that they i-desire fictional" (Doggett and Egan 2007, 10).

## 3 The case against

As the discussion of the previous section showed, proponents of desire-like imagination primarily make the case in favor of i-desires by arguing that several phenomena related to imagination can be explained only by the invocation of an imaginative analogue to desire. It's thus perhaps unsurprising that opponents of desire-like imagination primarily make the case against i-desires by showing that we can explain the phenomena in question in other ways, ways that do not involve the invocation of i-desire. Thus far in philosophical discussions of the issue – and remember that the debate about desire-like imagination is still a relatively new one, having started to receive serious attention only in the last decade – opponents of i-desires have focused their attention on the second two of the four phenomena that we considered in the previous section. My discussion here will thus largely be confined to the case against i-desires that stems from considering our emotional engagement with fiction and pretense behavior.

### *3.1 Emotional engagement with fiction*

In a sense, the proponents of desire-like imagination issue a challenge to their opponents: find me a desire that can adequately explain our engagement with fiction. The case for i-desires is built by offering reasons that this challenge cannot be met. In response, however, the opponents of desire-like imagination typically claim that such reasons appear plausible only if we assume an unreasonably strict conception of desire. Once we adopt a more suitable understanding of desire, the challenge can indeed be easily met.

Recall the three reasons that proponents of desire-like imagination offer to suggest that the conative state at work in producing affective response cannot be a desire: (1) any such conative state would violate the normative constraints governing desire; (2) any such conative state would not motivate action in the way that desires normally do; and (3) there is no adequate way to understand the content of the conative states if they are genuine desires.

Building on an influential discussion by Richard Moran (1994) in which he suggests that we can have all sorts of emotional responses to nonactual situations, Amy Kind argues that we can also have all sorts of desires concerning nonactual situations:

> We have all sorts of genuine desires about things that are not actual: desires about past events and existents, desires about future events and existents, desires about counterfactual events and existents, and so on. I might desire that I could introduce my children to their grandfather, who is no longer living; I might desire that my (not yet existing) grandchildren have healthy and happy lives; I might desire that a certain ballot proposition had been defeated in a recent election. In none of these cases is the reasonableness of the desire undercut by the fact that the object of the desire is non-actual.
>
> *(Kind 2011, 425)*

In this way, Kind argues that the plausibility of (1) depends on a mistaken account of the normative constraints governing desire. By reminding ourselves of the many different sorts of cases in which we have desires about nonactual entities and events, "we can more easily see that our desires about fictional entities and events are not especially peculiar; they simply lie along the same continuum as our desires about the past, the future, and the counterfactual" (Kind 2011, 425).

Responding to (2), Kind (2011) argues that the proponent of desire-like imagination mistakenly supposes that there must be a very tight connection between desire and its motivational tendencies. In actuality, however, there are cases (even if rare) in which desires are motivationally inert. The literature on desire contains a variety of examples: someone might want it to be a nice day (Marks 1984), someone heading to the airport to pick up her spouse might desire that his plane left on time (Mele 1995, 394), while someone else might desire that she had never been born, or that her parents had never met, or that a committee make a decision in her favor without her having to intervene (Schroeder 2004, 16–17). In none of these cases does the desire dispose the individual to any action. Another important consideration comes from Peter Carruthers, who has suggested that we don't act to stop fictional danger because "real desires will normally lead to real action only *when interacting with real beliefs*" (Carruthers 2006, 99). With respect to fictional danger, danger that has been imagined, we lack such real beliefs.

Finally, with respect to (3), opponents of i-desire might suggest that the relevant desire be about a fictional character – my desire that Charlotte survive is a desire that *the fictional character Charlotte* survive. Proponents of i-desires tend to dismiss this suggestion because they take it that having such a desire about the fictional character Charlotte "entails, or at the very least rationally requires, that one have the corresponding desire about the content of the fiction, since the only way for the fictional character to have the property that we desire [her] to have is for the content of the fiction to make it so" (Doggett and Egan 2007, 14). And as we have seen, a reader might desire that Charlotte survives without having this desire about the fiction.

In response, opponents of i-desire question the entailment. Such an entailment seems plausible only if one smuggles in a consistency requirement on desires. But given the frequency with which we all experience conflicting desires, it seems unlikely that we should accept such a consistency requirement. I might want to get some work done on Saturday and yet also want to spend the entire day with my children; I might want my elderly dog to live a long time and yet also want to put an end to his suffering. Thus, the reader of *Charlotte's Web* too might have conflicting desires – she desires one thing about Charlotte and yet another thing about the fiction. As Kind notes, "part of what's so hard about having desires is that we don't get to satisfy them all" (Kind 2011, 429).

### 3.2 Pretense

How might we account for pretense if we eschew desire-like imagination? One particularly influential account owes to Nichols and Stich (2003). On their view, we can explain pretense behavior in terms of (i) a desire to pretend, i.e., a desire to behave similarly to how one would behave were an imagined situation to be actual; and (ii) beliefs about what the relevant behavior would be in an actual situation. So, for example, a child who wants to pretend that she is a dog calls upon her beliefs about doglike behavior and behaves "more or less" as she would if she were a dog (see 39). Proponents of desire-like imagination fault this picture for several reasons, but we will here focus on three.[8]

First, Doggett and Egan (2007; see also Velleman 2000) worry that a pretender need not have any beliefs about what she's pretending to be. We can pretend to be undead even if we don't have any beliefs about how the undead really behave, and a child who doesn't know anything about cats might still pretend to be a cat. For many cases of pretending, however, this claim seems implausible. As Kind (2011, 433) notes, can someone pretend to be a vervet absent any beliefs about vervets? Perhaps the objection has more force with respect to the example of pretending to be undead. Here the pretender might really lack any beliefs about how the undead behave – rather, she calls upon her beliefs about the conventions for pretending to be undead. But this does not suggest that the Nichols–Stich schema for explaining pretense should be altogether discarded. Rather, it simply suggests that in some cases of pretense, slightly different belief–desire pairs might be operative. (For related discussion, see Schellenberg 2013.)

The second objection often leveled against the Nichols–Stich schema – and one we encountered briefly in Section 2.4 above – is that it requires pretenders to have the concept of pretense, a requirement that seems especially implausible when we consider that children begin to engage in pretend play at a very young age. Responding to this worry, Funkhouser and Spaulding argue that a proper understanding of the desire to pretend – as specified in (ii) above – requires only a behavioristic and not a mentalistic understanding of pretense: "Children have a behavioral understanding of pretense in that their desire to pretend that *p* is simply a desire to behave, loosely, as if *p* were the case" (Funkhouser and Spaulding 2009, 300; see also Nichols and Stich 2003).

Finally, recall Velleman's worry that a belief–desire explanation of pretense requires us to see the child engaged in pretend play as "depressingly unchildlike." The worry seems to be that, once we explain pretend behavior by postulating a motivation to pretend, we are forced to view the pretender as situated outside the pretend world. In response to this worry, both Funkhouser and Spaulding (2009) and Kind (2011) have argued that the relevant desire need not be a conscious one. Since the pretender need not be cognizant of her own motivations, she need not remain at a distance from what she is pretending. As Funkhouser and Spaulding also note, the fact that we distinguish pretend behavior from delusional behavior offers another reason in support of relying on a desire to pretend in explanations of the former (Funkhouser and Spaulding 2009, 301).

### 3.3 Other considerations

It is worth noting two more general considerations that have been raised as part of the case against desire-like imagination. The first is a phenomenological consideration. Typically, we can tell whether we are believing something or merely imagining it – we don't mistake our belief-like imaginings for beliefs. But we don't seem to have any way to tell whether we are desiring something or merely i-desiring it. Perhaps this should not bother the proponent of i-desires too much, i.e, perhaps it's just the case that i-desiring feels phenomenologically just like desiring. But since we normally take ourselves to be having genuine desires while, say, engaging with fiction, the postulation of desire-like imagination requires that we are systematically mistaken about our own mental states. (For further discussion, see Kind 2011, 429–430.)

The second consideration concerns our evaluative practices. We typically hold one another accountable for the kinds of responses we have to fiction. We are horrified if someone is rooting for Charlotte to die or for Bilbo to be viciously attacked by Smaug. We also hold ourselves accountable in the same way. Given that I am not generally sympathetic to mafia members, I thus might be puzzled as to why I want Tony Soprano to escape capture by the police. We likewise often hold people responsible for actions that they take when they are engaged in games of pretend. We would likely find it disturbing if Mirabel were to smother her doll, or if Imani were repeatedly to cast the unforgivable curses on her siblings. (See Aaron Smuts, "The ethics of imagination and fantasy," Chapter 28 of this volume.) In making their case against i-desires, opponents have charged that such evaluative practices make little sense unless the conative states we are evaluating are instances of genuine desire. (See Moran 1994 and Kind 2011 for further discussion.)

## 4 The state of the debate

As we have seen, the debate about i-desires has tended to focus on their potential explanatory role in several specific imaginative contexts. That said, there are some more general considerations that can be brought to bear on the debate – considerations that, on the whole, cut both ways. First, proponents of i-desires might note an instability at the heart of their opponents' position. In general, philosophers are more than willing to postulate an imaginative analogue of belief.[9] But then why shouldn't there be an imaginative analogue of desire? As Liao and Doggett (2014) put this point, there is a certain tension between being a "cognitive splitter" (someone who thinks that our cognitive states are split between belief and imagination) while also being a "conative lumper" (someone who thinks that our conative states are lumped in a single category). Thus we might think that the burden of proof is on the opponent of i-desires to show why there should be an important disanalogy between the belief/imagination relationship and the desire/imagination relationship. As yet, the opponents of i-desires have failed to carry this burden.

On the other hand, opponents of i-desires might note a different instability that threatens the case for i-desires. Here the problem stems from the motivational role that i-desires are supposed to play. In some contexts – as with simulation and our engagement with fiction – i-desires are supposed to help explain why we don't see the kind of action that we would expect were there a comparable desire in place. Consider the events that unfold in the second act of the musical *West Side Story* when Chino sets out to find Tony in order to avenge Bernardo's death. Normally, if we were to see someone with a gun heading out to kill somebody else, and we were to desire that the targeted individual stay safe, we would do something – warn that individual, call the police, or even (if we felt particularly brave) try to stop the shooting ourselves. But the theatergoers, despite pulling for Tony's safety and feeling distress about the unfolding action, don't do any of this; rather, they just stay in their seats. The invocation of i-desires is supposed to provide us with a nice explanation of their passivity: since the theatergoers do not desire that Tony stay safe but only i-desire it, we can explain why they are not motivated to take action. A similar explanation is offered for why, when simulating someone who desires revenge, the person doing the simulating isn't motivated to seek revenge herself. The mental states produced by the simulation are i-desires, and as such, they are blocked off from the action-generating system. As we have seen, however, there are other contexts such as pretense in which it is crucial to the explanatory power of i-desires that they not be blocked off in this way. We are supposed to be able to explain why Aadhya says "woof woof" and why Imani waves her tree branch in terms of their respective doglike and witchlike i-desires. In this context, it is critical that i-desires be connected to action. There is thus a tension at the core of the very concept of i-desire, a tension that proponents of desire-like imagining have so far not adequately addressed.

As noted above, the debate about desire-like imagination is still a relatively new one, and the next decade will likely bring increased attention to this issue. So how might we thus make progress in moving the conversation forward? Some have suggested that empirical research will help. There are various ways in which such research could be relevant. As we continue to achieve a better understanding of the neurological structures of the brain, this will undoubtedly prove relevant to the debate about cognitive architecture and, relatedly, to our understanding of the interactions between mental states and action. Alternatively, given the connections between counterfactual reasoning and imagining, further psychological research in this area could shed light on the role of imagining in both pretense and our engagement with fiction (see Liao and Gendler 2011, 90; see also Ruth M.J. Byrne "Imagination and rationality," Chapter 25 of this volume). But in addition to the insights that we might gain from future empirical studies, it seems clear that there is also considerable philosophical work to do. In recent years, research in aesthetics has increasingly been brought into contact with research in philosophy of mind, and vice versa. Given that the debate about desire-like imagining is a wide-ranging one – concerning issues from simulation to fiction to pretense – it will be important that such contact continue.

## Acknowledgments

Thanks to Clare Batty, Peter Kung, and Frank Menetrez for helpful comments on a previous draft of this essay.

## Notes

1 See Gendler 2011 for a discussion of imagining's direction of fit. For further discussion of the ways that imagining is and is not belief-like, see Currie and Ravenscroft 2002, 12–19, and Nichols 2006.
2 Currie had also previously used the term *desire*[i] to pick out this kind of state (see Currie 1997, 67).
3 In fact, simulation theorists often go even further than this. Goldman, for example, claims that in many mindreading contexts the use of simulation will also require the imaginative recreation of hopes, plans, and emotions in addition to the imaginative recreation of beliefs and desires (Goldman 2006, 48–49, 151). See also Walton 1997, 41–42.
4 Simulation theory is often extended to account for empathy in addition to mindreading. If this is right, then i-desires would be invoked to explain empathy as well. See Currie 1997, 66–68.
5 This way of characterizing the situation is employed in the title of Doggett and Egan 2007 – "Wanting Things You Don't Want." Currie (2002a, 211) also talks of desiring something you don't actually desire.

6 It's worth noting that not everyone agrees that belief-like imagination can play the same motivational role as belief; see, e.g., O'Brien 2005 and Funkhouser and Spaulding 2009.
7 For additional considerations against explaining pretense-behavior in belief–desire terms see Doggett and Egan 2007, 5–12.
8 See Funkhouser and Spaulding 2009 for a detailed rebuttal of a more comprehensive set of worries that might be raised by the proponent of desire-like imagination.
9 One notable exception is Langland-Hassan (2012), who argues for a "single attitude" account of imagination according to which imagination is just a form of believing.

## References

Altham, J.E.J. (1986) "The Legacy of Emotivism," in G. Macdonald and C. Wright (eds.) *Fact, Science, and Morality: Essays on A.J. Ayer's Language, Truth, and Logic*, Oxford: Blackwell, 275–288.
Carruthers, P. (2006) "Why Pretend?" in S. Nichols (ed.) *The Architecture of the Imagination*, Oxford: Oxford University Press, 89–109.
Churchland, P.M. (1981) "Eliminative Materialism and the Propositional Attitudes," *Journal of Philosophy* 78: 67–90.
Churchland, P.S. (1986) *Neurophilosophy: Toward a Unified Science of the Mind/Brain*, Cambridge, MA: MIT Press.
Currie, G. (1997) "The Paradox of Caring: Fiction and the Philosophy of Mind," in M. Hjort and S. Laver (eds.) *Emotion and the Arts*, Oxford: Oxford University Press, 63–77.
Currie, G. (2010) "Tragedy," *Analysis* 70(4): 632–638.
Currie, G. (2002a) "Desire in Imagination," in T.S. Gendler and J. Hawthorne (eds.) *Conceivability and Possibility*, Oxford: Oxford University Press, 201–221.
Currie, G. (2002b) "Imagination as Motivation," *Proceedings of the Aristotelian Society* 102(3): 201–216.
Currie, G., and I. Ravenscroft (2002) *Recreative Minds: Imagination in Philosophy and Psychology*, Oxford: Oxford University Press.
Doggett, T., and A. Egan (2007) "Wanting Things You Don't Want: The Case for an Imaginative Analogue of Desire," *Philosophers' Imprint* 7(9): 1–17.
Doggett, T., and A. Egan (2012) "How We Feel about Terrible, Non-existent Mafiosi," *Philosophy and Phenomenological Research* 84(2): 277–306.
Funkhouser, E., and S. Spaulding (2009) "Imagination and Other Scripts," *Philosophical Studies* 143(3): 291–314.
Gendler, T.S. (2000) "The Puzzle of Imaginative Resistance," *Journal of Philosophy* 97(2): 55–81.
Gendler, T.S. (2008a) "Alief and Belief," *Journal of Philosophy* 105(10): 634–663.
Gendler, T.S. (2008b) "Alief in Action (and Reaction)," *Mind & Language* 23(5): 552–585.
Gendler, T.S. (2011) "Imagination," in E.N. Zalta (ed.) *Stanford Encyclopedia of Philosophy* (Fall 2013 edition), <http://plato.stanford.edu/archives/fall2013/entries/imagination/>.
Goldman, A.I. (2006) *Simulating Minds: The Philosophy, Psychology, and Neuroscience of Mindreading*, Oxford: Oxford University Press.
Gopnik, A., and A. Meltzoff (1997) *Words, Thoughts, and Theories*, Cambridge, MA: MIT Press.
Gordon, R. (1986) "Folk Psychology as Simulation," *Mind & Language* 1: 158–171.
Heal, J. (1986) "Replication and Functionalism," in J. Butterfield (ed.) *Language, Mind, and Logic*, Cambridge: Cambridge University Press, 135–150.
Kind, A. (2011) "The Puzzle of Imaginative Desire," *Australasian Journal of Philosophy* 89(3): 421–439.
Langland-Hassan, P. (2012) "Pretense, Imagination, and Belief: The Single Attitude Theory," *Philosophical Studies* 159(2): 155–179.
Leslie, A. (1994) "Pretending and Believing: Issues the Theory of ToMM," *Cognition* 50: 211–238.
Liao, S., and T.S. Gendler (2011) "Pretense and Imagination," *Wiley Interdisciplinary Reviews* 2(1): 79–94.
Liao, S., and T. Doggett (2014) "The Imagination Box," *Journal of Philosophy* 111(5): 259–275.
Marks, J. (1984) "Motivation and Desire," in *Ways of Desire: New Essays in Philosophical Psychology on the Concept of Wanting*, Chicago: Precedent Publishing.
Mele, A. (1995) "Motivation: Essentially Motivation-Constituting Attitudes," *Philosophical Review* 104(3): 387–423.
Moran, R. (1994) "The Expression of Feeling in Imagination," *Philosophical Review* 103(1): 75–106.
Nichols, S. (2006) "Just the Imagination: Why Imagining Doesn't Behave Like Believing," *Mind & Language* 21(4): 459–474.

Nichols, S., and S. Stich (2003) *Mindreading: An Integrated Account of Pretence, Self-Awareness, and Understanding Other Minds*, Oxford: Oxford University Press.
O'Brien, L. (2005) "Imagination and the Motivational Role of Belief," *Analysis* 65(1): 55–62.
Ramsey, W. (2013) "Eliminative Materialism," in E.N. Zalta (ed.) *The Stanford Encyclopedia of Philosophy* (Summer 2013 edition), <http://plato.stanford.edu/archives/sum2013/entries/materialism-eliminative/>.
Schellenberg, S. (2013) "Belief and Desire in Imagination and Immersion," *Journal of Philosophy* 110(9): 497–517.
Schroeder, T. (2004) *Three Faces of Desire*, Oxford: Oxford University Press.
Velleman, J.D. (2000) "On the Aim of Belief," in *The Possibility of Practical Reason*, Oxford: Oxford University Press, 244–281.
Walton, K.L. (1990) *Mimesis as Make-Believe: On the Foundations of the Representational Arts*, Cambridge, MA: Harvard University Press.
Walton, K.L. (1994) "Morals in Fiction and Fictional Morality (I)," *Proceedings of the Aristotelian Society, Supplementary Volume* 68: 27–50.
Walton, K.L. (1997) "Spleunking, Simulation, and Slime: On Being Moved by Fiction," in M. Hjort and S. Laver (eds.) *Emotion and the Arts*, Oxford: Oxford University Press, 37–49.

# PART III

# Imagination in aesthetics

# 13
# ART AND IMAGINATION

*Nick Wiltsher and Aaron Meskin*

The histories of the terms 'art' and 'imagination' trace peculiarly parallel lines. Empiricists, rationalists, Kant, and post-Kantians all tended to think of imagination as a fundamental and unified human faculty, essentially enmeshed in conscious life. Similarly, early aestheticians thought that all the questions of art – its definition, its appreciation, its value, and its judgment – could be subsumed under one theory.

In the twentieth and twenty-first centuries, the trends have been toward fragmentation and particularity. The ambition of giving a single theory of art has been thwarted by its prolific diversification. Within the European artistic tradition, movements such as minimalism and conceptualism have challenged general claims about the nature of art. Awareness of other traditions, such as the Chinese and Native American, has brought further challenges. Art is now made in forms far beyond the traditional categories such as music, literature, and painting. And genres continue to multiply. All this adds to the complexity of the task, and various large-scale distinctions within the domain of art (between, for example, representational and nonrepresentational art, or fine and popular art) further complicate the picture.

Similarly, the idea that imagination is a single, unitary faculty has been challenged by the recognition that philosophers and folk alike ascribe to imagination a highly heterogeneous set of features, capabilities, and applications. One might thus doubt that a single sort of mental state or capacity is identified by the word "imagination" (Stevenson 2003; Kind 2014).

Accordingly, attempts to tease out the intuitively intimate links between art and imagination have become more modest. Where philosophers might once have used a general notion of imagination to underpin a grand theory of art, they now tend to argue that a specific kind or application of imagination can help to explain some particular element of art or artistic practice. And certainly, there are many questions of aesthetics where this is a promising approach. Making art is typically conceived of as the paradigmatically imaginative activity. We often praise works and artists for being imaginative, while criticizing others for being unimaginative (Grant 2012). The appreciation of art forms such as painting seems to involve something imagination-like: the appearance of things that are not really before us. Other works of art such as literary fictions, which do not seem to essentially traffic in these sorts of quasi-perceptual experiences are, nevertheless, typically understood as engaging and enriching our imaginations (Walton 1990; Nussbaum 1998).

Among the founders of modern aesthetics, Kant is most well-known for invoking imagination in his explanations of aesthetic phenomena. In the twentieth century, the grand and general approach is most closely associated with R.G. Collingwood (1938). For Collingwood, art is, by definition, imaginative expression of feeling. Unsurprisingly, Collingwood is forced to take a revisionary approach to the domain of art. But the comprehensive nature of his theories of art and imagination has placed his ideas at the heart of debates concerning them, and we will return repeatedly to them throughout this chapter.

Among many who deserve attention, perhaps the best-known contemporary exponent of the particularist approach is Kendall Walton. He argues that the representational arts are founded on make-believe, a special sort of imaginative activity. Unlike Collingwood, Walton is not aiming to be comprehensive; he does not try to define art, nor to give an account of its creation or ontology. Rather, he focuses only on certain sorts of art, and certain aspects of the artistic domain. In this respect, Walton serves as an exemplar of current thinking about art and imagination.

To structure our discussion, we will distinguish three domains in which art and imagination might be linked: production, ontology, and appreciation. In the first section of the chapter we explore what philosophers of art have said about the connections between artistic creation, creativity, and the imagination. In the second section, we engage with the view that artworks are imaginary objects. The third section of the chapter examines the problems of appreciation that face this approach to the ontology of art. In the fourth section, we address a number of other ways in which philosophers have seen the imagination as central to understanding and judging art. The final section of the chapter briefly draws attention to a miscellany of questions about imagination across the arts.

## 1 The creation of art

Imagination can be recreative; for example, we can use it to model other people's thoughts (Currie and Ravenscroft 2002). It can also be creative: we can conjure new things, or at least new ideas of things, into being. Art-making is, at least generically, a creative activity. So the temptation to link artistic creation to imagination is compelling. Berys Gaut, for example, argues that there is a significant (although inessential) link between creativity and the imagination (Gaut 2003). One way to understand the link is to think of the creation of art as a particular application of general creative capabilities. Much work on creativity in art takes this approach (e.g., Boden 2010).

However, several highly influential aestheticians have thought that artistic creativity is somehow special. Kant thinks that the greatest artists have a unique talent for producing and expressing "aesthetic ideas," which are ideas of the imagination which cannot be wholly brought under determinate concepts (Kant 1790, §§314–317). So very few people (only those endowed with genius) can produce creative and original art.

The Romantic movement that blossomed in Kant's wake enthusiastically endorsed the idea that artists have a special imaginative capacity that affords them insights and experiences unavailable to the ordinary person. Samuel Taylor Coleridge, for example, distinguishes between mere reproductive imagination, or "fancy," which everyone has, and the creative imaginative faculty, which only such people as poets possess, or employ to its fullest extent (Coleridge 1817, 167; for discussion, see Warnock 1976, pt. 3; Casey 1976, 182–188). This conception of artists as persons apart from others, with uncommon imaginative insights, imbues art and imagination alike with an air of mystery and exclusivity. It is the target of some of Collingwood's sharpest criticism (Collingwood 1938, ch. 6 §5). Collingwood conceives of creation as both explicable and available to all, and thinks that the cult of artistic genius founded by Kant is fraudulent. Nevertheless, he and Kant share some common ground on imagination and creativity.

Both Kant and Collingwood think of imagination as fundamental to conscious experience, though they differ over how it is therein involved. Kant, for example, thinks that perception depends on imagination, whereas Collingwood allows that at least some sort of perception is possible without imagination. More pertinently, they both think that imagination's involvement in artistic creation precludes the possibility that creativity is rule-governed. Kant thinks no rules govern true creation, and similarly Collingwood presents his own theory in contrast to the "technical theory" of art, according to which art is a craft: an artist skilfully makes something physical in order to achieve some particular, preconceived end, such as representation or amusement (Kant 1790, §§307–308; Collingwood 1938, chs. 2, 7). Collingwood only explicitly ascribes this theory to Plato, Aristotle, and Horace, but makes clear that, in some form or other, it informs a great deal of thinking about art. Collingwood agrees that artists make things, things that may represent or amuse, but argues that art proper involves creation: a special sort of making which can't have a preconceived end (Collingwood 1938, ch. 7). Creation is thus inimical to the technical theory. You cannot specify the end of a true creative process in advance. If art must involve creation, it must involve a process without a preconceived end. So you cannot specify in advance the rules that will get you to your artistic end. Since crafts involve specifying the end before the process of making begins, the essence of art is not craft (though a certain work can be a work both of craft and of art).

Creation, as Collingwood means it, is the imaginative expression of feeling. Art is the product of such creation, and art products are not ordinary physical things (Collingwood 1938, ch. 7). The middle third of *The Principles of Art* is dedicated to expounding a theory of imagination that underpins all this. According to Collingwood, human experience has three levels. At the "psychical level," experience consists in a constant, transient flux of "feelings," a term which encompasses perceptual sensation, affect, and emotion, all of which are often (perhaps always) co-occurrent in a particular feeling (Collingwood 1938, ch. 8). A feeling, an individual moment in this flux, may be consciously attended to. The act of attention lifts the feeling from the psychical level to the imaginative, where it is modified; it is clarified, brought into focus, perhaps vitiated somewhat, and becomes an idea of imagination, which unlike feelings at the psychical level may be retained and returned to (Collingwood takes himself to be improving upon Hume's division between impressions and ideas; Collingwood 1938, chs. 10–11). At the third level, thought, ideas of imagination are classified: they are accorded titles such as "real," put into relations with other ideas, and so on.

Collingwood thinks feelings are often complex, obscure, and difficult to understand. Consequently, the work of imagination in clarifying a particular feeling is far from trivial. Much effort may be required to establish just what a particular feeling is. Part of that effort is expressing the feeling. Expression is not an act subsequent to the identification of the feeling; rather, it is partially by expressing a feeling that one comes to know what it is. Bringing a feeling into focus in your imagination is precisely an act of expression. Thus, expression need not have a publicly visible aspect. So what imagination creates is an idea that expresses a particular feeling; the essence of art is this imaginative transformation of the stuff of sensation into the matter of thought (Collingwood 1938, chs. 10–11). Artists pin down the precise nature of feelings by expressing them using their imagination.

Exactly what Collingwood means by all this is the subject of debate, and no doubt the summary just given is tendentious (for discussion of how best to interpret Collingwood, see Ridley 1997; Dilworth 1998; Hausman 1998; Ridley 1998a, 1998b; Kemp 2003; D. Davies

2008). But whatever your interpretation, it is questionable whether Collingwood is really doing what he claims: making explicit something we all, intuitively, know already about art and imagination. Certainly, his neo-Humean theory of imagination is idiosyncratic. Again, we might think of imagination as sometimes creative, and sometimes recreative. Collingwood appears to simply deny that the latter is a sort of imagination. Now, you might reject this, and reject his particular account of how imagination is creative, while being attracted to the idea that imagination (somehow) is involved in artistic creation, and that this involvement has something to do with expression, which in turn is a matter of abstraction from and distillation of the everyday. Even so, while this is quite a plausible claim concerning a large class of artworks, it is implausible that it is true of all of what is ordinarily taken to be art. For example, construing all examples of conceptual art and minimalism as a matter of the expression of feeling, even on Collingwood's broad sense of "feeling," is something of a stretch. Admirable as the ambition is, in Collingwood's case a theory is perhaps stretched too thinly. Further criticism of Collingwood's view has generally centered on its implications for the ontology of art. We will discuss these, before turning to imagination's role in the appreciation of art.

## 2 The ontology of art

What do we actually make when we make art? Artworks, of course; but what sort of things are they? For several reasons, it has often been thought unsatisfactory to conclude that all artworks are physical things (Wollheim 1980a, 36–43). It is easy enough to think of painting and carved sculpture that the physical artifact just is the artwork, but this is hard to sustain when we think of artworks that are capable of multiple instantiation, such as plays, prints, or poems. One solution is to stop thinking that all artworks must be the same sort of thing. Perhaps there is just a diversity of ontological categories, and artworks are variously distributed among this happy plurality (Thomasson 2004, 2006). An alternative is to hold that artworks are all a certain sort of thing, but not a physical one: they are all imaginary objects.

The most naive version of this view would be that artworks exist in the minds of those appreciating them, consisting in a sort of imaginative state they enter. This would, quite implausibly, make the existence of an artwork dependent on the existence of that imaginative state. Collingwood is often interpreted as holding a more sophisticated version of this view, dubbed the "Ideal Theory." Even if he did not, some significant philosophers have certainly subscribed to it (e.g., Croce 1909; Sartre 1940, 188–192). The archetypal formulation of the Ideal Theory is that artworks are mental items, products of imagination, which can exist solely in the heads of the artist and appreciators. This is because the process of creating art is entirely an imaginative one, and so the true products of that process are entirely imaginary; they need not have any physical manifestation outside the mind of their creator, nor are they located, once created, in a sort of abstract realm of imaginary objects (nor, as a Meinongian might think, are they really discovered in that realm, rather than created). The Ideal Theory can be maintained even if it is also held that the process of creation involves expression (as it does on Collingwood's account), since such expression can be done internally. Writing, painting, sculpting, and so on are ancillary activities, not a necessary part of creation, and physical products like paintings should not be confused with the mental item that is the artwork proper. The relation between the mental item which is the artwork proper and any physical product is entirely contingent.

Criticisms of this theory are not hard to come by. Richard Wollheim's have been particularly influential (Wollheim 1973, 1980a, 36–43). He argues that the Ideal Theory mistakenly ignores the role of materials in the creation of artworks. If the theory is right, creation can take place entirely in the head; but manipulation of a physical medium is a vital part of creation, not a contingent adjunct to it. To deny this is to ignore the actual mechanics of creation, and to obviate the role of the audience in artistic practice. Further, the arguments for the Ideal Theory are based on a selective set of examples. While it might just about look plausible for poetry and music, it simply cannot be applied to painting and sculpture.

Such criticisms are typically taken to be fatal for the Ideal Theory. Now, as Ridley reads him, Collingwood never held anything like the Ideal Theory. Collingwood instead holds that expression must involve an external medium – precisely the claim that Wollheim makes against Collingwood. So though art is imaginative expression, that expression has a necessary public manifestation (Ridley 1997). Others deny that Collingwood can be read as anything other than an Ideal Theorist (Dilworth 1998; Kemp 2003).

A different line of defense is to adopt a more nuanced version of the Ideal Theory. Such a version might start from close examination of Collingwood's notion of an "imaginative experience of total activity" (Collingwood 1938, ch. 7 §6). This is what an artist undergoes when she creates an artwork, and it involves the employment of all her senses, and her motile capabilities too, or at least imaginative correlates of them (kinesthetic movements and the like). A sympathetic development of this idea might rescue the Ideal Theory from the criticisms above, though the key notion of the contingency of the physical product still seems present and still seems troublesome. (Wollheim also criticizes a "nuanced" version of the ideal theory, and those criticisms might likewise apply to the line just suggested.)

Further, this contingency generates a second set of criticisms of the Ideal Theory, concerned with the role of imagination in appreciation. We will examine these in the next section, before engaging with wider issues of imagination and appreciation.

## 3 Ideal appreciation

If you accept that artworks are (in some sense) imaginary, or the weaker thesis that to properly understand an artwork is to grasp the imaginative idea or process that gave rise to it, you face several closely related problems. One is that, on such a view, the physical manifestation of the artwork again seems contingent; it just occasions a sort of imaginative reverie, and any item that would allow you to grasp the right imaginative idea could be substituted for it. A second is that, if artworks are imaginary items, there appears to be no possibility of genuine critical disagreement. This is because every aspect of the artwork that we might usually think of as an interpretative imposition, over which we could disagree, is taken to be part of the work itself, part of the imaginative idea. And that means, if you and I find ourselves with different things in mind when we contemplate a painting, we are engaging with different artworks. Apparent disagreements between us are not disagreements with the same subject matter (Kemp 2003).

Ridley's response to these criticisms is to argue that Collingwood's account of how imagination is involved in appreciation avoids them. Ridley argues that imagination is what makes the difference between (for example) hearing a string of noises, and listening to music (Ridley 1997). The noises are necessary elements of the experience; the contribution of imagination is to associate those noises so as to construct in the listener's head the precise imaginative experience that the composer underwent when composing the music. If this is correct, there are actually quite strict constraints on what can possibly count as a valid interpretation of an artwork; as Ridley says, Collingwood seems to require an exact match between the artist's experience and the audience's, without offering anything more than an empirically grounded expectation that such a match can be achieved or verified.

If this is right, involving imagination in interpretation neither militates against genuine disagreement, nor renders physical artworks irrelevant. However, one might still think that the artwork is contingent in a weaker sense. If the aim of interpretation is to arrive at the relevant imaginative experience, anything that might occasion that experience would do equally well as another. Artworks thus become fungible. But there is a strong intuition that artworks are not fungible; what one artwork does, another cannot.

This is not a criticism that could be leveled at Collingwood, since he thinks that an imaginative idea and its expression are inseparable. Feelings are complex things for Collingwood, and the expression of a particular one can only be done one way. Therefore, the feeling expressed by a work in one medium simply cannot be expressed in another medium. However, the criticism could be made of any theory on which grasping a sort of idea is the ultimate aim of interpretation. And many people have thought that artworks engage our imagination, and that such engagement is a necessary condition of true understanding. Kant is plausibly read as holding a view of this sort. According to him, artists express aesthetic ideas, which are ideas of the imagination to which no idea of reason is adequate; crudely paraphrased, this means that aesthetic ideas are special ideas generated by the imagination which cannot wholly be described in words or captured by determinate concepts (Kant 1790, §§314–316). Proper interpretation involves grasping this aesthetic idea (though interpretation might involve more than just this). If this is so, it could be that any item which stimulates the imagination to generate the right aesthetic idea would do as well as any other item.

So the problem of how to reconcile something like the Ideal Theory with due respect for the materiality or autonomy of artworks is not just a problem for Collingwood. An intriguing alternative is to deny the apparently commonsense insight at the heart at the Ideal Theory. Where Kant, Collingwood, and others argue that aesthetic experience involves imagination more than perception does, Mikel Dufrenne argues that "aesthetic perception" involves *less* imagination than ordinary perception (Dufrenne 1953, ch. 12).

As the name suggests, aesthetic perception differs from ordinary perception. Both are intentional acts, directed toward intentional objects. In perception, the intentional object of your experience is some external object. There is often a question about what the intentional object of your experience might be, given the limited input from your senses. For example, on the basis of the same sensory experience, you might have a perceptual experience as of a real parrot, or as of a stuffed parrot. What makes the difference between the two, according to Dufrenne, is imagination. Imagination fills in the gaps and ambiguities of sensory experience so that we experience the world as filled with determinate objects which belong to particular sortal kinds.

However, in aesthetic perception, we perceive and consider a physical thing as a work of art: we treat the physical work as a special sort of thing, imbued with its own determinate meanings. If, in this act of aesthetic perception, we grasp properly the aesthetic object suggested by a work of art, all the work usually done by imagination in perception has been done for us already. The objects presented are already determinate; the picture tells us whether it is of a real parrot or a stuffed one. Thus, there are no gaps or ambiguities for imagination to complete (Dufrenne 1953, chs. 6, 12).

Dufrenne's position depends on a number of questionable doctrines, concerning (among other things) perception, the role of imagination in perception, and the existence of such things as aesthetic experiences and aesthetic perceptions. And of course, the view just sketched can't apply straightforwardly to music or literature, since they don't involve physical objects in the same ways that painting or sculpture do. (Needless to say, Dufrenne does have things to say about these art forms.) Nonetheless, the inversion of apparent commonsense that he suggests provides an interesting counterpoint to Kant and Collingwood.

## 4 Appreciating art imaginatively

Thus far, our discussion of appreciation has focused on the idea that proper appreciation of art is *constituted by* a particular sort of imaginative (or unimaginative) experience. In this section, we turn to the weaker idea that appreciation of (some) art *involves* imagination. For example, you might think that understanding what a representation represents requires an imaginative experience, or that the value of art depends on a certain sort of imaginative experience.

One need not even appeal to experience to think that imagination is somehow involved in the appreciation of art. For example, some think that interpreting art involves reconstructing the creative process (Wollheim 1980b). For another example, in the philosophy of literature, there is much debate over whether the best way to understand literature is in accordance with the intentions of the author, and whether that author may best be construed as a hypothetical figure whose intentions are to be divined from the text (see Levinson 1992 for the view, S. Davies 2006 for discussion). And similarly, some have proposed that the common practice of ascribing emotions to music can only be justified by positing a hypothetical person (or persona) who has those emotions; this is because music itself cannot literally have the emotions, but ascribing them to a real person (the composer or the performer) leads quickly to significant problems (Levinson 1996; Ridley 2007). Now, one does not necessarily have to invoke imagination to explain how we reconstruct a creative process, or hypothesize about authors' intentions, but it is natural to think that these things do involve the imagination. As ever, much depends on one's antecedent view of imagination; for example, whether one thinks that hypothesizing is an imaginative activity.

Beyond interpretation, some philosophers think that certain elements of art's value depend on the imagination, or even that judgments of its value are wholly contingent on the imaginative experiences it generates. The latter line is associated with Kant, and has been pursued in more recent times by several others. Anthony Savile, for example, explores the Kantian idea that art is valuable if, in experiencing it, we experience the beautiful or the sublime. We recognize that we are doing so by having a certain sort of experience, occasioned in the case of the beautiful by the fruitful interaction of the imagination and the understanding, and in the case of the sublime by a sort of antagonism between imagination and reason (Savile 1987, 2006). R.K. Elliott offers a slightly different line, less in thrall to Kant though recognizably Kantian in spirit, arguing that a certain sort of "imaginal" response conditions the qualities and values we attribute to art (Elliott 2006). The key to understanding the Kantian view here is perhaps understanding the "free play" between imagination and understanding that allows for judgments of beauty, and this has accordingly been the focus of much critical attention (Crowther 1989; Guyer 1979, 2006; Ginsborg 1997).

The former line, that some elements of art's value depend on some sort of imaginative experience, can be found in work on the moral aspects of art. If you think that part of art's value is that it can be morally enriching, you might also think that it manages that enrichment by engaging our moral imagination. Of course, someone arguing this needs a conception of what a moral imagination is. Amy Mullin provides such a conception, arguing that imagining is a matter of creatively reflecting on, reordering, and restructuring concepts, and moral imagination is just doing so with moral concepts. She then argues that the sorts of imagining which are morally significant are also aesthetically significant (Mullin 2004; see also Nussbaum 1998).

Mullin's conception of imagination owes something to Roger Scruton. He in turn owes something to Wittgenstein. Scruton conceives of the imagination as fundamentally a sort of unasserted thought, with appropriate unasserted analogues for perception. When we imagine, we entertain a thought, or a perceptual image, without asserting that it is true, or veridical, or should be believed. As explained in *Art and Imagination*, this theory is couched in an argumentative and conceptual framework derived from Wittgenstein and, hence, focuses on linguistic manifestations of imagination (that is, on what people might report about their imaginings). Nevertheless, Scruton thinks that there are special aesthetic experiences which require understanding a work, that imagination underpins understanding, and that imagination is thus crucial to expression, representation, and symbolism (Scruton 1974, 2009). Scruton has applied his ideas to experiences of architecture and of music (Scruton 1979, 1999).

Beyond the artworld, a role for imagination has been suggested in the appreciation of nature. For example, Emily Brady argues that to appreciate the beauty of natural objects and environments, one must engage imaginatively with them as well as perceiving them (Brady 1998). This is offered as a contrast to a scientific model according to which one appreciates natural things better the more one knows about them. The involvement of imagination, Brady argues, is necessary if appreciation here is going to be properly aesthetic, rather than ecological or cultural. Her model is, again, Kantian in spirit, if not in detail.

Back within the artworld, the most significant recent proposal for a role for imagination in appreciating art is Walton's, as presented in his *Mimesis as Make-Believe: On the Foundations of the Representational Arts* (Walton 1990). His view encompasses all the representational arts (where "representational" is understood broadly to include such things as nonfigurative painting), and so is not much narrower in scope than Collingwood's. In fact, since Walton is not interested in distinguishing "art falsities" from "art proper," the category of representations is plausibly broader along some dimensions than Collingwood's category of art. The larger structural difference between the two is that Walton is concerned only with a specific use of a specific capacity of imagination; he offers no general account of imagination, and seems unconvinced that one can be given (Walton 1990, 19).

Walton's key idea is that works of representational art (or "fictions" as he also calls them) are things which have the function of serving as props in games of make-believe. To make believe is to engage in a specific imaginative activity which uses such props. In a child's game of make-believe, tree stumps may function as props by mandating that participants in that game imagine various things related to bears (e.g., that there is a bear right there). In virtue of this, various things are fictionally true in that game of make-believe. (There are more bears around here than there used to be!) Similarly, props such as paintings and other representations invite us to engage in particular episodes of make-believe and, in virtue of so doing, make various things fictionally true in those works. Even a nonfigurative painting, such as one of Malevich's Suprematist canvases, mandates that we imagine various shapes spatially related to other shapes and, in so doing, make it fictionally the case that those shapes are spatially related that way (Walton 1990, 55). What is true in the world of the work depends on the features of the work, and relevant "principles of generation" (the rules by which fictional truths are generated from those features), which can vary among social contexts. To appreciate a work of representational art is to imagine correctly the propositions that are fictional in it, and in many cases, to imagine other things too; for example, to participate in a work by imagining emotional responses to events represented in it, or to imagine seeing things that a picture represents. Walton develops his view with particular reference to painting and to fiction, and uses the idea of make-believe to address questions about the ontology of fictional characters and the semantics of fictional names.

Though Walton's theory is presented holistically, criticism has tended to be piecemeal, focusing on one aspect or application of it. For example, much has been said about Walton's account of fiction, and his solution to the paradox of fiction, but since these are discussed elsewhere in this volume we shall concentrate on discussion of his view of pictorial representation (see Stacie Friend, "Fiction and emotion," Chapter 16 of this volume, and Kathleen Stock's Chapter 15, "Imagination and fiction").

According to Walton, a picture acts as a prop by inviting us to imagine (more accurately, make believe) that we are seeing whatever is in the picture (Walton 1990, ch. 8). Moreover, pictures mandate that we do this, as Walton says, "in a first-person manner" – we don't merely imagine *that* we are seeing those things, we imagine seeing those things, and imagine this "from the inside" (Walton 1990, 28–35, 346–348). Finally, this imagining is intimately linked to one's actual seeing of the picture – we imagine of our looking at the picture that its object is what the picture depicts. So representation in general is achieved through make-believe, and pictorial representation specifically is achieved by the complex employment of visual make-believe. Now, one way to argue against this view is to argue that representation is not secured by a sort of experience at all (perhaps it is secured by resemblance). Another way is to argue that Walton has the experience wrong.

For example, you might think that pictorial representation involves visual experience, but experience without imagination. Wollheim and Walton have a long history of debating this. Wollheim insists that depiction involves "seeing-in," which cannot be explained in terms of imagination. Walton insists that it can; he therefore sees his ideas as complementary to Wollheim's, while Wollheim sees them as incompatible (Walton 1991; Wollheim 1991, 2003; Nanay 2004). Alternatively, you might think that the account of imagination that Walton gives, or rather does not give, leads to ambiguities that undermine his account of seeing-in (Hopkins 1992). Or you might think that imagination is what gives us the occluded parts of depicted objects, and thus what makes them perceptually present, while denying that you imagine the whole object (Pettersson 2011).

In this section, we have moved gradually from thinking about appreciating art in general to appreciating certain art forms. In the next section, we consider a collection of further questions concerning the relationship between imagination and particular art forms.

## 5 Imagination across the arts

As mentioned at the beginning of this chapter, recent years have found philosophical aesthetics shifting from being almost exclusively focused on the general theory of art to a more "careful and imaginative scrutiny of the individual arts and their individual problems" (Kivy 1993, 131). This careful and imaginative scrutiny has discerned distinct questions and issues concerning the imagination and its role in the particular arts. In this section, we briefly sketch some recent debates about the role of imagination in three art forms: film, videogames, and literature.

What role does the imagination play in cinematic experience? Most contemporary philosophers of art reject the idea that cinematic experience is founded on illusion (Currie 1995, 19–47). We are not, according to them, fooled into thinking that we see the events that are depicted on the screen. (The question of whether cinematic motion is some sort of perceptual illusion is a related, albeit distinct, matter.) An alternative view, one which is sometimes rooted in Walton's general approach to depiction, holds that cinematic experience essentially involves imagined seeing. On Walton's account, when we watch a film we imagine of our seeing the film that we are seeing the objects and events depicted in it. In fact, it is usually the case that we imagine that we are seeing those events for the very first time, no matter how many times we have watched the film (Walton 1990, 264)! Similarly, George Wilson writes that "the spectator *knows* that he is in the theater, but *it is make-believe for him* that he is watching from within the space of the story" (Wilson 1986, 56). Alternatively, Gregory Currie argues that cinematic experience does not essentially involve this sort of imagined seeing but, rather, is rooted in impersonal "perceptually imagining"; we perceptually imagine the events depicted in the film without thereby imagining that we see those events (Currie 1995, 164–191). Currie is clear that perceptual imagining is akin to perceptual belief; that is, it is a cognitive belief-like state which exhibits a distinctive counterfactual dependence on the visual properties of certain objects (cinematic representations in the case in question) as well as distinctive structure and content (ibid., 181–185). (For a criticism of Currie's account, see Lopes 1998.)

Let us turn now to a different species of the moving image – videogames. Although some videogame scholars disagree (e.g., Aarseth 2007), it is natural to think of videogames, most videogames at least, as fictions in some broad sense (Tavinor 2009). And, as mentioned below, it is standardly, although not uniformly, thought that there is an intimate connection between fictionality and imagination. Hence, on a very common view of videogames, they are properly understood as depicting "situations with imagined existence only" and as reliant "on our cognitive abilities to imagine such things" (Tavinor 2009, 44). Engagement with videogames, then, appears to involve Waltonian make-believe or something very much like it. David Velleman is a notable recent dissenter from this view. In an article which focuses on Second Life, but which is clearly intended to apply to other videogames, Velleman argues that participation in the game involves what he calls "virtual play" rather than make-believe or pretend play (Velleman 2008, 407). Velleman points to a number of reasons for distinguishing such virtual play from make-believe, including: (1) the putatively recalcitrant and determinate nature of truth in videogame fictions (ibid., 407–409), (2) the nature of our affective engagement with videogames (ibid., 411–412), and (3) the peculiarly intimate relationship between characters and their avatars. So, for example, Velleman explicitly contrasts imagining a monster while engaging in ordinary pretend play with awareness of the objects of virtual worlds (such as those found in Second Life). He argues that the latter objects, but not the former, possess "the determinateness and recalcitrance characteristic of reality" (ibid., 411). More crucially, on Velleman's view, it is not the case that a user of Second Life merely fictionally does things in the world it represents (as, again, is the case with ordinary pretend play); rather, as he puts it, such a user "literally performs fictional actions" by means of their avatars (ibid., 407). In other words, when we engage in virtual play – as in Second Life – "a person really has a fictional body" (ibid., 414) which enables him or her to do things in the virtual world. But this is not the case with ordinary make-believe or pretend. In reply, Robson and Meskin (2012) argue against Velleman that videogame playing can after all be understood as involving make-believe in a fairly traditional Waltonian sense.

Most literature is fictional, so if one accepts the standard view that fiction and fictional engagement must be understood in terms of the cognitive imagination then one will be inclined to see the imagination as playing a central, if not essential, role in our engagement with literature. (For one recent version of the standard view, see Stock 2011; for criticism of the standard view, see Matravers 2014). But there is another way in which the imagination might be involved in our experience of literature: reading itself, it might be thought, has an essentially imaginative component. One traditional approach, often attributed to Joseph

Addison and Thomas Reid among others, is that silent reading of poetry (and literature more broadly) involves the perception-like experience of the situations described in those works. "Poetical description," Reid writes, "is painting to the Imagination" (Reid, quoted in Kivy 2006, 27). On Kivy's account, this perception-like experience is best understood as a sort of internal "performance" of the fiction – "the reading experience, in poetic or prose fiction is … the experience of 'seeing' and 'hearing' in the imagination, in the mind's eye, a dramatic representation: a theatrical production in the mind" (ibid., 29). Similarly, in *Zettel*, Wittgenstein considers the view that when he reads "the story pass[es] before me like pictures, like a cartoon story" (Wittgenstein 1968, 43).

There is plenty of empirical evidence that suggests that imagery can play a significant role in the experience of reading – so, for example, reading does produce some spontaneous imagery and training in the production of mental imagery can increase reading comprehension (Sadoski 1998). The philosophical question is whether reading essentially involves the production of imagery.

Kivy criticizes the "Addisonian" view of reading on largely introspective grounds ("simple introspection reveals that a running display of mental 'images' is palpably not what the silent reader of novels and other fictional narratives experiences"; Kivy 2006, 59) but, in its place, offers a very different "performance" account of literary reading. On Kivy's interpretation, silent reading of a literary work involves "hearing," in the imagination, an auditory performance of that work. As he puts it, reading involves "story telling in the mind's ear" (ibid., 63). So Kivy agrees that some sort of sensory imagination is involved in reading, but disagrees about the sensory modality.

This is just a taste of the interesting work being done on the role of the imagination in different art forms, but we hope it convinces the reader that there is much more work to be done in the area. (For an interesting discussion of the underexplored role of the imagination in the experience of comics see McCloud 1993, 60–69.)

## References

Aarseth, E. (2007) "Doors and Perception: Fiction vs. Simulation in Games," *Intermédialités: Histoire et théorie des arts, des lettres et des techniques /Intermediality: History and Theory of the Arts, Literature and Technologies* 9: 35–44.

Boden, M.A. (2010) *Creativity and Art: Three Roads to Surprise*, Oxford: Oxford University Press.

Brady, E. (1998) "Imagination and the Aesthetic Appreciation of Nature," *Journal of Aesthetics and Art Criticism* 56: 139–147.

Casey, E.S. (1976) *Imagining: A Phenomenological Study*, Bloomington: Indiana University Press.

Coleridge, S.T. (1817/1965) *Biographia Literaria*, ed. George Watson, London: Dent.

Collingwood, R.G. (1938) *The Principles of Art*, Oxford: Clarendon Press.

Croce, B. (1909/1922) *Aesthetic: As Science of Expression and General Linguistic*, trans. D. Ainslie, New York: Noonday.

Crowther, P. (1989) *The Kantian Sublime*, Oxford: Clarendon Press.

Currie, G. (1995) *Image and Mind*, Cambridge: Cambridge University Press.

Currie, G., and I. Ravenscroft (2002) *Recreative Minds: Imagination in Philosophy and Psychology*, Oxford: Oxford University Press.

Davies, D. (2008) "Collingwood's 'Performance' Theory of Art," *British Journal of Aesthetics* 48: 162–174.

Davies, S. (2006) "Authors' Intentions, Literary Interpretation, and Literary Value," *British Journal of Aesthetics* 46: 223–247.

Dilworth, J. (1998) "Is Ridley Charitable to Collingwood?" *Journal of Aesthetics and Art Criticism* 56: 393–396.

Dufrenne, M. (1953/1973) *The Phenomenology of Aesthetic Experience*, ed. E.S. Casey, trans. E.S. Casey, with A.A. Anderson, W. Domingo, and L. Jacobson, Evanston, IL: Northwestern University Press.

Elliott, R.K. (2006) *Aesthetics, Imagination, and the Unity of Experience*, ed. Paul Crowther, Farnham: Ashgate.

Gaut, B. (2003) "Creativity and Imagination," in B. Gaut and P. Livingston (eds.) *The Creation of Art: New Essays in Philosophical Aesthetics*, Cambridge: Cambridge University Press, 148–173.

Ginsborg, H. (1997) "Lawfulness without a Law: Kant on the Free Play of Imagination and Understanding," *Philosophical Topics* 25: 37–81.

Grant, J. (2012) "The Value of Imaginativeness," *Australasian Journal of Philosophy* 90: 275–289.

Guyer, P. (1979) *Kant and the Claims of Taste*, Cambridge, MA: Harvard University Press.

Guyer, P. (2006) "The Harmony of the Faculties Revisited," in R. Kukla (ed.) *Aesthetics and Cognition in Kant's Critical Philosophy*, Cambridge: Cambridge University Press, 162–193.

Hausman, C.R. (1998) "Aaron Ridley's Defense of Collingwood Pursued," *Journal of Aesthetics and Art Criticism* 56: 391–393.

Hopkins, R. (1992) Review of *Mimesis as Make-Believe: On the Foundations of the Representational Arts*, by K.L. Walton, *Philosophical Books* 33: 126–128.

Kant, I. (1790/2000) *Critique of the Power of Judgement*, ed. P. Guyer, trans. P. Guyer and E. Matthews, Cambridge: Cambridge University Press.

Kemp, G. (2003) "The Croce–Collingwood Theory as Theory," *Journal of Aesthetics and Art Criticism* 61: 171–193.

Kind, A. (2014) "The Heterogeneity of the Imagination," *Erkenntnis* 78: 141–159.

Kivy, P. (1993) "Differences," *Journal of Aesthetics and Art Criticism* 51: 123–132.

Kivy, P. (2006) *The Performance of Reading: An Essay in the Philosophy of Literature*, Oxford: Blackwell.

Levinson, J. (1992) "Intention and Interpretation: A Last Look," in G. Iseminger (ed.) *Intention and Interpretation*, Philadelphia: Temple University Press, 221–256.

Levinson, J. (1996) "Musical Expressiveness," in *The Pleasures of Aesthetics*, Ithaca: Cornell University Press, 90–125.

Levinson, J. (2010) "Defending Hypothetical Intentionalism," *British Journal of Aesthetics* 50: 139–150.

Lopes, D.M. (1998) "Imagination, Illusion and Experience in Film," *Philosophical Studies* 89: 343–353.

Matravers, D. (2014) *Fiction and Narrative*, Oxford: Oxford University Press.

McCloud, S. (1993) *Understanding Comics*, Northampton, MA: Kitchen Sink Press.

Mullin, A. (2004) "Moral Defects, Aesthetic Defects, and the Imagination," *Journal of Aesthetics and Art Criticism* 62: 249–261.

Nanay, B. (2004) "Taking Twofoldness Seriously: Walton on Imagination and Depiction," *Journal of Aesthetics and Art Criticism* 62: 285–289.

Nussbaum, M. (1998) "Exactly and Responsibly: A Defense of Ethical Criticism," *Philosophy and Literature* 22: 343–365.

Pettersson, M. (2011) "Seeing What Is Not There: Pictorial Experience, Imagination and Non-localization," *British Journal of Aesthetics* 51: 279–294.

Ridley, A. (1997) "Not Ideal: Collingwood's Expression Theory," *Journal of Aesthetics and Art Criticism* 55: 263–272.

Ridley, A. (1998a) "Collingwood's Commitments: A Reply to Hausman and Dilworth," *Journal of Aesthetics and Art Criticism* 56: 396–398.

Ridley, A. (1998b) *R.G. Collingwood: A Philosophy of Art*, London: Orion.

Ridley, A. (2007) "*Persona* Sometimes *Grata*: on the Appreciation of Expressive Music," in K. Stock (ed.) *Philosophers on Music: Experience, Meaning, and Work*, Oxford: Oxford University Press, 130–146.

Robson, J., and Meskin, A. (2012) "Videogames and the First-Person," in G. Currie, P. Kotako, and M. Pokorny (eds.) *Mimesis: Metaphysics, Cognition, Pragmatics*, London: College Publications.

Sadoski, M. (1998) "Mental Imagery in Reading: A Sampler of Some Significant Studies," *Reading Online*, <http://www.readingonline.org/past/past_index.asp?HREF=/research/Sadoski.html>.

Sartre, J.-P. (1940/2004) *The Imaginary*, trans. J. Webber, Abingdon: Routledge.

Savile, A. (1987) *Aesthetic Reconstructions: The Seminal Writings of Lessing, Kant, and Schiller*, Oxford: Blackwell.

Savile, A. (2006) "Imagination and Aesthetic Value," *British Journal of Aesthetics* 46: 248–258.

Scruton, R. (1974) *Art and Imagination*, London: Methuen.

Scruton, R. (1979) *The Aesthetics of Architecture*, Princeton: Princeton University Press.

Scruton, R. (1999) *The Aesthetics of Music*, Oxford: Oxford University Press.

Scruton, R. (2009) "Working towards Art," *British Journal of Aesthetics* 49: 317–325.

Stevenson, L.F. (2003) "Twelve Conceptions of Imagination," *British Journal of Aesthetics* 43: 238–259.

Stock, K. (2011) "Fiction and Imagination I," *Supplementary Proceedings of the Aristotelian Society* 85: 145–162.
Tavinor, G. (2009) *The Art of Videogames*, Oxford: Wiley-Blackwell.
Thomasson, A.L. (2004) "The Ontology of Art," in P. Kivy (ed.) *The Blackwell Guide to Aesthetics*, Oxford: Blackwell, 78–92.
Thomasson, A.L. (2006) "Debates about the Ontology of Art: What Are We Doing Here?" *Philosophy Compass* 1: 245–255.
Velleman, D. (2008) "Bodies, Selves," *American Imago* 65: 405–426.
Walton, K.L. (1990) *Mimesis as Make-Believe: On the Foundations of the Representational Arts*, Cambridge, MA: Harvard University Press.
Walton, K.L. (1991) "Reply to Reviewers," *Philosophy and Phenomenological Research* 51: 413–431.
Warnock, M. (1976) *Imagination*, Berkeley, CA: University of California Press.
Wilson, G. (1986) *Narration in Light: Studies in Cinematic Points of View*, Baltimore, MD: Johns Hopkins University Press.
Wittgenstein, L. (1968) *Zettel*, eds. G.E.M. Anscombe and G.H. von Wright, trans G.E.M. Anscombe, Oxford: Blackwell.
Wollheim, R. (1973) "On an Alleged Inconsistency in Collingwood's Aesthetic," in *On Art and the Mind*, London: Allen Lane, 250–260.
Wollheim, R. (1980a) *Art and Its Objects*, 2nd edn., Cambridge: Cambridge University Press.
Wollheim, R. (1980b) "Criticism as Retrieval," in *Art and Its Objects*, 2nd edn., Cambridge: Cambridge University Press, 185–204.
Wollheim, R. (1991) "A Note on *Mimesis as Make-Believe*," *Philosophy and Phenomenological Research* 51: 401–406.
Wollheim, R. (2003) "What Makes Representational Painting Truly Visual?" *Proceedings of the Aristotelian Society, Supplementary Volume* 77: 131–147.

# 14
# MUSIC AND IMAGINATION

*James O. Young*

## Introduction

Some musicians, musicologists and philosophers have defended the view that imagination plays a role in the apprehension of the expressive character of musical works. Many of these writers have argued that listeners imagine personae in music and that this is essential to grasping the full expressive character of music. Other writers, while denying that listeners imagine personae in music, have nevertheless held that imagination has an important role to play in understanding music. Philosophers who identify an important role for imagination are often reacting against certain influential views in philosophy of music. Consequently, in order to understand how imagination has come to play a role in some contemporary philosophy of music, it is necessary to know something about the current state of play in this philosophical subdiscipline.

This essay will focus on the philosophical literature on the role of imagination in listening to music. Some musicians have also emphasized the role of imagination in listening. For example, the distinguished American composer Aaron Copeland wrote that, "it is the freely imaginative mind that is at the core of all vital music making and music listening" (Copeland 1952, 7). Copeland does not, however, develop this point or fully describe the role that he thinks imagination plays in listening to music. There is also an emerging psychological literature on music and imagination. See, for example, the essays in Hargreaves et al. (2012). This psychological literature is, however, largely orthogonal to the philosophical literature. When psychologists say that imagination plays a role in listening to music, they seem to mean that the mind is active in listening. For example, they talk about how a listener's recall of other music can influence cognition of music. When philosophers say that imagination plays a role in listening to music they mean something quite different.

## The resemblance theory

A great deal of philosophy of music is concerned with the relationship between music and emotion. Music is often described using emotion predicates. A work of music is often characterized as, for example, joyful, agitated or melancholy. Some philosophers of music have regarded the use of such emotion predicates as misleading. These philosophers believe that emotion predicates, when applied to music, are used metaphorically and that music cannot be, in any literal sense, joyful, agitated or melancholy (Zangwill 2007). This is a minority position and most philosophers believe that when emotion predicates are used to describe music, these predicates are used in a way that is closely related to their normal, literal applications (Davies 2011, ch. 2). There are, however, many different views about the sense in which music is, say, triumphant, happy or sombre. Some philosophers believe that music is expressive of emotions, others believe that music expresses emotions, some believe that music arouses emotions, and still others believe that emotion is represented in music.

Understanding the distinction between music expressing emotion and music being expressive of emotion is important to understanding the role imagination plays in contemporary philosophy of music. To say that music expresses emotion is to say that music is a manifestation of, or revelatory of, someone's emotions. Often this person is taken to be the music's composer or performer. The view that music expresses the emotions of its composer (or performer) was held as early as the eighteenth century (Batteux 1746/2015) and was common in the nineteenth and early twentieth centuries (e.g., Collingwood 1938). This view fell into disfavor in the latter part of the twentieth century.

Some contemporary philosophers of music, notably Kivy (1989), have argued that music does not express emotion. Rather, they hold, music is expressive of emotion. To say that music is expressive of emotion is to say that it appears to manifest emotions without revealing an emotional state. Consider for example the drooping face of a basset hound. It appears to be sad, but may not express the dog's actual emotional state. On the contrary, the dog may have an uncommonly happy disposition. In short, the basset hound's face is expressive of sadness without expressing sadness. Music may similarly be expressive of some emotion without manifesting (and thus expressing) the emotion.

Music could be expressive of emotion by resembling expressive behavior. This sort of account of the relationship between music and emotion has been given a number of names: the "contour theory" (Kivy 1989), "appearance emotionalism" (Davies 1997), the "appearance-of-expression" view (Levinson 1996), and the "resemblance theory" (Cochrane 2010b). This article will speak of the resemblance theory.

The resemblance theory has a long pedigree and has its origins in the seventeenth century but it was given its classic statements by Kivy (1989) and Davies (1994). In essence, the resemblance theory is quite simple: a work of music *W* is expressive of emotion *E* iff properties of *W* resemble vocal or nonvocal behavior that is used in the expression of *E*. In other words, *W* possesses the property of being expressive of *E* only when it resembles behavior expressive of *E*. A basset hound's face is expressive of sadness since its face resembles a frown, which typically expresses sadness. A work of music is expressive of, say, melancholy since it resembles some vocal or nonvocal behavior that typically expresses melancholy. According to the resemblance theory, to say that a work of music is melancholy is to say that it is expressive of melancholy.

Some versions of the resemblance theory, notably Kivy (1989), are combined with skepticism about the capacity of music to express emotion. Kivy believes, rather implausibly, that the resemblance between music expressive of some emotion and behavior expressive of that emotion is accidental. Since, according to Kivy, composers do not intend to write music that is expressive of emotion, music does not express emotion. Nevertheless, the resemblance theory is compatible with the view that music can express emotion. So long as some composers intentionally compose music with features that make it expressive of emotion, the work may also be said to express emotion.

The resemblance theory enjoys considerable empirical support. Juslin and Laukka (2003) reviewed 140 studies and concluded that many musical works are experienced as resembling, in a variety of ways, human vocal behaviors that are expressive of various emotions. They conclude that many musical works are experienced as expressive of various emotions. Davies (1994) argues that experience of some music is also like experience of nonvocal behaviors expressive of emotion and that this makes this music expressive of these emotions. For example, the rhythm of a musical work may resemble the gait of a person in the grip of some emotion. This hypothesis also enjoys strong empirical support. For a review of the relevant empirical literature see Young (2014, 18–26).

As the resemblance theory is articulated by Davies (1994) and others, imagination plays little or no role in grasping that a work of music is expressive of *E*. Grasping that *W* is expressive of *E* is simply a matter of perceiving the resemblance between properties of *W* and behavior that is expressive of *E*. Some advocates of a resemblance theory hold that humans have a disposition to hear a resemblance between music and behavior expressive of emotions. That is, on some views we have a disposition to hear music as expressive of emotion or, as some writers say, to hear expressiveness in music. Kivy (1990) first suggested this possibility and it has since been developed by Levinson (1996).

The resemblance theory is compatible with both formalism and antiformalism. Formalism is the view that music is appreciated as pure musical form. That is, formalists hold that music is not about emotion or anything else, it does not express emotion, and does not represent anything. The resemblance theory makes possible what Kivy (1990) calls "enhanced formalism." Enhanced formalism is the view that music is pure musical form that happens (perhaps quite accidentally) to resemble human expressive behavior. At the same time, the resemblance theory can be incorporated into an antiformalist position, that is, one that holds that music is about or represents emotion (Young 2014).

Opponents of the resemblance theory typically do not reject it *in toto*. Rather, opponents typically hold that the theory is incomplete, as we will see in the next section. (Levinson [1996] explicitly says that his theory of musical expressiveness is a variety of resemblance theory.) Other writers hold that the sort of properties that Davies and others discuss, those that are expressive of emotion, are the basis for imaginings of various sorts. Listeners are, for example, prompted to imagine the existence of a persona who is expressing, say, melancholy when they hear music that (by resembling human expressive behavior) is expressive of that emotion.

Distinct from the questions of whether (and how) music is expressive of emotion or expresses emotion is the question of whether (and how) music arouses emotion. Kivy (1990) has influential views on the question of whether music arouses emotion. He is deeply skeptical about the view that music can arouse ordinary emotions such as joy, sadness or fear. (Kivy does allow that music may arouse a special "musical" emotion. This is a sort of awe or wonder in the face of musical beauty.) He is skeptical because he accepts a cognitive theory of emotions. According to this theory, a person cannot be in a particular emotional state without being in an appropriate corresponding belief state. For example, people cannot experience fear without believing that they face something dangerous. Since music does not put listeners in the appropriate belief states it cannot, Kivy believes, put them in the corresponding emotional states. (As will be noted below, this view is now widely regarded as incompatible with the available empirical evidence.) Believing that music cannot express or arouse emotion, Kivy also believes that music cannot represent emotion. Davies (1994), in contrast, does not deny that music can arouse some ordinary emotions and, in principle, the resemblance theory is compatible with music arousing a wide range of ordinary emotions.

The concept of imagination has been introduced into contemporary philosophy of music, at least in large part, as a result of a reaction against the views of Davies and, especially, Kivy. Some philosophers of music have rejected the view that we understand the full connection between music and emotion when we say that music is expressive of emotion (and can, perhaps, express emotion by being intended to be expressive of emotion). Some believe that music can represent emotion. Others have argued that music is expressive of emotions that the resemblance theory cannot explain. In the past, as we have noted, philosophers typically held that music expresses the emotions of an actual person (such as a composer). Often, this person was taken to be the composer or performer of the music. Philosophers of music who believe that music expresses emotion have usually not readopted this view. Instead, many philosophers arguing for the incompleteness of the resemblance theory have argued that the emotions expressed in music are of some imagined person or entity.

## Persona theories

When philosophers such as Robinson (2005) put a new emphasis on expression of emotion in their philosophies of music, they also introduced a major innovation. Music was no longer held to express the emotions of its composer or performer. Instead, these philosophers hold that a musical work, or a passage from such a work, expresses the emotions of some persona. A persona is the hypothetical person whose emotions are expressed in a work of music. A persona in music is distinct from the music's composer or performer. Sometimes personae are said to be *heard* in the music without the intervention of imagination. Other philosophers argue that personae are *imagined.*

Talk of personae in music can be traced back at least as far as the nineteenth century, but contemporary discussions of musical personae stem from the work of Cone (1974). On Cone's view, a work's persona is its composer. That is, his position can be seen as the continuation of the traditional view that music expresses its composer's emotions. Other writers, including Ridley (1995), Levinson (1996, 2006), Robinson (2005), Robinson and Hatten (2012) and Cochrane (2010a) distinguish persona in a work from its composer. I will refer to any view that personae play a role in appreciating or understanding music as a *persona theory*.

The suggestion that a complete account of musical expressiveness involves reference to personae gives rise to two questions. The first question concerns whether reference to personae is, in fact, part of a satisfactory account of the relationship between music and emotion. The second question asks whether imagination plays a role in the introduction of personae into a theory of musical expressiveness.

Several reasons have been advanced for introducing talk of personae in music. Some authors, including Cochrane (2010a) and Levinson (2006), have held that if music expresses an emotion, there must be a person whose emotions are expressed. After all, they reason, emotion cannot exist without a person who possesses the emotion. The resemblance theory has been charged with being unable to explain why listeners respond emotionally to works of music (Robinson and Hatten 2012). That is, the resemblance theory is thought to be incompatible with the fact that music arouses emotions such as joy and sadness. Robinson (2005) and Cochrane (2010a) have maintained that the resemblance theory cannot explain how music can be experienced as the expression of complex emotions, such as hope or jealousy, or sequences of emotions, such as anger that gives way to sorrow and then renewed joy. They do so on the grounds that certain emotions have no customary associated behavior. A persona theory has an advantage, it is held, because a persona is imagined to be a real person, with a full range of emotions.

Suppose for a moment that we have good reason to believe that personae play a role in understanding the relationship between music and emotion. We then need to ask whether imagination plays a role in the introduction of personae. Some of those committed to the existence of personae in music believe that personae are not imagined. As we have noted, Cone (1974) believes that personae in music are actual (the composers of the music) and not imagined. Ridley (1995) seems to have been among the first philosophers to talk about personae in music and to distinguish them from the composer. He does not say that personae are imagined. Instead, he speaks of hearing music as the expression of a persona. At other times he speaks of the "construction" of a persona. (To construct a persona may be to imagine it.) Levinson (1996) also seems committed to the view that listeners hear a persona in music without committing himself to the view that the persona is imagined. On his view, a passage *P* from a work of music is expressive of an emotion *E* iff *P* is heard as the expression of *E* by the music's persona. (This persona has no particular character.) For present purposes, the crucial words are "heard as": grasp of the expressive character of a composition does not require an act of imagination. Although Levinson (1996) contains no mention of imagination, Robinson and Hatten write that Levinson's analysis of musical expressiveness involves an "imagined persona" (Robinson and Hatten 2012, 78) and in one passage Levinson (2006, 193) speaks of "hearing an agent [i.e., persona] in the music ... or at least imagining such an agent." Nevertheless, Levinson's considered view seems to be that personae are heard in music, not imagined.

Other philosophers committed to the existence of personae in music explicitly hold that personae are imagined. Robinson and Hatten refer to "an imagined persona" (Robinson and Hatten 2012, 78). Cochrane is also clearly committed to the view that personae in music are imagined. While most defenders of a persona hypothesis are committed to a featureless persona, Cochrane advocates "imaginative fleshing out of the persona" (Cochrane 2010a, 267). We can imagine, for example, when listening to Beethoven's String Quartet No. 15, that we are hearing Beethoven recover from an illness and regain his vigor. Cochrane believes that this is a perfectly normal and acceptable sort of way to listen to music, given that humans tend to seek patterns and meaning in experience.

Trivedi (2001) adopts a position that is, in certain respects, similar to that adopted by writers who believe that listeners imagine personae in music. He holds that, "in hearing music as expressive we make-believedly animate the music itself so that the music *itself* is imaginatively experienced as *the very being* that is animate and whose emotions are being expressed musically" (414). The music itself is the persona on this view. Trivedi's reason for believing that listeners imagine that music is animate seems similar to a reason provided by persona theorists. Trivedi takes as an example the opening of Beethoven's Ninth Symphony. He holds that it is experienced as expressing exuberant joy. Trivedi suggests that there must be someone whose exuberant joy is expressed since joy cannot exist independently of someone who experiences the joy. Trivedi (2001) seems to take it as evident that the music, not a persona independent of the music, is imagined to be the possessor of the emotion. Trivedi does not explain how a work of music could possess some emotion.

Elsewhere Trivedi (2006) allows that an indefinite persona can be the imagined possessor of an emotion. He has also suggested that imagination has other roles in our experience of music. For example, he has suggested that listeners can imaginatively identify with the music and imagine that their own emotions are expressed. Trivedi also holds that listeners sometimes imagine that the happiness, say, expressed in a work of music belongs to the instruments on which the music is played. How this might be possible is not explained.

The view that personae are imagined in music needs to be distinguished from another use of imagination. There is a good deal of experimental evidence for the conclusion that some individuals engage in imaginings or form visual images while listening to music (Juslin and Västfjäll 2008). These imaginings arouse emotions and have an impact on how music is experienced. Philosophers have tended to discount this use of imagination in the experience of music. It is regarded as a sort of daydreaming, and not as a legitimate aesthetic response to a musical work. Kivy (2007) disparages it as "wool-gathering." Even someone such as Robinson (2008), who is committed to a role for imagination, denies that image formation contributes to the grasping of a work's expressive properties. On her view, listeners only imagine a persona. The emotional life of this persona is found in the music and not made up whole cloth.

Little attention has been paid to the question of why we should prefer the hypothesis that personae are imagined to the hypothesis that they are heard in music. Cochrane briefly considers this question. Suppose that listeners approach music with the belief that it has been designed by a human being. A persona would then be a "fairly automatic illusion" (Cochrane 2010b, 203). Since Cochrane believes that acts of imagination are deliberate, it follows that personae are not imagined but, rather, heard in the music. If listeners do not assume that works of music are designed by a human being, Cochrane suggests, a deliberate act of imagination will be needed to produce a persona. It is hard to see how listeners would not approach music with the belief that a composer has deliberately designed it. Nevertheless, as noted, Cochrane favors the view that personae are imagined.

In assessing the persona theory, we need to begin by asking whether the experience of music in emotion necessarily implies experience of an imagined persona who possesses the emotion. The form of the crucial argument of persona theorists is something rather like the form of a Kantian transcendental argument: a persona is a necessary condition of the existence of emotions and emotions exist, therefore a persona exists. This argument is less persuasive than it might be when we recall that no one suggests that emotion actually exists in a work of music. Rather, music contains only some sort of portrayal of emotions (or is somehow expressive of emotion). Some distinguished musicians have held that music portrays emotions. For example, Beethoven wrote that his Sixth Symphony is "a [record of] sentiments," that is, emotions (Beethoven 1951, 68). Similarly, Berlioz spoke of "depict[ing] a sentiment" in his music (Berlioz n.d., 52). Neither composer refers to a persona who possesses the sentiment (or emotion). If these composers are right, the question becomes whether a composer can provide a record or depiction of an emotion without depicting the person who has the emotion. This seems possible. A work of music could be about melancholy in general and not about the melancholy of anyone in particular. A listener could imagine a persona who is melancholy, but this does not seem to be prescribed by the music.

Next one might ask, by way of assessing the persona hypothesis, how commonly listeners hear or imagine a persona in music. Davies (1997) is skeptical about the claim that many listeners hear or imagine a persona in music. Presumably, however, some listeners, among them advocates of the persona theory, do hear or imagine personae in music. There is experimental evidence that some listeners engage in imaginings while listening to music but, at the same time, there is experimental evidence that many do not (DeNora 2000). Likely some listeners imagine personae in music and others do not.

Arguably the important question is whether hearing a persona in music is required for listeners to fully grasp the expressive content of a piece of music. Sometimes it is plausible to say that understanding of the expressive content a piece of music requires awareness of a persona. I would say that this is true in the case of Berlioz's *Symphonie Fantastique*. This work is, however, a piece of program music (that is, music with a text or program that explains what the music portrays) in which the composer intends a persona to be heard: it is not imagined. A similar point could be made about some music with lyrics. A setting of the *Stabat Mater* could be heard as an expression of Mary's emotions (she is the persona). Persona theorists want, however, to go further and hold, in effect, that all music is program music. One can wonder whether imagining a persona in music is part of the appreciation or understanding of a work of music, as opposed to free association, when a composer has not intended a persona to be heard in the music. Advocates of the persona hypothesis maintain, however, that unless listeners imagine a persona, part of the expressive character of music is lost.

One can wonder whether Robinson and Hatten (2012) are right in holding that only the persona theory can explain certain features of our experience of music. Consider, for a start, the suggestion that only a persona theory can explain our emotional engagement with music. The resemblance theory, one could hold, explains how we hear music as expressive of emotion but cannot explain the fact that listeners are themselves moved to feel emotions when they hear music. When listeners imagine a persona, however, they may be expected to feel emotions just as readers of a novel are moved to feel emotions by the tribulations of some fictional persona.

It is true that some versions of the resemblance theory (for example, Kivy 1989) are combined with the view that music cannot arouse ordinary emotions such as happiness and melancholy. The resemblance theory is, however, completely consistent with the view that music arouses ordinary emotions in listeners. Indeed, if music is expressive of emotion, it is to be expected that it will also arouse emotion. It will do so, for example, by means of mechanisms such as emotional contagion: experimental evidence suggests that listeners "catch" the emotions of which music is expressive. Several other ways in which music arouses emotion, all of them consistent with the resemblance theory, have been identified. See Juslin and Västfjäll (2008) for a discussion of the mechanisms by which music arouses emotions.

Robinson and Hatten (2012) argue that only when listeners imagine a persona can music express complex emotions such as yearning, resignation and nostalgia. The resemblance theory seems committed to the view that music can be expressive of (and thus potentially express) only emotions with associated expressive behavior. There are certain behaviors associated with, say, sadness: leaden movement, a voice that tails away, and so on. Music is plausibly held to be expressive of sadness when it resembles these behaviors. An emotion such as nostalgia, however, arguably has no associated behavior. One could conclude that the resemblance theory cannot explain how listeners can hear emotions such as nostalgia or resignation in music. And yet, Robinson and Hatten believe they can. They conclude that listeners imagine personae.

Two responses to this argument are available. Davies (1997) takes the first option when he expresses skepticism about music's capacity to be expressive of (or express) complex, sophisticated emotions such as nostalgia or jealousy. The other possibility is to argue that the resemblance theory can account for listeners' experience of music as, say, nostalgic, yearning or resigned. (There is experimental evidence that listeners hear music as nostalgic. Nostalgia is one of the emotions on the Geneva Emotional Music Scale, an instrument used in studying emotional responses to music. (See Zentner et al. 2008.) Arguably, complex emotions such as nostalgia and hope are the results of patterns of simpler emotions. If so, an advocate of the resemblance theory can argue that music is expressive of complex emotions by being expressive of patterns of simpler emotions.

A resemblance theory that allows that music can arouse emotion potentially has additional resources for explaining how music can be experienced as expressing complex emotions. It can be combined, for example, with the sort of theory that originates in Meyer (1956). Meyer indicates that familiarity with common musical patterns (such as the tendency in common practice composition for certain chords to be resolved in certain ways) can lead listeners to form musical expectations. The realization or frustration of these expectations may arouse a variety of complex emotions. Anxiety may be aroused when listeners doubt that an anticipated musical outcome will be attained. Hope can be aroused when listeners look forward to a desired musical outcome. Levinson (1990) argues in this way that music can be expressive of hope. Musical personae are incorporated into his argument, but the argument can be run without them. It is not clear that persona theory enjoys clear advantages over the resemblance theory.

The persona theory faces difficulties of its own. Davies (2011, ch. 1) has identified one of the most pressing of these difficulties. Davies charges that the properties of a musical work (or a musical performance) will be compatible with any number of accounts of a persona and narratives of its emotional life. One listener may imagine that a work is a persona's expression of joy while another listener takes the same work to be expressive of another persona's explosive anger. One listener may imagine that a work of music is expressive of a persona becoming increasingly despondent. Another listener may imagine that the work expresses the sadness of a series of personae, each more unhappy than the previous one. Nothing about a work, Davies maintains, makes the choice of one interpretation better than another. Advocates of the persona hypothesis will hold that Davies' worries are unfounded. They can maintain that a careful study of a piece of music will reveal that certain interpretations are correct and others wrong.

Arguably the debate between the resemblance theory and the persona hypothesis needs to be resolved by appeal to individual works of music. Advocates of the persona hypothesis recognize this and often support their view by nuanced interpretations of individual works. See, for example, the reading of Shostakovich's Tenth Symphony by Karl and Robinson (1995) or the reading of Mendelssohn's *The Hebrides* by Levinson (1990). If the best interpretations of many works require reference to personae, the persona hypothesis would enjoy strong confirmation.

Some of the concerns expressed here apply to any version of persona theory. The view that listeners imagine a persona in music faces an additional challenge. Arguably this hypothesis faces a dilemma, neither horn of which is attractive to advocates of the position. Suppose that we ask whether something in the music justifies the positing of a persona. The first possibility is that advocates of imagined personae answer this question affirmatively. That is, they grant that something is heard in works of music that suggests a persona. There are several reasons why this answer is attractive. A reason for holding that personae are part of our experience of music is that composers intend that personae be heard in their works and they craft their compositions in such a way as to make them audible. Moreover, advocates of imagined personae need a way to explain why personae are part of the experience of certain works but not others. This explanation will make reference to features of the music. It seems to follow that the persona is not imagined, but heard in the music. Obviously, persona theorists will find this conclusion anathema. Advocates of imagined personae could grasp the second horn of the dilemma and maintain that nothing in a work of music dictates the introduction of a persona. Imagination is then necessary to generate the persona and its emotional life, but this horn of the dilemma is as unattractive as the first. It seems then that the creation of a persona has nothing to do with a musical composition. A persona is not an apprehension of something in the music but simply a flight of fancy unrelated to the composition.

## Imagination without personae

Of the theories of musical expressiveness that have a role for imagination, persona theories have been most widely adopted in recent years. Several other theories of expressiveness have, however, emerged in which imagination plays an important role but personae do not. Here I will survey the theories of Walton (1994), Nussbaum (2007) and Noordhof (2008).

Walton holds that our "experiences of music seem shot through with imaginings" (Walton 1994, 52). In his view, the role imagination plays in the experience of music opens up the possibility that music is a representational art. (Walton holds that there is no hard and fast distinction between program music and absolute music. Presumably any music can be transformed into program music if one listens with imagination.) Walton's strategy is to apply his more general views on representation to the case of music. According to Walton (1990) a representation is a prop in a game of make-believe (see Kathleen Stock's Chapter 15 on "Imagination and fiction"). For example, a stick waved by a girl represents a magic wand because the girl makes believe (or imagines) that the stick is a magic wand in the game she is playing. Similarly, a drawing of a castle represents a castle because viewers of the drawing make believe that it is a castle.

A work of music is representational, Walton suggests, if it too is a prop in a game of make-believe. He entertains, only to reject, the possibility that musical works have fictional worlds in the way that, say, a novel does. So Walton rejects the suggestion that a description of (purely instrumental) musical works can justify narratives about persons moving through space. That is, music does not provide props for a game of make-believe in which persons move around a fictional world. Instead, Walton suggests that listeners imagine that they are experiencing certain emotions when hearing music.

It is doubtful that Walton succeeds in extending his account of representation to the case of music. On Walton's general view, something is a representation if someone make-believes or imagines something of it. In the examples just given, someone imagines that something is a magic wand or that it is a castle. But in the case of music, Walton seems to believe, listeners do not imagine anything about the music. Any imagining listeners do is about themselves and their emotions. So, according to Walton's general theory of representation, the music does not represent anything. If, as Walton believes, music is representational, it is not representational in the way described by Walton's general theory of representation. Walton's troubles are compounded by the fact there is no need for listeners to imagine that they are experiencing emotions when listening to music. Ample empirical evidence exists for the view that listeners actually experience emotions such as joy and sadness while listening to music. (For a review of the literature on the arousal of ordinary emotion by music, see Young 2014, ch. 2.)

Nussbaum (2007) presents a challenging account of the experience of music that is influenced by cognitive science and existential phenomenology. Like Walton, Nussbaum aims to show that music is a representational art. Nussbaum explicitly states that all music is program music. (At any rate, all Western art music composed since about 1650 is.) Nussbaum's account of representation in music provides an important role for imagination. He writes that "[t]he listener constructs models of layouts and scenarios in virtual musical space in which he moves in imagination" (Nussbaum 2007, 21). Nussbaum's position has been interpreted as a species of persona theory (Cochrane 2010a) but the position seems more akin to one that Walton considered and rejected. On Nussbaum's view, listeners do not imagine personae.

Rather they imagine themselves in motion through musical space. The negotiation of this musical space arouses emotions in listeners and Nussbaum concludes that music is a representation of "an emotionally charged virtual musical environment" (Nussbaum 2007, 251).

One can doubt whether listeners engage imaginatively with music in the way that Nussbaum suggests that they do. Empirical studies suggest that music is experienced as resembling motions expressive of certain emotions but I know of no experimental evidence for the claim that listeners imagine themselves moving through space while listening to music. Anecdotal evidence for Nussbaum's position is also limited. Even among philosophers who believe that imagination plays an important role in experience of music, Nussbaum appears to be alone (or in a small minority) in believing that listeners imagine themselves moving through an emotionally charged virtual musical space. More importantly, one can wonder whether imaginings of the sort that Nussbaum has in mind are sanctioned by expressive properties of works of music. If not, then any imaginings in which a listener engages are not part of an appreciation of a musical work.

Noordhof (2008) adopts another position according to which imagination plays a role in the recognition of music's expressive qualities. It has, perhaps, more in common with a persona theory than it has with the ideas of either Walton or Nussbaum. Noordhof's theory, like many others, begins from the perceived inadequacy (or incompleteness) of the resemblance theory: "A resemblance [between music and human expressive behavior], however strong, is not sufficient to explain how something is heard as expressing that which it resembles" (Noordhof 2008, 332). In order to hear the properties of music that resemble human expressive behavior as expressing emotion, listeners imagine a creative process that would result in the production of these properties. Listeners do not imagine they have certain emotions (as Walton holds) and listeners do not imagine a persona who has emotions (as Robinson and Cochrane believe).

Noordhof clarifies his proposal by reference to Collingwood (1938). Collingwood holds that an artist's expression of emotions amounts to the artist becoming clear about precisely which emotion he feels. Creating a work of art involves going through a process of clarifying one's emotions. Noordhof calls this process an emotion-guided creative process and it is this process that, he believes, listeners imagine when they hear a work of music as expressing some emotion. An example may also help clarify Noordhof's position. He asks us to suppose that listeners hear the Badinerie from Bach's Orchestral Suite No. 2, BWV 1067, as expressing joy. In this case, listeners "are imagining how joy may manifest itself in that way just as we see how someone's bodily behaviour expresses joy by imagining the twitch to prance about and caper" (Noordhof 2008, 339).

Noordhof allows that listeners can, say, hear a work of music as sad without imagining an emotion-guided creative process. (Presumably he means that listeners can hear music as expressive of sadness without imagining an emotion-guided creative process.) He simply denies that listeners can hear the work as *expressing* sadness (or any other emotion) without imagining this process. Philosophers who advocate the resemblance theory will not see the need to imagine an emotion-guided creative process. They can, like Kivy (1989), deny that music expresses emotion, or like Davies (1994) hold that they have a simpler and empirically supported account of how music expresses emotion.

All of the philosophers considered in this section draw attention to an important, and sometimes overlooked, feature of the experience of music. Music is experienced in different ways by different listeners, and by the same listener on different occasions and when listening to different pieces of music. If listeners approach music with the intention of hearing it as expressive of emotion or as representing emotion, they enhance their chances of hearing music in these ways. Whether this involves listening with imagination or merely listening with an ear for music's expressive properties can be debated. On the other hand, if listeners approach music with the intention of experiencing it as pure, contentless form, they are unlikely to find anything more than musical form.

## Conclusion

In recent years, various challenges have been mounted to the resemblance theory. Arguably these challenges have shown that the original resemblance theories of Kivy (1989) and Davies (1994) need, at least, to be supplemented. Many of these challenges maintain that imagination plays a role in listeners' experience of music. Frequently these theories maintain that, in grasping the expressive properties of music, listeners imagine personae whose emotions are expressed in the music. Other theories hold that listeners imagine creative processes or engage in imaginings about themselves, their emotions and their motions. Suggestions that imagination plays an important role in grasping the expressive character of music are all fairly recent developments. It remains to be seen which, if any, will prove to have enduring interest. The persona theory currently looks to have the best chance of enjoying philosophical longevity.

## References


Batteux, C. (1746/2015) *The Fine Arts Reduced to a Single Principle*, trans. J. Young, Oxford: Oxford University Press.

Beethoven, L. (1951) *Letters, Journals and Conversations*, trans. M. Hamburger, London: Jonathan Cape.

Berlioz, H. (n.d.) *Life of Hector Berlioz as Written by Himself in His Letters and Memories*, trans. K. Boult, London: J.M. Dent & Sons.

Cochrane, T. (2010a) "Using the Persona to Express Complex Emotions in Music," *Music Analysis* 29: 264–275.

Cochrane, T. (2010b) "A Simulation Theory of Musical Expressivity," *Australasian Journal of Philosophy* 88: 191–207.

Collingwood, R. (1938) *Principles of Art*, Oxford: Oxford University Press.

Cone, E. (1974) *The Composer's Voice*, Berkeley: University of California Press.

Copeland, A. (1952) *Music and Imagination*, Cambridge, MA: Harvard University Press.

Davies, S. (1994) *Musical Meaning and Expression*, Ithaca: Cornell University Press.

Davies, S. (1997) "Contra the Hypothetical Persona in Music," in M. Hjort and S. Laver (eds.) *Emotion and the Arts*, Oxford: Oxford University Press, 95–109.

Davies, S. (2011) *Musical Understandings and Other Essays on the Philosophy of Music*, Oxford: Oxford University Press.

DeNora, T. (2000) *Music in Everyday Life*, Cambridge: Cambridge University Press.

Hargreaves, D., D. Miell, and R. MacDonald (eds.) (2012) *Musical Imaginations: Multidisciplinary Perspectives on Creativity, Performance, and Perception*, Oxford: Oxford University Press.

Juslin, P., and P. Laukka (2003) "Communication of Emotions in Vocal Expression and Music Performance: Different Channels, Same Code?" *Psychological Bulletin* 129: 770–814.

Juslin, P., and D. Västfjäll (2008) "Emotional Responses to Music: The Need to Consider Underlying Mechanisms," *Behavioral and Brain Sciences* 31: 559–621.

Karl, G., and J. Robinson (1995) "Shostakovich's Tenth Symphony and the Musical Expression of Cognitively Complex Emotions," *Journal of Aesthetics and Art Criticism* 53: 401–415.

Kivy, P. (1989) *Sound Sentiment: An Essay on the Musical Emotions, Including the Complete Text of "The Corded Shell,"* Philadelphia, PA: Temple University Press.

Kivy, P. (1990) *Music Alone: Philosophical Reflections on the Purely Musical Experience*, Ithaca: Cornell University Press.

Kivy, P. (2007) "Moodophilia: A Response to Noël Carroll and Margaret Moore," *Journal of Aesthetics and Art Criticism* 65: 323–329.

Levinson, J. (1990) "Hope in *The Hebrides*," in *Music, Art, and Metaphysics: Essays in Philosophical Aesthetics*, Ithaca: Cornell University Press, 336–375.
Levinson, J. (1996) "Musical Expressiveness," in *The Pleasures of Aesthetics: Philosophical Essays*, Ithaca: Cornell University Press, pp. 90–125.
Levinson, J. (2006) "Musical Expressiveness as Hearability-as-Expression," in M. Kieran (ed.) *Contemporary Debates in Aesthetics and the Philosophy of Art*, Malden, MA: Blackwell, 192–204.
Meyer, L. (1956) *Emotion and Meaning in Music*, Chicago: University of Chicago Press.
Noordhof, P. (2008) "Expressive Perception as Projective Imagining," *Mind & Language* 23: 329–358.
Nussbaum, C. (2007) *The Musical Representation: Meaning, Ontology, and Emotion*, Cambridge, MA: MIT Press.
Ridley, A. (1995) *Music, Value and the Passions*, Ithaca: Cornell University Press.
Robinson, J. (2005) *Deeper than Reason: Emotion and its Role in Literature, Music, and Art*, Oxford: Clarendon Press.
Robinson, J. (2008) "Do All Musical Emotions Have the Music Itself as Their Intentional Object?" *Behavioral and Brain Science* 31: 392–393.
Robinson, J., and R. Hatten (2012) "Emotions in Music," *Music Theory Spectrum* 34: 71–106.
Trivedi, S. (2001) "Expressiveness as a Property of the Music Itself," *Journal of Aesthetics and Art Criticism* 59: 411–420.
Trivedi, S. (2006) "Imagination, Music, and the Emotions," *Revue Internationale de Philosophie* 4(238): 415–435.
Walton, K. (1990) *Mimesis as Make-Believe: On the Foundations of the Representational Arts*, Cambridge, MA: Harvard University Press.
Walton, K. (1994) "Listening with Imagination: Is Music Representational?" *Journal of Aesthetics and Art Criticism* 52: 47–61.
Young, J. (2014) *Critique of Pure Music*, Oxford: Oxford University Press.
Zangwill, N. (2007) "Music, Metaphor and Emotion," *Journal of Aesthetics and Art Criticism* 65: 391–400.
Zentner, M., D. Grandjean, and K. Scherer (2008) "Emotions Evoked by the Sound of Music: Characterization, Classification, and Measurement," *Emotion* 8: 494–521.

# 15
# IMAGINATION AND FICTION

*Kathleen Stock*

What is fiction? It permeates contemporary life: via novels we read, stories we tell, box-sets we watch, and, as philosophers, thought experiments we use. Many think it should be characterized in terms of a relation to the *imagination*. In this essay, I'll consider prominent expressions of this view, as well as rejections of it. Before this, I'll introduce two methodological approaches that it's helpful to distinguish.

## Methodology

One method of addressing "what is fiction?" is via conceptual analysis (CA). I identify this in terms of a goal: aiming to capture, in terms of a limited set of governing conditions, the thing identified by ordinary language/"the folk" as *fiction* (italicized to denote the concept). Objections to this approach tend to proceed by counterexample: looking for things counted as fictions by the folk but that don't satisfy any conditions offered as necessary; or, where sufficient conditions are offered, things that aren't counted as fictions, but do.

There are certain drawbacks to this approach. Ordinary language categorizations can be nonoptimal in various ways: messy, obfuscatory, reflecting the varying contexts of their application as usage expands. Most ordinary language concepts seem to be family resemblance concepts, governed by a potentially wide range of sufficient conditions, admitted into public language via the noticing of resemblances with established cases. To take Wittgenstein's famous case of *game*, it seems plausible to think that, when introduced, "computer games" were classed as *games* by resemblances with some subset of games (e.g., board games) but not others (e.g., cricket games), and not by reference to the possession of some esoteric essence shared with all games. There's little reason to think *fiction* will be different. This point might be accommodated, as it is in other discussions (e.g., Gaut 2000) by offering a "cluster account," i.e., a disjunctive list of sufficient conditions. However it isn't clear what benefit this would bring. An exhaustive list of the relatively diverse conditions sufficient for application of the concept *fiction* is not of obvious explanatory value.

Alternatively, one might offer an "explanatory theory" (ET). The primary goal of an explanatory theory is, unsurprisingly, to offer explanatory power. Examples might include: helping explain relations between entities in an enlightening way, and solving puzzles about them; fitting nicely with scientific discoveries about mind/behavior; or justifying some aspect(s) of our current practice. Ideally, the theory should also aim to display traditional theoretical virtues: for instance, to cover a wide range of interesting cases; and to be simple and elegant relative to rivals.

An ET of *x* aims to informatively supplement or even transform our understanding of a given phenomenon, via the relatively stipulative introduction of the term "*x*." Ideally an ET will at least fit with some uncontroversial cases of the original folk concept, in order to avoid the impression of talking past the original topic. However, the account may also permissibly include many items not ordinarily classified as "*x*," or exclude others ordinarily so classified. In effect, an ET may be taken as a provocation to redraw our classifications: even thoroughly so. In contrast, while CA permits occasional rejection of at least some ordinary intuitions about particular cases, it remains largely deferential to ordinary language usage; in so rejecting, the idea is to bring out what is already implicit in the folk concept (Jackson 2000, 35).

Should an explanatory theory be looking for a small set of necessary and jointly sufficient conditions? I suggest yes; not because of any residual superstition that the associated ordinary language concept must be governed by such conditions (after all, that isn't the target here), but because this makes for a more effective theory. To offer such conditions is to give a clear account of what the theoretical target is, and what it's differentiated from. This is a valuable goal.

As noted, in practice it may often be unclear (even to a view's own author) which methodological model is the goal. A familiar approach is to claim to be analyzing an existing concept, but to take some ordinary language commitments as "central" to the concept, and reject others. Whether this counts as CA or an ET in a given case depends on what goal the author is reasonably taken as most committed to: are the preferred commitments "central" because of their explanatory value, or "central" because deeply embedded in ordinary usage, at least implicitly? Sometimes, the answer might be "both," in which case it is even harder to distinguish. Importantly, the mere fact of a theory's sharing commitments with ordinary language concepts does not entail that it counts as CA rather than ET – this may be because those commitments offer great explanatory power in some respect, and are retained in the theory because of this fact.

I turn now to an examination of particular accounts of fiction. Where it's not easy to tell whether, broadly speaking, a CA or an ET is being offered, I will consider both interpretations.

## "Imagining Plus ..."

Here's a sketch of one popular approach to fiction. Broadly speaking, it's the approach of Gregory Currie, Peter Lamarque and Stein Olsen, and David Davies. I'll call it "Imagining Plus" or IP for short. The approach concerns fictional texts, though the approach might be extended to visual fictions too (Currie 1990, 39).

Though nomenclature varies,[1] the primary target of IP is "the fictive utterance" (Lamarque and Olsen 1994, 32–33; Davies 2007, 45–48; for a view which denies this, see Davies 2012). A "fictive utterance" is characterized as the sort of utterance where, if a sufficient number are present in a text, the whole counts, for that reason, as a fiction. That is, it's what we might call a "fiction-making unit" (my term). These accounts offer at least one necessary condition upon fiction, as a whole: it must contain fictive utterances. However, the primary aim of IP remains to offer necessary, jointly sufficient conditions for the fictive utterance, not for fiction (or not directly).

According to IP, it's a necessary condition upon a fictive utterance that the utterance *prescribes imagining*: in uttering, its author intends, and intends to communicate her intention, that the reader (or hearer) should imagine the utterance's content, as a response to understanding it (Currie 1990, 25; Lamarque and Olsen 1994, 77; Davies 2007, 42). A fictive utterance with content "*p*" (e.g., the sentence in Enid Blyton's *Five Go to Smuggler's Top* "George's father was a scientist, always working out new ideas") prescribes, in this sense, imagining that *p* (imagining that *George's father was a scientist, always working out new ideas*). So, on IP, fiction is characterized, partly at least, as originating in a particular kind of authorial intention: an intention that story content be imagined.

This commitment of IP has a forebear in Searle's claim that a fictive utterance necessarily involves its author pretending to assert its content (Searle 1975, 332). This has been criticized by proponents of IP (Currie 1990, 13–18; Lamarque and Olsen 1994, 41; Davies 2007, 38–41). Its most obvious problem is that, on any plausible notion of pretense, it seems empirically false that authors of fictions pretend to be asserting what they write. An act of pretense appears to require at least the thought of an audience for one's act; I can't pretend to, say, knit, unless I'm in front of an audience or at least imagining being witnessed. It is not plausible that all or even many authors of fictions imagine this as they write. Indeed, arguably authors needn't even imagine what they write is true, let alone pretend to assert it (Lamarque and Olsen 1994, 41).

It seems more promising to say that authors of fictions intend that their *readers* imagine things in response to their words, rather than pretend to do anything *themselves* via those words. As a necessary condition upon fictive utterance, this looks more attractive. It seems obvious that utterances in fictions ask us to consciously have some propositional attitude that involves thinking of the scenarios described as occurring, or as having occurred. But they don't seem to ask us (exclusively, anyway) to *believe* that content. This has looked to most like a kind of imagining.

So far, we have an account apparently similar-looking to a famous one offered by Kendall Walton. Walton (1990) offers a view according to which *x* is a fiction iff *x* functions as a prop in a game of imagining (he calls imagining "make-believe"). Because it makes a relation to imagining the only definitive feature of fiction, I'll call this sort of view "Imagining Only" (IO for short; I discuss a different version below). Walton's view has been extensively and clearly described by Friend (2008) and so I need not reduplicate details here. The main point to grasp for our purposes is that it differs from IP in two ways, as follows.

The first is that the relation to imagining cited by Walton as definitive of fiction is *functioning as a prop in a game of imagining*. This is a broader relation than the relation focused on IP, which is *being an utterance prescribing imagining*. An object may function as a prop in a game of imagining without being an utterance or being intended by any maker to prompt any particular response. For instance, a cloud or even cracks in a rock (Walton 1990, 86) may function for some imaginers in this way and so count as fiction on Walton's view. This leaves us with a very wide class of "fictions" indeed, a point exacerbated by Walton's reluctance to characterize imagining in any substantial way (Walton 1990, 19–21). As emphasized by Friend (2008) this is reasonably understood as an ET and not CA of fiction; it's not a strike against it, that it delineates a category considerably wider than the folk concept. However, what the theory gains in scope, it loses in ability to make satisfying distinctions: though it might be interesting to discover that clouds and novels appear in the same explanatory category, we presumably *also* want some more fine-grained category into which to put novels – along with some poems, short stories, thought experiments, and so on – but not clouds or photographs.

The second way in which IP differs from Walton's version of IO is one that promises to helpfully narrow down the theoretical target. That is, IP offers, in addition to a condition citing imagining, a *second* necessary condition upon fictive utterance in order to narrow the target (hence "Plus"). More precisely, each proponent of IP offers a slightly different extra condition. These respective conditions are at least partly motivated on the basis of four thought experiments originally introduced by Currie (1990, 42–44). In two, an author deliberately reproduces in a text what he knows to be factual, learnt from a newspaper in one case, and garnered from life experience in another. However, he intentionally prescribes imagining via the text, in the sense indicated above. In the other two, an author *unwittingly* produces a text that is factual – in one because he doesn't know his source is reliable, and in another because he has repressed memories of the events he describes – but again prescribes imagining via that text.

Currie thinks that ordinary usage would deny that these count as fictions, because in each case, the text is nonaccidentally true. In order to accommodate this, he makes it an additional condition upon fictive utterance "*p*" that "*p*" be false or at most accidentally true (Currie 1990, 46). Lamarque and Olsen read the same thought experiments differently: they think they reveal that "how things are (in the fiction) is determined by how they are described to be in a fictive utterance" and not by any correspondence with the world (Lamarque and Olsen 1994, 51). Presumably for related reasons, they claim as necessary for a fictive utterance "*p*" that any inference from it that the author believes that *p* would be inappropriate (Lamarque and Olsen 1994, 44). Davies argues that Currie's thought experiments show that for fictive utterance "*p*" the author's *reason* for uttering "*p*" cannot be to say something true, even if something true is thereby nonaccidentally said (Davies 2007, 46).

So to sum up so far: according to IP, a fiction is a thing that must contain some (unspecified) number of fictive utterances. Fictive utterances are utterances that: first, necessarily are intended by their author to prompt imagining of their content; and second, necessarily are false or only accidentally true (Currie); or intended not to be interpreted as reflecting the author's beliefs (Lamarque and Olsen); or whose reason for inclusion isn't truth-related (Davies). Taken jointly, satisfaction of these necessary conditions is deemed sufficient for a thing's counting as a fictive utterance, according to the respective accounts canvassed.[2]

Proponents of IP apparently see themselves as working within CA (Currie 1995, 1–2, 37; Lamarque and Olsen 1994, 15; Davies 2007, 33, 37). Moreover, as we've seen, IP strongly appeals to intuitions about thought experiments, in order to justify (in each case) its inclusion of a second necessary condition upon fiction. This too is strongly suggestive of CA.

A problem, however, is that the thought experiments discussed aren't central cases of fictional texts: they are peripheral and rare. Even if the goal were to do CA, it would seem counter-productive to hang so much on inevitably disputed cases. A further strike against IP counting as successful CA is that it's concerned to characterize what looks like a technically introduced notion – "fictive utterance" – unfamiliar to ordinary language users (Friend 2011, 166). Ordinary users certainly have the concept of the sentences that compose fictions, but they don't as a matter of course have the relatively technical concept of *fictive utterance* understood as a "fiction-making unit": a unit whose presence, in some number, in a text is what makes that text a fiction. This weakens any pretension to genuine CA.

So how does IP fare, considered instead as an ET (explanatory theory)? Perhaps we should read the notion of "fictive utterance" as an attempt to offer a theory with explanatory power; one that usefully helps us reconceptualize fiction, whether or not it fits exactly with public usage.

Here too though, there are problems with the use of thought experiments to justify introduction of each respective second necessary condition. The focus upon peripheral cases was problematic under the aegis of CA, since intuitions are bound to vary across users; a fortiori, for an ET, there can be little value in "intuitive" responses to the sorts of case described.

Leaving that point aside: considered broadly, IP has a number of virtues. Via its first necessary condition, it adverts to one of our main interests in fiction: its power to capture our imagination. Via the second conditions, it attempts to accommodate a widespread intuition of ordinary users of the term: that fictions stand, broadly speaking, in a negative relation to the truth and/or belief in the contents of the fiction. Though ETs don't have to slavishly capture common usage, as noted there's value in their squaring with uncontroversial folk intuitions. The theory covers a range of cases, unifying a complex field: large-scale novels, thought experiments, and short hypothetical sentences count as the same kind of thing, broadly speaking.

The main problem with IP, considered as an ET, is that it's silent about how many fictive utterances a fiction needs to contain to count as such, so unclear about precise conditions under which something counts as a fiction (Friend 2012, 186). This uncertainty infects any accompanying view of nonfiction: for if we don't know exactly when a thing is supposed to count as a fiction, we don't know when we have a nonfiction, either.

The reason for this incompleteness is as follows. According to IP, the fiction-making unit of explanatory value is the fictive utterance, defined in terms of the dual conditions of (i) prescribing imagining and (ii) standing in whatever negative relation to nonaccidental truth/authorial belief/truth-related reason for inclusion is specified by the particular proponent of the theory in question. Yet, often by authors' own admissions, many individual utterances within fictional texts *don't satisfy* the second of these conditions. Take the following passage from the fictional work *The Singapore Grip* by J.G. Farrell, which is true nonaccidentally (failing Currie's second condition), is manifestly something the author believes (failing Lamarque and Olsen's), and is reasonable to think included for its truth-value (failing Davies').

> The city of Singapore was not built up gradually, the way most cities are, by a natural deposit of commerce on the banks of some river or at a traditional confluence of trade routes. It was simply invented one morning early in the nineteenth century by a man looking at a map.
>
> *(Farrell 1992, 3)*

This admitted, we're left with the position that fiction is often a "patchwork" of fictive and nonfictive utterances (Currie 1990, 49). This leads to incompleteness, in tandem with understandable hesitancy to artificially name some proportion of fictive utterances the possession of which makes a text becomes fictional.

Taken as CA, it might be admissible that an account of fiction fails to specify the precise conditions under which a thing counts as a fiction: as admitted, the concept *fiction* is unlikely to be governed by any precise conditions. But taken as an ET, whose success stands or falls by its explanatory power, it's a severe defect to be unable to specify the conditions under which a thing counts as fiction or not.

A further possible worry about IP, at least for some, is that no explanation is given of what happens when a nonaccidentally true utterance, to be believed, is encountered in a fiction: how is it to be accounted for, in a way which doesn't implausibly entail a discontinuity in the reader's engagement with the narrative (Matravers 2014, 38)? After all, such utterances are not experienced as "interruptions in the fiction, interpolations of non-fiction woven into an otherwise fictional fabric" (Walton 1990, 79).

A third problem is that IP is relatively inelegant. Not only does it allow that a fiction can be composed of two types of utterance, only one of which is fiction-making, but it also makes the two specified conditions upon fictive utterance apparently unrelated in content. One pertains to imagining; the other pertains to a negative relation to truth/authorial belief/a truth-related reason for inclusion. No explanation is given of any connection between these.

I'll later consider how these flaws might be eradicated; meantime, I turn to a different approach. In recent years, an alternative to IP has emerged, which (again, broadly characterized) I'll call "No Imagining" (NI). I'll focus on two iterations.

## Friend's "No Imagining"

Stacie Friend denies that fiction has any governing set of necessary and sufficient conditions. In support, she argues that prescribing imagining isn't sufficient for fiction, since *nonfictions* regularly prescribe mental imagery and/or inferentially built models of what's the case according to the text, where both count as forms of imagining (Friend 2008, 154–156). They also sometimes contain wholly invented material, which one isn't supposed to believe (160). Equally, fictions often prescribe belief as well as imagining – either indirectly (158) or directly (159) – via the inclusion of nonaccidentally true statements (such as the one cited above, by Farrell).

None of this is obviously devastating to IP. If IP were claiming that it is necessary and sufficient *for a fiction* that it contain utterances which both (a) prescribe imagining and (b) stand in the relevant negative relation to truth/authorial belief/truth-related reason for inclusion, then Friend's observations would tell, since she shows that bits of nonfiction can satisfy both conditions. But IP is a view most directly about fictive utterance, not fiction, and as we've seen, it allows that fiction can be a "patchwork" of invented and nonaccidentally true material; by those lights, it presumably needn't deny that nonfiction can sometimes be a patchwork too, containing some invented, false material, intended to be imagined. Equally, her observation that bits of fiction can be nonaccidentally true, or otherwise fail to satisfy (b), is consistent with fiction being a patchwork of fictive and nonfictive utterances, which, as just reiterated, is allowed by IP.

Another thing to notice is that Friend provides no counterexample to *prescribing imagining* being a necessary condition either of fiction generally or of fictive utterance specifically. Even when explicitly considering this question, she doesn't give a definitive answer, focusing instead on whether fiction could be entirely nonaccidentally true (Friend 2012, 190).

Friend's positive view is that fiction and nonfiction are *genres*: more specifically, fiction is a "super-genre" (Friend 2012, 181) into which other genres such as pulp fiction and modernism fall. A genre is a way of classifying things which generates "expectations about the features of a work, and thereby determines appropriate standards of evaluation" (ibid.). Someone cognizant of a genre will grasp what features are standard (normal for the genre), contra-standard (tempting one to disqualify their possessor from membership) and variable (can vary happily), and be able to evaluate a work that falls within it appropriately. In Walton's example (Walton 1970), grasping what's standard for the genre of Roman busts allows us to appreciate them in a way not hampered by horror at the severance of the depicted subject's arms. So too, both fiction and nonfiction generate appreciative expectations: for instance, "memoirs" are expected to be true, while fact-based fiction is rarely seen as shockingly revelatory (Friend 2012, 179–180).

This doesn't yet give us the conditions under which a text counts as belonging to the genre in question. On one reading of Friend's view, there are no substantive necessary and sufficient conditions: rather, whether a text counts as fiction is determined by whether an entity satisfies some unspecified number of nonnecessary standard conditions for the genre (Friend 2012, 188). The standard features of fiction change over time (Friend 2012, 195; 2008, 162), but currently include things like: *prescribing imagining* (189); *including material which is invented or nonasserted* (ibid.); *using narrative and "certain literary devices"* (ibid.). An additional standard feature of fiction is that its author intends to write in a tradition that is publicly recognized as fiction at the time; or, at least, is recognized by some recipients as writing in such a tradition (193–194). Meanwhile, a nonfiction standardly includes "an effort to be faithful to the facts, references to real people, places and events; assertions that convey the author's views; and so on" (ibid.).

We are now in a position to assess. In some ways, this might seem quite close to a "family resemblance" account, and so engaged in CA. Friend's offer of a set of nonnecessary "standard" conditions for fiction, that in the right combination count as sufficient, makes her view look close to one that treats fiction as a cluster concept. Apparently lending to this reading is her observation that the conditions operative upon fiction can change over time, so that features that formerly were sufficient for nonfiction might come to typify fiction in a different intentional-historical context. This strengthens the comparison with a family resemblance concept, since ordinary language concepts tend to change their conditions over time in just this way, as usage expands and develops. She also tends to insist that what might look like controversial particular cases should just be treated as the folk (allegedly) treat them (Friend 2012, 203). Again this suggests CA as the favored approach.

Other points tell against this interpretation, however. One is the thought that the central idea – that fiction is a "genre" or "super-genre," of a kind with other genres like symbolist poetry or the modernist novel – looks startling, and so is unlikely to be one that the folk implicitly already accept.

Yet treating the view instead as an ET, a problem here is that it provides no clear conditions under which a fiction (or nonfiction) counts as such: it offers only standard but nonnecessary conditions, and moreover these conditions look explicitly time-indexed to the present context. Now, Friend can't rejoin that this is because there *aren't* any such clear conditions. That would be a return to the findings of CA. That the ordinary language concept *fiction* isn't governed by any small set of conditions is compatible with an ET positing some, since an ET aims to redraw categories, not simply uncover them. Moreover, an ET that doesn't posit any such conditions risks being vague about its theoretical target.

One might protest: Despite this vagueness, the view still does valuable explanatory work. Namely, it accounts for certain evaluative expectations about fiction and nonfiction, and reactions to texts that thwart expectations in these categories. Recall that Friend argues that, since (a) *prescribing imagining* and (b) *possessing invented or nonasserted content* both are standard features of fiction, readers expect to see them, and are surprised if they don't find them; equally, they are surprised when nonfiction exhibits them. Equally, she notes how, in reading a historically researched fiction, a reader may be disappointed on finding an apparent "fact" within the fiction is false (Friend 2012, 199), claiming it as a virtue of her view that it can account for this. She discusses other differences in treatment toward fiction and nonfiction, respectively, in terms of what formal features are considered standard (e.g., free indirect discourse is more visible in nonfiction because nonstandard; other stylistic features are treated as more integral to the work in fiction because standard) (198–200).

The problem is that this work can be done equally well by any explanatory theory that cites (a) and (b) as central to what fiction is – as indeed IP does, roughly. IP says that necessarily fictions contain utterances that prescribe imagining and (roughly) contain nonaccidentally true/nonasserted/non–truth-directed content – it can therefore account for a sense of failed expectation when the reader doesn't find this in a "fiction." Equally, since IP allows what count, on its terms, as nonfictive utterances within fictions, it can allow that readers may gain beliefs about the world from fictions and feel cheated when those beliefs are falsified. Since it has no pretensions to saying everything interesting about fiction, it can easily allow that there may be further context-relative standard nonnecessary conditions on fiction, for instance concerning form, with distinctive implications for appreciation. IP can also allow that, as Friend notes, what counts as standard features for fiction can develop over time, due to the inclusion, within particular works, of (at the time) contra-standard elements such as digressive narrative (Friend 2012, 192) and unreliability (191). This is easily compatible with the category of fiction being governed by necessary conditions throughout. In short, the explanatory work Friend's view does is available to its main rival, IP, and to other rivals too.

An alternative reading has Friend's view as, in effect, identifying the changing features of the ordinary concept of *fiction* across time as features of a stable, permanent social practice: one whose varying spatiotemporal conditions are a permanent feature of it.[3] Fiction is, on this reading, (permanently, necessarily) a social practice (or "genre") with context-dependent, historically and culturally varying conditions under which something gets to count as fiction. At the moment standard conditions upon fiction include that it *prescribes imagining* and *possesses invented or nonasserted content*; these conditions might change in the future and have not always been as important in the past. What's permanent, however, is that where the right intentional-historical context exists, and some number of other standard features are also present, then we will have fiction, on this theory.

This looks like an "institutional" account of fiction: roughly, what counts as fiction is what the dominant institutions call fiction.[4] Friend explicitly distances her account from an institutional reading, arguing that "[t]he role of standard and contra-standard features in genre classification" entails that hers isn't an institutional theory; in an institutional theory of art, for instance, "art status is conferred by relevant members of the 'artworld' with no internal constraint on the type of thing that qualifies" (Friend 2012, 193 n. 18). This attempted distancing is unconvincing: in an institutional theory of art, there needs to be room for time-indexed, nonpermanent but publicly recognized features that guide classification as art. That is, at a given time and cultural context, there are features which count as "standard" for art, as well as "contra-standard" and "variable." To deny this would be to suggest that art classification is wholly arbitrary and individualistic, something no institutional theorist could plausibly assert.

So how does an institutional reading of Friend's view fare, considered as an ET? One might worry that Friend's claim to capture our appreciative interest in fiction is now diluted, since in common with other institutional theories, the dominant focus is more upon the actual decisions fiction classifiers make, than the reasons for those decisions, which on this view are context-relative and change over time (though they still may be interestingly identified separately, as just noted). Space precludes me considering this further. In the meantime, I turn to a different variant of NI, that of Derek Matravers.

## Matravers' "No Imagining"

Matravers' version of NI says that the distinction between fiction and nonfiction does no explanatory work; we should abandon it. Instead, he introduces a "more fundamental" distinction between "confrontations" and "representations" (Matravers 2014, 53). This has the form of an ET par excellence (7–8), seeking to redraw categories in a more enlightened way than mere deference to ordinary usage would permit. A "confrontation" is a situation in one's egocentric space, to which one is directly perceptually related (50). What we currently think of as fictions *and* nonfictions are representations, as opposed to confrontations: they prompt thoughts of objects that aren't currently perceptually present and toward which no direct action is possible.

Matravers often talks as if the distinction between "confrontation" and "representation" is a rival to that of the distinction between "fiction" and "nonfiction." But fictions and nonfictions still both could count as representations in Matravers' technical sense, while there remained an interesting difference between them that did explanatory work. Matravers denies that there's any such difference. In particular, he denies the claim that the relevant difference concerns imagining.

As we saw, Friend doesn't deny that much of fiction standardly calls for an attitude – imagining – that isn't called for by much nonfiction, and vice versa. Rather, what she denies is that fiction can be defined in terms of this attitude. Matravers' position is much more radical – there's simply no difference in the attitudes prescribed, even standardly, by fiction and nonfiction. It's false that fiction prescribes imagining but nonfiction doesn't.

He considers at least two possible values for "imagining" here. According to one, "imagining" is interpreted as a kind of taking on of someone's perspective, in a vivacious or lively way (Matravers 2014, 16–17). He correctly argues that both fiction and nonfiction can prescribe this: autobiographies, for instance, can obviously do so.

He also considers imagining as "offline simulation" (Currie 1995). On this view, an imagining that *p* is negatively distinguished from a belief that *p*, in terms of typically having different perceptual causes, causal connections to accompanying mental states, and to behavioral outputs (Matravers 2014, 26–27). Yet, Matravers argues, the mental states which fiction makes appropriate don't differ in any of these three ways from those made appropriate by nonfiction. In particular: (A) there's no difference in kind in the perceptual inputs typically caused by fictions versus nonfictions; (B) there's no difference in kind in the behavioral outputs typically caused by fictions versus nonfictions; (C) there's no difference in the kinds of accompanying mental states typically caused by fictions versus nonfictions. In other words, fictions and nonfictions function exactly alike in the mental states they make appropriate, characterized in terms of inputs and outputs.

(A) looks true: all are of texts. (B) isn't strictly true, since possibilities of action exist toward actual particulars described in nonfiction that have no typical analogy in fiction. One could read a report about a homeless person, find her, and help her, for instance; whereas at most, a fiction might prompt a generalized desire to help homeless people (Matravers 2014, 28). What *is* true is that the possibilities of action toward (i) *invented* particulars characterized in fictions and (ii) *past* particulars, described in nonfiction but no longer existent, look similarly obstructed (though for different reasons), and hence we cannot easily distinguish fiction from nonfiction in terms of this factor alone.

The real trouble lies with (C). Why should we accept there's no difference in the kinds of accompanying mental states typically caused by fictions versus nonfictions? Matravers considers various possible accompanying states typically shared by responses to fictions and nonfiction (30–35), ignoring the most obvious: with exceptions as noted, the content of nonfiction tends to be stored, however briefly, as beliefs in the mind of the reader, whereas, with exceptions also noted, the content of fiction tends not to be. Moreover, when stored as beliefs, they tend to inferentially integrate with further stored beliefs in a way that imaginings don't. Matravers in fact acknowledges this, advocating a "two-stage" model of engaging with representations generally: "the first stage is neutral between non-fictional and fictional representations generally"; the mental model created in response to the text is "compartmentalized" from "pre-existing structures of belief" (90). However in the "second stage," in response to nonfiction, "the content of the mental model" is "integrated" into those structures, whereas in response to fiction, this occurs markedly less frequently with the utterances contained therein (95). Why deny that this integration, which takes place in one case but not the other (whether at a "second stage" or not), can form a basis for a distinction between fiction and nonfiction? To do so looks *ad hoc*, and Matravers himself seems explicitly worried by this accusation (95). There's no apparent reason not to include the inferences to which one is disposed, in reading a text, as part of the mental state appropriate to that sort of text. At least on the whole, fictions and nonfictions make different sorts of inference appropriate. So there's still room for a meaningful distinction here. In the final section, I'll explore exactly how that distinction can be made out.

## "Imagining Only"

I'll now argue that we can usefully characterize fiction in terms of its prescribing imagining, without citing any further condition, as IP did.

Earlier, I characterized Walton's theory of fiction as an IO ("Imagining Only") account: it offered a relation to imagining as both a necessary and sufficient condition of fiction. The relation in question was *functioning as a prop in a game of imagining*. The view was criticized for delineating too wide a group of things. This isn't to say that the general idea of IO cannot work, however. In my view it can, once we return to focusing, as IP did, on the relation of *being an utterance that prescribes imagining*, and characterize "imagining" more substantially (Stock 2011). In what follows, I intend to identify, under the aegis of an ET, one form of imagining, which need not be imagistic, and which can be identified as a familiar way of engaging with fiction. (I am not attempting CA either of fiction or imagining here, nor is the account supposed to be exhaustive of forms of imagining.)

Let's understand "imagining that *p*," in my sense, as having a necessary condition: it involves consciously thinking that *p*, in a way which represents *p* as occurring or as having occurred; as opposed, say, to the way that desire that *p* represents *p* as to-be-done, or "as dictating conditions to be achieved" (Velleman 2000, 111). It also involves a further necessary condition: one *either* doesn't believe that *p*, *or* believes that *p* and is disposed to inferentially connect the thought of *p* to further propositional content which one doesn't believe (Stock 2011, 152–153). For instance: I don't believe *I'm on the moon*. So according to the first disjunct, I can imagine *I'm on the moon*. I do believe *I'm typing at my computer*. According to the second disjunct, I can imagine *I'm typing at my computer*, even while I believe it, as long as I am disposed to inferentially connect the thought *I'm typing on my computer* with some further content I don't believe; for instance, that *I'm on the moon* (*and I'm typing on my computer*). I can believe that *p* and imagine that *p* simultaneously (Leslie 1994) as long as the total set of thoughts to which I'm disposed to be inferentially related is different, in each case.

Fictions, necessarily and sufficiently, prescribe imagining in this sense, with these conditions as operative. An author intends that the reader respond to that text by consciously thinking, and being disposed to inferentially conjoin, its total content, including at least some manifestly invented content that the reader is supposed to disbelieve. (Usually the proportion of manifestly invented content is high, but in "fact-based" stories it may not be.)

We now have a new proposal concerning the nature of fiction's negative relation to truth/belief: though parts of a fictional text can be believed true by the reader (and be true, and included for truth-related reasons), *the whole* cannot. For this would normally make it impossible for the reader to imagine its content, in my sense, short of inappropriately inventing further disbelieved content herself (e.g., making up new fates for characters), and inferentially relating it to the content of the text. IP's focus on a negative relation to truth at the level of the individual fictive utterance was misplaced: the correct focus is the text as a whole. This renders otiose any inelegant "second" condition upon fictive utterance, citing truth and/or belief, and apparently disconnected from the first condition offered. A further advantage of this over IP is that fictions are not patchworks: normally, every utterance within a fictional text satisfies the condition offered, including the ones included because they are true and to be believed, etc.

One objection made here is that it's "unanswerable" whether a given thought that *p* is inferentially connected to further propositional thought that isn't believed, given that such dispositions can be unactualized (Matravers 2014, 42). This looks overstated. My claim concerns thought-tokens, not thought-types. There are a familiar and limited list of ways two thought-tokens can be inferentially connected: conjoined, part of a *modus ponens*, part of a *modus tollens*, etc. To be freely associated, or merely contiguously experienced, is not to be inferentially connected. My claim is that an imagining is a current conscious propositional thought, representing a state of affairs as occurring or occurred, that is disposed to be inferentially connected to disbelieved content. Presumably, one should only attribute such a disposition with good reason: either because the imaginer *actually does* inferentially connect her current thought-token to disbelieved content, consciously, or because there's good reason to think she might. For instance, a good reason to think this would be that a reader, in consciously thinking that *p*, was responding to a text which included an utterance that "*p*" and which also included some manifestly invented content to be disbelieved; that she disbelieved it; and that she was signed up to the conventions of reading texts, including the convention that one should inferentially conjoin what one reads unless signaled otherwise.

This, however, leads to an apparently harder problem: many nonfictional texts contain some manifestly invented content, and so prescribe imagining in my sense (Friend 2011, 172; Matravers 2014, 42). Friend uses the example of "irony, hyperbole, questions, jokes, and so on, as well as quotations of sources who are not taken as reliable," and descriptions of possible future states of affairs or "alternative pasts" (172). Taking all of these at face value for the sake of argument, they can be accommodated, as long as we're happy to say that nonfictional texts can *contain fictions* – discrete passages of content to be imagined, in my sense, from which some conclusion to be believed may sometimes then be extracted. The extracted conclusion is to be inferentially integrated with the nonfictional parts of the texts, but the fiction itself is not.

More precisely, then: a fiction is any passage of text (or string of utterances) that prescribes imagining, in my sense, its total content (explicit and implicit), whether or not it prescribes believing some of that content. A nonfictional text (unlike "fiction," there isn't a natural interpretation of "nonfiction" which doesn't also apply to complete texts) is more complicated to characterize, but is, roughly, a text whose dominant purpose is to prescribe belief not imagining, though it may contain passages of fiction.

This is to admit that nonfictional text can be a "patchwork" of fiction and nonfictional parts – is this a problem, given that I denied the desirability of thinking of fiction as a patchwork? No. It fits the data. Fictions that prescribe the belief that *p also* prescribe imagining that *p*, so that there need be no discontinuity in attitude. Nonfictional texts that prescribe imagining that *p*, as in the cases offered by Friend, normally don't prescribe believing that *p*; at most, they prescribe us to believe something else, on the basis of imagining that *p*. There *is* discontinuity here. Hence the appropriateness of a "patchwork" of different kinds of statement, requiring different treatment.

What about those rare cases of alleged nonfictions that include invented elements: Tacitus' histories, and Edmund Morris' *Dutch*, the "biography" of Ronald Reagan that contains invented elements such as a "witness" narrator with no basis in actuality? These are treated by Friend as nonfiction, unambiguously (Friend 2011). Ordinary usage is confused about such peripheral cases; even less pressure, then, upon an explanatory theory to fit with (tendentious interpretations of) ordinary usage. But in any case, assuming the reader wasn't/isn't intended to believe the invented elements, they look like passages of fiction in a nonfiction, and can be treated as above. Alternatively, if the reader was supposed to believe them, then they look like deceptive nonfictional passages, unproblematically. Biographies and histories can lie without ceasing to be nonfictional, on my view.

Obviously there's much more to say here, and my opponents are unlikely to take the matter as settled. Meantime, we can summarize as follows. Earlier discussion revealed the following good-making features for an explanatory theory of fiction that cited imagining. It would be good to (i) cover at least noncontroversial applications of the folk concept; (ii) give clear conditions under which a whole text counts as fictional; (iii) give some substantive account of what's meant by "imagining" in a way which distinguishes it from the response typically called for by nonfiction; (iv) explain the widespread intuition that fiction tends to bear some negative relation to truth and/or to belief; (v) accommodate the inclusion of nonaccidental truths in a fiction, and explain reader response to them in a way which doesn't suggest discontinuity in the reader's experience; (vi) accommodate the presence in nonfictional texts of invented passages prescribing imagining; (vii) be simpler and more elegant than rivals; (viii) capture a range of cases; (ix) explain or at least be consistent with appreciative expectations concerning fiction. I have argued we can obtain much of this via a theory of fiction that cites prescribing imagining as its only necessary and sufficient condition.

## Notes

1 Currie (1990, 49) calls the fiction-making unit a "fictional statement," reserving "fictive utterance" for an utterance that satisfies only the condition that it prescribes imagining as an appropriate response to its content.
2 Lamarque and Olsen say that the "three main features" of fictive utterance are (i) the prescription to imagine, (ii) the reliance on an established social practice, and (iii) the blocking of inferences back to the writer's beliefs (Lamarque and Olsen 1994, 45–46). They examine whether these are sufficient, adding the condition cited above that "how things are (in the fiction) is determined by how they are described to be in a fictive utterance" (51). This looks very close to (iii) in any case.
3 In correspondence, Friend confirms this is a good reading of her view, though maintains distance from an institutional theory in Dickie's sense (see next note).
4 A famous institutional theory of art is offered by Dickie (1983).

## Further reading

Walton (1990) and Currie (1990) are the cornerstones of this literature, outlining positions that set the discursive agenda for years to follow. Lamarque and Olsen (1994) and Davies (2007) offer a welcome attention to particular cases, and wider literary culture, in their defenses of "Imagining Plus." In a range of stimulating articles, Friend challenges the orthodoxy about fiction and defends her own pleasingly unorthodox solution (Friend 2008, 2011, 2012). Matravers (2014) goes even further, pleading for an abandonment of the fiction/nonfiction distinction altogether.

## References

Currie, G. (1990) *The Nature of Fiction*, Cambridge: Cambridge University Press.
Currie, G. (1995) *Image and Mind*, Cambridge: Cambridge University Press.

Davies, D. (2007) *Aesthetics and Literature*, Basingstoke: Palgrave Macmillan.
Davies, D. (2012) "Fictionality, Fictive Utterance and the Assertive Author," in G. Currie, P. Kot'atko, and M. Pokorny (eds.) *Mimesis: Metaphysics, Cognition, Pragmatics*, London: College Publications, 61–85.
Dickie, G. (1983) "The New Institutional Theory of Art," *Proceedings of the 8th International Wittgenstein Symposium* 10: 57–64.
Farrell, J.G. (1992) *The Singapore Grip*, London: Orion.
Friend, S. (2008) "Imagining Fact and Fiction," in K. Stock and K. Thomson-Jones (eds.) *New Waves in Aesthetics*, Basingstoke: Palgrave Macmillan, 150–169.
Friend, S. (2011) "Fictive Utterance and Imagining II," *Proceedings of the Aristotelian Society, Supplementary Volume* 85: 163–180.
Friend, S. (2012) "Fiction as a Genre," *Proceedings of the Aristotelian Society* 112(2): 179–209.
Gaut, B. (2000) "'Art' as a Cluster Concept," in N. Carroll (ed.) *Theories of Art Today*, Madison: University of Wisconsin Press, 25–44.
Jackson, F. (2000) *From Metaphysics to Ethics: A Defence of Conceptual Analysis*, Oxford: Oxford University Press.
Lamarque, P., and S. Olsen (1994) *Truth, Fiction and Literature*, Oxford: Oxford University Press.
Leslie, A. (1994) "Pretending and Believing: Issues in the Theory of ToMM," *Cognition* 50: 211–238.
Matravers, D. (2014) *Fiction and Narrative*, Oxford: Oxford University Press.
Searle, J. (1975) "The Logical Status of Fictional Discourse," *New Literary History* 6(2): 319–332.
Stock, K. (2011) "Fictive Utterance and Imagining," *Aristotelian Society Supplementary Volume* 85(1): 145–161.
Velleman, D. (2000) *The Possibility of Practical Reason*, Oxford: Oxford University Press.
Walton, K. (1970) "Categories of Art," *Philosophical Review* 79(3): 334–367.
Walton, K. (1990) *Mimesis as Make-Believe: On the Foundations of the Representational Arts*, Cambridge, MA: Harvard University Press.

# 16

# FICTION AND EMOTION

*Stacie Friend*

Engagement with fiction often inspires emotional responses. We may pity Sethe while feeling ambivalent about her actions (in *Beloved*), fear for Ellen Ripley as she battles monstrous creatures (in *Alien*), get angry at Okonkwo for killing Ikemefuna (in *Things Fall Apart*), and hope that Kiyoaki and Satoko find love (in *Spring Snow*). Familiar as they are, these reactions are puzzling. Why do I respond emotionally if I do not believe that these individuals exist or that the events occurred? If I merely imagine that my best friend has betrayed me, I do not become angry with him; if I did, I would be considered irrational. Yet although beliefs seem to be necessary for emotions in other contexts, we respond to fiction without the relevant beliefs. These observations prompt two questions about our emotional responses to fiction (henceforth: *fictional emotions*). The first is *descriptive:* Should fictional emotions be classified as the same kind of emotions we experience in other contexts? The second is *normative:* Are fictional emotions irrational or otherwise inappropriate?

Both questions are typically framed in terms of the *paradox of fiction*, constituted by the following three statements:

1 We experience (genuine, ordinary) emotions toward fictional characters, situations, and events.
2 We do not experience (genuine, ordinary) emotions when we do not believe in the existence of the objects of emotion.
3 We do not believe in the existence of fictional characters, situations, and events.

Insofar as the three claims are individually intuitive but jointly incompatible, they cannot all be true. The debate over the descriptive question has focused on which claim to reject to resolve the paradox. The debate over the normative question has focused on whether all three claims must be accepted (though I question this approach below). I take each of these debates in turn.

## The descriptive question

The standard approach to the descriptive question assumes that one claim of the paradox of fiction must be rejected. The majority of philosophers reject either (1) or (2). Although the rejection of (3) is a possibility – and some philosophers have argued that we have the relevant beliefs, perhaps subconsciously or partially (Hartz 1999; Suits 2006) – I will focus on (1) and (2) because the disagreement between advocates of each position centers on the role of imagination in emotion.

It was Kendall Walton's (1978) rejection of (1) that prompted interest in the descriptive question (see also Walton 1990, ch. 7). Walton famously argued that moviegoer Charles, shrieking in terror of the on-screen blob coming straight at the camera, was not genuinely afraid. Instead, Charles's experience is better described as *make-believe* or *imagined* or *quasi*-fear, and similarly for our pity of Sethe, anger at Okonkwo, and so forth. On the face of it, this conclusion is counterintuitive. Walton is not, however, making the patently implausible claim that in fictional contexts we fake or pretend to have emotions, or that our experiences must be less intense or more easily controlled than in other contexts. To the contrary, Walton agrees that we experience emotions that share features with pity, fear, and so on; what he denies is that these are genuine pity and fear (i.e., emotions of just the same kind as ordinary pity and fear). Walton and his supporters point out that the responses occur in the context of imagining rather than believing the content of the fiction and, as a result, they possess features that distinguish them from other instances of emotion.

The vast majority of philosophers and psychologists nonetheless disagree with Walton's conclusion. Some argue that we need believe only that certain claims are fictionally true, rather than that the objects are real, to have genuine emotions (Neill 1991; Livingston and Mele 1997). But by far the most popular position is that no kind of belief is necessary for emotion, and in particular that imagination without belief is sufficient. Proponents of this position conclude that there is no good reason to deny that our responses to fiction are ordinary, genuine emotions. They therefore reject (2).

### *Rejecting (2)*

The debate over (2) is concerned with a particular form of *cognitivism* about the emotions. According to cognitivist theories, some kind of cognitive evaluation – often, but not necessarily, construed as a propositional attitude – constitutes an essential component of an emotion. In paradigm cases the attitude is a belief: in pity the belief that someone has suffered, in fear the belief that one is in danger, and so on. Many emotional states also have an affective component, involving phenomenological and physiological responses as well as associations with action. For example, fear usually involves a feeling of anxiety and an increase in heart rate and perspiration, along with a desire to flee. According to cognitivists, these aspects of an affective state or episode are insufficient by themselves to constitute an emotion. First, many emotions are associated with a similar physiological and phenomenological profile; the distinction between, say, fear and anger may simply be whether our feelings arise in evaluating a situation as dangerous or offensive. Second, these features do not distinguish emotions from moods – affective states lacking in content, as when I am anxious but not about anything in particular – or lower-level automatic responses, such as being startled by a loud noise. Emotions are open to rational assessment in ways that moods or reflex responses are not, and cognitivists explain this by pointing to the cognitive component.

Traditionally, the explanation assumed that the cognitive component was a belief (e.g., Lyons 1980; Oakley 1992), or even that emotions could be identified with judgments (e.g., Solomon 2003; Nussbaum 2001), so that the rationality of emotions was determined by the rationality of the relevant beliefs or judgments. Anyone who accepts this traditional, *narrow* form of cognitivism accepts (2). Significantly, narrow cognitivism does not require that the relevant belief be *true* for emotion to be possible. I will experience genuine fear if I believe a burglar is in my house, even if it turns out that I've only heard the wind rattle the door.

Those who reject (2) fall into two camps. In the first are those who agree with *broad cognitivism*, according to which emotions involve some form of cognitive evaluation, but not necessarily a belief (e.g., Stocker 1987; Greenspan 1988). From this perspective, pity involves the thought that someone suffers, fear the thought that one is in danger, and so on, but these thoughts can be entertained, supposed, imagined, or whatever. One motivation for this view is the existence of phobias, which appear to be cases of genuine fear in the absence of the belief that one is in danger. Another is the fact that the rationality of emotions departs in various ways from the rationality of beliefs (Greenspan 1980, 1988). Broad cognitivists who address the paradox of fiction, often called "thought theorists," argue that imagining in response to fiction is sufficient for genuine emotions (e.g., Lamarque 1981; Carroll 1990; Matravers 1998). In the second camp are *noncognitivists*, who deny that cognition of any kind is necessary for emotion. They argue that emotions can be triggered by stimuli that directly affect the amygdala, prompting an affective response prior to any signal's being sent to cortical areas of the brain (LeDoux 1996). In this way emotions involve an "affective" or "embodied" appraisal of a situation, which can arise without any intervening cognition (Robinson 2005 and Prinz 2004, respectively). For example, seeing a coiled shape in the dark or hearing a growl might prompt fear even before I have had a chance to process the stimulus. Given that no cognition is necessary for an emotion, noncognitivists such as Robinson and Prinz also reject (2).

Importantly, the disagreement between cognitivists and noncognitivists concerns only the *trigger* of emotion: whereas noncognitivists claim that emotions can be initiated without cognition, cognitivists only count a state or episode as an emotion once cognition is involved. But noncognitivists do not deny a role for cognition in emotion. First, they acknowledge that cognition plays a part in the development of emotions even when they are initiated more directly (Robinson 2005, 75–79). For instance, if I realize that the coiled shape is just a rope, my fear dissipates. Second, noncognitivism does not exclude the possibility of emotions triggered by cognitions; thinking of a sad incident can make me sad. Therefore noncognitivists agree with broad cognitivists that genuine emotions can occur when we merely imagine, but do not believe, the content of a fiction. Emotions can be triggered by mere imaginings, as with our pity of Sethe, our hope for Kiyoaki and Satoko, and so on. And imaginings can play a role in the development of emotions triggered noncognitively. Even if audiences of *Alien* experience fear as a gut reaction when the cat suddenly jumps out of its hiding place, this fear turns to relief once we recognize that the cat is not the alien. For this reason, the debate over (2) is not a debate between cognitivists and noncognitivists, but between narrow cognitivism and other theories of emotion. According to narrow cognitivists, genuine emotions are not possible when we do not believe that the objects of emotion exist. According to other theorists, they are.

Now, it is fair to say that narrow cognitivism is a minority position. Nearly everyone – philosophers, psychologists, neuroscientists, ordinary folk – agree that we can experience genuine emotions in the absence of relevant beliefs, often precisely because this seems to be the case in fiction. Contrary to the assumption of most parties to the debate, however, rejecting (2) does not settle the issue of how to classify fictional emotions. In particular, rejecting (2) does not entail accepting (1), for there may also be *other* reasons to deny that fictional emotions are genuine emotions (Stecker 2011). I consider these in the next section.

## Rejecting (1)

Among the reasons to reject (1) are the obvious dissimilarities between fictional emotions and emotions in other contexts. In ordinary circumstances there is a close relationship between our beliefs and central features of emotion that are missing in the fiction case. One is the connection between emotion and motivational force. Fear provokes a desire to flee, pity a desire to help, and so on. Ordinarily, if we believe that nothing endangers us, we do not desire to flee; if we believe that no one has suffered, we do not desire to help. Another is the way emotions are evaluated in light of our beliefs. If I do not believe that my friend has done anything wrong yet I am still angry at him, this response will be unjustified and perhaps even irrational. A third feature is the intentionality, or aboutness, of emotions. If you tell me about the terrible experiences of a friend I may pity her. If I then find out there is no such person, I can no longer experience pity *of your friend*, just as a child who knows there is no Santa Claus can no longer hope to meet *him*. (Notice that the problem is not merely that the object fails to exist. We may want to say that the Greeks worshipped Zeus even though there is no Zeus, given their false belief. Instead, the problem is the lack of any belief.) None of these features characterizes our emotions in response to fiction. Our pity of Sethe has no motivational force, we do not count ourselves unjustified in pitying someone we believe is unreal, and our feelings still seem directed toward Sethe despite her nonexistence. Fictional emotions thus depart in significant ways from emotions in ordinary circumstances.

Defenders of (1) argue that these disanalogies do not justify treating fictional emotions as a distinct kind. They draw attention to other instances of genuine emotions where beliefs are lacking. If phobic Jack is afraid of the gentle Fido even though he does not believe that Fido poses any danger to him, no one would deny that his fear is genuine. And Jill might fear walking on a glass platform over a deep drop, without believing that there is a genuine risk of falling (Gendler and Kovakovic 2006, 250). If these are genuine emotions, it looks as if belief is not required for fictional emotions to be so classified. However, fictional emotions cannot be assimilated to phobias and automatic reflex responses. Jack and Jill are likely to recognize that they have no good reason for their fears. By contrast, readers of Morrison's novel take themselves to have numerous reasons for pity. Moreover, if we take Jack and Jill as experiencing genuine emotions, this is only insofar as those emotions motivate action. If Jack did not avoid Fido or Jill was happy to step on the glass floor, we might doubt that they were afraid. Such motivations are lacking in the fiction case (Walton 1990, 201–202).

Proponents of (1) might then point to our emotional responses to some kinds of nonfiction representations: in these cases there is belief, but due to spatial or temporal distance no motivation to act. If something occurred a hundred years ago or a thousand miles away, we are as little capable of doing anything about it as we are in the case of fiction (Matravers 1998, 69–73; Gaut 2003). Moreover, they argue, our believing in the one case that the objects of emotion are (or were) real and in the other case that they are (or were) unreal has no impact on the experience. On the other hand, they must concede that by contrast with emotions directed at real individuals past or present, we cannot literally experience emotions *toward Sethe* if we believe there never was such a person (Lamarque 1981). The question is whether this is sufficient to show that the pity is of a distinct kind.

## Emotions and make-believe

It seems as if we have reached an impasse. After all, there is little disagreement about the features of fictional emotions themselves, which are widely acknowledged to be both similar to and different from emotions in other contexts. Now, an empirical approach might identify other, less obvious features of fictional emotions than those so far discussed (cf. Weinberg and Meskin 2006). For example, one psychological study suggests that emotional reactions to fiction are less intense than emotional responses to nonfiction (Cova et al., in prep.). But it is unlikely that the matter can be settled empirically. First, most empirical studies of emotion simply presuppose that emotions are all of a kind, insofar as psychologists and neuroscientists draw their conclusions from responses to fictional stimuli such as pictures and stories. Second, although empirical results may be illuminating in various ways, further data by themselves would not settle the issue; the data have to be interpreted.

If closer consideration of the emotions themselves will not shed more light on their classification, we must look instead at their context: the *fictional* aspect of fictional emotions. For the most persuasive arguments against (1) rely, not on a general background assumption of narrow cognitivism, but rather on the idea that emotions in response to fiction arise in the context of imaginative engagement. Indeed Walton's own account of fictional emotions makes sense only in the context of his theory of make-believe.

Starting from examples of novels, plays, films, paintings, and sculptures, Walton (1990) aims to construct a theory of what he calls *representational art* or *fiction*. Walton defines a work of fiction as a work whose function it is to act as props in certain games of make-believe. The connection with children's games of make-believe, where the props may be dolls and toy trucks, is intentional; for Walton there is continuity between the two types of games. The idea is that works of fiction are designed to prescribe imaginings about their content, and imagining what is prescribed is participating in the game of make-believe authorized by the work. What a work prescribes imagining is what is "true in the fiction," or simply *fictional*. On Walton's theory our imaginings about the content of a work – for instance, my imagining that Sethe suffers because her children are born into slavery – are generated by more basic games of make-believe that involve imagining about ourselves. Specifically, we make believe that in engaging with the fiction we are learning about actual fact, and we respond to the fictional events from within the scope of this imagining. In reality I am reading a novel; in imagination, in my game of make-believe, I am reading a true report about actual people and events. And it is within this context that I have emotional experiences.

Suppose that I am caught up in *Beloved* and I find myself pitying Sethe. I am perfectly aware that there is no such person. But my imagining is sufficiently vivid that I have a sinking sensation, tears well up, I find it hard to turn the page. According to Walton, facts about my real feelings – specifically, the phenomenological and physiological state I am in due to my imagining, which Walton calls *quasi-pity* – make it fictionally the case that I pity Sethe. From a perspective outside the game of make-believe, the experience does not count as genuine pity. Just as it is the fact that I (really) read a novel that makes it fictionally the case that I am learning about actual fact, it is the fact that I (really) experience quasi-pity that makes it fictionally the case that I experience pity. And because it is *only* fictionally the case that I am reading a true report and learning that Sethe suffers because she is separated from her children – the imaginings that explain my quasi-pity – it is *only* fictionally the case that I pity her. In short, Walton's introduction of quasi-emotions is a natural consequence of his theory of make-believe.

Now, most of Walton's opponents agree that when I read *Beloved* I imagine learning about actual fact. They also agree that it is within this imaginative context that my emotional experiences occur. However, they disagree with Walton's conclusion that the emotional experience is as much a part of the game as the events of the novel; for his opponents, the emotion falls outside the scope of the make-believe. To see what difference this makes, it is helpful to consider the distinction between imagining and believing.

### Quarantined emotions

The difference between imagining and believing is usually construed as a functional difference rather than a difference in content. So, for example, we can both believe and imagine that the sun is out; the contrast is not in the proposition believed or imagined, but rather in the function this content plays with respect to other cognitions, affective states, behavior, and so on. Two features of imagining are often noted, *mirroring* and *quarantining* (see Gendler 2003). Imagining *mirrors* belief to the extent that it is governed by similar inferential constraints. For example, if we imagine that the sun is out, we typically imagine that it is daytime. At the same time imagining is *quarantined* insofar as we treat its implications and effects as limited to a certain domain. For example, we do not take imagining that the sun is out to mean that we face an increased risk of skin cancer. The same applies to imagining in response to fiction. We draw conclusions about how Sethe feels based on what we know about people in general, but we do not expect to be able to meet her descendants or locate her grave. In short, at least some of what we imagine about Sethe remains compartmentalized from our beliefs about the world, so that it does not guide our ordinary actions. If Walton is correct that fictional emotions occur within the imaginative context, we should expect them similarly to be quarantined.

One way to test for the presence of quarantine is to see how we judge potential conflicts. In a pretend tea party, children playing with empty cups typically believe that the cups are empty while imagining that they are full. Because the imagining is quarantined from the belief, there is no conflict. Imagining in response to fiction works the same way. In reading *The Hitchhiker's Guide to the Galaxy* we imagine that the earth is an experiment designed by mice, while all the while believing that it is not. Quarantine prevents conflict; it also explains why scientists engage in astronomy and geology to explain the origins of the planet rather than trying to communicate with rodents.

There is some reason to think that the same applies to fictional emotions, as can be seen when we consider fictions about real individuals. Perhaps I believe that Richard III was a good king who did not murder his nephews in the Tower of London, but was instead the victim of Tudor propaganda. I admire him for his good deeds and pity him for the way he was killed. If I see a compelling production of Shakespeare's *Richard III*, I may well respond with very different emotions, condemning rather than admiring him, viewing his death as deserved rather than pitiable. Although some will disagree, I see no reason to deny that the Richard portrayed in Shakespeare's play is the real Richard; certainly the controversy about the portrayal, which Shakespeare borrows directly from Thomas More's history of Richard's reign, assumes that this is so (see also Friend 2003). In that case, if my fictional emotions do not conflict with my ordinary feelings about Richard, this is plausibly because they are quarantined. Whereas my admiration may prompt me to join the Richard III Society, it would make little sense for me to criticize the Society's views based on how I feel while watching the play. I might explain this difference by saying that I do not *really* condemn Richard; in reality I admire him.

There is, however, an objection to treating fictional emotions as quarantined within the imaginative context: that these experiences play a role in our ethical life that cannot be explained unless they are taken to be genuine emotions. If I read a description of a heinous murder in a novel I cannot be faulted for imagining an evil act, but it may seem that I can be faulted for responding with glee. The idea is that we are responsible for the emotions we experience in imagining, insofar as they reveal our characters in a way that the imaginings themselves do not (Moran 1994). In addition, we seem to be able to learn by responding emotionally to fiction, both by broadening the range of our emotional experiences and by acquiring ethical knowledge of the appropriate responses to various situations. If our experiences are not of genuine emotions, it is difficult to see how these kinds of learning are possible; in particular, nongenuine emotions would not seem capable of providing evidence for ethical conclusions (Gaut 2007, 206–207). So even if our imaginings in response to fiction are quarantined from our beliefs, the argument goes, our emotional responses to those imaginings cannot be.

These considerations are not entirely persuasive, however. First, not all responses in the fictional context reveal one's character, or else it would always be inappropriate to laugh at black comedies. It is true that in many cases fictional emotions mirror the emotions we would experience in response to similar, real-life situations; but mirroring of this sort is characteristic of imagining. Quarantine in the relevant sense does not mean total isolation. As for the possibility of learning, there is no doubt that we think of fiction as broadening our emotional experience, and that we sometimes transfer our emotional responses in the fictional context to real-life situations. The question, though, is whether or not these extrapolations are warranted. For whether or not the emotions are genuine they occur in response to imagined situations, and the move from the imagined to the real requires justification (Friend 2010). Ethical considerations therefore do not settle the answer to the descriptive question. They do, however, highlight the second issue concerning fictional emotions: the normative question.

## The normative question

Just as Walton's counterintuitive conclusion in "Fearing Fictions" prompted the debate over classification, Colin Radford's (1975) argument for a different counterintuitive conclusion prompted the debate over rationality. In "How Can We Be Moved by the Fate of Anna Karenina?" Radford argued that emotions in response to characters we know do not exist and events we know did not occur are "incoherent" and "inconsistent." The implication is that in responding emotionally to fictions we are irrational; though Radford himself does not use this terminology, this is how he is usually understood.

### *The standard interpretation*

According to the most popular interpretation of Radford's argument, the inconsistency he identifies is just our commitment to the three incompatible claims that constitute the paradox of fiction. Radford defends versions of the three claims in both his original paper and in subsequent replies to objections (e.g., Radford 1982, 1989, 1995, 2000). In accord with (1) he criticizes attempts to distinguish fictional emotions from ordinary emotions; even if they differ in some respects, they do not differ sufficiently to be subject to completely different considerations of consistency. In accord with (3) he argues that we do not, even temporarily, believe that the fiction is true; and if we did, we would have contradictory beliefs leading to a different form of incoherence. Finally he claims that "I can only be moved by someone's plight if I believe that something terrible has happened to him" (Radford 1975, 68). This is understood as a formulation of narrow cognitivism in defense of (2).

The usual reply to Radford's argument is to deny that we are, in fact, committed to all three claims in the paradox of fiction. Since the incoherence is supposed to stem from our commitment to these three inconsistent claims, this would avoid the charge of irrationality. From this perspective, the descriptive and normative questions are addressed in exactly the same way. Denying that fictional emotions are genuine, or arguing that emotions do not require beliefs, would on this interpretation remove the threat of maintaining inconsistent beliefs.

However, this interpretation fails to capture Radford's puzzle. Radford's ardent defense of (1) shows that he cannot be committed to narrow cognitivism. Rather, his claim in (2) is that *in ordinary contexts* we are not moved when we lack the relevant beliefs (cf. Teroni and Cova in prep.). This claim is consistent with both (1) and (3) and therefore produces no paradox. Radford argues for this claim with a series of examples. Most famously, he points out that if he hears a harrowing story about someone's sister he will be harrowed, but this feeling disappears – to be replaced perhaps by indignation – if he then learns that the sister does not exist. The surprise is not the key factor. If we know in advance that our friend is merely acting out the experience of pain, we will not pity her. In such cases, pity in the absence of relevant beliefs would not just be unwarranted, it would be incomprehensible. Yet in the fictional context we are systematically moved even though we do not believe anyone has suffered. That is what Radford finds puzzling.

### *Radford's normative argument*

If it is not the paradox of fiction that explains our inconsistency and incoherence, what is it? Radford's focus is the experience of fictional emotions themselves. Regardless of our theoretical position on the three claims that constitute the paradox of fiction – even if, for instance, we follow Walton in rejecting (1) – Radford claims that we would still be incoherent in responding emotionally to fiction. The explanation must be that in so responding we violate a *norm* that governs emotions (cf. Gendler and Kovakovich 2006). Radford's examples indicate that in ordinary contexts, we violate the norm when we do not believe that there exists an appropriate object for the emotion. So the relevant norm might be that an experience of an emotion presupposes that such an object, with the relevant properties, exists – or at least presupposes the belief that it exists – and is otherwise defective. If this is a genuine normative constraint on emotions, there is something deeply incoherent about having an emotion while believing that there is no appropriate object. It would be like intending to perform an action while believing oneself incapable of performing it.

It is widely accepted that emotions are subject to normative constraints. For example, to be appropriate an emotion must fit its formal object, the property ascribed to the target in normal occurrences of the emotion: fear for danger, pity for suffering, and so on. Emotional responses that fail to meet this condition, such as elation at the death of a close friend or terror of a teddy bear, are the ones most likely to be called irrational. An additional dimension of fit is proportionate intensity; mild annoyance may fit a situation that boiling anger does not. The fictional emotions that Radford discusses arguably meet this constraint. The problem with pity of Anna Karenina is not that it is directed at, say, a happy situation or one that invites only mild concern; the formal object is intense suffering, even if no actual object suffers.

A different condition for the appropriateness of emotions is correctness (also called "fittingness"; see D'Arms and Jacobson 2000), which is associated with objective rationality. An emotion is correct so long as the evaluation associated with the emotion is accurate.

I may have excellent reason to think that my friend Andrew betrayed me, but anger at him is incorrect if he is in fact innocent. Even if fictional emotions fail to meet this condition – since no appropriate object exists – this cannot be the source of Radford's claim that they are incoherent. My anger at Andrew coheres with my beliefs regardless of whether it turns out to be undeserved. Similarly, a child's feelings about Santa Claus may be incorrect since there is no Santa, but they make sense in light of her beliefs.

Radford seems rather to be concerned that fictional emotions fail to meet a condition of *justification* (sometimes also called "warrant"), associated with subjective rationality. An emotion is justified so long as the evaluation associated with it is adequately responsive to one's evidence about the situation. If I have good reasons to think I am in danger, or am sufficiently sensitive to danger cues, fear is justified; if I have every reason to think I am safe, fear is unjustified. Emotions may be more or less justified insofar as evidence is stronger or weaker. But they will seem irrational if the evidence is all on the opposite side. Once I know that Andrew is innocent, continuing anger would be entirely unjustified and probably irrational. Similarly, anyone who knows Santa does not exist but still harbors hopes of his largesse can be described as incoherent. Since this seems to be our position with fictional emotions – we are fully aware that no appropriate object exists – Radford takes them to violate this normative constraint.

## Objections to Radford

There are objections to accepting such a normative constraint on emotions, however. Coherence and consistency are clear requirements for rational belief, but the same does not seem to apply to emotion. For example, we often experience "mixed feelings," as when we are happy for a friend who wins a prize but unhappy because we would have liked to win. By contrast with beliefs, it may be more rational to maintain both emotions rather than trying to resolve the conflict, because doing so strikes the right balance between our interests in ourselves and in others (Greenspan 1980, 1988). In this way emotions in response to fiction might be "emotionally rational" insofar as they are socially adaptive, getting us to identify and sympathize with other people (Robinson 2005, 146–148). Their being rational in one sense is, however, consistent with their being irrational in a different sense, as Robinson herself points out. As we have seen, in ordinary contexts emotions without the relevant beliefs are unjustified. If fictional emotions are not subject to the same normative constraints as such emotions, this cannot be because of general features of emotional rationality.

A different objection to the normative constraint focuses on the role played by emotional responses to the merely imagined in reasoning. For example, successful planning typically involves imagining different possibilities and choosing among them, something we accomplish in part by responding affectively to the possible outcomes (Currie and Ravenscroft 2002, 98). Gendler and Kovakovich (2006) appeal to experiments by Antonio Damasio and his colleagues to argue that emotions in response to the merely imagined are essential to rational decision-making. The experiments compare normal individuals and patients with damage to the ventromedial prefontal cortex in a gambling task. Normal participants' performance improves once they begin to respond affectively in anticipation of high-risk choices as measured by skin conductance, even before they can explicitly identify which options are high-risk. The performance of the patients with damage, who fail to experience negative affect, never improves even when they are consciously aware that they are making high-risk choices. Gendler and Kovakovich conclude that because anticipatory affect plays a key role in decision-making, it contributes to rationality rather than undermining it.

These cases do not undermine Radford's claim that fictional emotions are unjustified, however. First, the low-level "gut reactions" described by Damasio are closer to reflex responses than to genuine emotions. Second, the results show only that certain affective responses are a precondition of making good decisions, not that they contribute to the goodness of those decisions. In other cases our gut reactions may lead us wildly astray. A similar point can be made about the use of heuristics in reasoning. Deploying simple heuristics is adaptive insofar as it results in quick judgments under conditions of uncertainty, but in at least some cases the heuristics generate wrong judgments, most notoriously with respect to probability (Tversky and Kahneman 1974). Finally, even if affective responses to imagined scenarios contributed positively to planning and decision-making in every case, this would indicate only that they were rational in the sense of being instrumentally valuable (cf. Kim 2010). Radford (1989) himself takes the experience of fictional emotions to constitute one of the great pleasures in life. As we have seen, it is consistent with Radford's argument that fictional emotions be rational in one sense but not in another.

A more significant concern is that we do not criticize ourselves or each other for responding emotionally to fiction (though overreactions might be subject to criticism). By itself this observation does not undermine Radford's argument, for we could be subject to norms we do not recognize. My beliefs should be consistent whether or not I realize this and my reasoning is constrained by the laws of probability whether I am aware of them or not. However, in the case of faulty reasoning or inconsistent beliefs, I can in principle be brought to see where I have gone wrong. In the case of fictional emotions, we remain convinced that our responses are unproblematic even upon reflection, when we are fully aware that the objects of emotion do not exist and thoroughly familiar with Radford's arguments. In other words, the norms governing fictional emotions seem to differ from those governing emotions in ordinary contexts. Saying this does not resolve the problem, though, without an explanation of why. In the absence of such an explanation we are simply distinguishing fictional emotions from other emotions on the grounds that only the latter require beliefs in existence; this looks like an *ad hoc* maneuver to avoid Radford's conclusion that fictional emotions are incoherent without such beliefs.

One explanation of why only certain emotional responses seem to be subject to a norm of consistency with beliefs might be the frequently noted connection between emotion and the motivation to act. In contexts where the demand for action is pressing or immediate, as when we are confronted directly with a situation, our emotional responses presuppose the existence of the appropriate objects. In fictions about purely invented characters and events, where action is impossible, we are not subject to the same constraint.

If this is right, rather than a dichotomy between emotions in the fictional context and emotions in other contexts we should find a range of cases between the two extremes. For instance, although direct action is typically ruled out in engagement with nonfiction representations, indirect actions are possible and subject to a justification condition. In response to a sympathetic history of Richard III (or even a historically researched fiction) I might decide to join the Richard III Society and work to exonerate him; this only makes sense if I believe the work to be accurate. Similarly, even though planning involves the imagination of potential outcomes, insofar as action is the goal our affective responses must be constrained by beliefs about what is possible. In planning a dinner party I might be elated picturing myself creating wonderful dishes with a *Bewitched*-style crinkle of the nose, but it would be irrational to take this feeling as a guide to action. On this picture, if Radford is wrong it is not because no emotions are constrained by beliefs, but rather because fictional emotions typically lack the connections to action that characterize emotions in other contexts.

### *Norms for fiction*

Although fictional emotions are not subject to the same norms of consistency with beliefs as other emotions, they are subject to other norms (cf. Gilmore 2011). We have already seen that such emotions should fit their formal objects. Pitying Ivan Denisovich is appropriate, whereas envying his life in the gulag is not. In addition, we can specify versions of the conditions of justification and correctness for the fictional context (Friend 2010). An emotion counts as fictionally justified so long as it is reasonable in light of one's fictional information; justification reflects competence at deploying the "principles of generation" (Walton 1990) that generate fictional truths. An emotion is fictionally correct so long as the associated evaluation accurately represents the fictional situation, even if one is unaware of this. Being worried that Mr. Hyde will harm Dr. Jekyll is fictionally justified up to a certain point in Stevenson's novella, but given that they are the same person it is fictionally incorrect. By contrast detesting Sethe for killing all her children (rather than just Beloved) is neither correct nor justified.

These normative constraints reflect the idea that our emotional responses to fiction typically follow our emotional responses to real life. But there are further conditions that fictional emotions may need to meet that do not apply to emotions in other contexts (Currie 1990, 213–215; Livingston and Mele 1997). For example, genre conventions play a role. Feeling depressed because of the death and destruction wrought by the Killer Rabbit in Monty Python's *The Holy Grail* is inappropriate, even if such carnage would warrant bleak despair and terror in reality. Black comedies typically invite responses such as amusement that are neither justified nor correct in light of the fictional truth (Currie 1990, 213). Similarly, artistic skill is relevant. The justified and correct response to a scene of someone dying of a terminal illness might be sadness, but if the film is mere sentimental rubbish this response will not be appropriate. Some philosophers also take moral considerations to be relevant. If a story invites us to sympathize with an evil character, we might treat this response as "unmerited" insofar as it is unethical (Gaut 1998). Others argue, though, that entering into immoral points of view, and experiencing the attendant emotions, is a potentially valuable feature of engaging with fiction (Jacobson 1997; Kieran 2003; Eaton 2012). If this is right, it is another way in which the normative constraints on fictional emotions depart from the constraints on emotions in other contexts.

## Conclusion

Emotional responses to fiction raise two distinct questions: the descriptive question, which concerns whether these responses constitute genuine emotions of the same sort as emotions in other contexts; and the normative question, which concerns the rationality or appropriateness of these emotions. According to the standard interpretation, both questions can be answered by rejecting one of the three claims that constitute the paradox of fiction. I have argued, however, that although resolving the paradox is relevant to the descriptive question, it is not the right strategy for addressing the normative question. Nonetheless imagination plays a key role in how we approach both questions, by providing a context within which fictional emotions may be quarantined and by generating distinctive norms for evaluating those emotions.

## Acknowledgments

I would like to thank Amy Kind and Shen-yi Liao for helpful comments on a previous draft. I would also like to thank audiences at conferences in Paris, Leeds, and Ann Arbor, Michigan, for discussion of related material.

## References

Carroll, N. (1990) *The Philosophy of Horror: Or, Paradoxes of the Heart*, New York: Routledge.
Cova, F., A. García, and V. Sennwald (In prep.) "Is What I'm Feeling Really Genuine? Fiction vs. Reality."
Currie, G. (1990) *The Nature of Fiction*, Cambridge: Cambridge University Press.
Currie, G., and I. Ravenscroft (2002) *Recreative Minds: Imagination in Philosophy and Psychology*, Oxford: Oxford University Press.
D'Arms, J., and D. Jacobson (2000) "The Moralistic Fallacy: On the 'Appropriateness' of Emotions," *Philosophy and Phenomenological Research* 61: 65–90.
Eaton, A.W. (2012) "Robust Immoralism," *Journal of Aesthetics and Art Criticism* 70: 281–292.
Friend, S. (2003) "How I Really Feel about JFK," in M. Kieran and D.M. Lopes (eds.) *Imagination, Philosophy, and the Arts*, London: Routledge, 35–53.
Friend, S. (2010) "Getting Carried Away," in *Film and the Emotions*, special issue, *Midwest Studies in Philosophy* 34: 77–105.
Gaut, B. (1998) "The Ethical Criticism of Art," in J. Levinson (ed.) *Aesthetics and Ethics: Essays at the Intersection*, Cambridge: Cambridge University Press, 182–203.
Gaut, B. (2003) "Reasons, Emotions, and Fictions," in M. Kieran and D.M. Lopes (eds.) *Imagination, Philosophy, and the Arts*, New York: Routledge, 14–34.
Gaut, B. (2007) *Art, Emotion and Ethics*, Oxford: Oxford University Press.
Gendler, T.S. (2003) "On the Relation between Pretense and Belief," in M. Kieran and D.M. Lopes (eds.) *Imagination, Philosophy, and the Arts*, London: Routledge, 125–141.
Gendler, T.S., and K. Kovakovich (2006) "Genuine Rational Fictional Emotions," in M. Kieran (ed.) *Contemporary Debates in Aesthetics and the Philosophy of Art*, Oxford: Blackwell, 241–253.
Gilmore, J. (2011) "Aptness of Emotions for Fictions and Imaginings," *Pacific Philosophical Quarterly* 92: 468–489.
Greenspan, P.S. (1980) "A Case of Mixed Feelings: Ambivalence and the Logic of Emotion," in A.O. Rorty (ed.) *Explaining Emotions*, Berkeley and Los Angeles: University of California Press, 223–250.
Greenspan, P.S. (1988) *Emotions and Reasons: An Inquiry into Emotional Justification*, New York: Routledge.
Hartz, G.A. (1999) "How We Can Be Moved by Anna Karenina, Green Slime, and a Red Pony," *Philosophy* 74: 557–578.
Jacobson, D. (1997) "In Praise of Immoral Art," *Philosophical Topics* 25: 155–199.
Kieran, M. (2003) "Forbidden Knowledge: The Challenge of Immoralism," in J.L. Bermúdez and Sebastian Gardner (eds.) *Art and Morality*, London: Routledge, 56–73.
Kim, S. (2010) "The Rationality of Emotion toward Fiction," in *Film and the Emotions*, special issue, *Midwest Studies in Philosophy* 34: 106–119.
Lamarque, P. (1981) "How Can We Fear and Pity Fictions?" *British Journal of Aesthetics* 21: 291–304.
LeDoux, J. (1996) *The Emotional Brain: The Mysterious Underpinnings of Emotional Life*, New York: Simon & Schuster.
Livingston, P., and A.L. Mele (1997) "Evaluating Emotional Responses to Fiction," in M. Hjort and S. Laver (eds.) *Emotion and the Arts*, New York: Oxford University Press, 157–176.
Lyons, W.E. (1980) *Emotion*, Cambridge: Cambridge University Press.
Matravers, D. (1998) *Art and Emotion*, Oxford: Oxford University Press.
Moran, R. (1994) "The Expression of Feeling in Imagination," *Philosophical Review* 103: 75–106.
Neill, A. (1991) "Fear, Fiction and Make-Believe," *Journal of Aesthetics and Art Criticism* 49: 47–56.
Nussbaum, M.C. (2001) *Upheavals of Thought: The Intelligence of Emotions*, Cambridge: Cambridge University Press.
Oakley, J. (1992) *Morality and the Emotions*, London: Routledge.
Prinz, J.J. (2004) *Gut Reactions: A Perceptual Theory of Emotion*, New York: Oxford University Press.
Radford, C. (1975) "How Can We Be Moved by the Fate of Anna Karenina?" *Proceedings of the Aristotelian Society, Supplementary Volume* 49: 67–80.
Radford, C. (1982) "Stuffed Tigers: A Reply to H.O. Mounce," *Philosophy* 57: 529–532.
Radford, C. (1989) "Replies to Three Critics," *Philosophy* 64: 93–97.
Radford, C. (1995) "Fiction, Pity, Fear, and Jealousy," *Journal of Aesthetics and Art Criticism* 53: 71–75.
Radford, C. (2000) "Neuroscience and Anna: A Reply to Glenn Hartz," *Philosophy* 75: 437–440.
Robinson, J. (2005) *Deeper than Reason: Emotion and Its Role in Literature, Music, and Art*, Oxford: Oxford University Press.

Solomon, R.C. (2003) *Not Passion's Slave: Emotions and Choice*, New York: Oxford University Press.
Stecker, R. (2011) "Should We Still Care about the Paradox of Fiction?" *British Journal of Aesthetics* 51: 295–308.
Stocker, M. (1987) "Emotional Thoughts," *American Philosophical Quarterly* 24: 59–69.
Suits, D.B. (2006) "Really Believing in Fiction," *Pacific Philosophical Quarterly* 87: 369–386.
Teroni, F., and F. Cova (In prep.) "Why There Still Is a Paradox of Fiction."
Tversky, A., and D. Kahneman (1974) "Judgment under Uncertainty: Heuristics and Biases," *Science* 185: 1124–1131.
Walton, K.L. (1978) "Fearing Fictions," *Journal of Philosophy* 75: 5–27.
Walton, K.L. (1990) *Mimesis as Make-Believe: On the Foundations of the Representational Arts*, Cambridge, MA: Harvard University Press.
Weinberg, J.M., and A. Meskin (2006) "Puzzling over the Imagination: Philosophical Problems, Architectural Solutions," in S. Nichols (ed.) *The Architecture of the Imagination: New Essays on Pretence, Possibility, and Fiction*, Oxford: Oxford University Press, 175–202.

# PART IV

# Imagination in philosophy of mind and cognitive science

# 17

# THE COGNITIVE ARCHITECTURE OF IMAGINATIVE RESISTANCE

*Kengo Miyazono and Shen-yi Liao*

Very roughly, *imagination* is the attitude with which we think about possibilities, reason counterfactually, construct pretense scenarios, and engage with stories and other representational artworks. As a part of our mental repertoire, it interacts with beliefs, desires, emotions, and other attitudes and processes to allow us to engage in a rich array of activities. (We will say more about imagination in Section 1.)

Very roughly, *imaginative resistance* is the phenomenon in which we, who are otherwise competent imaginers, experience a constraint in taking part in an imaginative activity. Philosophers have focused primarily on when people experience imaginative resistance in response to stories. For example, if a story simply states that "in killing her baby, Giselda did the right thing; after all, it was a girl" without any additional context, then many readers are likely to experience a constraint in imaginatively engaging with this story. (We will say more about imaginative resistance in Section 2.)

So, where is imagination in imaginative resistance?

In this chapter, we seek to answer this question by connecting two ongoing lines of inquiry in different subfields of philosophy. In philosophy of mind, philosophers have been trying to understand imagination's place in cognitive architecture. In aesthetics, philosophers have been trying to understand the phenomenon of imaginative resistance, especially in connection with fictional narratives. By connecting these two lines of inquiry, we hope to achieve mutual illumination of an attitude and a phenomenon that have vexed philosophers.

Our strategy is to reorient the imaginative resistance literature from the perspective of cognitive architecture.[1] Existing taxonomies of positions in the imaginative resistance literature (e.g., Liao and Gendler forthcoming) have focused on disagreements over the *source* and *scope* of the phenomenon – mainly, with respect to the question of when imaginative resistance arises. In contrast, our proposed taxonomy focuses on the *psychological components* necessary for explaining imaginative resistance.

We start by characterizing the attitude and the phenomenon under discussion. In Section 1, we explain the cognitive architectural framework that guides this chapter, and clarify the sense of imagination that is relevant to our discussion. In Section 2, we give an overview of imaginative resistance. We then offer a new taxonomy of accounts of imaginative resistance based on their cognitive architectural commitments. In Section 3, we examine cognitive imagination (or belief-like imagination) accounts. In Section 4, we examine conative imagination (or desire-like imagination) accounts. In Section 5, we examine accounts of imaginative resistance that do not fundamentally involve any imaginative attitudes. We conclude, in Section 6, by gesturing toward directions for further research.

## 1 Imagination

### *1.1 Imagination as a propositional attitude*

Imagination's nature is surprisingly mysterious. Surprising because it is so widely discussed and invoked in theories – in philosophy of mind, in epistemology, in aesthetics, and in ethics (Gendler 2011). Mysterious because even the experts have a hard time finding a unifying concept from the various uses. For example, in *Mimesis as Make-Believe*, the text that has arguably become the reference point for contemporary philosophical discussions of imagination, Kendall Walton (1990, 19) writes,

> What is it to imagine? We have examined a number of dimensions along which imaginings can vary; shouldn't we now spell out what they have in common? – Yes, if we can. But I can't.

In this dispiriting spirit, numerous other philosophers – including Gendler (2011), Kind (2013), and Van Leeuwen (2013) – have commented on the heterogeneity of imagination. Hence, instead of tackling the incredibly difficult, if not impossible, project of delineating a central concept of imagination, we will simply stipulate the sense of imagination that will be relevant to our discussion.

We will talk about *imagination* in its *attitudinal* sense – as a component of one's cognitive architecture. As an attitude, imagination is located at the same explanatory level as other commonly recognized folk psychological attitudes such as belief and desire. Specifically, we will talk about imagination as a *propositional* attitude – it, like belief and desire, takes propositions as its content. Of course, there are many other senses of imagination (see Gendler 2011 and Van Leeuwen 2013 for a sample), but we will set them aside in this chapter. Even with this narrow focus, there remain significant and substantial debates about the nature of imagination; these are debates about imagination's place in cognitive architecture.

### *1.2 Cognitive architecture*

A *cognitive architecture* is a theory about the mind at the functional – as opposed to, say, neurological or biological – level that aims to explain relevant psychological phenomena. By (literally) drawing out the functional connections between various components of the mind – a practice that is sometimes (derisively) called "boxology" – a cognitive architecture highlights psychological laws at the functional level.[2]

On a familiar analogy, *attitudes* – such as belief, desire, and imagination – are containers of content. Each attitude is associated with a set of characteristic functions, or inputs and outputs. *Mental states* – such as specific beliefs, desires, and imaginings – are combinations of a container and a content, which is typically a proposition. Note that the container metaphor is misleading in one respect: not every mental state can be neatly slotted into a container. Instead, a mental state only needs to exhibit enough of the characteristic functions of an attitude to count, and ambiguous cases are common.

### *1.3 Cognitive architectural debates about the imagination*

In contemporary discussion, there are two prominent debates about imagination as a component of cognitive architecture (Liao and Doggett 2014). The first debate concerns the existence of an imaginative attitude that is "belief-like," which we will call *cognitive imagination*. The second debate concerns the existence of an imaginative attitude that is "desire-like," which we will call *conative imagination*. For an example of each, consider what happens when one pretends to be Romeo in the final act of *Romeo and Juliet*: one cognitively imagines that Juliet is dead, and consequently one also conatively imagines that Romeo is dead too.

There are a number of features that can make these respective imaginative attitudes belief-like or desire like, such as functional roles, inferential patterns, and directions-of-fit. For example, some defenders of both cognitive and conative imagination say that pairs of cognitive and conative imaginings can generate actions and emotions in the same way that pairs of beliefs and desires can; and that's the sense in which these imaginative attitudes are, respectively, belief-like and desire-like (Doggett and Egan 2007, 2012).

The dominant position in this literature accepts cognitive imagination but rejects conative imagination (e.g., Funkhouser and Spaulding 2009; Nichols and Stich 2003; Kind 2011; Weinberg and Meskin 2006a, 2006b). A notable minority accepts both cognitive and conative imagination (e.g., Doggett and Egan 2007, 2012; Currie and Ravenscroft 2002). Another notable minority rejects both cognitive and conative imagination as distinctive, *sui generis* attitudes (e.g., Langland-Hassan 2012, 2014; Leslie 1987, 1994; and plausibly also Gendler 2008a, 2008b). As far as we know, despite the logical possibility, no one accepts conative imagination but rejects cognitive imagination. Finally, of course, there exist a variety of positions that do not fall neatly into this taxonomy (e.g., Schellenberg 2013; Van Leeuwen 2011).

The broader debate between these positions on imaginative attitudes primarily turns on the respective cognitive architectures' ability to explain relevant psychological phenomena. In the context of this broader debate, imaginative resistance is one psychological phenomenon that can be used to test different cognitive architectures' explanatory power and empirical adequacy. For example, all else being equal, if it turns out that the best explanation of imaginative resistance invokes cognitive imagination but not conative imagination, then imaginative resistance functions as a data point that pushes us, if only weakly, toward the currently dominant position.

With this broader debate in mind, we will examine different accounts of imaginative resistance and draw out their cognitive architectural commitments in Sections 3–5. Specifically, we will focus on where in the mind different accounts locate the experienced constraint that characterizes imaginative resistance. Before we can do so, we will give an overview of the puzzling psychological phenomenon in question.

## 2 Imaginative resistance

### *2.1 Phenomenon and puzzles*

Arguably, contemporary philosophical discussions of imaginative resistance began with Walton (1994, 31; but see also Walton 1990; Moran 1994; Gendler 2000), who noted a curious asymmetry while echoing a passage from David Hume (1757):

> If we find the perspective presented in a story [morally] offensive enough, we may object even to imagining taking it up. We might refuse to empathize with a

character who accepts it, to put ourselves imaginatively in her shoes. We usually don't flinch at imagining accepting as true nonmoral propositions that we firmly believe to be false: the proposition that there is a ring that makes its wearer invisible, or that a village in Scotland appears and disappears every hundred years.

On a first pass, the asymmetry that Walton points to is that we do not resist imagining nonmoral propositions that we do not believe in, but we do resist imagining moral propositions we do not believe in.

What is an example of a moral proposition that we resist imagining? Walton (1994) offers the following:

*Giselda*: In killing her baby, Giselda did the right thing; after all, it was a girl.

Suppose the reader reads this sentence as part of a story's text (hereafter, when the reader *encounters* "*Giselda*"). The reader is likely to have several related reactions that give rise to distinctive philosophical puzzles (Liao and Gendler forthcoming; see also Weatherson 2004 and Walton 2006):

1 Imaginative puzzle: Why does the reader have difficulty *imagining* that Giselda really did the morally right thing?
2 Fictionality puzzle: Why does the reader have difficulty accepting that it is *fictional*, or true in the story world, that Giselda really did the right thing?
3 Phenomenological puzzle: Why does the reader *experience* a sense of jarring confusion in response to the sentence?
4 Aesthetic value puzzle: Why does the reader think or judge that the story would be *aesthetically* superior if this sentence were omitted?

Given the complexity of imaginative resistance, it is no wonder that Walton (2006) wryly remarks "the puzzle of imaginative resistance" is composed of a series of misnomers, except the word "of"; it is not just one puzzle, but several puzzles, and not all of them have to do with imagination or with resistance.[3] We will focus on the puzzles that have to do with psychological aspects of imaginative resistance, namely, the imaginative and phenomenological puzzles.[4] Both are concerned with how readers psychologically respond to sentences like the one above, which evoke imaginative resistance.

Imaginative resistance should be distinguished from the related phenomenon of *hermeneutic recalibration*, which is a common literary technique of temporarily puzzling the reader so as to cause her to reconsider and reinterpret the imaginative prompt (Liao 2013). In cases of hermeneutic recalibration, one eventually comes to a relatively stable understanding of the imaginative prompt. For example, one can feel like one can finally make sense of an initially puzzling sentence. However, in cases of imaginative resistance, even after multiple attempts to reconsider and reinterpret the imaginative prompt, the characteristic reactions – the difficulties with imagining and accepting the puzzling proposition, the experience of jarring confusion, and the thought that the work would be aesthetically better off without the puzzling proposition – persist.

Even if we restrict our discussion to cases involving persistent perplexity, there remain disagreements about the scope of the phenomenon. For example, while Tamar Szabó Gendler (2000, 2006) argues for the centrality of moral deviance to resistance phenomena, others think that imaginative resistance can also arise with cases of aesthetic deviance, epistemic deviance, etc. (e.g., Walton 1994, 2006; Weatherson 2004; Yablo 2002). Hence, our first pass at the asymmetry that defines imaginative resistance will have to be refined accordingly to reflect these scope disagreements. Moreover, these disagreements about the exact explanandum constitute one source for the conflicting explanans of imaginative resistance. Indeed, as we will see next, these disagreements about scope can even make other philosophers doubt the existence of the whole phenomenon.

### *2.2 Skepticism about imaginative resistance*

On our treatment, the phenomenon of imaginative resistance functions as a data point in resolving cognitive architectural debates about imagination. However, it is only fair to note that whether it really counts as a data point is in contention. There exists a group of philosophers – call them *imaginative resistance doubters* – who have expressed skepticism about the very existence of a philosophical problem in the vicinity.

Imaginative resistance doubters contend that there is no such thing as imaginative resistance per se. Rather, they maintain, the appearance of a philosophical problem arises from the bizarre so-called stories that philosophers have concocted. Nothing like the imaginative or phenomenological puzzles arises with narratives we ordinarily encounter in nonphilosophical contexts. Consider the following statement, from Mary Mothersill (2003, 90):

> a fictional world is not created by a single proposition and hence that whether that proposition is or is not imaginable is otiose. … to grasp the moral content of a novel, you have to read the whole novel.

Imaginative resistance, the doubters contend, can at most be found in philosophers' poor attempts at literature. It is only because they have focused on single propositions divorced from context – or one-page stories constructed for the sake of making a philosophical point – that philosophers think there is a problem to be explained (Todd 2009; cf. Tanner 1994). The doubters contend that propositions that are alleged to evoke imaginative resistance typically cease to do so once appropriate context is given (modulo some relativity regarding general imaginative capacity).

There is a core insight that can be gleaned from the doubters' arguments: imaginative resistance is not a phenomenon about particular propositions; instead it is a phenomenon about the interactions between particular propositions and particular contexts. While affirming the existence of the phenomenon, recent accounts of imaginative resistance have incorporated the core insight of the doubters to refine the puzzles and solutions associated with the phenomenon (see, e.g., Brock 2012 and Liao et al. 2014).

## 3 Cognitive imagination accounts

Cognitive imagination accounts typically invoke cognitive imagination *in conjunction with* other relatively uncontroversial attitudes or processes (e.g., belief and desire) in their explanations of imaginative resistance. Given that these explanations appeal to cognitive imagination *and* other attitudes or processes, these accounts can vary with respect to the degree to which cognitive imagination is central to explaining the phenomenon. However, despite such differences, they nevertheless share the core feature of placing the constraint that one experiences during imaginative resistance on cognitive imagination.

Although they are not always explicit, these accounts typically take conative imagination to be unnecessary for explaining imaginative resistance. Hence, insofar as these accounts are successful, they push us toward the position in the cognitive architectural debate that accepts cognitive imagination and rejects conative imagination.

We discuss four types of cognitive imagination accounts below. The distinction between these accounts does not necessarily imply strict incompatibility between them. For example, it might turn out that different accounts provide plausible descriptions of different aspects of the phenomenon of imaginative resistance. Or, it might turn out that an account is plausible at one level of description (e.g., the personal level), while another is plausible at another level of description (e.g., the subpersonal level).

### *3.1 Single code for cognitive imagination and belief*

One type of cognitive imagination account appeals to the functional and representational similarities between cognitive imagination and belief to explain imaginative resistance.

According to a now widely accepted hypothesis, cognitive imagination and believe operate on a *single code*: they share three key characteristics (Nichols 2004, 2006). First, cognitive imagination has belief-like propositional content. The same proposition, such as <Mitt Romney is the President of the United States>, can be taken on by both cognitive imagination and belief. Second, cognitive imagination displays belief-like inferential regularities (Leslie 1987). When one believes the proposition <if a cup filled with water is upturned, it is now empty> and the proposition <a cup filled with water is upturned>, then one is strongly disposed to believe the proposition <the cup is now empty>. Similarly, when one cognitively imagines the proposition <if a cup filled with water is upturned, it is now empty> and the proposition <a cup filled with water is upturned>, then one is strongly disposed to cognitively imagine the proposition <the cup is now empty>. Third, and most importantly, cognitive imagination has belief-like functional connections to moral and affect systems – as we will quickly see below.

Shaun Nichols (2004, 2006) argues, on the basis of this picture, that imaginative resistance is best explained by the hypothesis that cognitive imaginings are processed by a moral system in the same way that analogous beliefs are processed. When one believes that a mother kills her baby merely because the baby is a girl, one's moral system typically produces responses of condemnation. Similarly, when one cognitively imagines – when encountering *Giselda* – that a mother kills her baby merely because the baby is a girl, one's moral system typically produces responses of condemnation too. Given these responses of condemnation, one encounters difficulties with cognitively imagining – when encountering *Giselda* – that the mother did the morally right thing.

Jonathan Weinberg and Aaron Meskin (Weinberg and Meskin 2006b; see also Meskin and Weinberg 2011) propose a similar idea. On their explanation, imaginative resistance arises from a conflict between different cognitive systems. When one encounters *Giselda*, there exists a conflict between one's representation input system – cognitive imagination – that takes in the explicitly stipulated moral deviance (namely, Giselda did the morally right thing) as its content, and one's moral system that makes an independent judgment (namely, Giselda did not do the morally right thing) on the basis of the fictional scenario's relevant nonmoral features. The account by Weinberg and Meskin is peculiar in that it allows for the cases where there is moral deviance but imaginative resistance does not arise (see also Weinberg 2008). On their explanation, these cases are possible because under certain circumstances either the relevant representation input system or the relevant processes within the moral system can be locally suspended so that no psychological conflict arises. (We will say more about these cases in Section 3.3.)

### *3.2 Cognitive imagination plus belief about the world*

Another type of cognitive imagination account appeals to the *interactions* between cognitive imagination and belief to explain imaginative resistance. To start, we will focus on accounts that focus on interactions between cognitive imaginings and *beliefs about the real world* (as opposed to beliefs about the imaginative prompt itself).

In particular, many of these accounts focus on the supervenience relationships that hold in the real world. On their diagnoses, imaginative resistance is the manifestation of the inability to cognitively imagine stories that involve *higher-lower inconsistencies* (Walton 1994; Weatherson 2004; Miyazono in prep.; Stear forthcoming). These inconsistencies can arise with propositions that are true, when they are true, in virtue of the truth of other propositions. For example, some philosophers think that a proposition about an action's moral status is true, when it is true, in virtue of the truth of other propositions about nonmoral features of that action, such as propositions about the harms that the action causes. In this example, the moral propositions are *higher-level* and the nonmoral propositions are *lower-level.* What is peculiar about prompts that evoke imaginative resistance, such as *Giselda,* is that they involve inconsistencies between the higher- and lower-level propositions that one is supposed to cognitively imagine.

Higher-lower inconsistencies arise because we have beliefs about how higher-level propositions should relate to lower-level propositions, which we import into our imaginative engagements. For example, we might think that, insofar as female infanticide can be the morally right thing to do in some cases, it is only *because* of some explicable reason like not committing the female infanticide would cause more deaths. When one encounters *Giselda* without additional context, no such explicable reason is present, and so given our belief in the relationship between moral and nonmoral propositions, we cannot cognitively imagine the higher-level moral proposition (namely, Giselda did the morally right thing) given what we have cognitively imagined at the lower level (namely, Giselda killed the baby just because the baby is a girl). As Brian Weatherson (2004, 21) notes, "we can imagine the higher-level claim only some way or another, just as we imagine a chair only as some chair or other." We cannot cognitively imagine the moral proposition, because the nonmoral propositions we cognitively imagined do not constitute one of the ways of realizing the moral rightness of female infanticide.

Of course, the relevant beliefs about the world that affect our cognitive imaginings need not be beliefs about supervenience relationships. For example, Cain Todd (2009) speculates that deontologists and utilitarians might respond differently to the same stories that are alleged to evoke imaginative resistance. More generally, one's background belief about (meta)ethical issues might shape one's cognitive imaginings differently. Difference in background beliefs about (meta)ethical issues might help to explain some individual differences in imaginative resistance that some philosophers have observed.

### *3.3 Cognitive imagination plus belief about the imaginative prompt*

Continuing our focus on accounts that use interactions between cognitive imagination and belief to explain imaginative resistance, we now turn to accounts that focus on interactions between cognitive imaginings and *beliefs about the imaginative prompt* (as opposed to beliefs about the real world). On these accounts, during imaginative engagements with particular prompts, our cognitive imaginings are shaped by beliefs that we have about the prompts.

The most notable variant of this type of account appeals to beliefs about genre conventions that govern stories (Gendler 2000; Weinberg 2008; Nanay 2010; Liao 2011; Willard in prep.). On their diagnoses, the relevant constraints on cognitive imagination do not come from beliefs about the real world, but beliefs about fictional worlds. For example, while few people believe that divine command theory is true of the real world, many more believe that divine command theory is true of fictional worlds of creation myths and other religious stories. As such, while few people believe that the truth of moral propositions supervene on the truth of nonmoral propositions about God or gods' pronouncements, many more believe that the fictional truth of moral propositions supervene on the fictional truth of nonmoral propositions about God or gods' pronouncements, when it comes to creation myths and other religious stories. The belief about divine command theory being true in creation myths and other religious stories is an example of a belief about genre conventions. These accounts can explain why the same proposition can be puzzling in one story but not another, when two stories belong to different genres and so are governed by different conventions.

It is possible to incorporate the role of beliefs about the imaginative prompt into accounts of imaginative resistance discussed earlier. For example, Weinberg (2008) modifies the earlier account in Weinberg and Meskin (2006b) to make explicit the role of beliefs about genre conventions. Recall that on Weinberg and Meskin's original account, imaginative resistance arises from a conflict between cognitive systems, but conflicts can be avoided when one cognitive system can be "locally suspended." According to Weinberg (2008), beliefs about genre conventions constitute one way to locally suspend the moral system – or, more precisely, to locally suspend the typical connection between cognitive imagination and the moral system – such that no conflict arises.

This type of imaginative resistance account has recently received some support regarding its empirical adequacy. Shen-yi Liao, Nina Strohminger, and Chandra Sekhar Sripada (Liao et al. 2014) report two empirical studies they conducted to show that beliefs of genre conventions can influence one's imaginative responses to fictions. Study 1 shows that there is a correlation between one's familiarity with a genre, which affects the likelihood that one correctly believes the relevant genre conventions, and one's experienced difficulty in cognitively imagining a morally deviant proposition. Study 2 finds that manipulating governing genre conventions makes the same morally deviant proposition relatively difficult to cognitively imagine in one story but not in another.

### 3.4 Cognitive imagination plus desire

The final type of cognitive imagination account appeals to the interactions between cognitive imagination and desire to explain imaginative resistance. According to these accounts, the difficulty with cognitively imagining puzzling propositions is not a kind of inability, but a kind of unwillingness.

Gendler (2000, 2006) provides the paradigmatic example of this type of account. Gendler (2000) notes that resistance-evoking stories are what she calls "non-distorting fictions." Something that is true in the real world is likely to be true in these fictional worlds, and more importantly, something that is true in these fictional worlds is likely to be true in the real world. Hence, if we judge something as true in these stories, there is a prima facie demand that we judge it as true in the real world as well. For example, if we are to cognitively imagine that Giselda's female infanticide is morally right, then there is pressure on us to believe that analogous cases of female infanticide in the real world are morally right as well. However, as Gendler notes, we have strong desire not to believe that analogous cases of female infanticide are morally right in reality, and so this in turn pressures us not to cognitively imagine that Giselda's female infanticide is morally right. As Gendler (2000, 77) puts the point: "my hypothesis is that cases that evoke genuine imaginative resistance will be cases where the reader feels that she is being asked to export a way of looking at the actual world which she does not wish to add to her conceptual repertoire."

Gendler (2006) provides a refinement of the earlier account on which desire plays a less central role in explaining imaginative resistance. Moran (1994) and Currie (2011) can also be seen as proponents of accounts that give desire a significant role in explaining imaginative resistance, sometimes via emotions that are generated by the relevant desires.

## 4 Conative imagination accounts

Conative imagination accounts invoke both cognitive and conative imagination in their explanations of imaginative resistance. As the name indicates, a core feature that these accounts share is that they place the constraint that one experiences during imaginative resistance on conative imagination. Insofar as these accounts are successful, they push us toward the position in the cognitive architectural debate that accepts both cognitive and conative imagination.

### *4.1 Desire-like imagination*

There seems to be an asymmetry between *supposing* and *imagining* a morally deviant proposition. We seem to have no trouble supposing that female infanticide is morally right without any further explanation for the purpose of, say, philosophical arguments. However, as our responses to *Giselda* show, we do have trouble imagining that female infanticide is morally right, absent some explanation.

Gregory Currie (2002) gives an interpretation of this asymmetry at the cognitive architectural level. What we ordinarily call "imagination" is the use of both cognitive and conative imagination. In contrast, what we ordinarily call "supposition" is the use of cognitive imagination without the accompaniment of conative imagination. On this interpretation, the fact that we can easily suppose the moral rightness of female infanticide but cannot easily imagine so is evidence that cognitive imagination does not play a central role in explaining imaginative resistance. In fact, the explanatory work is done by a specific version of conative imagination that he calls "desire-like imagination."

Whereas to desire something is to want it to be the case in the real world, to desire-like imagine something is to want it to be the case in some imagined or fictional world. However, Currie says that there is an important difference between the dissociability of cognitive imagining and belief and the dissociability of desire-like imagining and desire. While we can easily cognitively imagine something we do not believe, we cannot easily desire-like imagine something we do not desire. Hence, for the majority of people who do not in fact desire that female infanticide for no obvious reason is morally right, it is difficult to desire-like imagine that female infanticide for no obvious reason is morally right. And this difficulty to desire-like imagine so is what explains the difficulty with imagination that *Giselda* brings out.

### *4.2 Value-like imagination*

Dustin Stokes (2006) revises Currie's account and argues that the relevant conative imaginative attitude is not Currie's desire-like imagination but what he calls "value-like imagination." Stokes relies on David Lewis's (1989) picture of valuing, on which to value something is to have a second-order desire of that thing: to value *x* is to desire that one desires *x*. On Stokes's account, imaginative resistance is best explained by value-like imagination, an attitude to want oneself to want something to be the case in some imagined or fictional world.

Stokes argues that desire-like imagination is insufficient to explain imaginative resistance. For example, it is not clear how Currie's view explains why we experience imaginative resistance with a story that says that a really dumb Knock-Knock joke is hilariously funny (Walton 1994). We have no actual desire about the joke and its funniness. So there is no reason to think that our desire-like imagination is constrained by any actual desire in this case. However, there is reason to think that it would be a part of our value system that the dumb joke is not hilariously funny: we do not want it to be true of ourselves that we want the dumb joke to be funny. Hence, given the relatively low dissociability of value-like imagining and value, we cannot easily value-imagine that a really dumb Knock-Knock joke is hilariously funny.

## 5 No-imagination accounts

No-imagination accounts bypass imaginative attitudes altogether in their explanations of imaginative resistance. In other words, on these accounts neither cognitive nor conative imagination – as they are standardly characterized – factor in understanding the psychology of imaginative resistance at the fundamental level. They place the constraint that one experiences during imaginative resistance on neither cognitive nor conative imagination, but elsewhere in cognitive architecture. Hence, insofar as these accounts are successful, they push us toward the position in the cognitive architectural debate that rejects both cognitive and conative imagination.

### *5.1 Alief*

In an evolution of her earlier views, Gendler (2008a, 2008b) argues that *imaginative contagion*, cases where (merely) imaginative engagement with fictions can reshape our real-world moral views, may ultimately be traced to a novel psychological state that she calls "alief." Roughly, *aliefs* are innate or habitual propensities to respond to apparent stimuli in automatic and associative ways. According to Gendler (2008b), aliefs are antecedent to other cognitive attitudes, including belief and cognitive imagination: "Indeed, one might even argue that it is out of these *more primitive* association patterns [that constitute aliefs] … that the *less fundamental* differentiated attitudes like belief, desire, and imagination are constructed" (643; our emphases). Alief is unlike imagination in some ways; for example, aliefs tend to be opaque to the subject: they are not generally available for introspective access. However, alief is also like imagination in other ways; for example, they are both to a degree source-insensitive: they need not track how the subject consciously conceives of the world.

Although Gendler never explicitly spells out, in print, the implication of alief for explaining imaginative resistance, the relative source-insensitivity of aliefs suggests a relatively straightforward proposal. Since aliefs are source-insensitive, even contents we consciously recognize as purely imaginary can produce powerful emotional and cognitive responses of the sort that underpin imaginative contagion. Not all contents do so, of course. However, plausibly our deeply held moral commitments are just the sort of content that would be encoded in aliefs, such that being asked to imagine that Giselda's female infanticide is morally right would trigger psychological responses that are characteristic of imaginative resistance. Given the importance Gendler now places on aliefs, it is plausible that she thinks that, at least for some questions concerning imaginative resistance, a psychological framework at the level of aliefs can provide better explanations than a psychological framework at the level of cognitive imaginings.

If Gendler is right that alief is more primitive and fundamental than cognitive imagination, then the most fundamental cognitive architecture no longer contains cognitive imagination or belief as *sui generis* attitudes. In turn, a psychological explanation of imaginative resistance at this fundamental cognitive architectural level does not locate the constraint that one experiences during imaginative resistance in cognitive imagination (or conative imagination, for that matter); instead, it locates that constraint in alief. Hence, we count this a no-imagination account because it plausibly bypasses all imaginative attitudes in explaining imaginative resistance.

Considering how Gendler's most recent account differs from her earlier ones is also useful for bringing out the theoretical value of our cognitive architectural reorientation of the imaginative resistance literature. Although Gendler's understanding of the phenomenon of imaginative resistance itself has only subtly evolved throughout the years, the alief-based account is a substantial departure from the imagination-based account at the cognitive architectural level. It would be harder to detect this substantial change in her overall position using existing taxonomies of positions in the imaginative resistance debate.

### *5.2 Emotion*

Ronald de Sousa (2010) argues that emotion plays a central role in generating imaginative resistance. On this view, imagination is unconstrained, but emotional responses to imaginings are constrained. Imaginative resistance is the product of constraints on emotional responses: "what is really going on in these cases is not so much an inability to imagine, but to experience a certain emotional response (or an absence of emotional response) to something imagined" (De Sousa 2010, 108).

On this account, a story evokes imaginative resistance when (1) one part of the story generates some emotional response that does not fit with what another part of the story asks us to imagine, or (2) when one part of the story fails to generate some emotional response that fits with what another part of the story asks us to imagine. For an example of (1), we can revisit what happens when one encounters *Giselda*. We respond to the claim that Giselda killed her baby just because the baby was a girl with disapprobation and disgust, which does not fit with also imagining that what she did is morally right. For an example of (2), we can revisit the Knock-Knock joke story. We fail to respond to the dumb Knock-Knock joke with mirth, which is the emotion that fits with imagining that the joke is hilariously funny.

Note that De Sousa's account is distinct from other accounts that invoke emotion in connection with cognitive imagination and other attitudes (Moran 1994; Currie 2011; Van Leeuwen forthcoming). On these other accounts, it is still imagination, perhaps in interaction with other attitudes such as desire, that ultimately explains imaginative resistance; emotions are just mediators in the explanation. However, on De Sousa's account, the experienced constraint that characterizes imaginative resistance directly comes from constraints on emotions. Hence, we count this as a no-imagination account too.

## 6 Directions for future research

In this chapter, we have given an introduction to the phenomenon of imaginative resistance from the perspective of cognitive architecture, with special attention to imaginative attitudes' role in explaining this phenomenon. By dividing up accounts of imaginative resistance based on their psychological commitments, we have also laid the groundwork for theorizing about the mind using the phenomenon of imaginative resistance.

Of course, the task of theorizing the mind using the phenomenon of imaginative resistance may be complicated by the very nature of imaginative resistance. Although we have treated imaginative resistance as a unified phenomenon, ongoing disagreements about its scope suggests that there may be multiple related phenomena in the vicinity that demand different psychological explanations (Currie and Ichino 2013). If that were the case, then we must approach the task piecemeal and consider the different cognitive architectural implications of different psychological explanations.

The new orientation we have developed in this chapter can spur further progress on the elusive phenomenon of imaginative resistance and the equally elusive attitude(s) of imagination in other ways:

- Aestheticians who work on imaginative resistance can be more explicit about their cognitive architectural commitments and also about cognitive architectural commitments of competing explanations.
- Philosophers of mind who work on imagination can make holistic assessments of competing cognitive architectures by examining a wide range of psychological phenomena that are primarily discussed in cognate subfields.
- Psychologists and experimental philosophers can design better studies of imaginative resistance by considering its potential psychological commitments, which can lead to new discoveries about aspects of imaginative resistance that are less readily accessible to introspection or intuition.

## Acknowledgments

The authors are equal contributors; they are listed reverse-alphabetically. We thank Adriana Clavel Vázquez, Anna Ichino, Amy Kind, Shannon Spaulding, and Nils-Hennes Stear for their careful, incisive comments on earlier versions of this chapter.

## Notes

1 We are inspired by the approach that Jonathan Weinberg and Aaron Meskin (2006b) take to puzzles that involve imagination: "it should hardly be surprising that many puzzles of the imagination might begin to dissolve with the appropriate application of cognitive science. The imagination, after all, is a faculty that creatures like us contingently possess and deploy in distinctive ways" (177). Currie and Ichino (2013) also pursue this strategy in their brief discussion of imaginative resistance.

2 The name "boxology" comes from diagrammatic representations of cognitive architectures, in which attitudes are typically represented by boxes and their functions are typically represented by arrows from one box to another. The deployment of cognitive architecture in psychological explanations involves some assumptions that are controversial in the broader context of philosophy of mind. Most glaringly, this discussion assumes that it makes sense to theorize about the mind – at least with respect to propositional attitudes – at the functional level. That is, this discussion assumes that attitudes can be, at least partially, characterized by their *functional roles* – their dispositions to causally interact with other components of the mind in particular ways. However, since all discussions of the psychology of imaginative resistance occur at the functional – as opposed to, say, neurological or biological – level, these assumptions can be safely adopted in the present context.

3 In fact, nothing hangs on the name "imaginative puzzle." We are merely using it as a placeholder for the puzzle in this vicinity that is concerned with the reader's psychological attitudes toward puzzling stories like *Giselda*. As we will see in Section 5, it could turn out that, on the best overall explanation of imaginative resistance, imagination plays no fundamental role in explaining the so-called imaginative puzzle.

4 On an alternative formulation, the imaginative puzzle too has a normative dimension and is perhaps better characterized as the imagin*ability* puzzle (Liao 2011; Liao and Gendler forthcoming; Stear forthcoming.; Todd 2009). On this alternative formulation, the emphasis is on why the reader *ought not* imagine that Giselda really did the morally right thing while imaginatively engaging with the story, regardless of the reader's actual difficulty with imagining so. On this alternative formulation, there is a close relationship between the imaginative puzzle and the fictionality puzzle because what is fictional is equivalent to what is to be imagined (see Walton 1990; but see also the caveats added by Walton 2013).

## References


Brock, S. (2012) "The Puzzle of Imaginative Failure," *Philosophical Quarterly* 62: 443–463.

Currie, G. (2002) "Desire in Imagination," in T.S. Gendler and J. Hawthorne (eds.) *Conceivability and Possibility*, New York: Oxford University Press, 201–221.

Currie, G. (2011) *Narratives and Narrators: A Philosophy of Stories*, New York: Oxford University Press.

Currie, G., and I. Ravenscroft (2002) *Recreative Minds: Imagination in Philosophy and Psychology*, New York: Oxford University Press.

Currie, G., and A. Ichino (2013) "Imagination and Make-Believe," in B. Gaut and D.M. Lopez (eds.) *The Routledge Companion to Aesthetics*, 3rd edn., London: Routledge, 320–329.

De Sousa, R. (2010) "The Mind's Bermuda Triangle: Philosophy of Emotions and Empirical Science," in P. Goldie (ed.) *The Oxford Handbook of Philosophy of Emotion*, New York: Oxford University Press, 95–117.

Doggett, T., and A. Egan (2007) "Wanting Things You Don't Want," *Philosophers' Imprint* 7(9): 1–17.

Doggett, T., and A. Egan (2012) "How We Feel about Terrible, Non-existent Mafiosi," *Philosophy and Phenomenological Research* 84(2): 277–306.

Funkhouser, E., and S. Spaulding (2009) "Imagination and Other Scripts," *Philosophical Studies* 143(3): 291–314.

Gendler, T.S. (2000) "The Puzzle of Imaginative Resistance," *Journal of Philosophy* 97(2): 55–81.

Gendler, T.S. (2006) "Imaginative Resistance Revisited," in S. Nichols (ed.) *The Architecture of the Imagination: New Essays on Pretence, Possibility, and Fiction*, New York: Oxford University Press, 149–173.

Gendler, T.S. (2008a) "Alief and Belief," *Journal of Philosophy* 105(10): 634–663.

Gendler, T.S. (2008b) "Alief in Action (and Reaction)," *Mind & Language* 23(5): 552–585.

Gendler, T.S. (2011) "Imagination," in E.N. Zalta (ed.) *Stanford Encyclopedia of Philosophy* (Spring 2011 edition), <http://plato.stanford.edu/archives/fall2011/entries/imagination/>.

Hume, D. (1757/1889) "Of the Standard of Taste," in *Essays: Moral, Political and Literary*, vol. 1, London: Longmans, Green & Co, 231–258.

Kind, A. (2011) "The Puzzle of Imaginative Desire," *Australasian Journal of Philosophy* 89(3): 421–439.

Kind, A. (2013) "The Heterogeneity of the Imagination," *Erkenntnis* 78(1): 141–159.

Langland-Hassan, P. (2012) "Pretense, Imagination, and Belief: The Single Attitude Theory," *Philosophical Studies* 159(2): 155–179.

Langland-Hassan, P. (2014) "What It Is To Pretend," *Pacific Philosophical Quarterly* 95(1): 397–420.

Leslie, A. (1987) "Pretense and Representation," *Psychological Review* 94(4): 412–426.

Leslie, A. (1994) "Pretending and Believing," *Cognition* 50: 211–238.

Lewis, D. (1989) "Dispositional Theories of Value," *Proceedings of the Aristotelian Society, Supplementary Volume* 63: 113–137.

Liao, S. (2011) "On Morals, Fictions, and Genres," PhD diss., University of Michigan.

Liao, S. (2013) "Moral Persuasion and the Diversity of Fictions," *Pacific Philosophical Quarterly* 94(3): 269–289.

Liao, S., and T. Doggett (2014) "The Imagination Box," *Journal of Philosophy* 111(5): 259–275.

Liao, S., and T.S. Gendler (Forthcoming) "The Problem of Imaginative Resistance," in J. Gibson and N. Carroll (eds.) *The Routledge Companion to Philosophy of Literature*, New York: Routledge.

Liao, S., N. Strohminger, and C.S. Sripada (2014) "Empirically Investigating Imaginative Resistance," *British Journal of Aesthetics* 54(3): 339–355.

Meskin, A., and J. Weinberg (2011) "Imagination Unblocked," in E. Schellekens and P. Goldie (eds.) *The Aesthetic Mind: Philosophy and Psychology*, New York: Oxford University Press, 239–253.

Miyazono, K. (In prep.) "Unstable Imaginative Resistance," University of Birmingham.
Moran, R. (1994) "The Expression of Feeling in Imagination," *Philosophical Review* 103(1): 75–106.
Mothersill, M. (2003) "Make-Believe Morality and Fictional Worlds," in J.L. Bermúdez and S. Gardner (eds.) *Arts and Morality*, New York: Routledge, 74–94.
Nanay, B. (2010) "Imaginative Resistance and Conversational Implicatures," *Philosophical Quarterly* 60: 586–600.
Nichols, S. (2004) "Imagining and Believing: The Promise of a Single Code," *Journal of Aesthetics and Art Criticism* 62(2): 129–139.
Nichols, S. (2006) "Just the Imagination: Why Imagining Doesn't Behave Like Believing," *Mind & Language* 21(4): 459–474.
Nichols, S., and S. Stich (2003) *Mindreading: An Integrated Account of Pretense, Self-Awareness, and Understanding Other Minds*, New York: Oxford University Press.
Schellenberg, S. (2013) "Belief and Desire in Imagination and Immersion," *Journal of Philosophy* 110(9): 497–517.
Stear, N. (forthcoming) "On the Imaginative and Fictionality Puzzles," *Philosophers' Imprint*.
Stokes, D. (2006) "The Evaluative Character of Imaginative Resistance," *British Journal of Aesthetics* 46(4): 387–405.
Tanner, M. (1994) "Morals in Fiction and Fictional Morality (II)," *Supplement to the Proceedings of the Aristotelian Society* 68: 51–66.
Todd, C. (2009) "Imaginability, Morality, and Fictional Truth: Dissolving the Puzzle of 'Imaginative Resistance,'" *Philosophical Studies* 143(2): 187–211.
Van Leeuwen, N. (2011) "Imagination Is Where the Action Is," *Journal of Philosophy* 108(2): 55–77.
Van Leeuwen, N. (2013) "The Meanings of 'Imagine' Part 1: Constructive Imagination," *Philosophy Compass* 8(3): 220–230.
Van Leeuwen, N. (Forthcoming) "The Imaginative Agent," in A. Kind and P. Kung (eds.) *Knowledge through Imagination*, New York: Oxford University Press.
Walton, K.L. (1990) *Mimesis as Make-Believe: On the Foundations of the Representational Arts*, Cambridge: Harvard University Press.
Walton, K.L. (1994) "Morals in Fiction and Fictional Morality (I)," *Supplement to the Proceedings of the Aristotelian Society* 68: 27–50.
Walton, K.L. (2006) "On the (So-called) Puzzle of Imaginative Resistance," in S. Nichols (ed.) *The Architecture of the Imagination: New Essays on Pretence, Possibility, and Fiction*, New York: Oxford University Press, 137–148.
Walton, K.L. (2013) "Fictionality and Imagination Reconsidered," in C. Barbero, M. Ferraris, and A. Voltolini (eds.) *From Fictionalism to Realism*, Newcastle upon Tyne: Cambridge Scholars Publishing, 9–26.
Weatherson, B. (2004) "Morality, Fiction, and Possibility," *Philosophers' Imprint* 4(3): 1–27.
Weinberg, J.M. (2008) "Configuring the Cognitive Imagination," in K. Stock and K. Thomsen-Jones (eds.) *New Waves in Aesthetics*, New York: Palgrave Macmillan, 203–223.
Weinberg, J., and A. Meskin (2006a) "Imagine That!" in M. Kieran (ed.) *Contemporary Debates in Aesthetics and the Philosophy of Art*, Cambridge: Blackwell, 222–235.
Weinberg, J., and A. Meskin (2006b) "Puzzling over the Imagination," in S. Nichols (ed.) *The Architecture of the Imagination: New Essays on Pretence, Possibility, and Fiction*, New York: Oxford University Press, 175–202.
Willard, M.B. (In prep.) "Stop Over-Analyzing It: The Puzzle of Historical Inaccuracy and the Pragmatic Interpretation of Imaginative Resistance," Weber State University.
Yablo, S. (2002) "Coulda, Woulda, Shoulda," in T. S. Gendler and J. Hawthorne (eds.) *Conceivability and Possibility*, New York: Oxford University Press, 441–492.

# 18
# IMAGINATION AND CREATIVITY

*Dustin Stokes*

If I ask you to imagine the sun setting over the sea, you will easily comply; and there is nothing creative about this familiar image. But while imagination and creative behavior come apart, it is nonetheless true that some of our most creative minds are also some of our most imaginative minds. This chapter attempts to identify some of the central ways that they relate by asking what roles imagination plausibly plays in human creativity.

For purposes of this discussion, a liberal characterization of the concept of imagination can be assumed. Imagination is typically, though not always, a voluntary mental activity that involves mental representation of subjectively nonpresent objects and events. It often involves an image, sensory in character, but perhaps it need not. That is, perhaps there is imageless propositional imagination.

"Creativity" requires a bit more clarification, but here again commitments can be kept sparse. Competent users of the concept will attribute "creative" to persons (the artist, the scientist), to products (the artwork, the theory), and to processes (whatever means by which the individual made the product). In each case, there is a convergence in the historical and contemporary literature upon two conditions for creativity attribution. First, creativity requires novelty. To be creative, an *x* must be novel *relative to* some comparison class. Note that this last qualification affords flexibility: some *x* might be novel relative to human history, or to some particular spatial or temporal locale, or even to an individual's history of thought.[1] And this flexibility implies that creativity is a degree concept: the *x* that is novel relative to the whole of human history is *more* creative than an *x* novel relative only to some smaller comparison class. Secondly, most theorists maintain that creativity requires value. As Kant put it, "there can also be original nonsense" (Kant 1781/2000, 186), and nonsense is not creative. So, creativity requires, in addition to novelty, that an *x* be of some value to its maker and/or its context of making.[2] Beyond a novelty and a value condition, theorists vary substantially. Some argue that creativity requires agency: there are no accidental instances of creativity.[3] Some argue that creativity must involve some substantial psychological or computational breakthrough, perhaps where the individual manages to think or do something that she *could* not have done before.[4] Some recent accounts isolate the creative process, and argue that what's distinctive about it is the way it is experienced or acted.[5] Here only the novelty and value conditions are assumed.[6]

While there has recently been some increase in philosophical research on creativity, it remains a largely underexplored subject matter. Similarly, research on imagination focuses largely on its use for *recreating*, as one does when imagining along with a narrative or thinking of a pleasurable past event, rather than its uses for creating something new and valuable.[7] Plausibly, the same (broadly typed) imaginative processes can be *used* in these two different ways: in ways guided by a goal of mentally mirroring or recreating, or as motivated to some end of creativity or discovery. This is an important qualification for anyone interested in researching creativity: much of recent philosophical and psychological work on imagination (in either use) is plausibly relevant to the more neglected topic of the two.

The chapter proceeds as follows. Sections 1 and 2 focus on two traditional philosophical treatments of imagination and creativity. Section 3 focuses on imagination in the context of science. Section 4 concludes with a brief review of some recent work on conceptual and empirical relations between imagination and creativity.

## 1 Kant

Immanuel Kant's discussion of creativity focuses centrally on artistic genius. Artistic creativity essentially involves originality for Kant, and accordingly the genius engages in non-rule-bound imaginative activity. Kant suggests that the faculty for creativity in art is innate and unteachable, and that processes of artistic creation are ineffable to artist and audience both. In one famous passage, Kant writes:

> Genius is the talent (natural gift) that gives the rule to art. Since the talent, as an inborn productive faculty of the artist, itself belongs to nature, this could also be expressed thus: Genius is the inborn predisposition of the mind (*ingenium*) through which nature gives the rule to art.
>
> *(Kant 1781/2000, 186)*

Here Kant echoes an idea traceable to Plato, namely, that the creative individual is a conduit for some kind of uncontrolled force, be it a deity or nature. Accordingly, creativity cannot be learned, and it cannot be explained. This general claim – that creativity is inexplicable if not magical – influenced much romantic theorizing about creativity in the two centuries that followed, accordingly discouraging theorists of an analytic, naturalistic, or generally scientific approach.[8] That said, Kant's analysis of creativity is rich and varied, and lessons for explaining creativity can still be learned from his discussion of imagination in creative behavior.[9]

In many respects, Kant's account of artistic creativity mirrors his account of aesthetic judgment. To begin, note that Kant claims that judgments of taste – that an object is beautiful – are importantly different from cognitive judgments. When one judges that, say, an event is a sunset, one places one's sensory impressions under a concept, following a kind of rule. By contrast, when one judges beautiful a sunset or a painting of a sunset, this judgment does not itself involve application of any rule or concept. Instead, one recognizes the "purposiveness of form" of the object. In the case of an art object, one represents the object's form as exemplifying a kind of purpose but, necessarily, without identifying any particular purpose – as Kant sometimes puts it, "*as if* it were a mere product of nature" (Kant 1781/2000, 185; emphasis added). And this mental representation involves a balanced use of imagination and understanding which, as we will see, is the "free play" also required of the creative artist.

Before discussing how this account of aesthetic judgment informs the account of artistic creativity, it is worth briefly noting how some of the same claims serve to exclude scientists from the realm of genius. Kant takes as a platitude that acts of genius, since they essentially involve originality, logically oppose acts of imitation. He then argues:

> [S]ince learning is nothing but imitation, even the greatest aptitude for learning, facility for learning (capacity) as such, still does not count as genius. But even if one thinks or writes for himself, and does not merely take up what others have thought, indeed even if he invents a great deal for art and science, this is still not a proper reason for calling such a great mind … a genius, since just this sort of thing could also have been learned, and thus still lies on the natural path of inquiry and reflection in accordance with rules, and is not specifically distinct from that which can be acquired by means of imitation.
>
> *(Kant 1781/2000, 187)*

From this line of thought, Kant concludes that a scientist like Newton, although possessing "a great mind," is not a genius. Newton's discovery can be recounted in stepwise fashion, and accordingly learned and codified into rules. By contrast, great art, although based in some fundamental skill, falls under no determinate rules and so cannot be imitated, taught, or learned.

Whatever this argument's success,[10] let us grant that there *are* geniuses in the context of art making, and then ask about the theory of mind Kant offers. So, Kant does acknowledge that the artist must learn some skills, namely, those foundational to her chosen artistic medium. In addition to this cognitive understanding, the artist must execute aesthetic judgment (understood as per above). Indeed, the artist is the first to judge the beauty of the work, and for Kant this judgment is

> the discipline … of genius, clipping its wings and making it well behaved or polished; … it gives genius guidance as to where and how far it should extend itself if it is to remain purposive; and by introducing clarity and order into the abundance of thoughts it makes the ideas tenable, capable of enduring and universal approval …
>
> *(Kant 1781/2000, 197)*

Although not wholly rule-bound then, understanding and judgment constrain the artist's process; in particular, they constrain her *productive imagination*.

The *reproductive imagination* is, for Kant, largely the traditional empiricist imagination: it involves mental representation of an object or event that is not present to the senses. It further involves placing items from the sensory manifold under concepts and so is essential for knowledge acquisition and bound by empirical laws. Productive imagination, by contrast, is comparably unconstrained, involving what Kant often calls "rapid" and "free play," and transcends concept and language.[11] It is the "spirit" of genius, animating the artistic mind and providing new materials for cognizing, materials that are not amenable to strict conceptualization. Kant calls these materials "aesthetic ideas," which eventually make up the ineffable content of a work of art. The genius is able to harness this raw and unwieldy material, through her understanding and taste, and thereby to "express what is unnameable … to make it universally communicable, whether the expression consist in language, or painting, or in plastic art" (Kant 1781/2000, 195). In turn, this expressive content is what one properly appreciates in judging the work as beautiful, a purposiveness without an applicable concept.

For Kant, what distinguishes the mental activity of genius, then, is this exceptionally free play between imagination and understanding. This is richly productive imagination, enjoyed only by the artistic genius by contrast to the merely competent artist. Without it, one will fail to create a work that is both original and appropriate for the Kantian judgment of beauty – one of wide if not universal appeal that provides "a standard … for judging" (Kant 1781/2000,

187). It is here that Kant departs most clearly from his empiricist predecessors. The productive imagination of the genius is transcendental and a priori: it goes beyond what has been previously given in experience and provides new concepts (Kant even sometimes says "rules") for experience without being determined by any existing concepts.[12] And it is neither willed nor predicted, but instead the inspiration provided by nature. The romantic goes too far, however, if she generalizes this feature to Kant's entire account. The artistic genius manages to guide these materials into a finished product using the imagination "powerful in creating, as it were, another nature, out of the material which the real one gives it" (Kant 1781/2000, 192). So while artistic creativity involves for Kant some uncontrolled inspiration, it also involves what some have called a "mastery of nature."[13]

## 2 Sartre

There are some surprising points of overlap between Kant's analysis and the one given by Jean-Paul Sartre in his various texts on the imagination.[14] Sartre also distinguishes the (empiricist) reproductive imagination from a productive imagination, and further argues that it is the latter that enjoys the flexibility needed for creativity. And, like Kant, Sartre maintains that the imagination serves a role in everyday activity, for example in our aesthetic appreciation of artworks and literature. Unlike Kant, however, Sartre maintains that the latter kind of activity – say, reading a novel – is a genuinely creative one. And this activity exemplifies a much bigger and more important existentialist role for the imagination, namely, the creation of the self.

Part of Sartre's project is to distinguish imagination from perception, but in a way that does not commit to the reification that Sartre charges early modern analyses with. Descartes, Leibniz, and Hume all committed to what Sartre called "thingism," an assumption that mental images are, like the environmental objects that we perceptually experience, *things* in their own right. This assumption is then echoed, as Sartre traces it, throughout nineteenth- and twentieth-century philosophical and psychological theorizing.[15] Sartre's view is that once this assumption is made, there is no logically consistent method to vindicate our pretheoretic, phenomenologically grounded distinction between perception and imagination. And so we must reject the assumption – the only objects are the objects of perception: people, tables, chairs, and so on – and mark the distinction in some other way.

Sartre identifies four characteristics of images. His starting assumption anticipates what philosophers of perception today call the "transparency of experience."

> [I]t is certain that when I produce in myself the image of Pierre, it is Pierre who is the object of my current consciousness. So long as that consciousness remains unaltered, I can give a description of the object as it appears to me as imaged, but not of the image as such. To determine the characteristics of the image as image, it is necessary to turn to a new act of consciousness: it is necessary to *reflect*. So the image as image is describable only by a second-order act in which the look is turned away from the object and directed at the way in which the object is given.
>
> *(Sartre 1940/2004, 4)*

So a mental image for Sartre is an intentional relation: a way of being conscious *of* an object or event, where this awareness is transparent in the first order. One enjoys an "imaging consciousness of" – rather than *perceptual* consciousness of – Pierre. Second, imagery is *quasi-observational*; an image is impoverished relative to a perceptual experience in the sense that it contains only those features that the imaginer gives it, while perceived objects "overflow consciousness" in their features. Third, perceived objects come as present to oneself, while images give their objects, phenomenally, as a "nothingness," as not being present (to the imaginer). Fourth, and as a counterpart to this last feature of images, Sartre contrasts the passivity of perception with the voluntary spontaneity of imagination, claiming that "an imaging consciousness gives itself to itself as an imaging consciousness, which is to say as a spontaneity that produces and conserves the object as imaged" (Sartre 1940/2004, 14).

It is the combination of these four characteristics that gives images, for Sartre, their distinctively creative power. Absent the phenomenal commitment to the presence of an imaged object, the imaginer engages in the voluntary production of objects-as-imaged, as existing or nonexisting, but never as present. The freedom that allegedly comes with the active *doing* of imagining comports well with a pretheoretical feature of imagining, namely, that it is richly playful. Furthermore, because imaged contents are quasi-observational, one is responsible for them in a way different from the contents of perception and thought. And because imagery is transparent, imaged contents enjoy similar mental consequence, where one can become attentively and emotionally engaged with one's own imaginative productions. Thus,

> The consciousness appears to itself as creative, but without positing as object this creative character. It is thanks to this vague and fugitive quality that the image consciousness is not given as a piece of wood that floats on the sea, but as a wave among the waves. It feels itself to be consciousness through and through and homogeneous with the other consciousnesses that have preceded it and with which it is synthetically united.
>
> *(Sartre 1940/2004, 14)*

Representing in imagination, then, is a creative conscious activity for Sartre: "In the image, that [representative] element … is the product of a conscious activity, is shot through with a flow of creative will" (15).

Sartre applies this account to our uptake of literary and performance arts. When one reads a novel, there is a series of explicit statements describing the characters and events of the story. But as many contemporary philosophers have noted, the story is not exhausted by these descriptions. Rather, the author will rely upon the reader to "fill in" details left out of the explicit descriptions. For example, it may never be stated in a story that a human character's blood is red, but if the reader is explicitly told that the character entered the room with blood stains on her shirt, the reader will infer that there are red stains on the character's shirt.[16] Sartre anticipates this in his own theorizing, but also notes how the reader bears, for her own conscious experience, the responsibility for filling out the sensible details like those that give an analogous nonfictional situation its rich character or, as Sartre would say, its irreality. He writes, "To read is to realize contact with the irreal world on the signs. In this world there are plants, animals, fields, towns, people: initially those mentioned in the book and then a host of others that are not named but are in the background and give this world its depth …" (Sartre 1940/2004, 64). Importantly for Sartre, this imaginative activity, although guided by the text (by "the signs" or "words"), is richly creative. The artist's creative act is "an incomplete and abstract moment in the production of a work" (Sartre 1947b/1988, 52). The completed work requires the reader to be complicit in creation of the fictional world. This creative collaboration explains why different readers sometimes enjoy markedly different experiences of the same text. It also explains, given Sartre's account of imagination as described just above, why our engagement with narrative arts can be so powerful.

Productive imagination is free and spontaneous, allowing for much flexibility even when guided by a narrative. But it is also transparent in the sense described above, so that we "see through" our images to the irreal world partly of our own creation.

The creative imagination is of even deeper importance for Sartre's broader philosophy. A central subject for discussion in *Being and Nothingness* (Sartre 1948) is "bad faith," where individuals practice methods of self-deception in order to avoid the responsibility that comes with free will. This practice is enabled by the imagined scenarios and roles that an individual creates in order to "blind" oneself from the reality of free choice. But in a positive light, imagination also seems essential to how we become, how we create and identify as, individual selves. The world comes to us in a certain way, but on Sartre's view we are free and accordingly how we organize our experiences of the world, and how we identify as selves in that world, are a constant opportunity for creativity. As Jonathan Webber describes it, freedom for Sartre is intimately bound up with imagination: "We can imagine the world or any part of it being different from the way it in fact is. This ability is necessary to motivate changing the world. We can imagine it, moreover, as being different in any number of ways, and so can present ourselves with any number of ways that we might try to mould it. We are therefore not compelled to live in the world as we find it. We can and do act to change it, and this involves imagination" (Webber 2004, xxvi). In turn, these imaginative doings are central to how we create, through an imagined narrative, our selves. Therefore, imagination plays a core role in Sartre's existentialist philosophy.[17]

## 3 Imagination, scientific discovery, and experiment

As discussed above, Kant excluded scientists from the category of genius which, by Kant's analysis, was to exclude them from acting in any richly creative ways. One of Kant's arguments is that scientific discovery can be described procedurally and therefore learned. Newton, Kant suggested, could "make all the steps that he had to take, from the first elements of geometry to his great and profound discoveries, entirely intuitive not only to himself but also to everyone else, and thus set them out for posterity quite determinately" (Kant 1781/2000, 187). Great artists, by contrast, act in ways that are not captured in steps or rules, and so are not teachable.

A fundamental point for Kant was that the scientist's discovery is perfectly rational. This connects in interesting ways with a distinction familiar in early twentieth-century philosophy of science. As first explicitly marked by Hans Reichenbach (1938), one can distinguish the *context of discovery* from the *context of justification*. The insights involved in constructing a new scientific hypothesis or theory are of mere psychological or sociological interest, but not of genuine import to the epistemic value of the resultant theory. As Karl Popper (1934/1959) understood it, a philosophy of science should focus not on the insight stage of discovery involving creator and context, but instead only on the context of justification where an hypothesis is made testable and the logical relations between evidence and hypothesis can be independently evaluated. Notice how this is grounded in a reason that inverts Kant's: the stage of scientific insight according to these theorists is rationally unconstrained. What's common to both is that scientific discovery, at the stage of insight and innovation, is not particularly interesting vis-à-vis creativity – for Kant, because it is simply procedural, for Reichenbach and others, because it is simply too unconstrained.

From the perspective of philosophy of mind, both hypotheses are unsatisfying since, in a clear sense, the insight stage is where much of the mental action occurs. And philosophers of science too, especially beginning in the 1960s, have rejected the discovery/justification distinction, at least in the sense that the study of science will be impoverished if and to the degree that it eschews any discussion of the psychology and sociology that, as a matter of fact, underpin scientific innovation. This is perhaps most famously argued by Thomas Kuhn (1962) in his work on scientific revolutions, but there are some less frequently discussed theorists, and ones that well highlight the possible role of imagination in scientific discovery.

Michael Polanyi's work casts doubt on both Kant and Reichenbach. He denies the Kantian view that a scientific discovery is rational and stepwise. And Polanyi resists the assumption that theory commitment and explanation in science is a strictly logical matter. Across nearly four decades of publications, through consideration of examples from Copernicus to Kepler, Einstein to Planck, Darwin to Mendel, Polanyi motivates the claim that "the capacity rightly to *choose* a line of thought the end of which is vastly *indeterminate*, is as much part of the scientific method as the power of assuring the exactitude of the conclusions eventually arrived at" (Polanyi 1974, 62; emphasis added). Two important bases for Polanyi's analysis are these: (1) theoretical decisions are often underdetermined, both in terms of the exactness of the problem and in terms of the relation between observation and hypothesis; (2) scientific theories have been, on countless occasion across the history of science, accepted as "fact" or as "true" on rather shaky evidential ground. The first is a version of the now-called Quine–Duhem thesis of underdetermination, the second mirrors a broadly Kuhnian claim about scientific change.[18]

Throughout his work, Polanyi describes science as an extension of perception, describing scientific discovery as a kind of "indeterminate vision." Of Copernicus, he writes, "The vast indeterminacy of the Copernican vision showed itself in the fact that discoveries made later, in the light of this vision, would have horrified its author. Copernicus would have rejected the elliptic planetary paths of Kepler and, likewise, the extension of terrestrial mechanics to the planets by Galileo and Newton" (Polanyi 1966/2009, 149). Polanyi then generalizes this suggestion in a number of ways: scientific vision is responsive to the hidden reality of nature, vision can be shared or "picked up" and extended by later scientists, and the clues that trigger and guide the vision are themselves indeterminate.

Plausibly, science is indeterminate all the way down. So, theory commitment, hypothesis verification or falsification, and observation are none of them exact or, as we might say, deductively closed. But this is also true, Polanyi argues, at the earliest stages, where the scientist is identifying a problem and possible means for solution. The general puzzle here can be traced to Plato's *Meno*. One cannot inquire into what one does not know since one does not know what one seeks, and one cannot inquire into what one knows since one already knows it; thus genuine inquiry appears impossible. Meno's alleged paradox applies no less to scientific innovation, since in identifying and solving a new problem, the scientist must somehow cross this abyss between known and unknown and land on something sufficiently stable for commitment, some new theory or hypothesis that is cogent and coherent. This suggests a role to be played by some mental faculty or faculties and Polanyi's suggestion is that this role is served by imagination and intuition. Polanyi understood imagination broadly as thoughts about nonpresent events or actions. And he understood intuition, as a skill "for guessing with a reasonable chance of guessing right, a skill guided by an innate sensibility to coherence" (Polanyi 1966/2009, 155).

Polanyi offers frequent analogies with both muscle learning and visual perception. Consider a child learning to ride a bike. The child forms an intention to ride the bicycle, but of course because she doesn't yet know how to do this, she has only a loose imagining of the aim or outcome. This "imaginative intention" is a rough, nonstepwise way of pushing the agent toward her goal, aided by the feedback that comes with combining different actions (turning the handlebar this way or that, pedaling versus not pedaling), plus losing her balance, falling, managing some distance without falling, and so on. As one may recall, at some point, something spontaneous happens, something clicks. All of this feedback between world and agent provides clues (most of which the average person could never articulate) and these clues guide one closer to the aim, toward a coherent method for riding the bicycle. According to Polanyi, intuition is the faculty that responds to these clues, and that ultimately provides the spontaneous click – the "this is how I do it!" for the learner. Polanyi identifies the same structure in visual perception. Consider perceiving some ambiguous figure. One imagines that there is *some* appropriate interpretation and this narrows the scope of possible visual interpretations. Intuition then guides one toward a coherent interpretation, responsive to clues that are many of them below the surface of conscious awareness. One's deliberate efforts eventually effect a spontaneous, coherent visual experience (one suddenly sees the Dalmatian in the ambiguous figure). So, even at this mundane level, one breaks out of Meno's paradox through the use of imagination and intuition.

Polanyi identifies this same structure, involving the interplay of imagination and intuition, as crucial to scientific discovery. The scientist has some vague vision of a problem and solution space. Imagination serves the role of fixing attention on some global, but yet unknown, result. Intuition serves the role of guiding the scientist's pursuit, in two senses. *Strategic intuition* clues in on the long-range viability of attempting to solve certain (sub)problems, which lines of inquiry to pursue, and so on. *Dynamic intuition* is responsive to the clues provided by nature, and moves the scientist toward deepening coherence, to understanding some reality hidden to ordinary observation. Imagination then refines the pursuit in a way sensitive to what insight clues in on. This interplay between imagination and intuition will continue for some time until, in the best of cases, the scientist lights on something that completes the coherence, that amounts to some full-fledged discovery (recall the bicycle analogy). Polanyi describes the process as follows.

> Discovery is made therefore in two moves: one deliberate, the other spontaneous, the spontaneous move being evoked in ourselves by the action of deliberate effort. The deliberate thrust is a focal act of the imagination, while the spontaneous response to it, which brings discovery, belongs to the same class as the spontaneous coordination of muscles responding to our intention to lift our arm, or the spontaneous coordination of visual clues in response to our looking at something. This spontaneous act of discovery deserves to be recognized as *creative intuition*.
>
> *(Polanyi 1966/2009, 159)*

In some respects, Polanyi's picture has an air of mystery to it, but in fact the motivation for his account lies in its explanatory power. The "focal" use of imagination explains how a scientist sets out on a pursuit, in a context involving so much indeterminacy, with only a rough vision of the problem and perhaps none of the solution. It also explains the phenomenology of sustaining this pursuit, where even in spite of still lacking a clearly coherent understanding, the scientist feels some kind of "hunch" or a feeling of getting closer to solution. Polanyi offers as one example Einstein's self-reports regarding years of pursuing the discovery of relativity: "there was a feeling of direction, of going straight towards something definite … clearly to be distinguished from later thoughts about the rational form of the solution" (Polanyi 1966/2009, 157). Polanyi's account explains this as the interplay of imagination and intuition: imagination refines and narrows the vaguely understood solution space in response to the coherence sensed by intuition, and this reflexive process continues as the coherence deepens. This largely deliberate effort, "racking our brain," as encouraged by the feeling of getting closer, ultimately gives way to some spontaneous insight – an Ah-ha! moment. On Polanyi's account, this feeling that the idea has come unbidden is analogous to the spontaneous bit of muscle learning or perceptual disambiguation; it is the result of the refinement – the narrowing of appropriate "moves" – afforded by imagination and intuition. It is the final hunch or clue. Importantly, its causal ancestral structure is the same in kind as these more basic cases as well. Learning to ride a bicycle and discovering relativity both involve a great deal of deliberate toil, regular use of the imagination, and intuitive judgments. So although the final insight may involve a phenomenology of spontaneity, it is causally dependent upon work for which the agent is responsible. This keeps creative discovery in the realm of naturalistic explanation.[19]

Finally, Polanyi's account goes some way to explaining the backlash that many of our greatest scientific discoveries suffer upon initial presentation. Copernicus, Kepler, Darwin, Einstein, and countless others did not immediately succeed in convincing the folk *nor* scientific community of their most important hypotheses. If Polanyi is right, this gap in understanding (which comes close to what Kuhn and others sometimes mean by "incommensurability") is a result of a gap in imagination and intuition between discoverer and the rest of the community. These creative discoveries involved applications of learned skills, theoretical principles, and so on, but they were not, contrary to Kant's claims, rational, stepwise cognitive achievements. Crossing the abyss to scientific discovery, with all of its indeterminacy, requires a probing imagination and highly sensitive intuition. On Polanyi's account, this is what the richly creative scientist – the genius – possesses and others lack. Accordingly, receipt of a discovery achieved by and imbued with such imagination will not be immediately well understood by the less imaginative.

Polanyi's emphasis, and one standard in much of the literature on scientific discovery, is on insight involving some hypothesis or other theoretical postulate. But scientific discovery typically involves experimentation, both in thought and in the laboratory, and here too imagination is greatly important. Consider thought experiments first. Much of the literature focuses on how a thought experiment is used to criticize an existing theory, or to argue for or present a new theory.[20] But thought experiments can be an indispensable component of the discovery process as well.

Tim De Mey (2006) offers an extended analysis of William Harvey's "quantitative argument," arguing that it is not merely a presentation of but an essential component in Harvey's discovery of the circulation of blood in humans. Harvey challenged Galen's long-dominant model, which maintained two kinds of blood, one originating at the liver and transmitted through the veins and the other originating at the heart and distributed through the arteries, all of it supposedly regularly consumed by the body. In attempting to square this model with anatomical observation (including rapidity of blood loss upon incision), Harvey inquired how this system could possibly create and distribute a sufficient amount of blood, and sufficiently quickly. Harvey famously suggests that after much reflection, he encountered the following dilemma. On Galen's model "we would have veins empty and altogether drained dry and arteries, on the other hand, burst open with the too great intrusion of blood, unless this blood should somehow flow back out of the arteries once more into the veins and return to the right ventricle of the heart" (Harvey 1628/1976, 74–75, cited in De Mey 2006, 233–234). Although informed by observational data from medical examination, Harvey's considerations were performed in thought. At this stage of medical knowledge, the dilemma can be solved only by use of the imagination. Harvey reports this imagining, "I began to bethink myself whether it might not have a kind of movement as it were in a circle" (ibid., 234). And this merely imagined possibility is then later confirmed by empirical investigation, Harvey thus being the first to discover the human cardiovascular system.[21]

As De Mey notes, it is controversial among historians and philosophers of science whether Harvey has accurately reported his methods of investigation and discovery. But for our purposes it suffices as at least a possible example of how imagination and thought experiment might contribute to creative scientific discovery. In Polanyi's terms, Harvey was able to make coherent his vision of the phenomenon by imagining some novel possibility, then sustaining and closing the inquiry by some intuitive sense for the ultimately coherent theory he devised. Imagination, in the form of thought experimentation, is plausibly essential to this creative discovery.

Now consider what we might call, for lack of a better term, empirical experimentation, taking perceptual psychology as the example. Experimental psychologists are regularly faced with challenges that can be placed under the broad rubric of *experimental confounds*. The human mind is a complex and a messy thing, and often enough the phenomenon that one would like to isolate is not easily separated from other observable phenomena, and/or the data that one collects is consistent with a variety of explanations. Accordingly, the experimenter must devise ever more sophisticated ways to *control for* those variables that are possible confounds in a way that ideally isolates the target phenomenon. These methods are far from straightforward. They are often remarkably innovative, and on at least two distinct levels. First, once possible confounds have been identified, the experimenter must imagine possible ways to work around them. And because time and resources are always limited, she must imagine how these possible ways of experimenting are likely to play out. Second, often enough the methods envisaged are not embodied by some existing technologies. And so the experimenter must, literally, build new technology. In this way, it is appropriate to describe the experimental psychologist as a kind of tinkerer: she tinkers with both experimental strategy and technology construction. And this tinkering often involves imagination.

Of course one might note that in the psychological sciences, like any other science, there are standard experimental methods or "paradigms." And these can often be used to address confounds. But these do not come ready-made by nature. For example, the now standard method of *visual masking* had to be initially envisaged and then constructed into a workable technology.[22] In its most general form, the technique involves augmentation of visual awareness of an initially presented target stimulus by presenting a second "masking" stimulus. The broad method is now widely used to study a wide range of perceptual phenomena, including, scene and face recognition, cognitive, emotional and attentional effects on vision, and conscious versus unconscious visual information-processing. So visual masking has been put into service of discoveries about the human visual system, but it is itself a creative innovation in its own right. This subject matter – creativity in experimental method – is one ripe for new research.[23]

## 4 Conceptual and empirical relations

This final concluding section briefly discusses recent philosophical analyses that offer some additional treatment of the question *why* imagination may serve in the various creative roles as described above.

Berys Gaut (2003, 2009, 2010) and Dustin Stokes (2014) have both recently argued, on conceptual grounds, that imagination is especially well-suited to creative behavior (while remaining cautious about any necessary conceptual connection). Gaut's emphasis is on instances of creativity where one is actively pursuing a solution or a new idea. Both theorists agree that imagination is "non-truth-bound" (Stokes 2014) and decoupled from action (Gaut 2003). This freedom or playfulness of imagination is crucial to the novelty required of creativity, since it allows one to safely "try out" hypotheses, conceptual combinations, strategies for solution, and so on, without epistemic or behavioral commitment. And because imagination connects in important ways with inferential systems, as well as affective systems, the thoughts it produces can often be integrated with knowledge and skills to formulate an innovative strategy or solution to a problem. Finally, as Stokes argues, this role for imagination in creativity is not exclusive to the rich creativity of artists and scientists, but indeed seems to characterize the minimally creative behavior that we all enjoy. This claim is partly motivated by empirical research on cross-category task performance (e.g., drawing a house with person-like features) and learning of figurative language in children. Here, as in the more radical cases, instances of novel achievement or learning by subjects requires more than rote memorization; it requires "cognitive manipulation" of the information in the relevant conceptual space (e.g., combining concepts about houses and persons). This kind of cognitive activity is best done by using the imagination.[24]

Peter Carruthers (2002, 2006; see also Picciuto and Carruthers 2014) argues for connections between imagination and creativity on evolutionary grounds. He too focuses on the playfulness of imagination. Pretend play normally develops early in childhood in humans.[25] And imagination in adults, as also argued by the above theorists, provides an appropriate mental mechanism for generating and exploring ideas.[26] Carruthers hypothesizes that imagination serves the evolutionary function for practice of adult creativity – and may have been accordingly selected for in a way that accords with the putative creativity explosion of 40,000 years ago. To his mind, this is the most parsimonious explanation of both the emergence and the ubiquity of creativity in the human species.[27]

Carruthers (2011) also offers a related but distinctive "act-first" account of creativity. Again drawing on recent empirical evidence, Carruthers suggests that a locus of creativity is in action – the construction and conscious activation of action schemata – rather than conceptual thought. These schemata involve mental imagery of motor sequences for bodily movement, and good evidence suggests that this occurs without any prior cognitive planning in the form of beliefs or intentions. Carruthers suggests that, at the very least, this model will better explain the presentation and phenomenology of the kind of "online" creative behavior found in musical improvisation and dance performance. He further suggests that the act-first model might even be extended to explain all of human creativity.

## Conclusion

This last discussion was brief for one simple reason: there has been little recent philosophical research on imagination and creativity. However, as this chapter as a whole suggests, this neglect is not for lack of interesting subject matter nor interesting theoretical precedent to be revived and studied. The pictures given by Kant, Sartre, and Polanyi are vastly different. However, one common thread which runs from Kant all the way through the contemporary theorists just discussed is that imagination can be remarkably productive, and productive *because* playful. Kant isolated this creative productivity to the artistic genius, but his arguments for excluding scientists, among others, are questionable. Polanyi provides one plausible counterexample, with an emphasis on scientific discovery in a context riddled with indeterminacy. Sartre is the most emphatic in bringing creativity down to the ground level, but does not thereby acquiesce in its being banal or trivial: on his theory, we are regular creators of the original narratives that frame our lives and determine how we self-identify. In each case, the imagination is central to this kind of productivity. And the recent theorists discussed offer additional conceptual and empirical reasons to think that this very playfulness is partly explanatory of the imagination's workfulness: from the everyday to the historically monumental, the imagination has unparalleled powers to create, to enable thoughts, actions, and products that are both novel and valuable.

## Acknowledgements

Thank you to Amy Kind and Samantha Matherne for helpful critical feedback on an earlier draft, and to Steve Downes and Melinda Fagan for helpful discussion.

## Notes

1 Margaret Boden (1990/2004) marks this distinction in one clear way, distinguishing *historical creativity* from *psychological creativity*. The first involves novelty relative to the history of ideas, while the second involves novelty only relative to the psychology of the agent in question. The fundamental point is that an *x* is novel relative only to some comparison class, and this can vary substantially in broadness.

2 Some have been critical of inclusion of a value condition for creativity. See Stokes 2011 and Runco 2010.

3 See Gaut 2010, 2012; Stokes 2007, 2011, 2014.

4 See Boden 1990/2004; Stokes 2011.

5 See Nanay 2014; Carruthers 2011.

6 Attribution of "creativity" to persons requires some qualification. It isn't that the person herself is judged novel and/or valuable, at least not centrally, but rather that she regularly engages in a process, or produces products, that satisfy the discussed conditions of creativity.

7 For example, see Currie and Ravenscroft (2002), who explicitly draw the distinction between creative and recreative imagination and then focus exclusively on the latter.

8 "Romantic" here is used not to denote a particular school of thought or criticism, but a broad category of theorizing creativity whereby it comes out as largely magical or inexplicable. Examples include Bergson 1911/1998, 1942/1992; Collingwood 1938; Dewey 1958; Schelling 1809/1936; Schopenhauer 1969. More recently, see Hospers 1985 and Kivy 2001.

9 For extended discussion of Kant's theory of imagination, see Samantha Matherne's Chapter 4, in this volume.

10 For two recent examples of criticism, see Cohen 2003 and Gaut 2014. The topic of imagination and scientific discovery will be discussed again, and in a more positive light, in Section 3.

11 Again, with the exception of constraints imposed by understanding of the chosen artistic media, and a non-rule-bound judgment of purposiveness of form.

12 See Crawford 1982 for discussion of this point.

13 On this last point see Crawford 1982, see also his 2001. For other recent commentary on Kant and the creative imagination, see Cohen 2003; Gaut 2003; Guyer 2005; Kivy 2001; Ostaric 2012.

14 Sartre wrote two texts, typically neglected by analytic philosophers, devoted exclusively to imagination and imagery. Both have been recently retranslated into English, with helpful introductions from the translators/editors. The first, *The Imagination*, was originally published in 1936 and recently translated by Kenneth Williford and David Rudrauf (Sartre 1936/2012). This text is a largely critical examination of philosophical and psychological theories of imagination, with a final positive section focused on Husserl. The second, *The Imaginary*, was originally published in 1940 and recently translated by Jonathan Webber (Sartre 1940/2004). This text attempts to provide a comprehensive theory of imagination, mental images, and imagistic representation generally. There are additional places throughout Sartre's writing where he discusses the imagination (as suggested below, it is arguably essential to his existentialism), but one text of clear significance (and one that influenced the discussion in this chapter) is his *What Is Literature?* (Sartre 1947a/1988).

15 Indeed, one might think of sense-datum theories of perception as making the same commitment, some of these theories articulated after Sartre's 1936 analysis.

16 For philosophical discussion of truth in fiction, and fiction generally, see Searle 1975; Lewis 1983; Currie 1990; Walton 1990. See also Kathleen Stock's Chapter 15, in this volume.

17 For more on Sartre and imagination, see Robert Hopkins' Chapter 6, in this volume, and Levy 2014.

18 One should not assume, however, that Polanyi just borrowed these points from such figures and their writings. Indeed, some of his publications, with these very insights, predated (or were at least closely contemporary with) the publications most commonly credited. In addition to those publications discussed explicitly above and below, see Polanyi 1936, 1946, 1950, 1958.
19 See Kronfeldner 2009; Stokes 2007, 2011; Stokes and Paul forthcoming. See also various papers in Paul and Kaufman 2014.
20 For general discussion of imagination and thought experiments, see Roy Sorensen's Chapter 31, in this volume.
21 For more detailed historical and philosophical discussion of Harvey's discovery, see De Mey 2006; Mowry 1985; and Wear 1990.
22 Breitmeyer and Öğmen's *Visual Masking* (Breitmeyer and Öğmen 2006) discusses both the history and the state of the art of the method. They cite McDougal (1904), Sherrington (1897), and Stigler (1910) as the innovators of the method in the late nineteenth and early twentieth century.
23 To qualify, there has been a good deal of related work in the history and philosophy of science, on experiment in science generally (though rarely with explicit emphasis on creativity and/or imagination). For two original monographs, see Hacking 1983 and Galison 1987. And for a collection of original papers, see Gooding et al. 1989.
24 Stokes also attempts to extend the account of imagination's role in creativity to Ah-ha moments, or what Gaut calls "passive creativity." See Stokes 2014, 170–178.
25 For discussion of pretending, see Elizabeth Picciuto and Peter Carruthers' Chapter 23, in this volume; and for imagination in children, see Deena Skolnick Weisberg, Chapter 22.
26 Carruthers endorses the "geneplore" model of creative ideas. See Finke et al. 1992 and Ward et al. 1999.
27 See Gaut 2009 for a critique of Carruthers' analysis.

## References


Bergson, H. (1911/1998) *Creative Evolution*, trans. A. Mitchell, New York: Dover.

Bergson, H. (1942/1992) *The Creative Mind*, trans. M. Andison, New York: Citadel Press.

Boden, M. (1990/2004) *The Creative Mind*, London: Routledge.

Breitmeyer, B.G., and H. Öğmen (2006) *Visual Masking: Time Slices through Conscious and Unconscious Vision*, Oxford: Oxford University Press.

Carruthers, P. (2002) "Human Creativity: Its Cognitive Basis, Its Evolution, and Its Connections with Childhood Pretence," *British Journal for the Philosophy of Science* 53: 225–249.

Carruthers, P. (2006) *The Architecture of the Mind: Massive Modularity and the Flexibility of Thought*, Oxford: Oxford University Press.

Carruthers, P. (2011) "Creative Action in Mind," *Philosophical Psychology* 24(4): 437–461.

Cohen, T. (2003) "The Inexplicable: Some Thoughts after Kant," in B. Gaut and P. Livingston (eds.) *The Creation of Art*, Cambridge: Cambridge University Press.

Collingwood, R.G. (1938) *The Principles of Art*, London: Oxford University Press.

Crawford, D. (1982) "Kant's Theory of Creative Imagination," in T. Cohen and P. Guyer (eds.) *Essays in Kant's Aesthetics*, Chicago: Chicago University Press, 151–178.

Crawford, D. (2001) "Kant," in B. Gaut and D.M. Lopes (eds.) *The Routledge Companion to Aesthetics*, London: Routledge.

Currie, G. (1990) *The Nature of Fiction*, Cambridge: Cambridge University Press.

Currie, G., and I. Ravenscroft (2002) *Recreative Minds: Imagination in Philosophy and Psychology*, Oxford: Oxford University Press.

De Mey, T. (2006) "Imagination's Grip on Science," *Metaphilosophy* 37(2): 222–239.

Dewey, J. (1958) *Art as Experience*, New York: Capricorn.

Finke, R., T. Ward, and S. Smith (1992) *Creative Cognition*, Cambridge, MA: MIT Press.

Galison, P. (1987) *How Experiments End*, Chicago: University of Chicago Press.

Gaut, B. (2003) "Creativity and Imagination," in B. Gaut and P. Livingston (eds.) *The Creation of Art*, Cambridge: Cambridge University Press.

Gaut, B. (2009) "Creativity and Skill," in K. Bardsley, D. Dutton, and M. Krausz (eds.) *The Idea of Creativity*, Leiden: Brill, 83–103.

Gaut, B. (2010) "The Philosophy of Creativity," *Philosophy Compass* 5: 1034–1046.

Gaut, B. (2012) "Creativity and Rationality," *Journal of Aesthetics and Art Criticism* 70: 259–270.

Gaut, B. (2014) "Educating for Creativity," in E.S. Paul and S.B. Kaufman (eds.) *The Philosophy of Creativity: New Essays*, New York: Oxford University Press, 265–287.
Gooding, D., T. Pinch, and S. Schaffer (eds.) (1989) *The Use of Experiment*, Cambridge: Cambridge University Press.
Guyer, P. (2005) "Exemplary Originality: Genius, Universality, and Individuality," in *Values of Beauty: Historical Essays in Aesthetics*, Cambridge: Cambridge University Press, 242–262.
Hacking, I. (1983) *Representing and Intervening*, Cambridge: Cambridge University Press.
Harvey, W. (1628/1976) *An Anatomical Disputation concerning the Movement of the Heart and the Blood in Living Creatures*, trans. G. Whitteridge, Oxford: Blackwell.
Hospers, J. (1985) "Artistic Creativity," *Journal of Aesthetics and Art Criticism* 43: 243–255.
Kant, I. (1781/2000) *Critique of the Power of Judgment*, trans. P. Guyer and E. Matthews, Cambridge: Cambridge University Press.
Kivy, P. (2001) *The Possessor and the Possessed*, New Haven: Yale University Press.
Kronfeldner, M.E. (2009) "Creativity Naturalized," *Philosophical Quarterly* 59: 577–592.
Kuhn, T. (1962) *The Structure of Scientific Revolutions*, Chicago: Chicago University Press.
Levy, L. (2014) "Sartre and Ricoeur on Productive Imagination," *Southern Journal of Philosophy* 52: 43–60.
Lewis, D. (1983) "Truth in Fiction," in *Philosophical Papers*, New York: Oxford University Press.
McDougall, W. (1904) "The Sensations Excited by a Single Momentary Stimulation of the Eye," *British Journal of Psychology* 1: 78–113.
Mowry, B. (1985) "From Galen's Theory to William Harvey's Theory: A Case Study in the Rationality of Scientific Theory Change," *Studies in History and Philosophy of Science Part A* 16(1): 49–82.
Nanay, B. (2014) "An Experiential Account of Creativity," in E.S. Paul and S.B. Kaufman (eds.) *The Philosophy of Creativity*, New York: Oxford University Press.
Ostaric, L. (2012) "Kant on the Normativity of Creative Production," *Kantian Review* 17: 75–107.
Paul, E.S., and S.B. Kaufman (eds.) (2014) *The Philosophy of Creativity*, New York: Oxford University Press.
Picciuto, E., and P. Carruthers (2014) "The Origins of Creativity," in E.S. Paul and S.B. Kaufman (eds.) *The Philosophy of Creativity*, New York: Oxford University Press.
Polanyi, M. (1936) "The Value of the Inexact," *Philosophy of Science* 3: 233–234.
Polanyi, M. (1946) "Science and Reality," *Synthese* 5: 177–196.
Polanyi, M. (1950) "Scientific Beliefs," *Ethics* 61: 27–37.
Polanyi, M. (1958) *Personal Knowledge*, Chicago: University of Chicago Press.
Polanyi, M. (1966/2009) "Creative Imagination," repr. in K. Bardsley, D. Dutton, and M. Krausz (eds.) *The Idea of Creativity*, Leiden: Brill, 147–163.
Polanyi, M. (1974) "Genius in Science," in R.S. Cohen and Marx W. Wartofsky (eds.) *Methodological and Historical Essays in the Natural and Social Sciences*, Boston: Reidel, 57–71.
Popper, K. (1934/1959) *The Logic of Scientific Discovery*, London: Routledge.
Reichenbach, H. (1938) *Experience and Prediction*, Chicago: University of Chicago Press.
Runco, M. (2010) "Parsimonious Creativity and Its Measurement," in E. Villaba (ed.) *Measuring Creativity: Proceedings of the European Council Meeting on Creativity and Innovation*, Luxembourg: Publications Office of the European Union.
Sartre, J.-P. (1936/2012) *The Imagination*, trans. K. Williford and D. Rudrauf, London: Routledge.
Sartre, J.-P. (1940/2004) *The Imaginary*, trans. J. Webber, London: Routledge.
Sartre, J.-P. (1947a/1988) "What Is Literature?," in *What Is Literature? And Other Essays*, trans. B. Frechtman, Cambridge, MA: Harvard University Press.
Sartre, J.-P. (1947b/1988) "Why Write?" in *What Is Literature? And Other Essays*, trans. B. Frechtman, Cambridge, MA: Harvard University Press.
Sartre, J.P. (1948) *Being and Nothingness*, trans. H.E. Barnes, New York: Philosophical Library.
Schelling, F.W.J. (1809/1936) *Of Human Freedom*, trans. J. Guntman, Chicago: Open Court.
Schopenhauer, A. (1969) *The World as Will and Representation*, vols. 1 and 2, trans. E.F.J. Payne, New York: Dover.
Searle, J. (1975) "The Logical Status of Fictional Discourse," *New Literary History* 6: 319–332.
Sherrington, C.S. (1897) "On the Reciprocal Action in the Retina as Studied by Means of Some Rotating Discs," *Journal of Physiology* 21: 33–54.
Stigler, R. (1910) "Chronotopische Studien über den Umgebungskontrast," *Pflügers Archiv für die gesamte Physiologie* 135: 365–435.

Stokes, D. (2007) "Incubated Cognition and Creativity," *Journal of Consciousness Studies* 14: 83–100.
Stokes, D. (2008) "A Metaphysics of Creativity," in K. Stock and K. Thomson Jones (eds.) *New Waves in Aesthetics*, Basingstoke: Palgrave Macmillan.
Stokes, D. (2011) "Minimally Creative Thought," *Metaphilosophy* 42(5): 658–681.
Stokes, D. (2014) "The Role of Imagination in Creativity," in E.S. Paul and S.B. Kaufman (eds.) *The Philosophy of Creativity*, New York: Oxford University Press.
Stokes, D., and E. Paul (Forthcoming) "Naturalistic Approaches to Creativity," in J. Sytsma and W. Buckwalter (eds.) *The Blackwell Companion to Experimental Philosophy*, Oxford: Blackwell.
Walton, K. (1990) *Mimesis as Make-Believe: On the Foundations of the Representational Arts*, Cambridge, MA: Harvard University Press.
Ward, T., S. Smith, and R. Finke (1999) "Creative Cognition," in R. Sternberg (ed.) *Handbook of Creativity*, Cambridge: Cambridge University Press.
Wear, A. (1990) "The Heart and Blood from Vesalius to Harvey," in R.C. Olby, G.N. Cantor, J.R.R. Christie, and M.J.S. Hodge (eds.) *Companion to the History of Modern Science*, London: Routledge, 571–574.
Webber, J. (2004) "Philosophical Introduction," in J.-P. Sartre, *The Imaginary*, trans. J. Webber, London: Routledge.

# 19
# SIMULATION THEORY

*Shannon Spaulding*

## 1 Introduction

The Simulation Theory (ST) is an account of how we understand other people. In brief, the theory holds that we understand others by mentally simulating being them. Observing your behavior, I imagine what I would think, feel, and do in your situation. On the basis of this imaginative simulation, I make an inference about what you think, feel, and will do.

Originally, ST was advanced as a theory of mindreading, i.e., as a theory about how we attribute mental states to others in order to explain and predict their behavior (Goldman 2006b, 1986). The theory has been co-opted to explain pretense (Currie and Ravenscroft 2002), engagement with fiction (Currie 2010; Goldman 2006a), imitation (Hurley 2005), and other cognitive feats (Davies and Stone 1995b). In each of these roles, simulation crucially involves imagination. In this chapter, I will focus on ST as a theory of mindreading. However, when appropriate, I will draw connections with these other uses of the theory.

Mindreading consists in attributing a mental state to a target in order to understand the target's behavior and anticipate future behavior. Mindreading theorists typically fall into two distinct camps: Theory Theory (TT) and ST. Theory theorists argue that we understand others by employing a folk psychological theory to explain and predict others' behaviors (Carruthers and Smith 1996; Davies and Stone 1995a). In contrast, simulation theorists argue that we do not need to employ a *theory* about folk psychology to understand others. The theory theorists overintellectualize this process. To understand a target's behavior, all we need to do is imagine what *we* would think, feel, and do in the target's situation, and on that basis we come to understand what the target thinks, feels, and will do (Davies and Stone 1995b).

There are two kinds of simulational mindreading, which often work together. The first kind is *retrodictive* simulation. We simulate the target to figure out what the target's mental states could have been to cause the observed behavior. That is, we imagine ourselves in the target's situation and imagine what mental states could have caused us to act in the way the target acts. The result of the retrodictive simulation is an explanation of the target's behavior. The second kind is *projective* simulation, which can take as input the output of the retrodictive simulation. We imagine that we have the target's beliefs and desires, and we imagine what we would do next in that situation. We take the resulting conclusion and attribute it to the target. The result of the projective simulation is a prediction of what the target will do next.

ST is sometimes characterized as an *information-poor* mindreading process. It does not require access to large bodies of information about folk psychology. We do not need theoretical knowledge about causal relations between mental states and behavior. Simulation requires the ability to imagine oneself in a target's situation and figure out what one would feel, think, and do in that position. One simply redeploys one's own cognitive mechanisms for the purpose of mindreading. It is in this sense that ST is an information-*poor* mindreading process (Goldman 2006b).

Simulational mindreading can be either "high-level" or "low-level." For high-level mindreading, the mental states involved are beliefs and other propositional attitudes, and the mindreading process is consciously and voluntarily mediated. For low-level mindreading, the mental states involved are nonpropositional attitudes, such as emotions and basic intentions, and the mindreading process is largely automatic and nonconscious.[1]

In this chapter, I discuss three aspects of ST: the concept of simulation and high- and low-level simulation. In the next section, I argue for a more precise characterization of the concept of simulation. In Sections 3 and 4, I discuss high- and low-level simulation, which are quite different in some respects. High-level simulation involves imagination in the conventional sense. The process and product of high-level simulation are consciously accessible and potentially under the control of the agent. In contrast, low-level simulation involves an unconventional sense of imagination, and the process and product of low-level simulation are involuntary and not consciously accessible. I discuss the features and potential limitations of both high- and low-level simulation.

## 2 The concept of simulation

One difficulty in assessing ST is that the concept of simulation is often not well defined. There is no unified conception of simulation across the sciences. Computer simulations, physical simulations, abstract simulations in scientific modeling, and mental simulations have little in common. There is no consensus on what exactly simulation is in the cognitive sciences, not even in the area of mindreading. As a result, some theorists have called for a moratorium on the term (Nichols and Stich 2003, 134).

Within the field of mindreading, Alvin Goldman has done the most to advance the concept of simulation. My exploration of ST will be based on Goldman's influential work. Goldman defines simulation in the following way: Process $P$ simulates process $P'$ iff (1) $P$ duplicates, replicates, or resembles $P'$ in some significant respect and (2) in its duplication of $P'$, $P$ fulfills one of its purposes or functions. For mindreading simulation, $P$ and $P'$ are mental processes and the purpose or function of $P$ – the simulating process – is to understand a target's mental states (Goldman 2006b).

This definition of simulation is vague.[2] With respect to (1), it is unclear what it is for a process to duplicate, replicate, or resemble another process *in some significant respect*. Following Justin Fisher (2006), let us distinguish *concrete* and *abstract* replications. When event $A$ concretely replicates event $B$, $A$ and $B$ involve the same types of systems and exhibit similar fine-grained details. Building a functional model rocket is an example of concrete replication. The model rocket reproduces the parts of the rocket and the relations between those parts and the environment. An accurate model rocket will replicate, in proportion, the concrete details of the actual rocket. When using a model rocket to explain or predict the behavior of an actual rocket, the success of the replication *depends on* reproducing the fine-grained details of the actual rocket and its environment.

In contrast, when event $A$ abstractly replicates event $B$, $A$ and $B$ need not involve the same types of systems or fine-grained details. For example, the mathematical process in my head when I add 2 and 3 abstractly resembles a calculator's mathematical process of adding 2 and 3. Both the system underlying the calculator's mathematical process and the fine-grained details of the process differ from the cognitive system underlying, and the fine-grained details of, my mathematical process.

The central difference between abstract and concrete replication is that successful abstract replication does not require sameness of system and fine-grained process similarity, whereas successful concrete replication does.[3] The calculator may successfully replicate my mathematical process – that is, it may perform a mathematical process the output of which is the same as the output of the mathematical process that occurs in me – without matching the fine-grained details of my cognitive process. Crucially, when *A* abstractly replicates *B*, *A* and *B* may in fact be the same type of process and share the same fine-grained details, but the success of the replication – equifinality – does not depend on this similarity. This point will be important later.

I suggest that when Goldman claims that simulation requires that process *P* replicates, duplicates, or resembles process *P′* *in some significant respect*, this ought to mean that *P concretely* replicates *P′*. Abstract replications do not count as significant replications, because they are ubiquitous. Using a calculator, an abacus, a look-up table, counting on one's fingers, and the operations of a particular Turing machine are all abstract replications of the mathematical process that occurs in my mind when I add 2 and 3. At a coarse-grained level they resemble the mathematical process that occurs in my brain when I add 2 and 3. In contrast, concrete replications are generally far less common than abstract replications (because the criteria for concrete replications are more stringent), and the replicational aspect plays a central role in their success. If ST is to offer an interesting, distinctive claim about how mindreading operates, it ought to be restricted to concrete replications.

Another reason that simulation should require concrete replication is that some versions of TT entail abstract replication (Fisher 2006, 422). For example, in predicting whether you will decide to go to the party on Friday night, I call on my knowledge that you enjoy parties, you like the people who are attending the party, you have had a difficult week and desire to go out, and you know that you have been invited to a party on Friday night. I *theorize* that you believe there is a party on Friday night and desire to go to the party, and that you do not have a competing desire not to attend the party. Thus, I predict that you will go to the party. Suppose that my reasoning process just so happens to resemble your reasoning process. We both weigh various considerations, decide how to maximize preferences, etc. Despite the fact that I am *theorizing* about your behavior, my cognitive system merely *abstractly* replicates your decision-making process. My reasoning process has only *accidentally* resembled your reasoning process.[4] You may have employed a very different sort of reasoning to get to the conclusion that you will go to the party. The success of my prediction does not *depend* on a fine-grained similarity between my cognitive process and yours. Thus, TT entails abstract replications.

Given that abstract replications are so easy to come by, and that TT entails them, ST needs a more restrictive account of simulation. ST needs to be restricted to concrete replications, which are not ubiquitous and not entailed by TT. This means that simulation theorists must show that their examples of simulational mindreading are cases in which the mindreader's mental process replicates the actual mental process the target goes through, and that the nonaccidental success of the simulation *depends on* replicating that mental process. This is not an overly burdensome requirement, but it will limit what counts as simulational mindreading (Fisher 2006).

Goldman's second criterion for a process *P* to simulate *P′* is that in its duplication of *P′*, *P* fulfills one of the purposes or functions of *P*. How can we tell when a process has the function of (concretely) replicating another process? Simulation theorists do not provide many details, but they give examples of what they take to be simulational processes. These examples include using one's own inference mechanisms to determine what a target believes (Nichols and Stich 2003, 135), using one's own inference mechanism to predict the kind of inferences others will make (Stich and Nichols 1995); using one's own grammaticality system to determine whether a target will judge a particular sentence to be grammatical (Harris 1995); using our knowledge of a scientific theory to predict what other experts in the field believe (Heal 1995); using our arithmetical skills to figure out how a target will answer an arithmetic question (Heal 2003).

The problem with these examples is that they do not discriminate cases in which a process *happens* to replicate another process from cases in which replication is the *function* of the process. Consider the following case, which shares the same form as the other examples but is not a case of simulational mindreading (Ramsey 2010). In watching a baseball game, I predict that the pitcher will throw to first base. I see that the runner has strayed too far off base, I see that the pitcher sees this, and I infer that since the pitcher sees that the runner has strayed too far off base that he believes this. This belief, plus the attributed belief that runners who stray too far off base are easy to throw out, and the attributed desire to throw out runners, lead me to predict that the pitcher will throw to first base. I theorize about what the pitcher will do and why. When I see what the pitcher sees, I reason as the pitcher reasons. My perceptual system generates a belief about the status of the runner, as does the pitcher's perceptual system. But this does not mean that I am simulating the pitcher's visual system and decision-making processes. In this case I am using my visual system in the way that it is normally used, to ascertain various facts about the world that I can use in my reasoning. I employ these facts in reasoning about where the pitcher ought to throw. The fact that the states of my perceptual system and reasoning process about where the ball needs to be thrown resemble the processes taking place in the pitcher's mind does not entail that I am simulating the pitcher. I am simply using my cognitive capacities as I normally do, i.e., as fact finders, and on the basis of the facts I know about the world and the pitcher, I predict that the pitcher will throw to first base (Ramsey 2010).

We must distinguish when our cognitive mechanisms are being used as they normally are – as *fact finders* that merely happen to replicate the cognitive processes in a target – from when they are being used to simulate a target's cognitive processes. In other words, we need a way to determine when a process has the *function* of concretely replicating another process. In order to determine this, we need to look at two features of the cognitive process in question: how it operates and its content (Nichols and Stich 2003, 132–135; Ramsey 2010). Genuine mental simulation requires that the cognitive process be taken "offline" and provided with nonstandard inputs.[5]

The first criterion for a process $P$ to have the function of replicating $P'$ is that $P$ is taken "offline" in its simulating role. When I am genuinely simulating a target's cognitive processes, I use my own cognitive mechanisms but the process does not result in an action, decision, etc., as it does when I am using my cognitive mechanisms "online." Rather, it is merely an imagined action, decision, etc. Importantly, this criterion is neutral with respect to whether $P$ in its offline role is conscious and voluntary or unconscious and involuntary.

The second criterion is that the content (i.e., the input and output) of my simulational cognitive process is (or aims to be) the content of the target's cognitive process. In other words, inputs and outputs of the simulational process are nonstandard; they are imaginative representational surrogates for the target's mental states. This criterion is neutral with respect to the kind of representational surrogates involved. These may be propositional attitudes or nonpropositional mental states like emotions or images.

These two criteria for figuring out whether P has the function of simulating $P'$ – offline operation and representational surrogates – allow for processes that are conscious, voluntary, and involve propositional attitudes *and* processes that are unconscious, nonvoluntary, and involve nonpropositional attitudes. This means that these requirements for simulation apply both to *low-level* and *high-level* mindreading.

Putting this all together, we have the following definition of simulation:

1 *P* concretely resembles $P'$, which requires that:

  a *P* and $P'$ involve the same type of system;
  b *P* and $P'$ exhibit similar fine-grained details.

2 In resembling $P'$, *P* fulfills one of its functions, which requires that:

  a The success of the simulation depends on *P* concretely resembling $P'$;
  b *P* is taken "offline" in its simulating role;
  c The input and output of *P* are representational surrogates for the input and output of $P'$.

Consider again some of the examples discussed so far. On this definition, the way in which I determined that you would attend the party on Friday night – theorizing about what you would do in a way that just so happened to resemble your own reasoning process – does not count as a simulation, because it does not meet (2a), (2b), or (2c). My prediction that the pitcher will throw to first base is not the result of a simulation, because it does not meet (2a), (2b), or (2c), either. A legitimate case of simulation is one where I use my cognitive system to concretely replicate your mental process, i.e., I adopt representational surrogates for your mental states and run them through my own offline cognitive mechanisms, and the success of this process depends on replicating the mental process that you actually go through.

We ought to adopt this more precise conception of simulation. Though it is more demanding than Goldman's generic conception discussed above, the problem with the generic conception is that it is far too lax. This more precise account of simulation rules out those illegitimate examples of simulation and captures what is truly distinctive about legitimate cases of simulation. Moreover, it offers a unified conception of simulation that is appropriate both for high- and for low-level simulation.

## 3 High-level simulation

Now that we have clarified the concept of simulation, we can discuss high- and low-level simulation. Before philosophers and cognitive scientists conceived of the concept of low-level mental simulation, all simulational mindreading was considered high level, i.e., consciously accessible and voluntarily mediated. In this section, I describe exactly how high-level simulation mindreading is meant to work and identify some theoretical worries about it.

Recall the two kinds of simulational mindreading. First the subject retrodictively simulates the target in order to figure out what mental states could have caused that behavior, and then the subject projectively simulates in order to figure out what the target will do next. Suppose I have a guest lecturer in my class one day and a student comes in late. She slowly opens the door, looks to the front of the room and leaves. According to ST, first I imagine myself in the student's situation. I imagine that I am coming in late to class, I see a stranger at the front of the room, and I walk out. I imagine what I would think in this situation. Perhaps I would think that in my rush to get to class, I walked into the wrong classroom. Or maybe I would think a guest lecturer is not worth my time, so I leave. Or perhaps I know and dislike the guest lecturer, so I prefer not listen to him. I imaginatively adopt these mental states to see if they would explain the observed behavior. I determine that if I were in that situation, I would think that I walked into the wrong class. Thus, I attribute to the student the desire to attend my class and the false belief that she has walked into the wrong classroom.

For the projective simulation, the subject takes the results of the retrodictive simulation and imagines what she would do next if she were in the target's situation. In our example, I imaginatively adopt the desire to attend class and the belief that I have walked into the wrong classroom, and I run this information through my own decision-making mechanisms. I imaginatively decide to check the classroom location on the syllabus, which as a good student I always carry with me. I imagine that having done this, I would realize that I did not walk into the wrong classroom. I imaginatively decide to peek into the classroom again to see if I recognize the other students in the room. I imagine that doing this would result in the realization that all of my classmates are in the room, and that the person at the front of the room is just a guest lecturer, and as a result I would come back into the classroom. Thus, through this simulational process, I generate a prediction about what the student will do. I predict that she will check her syllabus, realize that she did not make a mistake, and then come back into the classroom.

This example highlights several facts about high-level simulational mindreading. First, high-level simulation involves imagination in the conventional sense. In both retrodictive and projective simulation, I consciously and deliberatively imagine myself in the target's circumstances. Second, high-level simulation can easily be co-opted to explain our engagement with fiction (Currie and Ravenscroft 2002; Doggett and Egan 2012). I simply put myself in the fictional character's position and imagine what I would think, feel, and do in that situation. I imaginatively adopt the beliefs and desires of the character and in some circumstances even have affective responses to the fictional events. When Othello approaches Desdemona in a murderous rage, I feel something like fear and horror at this impending fictional murder.[6] Third, this account of simulational mindreading could be co-opted to explain how some thought experiments work (Williamson forthcoming). In some thought experiments, you imagine being in a particular situation and then you entertain a question about what you would think or do in that situation. In this way, you could potentially get knowledge through simulational imagination.[7]

One worry about ST is about whether it is computationally tractable. For ST, explanation requires identifying what the possible relevant mental states of the target could have been in order to cause the observed behavior, running the imagined mental states through one's own (offline) decision-making mechanism and, once plausible candidate mental states are identified, attributing the computed imagined decision to the target as an explanation of past behavior and prediction for future behavior. For social interactions that involve a range of people and behaviors, one would first need to identify the possible relevant mental states of all the participants and run the simulations simultaneously to come up with a coherent explanation of the participants' behaviors and then use this explanation to imaginatively simulate the decisions of the participants. It is an open question whether it is possible to run multiple simultaneous simulations through one's own decision-making mechanism. However the more serious problem is that the targets' behavior and mental states will be interdependent. ST's simultaneous, interdependent simulations, if they are even possible, would be computationally intractable (Bermúdez 2003, 31–34).

Another theoretical limitation of the ST is what is known as the "threat of collapse" (Davies and Stone 1995b). To retrodictively simulate my student, I observe her walking out of class upon seeing the guest speaker, imagine myself in her situation, generate hypothetical beliefs and desires that would explain why I would walk out of class if I were in that situation, and then attribute those mental states to my student. The difficulty here is that there are indefinitely many mental state combinations that would explain the observed behavior. If we were to try to figure out, with simulation resources only, what our mental states could have been to cause us to behave like the target, our retrodictive simulation would have no way to decide between radically different belief–desire combinations that would explain the behavior. Moreover, there would be no stopping point for the retrodictive simulation. The simulation itself provides no way to determine when we have landed on a good enough explanation of the observed behavior and can stop simulating.

This problem is called the threat of collapse because, upon inspection of imagination-based simulation, it is evident that ST needs the theoretical knowledge posited by TT. Thus, it is argued, perhaps hyperbolically, that ST simply collapses into TT. Retrodictive simulation reveals some of the possible mental states that a target may have, but it cannot, all by itself, provide knowledge of other minds. Theoretical information is required to move from identifying possible mental states to knowing a target's mental states. Most simulation theorists these days recognize this problem and as a result endorse hybrid ST/TT models (Davies and Stone 1995b; Goldman 2006b; Heal 1998; Nichols and Stich 2003). The hybrid models handle the threat of collapse, and they may also alleviate the computational worries about running multiple, interdependent simulations.

## 4 Low-level simulation

Like high-level simulation, low-level simulational mindreading involves both retrodictive and projective simulation. One central difference between high- and low-level simulation is that one has neither conscious access to nor control over the process or product of low-level simulational mindreading. Low-level simulation involves an unconventional conception of imagination. In the context of low-level simulation, imagination operates unconsciously and automatically.

The ordinary, folk conception of imagination is that it is conscious and potentially under the agent's voluntary control. However, several theorists have argued that imagination may be nonconscious and nonvoluntary (Church 2008; Goldman 2006b; Nanay 2013; Van Leeuwen 2014; Walton 1990). Kendall Walton, for example, posits nonoccurrent imaginings that do not occupy the subject's attention. Bence Nanay's conception of pragmatic mental imagery involves spatially rich representations that may or may not involve conscious visualization. Jennifer Church argues that several ordinary cases of imagining are most plausibly explained by unconscious imagining. She considers several objections to the idea that imagination can be nonconscious and develops her own account of unconscious imagining. In each of these cases, imagination involves imagery, but this imagery may not be conscious and it need not be under the voluntary control of the subject. Although the notion of unconscious imagining is unconventional, it is not unprecedented. Several prominent figures in the philosophy of imagination argue for it. Thus, it is appropriate to hold that low-level simulation involves imagination.

I argued above that high- and low-level simulation have the same basic requirements. It is worth pausing to consider an objection to my claim that the above requirements apply to high- *and* low-level simulation. Goldman argues that (2b) (offline operation) and (2c) (representational surrogates) are required only for *high-level* simulational mindreading. These two criteria require using pretense or imagination, which Goldman argues are high-level activities that are potentially and intermittently under intentional guidance or control. Low-level simulational mindreading is supposed to be fully automatic, though (Goldman 2006b, 131–132).

The definition of simulation I offer can accommodate Goldman's claims about low-level mindreading. Imagination is required to produce representational surrogates for low-level simulation, but above I cite several prominent theorists who allow for unconscious, involuntary imagination. Even by Goldman's own lights, imagination need not be a conscious, voluntary process. In characterizing *E-imagination* (his prototype for high-level simulational mindreading), Goldman cautions against adopting the naive conception of imagination, which is restricted to the sphere of consciousness and the control of the will. "E-imagination is introduced here as a psychological construct, the referents of which can either be conscious or covert, voluntary or automatic, and these properties can hold for both the generating process and the products so generated" (Goldman 2006b, 151). We can say that low-level simulation involves psychological surrogates (nonconsciously and automatically produced by imagination) that are run through one's offline cognitive mechanisms. Thus, these criteria for simulation can be applied to low-level simulation, as well.

Moreover, rejecting the stricter criteria comes at a significant cost. If we adopt Goldman's generic definition of simulation for high- and low-level simulation, then simulation just is process resemblance. However, process resemblance does not discriminate simulational from nonsimulational processes. Predicting that you will go to the party or that the pitcher will throw to first base both involve process resemblance, but these are cases of theorizing, not simulating. Adopting the generic conception for high- and low-level simulation would obscure the distinction between simulation and theory.

Alternatively, if one adopts the stricter criteria for high-level simulation but the generic definition for low-level, then low- and high-level simulation would end up looking quite different. High-level simulation would involve concrete resemblance, offline processing, and representational surrogates, whereas low-level simulation would involve none of these features. Low-level simulation would simply be process resemblance. The criteria for low-level simulation would be significantly weaker and different than for high-level simulation. Adopting different criteria for low- and high-level simulation threatens the idea that there is a unified conception of simulation. "Low-level simulation" would be a different sort of thing altogether, and evidence of "low-level simulation" would not be evidence for ST in general. Fragmenting simulation in this way would seriously damage ST. Thus, there are several good reasons to adopt the stricter criteria for high- *and* low-level simulation.

By far the most discussed example of low-level simulational mindreading is mirror neurons. Mirror neurons are neurons that fire, or activate, when a subject acts, emotes, or experiences a certain sensation, and also when a subject observes a target acting, emoting, or experiencing a certain sensation. For example, a host of neurons in the premotor cortex and posterior parietal cortex fires when I grasp an object, and this same host of neurons fires when I observe another person grasping an object (Rizzolatti and Craighero 2004). There are similar mirror neuron systems for experiencing and observing certain emotions. When I experience disgust and when I observe another person experiencing disgust the same collection of neurons in the insula fires (Calder et al. 2000; Wicker et al. 2003). Similar findings hold for the experience and observation of fear (Adolphs et al. 1994), anger (Lawrence et al. 2002), pain (Singer et al. 2004) and touch (Keysers and Perrett 2004). In each of these cases, groups of neurons are endogenously activated when the subject acts, emotes, or feels a certain way, and these same groups of neurons are exogenously activated (at an attenuated level) when the subject observes another acting, emoting, or feeling in those same ways.

Some theorists propose that mirror neurons are the basis for our ability to understand and interact successfully with other people (Gallese 2007; Gallese et al. 2004; Hurley 2005; Keysers and Gazzola 2009; Oberman and Ramachandran 2009). The argument goes like this. How is it that we understand what other people are doing, why they are doing it, what they are going to do next? Mirror neuron studies demonstrate that parts of our brains fire in the same ways when we observe an action, emotion, or sensation and when we act, emote, or sense in the same way. The suggestion is that we understand what another person is doing, feeling, and experiencing because when we observe the other person, parts of our brains are activating as if *we* were doing what the other person is doing. Our brain activity mirrors – that is, simulates – the other person's brain activity such that it is *as if* we are acting, feeling, or experiencing as the target is acting, feeling, or experiencing.

Controversy surrounds many aspects of mirror neurons (Hickok 2009). In fact, it is not even clear whether the empirical facts support the claim that mirror neurons are simulational in the relevant respect (Herschbach 2012; Spaulding 2012, 2013). In this context, however, we need not concern ourselves so much with these controversies. Mirror neurons are a common example of how low-level simulation works. Mirror neurons are supposed to be an example of a neural mechanism that has the function of concretely replicating a target's experience. We do not need to worry about whether this particular neural mechanism actually meets all the criteria in order to use it as an illustrative example.

Low-level simulation faces a version of the threat of collapse (Spaulding 2012, forthcoming). The threat of collapse for high-level simulation is that indefinitely many propositional attitude combinations are compatible with the observed behavior, and simulation itself provides no way to determine when we have landed on a plausible, good enough explanation of the observed behavior. The threat of collapse for high-level simulation concerns propositional attitudes. Low-level simulation involves nonpropositional attitudes, such as basic intentions and emotions. I will use mirror neurons to illustrate the threat of collapse for low-level simulation. Again, though there are genuine concerns about whether the empirical data support the claim that mirror neurons are simulational in the relevant respect, let us set aside those concerns for now.

The threat of collapse for low-level simulation is that an observed behavior or facial expression is compatible with a number of different basic intentions or emotions. A blush may indicate embarrassment, happiness, anger, or even just a hot flash. The same applies even more clearly for basic intentions. A given behavioral movement may indicate an intention to eat, give, tease, throw, play with, put away, etc. We need more information than the simulation heuristic provides in order to be justified in attributing to a target a particular intention or emotion.

The observed behavior is compatible with a number of mental states, and the low-level simulation itself provides no way to determine the plausibility of the candidate emotions or intentions. That is, there is no sufficing heuristic or stopping point built into the operation of the low-level simulation. We need other information to discriminate between the intentions that could cause the behavior, or the emotions that could cause the blush. This may be information about the target's recent history, her personality, how certain situations make her feel, folk psychological platitudes about how behaviors relate to mental states, etc.

One way to mediate the threat of collapse for high-level simulation is to endorse a hybrid ST/TT model. TT provides the theoretical information required to move from identifying possible mental states to knowing a target's mental states. There is an analogous move for low-level simulation. One could hold that low-level simulational mechanisms receive input from and send output to nonsimulational mechanisms. In fact, functional anatomical evidence supports the idea that simulational and nonsimulational mechanisms are integrated in this way.

During action observation, mirror neurons receive input from the superior temporal sulcus (STS), an area independently associated with perception of social stimuli, mentalizing, and action understanding (Rizzolatti and Craighero 2004, 172). Mirror neuron regions send output to the primary and secondary somatosensory cortices and the middle temporal lobe (Rizzolatti and Sinigaglia 2010, 265). The STS, mirror neuron areas, and somatosensory cortices are informationally integrated. These neural regions, in addition to the aFMC (anterior fronto-median cortex), posterior STS, and temporal parietal junction, are involved in perception of social stimuli, action understanding, and mentalizing (Brass et al. 2007).

These data show that there are several neural regions informationally integrated with mirror neurons that are involved with the same functions that mirror neurons are alleged to be involved in. Importantly, these other regions do not operate by neural reuse. Thus, one empirically and theoretically plausible way to address the threat of collapse for low-level simulation is to conceive of the low-level simulational mechanism as informationally integrated with other nonsimulational mechanisms. These nonsimulational mechanisms supplement the simulational in the same way that theoretical knowledge supplements high-level simulation.

## 5 Conclusion

There has been much philosophical and empirical work on ST in the last decade or so, and as a result it is a flourishing theory. My discussion in this chapter attempts to clarify some aspects of ST, specifically the concept of simulation, high-level simulation, and low-level simulation. I argued that we have good reasons to adopt a more precise conception of simulation for high- and low-level simulation. The stricter criteria rule out some illegitimate examples of simulation, and they also capture what is truly distinctive about legitimate cases. I hope this more precise conception of simulation will contribute to the flourishing of ST.

## Notes

1 The distinction between low- and high-level simulation need not take a stand on propositionalism, the view that all attitudes are propositional. If your view is that all attitudes are propositional, then on your view low-level simulation involves propositional attitudes. Throughout this chapter I will assume that there are nonpropositional attitudes, but my arguments do not hang on this assumption.

2 This discussion of the concept of simulation is based on previous work. See Spaulding 2012 for a more in-depth discussion.

3 What counts as a successful replication depends on the particular replication at hand. For the mathematical process, it is coming up with the same result. For the rocket, it is duplicating the conditions of the actual rocket.

4 It would count as abstract replication even if the resemblance were nonaccidental. I emphasize accidental resemblance in the main text to highlight the fact that the success of an abstract replication does not depend on any fine-grained similarities between the processes. This is further evidence that abstract replication is too liberal for ST.

5 Though these criteria are standard for ST, Goldman has argued that they are required only for high-level simulation (Goldman 2006b, 131). I consider this argument in Section 4 below.

6 The characterization of these affective responses is a matter of much dispute. Some argue that the affective responses simply are emotions (Carroll 1990; Gendler 2008; Weinberg and Meskin 2006), whereas others argue that they are best characterized as imaginative emotions (Goldman 2006a; Velleman 2000; Walton 1990). Simulation theorists tend to fall into the latter category, but we need not take a stance on that issue here.

7 See Spaulding forthcoming for a discussion of how exactly we can and do get knowledge through imagination.

## References

Adolphs, R., D. Tranel, H. Damasio, and A. Damasio (1994) "Impaired Recognition of Emotion in Facial Expressions Following Bilateral Damage to the Human Amygdala," *Nature* 372(6507): 669–672.
Bermúdez, J.L. (2003) "The Domain of Folk Psychology," in A. O'Hear (ed.) *Minds and Persons*, Cambridge: Cambridge University Press, 25–48.
Brass, M., R.M. Schmitt, S. Spengler, and G. Gergely (2007) "Investigating Action Understanding: Inferential Processes versus Action Simulation,"*Current Biology* 17(24): 2117–2121.
Calder, A.J., J. Keane, F. Manes, N. Antoun, and A.W. Young (2000) "Impaired Recognition and Experience of Disgust Following Brain Injury," *Nature Neuroscience* 3(11): 1077–1078.
Carroll, N. (1990) *The Philosophy of Horror*, New York: Routledge.
Carruthers, P., and P.K. Smith (1996) *Theories of Theories of Mind*, Cambridge: Cambridge University Press.
Church, J. (2008) "The Hidden Image: A Defense of Unconscious Imagining and Its Importance," *American Imago* 65(3): 379–404.
Currie, G. (2010) "Tragedy," *Analysis* 70(4): 632–638.
Currie, G., and I. Ravenscroft (2002) *Recreative Minds: Imagination in Philosophy and Psychology*, Oxford: Oxford University Press.
Davies, M., and T. Stone (1995a) *Folk Psychology: The Theory of Mind Debate*, Oxford: Blackwell.
Davies, M., and T. Stone (1995b) *Mental Simulation: Evaluations and Applications*, Oxford: Blackwell.
Doggett, T., and A. Egan (2012) "How We Feel about Terrible, Non-existent Mafiosi," *Philosophy and Phenomenological Research* 84(2): 277–306.
Fisher, J.C. (2006) "Does Simulation Theory Really Involve Simulation?" *Philosophical Psychology* 19(4): 417–432.
Gallese, V. (2007) "Before and Below Theory of Mind: Embodied Simulation and the Neural Correlates of Social Cognition," *Philosophical Transactions of the Royal Society* 362(1480): 659–669.
Gallese, V., C. Keysers, and G. Rizzolatti (2004) "A Unifying View of the Basis of Social Cognition," *Trends in Cognitive Sciences* 8(9): 396–403.
Gendler, T.S. (2008) "Alief and Belief," *Journal of Philosophy* 105(10): 634–663.
Goldman, A.I. (2006a) "Imagination and Simulation in Audience Responses to Fiction," in S. Nichols (ed.) *The Architecture of the Imagination*, Oxford: Oxford University Press, 41–56.
Goldman, A.I. (2006b) *Simulating Minds: The Philosophy, Psychology, and Neuroscience of Mindreading*, New York: Oxford University Press.
Gordon, R.M. (1986) "Folk Psychology as Simulation," *Mind & Language* 1: 158–171.
Harris, P. (1995) "From Simulation to Folk Psychology: The Case for Development," in M. Davies and T. Stone (eds.) *Folk Psychology*, Oxford: Blackwell, 207–231.
Heal, J. (1995) "How to Think about Thinking," in M. Stone and M. Davies (eds.) *Mental Simulation: Evaluations and Applications*, Oxford: Blackwell.
Heal, J. (1998) "Co-cognition and Off-Line Simulation: Two Ways of Understanding the Simulation Approach," *Mind & Language* 13(4): 477–498.
Heal, J. (2003) *Mind, Reason and Imagination*, Cambridge: Cambridge University Press.
Herschbach, M. (2012) "Mirroring versus Simulation: On the Representational Function of Simulation," *Synthese* 189(3): 483–514.
Hickok, G. (2009) "Eight Problems for the Mirror Neuron Theory of Action Understanding in Monkeys and Humans," *Journal of Cognitive Neuroscience* 21(7): 1229–1243.
Hurley, S. (2005) "The Shared Circuits Hypothesis: A Unified Functional Architecture for Control, Imitation, and Simulation," in S. Hurley and N. Chater (eds.) *Perspectives on Imitation: From Neuroscience to Social Science*, Cambridge, MA: MIT Press.
Keysers, C., and D.I. Perrett (2004) "Demystifying Social Cognition: A Hebbian Perspective," *Trends in Cognitive Sciences* 8(11): 501–507.
Keysers, C., and V. Gazzola (2009) "Unifying Social Cognition," in J.A. Pineda (ed.) *Mirror Neuron Systems*, New York: Humana, 1–35.
Lawrence, A.D., A.J. Calder, S.W. McGowan, and P.M. Grasby (2002) "Selective Disruption of the Recognition of Facial Expressions of Anger," *Neuroreport* 13(6): 881–884.
Nanay, B. (2013) "*Between Perception and Action*, Oxford: Oxford University Press.
Nichols, S., and S. Stich (2003) *Mindreading: An Integrated Account of Pretence, Self-Awareness, and Understanding Other Minds*, Oxford: Oxford University Press.

Oberman, L.M., and V.S. Ramachandran (2009) "Reflections on the Mirror Neuron System: Their Evolutionary Functions beyond Motor Representation," in J.A. Pineda (ed.) *Mirror Neuron Systems*, New York: Humana, 39–62.
Ramsey, W.M. (2010) "How Not to Build a Hybrid: Simulation vs. Fact-Finding," *Philosophical Psychology* 23(6): 775–795.
Rizzolatti, G., and L. Craighero (2004) "The Mirror-Neuron System," *Annual Review of Neuroscience* 27(1): 169–192.
Rizzolatti, G., and C. Sinigaglia (2010) "The Functional Role of the Parieto-Frontal Mirror Circuit: Interpretations and Misinterpretations," *Nature Reviews Neuroscience* 11(4): 264–274.
Singer, T., B. Seymour, J. O'Doherty, H. Kaube, R.J. Dolan, and C.D. Frith (2004) "Empathy for Pain Involves the Affective but Not Sensory Components of Pain," *Science* 303(5661): 1157–1162.
Spaulding, S. (2012) "Mirror Neurons Are Not Evidence for the Simulation Theory," *Synthese* 189(3): 515–534.
Spaulding, S. (2013) "Mirror Neurons and Social Cognition," *Mind & Language* 28(2): 233–257.
Spaulding, S. (Forthcoming) "Imagination through Knowledge," in A. Kind and P. Kung (eds.) *Knowledge through Imagination*, Oxford: Oxford University Press.
Stich, S., and S. Nichols (1995) "Second Thoughts on Simulation," in M. Davies and M. Stone (eds.) *Mental Simulation: Evaluations and Applications*, Oxford: Oxford University Press.
Van Leeuwen, N. (2014) "The Meanings of 'Imagine' Part II: Attitude and Action," *Philosophy Compass* 9(11): 791–802.
Velleman, J.D. (2000) "On the Aim of Belief," in *The Possibility of Practical Reason*, Oxford: Oxford University Press, 244–281.
Walton, K.L. (1990) *Mimesis as Make-Believe: On the Foundations of the Representational Arts*, Cambridge, MA: Harvard University Press.
Weinberg, J.M., and A. Meskin (2006) "Puzzling over the Imagination: Philosophical Problems, Architectural Solutions," in S. Nichols (ed.) *The Architecture of the Imagination: New Essays on Pretence, Possibility, and Fiction*, Oxford: Oxford University Press, 175–202.
Wicker, B., C. Keysers, J. Plailly, J.P. Royet, V. Gallese, and G. Rizzolatti (2003) "Both of Us Disgusted in My Insula: The Common Neural Basis of Seeing and Feeling Disgust," *Neuron* 40(3): 655–664.
Williamson, T. (Forthcoming) "Knowing by Imagining," in A. Kind and P. Kung (eds.) *Knowledge through Imagination*, Oxford: Oxford University Press.

# 20
# IMAGINATION AND THE SELF

*Dilip Ninan*

## 1 Introduction

Imagine for a moment that you are Napoleon; that is, imagine *being Napoleon.* You are looking out on the desolation of Austerlitz, tucking your right hand into your tunic, wondering whether or not to declare your brother King of Spain. (If Napoleon is too distant or unfamiliar a figure, pick another.) The main issue philosophers have discussed under the rubric "imagination and the self" concerns this sort of imaginative exercise: imagining oneself to be another.

Imaginings of this sort were taken up by Bernard Williams in his paper "Imagination and the Self" (Williams 1973). Williams took such imaginings – or our manner of describing them – to raise something of a puzzle. It seems unproblematic for me to imagine that I am Napoleon; asked to do this, I know roughly how to comply. (Contrast this with the instruction to imagine that someone else – Abraham Lincoln, say – is Napoleon; here it is much less clear how to proceed.) But if imagining is a guide to possibility, my imagining may lead me to a further, more metaphysical thought: the thought that *I could have been Napoleon.* And it is this that Williams finds puzzling: "I do not understand, and could not possibly understand, what it would be for me to have been Napoleon" (Williams 1973, 45). How could I (or Williams or anyone other than Napoleon) have been Napoleon? Surely only Napoleon could have been Napoleon.

In Section 2, I examine Williams's puzzle in more detail. Section 3 then considers the dominant response to the puzzle found in the literature, which is to deny that an imagining that I would report by saying, "I am Napoleon" – a *Napoleonic imagining,* for short – is an imagining whose content is the proposition that I am Napoleon. Section 4 takes up a variation on this response, one couched in terms of the *property theory* of *de se* attitudes (see Lewis 1979). In Section 5, I discuss *Lakoff cases,* another puzzling class of imaginings (and a class not much discussed in the literature emerging out of Williams's article). Finally, I close in Section 6 with a brief discussion of two further issues, one concerning the relationship between Napoleonic imaginings and mental imagery, another concerning temporal aspects of imagination.

## 2 Williams's puzzle

Williams has a bit more to say about why we should deny that I (or anyone other than Napoleon) could have been Napoleon. Note first that when I imagine that I am Napoleon – when

I imagine *being Napoleon* – I do not (have to) imagine that my biography is intertwined with Napoleon's. I do not (have to) imagine *discovering* that I am Napoleon, through some freakish twist in history.[1] Rather, I simply imagine that I am Napoleon by taking on his biography and characteristics and abandoning my own.

So the putative possibility that I am contemplating when I contemplate my being Napoleon appears to be a possibility in which I do not have my particular body nor my particular history nor my particular origins. Williams thus worries that if we take such imaginings as indications of possibility, we will quickly be led to a form of Cartesianism about the self:

> If we press hard enough, we readily get the idea that it is not necessary to being *me* that I should have any of the individuating properties that I do have, this body, these memories, etc. ... The limiting state of this progress is the Cartesian consciousness: an "I" without body, past, or character.
>
> *(Williams 1973, 41)*

Williams is not completely explicit about what a "Cartesian consciousness" is supposed to be. But presumably he has in mind some sort of substance dualism according to which minds are distinct from – and can exist without – bodies. Thus, Williams appears to be suggesting that taking my Napoleonic imagining seriously leads to a form of dualism about the mind. Many contemporary philosophers will already be troubled by this result, but Williams thinks a few more steps are needed in order to reach something really problematic.

It seems true that I (or Williams or you) might not have existed. But if I am a Cartesian consciousness then my not existing is not simply this body not existing nor someone with this psychology not existing, but rather this consciousness not existing. But since there is nothing to distinguish my Cartesian consciousness from any other, "it is impossible to see any more what would be subtracted from the universe by the removal of *me*" (Williams 1973, 42). The objection is that there is a difference between my existing and my not existing, but on the present approach it is hard to see what this difference could consist in.

Williams's discussion here is a bit confusing. The putative possibility we are supposed to be considering is one in which I am Napoleon. But presumably on the Cartesian picture, I am a certain Cartesian consciousness *d*. Thus, nothing is identical to me unless it is identical to *d*. Napoleon, on the other hand, is a distinct Cartesian consciousness *n*, and nothing is identical to Napoleon unless it is identical to *n*. But then it cannot be that what it is for me to be Napoleon is for my Cartesian consciousness *d* to be associated with Napoleon's history, body, and experiences. For the resulting person would not be Napoleon since – as we just agreed – nothing could be Napoleon unless it was identical to Napoleon's Cartesian consciousness *n*, and, in the envisioned scenario, I am still identical to *my* Cartesian consciousness *d*, not to *n*. So it would appear that Williams's objection is not an objection to my being Napoleon but rather to my Cartesian self being associated with Napoleon's history, body, and experiences. If that is correct, then nothing has so far been said against the possibility of *my* being Napoleon.

Williams's thought might be rescued as follows. Perhaps on the Cartesian approach, we should regard ordinary referring expressions like 'I' and 'Napoleon' as ambiguous (even relative to a context of utterance): on one reading they refer to an "empirical self" (to use Williams's phrase), on another they refer to a Cartesian self.[2] Cartesian selves and empirical selves are connected, but only contingently so. The Cartesian self I refer to with the first-person pronoun is associated with the empirical self that I refer to with 'Dilip Ninan' rather than with the one I refer to with 'Napoleon,' but this needn't have been the case. The putative possibility in which I am Napoleon is a situation in which my Cartesian self is associated with Napoleon's empirical self. Perhaps it is a picture like this to which Williams is objecting.

So Williams's puzzle is this. It seems easy for to me imagine being Napoleon. But if imagining is a guide to possibility, then we should have to admit that I could have been Napoleon. This might be objectionable in and of itself, perhaps because it contravenes the necessity of identity. But if Williams is right, it is also objectionable since it leads to a Cartesian picture of the self, a picture that may be regarded as unappealing for a number of different reasons.

## 3 The naive view and its critics

It might seem that the way out of the puzzle is clear enough: deny the move from *imaginability* to *possibility*. The mere fact that I can imagine that I am Napoleon is not a good reason to judge this possible. I think that I can imagine Lavoisier discovering that water had a chemical composition other than $H_2O$: I imagine the experiments going differently, the relevant publications making different claims, and so on and so forth. But that doesn't lead to me think that it is metaphysically possible for water to have had some other chemical composition. Imaginability may be a guide to possibility, but it is surely a fallible guide. We see its limitations in all sorts of cases.

I am less sanguine than many philosophers in accepting this familiar line about the gap between imaginability and possibility. The problem is that it is very difficult to see how *else* it is we come by our modal knowledge. As Stephen Yablo writes:

> No one would doubt of herself that (e.g.) she could have born on a different day than actually, or lived in different places ... But how do we know [these things], if not by attempting to conceive ourselves with the relevant characteristics and finding that this presents no difficulties?
>
> *(Yablo 1993, 16)*

A more subtle move would be to deny that *apparent* imaginability is a guide to possibility. It seems that I can imagine that I am Napoleon. I might be tempted to conclude from this that I could have been Napoleon. But this inference might fail not because of any gap between imaginability and possibility, but simply because I am mistaken about what it is that I am really imagining. It *seems* to me that I'm imagining my being identical to Napoleon, but perhaps this appearance is misleading.

This strategy is reminiscent of a familiar approach to the water-$H_2O$ case, a strategy that has its roots in Kripke (1980). The approach I have in mind says that, in the aforementioned case, I am, strictly speaking, not imagining a situation in which *water* is not $H_2O$. Rather, I am imagining a world very much like ours but in which the substance that falls from the sky and flows in the rivers – the "watery stuff" – is discovered to have a chemical composition other than $H_2O$. And this may well be possible, even if water could not have failed to be $H_2O$. The mistake is not in assuming that imaginability is evidence of possibility; the mistake concerns the correct description of what has actually been imagined.[3]

Williams – like many subsequent commentators – seems to adopt something like this line in response to his initial puzzle. Rather than denying (or rather than *merely* denying) the move from imaginability to possibility, he argues that when I have a Napoleonic imagining, the content of this imagining is not what it would seem to be, namely the proposition that

I am identical to Napoleon. Indeed, Williams thinks reporting such an imagining by saying "I imagined that I was Napoleon" is a bit misleading; he prefers reporting the imagining with a different construction: "I imagined *being* Napoleon" (Williams 1973, 44).

Let's call the view that when one imagines being Napoleon one imagines the proposition that one is identical to Napoleon *the naive view*. (In naming it thus, I mean no disrespect; my own sympathies lie with something like this view.) One theme in the literature on "imagination and the self" is that the naive view is wrong. Consider these passages from Zeno Vendler and Steven Reynolds:

> in imagining being someone else, the object of the exercise cannot be fancying *me* (Z.V.) being identical with that person. In imagining, for instance, being Ronald Reagan, I cannot be imagining the identity of Z.V. with R.R., for it is patently impossible for these two men to be one and the same, and the patently impossible cannot be imagined.
>
> *(Vendler 1984, 105)*

> It ... seems that the content apparently imagined is not the content really imagined. In saying "I imagine that I am Napoleon" I am not reporting having imagined that a false identity statement is true.
>
> *(Reynolds 1989, 618)*

But while Williams and subsequent commentators are clear in their rejection of the naive view, they are often less clear about what they take to be its proper replacement. That said, two (compatible) ideas emerge from this literature. The first is that when I imagine being Napoleon, *I* do not figure in the content of my imagining, only Napoleon does. The second is that when I imagine being Napoleon, *the relation of identity* does not figure in the content of my imagining, another relation does. Both proposals are ways of denying the naive view.

I'll return to the first proposal shortly, but let me begin by taking up the second. This idea is advanced by Richard Wollheim who argues as follows:

> I can say – there is such an idiom – that I imagine myself being Sultan Mahomet II. But in this idiom, appearances notwithstanding, identity does not occur: I am not saying that I imagine myself being identical with Sultan Mahomet II. And this we can see from the fact that, though identity is symmetrical, "imagining myself being Sultan Mahomet II" and "imagining Sultan Mahomet II being me" are not synonyms. They are used to pick out two different imaginative projects.
>
> *(Wollheim 1984, 75)*[4]

While Wollheim's observation strikes me as both correct and significant, it isn't clear that the conclusion he draws from it – "identity does not occur" – is warranted. For, as Kendall Walton (1990, 33) points out, it might be that normally when I imagine that *a* is *b*, I imagine (i) that *a* is identical to *b*, and (ii) that *a* has some *b*-ish properties; and when I imagine that *b* is *a*, I imagine (i) that *b* is identical to *a*, and (ii) that *b* has some *a*-ish properties. So for example, when I imagine that I am Napoleon, it might be that I imagine that I am identical to Napoleon, *and* that I have certain Napoleonic characteristics, e.g. commanding French armies and longing for Maria Walewska. Assuming it even makes sense for me to imagine Napoleon being me (something many authors deny), it might be that I imagine that

Napoleon is identical to me, *and* that Napoleon has certain D.N.-properties, e.g. sipping coffee while grading a stack of logic exams. Walton's suggestion would make sense of the subject–object asymmetry that Wollheim observes without requiring us to relinquish the view that the identity relation figures in the content of such imaginings. Of course, Walton's point does not establish that identity *does* occur in the content of such imaginings; it merely shows that Wollheim's observation is not sufficient to establish that it does not.[5]

What about the idea that *I* do not figure in the content of my Napoleonic imaginings? This view is usually attributed to Williams, who claims that when I imagine being Napoleon "what I am doing, in fantasy, is something like playing the role of Napoleon" (Williams 1973, 44). Williams's proposal is not entirely straightforward. At various points, Williams suggests that imagining being Napoleon is akin to *pretending* to be Napoleon. This is undoubtedly correct on some construal. But it would appear to offer us little guidance on the matter at hand, since it simply raises the further question of what it is to pretend to be Napoleon. What is the content of such a pretending (assuming, as seems natural, that pretendings are content-bearing states)? Moreover, while imagination and pretense are surely similar in important respects, there are some disanalogies that seem relevant to the issues at hand.[6] For example: just as I can pretend that I am Napoleon, I can pretend that *you* are the Duke of Wellington, defeating me/Napoleon at Waterloo. But many commentators in the literature – including Williams himself – think that while it is clearly possible for me to imagine being Napoleon, it is not so clear that I can imagine your being the Duke of Wellington.[7] If this is right, then while there is a certain first-person/third-person asymmetry when it comes to imagining, it is not so clear that there is a similar one when it comes to pretending. That at least suggests that getting clear on the nature of pretending will not by itself resolve all of the relevant issues concerning imagination and the self.

In any case, one thing that emerges from Williams's discussion is the thought that my Napoleonic imagining concerns only Napoleon and not myself (Williams 1973, 44–45). While this thought is often endorsed in the literature,[8] little has been done to develop it in detail. On the simplest interpretation of this proposal, when I imagine that I am Napoleon, gazing out upon the desolation at Austerlitz, the content of my imagining is simply the proposition that Napoleon is gazing out upon the desolation at Austerlitz. But this proposal raises at least two questions.

First, there is a difference between imagining *being* Napoleon at Austerlitz and merely imagining a scenario in which Napoleon is at Austerlitz, e.g. imagining a scenario in which Napoleon is at Austerlitz and is "seen" from the outside. But on the present proposal, this is not a difference in the content of the two imaginings. So how, on the present proposal, do the two imaginings differ? After all, as Fodor (1987, 11) observes, "the canonical way of picking out an attitude is to say (a) what sort of attitude it is (a belief, a desire, a hunch, or whatever); and (b) what the content of the attitude is …" But if imaginings are not individuated in the canonical way, how are they to be individuated?[9]

A second question that arises is why such imaginings are reported using the first-person pronoun.[10] If I do not figure in the content of such imaginings, why can I report my imagining by saying, "I imagined that I was Napoleon"? Of course, Williams regards such reports as misleading, as we noted above. But his suggestion that we pay attention to the corresponding reports with nonfinite clauses (e.g. "I imagined being Napoleon") does not help matters much. For on influential accounts of the structure and meaning of such sentences, they are true only if the subject $x$ of the attitude report has an attitude whose content $p$ is such that $x$ could express $p$ using a sentence containing a first-person pronoun (e.g., "I am Napoleon").[11] Is Williams's proposal about the content of Napoleonic imaginings compatible with any reasonable account of the syntax and compositional semantics of such sentences?

## 4 Contents as properties

François Recanati (2007, 203–210) puts forward a proposal that retains something of Williams's idea, while avoiding the preceding objections. On Recanati's approach, when I imagine that I am Napoleon, the content of my imagining is a *property* – in this particular case, the property of being Napoleon. Recanati here builds on an approach to the content of first-person (*de se*) thought, according to which the contents of so-called "propositional attitudes" (beliefs, desires, etc.) are taken to be properties rather than classical propositions (Loar 1976; Lewis 1979; Chisholm 1981). An individual believes a property *p* just in case she "self-ascribes" *p*, i.e. she believes *de se* that she has *p*. Properties are construed as things that vary in truth value across worlds, times, and individuals. A triple of a world, time, and individual is a *centered world*. A property *p* is *true* at a centered world (*w, t, x*) iff the individual *x* has *p* at time *t* in world *w*. David Lewis (1979) is often understood as identifying a property with the set of centered worlds at which it is true.

Recanati's property account avoids the two problems discussed above. Firstly, it has the resources to distinguish imagining being Napoleon at Austerlitz, on the one hand, and simply imagining "from the outside" a scenario in which Napoleon is at Austerlitz. The content of the first imagining would be the property of *being Napoleon at Austerlitz*, while the content of the second would (e.g.) be the property of *being such that Napoleon is at Austerlitz*. These are different properties, since only Napoleon had the first, whereas many people had the second. Secondly, the property account dovetails nicely with an approach to attitude reports that features prominently in the formal semantics literature. Several accounts of attitude reports like "I imagined being Napoleon" have been offered, all of which would predict that the sentence is true (relative to a context) iff the speaker had an imagining whose content is the property of being Napoleon (see, e.g., Chierchia 1989; Schlenker 2003; Anand and Nevins 2004; Ninan 2008, 2009). The details of such proposals needn't detain us here, but it is worth observing that Recanati's approach enjoys this apparent advantage over the accounts discussed earlier.

How should we understand the link between imaginability and possibility once we move to the property view of content? Having an imagining whose content is property *p* is imagining that you yourself have *p*. So it would be natural to think that such an imagining is evidence that it is possible for you to have *p*. If this is correct, then Recanati's approach seems similar to the naive view, insofar as both views yield the result that if imagining is a guide to possibility, then my Napoleonic imaginings are evidence that I could have been Napoleon.

Recanati does not wish to challenge the link between imaginability and possibility, but nor does he wish to accept the conclusion that anyone other than Napoleon could have been Napoleon. He manages to maintain this position by rejecting the claim I made above about what my Napoleonic imagining is evidence for: it is not evidence that *I* could have been Napoleon, but only that Napoleon could have been Napoleon. To understand how Recanati achieves this result, we need to understand a further feature of his overall framework.

On a traditional approach to attitude content, the content of an attitude is a proposition, something that is true or false *simpliciter*. A token belief can then be said to be true (false) just in case its content is true (false). Since properties are not true or false *simpliciter*, more needs to be said about how the truth of a belief is to be characterized on the property account. To resolve this problem, Recanati introduces the notion of the *circumstance of evaluation* of a (token) belief: given a token belief *b* possessed by individual *x* at time *t* in world *w*, *b*'s *circumstance of evaluation* is ($w$, $t$, $x$). A token belief with content $p$ and circumstance of evaluation ($w$, $t$, $x$) can then be said to true *simpliciter* iff $p$ is true at ($w$, $t$, $x$).[12] So if Joe believes, at a particular time $t$ in the actual world, that he is in danger, then his belief is true iff Joe is in danger at that time $t$ in the actual world.

Recanati's account of imagination has two relevant features. The first is that the circumstance of evaluation of an *imagining* needn't contain the imaginer himself; in this respect, imaginings differ from beliefs. More specifically, Recanati implements Williams's idea that my Napoleonic imagining concerns Napoleon and not myself by claiming that the circumstance of evaluation of my imagining does not consist of a world, a time, and *me* (D.N.), but rather of a world, a time, and *Napoleon*:[13]

> It is to *Napoleon himself* that the imagined properties and experiences are ascribed ... I – the actual imaginer – do not come into the picture. The content of the imagination is assumed to hold in *Napoleon's* situation.
>
> *(Recanati 2007, 205–206)*

The second feature of Recanati's proposal concerns how to interpret the imaginability–possibility link within this framework. Given a token imagining $i$ with content $p$ and circumstance ($w$, $t$, $x$), Recanati claims that the fact that $p$ is imaginable is evidence for the possibility of *$x$'s having $p$*. Note that since $x$ needn't be the imaginer, this is not necessarily evidence that the imaginer could have had $p$. In particular, when I imagine that I am Napoleon – when I imagine the property of being Napoleon – this is only evidence that Napoleon could have had that property, not that *I* could have that property. In this way, Recanati avoids having to say that my Napoleonic imagining is evidence that I could have been Napoleon.

This is a very interesting proposal, and perhaps the most sophisticated development of Williams's line of thought. That said, one worry for Recanati's proposal runs as follows. On the property account of attitudes, circumstances of evaluation are needed to evaluate a token belief for truth or falsity. But what is the role of the circumstance of evaluation of an *imagining*? We do not ordinarily think of imaginings as things that can be evaluated for truth or falsity, since imaginings (unlike beliefs) do not appear to have correctness conditions.[14] What then is meant by talking about the circumstance of evaluation of an imagining? Why do we need it, other than to avoid the result that Recanati wishes to avoid?[15]

A second question is how the circumstance of evaluation of an arbitrary imagining is to be determined. Given a token belief $b$ possessed by $x$ at $t$ in $w$, the circumstance of $b$ is ($w$, $t$, $x$). This is something we know even before we know anything about the content of $b$. But what is the circumstance of a token imagining $i$ possessed by $x$ at $t$ in $w$? It seems that on Recanati's picture, we cannot answer this question until we know more about the content of $i$; for presumably the circumstance associated with imagining being Napoleon will differ from the circumstance associated with imagining being Hillary Clinton. Perhaps this is an acceptable asymmetry between belief and imagination. But it takes us back to the question we raised before: what does it mean to say that a token imagining has a particular circumstance of evaluation? What aspect of an imagining are we attempting to capture when we say that it has such-and-such a circumstance of evaluation?

## 5 Lakoff cases

Having explored alternatives to the naive view, let us return to it. Williams's particular objection to that view, recall, depends to some extent on a particular interpretation of it.

Williams seems to assume that if the naive view is true, then when I imagine that I am Napoleon, I am imagining that my Cartesian self is associated with Napoleon's empirical self. But that is not so obvious. For example, a Fregean about mental content might instead hold that when I imagine that I am Napoleon, the content of my imagining is a thought that contains a certain mode of presentation of myself and a certain mode of presentation of Napoleon. This account appears to make no mention of Cartesian or empirical selves. Or, as we noted above, an advocate of the property view might hold that the content of this imagining is simply the property of being Napoleon. Again, no mention of "selves," Cartesian or otherwise.

Of course, on either of these versions of the naive view, there remains the question of how to understand the relation between imaginability and possibility. If we accept that such imaginings are indications of possibility, then we might be tempted to conclude that I really could have been Napoleon. Williams objects to this claim by objecting to a particular Cartesian interpretation of it. So perhaps we can avoid the objection by offering an alternative interpretation.

Here is one. Suppose we accept the property view of content. How then should we understand the link between imaginability and possibility? Suppose, contra Recanati, we say this: if $x$ imagines property $p$, this is evidence that $x$ could have had $p$. Since I can imagine the property of being Napoleon, this is evidence that I could have had that property. But many philosophers will reject the idea that there is any *possible world* in which I am identical to Napoleon. Perhaps this is correct. Then what we need is an alternative way to analyze such a possibility claim. One alternative is to analyze it in terms of quantification over *centered worlds*: I could have been Napoleon just in case there is a centered world ($w$, $t$, $x$) accessible from me such that $x$ is Napoleon (see Ninan 2008, 2009). Alternatively, we might attempt to analyze the relevant possibility claims using some version of counterpart theory (see Lewis 1986, 230ff.) (though perhaps these two options come to the same thing once they are spelled out in more detail).[16]

In any case, I want to put aside these issues concerning imagination and possibility for the moment in order to focus on a different problem for the naive view. The problem arises in connection with what we might call "Lakoff cases," since they are inspired by similar examples due to the linguist George Lakoff. Lakoff (1972) was interested in *dream reports* like "I dreamt that I was Brigitte Bardot and that I kissed me." Here we consider the corresponding imagination reports: "I imagined that I was Brigitte Bardot and that I kissed me." The interpretation to focus on here is not one in which Bardot engages in an act of self-kissing, but in which the speaker imagines being Bardot and then kissing the speaker.

I will presently argue that such imaginings pose a problem for the naive view, but I first want to respond to an objection sometimes directed at Lakoff cases, namely that these cases are too weird or obscure to merit serious attention. I myself have little sympathy with this objection, at least if one has already granted that it is possible to imagine being someone else. For if that is possible, then surely it is possible to imagine being (e.g.) Bardot and interacting with other people. Suppose, for example, that I point at a figure I see a few feet from me, and decide to imagine being Bardot and kissing that person. Lo and behold, I suddenly realize that that person is me: the figure in question is my image reflected in a cleverly placed mirror. Does this discovery now render it impossible for me to imagine being Bardot and kissing that person? I can't see why it should. If it doesn't, then it seems possible to imagine being Bardot and kissing me. Moreover, if it is possible in this case, then surely it is possible even when I haven't recently been involved in a confusion about my identity. Sitting here now in my mirrorless office, I can imagine being Bardot and kissing me.

What problem do the Lakoff cases pose for the naive view? Consider, for example, a Fregean version of that view. The Fregean might say that the content of my imagining is a thought that involves two modes of presentation of me, and one of Bardot. To appreciate the proposal, consider the following sentence, noting the underlining and the italics:

(⋆) I imagined that I was Bardot and that I kissed *me*.

The mode of presentation associated with the underlined occurrences of the first-person pronoun in (⋆) would be a first-person mode of presentation; the mode associated with the italicized occurrence of that pronoun in (⋆) would be a third-person mode, perhaps the one I associate with the name 'Dilip Ninan.'

The difficulty with such a proposal is that "I imagined that I was Brigitte Bardot and that I kissed me" (as uttered by me) is not equivalent to "I imagined that I was Brigitte Bardot and that I kissed D.N." (Ninan 2008, ch. 1). In a situation in which I fail to realize that I am D.N., these would appear to report different imaginings.[17] Moreover, if one accepts the arguments of Perry (1977, 1979) and Lewis (1979), it would appear doubtful that we will be able to find any third-person mode of presentation to associate with the italicized first-person pronoun in (⋆). For suppose I awake from surgery with a serious case of amnesia. I know that I am not Bardot (perhaps you tell me this), but I have no idea who I am. Despite my confusion, I am still able to imagine that I am Bardot and that I'm kissing me. I know that I am a certain objective person in the world, and I can imagine being Bardot and kissing *that person*, whoever it is he or she may be. I needn't possess any third-person way of thinking about myself in order to engage in this sort of imagining.

A parallel problem arises for the property view. What is the content of my "Bardot imagining" according to that view? The property of being Bardot and kissing D.N.? But, again, what if I do not realize that I am D.N.? In that case, imagining that I am Bardot and kissing me would appear to be different from imagining that I am Bardot and kissing D.N. But it isn't clear how the property view would distinguish these.[18]

A Fregean might claim that what this shows is that, when it comes to the imagination, there are *two* first-person modes of presentation, one associated with the underlined occurrences of the first-person pronoun in (⋆), another with the italicized occurrence of that pronoun in (⋆). But unless more is said about how to understand these two modes of presentation, such a proposal appears highly schematic. And it isn't clear how to reconcile this idea with the best-developed Fregean accounts of content, such as the one presented in Evans (1981).

Ninan (2008, ch. 2) offers a different solution, one that involves modifying Lewis's centered worlds version of the property account. On the standard centered worlds account, the content of an attitude is a set of centered worlds. On the modified account, the content of a *belief* is still a set of centered worlds, but the content of an *imagining* is a *function* from a centered world to a set of centered worlds, i.e. a *two-dimensional intension*. The idea is that states of imagining are "anaphoric" or "parasitic" on states of belief: given a centered world $c$ compatible with what I believe, we can characterize a set of centered imagination worlds relative to $c$. This gives us "two centers" with which to characterize an imagining: a belief center and an imagination center. So the content of my Bardot imagining would be a function that maps one of my centered belief worlds $(w, t, x)$ to the set of centered worlds $(w', t', x')$ such that $x'$ is Bardot and $x'$ is kissing $x$ at $t'$ in $w'$. This is a coherent (i.e. nonempty) two-dimensional intension. Furthermore, the proposal respects the fact that I can engage in a Bardot imagining even if I lack any third-person way of thinking of myself.[19] I leave as topic for future inquiry how one ought to think about the connection between imaginability and possibility if one adopts this two-dimensional view of the content of imaginings.

## 6 Further issues

I close the discussion by mentioning two further issues: the relationship between Napoleonic imaginings and imagery, and a parallel issue that arises in connection with imagination and *time*.

We have yet to say much about the sort of imagery involved in imagining oneself to be another. Much of the literature follows Williams in holding that, when I imagine being Napoleon, my imagining will usually involve "looking" at the imaginary scenario through Napoleon's eyes:

> Images of myself being Napoleon can scarcely merely be images of the physical figure of Napoleon … They will rather be imagines of, for instance, the desolation of Austerlitz as viewed by me vaguely aware of my short stature and my cockaded hat, my hand in my tunic.
>
> *(Williams 1973, 43)*

Of course, as Williams hints, *some* of the imagery may be "from the outside." For example, suppose I imagine being the race-car driver Danica Patrick. I imagine feeling tense, my body jolted around, hands clasped tightly around the steering wheel; then I picture a car – my car – zooming across the finish line; and then my garlanded neck and beaming face on *ESPN*. I am imagining being Patrick even though not *all* of the associated imagery is from Patrick's visual point of view.

There are further subtleties concerning the precise connection between imagery and imagining oneself to be another. I can imagine being Napoleon, sitting in a pitch-black and completely quiet room, and I can do this by visualizing a featureless black expanse; I can also imagine that the universe contains nothing by visualizing a featureless black expanse. Obviously, in the former case I am imagining myself to be another, while in the latter I am not, even though the imagery associated with both imaginings is exactly the same.[20]

Our discussion has focused, of course, on certain imaginings that the imaginer could report using the indexical 'I.' But other indexicals appear to raise similar issues: just as I can imagine being someone else, I can imagine it being a different time. For example, I can imagine that it is now 2065, perhaps by imagining self-driving cars and the like. We can also produce Lakoff-style examples for the temporal case. Suppose I have no idea what year it is; I can nevertheless imagine that it is now fifty years from now. The first occurrence of 'now' in that imagination report indicates the time of the imagined scenario; the second indicates the time at which the imagining occurs. These cases would appear to raise similar issues for theories of imaginative content.[21]

## Notes

1 I do not, for example, have to imagine a scenario in which Napoleon was cryogenically frozen at birth, put on ice for some 200 years, and then handed over to an unsuspecting Mrs. Ninan (see Velleman 1996, n. 2).

2 Williams is not explicit about what he means by an "empirical self." Perhaps it is simply a body, or a body together with certain essential characteristics of the relevant person.

3 See Peter Kung, "Imagination and modal epistemology," Chapter 32 of this volume, for further discussion of the relationship between imagination and possibility.
4 See also Wollheim 1974, 80.
5 Wollheim's observation raises an interesting linguistic question: why do we see subject-object asymmetries of this sort in imagination reports? The issue is not in fact specific to *imagination* reports per se (as Wollheim seems to think), since similar asymmetries occur with belief reports. See Cumming 2008 for some examples of the latter.
6 For some relevant discussion of the relationship between imagining and pretending, see Kind 2001, 96–97, and Elizabeth Picciuto and Peter Carruthers, "Imagination and pretense," Chapter 23 of this volume.
7 See, for example, Wollheim 1974, 80–81, and Nichols 2008, 519. On the other hand, Walton (1990, 25–27) seems to take it for granted that I *can* (for example) imagine your being the Duke of Wellington. But his examples suggest to me that there may be a sense of "imagine" on which it is more or less equivalent to "pretend," at least in some dialects of English.
8 See, for example, Reynolds 1989, 625; Velleman 1996, 39–40; Blackburn 1997, 196; and Nichols 2008, 528.
9 If the relevant sorts of imaginings are a type of phenomenal experience, then the present approach would appear to be committed to denying *representationalism* about experience, the thesis that the phenomenal feel of an experience is determined by its content. See Byrne 2001 for an explication and defense of this thesis.
10 This question is taken up in Reynolds 1989.
11 See, for example, Chierchia 1989.
12 The expression "circumstance of evaluation" is used by Kaplan (1989) in his theory of languages containing indexicals. Recanati extends the notion into the philosophy of mind.
13 Recanati does not say how the world and time of the circumstance of my imagining are determined. Presumably the world of the circumstance is the actual world, and the time is either the time of the imagining or a time at which Napoleon lived.
14 For relevant discussion, see Neil Sinhababu, "Imagination and belief," Chapter 8 of this volume.
15 If I imagine being Napoleon at Austerlitz with the aim of trying to understand what it was like to be Napoleon at Austerlitz, my imaginative project would seem to have correctness conditions: it is correct just in case *that* is what it was like to be Napoleon at Austerlitz. But not all imaginative projects come with such a goal: I can imagine being Napoleon and landing on the moon, without attempting to understand what it was (or would be) like for Napoleon to land on the moon (see Walton 1990, 39).
16 See Hare 2009, ch. 6, for yet another analysis that renders some utterances of "I could have been Napoleon" true.
17 That is, there are many contexts (in which I am the speaker) in which these two reports would convey different information about what I was imagining. This is true even if these reports have the same truth conditions, as some philosophers of language hold.
18 The account of *de re* attitudes presented in Lewis 1979, 358ff., is of little help here, since it seems that I can imagine that I am Bardot and that I am kissing me without there being any acquaintance relation $R$ such that (a) I bear $R$ uniquely to myself, and (b) I imagine the property of being an $x$ such that $x$ is Bardot and $x$ is kissing the one to whom $x$ bears $R$. One problem is connected to the issues discussed in the previous paragraph; another is that Lewis's account of *de re* attitudes faces independent problems when extended to the imagination (see Ninan 2012, 2013).
19 Chalmers (2002, n. 27) suggests that the "epistemic content" of certain desires or wishes ("I wish I were two inches taller than I am") should be identified with a similar sort of two-dimensional intension.
20 For further discussion of distinct imaginings with identical imagery, see Kind 2001 and Dominic Gregory, "Imagination and mental imagery," Chapter 7 of this volume.
21 See Moss 2012 for a discussion of related issues.

## References

Anand, P., and A. Nevins (2004) "Shifty Operators in Changing Contexts," in R. Young (ed.) *Proceedings of SALT 14*, Ithaca: Cornell University Press.
Blackburn, S. (1997) "Has Kant Refuted Parfit?" in J. Dancy (ed.) *Reading Parfit*, Oxford: Blackwell.
Byrne, A. (2001) "Intentionalism Defended," *Philosophical Review* 110(2): 199–240.

Chalmers, D. (2002) "The Components of Content," in D. Chalmers (ed.) *Philosophy of Mind: Classical and Contemporary Readings*, Oxford: Oxford University Press.

Chierchia, G. (1989) "Anaphora and Attitudes *De Se*," in R. Bartsch, J. van Benthem, and P. van Emde Boas (eds.) *Semantics and Contextual Expression*, Dordrecht: Foris.

Chisholm, R. (1981) *The First Person*, Brighton: Harvester Press.

Cumming, S. (2008) "Variabilism," *Philosophical Review* 117(4): 525–554.

Evans, G. (1981) "Understanding Demonstratives," in H. Parret (ed.) *Meaning and Understanding*, Oxford: Clarendon Press.

Fodor, J. (1987) *Psychosemantics: The Problem of Meaning in the Philosophy of Mind*, Cambridge: MIT Press.

Hare, C. (2009) *On Myself and Other, Less Important Subjects*, Princeton: Princeton University Press.

Kaplan, D. (1989) "Demonstratives," in J. Almog, J. Perry, and H. Wettstein (eds.) *Themes from Kaplan*, Oxford: Oxford University Press.

Kind, A. (2001) "Putting the Image Back in Imagination," *Philosophy and Phenomenological Research* 62(1): 85–109.

Kripke, S. (1980) *Naming and Necessity*, Cambridge: Harvard University Press.

Lakoff, G. (1972) "Linguistics and Natural Logic," in D. Davidson and G. Harman (eds.) *Semantics of Natural Language*, Dordrecht: D. Reidel Publishing Co.

Lewis, D. (1979) "Attitudes, *De Dicto* and *De Se*," *Philosophical Review* 88(4): 513–543.

Lewis, D. (1986) *On the Plurality of Worlds*, Oxford: Blackwell.

Loar, B. (1976) "The Semantics of Singular Terms," *Philosophical Studies* 30(6): 353–377.

Moss, S. (2012) "Updating as Communication," *Philosophy and Phenomenological Research* 85(2): 225–248.

Nichols, S. (2008) "Imagination and the *I*," *Mind & Language* 23(5): 518–535.

Ninan, D. (2008) "Imagination, Content, and the Self," PhD diss., MIT.

Ninan, D. (2009) "Persistence and the First-Person Perspective," *Philosophical Review* 118(4): 425–464.

Ninan, D. (2012) "Counterfactual Attitudes and Multi-Centered Worlds," *Semantics and Pragmatics* 5(5): 1–57.

Ninan, D. (2013) "Self-Location and Other-Location," *Philosophy and Phenomenological Research* 87(2): 301–331.

Perry, J. (1977) "Frege on Demonstratives," *Philosophical Review* 86(4): 474–497.

Perry, J. (1979) "The Problem of the Essential Indexical," *Noûs* 13(1): 3–21.

Recanati, F. (2007) *Perspectival Thought: A Plea for (Moderate) Relativism*, Oxford: Oxford University Press.

Reynolds, S. (1989) "Imagining Oneself to Be Another," *Noûs* 23(5): 615–633.

Schlenker, P. (2003) "A Plea for Monsters," *Linguistics and Philosophy* 26(1): 29–120.

Velleman, D. (1996) "Self to Self," *Philosophical Review* 105(1): 39–76.

Vendler, Z. (1984) *The Matter of Minds*, Oxford: Clarendon Press.

Walton, K. (1990) *Mimesis as Make-Believe: On the Foundations of the Representational Arts*, Cambridge: Harvard University Press.

Williams, B. (1973) "Imagination and the Self," in *Problems of the Self*, Cambridge: Cambridge University Press.

Wollheim, R. (1974) "Imagination and Identification," in *On Art and the Mind*, Cambridge: Harvard University Press.

Wollheim, R. (1984) *The Thread of Life*, Cambridge: Harvard University Press.

Yablo, S. (1993) "Is Conceivability a Guide to Possibility," *Philosophy and Phenomenological Research* 53(1): 1–42.

# 21
# IMAGINATION AND ACTION

*Neil Van Leeuwen*

## Introduction: why imagination matters

Philosophy and common sense both distinguish actions from mere happenings. Having an apple fall on your head is a mere happening. Jumping over a crack in the sidewalk is an action. We also distinguish actions – properly so-called – from *mere* behaviors, which are not mere happenings but also don't rise to the level of actions. Reflexively scrunching your face when you see a disgusting picture involves emotion and information-processing, so it is more than a mere happening. But it unfolds automatically and often without awareness, making it less than action. Actions form a proper subset of behaviors, which form a proper subset of happenings.

Philosophy of action, as one would expect, seeks to answer at least two questions. What *constitutes* action? What *causes* action?

To date, the most prevalent theory of action – both its constitution and its etiology – is belief-desire explanation, which emerges from works of David Hume and Donald Davidson; it is also the basic framework for decision theory. Beliefs and desires, on this theory, cause and rationalize actions that can be expected to satisfy the desires, if the beliefs are true. *Example.* Belief: *pushing COKE releases a soda from the machine.* Desire: *I drink soda.* Caused action: pushing COKE. Thus are actions caused. Furthermore, many think this is a constitutive theory of action as well. Actions are those events caused in this fashion. (Reflexively scrunching your face seems not to have a belief-desire explanation; nor does it seem to deserve the label "action"; so the belief-desire theory seems to classify it correctly. Conversely, pushing COKE is an action.)

The belief-desire theory looms so large that one is tempted to ignore or deny the possibility that *other* mental states are central to the etiology or constitution of action. Much literature scarcely mentions other mental states. And some papers even argue *against* positing other mental states as contributors to action. Neil Sinhababu (2013), for example, argues against positing *intention* over and above beliefs and desires. And Peter Langland-Hassan (2012) argues that actions involved in pretending, which would seem to *require* imagining, don't in fact employ a distinct cognitive attitude of imagining; he thinks one can make do with positing only conditional beliefs and desires.[1]

I think we shouldn't limit our ontology in this fashion. Mental states underlying human action are various and interesting. Thus, this entry discusses how different sorts of *imagining* – a term I'll clarify – play critical roles in causing and even (for some sorts of action) constituting actions.

I proceed as follows. Since Elizabeth Picciuto and Peter Carruthers (Chapter 23, in this volume) discuss pretending specifically, I won't focus on it, except to illustrate some relations between pretense and action generally. Imagination supports many forms of action, and my topic is this broader class. In Section 1, I describe how imagistic imagining (mental imagery) helps structure actions. In Section 2, I discuss propositional imagining (which I've also called *attitude imagining*) and present some still-controversial ideas about how it figures in action. In Section 3, I explain how *constructive imagination* is necessary for actions in which the agent considers more than one option.

## 1 Imagery-oriented action

Let's start with an example.

Now that Frank has a yard, he goes to the shelter for a dog to rescue. "How big of a dog?" asks the keeper. Frank says, "About this_______ big." As he says "this_______" he gestures with his hand a certain height off the ground – about 2 feet – visualizing his future dog, who would be too big to lay comfortably on his lap but small enough to sit with him on the couch. As he answers the keeper's question, he imagines the fantasy dog in the space next to him and puts his hand on top of its imagined back.

This example highlights one of two important roles mental imagery, or *imagistic imagining*, can play in guiding action. Mental imagery is internal mental representation that is structured like percepts and is to some extent phenomenologically similar to perception (see Bence Nanay, Chapter 9 of this volume; Dominic Gregory, Chapter 7). Visual imagery resembles visual perception; auditory imagery resembles auditory perception – and so on.

Imagery is uniquely suited to guiding actions on *possible objects or properties* that are projected into the agent's surrounding environment.[2] Imaged content can take the *object-acted-on role* in the causation and constitution of action.

Let's call the type of action we're discussing here *imagery-guided action*. (It's the first of two types of action that fall under the broader heading of *imagery-oriented action*.) *Petting an imagined cat, pinning the tail on the donkey, avoiding the armchair when you walk to the bathroom in the dark of the night, pantomiming turning a doorknob*, and *holding a shirt up in front of an imagined friend for whom you're buying a present*, etc., are all imagery-guided action, since mental imagery is used to represent the spatial structure of potential objects in one's surrounding environment in relation to which one acts.

Imagistic imagining contributes to imagery-guided action in four ways:

1. Imagistic imagining represents an object or property as having a location in space. In the visual case, it represents shape too.
2. The imaged object or property is not present to current perception.
3. The imagistic imagining integrates with perception insofar as the projected object or property is represented as being in the agent's perceived surrounding space.
4. The agent directs bodily movement toward or away from the object projected by the imagery, using the imagery jointly with perception as a guide.[3]

Perceptual memory makes these features possible by encoding a rich body of information that can be retrieved and manipulated in imagistic imagining (Schacter and Addis 2007), which can then guide action in the actual space surrounding the agent.

The examples I gave include pretend actions (petting the imagined cat) and ordinary or "plain" actions (avoiding the armchair). But one might be tempted to think that, since it is a form of "imagining," imagery can only generate pretense. How is it possible that imagery-guided action can be of both types (pretend and ordinary action)? The answer is that mental imagery can figure in the constituent structure of many sorts of propositional attitudes, including both beliefs and propositional imaginings (see below). When we talk about propositional attitudes, we talk about the *attitude* in question, the *representation* in question, and the *content* of said representation. On the attitude dimension, we distinguish *belief* (taking a proposition to describe reality, roughly) from *fictional* or *propositional imagining* (taking a proposition to describe a fictional state of affairs, roughly). Importantly, since the representational dimension of a mental state is independent of the attitude dimension (you can believe *r* or hypothesize *r* or whatever-attitude *r* for any propositional representation *r*), and since mental imagery is a value on the representational dimension, mental imagery can figure as constituent(s) both in beliefs and in propositional imaginings, like beliefs about the location of an armchair in the bedroom and imaginings about the shape of an imagined cat (see Langland-Hassan 2015 for more detail on this point). The ability of imagery to figure in attitudes of either type allows imagery-guided action to include some ordinary actions (avoiding the armchair), where the imagery is encoded in *beliefs*, and some pretense actions (petting the imagined cat), where the imagery is encoded in propositional imaginings. Thus, *imagery-guided action* crosscuts the categories of pretend and ordinary action.

It should be clear how imagery helps *cause* imagery-guided actions: the spatially rich structure of imagery guides spatially rich action. But why say imagery can be *constitutive of* actions? There is more to be said on this topic than is appropriate for this entry, but an example, which can be multiplied, is worth mentioning. Say you are showing a friend the size of an animal you saw. "It's about this_______ big," you say with a gesture. You don't know the name of the animal, but you visually remember it and hence can imagistically imagine its dimensions. If the animal you visualize happens to be a groundhog, then your action *is* gesturing the size of a groundhog; if the animal you visualize happens to be a porcupine, then your action *is* gesturing the size of a porcupine. This will be so, even if the motions you make with your hands in either case are physically type identical to those in the other case. Furthermore, you may have no other representations in mind, aside from imagery, that track the difference between the animals. So since the action types in either case are different (*gesturing the size of a groundhog* vs. *gesturing the size of a porcupine*), and since the only mentalistic (or physical) difference is in the imagery, the difference in action type must be constituted by the difference in imagery.

Now that we've addressed imagery-guided action, let's turn to the second major way imagistic imagining can be used to control action. Say you're doing an impression of the characteristic hand gestures of Don Corleone, as played by Marlon Brando. You're likely to visualize Don Corleone's gestures, recalling visual memories formed watching *The Godfather*, and then *imitate* what you visualize. Further examples include gestures in playing charades, such as imitating – in forelimb posture and jumping motion – an imagistically imagined kangaroo. This category also includes many actions used to communicate with others when words are lacking. Say you want to refer to a woman from last night's party and have forgotten her name. "The woman who walked like this_______," you say, accompanying "this_______" with a walking motion that imitates that which you visualize (see Kaplan

1968). This action type doesn't just include imitation of visual imagery; it can include auditory imagery, as when you do an impression of someone's voice, and even tactile imagery, as when you demonstrate a massage technique you learned on a friend. Let's call this type *imagery-imitating action*.

We can, as mentioned, put imagery-guided action and imagery-imitating action under a broader type: imagery-*oriented* action. What explains the existence of imagery-oriented action? It is a cousin of perception-oriented action. When you grasp a cup or copy the motions of someone you're looking at in a game of "Simon Says," your perceptual states provide control structures for your action. As you reach for the cup, you do not form a series of abstract beliefs of the form *now the cup is 8 inches from my hand, now the cup is 7 inches from my hand, now the cup is 6* ... Rather, your visual perception of the relation between cup and hand forms the input into your motor system that allows your muscles to contract such that you ultimately grasp the cup.[4] Granted, beliefs and desires – believing there's water in the cup and desiring water – may figure into the initiation of the action, but perceptual states are the cognitive input into its more immediate guidance. Likewise, in imitating what one sees, one lets visual percepts shape one's bodily movement, a process that sidesteps mediating beliefs and desires. Evidence that beliefs and desires are left out of the immediate structuring of perception-oriented imitative action is as follows: in playing "Simon Says," one is easily "tricked" into imitating an action one does *not* want to imitate and that goes contrary to what one believes the rules of the game to be, simply because the leader issues a command and performs in full view an action to be copied after the imitative process has been started. In such a case, percepts control the actions directly, for the most part bypassing the mediating influence of beliefs and desires (otherwise put, the mistakes one makes in Simon Says are evidence that such bypassing occurs).

Imagery-oriented action exists in virtue of the same action-structuring pathways that account for perception-oriented action. Imagistic imagining can replace perception as the structuring representation. Often enough, we find ourselves in need of the sorts of action-structuring that percepts give in virtue of their spatial and temporal richness, even though at that moment we lack the full complement of perceptual states that would facilitate the action we wish to perform. So we rely on imagery instead, which employs the same representational formats as perception and is processed largely in perceptual cortices of the brain (Kosslyn et al. 2006).

This brings us to our first lesson.

Lesson 1: Imagistic imagining can structure actions in the same manners as percepts do, in absence of percepts that would otherwise structure the action.

Insofar as imagery falls under the broad heading of *imagination*, Lesson 1 identifies an important contribution imagination makes to the causation and constitution of action. It is a form of action causation in which beliefs and desires are not the mental states most immediate; rather, any influence that beliefs and desires have is mediated by imagery, which structures the action more directly. And since the contents of the imagery can play a role in determining what the actions even are, imagery has a constitutive role in some actions as well.

## 2 Imaginative attitudes and desires in action

In addition to imagery, another mental state falls under the term "imagination," typically called *propositional imagining*. This is a cognitive attitude distinct from belief that (according to most scholars; see below for the controversy) underlies abilities to pretend and to follow fiction. Mental imagery *can* be part of the constituent structure of propositional imagining. But many scholars think that there can be propositional imagining without imagery and imagery without propositional imagining.[5] In any case, it is fair to say that propositional imagining makes contributions to action of its own kind. (Note here that I am distinguishing propositional imagining, which figures in pretend play and cognition of fiction, from supposition, which is used more in inference, argument, and verbal behavior. Making that distinction rigorous is another project.)

We can start by contrasting the contribution of propositional imagining with the contribution of belief, or what I (Van Leeuwen 2014b) call *factual belief*, to pretend action.

In guiding pretense, factual belief and propositional imagining combine to form a two-map cognitive structure, where each layer or "map" in the cognitive structure makes its own sort of contribution. In pretending a sofa is a spaceship, you might have the following cluster of factual beliefs.

FB: the sofa is in the living room.
FB: the sofa is made of fabric, wood, and cushioning.
FB: the sofa is of normal dimensions, about $3' \times 3' \times 6'$.

Those factual beliefs and others constitute the first map. (Note that these beliefs can't just be identified as percepts, since you'd continue to hold them even with your eyes closed. If one wishes, however, one can include percepts in the first map; this won't change the present point.) You might then have the following propositional imaginings, which constitute the second map.

PI: the sofa is a spaceship in outer space.
PI: the spaceship is made of light, durable metal and has controls for flying.
PI: the spaceship is about the size of a medium-sized airplane.

Kendall Walton (1990) would point out that we get *to* many of the elements in the second map *from* elements in the first map by way of "principles of generation": principles of a given game of make-believe that prescribe certain imaginings, given certain inputs or beliefs about the props in one's environment. But the present point is that both maps help guide your subsequent bodily movements. When you say, "Let's go to the control room" and then move to the other end of the sofa, your movement on the "spaceship" will be guided by (1) factual beliefs you have about the shape and structure of the actual sofa, since that is where you have to move your body, and by (2) propositional imaginings, since they represent controls on part of the "spaceship."

That both maps are used in guiding pretense is an elementary point, but it's easy to miss. Some theorists write as if, in pretend play, *only* imaginings are implicated in guiding the actions.[6] Other theorists hold that beliefs are the only propositional attitudes that can be the direct cognitive input into choosing bodily movements, even in pretense. The first mistake, I think, is fueled by an intense focus on imagination – a good focus to have – coupled with the fact that the relevant factual beliefs are often mundane and unnoticeable. (One doesn't think about the fact that one believes the sofa is in the living room.) The second mistake is fueled, I think, by the prominence belief is given in explaining action. Shaun Nichols and Stephen Stich (Nichols and Stich 2003), for example, hold that imaginings cause conditional beliefs, and that these conditional beliefs, combined with desires, produce action; so for them, imaginings guide action *only* indirectly, mediated by beliefs. Langland-Hassan (2012) goes further. He holds that there is *no* distinct cognitive attitude of imagining at all that figures in the etiology of pretense; rather, conditional beliefs do all the work. As an antidote to both mistakes, we can keep in mind that (for example) the pretender represents a "cockpit" *at* some specific location on the actual sofa. That is, the pretender *propositionally imagines* there is a cockpit at a place on the sofa, where the shape of the sofa is tracked by beliefs. Both layers in the two-map cognitive structure help guide the action.

Lesson 2: Actions that express propositional imaginings rely also on factual beliefs to guide them, since those actions take place within the confines of the real world and agents use factual beliefs to track reality.

Some research in the developmental psychology of pretend play helps cement this point (see Deena Skolnick Weisberg, Chapter 22 of this volume). Claire Golomb and Regina Kuersten (Golomb and Kuersten 1996) had children play with adults at making "cookies" out of playdough. To test whether the children ever really lost track of the reality/fantasy distinction, the adult experimenters would take an *actual* bite out of the playdough "cookie." If the children had lost track of the fact that the playdough was not really a cookie, this would not have surprised them. But they typically were surprised, which shows that they were tracking the identity of the playdough all along (factual belief), while simultaneously labeling it as being a cookie (propositional imagining).

> On the basis of our findings it seems likely that the world of pretence and reality are not mutually exclusive. The playing child monitors events occurring in reality and maintains the duality between the two modes of thought. In this model of play, thoughts about reality run parallel to thoughts about pretence, although pretence would be the predominant mode of thinking during play.
>
> *(215)*

Furthermore, in order to interact with playdough with their hands, children have to rely on their ordinary factual beliefs about the shape, texture, and consistency of *actual* playdough.[7]

Having established Lesson 2, we can further inquire exactly *how* propositional imaginings generate actions. In particular, how do they interact with desires or motivation generally speaking?

One suggestion, which I (Van Leeuwen 2009) think is partially correct, comes from David Velleman (2000). Velleman holds that propositional imaginings cause a wide variety of actions – not just pretense – in the same way that beliefs do. Just as we perform actions that would satisfy our desires if our beliefs are true, so too we perform actions that would satisfy our desires (or "wishes") if our imaginings were true. Velleman develops several examples, but walking through his extension of an example from Hume will suffice to illustrate the idea. His treatment of this particular case can be debated (see note 11, p. 298), but I think it is fair to say that at least some actions will have roughly the etiology Velleman describes. Hume (1740/1978, 148) describes a man suspended high above the ground in a cage, from which he knows (and hence believes) there is no chance he'll actually fall, who nevertheless feels a great amount of fear. Velleman extends this case to one in which the man also clings to the bars as if he's about to fall and parses the example as follows. The man *imagines* that if he let's go, he'll fall. This imagining (in conjunction with the desire not to fall) causes clinging behavior that is like the behavior he would have performed if he believed that if he let go, he'd fall. For Velleman, this illustrates how imagining (as a propositional attitude) makes the same contribution to action that belief does. Furthermore, Nishi Shah and David Velleman (Shah and Velleman 2005) extend this view to *all* cognitive attitudes, a class of propositional attitudes that includes hypotheses, assumptions, imaginings, and any attitude that represents the world as being a certain way. Effectively, they replace the formula agents perform actions that will satisfy their desires if the relevant beliefs are true (other things equal) with

> agents perform actions that will satisfy their desires (or wishes) if the relevant cognitive attitudes are true (other things equal).[8]

As mentioned, I think there is something right about this generalization of the Davidsonian view of action causation, even if it needs to be qualified. I'll start with the sorts of case for which it seems right and then proceed to the qualification.

The categories of action for which Velleman's picture seems most plausible are explicit pretense and some forms of expressive action.

Consider pretending to stab a monster with a make-believe sword. Let's say I'm imagining that a pillow is the monster and that the ruler I'm holding is a sword. The action involves shoving one end of the ruler into the pillow. Now we ask: what *motivates* this action? Otherwise put, what do I *want* such that I perform the action I do? (If I had had *other* motivations than whatever ones I did have, I might have pretended to give the monster a haircut with the blade of the sword, as opposed to stabbing it.)

The Velleman picture seems to work for this action. Arguably, the following propositional attitudes are at work.

Imagining: This{ruler} is a sword.
Imagining: This{pillow} is a monster.
Imgagining: Thrusting my sword into the monster will kill it.
Desire: I kill the monster.

Velleman's view is compelling enough that others extend and defend it. Some, like Tyler Doggett and Andy Egan (Doggett and Egan 2007, 2012) even posit a special *kind* of imaginative desire that interacts with imagining in this fashion, which typically gets called *i-desire*. There has been some controversy around whether it's a good idea to posit a separate kind of desire, with Amy Kind (2011) and Shannon Spaulding (forthcoming), and I (Van Leeuwen 2011, 2014a) holding that the posit is undermotivated and superfluous (see also Amy Kind, Chapter 12 of this volume). Shen-yi Liao and Tyler Doggett (Liao and Doggett 2014) would reply that reasons to posit propositional imagining as separate from belief are at least prima facie reasons for positing i-desires as separate from desires. So the debate is still unresolved. But even though the question of i-desires is unsettled, it's fair to say that even those who reject i-desires don't necessarily reject the idea that imaginings can interact with desires *of some sort* to produce pretense actions. And once we set the question of regular desires vs. i-desires aside, Velleman's initial account has gone largely unchallenged.

The other category of action in which imaginings seem to interact with desires in the way Velleman describes is *expressive action*. This is something of a vague category, but the following example gives a sense of it: I was sitting on the A Train in New York one summer's day, when I noticed a woman reading a magazine. From where I was sitting, I could also see the pictures on the pages. At one point, she turned the page to reveal a two-page Louis Vuitton advertisement, featuring Sean Connery lying on his side on the beach. At once, on seeing this image, she exclaimed (under her breath), "Oh, Sean Connery!," and proceeded eagerly to kiss the face of Sean Connery in the picture, after which she stroked his cheek gently. (In expressive actions generally, certain desires or emotions take on a higher-than-usual salience in motivating action.)

Now, as Rosalind Hursthouse (1991) would point out, a belief-desire explanation of this expressive action (or *arational action*, as she would put it) looks implausible, no matter how we flesh it out. We could say that the woman was temporarily deluded and hence *believed* Sean Connery was in front of her, and that desiring to kiss Sean Connery she then planted the kiss on the picture. But the woman need not have been insane; nor need one be generally in expressive action. Alternatively, we could try to posit a desire *that I feel good* and a belief *that by kissing this image of Sean Connery I will feel good*. But this seems to posit the wrong desire. If she really had an operative desire to feel good, why was she on the train instead of out buying ice cream?

A more plausible suggestion than the belief-desire explanation presents itself. Rather, we can say that the woman on the A Train had the following pair of mental states:

Imagining: Sean Connery is before me.
Desire: I kiss Sean Connery.

This pair then causes the action that is *similar to* the action she would have performed had she had the following pair.

Belief: Sean Connery is before me.
Desire: I kiss Sean Connery.

Imagining, then, can stand in for belief in the causation of this kind of expressive action. We can now state our third lesson.

Lesson 3: Propositional imaginings can, under certain conditions, take on a belief-like role in guiding actions that are motivated by desires, where that role is specified by the standard belief-desire explanation form.

Now we ask: under what conditions? In my view, there has not been enough of an attempt in the philosophical literature to date at answering this question. So what follows is still a preliminary sketch.

Humans are adept at setting up play situations. When parents adopt high-pitched voices and give knowing looks to their children before engaging in what would otherwise be a silly or confused action, like "drinking" from an empty cup, they've set up one such situation, or *practical setting* as I call it. In this case, it's the practical setting of make-believe. The proposal, then, is that being in the practical setting of make-believe allows imaginings to take on a belief-like role in relation to desires in guiding actions, where it is the agent's awareness of that setting that constitutes the actions as full pretense.[9]

The setting of make-believe is constituted by a cluster of three shared expectations that agents have, when they are pretending together. The first expectation is that episodes of make-believe will be of limited duration; whatever imaginary actions and events occur during the episode will not be regarded as having occurred once the episode is over (Harris

2000). The second expectation is that certain signals trigger the start and stop of any episode of make-believe (unless it is an instance of solo pretense). Some of the signals may be innate, since they arise early in childhood (Lillard and Witherington 2004), but the signals are many and various and, after a certain point, determined by culture. Signals include anything from higher-pitched, slower voices and knowing looks (in childhood pretense) to verbal cues ("Let's play *X*!") or physical events, like lights going down on the stage. The third expectation is that some objects, spaces, properties, and events will be assigned identities other than what they are factually believed to be (Leslie 1987): a sofa will be a spaceship; an empty space will be a lion; red will be hot – etc. This third expectation is the most substantive in defining the practical setting of make-believe, since the other two make reference to that setting itself (an episode of *the setting of make-believe* will be of limited duration; there will be certain signals that trigger the start and stop of *the setting of make-believe*), though they are still informative insofar as they put constraints on the nature of the setting.

Our qualification of Lesson 3 then is this: imaginings have a belief-like role in guiding action *in the setting of make-believe* and not otherwise.

Though I think this qualification is broadly right, a difficulty arises. In expressive action, there seems to be no signal that sets up make-believe; nor is it clear what the duration is. So it seems that the belief-like role that imagining can play in guiding action spills over from the setting of make-believe into other moments in life. This realization may be what led Velleman to think that the motivational role of imagining was the same as that of belief *simpliciter*.

The problem is tricky because the extension of the term "expressive action" is fuzzy. But I think we can say the following in favor of our qualification on Lesson 3: in cases where expressive action clearly does involve propositional imagining in a belief-like role in relation to desire, there does seem to be a practical setting of make-believe that gets briefly set up by the agent, or at least something like one. Returning to the example of the woman on the A Train, she seems to have set up a spontaneous, brief make-believe setting after all. The fact that she knew perfectly well that the picture was a picture shows that she was aware that she was assigning an object a value other than what it was in reality (the third expectation), treating a portion of picture as a man. And the fact that she stopped after less than 2 seconds shows that the episode *was* of limited duration (the first expectation). So the only expectation lacking is the signal that initiates the make-believe, and presumably such a signal wasn't needed, since there were no other real people involved in her episode of expressive action. On this view, much (not all) expressive action is unsignaled pretense, though it is spontaneous and unreflective enough that it is not thought of as pretense and certainly differs from paradigmatic cases of pretense in that it is not as deliberate. Let's call this category of expressive actions *mimetic expressive actions*.[10,11]

Insofar as such mimetic expressive actions are woven throughout daily life, a certain amount of pretending is woven throughout daily life. Most adults do not set up explicit, signaled episodes of pretense as often as children do. But the tendency to pretend often doesn't really go away. Herbert Clark and Richard Gerrig (Clark and Gerrig 1984) argue that ironic speech, such as "*He*'s a smart one" (said of someone thought to be unintelligent), is a form of pretense, where the speaker is *pretending* to be someone who thinks what is said and is speaking to an audience who will receive the message. If they're right, this is another form of low-level pretending, in addition to mimetic expressive action, that pervades regular life without often being noticed as such.

To sum up, humans often represent objects, spaces, properties, and events as other than what they believe them to be. Propositional imagining can function as a secondary map to represent these alternate identities. And in certain settings, propositional imagining guides action, often in a belief-like way in relation to desire. But throughout such actions, factual beliefs retain their usual role in representing the states of affairs in the physical world with which the agent must continue to interact in order to execute the many forms of pretense at all.[12]

## 3 Constructive imagination and action choice

Temple Grandin (Grandin and Panek 2014) has recently criticized the designers of the Fukishima nuclear power plants, which had a meltdown in the wake of the tsunami of 2011, along the following lines:

> During the Japanese tsunami catastrophe of 2011, the Fukushima nuclear power plants melted down because the tidal wave that came over the seawall flooded not only the main generator but its backup. And where was the backup located? In the basement – the basement of a nuclear power plant that is located next to the sea. As I read many descriptions of the accident, I could *see* the water flowing into the plant, and I could *see* the emergency generators disappearing under the water.
>
> *(169; Grandin's italics)*

In short, the power plant where the meltdown occurred had a cooling system that ran on electricity; both the power grid and the backup generators lost function due to the tsunami; so the cooling system failed and there was a meltdown.

Grandin's point, as I interpret it, is that whoever designed the plant *failed to imagine* the possibility that the basement, where the backup generators were, would flood, and her implication is that this failure of imagination is in part responsible for the failure to act.

Grandin is very much talking about mental imagery, but there is another sense of the term "imagination" that we have not canvassed so far that is critical to seeing a more fundamental point. The term "imagination" can refer to the capacity to generate novel representations that are not arrived at simply by remembering or by perception of the nearby environment. To disambiguate, I call this capacity *constructive imagination*. (Constructive imagination does not entail propositional imagining or mental imagery, though it may involve either or both.[13])

Grandin's main point is that certain possibilities are more likely to be arrived at by visual or (as she puts it) "artistic" minds than by mathematical minds, which is why "different kinds of minds" are needed. This is a substantive thesis about the relationship between imagistic imagining and constructive imagining. But for purposes of the present entry, we should extract two more general morals about the relationship between constructive imagination and action. First, constructive imagination generates representations of possible states of the world – ways the world might be – on the basis of which we might choose actions. Second, constructive imagination generates representations of possible actions to take. If one's imagination fails to generate a possibility of either sort that it *should*, then we describe this failure as a failure of imagination.

Some basic decision theory will help make these two points precise. In the top row of a typical decision table, possible states of the world (relevant to the action choice) are listed, along with probabilities assigned to them (which sum to one). In the first column of the table, possible actions are listed. In the body of the decision table are the expected outcomes of each action, for any given possible state of the world (often called "state of nature"), along with the values of the outcomes. One then chooses actions by weighting those values according to the probabilities of each possible state of the world in a function that gives an *expected* value for each action. We have the following structure:

| | *Possible state of the world 1 ($p_1$)* | ... | *Possible state of the world n ($p_n$)* | *Expected value of Action* |
|---|---|---|---|---|
| **Action 1** | Outcome / value$_{1,1}$ | ... | Outcome / value$_{1,n}$ | $f(p_1,\ldots, p_n, \text{value}_{1,1},\ldots, \text{value}_{1,n})$ = expected value of Action 1 |
| ... | ... | ... | ... | ... |
| **Action *m*** | Outcome / value$_{m,1}$ | ... | Outcome / value$_{m,n}$ | $f(p_1,\ldots, p_n, \text{value}_{m,1},\ldots, \text{value}_{m,n})$ = expected value of Action *m* |

Let us suppose that in the above table the probabilities have been carefully assigned and the expected values carefully calculated. Is this sufficient for making a good decision on how to act? No, a problem arises: what if we *failed to imagine* a possible way the world might be? That is, a better imaginer might have come up not with *n* possible ways the world might be, but rather $n+1$. Arguably, something like this is precisely what happened in Fukushima. No doubt the "mathematical minds" had carefully figured out the probability of each of the *n* possible states of the world that they did imagine – and good for them – but they failed to imagine possibility $n+1$: the flooding of the basement. And since they never imagined it in the first place, they couldn't assign it a probability in their decisions about how to act.

Likewise for actions. If one doesn't imagine buying a watertight door, then one can't assign a value to the outcomes of this action, given the ways the world might be. Grandin's recent work emphasizes that, where one lacks a certain kind of constructive imagination, one should rely on another kind of mind, one that has the requisite form of constructive imagination, to be able to make good decisions and take appropriate actions. This brings us to Lesson 4, which generalizes Grandin's point.

Lesson 4: Constructive imagination is a necessary precursor to choices that select among multiple possible actions, given multiple possible states of the world, since possibilities must be first *represented* before they can be assigned probabilities and values.[14]

## Conclusion: acting in relation to *possibilia*

Let's take stock. We've seen that the terms "imagine" and "imagination" can be taken in three ways, with each kind of imagining making its own characteristic contributions to action.

*Imagistic imagining* (or *mental imagery*) involves percept-like representational structures that can integrate with the perceptual manifold and substitute for percepts in guiding bodily movements (Lesson 1). This is a causal contribution, but we saw that the contents of the imagery can also constitute otherwise identical bodily movements as distinct action types, as in gesturing the size of a porcupine as opposed to a hedgehog. Mental imagery figures in *imagery-oriented action*, which divides (at least) into *imagery-guided action* and *imagery-imitating action*.

*Propositional imagining* is an attitude distinct from belief, where to imagine (in this sense) that *p* is to regard that content as fictional as opposed to real. We saw that people do act on their propositional imaginings in explicit make-believe and mimetic expressive action and that they do so in manners similar to how they would have, if they had believed the contents of those very imaginings (Lesson 3). But when people do act on propositional imaginings, they continue to track what their surrounding environment is actually like by using factual beliefs (Lesson 2).

*Constructive imagining* is the capacity (or, more likely, cluster of capacities) for coming up with representations that go beyond the deliveries of one's perceptions of the nearby environment. Constructive imagination figures in action choice as follows. When one chooses actions, one represents various ways the world might be for the sake of predicting and valuing likely outcomes of the actions. But one can't act on a possibility one has failed to imagine in the first place, and one can't assign values to the outcomes of actions that never occurred to one. A failure of either sort is a failure of imagination. Thus, not only is constructive imagination involved in the psychology of action choice, but it is also an underexplored dimension that can be normatively appraised.[15]

What these three notions of imagination all have in common is this: Humans perform actions not just on what we take to exist in our immediate environment. We also act in relation to objects, spaces, properties, and events that are remote in time, actual space, possibility space, or epistemic space. We gesture the size of creatures that are not before us and operate control panels that only exist in fictions. When we don't know which possibility is actual, we represent the ones that are relevant,[16] if we imagine well, and then act. Thus, various forms of imagining surround humans with *possibilia*, representations of which guide action in the world.

## Acknowledgments

For helpful exchanges, I'd like to thank Kenny Easwaran, Amy Kind, Shen-yi Liao, Rachel McKinnon, Bence Nanay, Joëlle Proust, and David Spurrett.

## Notes

1 Matravers (2010) is similar in spirit to Langland-Hassan, except Matravers has two differences: (1) He's dealing with cognition of fiction as opposed to pretend action; (2) instead of positing conditional beliefs, he posits beliefs with an in-the-story operator as a replacement for imagining. Nichols and Stich (2003), who are in many ways the inspiration for Langland-Hassan, also implicitly have a belief-desire psychology for pretending, since they see imaginings as causing conditional beliefs, which then cause pretense actions in conjunction with desires. See Nanay's (forthcoming) introduction for an overview of various critiques of the belief-desire theory of action not canvassed in this entry.

2 As I argue in Van Leeuwen 2011.

3 These features bring together ideas from Van Leeuwen 2011, Nanay 2013, and Briscoe forthcoming.

4 Note that the percepts guiding the movement aren't necessarily the conscious ones (Milner and Goodale 1995; Nanay 2013).

5 There is some disagreement here, though this particular issue is not hotly debated. Kind (2001), for example, argues that propositional imagining requires mental imagery. I know of no one, however, who thinks mental imagery requires propositional imagining.

6 Bach (2010), for example, seems guilty of this.

7 Gendler (2003) and Liao and Doggett (2014) make much the same point.

8 My formulation, not theirs.

9 This is the view I argue for in Van Leeuwen 2009.

10 Mimetic expressive action overlaps with but doesn't have the same extension as semipretense, which I define in Van Leeuwen 2011. In much mimetic expressive action, the agent is aware of the pretense-like character of her action, which is not true of semipretense. So not all mimetic expressive action is semipretense. Is all semipretense mimetic expressive action? This is trickier, but it appears it is not,

since much semipretense isn't the expression of any desire or emotion at all; one may simply be "going through the motions" and be influenced by a mental image in so doing.

11 The one case that appears truly problematic for the present qualification on Lesson 3 is the case of the man clinging to the bars of the cage, since it seems that he is in no sense in a setting of make-believe; yet he acts on his desires in conjunction with imagining he is going to fall anyway – at least this is how Velleman treats the case. But I think what we can say here, contra Velleman, is that it is most likely perception that is doing the work, rather than propositional imagining, in supplying the cognitive input into the clinging behavior: the mere sight of the ground so far below sparks fear and the clinging that is an expression thereof. So this is not a counterinstance to the qualification after all. See Gendler (2008a, 2008b) for a different treatment of this kind of case.

12 Exercise for the reader: how do the notions of practical setting and belief-like role in action allow us to solve the problem of distinguishing propositional imagining from mere supposition?

13 See Van Leeuwen 2013 for further clarification.

14 Nanay (forthcoming) presents a model of decision-making that also emphasizes the role of imagination; his paper makes much the same point about the need to supplement the traditional belief-desire model of action.

15 Note that constructive imagining is not merely the capacity to generate imagistic imagining and propositional imagining, since constructive imagining can also figure in generating novel propositional beliefs as well.

16 Joëlle Proust informs me (pers. commun.) that she regards *relevance* as a norm for imagining.

## Further reading

In addition to the pieces already cited here, I recommend the following as entrance points into research relating to imagination and action: M.E. Bratman, "Practical Reasoning and Acceptance in a Context," *Mind* 101 (1992): 1–15, explores how acceptance in a context – a nonbelief cognitive attitude – can be the cognitive input into action choice. A wide-ranging simulationist account of imagination that also explores links to action is found in G. Currie and I. Ravenscroft, *Recreative Minds: Imagination in Philosophy and Psychology* (Oxford: Oxford University Press, 2002). A. Egan, "Imagination, Delusion, and Self-Deception," in T. Bayne and J. Fernández (eds.) *Delusions, Self-Deception, and Affective Influences on Belief-Formation* (Hove: Psychology Press, 2009) discusses delusions as states in between believing and imagining and uses links to action to motivate this position. E. Funkhouser and S. Spaulding, "Imagination and Other Scripts," *Philosophical Studies* 143(3) (2009): 291–314, explores various ways imagination can be a script for guiding action. And J. Proust, "Time and Action: Impulsivity, Habit, Strategy," *Review of Philosophy and Psychology* (forthcoming), explores the question of what the immediate mental antecedents to action are.

## References


Bach, T. (2010) "The Objects of Pretense," paper presented at the One Hundred and Second Annual Conference of the Southern Society of Philosophy and Psychology, 15–17 April, Atlanta.

Briscoe, R. (Forthcoming) "On the Uses of Make-Perceive," in F. Macpherson and F. Dorsch (eds.) *Perceptual Memory and Perceptual Imagination*, Oxford: Oxford University Press.

Clark, H., and R. Gerrig (1984) "On the Pretense Theory of Irony," *Journal of Experimental Psychology* 113(1): 121–126.

Davidson, D. (1963) "Actions, Reasons, and Causes," *Journal of Philosophy* 60(23): 685–700.

Doggett, T., and A. Egan (2007) "Wanting Things You Don't Want: The Case for an Imaginative Analogue of Desire," *Philosopher's Imprint* 7(9): 1–17.

Doggett, T., and A. Egan (2012) "How We Feel about Terrible, Non-existent Mafiosi," *Philosophy and Phenomenological Research* 84(2): 277–306.

Gendler, T.S. (2003) "On the Relation between Pretense and Belief," in M. Kieran and D.M. Lopes (eds.) *Imagination, Philosophy, and the Arts*, London: Routledge, 125–141.

Gendler, T.S. (2008a) "Alief and Belief," *Journal of Philosophy* 105: 634–663.

Gendler, T.S. (2008b) "Alief in Action (and Reaction)," *Mind & Language* 23: 552–585.

Golomb, C., and R. Kuersten (1996) "On the Transition from Pretense Play to Reality: What Are the Rules of the Game?" *British Journal of Developmental Psychology* 14: 203–217.

Grandin, T., with R. Panek (2014) *The Autistic Brain*, New York: Houghton Mifflin Harcourt.
Harris, P. (2000) *The Work of the Imagination*, Oxford: Blackwell.
Hume, D. (1740/1978) *A Treatise of Human Nature*, eds. L.A. Selby-Bigge and P.H. Nidditch, Oxford, Oxford Clarendon Press.
Hursthouse, R. (1991) "Arational Actions," *Journal of Philosophy* 88(2): 57–68.
Kaplan, D. (1968) "Quantifying In," *Synthese* 19: 178–214.
Kind, A. (2001) "Putting the Image Back in Imagination," *Philosophy and Phenomenological Research* 62(1): 85–110.
Kind, A. (2011) "The Puzzle of Imaginative Desire," *Australasian Journal of Philosophy* 89(3): 421–439.
Kosslyn, S., W. Thompson, and G. Ganis (2006) *The Case for Mental Imagery*, Oxford: Oxford University Press.
Langland-Hassan, P. (2012) "Pretense, Imagination, and Belief: The Single Attitude Theory," *Philosophical Studies* 159: 155–179.
Langland-Hassan, P. (2015) "Imaginative Attitudes," *Philosophy and Phenomenological Research* 90(3): 664–686.
Leslie, A.M. (1987) "Pretense and Representation: The Origins of 'Theory of Mind,'" *Psychological Review* 94: 412–426.
Liao, S., and T. Doggett (2014) "The Imagination Box," *Journal of Philosophy* 111(5): 259–275.
Lillard, A.S., and D.C. Witherington (2004) "Mothers' Behavior Modifications during Pretense and Their Possible Signal Value for Toddlers," *Developmental Psychology* 40(1): 95–113.
Matravers, D. (2010) "Why We Should Give Up on the Imagination," *Midwest Studies in Philosophy* 34(1): 190–199.
Milner, A.D., and M.A. Goodale (1995) *The Visual Brain in Action*, Oxford: Oxford University Press.
Nanay, B. (2013) *Between Perception and Action*, Oxford: Oxford University Press.
Nanay, B. (Forthcoming) "The Role of Imagination in Decision-Making," *Mind & Language*.
Nichols, S., and S. Stich (2003) *Mindreading*, Oxford: Oxford University Press.
Schacter, D.L., and D.R. Addis (2007) "The Cognitive Neuroscience of Constructive Memory: Remembering the Past and Imagining the Future," *Philosophical Transactions of the Royal Society B: Biological Sciences* 362(1481): 773–786.
Shah, N., and J.D. Velleman (2005) "Doxastic Deliberation," *Philosophical Review* 114(4): 497–534.
Sinhababu, N. (2013) "The Desire-Belief Account of Intention Explains Everything," *Noûs* 47(4): 680–696.
Spaulding, S. (forthcoming) "Imagination, Desire, and Rationality," *Journal of Philosophy*.
Van Leeuwen, N. (2009) "The Motivational Role of Belief," *Philosophical Papers* 38(2): 219–246.
Van Leeuwen, N. (2011) "Imagination Is Where the Action Is," *Journal of Philosophy* 108(2): 55–77.
Van Leeuwen, N. (2013) "The Meanings of 'Imagine' Part I: Constructive Imagination," *Philosophy Compass* 8(3): 220–230.
Van Leeuwen, N. (2014a) "The Meanings of 'Imagine' Part II: Attitude and Action," *Philosophy Compass* 9(11): 791–802.
Van Leeuwen, N. (2014b) "Religious Credence Is Not Factual Belief," *Cognition* 133(3): 698–715.
Velleman, J.D. (2000) "On the Aim of Belief," in *The Possibility of Practical Reason*, Oxford: Oxford University Press, 244–281.
Walton, K. (1990) *Mimesis as Make-Believe: On the Foundations of the Representational Arts*, Cambridge: Harvard University Press.

# 22
# IMAGINATION AND CHILD DEVELOPMENT

*Deena Skolnick Weisberg*

## Studying development can be informative for philosophy

There are four general reasons why the study of human development can help to provide philosophers with insights into questions about imagination.

- Looking at how aspects of the imagination develop can provide information about how different imaginative processes relate to each other. This may suggest which imaginative processes arise earlier in development. In turn, establishing the developmental sequence can suggest which imaginative abilities are prerequisite for others, and hence may be conceptually more basic.
- Examining how imaginative processes interact with other cognitive processes in development can help to explain our cognitive architecture: the way in which our mental processes are organized relative to each other and communicate with each other.
- Understanding the ways in which children use their imaginations may be crucially important to understanding how adults think and reason. Children's reasoning processes are different from adults' in a variety of ways, but the sorts of errors that children make or biases that they hold may persist into adulthood. This means that deepening our understanding of what children do can help to explain why adults reason as they do and how their imaginative processes work.
- Learning more about how children pretend, and particularly about the constraints that children place on their pretend games, can help to explain aspects of adults' aesthetic experiences. This suggestion is based on Kendall Walton's theory of mimesis as make-believe, which posits that the way in which adults interact with art is an exact parallel to the way in which children construct pretend games in development (Walton 1990).

For all of these reasons, the development of imagination can be a valuable tool for probing aspects of the philosophy of imagination. The current chapter aims to assist with this endeavor by reviewing the developmental trajectories of the three main forms of imagination that have been studied in children: pretend play games, counterfactual scenarios, and fictional stories. It also considers several theoretical issues related to the imagination in development, including whether children can distinguish between imagination and reality, whether children with autism spectrum disorder (ASD) have impairments to their imaginative capacities, and how different forms of imaginative endeavors relate to each other and to other cognitive abilities.

## Pretend play

### *Pretend play across development*

Pretend play is the first form of imaginative activity that appears in development, and it is the one that has received the most attention in the developmental literature. Although the exact time-course of this ability varies across children, pretend play behaviors begin to appear roughly around 18 months (Fein 1981; Lillard et al. 2011). These early pretending behaviors are generally object-substitution pretense, which involves using one object as a stand-in for another, as when a toddler picks up a television remote and holds it to his ear as if it were a telephone (McCune-Nicolich 1981). At this age, pretend games often consist of little more than this simple object substitution, recapitulating known action sequences with props or replica objects. In addition, the kinds of props used in early pretense tend to match their referents quite closely – both the television remote (prop) and the phone (referent) are rectangular and have buttons. Later, around 2 years, children begin to pretend with a wider range of props that are not as perceptually tied to their referents, like using a building block or a spoon as a telephone. Pretense with entirely invisible objects (holding one's hand to one's ear without a prop) appears at yet a later stage of development, between the ages of 4 and 6 (Jackowitz and Watson 1980; Overton and Jackson 1973; Taylor and Carlson 1997).

Pretending at older ages not only uses more invisible props, it also incorporates longer and more complex action routines and narratives and becomes more social. Rather than being a pretense-specific development, these changes reflect children's growing abilities to construct narratives and their burgeoning social skills. Indeed, research on preschool-aged children has shown that they understand that pretending is a form of social convention, and as such it should obey internal rules and be sensitive to the knowledge state of the players (Rakoczy 2008). One consequence of this understanding is the fact that children separate different pretend episodes from each other and think of objects' pretend identities as existing only relative to a particular game with a particular set of participants. For example, children understand that if someone was not present when a prop was established, they shouldn't be expected to use that prop correctly in the pretend world (Gopnik and Slaughter 1991; Harris and Kavanaugh 1993; Weisberg and Bloom 2009; Wyman et al. 2009a, 2009b).

One of the more involved forms of play is the phenomenon of imaginary companions (Gleason 2013; Taylor 1999). While these imagined entities were once seen as a sign of a withdrawn or disordered child, it is now known that children who create imaginary companions are nearly always perfectly psychologically healthy. They may even be more well-adjusted than their peers. Indeed, insofar as there are any differences between children with imaginary companions and children without, children with imaginary companions tend to have better theory of mind skills and more advanced language skills (Jersild et al. 1933; D.G. Singer and Singer 1990; Taylor and Carlson 1997; Taylor 1999). This phenomenon tends to arise in preschool and reaches its peak prevalence in early elementary school, when children are around 6 or 7 years old. Older children may be involved in playing with paracosms: entire imaginary worlds that obey their own internal rules (Root-Bernstein 2013). This phenomenon is not necessarily connected to imaginary companions. While some children do expand their interactions with their imaginary companions into a full world, other children have only one or the other. But both types of play are highly involving, extended through time, and crucially engage the child as the creator of the ongoing imagined entity. As such, imaginary-companion and paracosm play are associated with creativity in adulthood (Root-Bernstein and Root-Bernstein 2006).

Around middle childhood (9–11 years old), pretend play seems to go dormant or underground (Smith and Lillard 2012; see also Taylor 1999, ch. 6). It's not yet entirely clear why this happens. Of course the mental capacity to pretend still exists – indeed, we pretend as adults and certainly use our imaginations in other ways, as will be reviewed later. One suggestion for the disappearance of play, at least for children in Western cultures, is that children become involved in other activities and schoolwork and have less unstructured time for play. A different suggestion is that they continue to engage in play, but hide it from their parents and peers (and researchers), because they have absorbed the general cultural view that play is childish.

Establishing the developmental sequence of pretend play is important in its own right, but it may also help us to determine how the imagination develops in general. As noted in the introduction, the developmental priority of particular kinds of abilities may relate to the conceptual priority of these abilities. The fact that children are able to pretend with props before they can pretend with invisible objects, for example, suggests that engaging in prop-based imagination (see Walton 1990) may be a necessary condition for engaging in more free-flowing forms of imagination.

## *Cognitive and social foundations of pretense*

Some researchers have argued that the developmental trajectory described above represents increasing levels of maturity in children's pretend play (Fein 1981; Jackowitz and Watson 1980). While it seems sensible that more complex forms of pretense appear later in development, little research has addressed this issue directly. Further complicating attempts at fully establishing which types of pretense are more or less sophisticated is the fact that some researchers have examined children's production of pretend actions (Elder and Pederson 1978) while others have examined children's comprehension of these actions in others (Bigham and Bourchier-Sutton 2007). These two processes are likely to be distinct, because comprehension requires only observation and understanding and does not additionally require the child to produce a series of actions to a certain standard (Hopkins et al. forthcoming).

Considering this general issue of production and comprehension leads to the question of when children develop the representational capacities to understand pretend play at all, and how this ability relates to their development of pretend actions. Onishi et al. (2007) examined the first of these issues directly, and found that 15-month-olds are able to understand pretend sequences even before they are able to produce them. Along these lines, other researchers have examined what signals babies and children might use to distinguish real-world actions from pretend actions (Lillard and Witherington 2004; Richert and Lillard 2004). These studies found that pretend actions tend to be faster and accompanied by more positive affect than nonpretend actions. Children may be able to determine which actions are and are not pretense on the basis of what they perceive even if they are unable to produce these kinds of actions themselves.

Given the focus on pretend actions and the way in which young children's play manifests itself primarily in behaviors, many researchers have attempted to determine whether play is properly characterized as a behavior or as a mental state (Friedman and Leslie 2007; Friedman 2013; Weisberg 2015; see also Elizabeth Picciuto and Peter Carruthers, Chapter 23 of this volume). Researchers in this debate disagree both about whether pretending requires the child to have a particular kind of mental state, and also about whether the process of understanding and engaging in pretense requires that the child be able to attribute a particular kind of mental state (to herself or to others). Some argue that pretending is a form of behaving-as-if, not necessarily a mental state. On this view, the child's actions are more important than whether the child can conceptualize play as a kind of mental state (Jarrold et al. 1994; Nichols and Stich 2003; Perner 1991). These researchers claim that a behavioral account is sufficient to describe young children's actions in pretend settings, even when other people are involved, because children only need to understand that the actions are meant to be nonliteral: "[The child] may be able to make sense of the pretence … by realizing that the event being acted out is not 'for real,' whether from maternal cues or because of the inherent strangeness of the behavior … [The child] could then join in by relying on scripted or stereotyped knowledge" (Jarrold et al. 1994, 463). This account is parsimonious in terms of the kind of cognitive and social skills attributed to the child. It also makes sense of children's pretend behaviors, which do conform to scripts and general knowledge a majority of the time, as discussed above.

However, others point to the crucial role of mental states in making a particular action pretend. One could engage in the same physical activity both in pretense and in reality, meaning that it is only one's intention to pretend that could set them apart. Further, characterizing pretending as a representational mental state makes sense of cases reviewed above, where multiple actors engage in different games of pretense with the same object; it is their different beliefs about what the object is in each game that requires a separation between games. This line of argument also makes sense of recent work showing that children understand pretense even when the actions are more than merely nonliteral behaviors directed at props, as when one uses replica objects or speaks in a different voice when one is pretending that a stuffed animal is speaking. In order to understand these cases, children must interpret the "vroom" noises directed at a pen or the funny voice in the presence of a teddy bear as coming from the pen or teddy bear in the pretense, and not just as a behavior that doesn't match reality (Friedman et al. 2010). This debate has not yet been settled, but it brings to the fore issues of how mental states bear on behaviors and how much of our understanding of others' behaviors requires mental states for drawing correct conclusions.

It is important to consider not only the underlying mental representation of pretense, but also its function in children's lives. Although children's pretend actions and action sequences become more complex through development, children's immediate goals when engaging in pretense remain consistent: Young children use pretending as a way to work through their experiences and emotions and to try out variations on the events that they have seen. Through play, children scale the world down and develop ways of understanding and working out their problems and feelings (Bruner 1986; D.G. Singer and Singer 1990). This is especially true during the preschool years (roughly 3 to 5), when pretending becomes a major way that children try out new social, cognitive, and linguistic skills (Hirsh-Pasek et al. 2008; D.G. Singer et al. 2006; Weisberg, Hirsh-Pasek et al. 2013). There is evidence that this practice has benefits: Correlational studies have found that children who play more have better language skills (Weisberg, Zosh et al. 2013), self-control abilities (J.L. Singer 1961), and theory of mind skills (Lillard 1993; Schwebel et al. 1999). While we should be cautious not to place too much value on pretend play as a uniquely effective learning environment (Lillard et al. 2013), it's clear that play is an activity that incorporates the workings of many systems and that children use it for learning. Indeed, the concept of play therapy relies on this being the case. In play therapy, children are encouraged to pretend about themes that are troubling to them or situations that they are struggling with in real life. These sessions use children's proclivity for play and for working out issues through play to help therapists understand how children are feeling and interpreting situations, and can provide an environment to allow children to resolve these issues (Russ and Fehr 2013).

## Counterfactual reasoning

Another use of imagination in development (and at maturity, of course) is counterfactual reasoning. Less is known about the developmental trajectory of counterfactual thinking than about pretending, but several studies have shown that children have some basic ability to compute simple counterfactuals by around age 4. For example, one study gave 3- and 4-year-olds scenarios in which a character causes a certain outcome (e.g., Teddy paints a clean floor with red paint). Children were then asked to evaluate a counterfactual: If Teddy hadn't painted the floor, would it be clean or dirty? The researchers found that children were generally good at this task, answering the counterfactual questions correctly (Harris et al. 1996; Kavanaugh et al. 1995).

However, children struggle when asked to reason on the basis of a counterfactual syllogism (Dias and Harris 1988, 1990; Scott et al. 1999). In these studies, children are generally asked to take on a premise that contradicts reality, like "all cats bark." They are then given a fact, like "Fluffy is a cat," and are then to draw a conclusion from this pair of premises about what Fluffy will say. Preschool-aged children usually report that the cat will say "meow." That is, they fail to take on the counterfactual premise and reason from it, instead using their real-world knowledge to answer the question. However, framing the same task in terms of a pretend game or as taking place in a fictional world dramatically improves their performance. Under these circumstances (e.g., "Let's pretend that all cats bark"), children draw the appropriate conclusion (Fluffy barks).

These studies show that children do have the ability to reason counterfactually, but this ability only reveals itself in situations in which there is enough contextual support to allow children to recognize the need to adopt the counterfactual premises independently of their empirical knowledge. Pretend play provides one such situation, likely due to its social nature. A child who engages in a pretend game with a parent or peer can rely on feedback from the partner's actions and from his or her own responses to support the otherwise difficult task of thinking about a scenario that is not literally true (Amsel and Smalley 2000; Leslie 1994). What changes across development, then, is the ability to recognize these cases as being instances where one needs to inhibit prior knowledge, as well as the suite of abilities necessary for actually performing this inhibition process.

These links between pretending and counterfactual reasoning have led many theorists to argue that the underlying mental capacities for engaging in pretense and creating counterfactuals are the same (Amsel and Smalley 2000; Gopnik 2009; Harris 2000; Lillard 2001). Like pretending, these abilities involve representing possible worlds – imagining that things happened or will happen in a certain way even if that doesn't match the current or past state of reality. This line of reasoning additionally suggests that one of the purposes of pretend play in development is to practice counterfactual reasoning (Buchsbam et al. 2012; Weisberg and Gopnik 2013), although direct evidence for this claim is lacking.

One reason to be skeptical of this tight connection between pretending and counterfactual reasoning is evidence showing that children are not actually able to compute true counterfactuals until around the age of 7 or 8, contrary to the work reviewed above. In these studies, children failed to explicitly construct an alternative possibility that contradicted the true chain of past events (Rafetseder et al. 2010; see also Beck et al. 2006). For example, when children saw an action sequence in which a tall character retrieved a treat from a high shelf, they had trouble reasoning about what would have happened if a short character had come to get the treat instead. Some researchers have used such results to argue that young children are actually unable to reason counterfactually. On this view, children appear able to succeed on other counterfactual reasoning tasks because they are using conditional reasoning to construct general response rules, not because they are genuinely creating alternatives to reality.

It is not yet clear how to reconcile the two positions presented here. Children may be unable to conceptualize conflicting alternatives, but the similarities between creating possible worlds in pretense and doing so for thinking about counterfactual alternatives are hard to explain away – especially since, in pretense, children do seem to be suppressing current reality (e.g., the exact physical features of a prop, like the size of a pen) in order to consider a conflicting alternative (e.g., the pen is a car). One possibility is that children's counterfactual reasoning abilities are present but are weak, requiring contextual or physical support to help them in overcoming a reliance on reality. In addition, pretense tends to be more self-directed and less scripted than the experimental tasks used to study counterfactual reasoning, and may require less suppression of reality. This remains an active area of research, and one that can potentially shed light on various aspects of our cognitive architecture, such as the relationship between counterfactual and conditional thinking.

## Fictional stories

One final form of imagination that has been widely studied in development is children's understanding of fictional stories. Children listen to many fictional stories, and watching movies and television shows that present fictional situations is a major activity in development. As with pretending, the earliest children's books are simple and highly iconic in their representations. Later, books and other forms of media incorporate more intricate plots and social issues. However, looking at children's books tells us primarily about the sorts of stories and situations that adults assume children will like and comprehend, and not necessarily about children's actual liking or comprehension.

To test these issues more directly, researchers in this area have tended to write their own stories with a variety of features in order to determine how children think about fictional narratives. For example, some work from my lab has examined whether children construct internally consistent stories: If they are given the beginning of a story that is either realistic or fantastical, will they choose a realistic or fantastical event to come next in the story? Surprisingly, children in these circumstances will tend to choose the realistic event, regardless of how the story started (Sobel and Weisberg 2014; Weisberg, Bloom et al. 2013; Weisberg and Sobel 2012). Such results can inform our understanding of creativity in childhood and adulthood, since they imply that it's difficult for children (and adults: Ward 1994) to stray too far from the rules that govern how things work in reality. Conversely, examining which rules children will leave behind in reality when they construct fictional worlds can inform our understanding of how children think about reality and which types of structures they consider fundamental to the way things work. In turn, that can tell us about phenomena like imaginative resistance, which occurs (on some views) because an imaginer has trouble with precisely this process: leaving behind the rules of reality to take on the premises presented in a story that contradict one's deeply held beliefs (Gendler 2000; Kengo Miyazono and Shen-yi Liao, Chapter 17 of this volume). As with pretense and counterfactual reasoning, then, the development of these skills and the content that children choose for their stories gives us valuable insight into their cognitive and social development in general, and, in turn, into adults' thinking processes.

A second body of literature in this area has examined children's learning from fictional stories, that is, how and under what circumstances children will transfer information from a fictional world into their real-world knowledge base. Children can learn object labels from picture books starting at around 18 months (Ganea et al. 2008; Keates et al. 2014; Khu et al. 2014). However, although these books are clearly representational, it's unclear whether they are actually fictional, since they consist of little more than isolated pictures of the target objects accompanied by one-word labels. Older children do export a wide variety of information from genuinely fictional stories, including facts (Fazio and Marsh 2008), information about plants and animals (Ganea et al. 2014; Ganea et al. 2011; Walker et al. 2015), and causal sequences that can be used to solve problems (Hopkins and Lillard in prep.; Richert et al. 2009; Richert and Smith 2011). Starting in preschool, then, children have some way of solving the "reader's dilemma" – the problem of separating which information presented in the context of a fictional story is purely fiction, and which information can accurately apply to reality (Gerrig and Prentice 1991). Indeed, this is part of the utility of the imagination in general: providing a way to simulate reality without the risk of real-world consequences so that one can learn about the structure of reality or decide what to do (Gopnik 2009; Weisberg 2009).

Both of these research programs have examined children's comprehension of the stories with which they are presented. But, as discussed above with respect to pretense, there are more and more complex processes involved in production than in comprehension. Fortunately, there is also work on children's production of stories and the development of their abilities to construct narratives. To conduct these studies, some researchers use a wordless book to elicit narratives from children (e.g., Berman and Slobin 1994), while others simply ask children to tell stories on a topic of their choosing (e.g., Nicolopoulou 2008). Researchers then examine the types of events children describe and the language they use in these descriptions. The developmental trajectory revealed by such studies parallels that of pretense. Children begin with concrete and familiar events, and, over time, their growing linguistic and cognitive skills allow them to string together longer and more complex events. However, it is important to note that these studies have primarily examined the development of children's narrative abilities, which are used in service of imaginative endeavors but which are not uniquely imagination-related. Future work should determine if there is any difference between how children tell stories about fictional events as opposed to about true events.

## The imagination/reality distinction

One of the first issues that arises in any discussion of children's imagination is the question of whether children can tell the difference between imagination and reality. Although Jean Piaget (and many parents!) feared that children were unable to understand that some entities and events were merely imaginary (Piaget 1962), recent research has shown that this is not the case. Older preschoolers are somewhat better at making this distinction and do so for a broader range of cases, but even 3-year-olds can report accurately on the ontological status of their pretend games and the characters and events in stories (Weisberg 2013).

That is not to say that the boundary between reality and fiction is always sharply drawn for children. Strong emotional responses can lead to inconsistent or inaccurate reporting. For example, children may mistakenly report that events they find scary can't happen (Carrick and Quas 2006; Dierker and Sanders 1996) or behave as if something that they have imagined can become real (Bourchier and Davis 2002; Harris et al. 1991). And children are genuinely afraid of the monsters that might be under their beds. However, there are cases in which adults make similar errors, as when we leave the lights on after watching a horror movie (Gergely 2002; Harris 2002). It therefore makes more sense to think of children's behavior differing from adults' behavior only quantitatively, not qualitatively. Indeed, this provides a perfect example of a case in which the errors children make in seemingly failing to distinguish reality from fiction can give us insight into the variables that lead to this kind of confusion in adults: strong emotions, mental availability, and motivated cognition, among others.

Further, as noted above, one of the main ways in which the imagination functions is as a learning tool, allowing us to draw real-life lessons from hypothetical and counterfactual scenarios and to learn true facts about reality from fictional stories. So while some imagined information should surely remain quarantined, some must flow through the boundary. This makes it difficult to determine where the boundary should be for all cases a priori.

## Imagination in ASD

Children with ASD (autism spectrum disorder) provide an interesting population for testing questions of imagination in development, because part of their impairment seems to involve a deficit to their imaginative capacities, manifested primarily though a lack of pretend play. Although children with ASD likely do not lack all forms of representational abilities, they do show a marked impairment in the type and frequency of their pretend play when compared with typically developing controls and with matched clinical controls with other types of developmental disorders, such as Down syndrome (Baron-Cohen 1987; Rutherford and Rogers 2003). Children with ASD also tend not to engage in pretend play spontaneously, as their peers do (Charman et al. 1997; Jarrold et al. 1993; Lewis and Boucher 1988).

Why is this the case? Many researchers have suggested that the root cause of ASD is impairment to the individual's ability to create decoupled representations, that is, representations that are separated from reality and that may not necessarily reflect literal truths (Baron-Cohen et al. 1985; Baron-Cohen 1995; Leslie 1987, 1988). These researchers theorize that understanding both pretense and belief requires a decoupling between a statement and reality (e.g., "there is tea in that cup" vs. "she pretends/believes that there is tea in that cup"). Because of this impairment, children with ASD fail to display the pretend behavior that is characteristic of typically developing children; they have difficulty with understanding simple object substitutions, like the use of a banana as a telephone. In addition, because they cannot create such decoupled representations, they are unable to understand false beliefs or to take others' points of view, since these activities require representing something other than what the child himself or herself believes is to be true in reality.

If this is the correct explanation for the imagination impairment in ASD, then these children's abilities to reason counterfactually and to understand stories should be damaged as well, since these arguably rely on the same mental capacities. As noted above, counterfactual reasoning and thinking about stories involve the same sort of movement into a representation as pretend play does; none of these scenarios are accurate reflections of reality, hence all involve the ability to decouple a statement from reality and to form beliefs about a nonreal representation. If children with ASD have difficulty with precisely this kind of decoupled representation, then they should fail to reason accurately from explicit counterfactual premises and to engage appropriately with fictional stories, just as they fail to play pretend games. Indeed, studies of adults with ASD reveal that the narratives they construct differ from those of neurotypical controls (Barnes and Baron-Cohen 2012), suggesting that their understanding of fictional stories may be impaired as well.

A different possibility is that children with ASD fail to pretend because they lack a motivation to (Jarrold et al. 1993; Russell 1997). As support for this view, children with ASD seem to have difficulty engaging in play behavior more generally, not just in symbolic or representational play. Rather than engaging with toys both functionally and symbolically, as typically developing children do, children with ASD demonstrate repetitive, ingrained action routines in their interactions with objects. These results may be best explained by positing a malfunction to their central executive processing abilities, which does not allow them to overcome these routines to engage in either functional or symbolic play.

If this is the best way to understand the impairment in pretend play in ASD, then children with ASD may demonstrate an intact ability to reason counterfactually or understand stories. Their difficulty with pretending is not with decoupling representations per se, but rather in a general difficulty with engaging their intact representational abilities in service of pretend play. But because some degree of inhibiting current reality is necessary for counterfactual reasoning, as argued above, children with ASD may only demonstrate intact reasoning abilities in situations that have provided them with enough support to overcome a focus on what is true in reality.

Unfortunately, the psychological literature provides evidence for both views of the nature of autistic children's abilities in counterfactual reasoning. For example, Leevers and Harris (2000) found that children with ASD failed to solve counterfactual syllogisms, while Scott et al. (1999) found that they succeeded. Given that each of these two theories of the nature of the imaginative impairment in ASD have studies to support them, the question of the exact nature of this impairment is far from settled. It is still unclear whether children with ASD lack the ability to understand counterfactual scenarios and fictional stories, and what is the nature of their deficit with pretend scenarios. Because of this, the precise nature of the links among all three imaginative abilities is also unclear, but further work with this population could serve to elucidate them.

## Linking imaginative abilities with each other and other capacities

One major theoretical concern within developmental psychology has been to map out the relations among the different imaginative abilities reviewed above. While it seems reasonable to assume that engaging in pretense, reasoning counterfactually, and thinking about fictional stories share some common elements, it is not yet clear which elements are shared and which elements might be unique to these activities. For example, while pretending and counterfactual reasoning may share a common core, pretend scenarios are acted out while counterfactual scenarios are not. The extant research does not yet allow us to determine whether this difference is merely a surface feature or reflects a deeper divide between these two activities. More generally, although some aspect of the imagination is indeed implicated in the three activities reviewed above, it is not yet known how exactly this kernel of commonality manifests itself in the three cases, and whether it does so differently depending on the use to which it is being put.

Further, as should be clear from the previous section, a second major theoretical concern is to determine how imaginative abilities relate to other developing mental skills. The question of how pretend play relates to theory of mind is one of the foremost areas of research in this field, based on the proposal that both pretending and theory of mind rely on the ability to create a metarepresentation of another person's (or one's own) mental state (Leslie 1987,

1994). For example, in the case of pretense, one represents one's partner's mental state about the prop, even though it doesn't match reality: Mom pretends that the banana is a telephone, even though it's really a banana. In the case of belief, one does the same thing: Mom thinks that the banana is on the table, even though it's really in the fruit bowl. Evidence from children with ASD, who seem to lack both the ability to pretend and to consider others' mental states, provides support for this argument. However, some have taken issue with this characterization of pretending and theory of mind, claiming both that it might not be necessary to represent others' mental states in order to understand and engage in pretending, and that the pretense impairment in ASD may be due to factors other than a failure of metarepresentation. Further research is needed to more fully determine the nature of this link.

A second example of a purported link between imaginative abilities and other mental processes is language. Both language and pretend play involve symbolic thinking: the ability to match objects in the world with symbols representing them, which may be more or less iconic. Because symbolic capacities like language develop concurrently with pretend play, looking at the links between them might give insight into whether a more general symbolic reasoning capacity underlies both. As noted above, children who play more do tend to have better linguistic skills, suggesting that using both props and words as stand-ins for real objects might share a developmental trajectory. On the basis of such findings, some researchers have claimed that pretending can provide training for children's developing symbolic thinking capacities, leading to better language skills (McCune 1995; Miller and Almon 2009; Vygotsky 1977). However, studies of this issue are almost invariably correlational, leaving it unclear whether this direction of causality is correct or whether a different variable explains the connection between pretending and language.

Finally, imagination is also likely to be related to the set of skills under the collective heading of "executive functioning." These skills involve the abilities to create strategies for performing a sequence of actions, to flexibly deploy these strategies as the situation requires, and to inhibit responses that may not be appropriate (Baddeley 1986). These are precisely the skills required for most cases of imagining, particularly counterfactual reasoning, since children must inhibit their knowledge of the true state of affairs in order to adopt a counterfactual premise. Interestingly, these skills are also involved in theory of mind reasoning, which requires that children set aside their own knowledge in order to think about someone else's knowledge. This provides some additional evidence that imagining and thinking about others' mental states share some commonalities, but again the precise nature of these commonalities have not yet been determined.

## Conclusion

Although this review has focused on issues that pertain directly to children and the development of their imaginative skills, part of the utility of thinking about these issues is the insight that they can provide into the adult system. For example, knowing that children tend not to create stories that stray too far from reality, as reviewed above, can explain why adults experience imaginative resistance and have difficulty thinking creatively. As another example, understanding which mental capacities are shared by pretend play and theory of mind can explain the nature of adults' reasoning about other people and how they may use mental simulation to understand others' actions (Goldman 2006). Further, because counterfactual reasoning has been linked strongly to causal reasoning (Gopnik et al. 2004; Mackie 1974), looking to the development of this capacity can help in our understanding of the nature of causation. Finally, philosophical thought experiments may be thought of as counterfactual scenarios or fictional stories, so gaining additional understanding into how people think counterfactually and understand stories can shed light on this important philosophical reasoning tool. In general, then, developmental psychology has much to offer to the philosophy of imagination. And philosophy of imagination has much to offer to developmental psychology, especially considering that many important questions about the nature and development of the imaginative abilities reviewed here have yet to be settled. Stronger partnerships between these disciplines can thereby lead to advantages for all, and to a deeper understanding of how the imagination works.

## References

Amsel, E., and J.D. Smalley (2000) "Beyond Really and Truly: Children's Counterfactual Thinking about Pretend and Possible Worlds," in P. Mitchell and K.J. Riggs (eds.) *Children's Reasoning and the Mind*, Hove: Psychology Press, 121–147.

Baddeley, A.D. (1986) *Working Memory*, Oxford: Clarendon Press.

Barnes, J.L., and S. Baron-Cohen (2012) "The Big Picture: Storytelling Ability in Adults with Autism Spectrum Conditions," *Journal of Autism and Developmental Disorders* 42(8): 1557–1565.

Baron-Cohen, S. (1987) "Autism and Symbolic Play," *British Journal of Developmental Psychology* 5(2): 139–148.

Baron-Cohen, S. (1995) *Mindblindness*, Cambridge, MA: MIT Press.

Baron-Cohen, S., A.M. Leslie, and U. Frith (1985) "Does the Autistic Child Have a 'Theory of Mind'?" *Cognition* 21: 37–46.

Beck, S.R., E.J. Robinson, D.J. Carroll, and I.A. Apperly (2006) "Children's Thinking about Counterfactuals and Hypotheticals as Possibilities," *Child Development* 77(2): 413–423.

Berman, R., and D. Slobin (1994) *Relating Events in Narrative: A Crosslinguistic Developmental Study*, Hillsdale, NJ: Erlbaum.

Bigham, S., and A. Bourchier-Sutton (2007) "The Decontextualization of Form and Function in the Development of Pretence," *British Journal of Developmental Psychology* 25(3): 335–351.

Bourchier, A., and A. Davis (2002) "The Pretence–Reality Distinction – Confusion, Emotion, and Source Monitoring," *Developmental Science* 5(4): 422–426.

Bruner, J. (1986) *Actual Minds, Possible Worlds*, Cambridge, MA: Harvard University Press.

Buchsbam, D., S. Bridgers, D.S. Weisberg, and A. Gopnik (2012) "The Power of Possibility: Causal Learning, Counterfactual Reasoning, and Pretend Play," *Philosophical Transactions of the Royal Society B: Biological Sciences* 367: 2202–2212.

Carrick, N., and J.A. Quas (2006) "Effects of Discrete Emotions on Young Children's Ability to Discern Fantasy and Reality," *Developmental Psychology* 42(6): 1278–1288.

Charman, T., J. Swettenham, S. Baron-Cohen, A. Cox, G. Baird, and A. Drew (1997) "Infants with Autism: An Investigation of Empathy, Pretend Play, Joint Attention, and Imitation," *Developmental Psychology* 33(5): 781–789.

Dias, M.G., and P.L. Harris (1988) "The Effect of Make-Believe Play on Deductive Reasoning," *British Journal of Developmental Psychology* 6: 207–221.

Dias, M.G., and P.L. Harris (1990) "The Influence of the Imagination on Reasoning by Young Children," *British Journal of Developmental Psychology* 8: 305–318.

Dierker, L.C., and B. Sanders (1996) "Developmental and Individual Differences in Children's Ability to Distinguish Reality from Fantasy," *Imagination, Cognition, and Personality* 16: 25–49.

Elder, J.L., and D.R. Pederson (1978) "Preschool Children's Use of Objects in Symbolic Play," *Child Development* 49(2): 500–504.

Fazio, L.K., and E.J. Marsh (2008) "Older, Not Younger, Children Learn More False Facts from Stories," *Cognition* 106(2): 1081–1089.

Fein, G.G. (1981) "Pretend Play in Childhood: An Integrative Review," *Child Development* 52(4): 1095–1118.

Friedman, O. (2013) "How Do Children Represent Pretend Play?" in M. Taylor (ed.) *Oxford Handbook of the Development of Imagination*, New York: Oxford University Press, 186–195.

Friedman, O., and A.M. Leslie (2007) "The Conceptual Underpinnings of Pretense: Pretending Is Not 'Behaving-As-If'," *Cognition 105*(1): 103–124.

Friedman, O., K.R. Neary, C.L. Burnstein, and A. Leslie (2010) "Is Young Children's Recognition of Pretense Metarepresentational or Merely Behavioral? Evidence from 2- and 3-Year-Olds' Understanding of Pretend Sounds and Speech," *Cognition 115*: 314–319.

Ganea, P.A., M.B. Pickard, and J.S. DeLoache (2008) "Transfer between Picture Books and the Real World by Very Young Children," *Journal of Cognition and Development* 9(1): 46–66.

Ganea, P.A., L. Ma, and J.S. DeLoache (2011) "Young Children's Learning and Transfer of Biological Information from Picture Books to Real Animals," *Child Development* 82(5): 1421–1433.

Ganea, P.A., C.F. Canfield, K. Simons-Ghafari, and T. Chou (2014) "Do Cavies Talk? The Effect of Anthropomorphic Picture Books on Children's Knowledge about Animals," *Frontiers in Psychology* 5: 283, doi:10.3389/fpsyg.2014.00283.

Gendler, T.S. (2000) "The Puzzle of Imaginative Resistance," *Journal of Philosophy* 97(2): 55–81.

Gergely, G. (2002) "Some Confusion about Pretence–Reality Confusions," *Developmental Science* 5(4): 417–419.

Gerrig, R.J., and D.A. Prentice (1991) "The Representation of Fictional Information," *Psychological Science* 2: 336–340.

Gleason, T.R. (2013) "Imaginary Relationships," in M. Taylor (ed.) *Oxford Handbook of the Development of Imagination*, New York: Oxford University Press, 251–271.

Goldman, A.I. (2006) *Simulating Minds: The Philosophy, Psychology, and Neuroscience of Mindreading*, Oxford: Oxford University Press.

Gopnik, A. (2009) *The Philosophical Baby: What Children's Minds Tell Us about Truth, Love, and the Meaning of Life*, New York: Farrar, Straus & Giroux.

Gopnik, A., and V. Slaughter (1991) "Young Children's Understanding of Changes in Their Mental States," *Child Development* 62: 98–110.

Gopnik, A., C. Glymour, D.M. Sobel, L.E. Schulz, T. Kushnir, and D. Danks (2004) "A Theory of Causal Learning in Children: Causal Maps and Bayes Nets," *Psychological Review* 111(1): 3–32.

Harris, P.L. (2000) *The Work of the Imagination*, Oxford: Blackwell.

Harris, P.L. (2002) "Delving into Uncle Albert's Cabinet: Further Thoughts on the Pretence–Reality Distinction," *Developmental Science* 5(4): 419–421.

Harris, P.L., and R.D. Kavanaugh (1993) "Young Children's Understanding of Pretense," *Monographs of the Society for Research in Child Development* 58(1).

Harris, P.L., E. Brown, C. Marriot, S. Whittal, and S. Harmer (1991) "Monsters, Ghosts, and Witches: Testing the Limits of the Fantasy–Reality Distinction in Young Children," *British Journal of Developmental Psychology* 9(1): 105–123.

Harris, P.L., T. German, and P. Mills (1996) "Children's Use of Counterfactual Thinking in Causal Reasoning," *Cognition* 61: 233–259.

Hirsh-Pasek, K., R.M. Golinkoff, L.E. Berk, and D.G. Singer (2008) *A Mandate for Playful Learning in Preschool: Applying the Scientific Evidence*, Oxford: Oxford University Press.

Hopkins, E.J., and A.S. Lillard (In prep.) "The Effect of Story Framing on Analogical Transfer from Fantasy."

Hopkins, E.J., E.D. Smith, D.S. Weisberg, and A.S. Lillard (forthcoming) "The Development of Substitute Object Pretense: The Differential Importance of Form and Function." *Journal of Cognition and Development.*

Jackowitz, E.R., and M.W. Watson (1980) "Development of Object Transformations in Early Pretend Play," *Developmental Psychology* 16(6): 543–549.

Jarrold, C., J. Boucher, and P. Smith (1993) "Symbolic Play in Autism: A Review," *Journal of Autism and Developmental Disorders* 23(2): 281–307.

Jarrold, C., P. Carruthers, P.K. Smith, and J. Boucher (1994) "Pretend Play: Is It Metarepresentational?" *Mind & Language* 9(4): 445–468.

Jersild, A., F. Markey, and C. Jersild (1933) "Children's Fears, Dreams, Wishes, Daydreams, Likes, Dislikes, Pleasant and Unpleasant Memories," *Child Development Monographs*, vol. 12, New York: Teachers College, Columbia University.

Kavanaugh, R.D., T. Goodrich, and P.L. Harris (1995) "Counterfactual Reasoning in Two-Year-Olds," paper presented at the 7th European Conference on Developmental Psychology, Krakow, Poland, August.

Keates, J., S.A. Graham, and P.A. Ganea (2014) "Infants Transfer Nonobvious Properties from Pictures to Real-World Objects," *Journal of Experimental Child Psychology* 125: 35–47.

Khu, M., S.A. Graham, and P.A. Ganea (2014) "Learning from Picture Books: Infants' Use of Naming Information," *Frontiers in Psychology* 5: 144, doi:10.3389/fpsyg.2014.00144.

Leevers, H.J., and P.L. Harris (2000) "Counterfactual Syllogistic Reasoning in Normal 4-Year-Olds, Children with Learning Disabilities, and Children with Autism," *Journal of Experimental Child Psychology* 76(1): 64–87.
Leslie, A.M. (1987) "Pretense and Representation: The Origins of 'Theory of Mind,'" *Psychological Review* 94(4): 412–422.
Leslie, A.M. (1988) "Some Implications of Pretense for Mechanisms underlying the Child's Theory of Mind," in J.W. Astington, P.L. Harris, and D.R. Olson (eds.) *Developing Theories of Mind*, Cambridge: Cambridge University Press, 19–46.
Leslie, A.M. (1994) "Pretending and Believing: Issues in the Theory of ToMM," *Cognition* 50(1–3): 211–238.
Lewis, V., and J. Boucher (1988) "Spontaneous, Instructed and Elicited Play in Relatively Able Autistic Children," *British Journal of Developmental Psychology* 6(4): 325–339.
Lillard, A.S. (1993) "Pretend Play Skills and the Child's Theory of Mind," *Child Development* 64: 348–371.
Lillard, A.S. (2001) "Pretend Play as Twin Earth: A Social-Cognitive Analysis," *Developmental Review* 21(4): 495–531.
Lillard, A.S., and D.C. Witherington (2004) "Mothers' Behavior Modifications during Pretense and Their Possible Signal Value for Toddlers," *Developmental Psychology* 40(1): 95–113.
Lillard, A.S., A.M. Pinkham, and E.D. Smith (2011) "Pretend Play and Cognitive Development," in U. Goswami (ed.) *The Wiley-Blackwell Handbook of Childhood Cognitive Development*, 2nd edn., London: Wiley-Blackwell, 285–311.
Lillard, A.S., M.D. Lerner, E.J. Hopkins, R.A. Dore, E.D. Smith, and C.M. Palmquist (2013) "The Impact of Pretend Play on Children's Development: A Review of the Evidence," *Psychological Bulletin* 139(1): 1–34.
Mackie, J.L. (1974) *The Cement of the Universe: A Study of Causation*, Oxford: Oxford University Press.
McCune, L. (1995) "A Normative Study of Representational Play in the Transition to Language," *Developmental Psychology* 31(2): 198–206.
McCune-Nicolich, L. (1981) "Toward Symbolic Functioning: Structure of Early Pretend Games and Potential Parallels with Language,"*Child Development* 52(3): 785–797.
Miller, E., and J. Almon (2009) *Crisis in the Kindergarten: Why Children Need to Play in School*, Alliance for Childhood (NJ3a), College Park, MD: Alliance for Childhood.
Nichols, S., and S.P. Stich (2003) *Mindreading: An Integrated Account of Pretense, Self-Awareness, and Understanding Other Minds*, New York: Oxford University Press.
Nicolopoulou, A. (2008) "The Elementary Forms of Narrative Coherence in Young Children's Storytelling," *Narrative Inquiry* 18(2): 299–325.
Onishi, K.H., R. Baillargeon, and A.M. Leslie (2007) "15-Month-Old Infants Detect Violations in Pretend Scenarios," *Acta Psychologica* 124(1): 106–128.
Overton, W.F., and J.P. Jackson (1973) "The Representation of Imagined Objects in Action Sequences: A Developmental Study," *Child Development* 44(2): 309–314.
Perner, J. (1991) *Understanding the Representational Mind: Learning, Development, and Conceptual Change*, Cambridge, MA: MIT Press.
Piaget, J. (1962) *Play, Dreams, and Imitation in Childhood*, New York: Norton.
Rafetseder, E., R. Cristi-Vargas, and J. Perner (2010) "Counterfactual Reasoning: Developing a Sense of 'Nearest Possible World,'" *Child Development* 81(1): 376–389.
Rakoczy, H. (2008) "Taking Fiction Seriously: Young Children Understand the Normative Structure of Joint Pretence Games," *Developmental Psychology* 44(4): 1195–1201.
Richert, R.A., and A.S. Lillard (2004) "Observers' Proficiency at Identifying Pretense Acts Based on Behavioral Cues," *Cognitive Development* 19(2): 223–240.
Richert, R.A., and E.I. Smith (2011) "Preschoolers' Quarantining of Fantasy Stories," *Child Development* 82(4): 1106–1119.
Richert, R.A., A.B. Shawber, R.E. Hoffman, and M. Taylor (2009) "Learning from Fantasy and Real Characters in Preschool and Kindergarten," *Journal of Cognition and Development* 10(1–2): 41–66.
Root-Bernstein, M. (2013) "The Creation of Imaginary Worlds," in M. Taylor (ed.) *The Oxford Handbook of the Development of Imagination*, New York: Oxford University Press, 417–437.
Root-Bernstein, M., and R. Root-Bernstein (2006) "Imaginary Worldplay in Childhood and Maturity and Its Impact on Adult Creativity," *Creativity Research Journal* 18(4): 405–425.
Russ, S.W., and K.K. Fehr (2013) "The Role of Pretend Play in Child Psychotherapy," in M. Taylor (ed.) *The Oxford Handbook of the Development of Imagination*, New York: Oxford University Press, 516–528.

Russell, J. (ed.) (1997) *Autism as an Executive Disorder*, Oxford: Oxford University Press.
Rutherford, M.D., and S.J. Rogers (2003) "Cognitive Underpinnings of Pretend Play in Autism," *Journal of Autism and Developmental Disorders* 33(3): 289–302.
Schwebel, D.C., C.S. Rosen, and J.L. Singer (1999) "Preschoolers' Pretend Play and Theory of Mind: The Role of Jointly Conducted Pretense," *British Journal of Developmental Psychology* 17: 333–348.
Scott, F.J., S. Baron-Cohen, and A. Leslie (1999) "If Pigs Could Fly: A Test of Counterfactual Reasoning and Pretence in Children with Autism," *British Journal of Developmental Psychology* 17: 349–362.
Singer, D.G., and J.L. Singer (1990) *The House of Make-Believe: Children's Play and the Developing Imagination*, Cambridge, MA: Harvard University Press.
Singer, D.G., R.M. Golinkoff, and K. Hirsh-Pasek (eds.) (2006) *Play = Learning: How Play Motivates and Enhances Children's Cognitive and Social-Emotional Growth*, New York: Oxford University Press.
Singer, J.L. (1961) "Imagination and Waiting Ability in Young Children," *Journal of Personality* 29(4): 396–413.
Smith, E.D., and A.S. Lillard (2012) "Play on: Retrospective Reports of the Persistence of Pretend Play into Middle Childhood," *Journal of Cognition and Development* 13(4): 524–549.
Sobel, D.M., and D.S. Weisberg (2014) "Tell Me a Story: How Children's Developing Domain Knowledge Affects Their Story Construction," *Journal of Cognition and Development* 15(3): 465–478.
Taylor, M. (1999) *Imaginary Companions and the Children Who Create Them*, New York: Oxford University Press.
Taylor, M., and S.M. Carlson (1997) "The Relation between Individual Differences in Fantasy and Theory of Mind," *Child Development* 68: 436–455.
Vygotsky, L.S. (1977) "Play and Its Role in the Mental Development of the Child," *Soviet Psychology* 5: 6–18.
Walker, C.M., A. Gopnik, and P.A. Ganea (2015) "Learning to Learn from Stories: Children's Developing Sensitivity to the Causal Structure of Fictional Worlds," *Child Development* 86(1): 310–318.
Walton, K.L. (1990) *Mimesis as Make-Believe: On the Foundations of the Representational Arts*, Cambridge, MA: Harvard University Press.
Ward, T.B. (1994) "Structured Imagination: The Role of Category Structure in Exemplar Generation,"*Cognitive Psychology* 27(1): 1–40.
Weisberg, D.S. (2009) "The Vital Importance of Imagination," in M. Brockman (ed.) *What's Next? Dispatches on the Future of Science*, New York: Vintage Books.
Weisberg, D.S. (2013) "Distinguishing Imagination from Reality," in M. Taylor (ed.) *Oxford Handbook of the Development of Imagination*, New York: Oxford University Press, 75–93.
Weisberg, D.S. (2015) "Pretend Play," *WIREs Cognitive Science* 6(3): 249–261.
Weisberg, D.S., and P. Bloom (2009) "Young Children Separate Multiple Pretend Worlds," *Developmental Science* 12(5): 699–705.
Weisberg, D.S., and D.M. Sobel (2012) "Young Children Discriminate Improbable from Impossible Events in Fiction," *Cognitive Development* 27(1): 90–98.
Weisberg, D.S., and A. Gopnik (2013) "Pretense, Counterfactuals, and Bayesian Causal Models: Why What Is Not Real Really Matters," *Cognitive Science* 37(7): 1368–1381.
Weisberg, D.S., P. Bloom, D.M. Sobel, and J. Goodstein (2013) "Young Children are Reality-Prone When Thinking about Stories," *Journal of Cognition and Culture* 13(3–4): 383–407.
Weisberg, D.S., K. Hirsh-Pasek, and R.M. Golinkoff (2013) "Guided Play: Where Curricular Goals Meet a Playful Pedagogy," *Mind, Brain, and Education* 7(2): 104–112.
Weisberg, D.S., J.M. Zosh, K. Hirsh-Pasek, and R.M. Golinkoff (2013) "Talking It Up: Play, Langauge, and the Role of Adult Support," *American Journal of Play* 6(1): 39–54.
Wyman, E., H. Rakoczy, and M. Tomasello (2009a) "Normativity and Context in Young Children's Pretend Play," *Cognitive Development* 24: 146–155.
Wyman, E., H. Rakoczy, and M. Tomasello (2009b) "Young Children Understand Multiple Pretend Identities in Their Object Play," *British Journal of Developmental Psychology* 27: 385–404.

# 23
# IMAGINATION AND PRETENSE

*Elizabeth Picciuto and Peter Carruthers*

In this chapter we argue that pretense is a form of embodied imagination. We also examine what pretense is for (both proximally and distally). In doing so we consider whether nonhuman animals who have the requisite imaginative abilities likewise engage in pretense. We suggest that pretense in humans may be an adaptation to encourage and develop adult forms of creativity.

## 1 What is pretense?

Pretend play (sometimes called "symbolic play") is early to develop and universal among humans (Haight et al. 1999). Around the middle of the second year of life all typically developing children start to pretend that one thing is another. They pretend that a banana is a telephone, for example, and act accordingly; or they pretend that they themselves are Superman, and rush around the room wearing a cape – and so on. In Section 3 we will consider whether such behavior is not only *universal* to humans, but *unique* to humans. At the very least it can be said that human children are unique in the extent and variety of their pretend play. In the present section we attempt to characterize what pretense itself *is*.

If one is to pretend that one thing is another, then of course one should not *believe* that it *is* the other. This is what distinguishes pretense from delusion. Someone who rushes around wearing a cape because he believes he *is* Superman is not pretending, but delusional. One might propose, then, that *pretense that P* is behavior *as if P*, or behavior that *resembles* the behavior of someone who believes *P*, but where the agent does *not* believe that *P*.

One thing this proposal gets right is that it characterizes pretense as embodied. In our view, you cannot pretend without overtly doing anything. Someone who is imagining hiking in the Smoky Mountains purely internally (without her bodily actions making any contribution to the imaginative episode) is indeed *imagining* hiking or *supposing* that she is in the Smoky Mountains; but she is not *pretending* to be there. However, it is not necessary that one actually moves one's body to pretend; it may suffice to adopt a certain bodily posture. Someone who is pretending may hold her body perfectly still, such as the child who pretends to be a dead cat (see Nichols and Stich 2003). Sometimes exhausted parents will initiate a game for their children by saying, "Let's pretend to be sleeping lions." Presumably the motionless children *are* pretending to be sleeping lions (until they actually – and mercifully – fall asleep).

Accounts of pretense as *behavior as if P in the absence of a belief that P* or *behavior that resembles P in the absence of a belief that P* are too simple, however (Friedman et al. 2010). The bodily actions and postures of a person pretending *X* do not need to *resemble* the bodily actions of someone doing *X*. A child who enacts a family dinner scene with dolls is not moving her body as she would if *she* were eating dinner. She is using her body to manipulate external symbols of her imaginings. Someone playing a game of Risk may (or may not) be imagining that she is directing battles so as to conquer the world. Her body movements are not similar to an actual general directing battles. Yet, while imagining directing a battle, she may use her body to pretend that one object (a game piece) is another (an army).

Moreover, consider two fencers who often spar with one another competitively. Although their behavior resembles that of two pirates fighting, and although they do not believe that they are pirates, they are not pretending to be pirates fighting. Nor, in our view, are they pretending to do or to be anything else. Rather, they are participating in a sport that has rules and constraints, as well as criteria for what constitutes winning. Each is trying to contact the other's torso with her foil, while attempting to avoid being similarly contacted by the other's foil. This point generalizes. There are many sports and games that resemble another activity, yet are not games of pretense. Someone playing a tennis videogame might be swiping the controller in a movement that roughly resembles forehands and backhands. However, she may or may not be pretending to play an actual game of tennis. Such a person may just be trying to win the videogame. Her focus is not on imagining a game of tennis, but on gaining points.

In fact, the very same behavior might constitute pretense on one occasion but not on another (in both cases in the absence of belief). For example, our two fencers might go through the very same sequence of motions while they *are* pretending to be pirates. Imagine them attending a child's birthday party and being begged by one of the children, "Please Aunt Joan and Aunt Jill, pretend to be pirates." When they pick up their foils and begin to spar, *then* they are (probably) pretending (unless they forget their intended roles in the heat of a familiar form of competition). They may be pretending even if an observer with no knowledge of the context would be unable to distinguish their behavior from that involved in one of their regular, unpretended, sparring sessions.

What is distinctive of pretending that *P*, in contrast with merely acting as if *P*, we suggest, is that the agent *represents* what she is doing *as* an action or as symbolic of an action of the sort *P* (while not believing that *P* is true, of course). Someone who is sparring with a partner while pretending to be a pirate represents her movements *as* the actions of one pirate fighting another. Often this might result in forms of behavior that would distinguish it from a regular bout of fencing, as when she yells, "Take that you scurvy dog!" or, "I've got you now Captain Hook!" But it need not do so. It is enough that the person *supposes* herself to be a pirate while fighting, or *imagines* herself as a pirate while fighting.

Notice, however, that someone can pretend that *P* while representing only some aspects of her behavior as being of the kind *P*, and without attempting to replicate all aspects of the behavior appropriate for *P*. Aunt Jill's mental representation of herself as pirate, as well as her pretense behavior, might be very different from that of a real pirate: she might make overly dramatic flourishes, for example, and she might joshingly pretend to fight off a vicious goldfish that has leaped aboard her ship. Moreover, pretense can vary in richness and degree depending on the amount of detail present in the accompanying mental representations. At the birthday party, Aunt Jill and Aunt Joan may not devote as much of their working memory to representing themselves as pirates as do their nieces Mia and Madison when they pick up sticks and begin to spar. The aunts may be more occupied with the task of entertaining the children, and may fail to represent themselves as being on the deck of a sailing ship, for example.

In what sense is *imagination* involved in pretense, on this account? Imagination is a form of non-truth-directed thought. While one can, of course, imagine something in an attempt to get it right, this will be a distal use of imagination, not constitutive of the activity of imagining itself. Put differently: in imagining something, one is not thereby committed to the truth of what one imagines. (This distinguishes imagination from belief and episodic memory.) To imagine something, then, is to entertain a representation of an event or state of affairs without believing that it exists. Sometimes these representations are produced creatively, as when one notices a roll of duct tape and imagines a novel use for it: to replace the binding on one's favorite book. Sometimes the content of what one imagines is given by features of the context, as when one is asked whether one would rather go to the museum or go hiking, and imagines and responds affectively to each before reaching a decision. (Here we see one of the central uses of imagination, in so-called *prospection* of the future; see Damasio 1994; Gendler and Kovakovich 2005; Gilbert and Wilson 2007.) At yet other times one allows the content of what one imagines to be given to one by others, as when watching a movie or reading a novel.

We take a broad view of what constitutes imagination in this chapter. First, we will not distinguish between imagination and supposition (contra Gendler 2000 and Weinberg and Meskin 2006). On our view, imagination may involve the generation of mental imagery, or it may mean the entertaining of a proposition. Someone may create a mental image of a unicorn, or simply entertain the proposition (without believing it) that *there is a unicorn*: in both cases, the person imagines a unicorn. Similarly, we do not insist that imagination, as such, requires one to entertain imaginative representations of possible experiences. In some cases, of course, one's imaginings include representations of experience. One might imagine that one is listening to Beethoven's Ninth Symphony, that one is flying, or that one is a football player who is leaping to catch a long pass in the end zone. In these cases one represents sequences of auditory, visual, or proprioceptive experience respectively. However, the content of what one imagines need not be related to experiences at all. For example, one might merely imagine that Santa Claus exists, without also imagining that one perceives him or is interacting with him. (Currie and Ravenscroft [2002] call this *belief-like imagining*.)

What distinguishes imagining from states such as intending, wanting, hoping, and dreading, however? For in these latter cases, too, one might generate and entertain a representation of a nonactual state of affairs while believing that it does not (yet) exist. If one wants to go hiking or decides to go hiking, then one has a representation of oneself as hiking without believing that one is. In fact standing-state – or stored – intentions, desires, and other such states are easy to distinguish from acts of imagination. For imaginings are *events* that occupy specific periods of time, whereas stored intentions and desires are *states*. It is only when these states are activated that they *become* events involving a representation of something nonexistent. One may have a nonoccurrent desire or intention, of course; it makes much less sense to say one has a nonoccurrent imagining.

Another difference between imaginings and states such as intention or desire is the role each plays in motivation. Intentions, desires, and hopes are intimately bound with motivation. They are apt to get one to do the things represented, or to bring about the states of affairs represented, or to avoid those states of affairs. Even if a given hope (say) does not actually motivate behavior, one likely considers and rejects doing things that bring about the hoped-for state of affairs. One might hope to be rolling in money but decide for other reasons not to buy a lottery ticket. In the case of dread, one may take steps to avoid the state of affairs that one fears. Such states are intrinsically motivating. Imaginings, however, can be motivationally neutral, or they may motivate attractively or repulsively depending on our emotional response to them. What starts as just an imagining of oneself on a Caribbean beach may swiftly turn into a desire to be there. And imaginings can *cause* novel desires, intentions, or beliefs, of course. When one prospectively imagines the alternatives of a museum visit or a hike, one's affective reactions to those representations may issue in both a desire and subsequent intention to go hiking.

Returning now to the question of the relationship between pretense and imagination, we suggest that to pretend that *P* is to act as if *P* (without believing it) *while imagining that P*. A child who pretends that the banana is a telephone needs to suppose that the banana is a telephone, or to imagine the banana *as* a telephone, and act accordingly. While acting (making dialing movements, saying things that would initiate a conversation with the person dialed) the child acts within the scope of the initial supposition. This means that she represents her actions *as* the actions of someone who dials a number and then starts a conversation when the call is answered. Similarly, someone pretending to be a pirate represents the actions in which she is engaged *as* those of a pirate.

Pretending, then, is a kind of embodied imagination. (Currie and Ravenscroft [2002], in contrast, regard imagining and pretending as excluding one another. We mention further alternatives below.) Indeed, when pretending one performs an action of one sort (holding a banana to one's ear, say) not only *while* imagining it as an action of a different sort (talking on a telephone), but *because* one does so. For this reason we think that pretending only lasts for as long as imagination actively guides one's movements. Thus a child might set out on Halloween night not only dressed as a witch but pretending to be a witch. Yet as she walks around the neighborhood chatting with her friends, she may no longer be imagining herself as a witch. In that case, although she is dressed as a witch she is not pretending to be a witch. She is just a child dressed as a witch who is talking with friends. And this remains true even if at some point she forms an image of a witch riding a broomstick, provided this does not guide her own behavior.

If to pretend that *P* is to act as if *P* while guided by one's imagining that *P*, then an important question to consider is what sets the *limits* of pretense? Someone pretending that *P* does not generally act *entirely* as if *P* were true. Children pretending to make (mud) pies do not normally eat them. And someone pretending to be Superman will not normally leap from the balcony of a third-floor apartment. So what is it that determines where pretending ends and reality begins? One possibility is that the limits of pretense are set by one's real countervailing motivations. Because children generally understand that mud does not taste nice, they stop short of actually eating the pies. And because one does not want to suffer severe injury one usually does not actually attempt to fly.

This account of the limits of pretense is entirely first order in character (Nichols and Stich 2003). That is, it does not require the mental states involved in pretense to be meta-represresentational ones. A child, on this account, might be motivated to act as Superman does (see our discussion in Section 2), but also be motivated to avoid injury. These two motivations battle it out between themselves, and the child behaves accordingly (generally by limiting the pretense; but note that children sometimes *do* eat their pretend creations and sometimes *do* jump from high places, occasionally with tragic consequences). An alternative account, however, is that children are aware *that* they are only pretending (Leslie 1987), and are thus aware of the difference between imagination and reality. This account is a meta-representational one, requiring that pretense is not merely action as if *P* guided by imagination of *P*, but is also action guided by one's meta-awareness that one is imagining or pretending.

Which account should we prefer? Each is possible. In particular, children's third-person understanding of pretense emerges at about the same age as their own pretense behavior begins (Onishi et al. 2007); so they have the conceptual resources for the metarepresentational account to be true. Yet on the other hand, the metarepresentational view makes pretense unique among attitudes. Children and nonhuman animals can want things without representing themselves *as* wanting them, and they can believe things without representing themselves *as* believing them. So why should pretense be any different? Why should pretense, and only pretense, require metarepresentational awareness of the presence of that attitude? It might be replied that on our account a child pretending to be Superman must be aware that he is behaving *as* Superman, while of course believing that he is not. This comes quite close, at least, to saying that he must be aware of pretending to be Superman. Whatever might be true of the essence of pretense, what is surely true is that children are, as a matter of fact, often aware that they are pretending while they pretend. So a metarepresentational account of the limits of pretense is at least likely to be partly correct.

## 2 The proximal function of pretense

Why do people (primarily but by no means exclusively children) pretend? The question can be interpreted proximally (as one about motivations) or distally (as a question about adaptive or evolutionary function). We will address the distal version of the question in Section 4. Here we focus on the question of motives.

There are probably a multitude of ways in which pretense can be experienced as rewarding or enjoyable. Children often pretend to do or to be things they find intrinsically desirable or admirable. If one admires Superman and thinks it would be wonderful to fly through the air, then when one pretends to be Superman one will represent oneself as someone admirable doing something wonderful. But this is unlikely to constitute a full explanation. For example, we rather doubt that the child pretending to be a dead cat is doing it because she thinks dead cats are admirable or that it is desirable to be a dead cat. In this case the motivations might be social, however. The child pretends something with the goal that it should be found amusing by others. Moreover, when children engage in *joint* pretense, the rewards might derive in part from the mere fact of doing something jointly with another person. For children (and adults) appear to find joint attention and joint action intrinsically rewarding (Tomasello et al. 2005).

Beyond all this, however, we think that the mere fact of imagining something is intrinsically rewarding. As one of us has argued elsewhere (Picciuto 2009), people don't only enjoy imagining things that would make them happy if true. They also enjoy imagining things that they wouldn't want to be actual: that they are being eaten by monsters, that they are vicious bad guys, that they are throwing up, that they are dangling by a rope above a pit full of snakes. Children's pretense is full of blood and guts and pain; it can be variously disgusting and scary and sad. The same is true of adult imagining in fiction and film. It seems that imagining provides rewards regardless of the representational content of the imagining.

These points about the rewards of imagination issue in a puzzle for the account of pretend play outlined in Section 1, however. For if the rewards of pretending derive from those of imagining, why do children bother to pretend at all? Why do they perform any overt pretend activities? Why not just imagine the same things in their heads, thereby deriving the same enjoyment? One might think that a partial solution to this puzzle would involve noting that *social* pretense is an intrinsically overt activity. It might be said that one cannot share an imaginative episode with someone unless that episode is externalized somehow, either in storytelling or in pretense. But on reflection this may merely beg the question at issue. For one can of course *imagine* that one is engaging in a shared activity with someone else. If the rewards derive from the imagining, then why should it matter whether one is *really* sharing an activity with someone?

Our answer to this puzzle is one that simultaneously explains why pretense tends only to be seen in children or among those who are interacting with children. Children's immature executive functions and limited working memory capacities mean that they are incapable of sustaining rich imaginative representations purely internally. The executive demands of covert imagination are generally much greater than those involved in pretense. For in the case of the latter, most of the representational burden can be offloaded onto perception of one's own actions. So the representations don't need to be endogenously generated and sustained, as they would have to be if they were created purely internally. Once a decision has been taken to imagine being Superman, if one's imagination takes the form of pretending then one merely has to impose the content *this is me being Superman* on one's perception of the actions that one undertakes as a result. If one were to imagine being Superman without pretending, in contrast, then one would also have to construct an extended sequence of images for oneself, roughly corresponding to the content of those perceptions. (Adults do still frequently offload the representational burdens of imagining by engaging in fictions, of course. It may be that adults, even with their greater capacity for working memory, still appreciate the representational assistance offered by fiction, while not requiring the more substantial representational work provided by the body when pretending.)

## 3 Do animals pretend?

We know that many animals not only *have* imagination, but make adaptive use of it. For example, both corvids (rooks, crows, jays, and the like) and chimpanzees can engage in prospective reasoning of a sort similar to that used by humans, imaginatively representing potential actions and formulating plans or reaching decisions as a result. (See Carruthers 2015 for review and discussion. See also Chapter 24 of this volume.) If humans are nevertheless unique in engaging in pretend play, then this would set up another puzzle. For pretending, as we have just seen, makes imagining easier, not harder. The question of the evolutionary function of pretense will be taken up in Section 4. Here we focus on the question whether nonhuman animals actually engage in pretense.

Many animals engage in forms of rough-and-tumble play, or else play that seems designed to mimic adult mating or hunting behavior. Think here of lambs butting heads in the spring, of puppies play fighting, and of a kitten stalking and pouncing on a piece of string. The question is whether the lambs are pretending to be males competing for mates in the rutting season, whether the puppies are pretending to fight for dominance in the pack, and whether the kitten is pretending to hunt and kill prey.

One thing that can be said in light of our earlier discussion is that if animals are to pretend to do these things, then they must possess the corresponding concepts. (Indeed, if Leslie's metarepresentational account of pretense is true, then they must possess not just concepts, but the concept *pretense* itself.) In order to pretend to do or to be something, one must have the concept of that action or kind. One can't pretend to be Superman without having the concept *Superman*, and one can't pretend to be a pirate without having the concept *pirate*. This result provides an obvious opening for those wanting to deny pretend play to animals, since many philosophers deny that animals have concepts at all (Dummett 1991; Brandom 1994; McDowell 1994; Bermúdez 2003; Hurley 2006). Their grounds for doing so, however, are that the putative concepts of animals don't satisfy the so-called *generality constraint*, which is said to be a constraint on genuine concept possession (Evans 1982). The generality constraint states that any concept that one possesses should be capable of combining together with any other concept that one possesses (of appropriate adicity) to constitute a new thought. Since it is assumed (very plausibly) that animals are *not* capable of fully recombinatorial thought, it then follows that they lack concepts altogether. And if they lack concepts, then they must be incapable of pretend play. Or so it might be claimed.

One of us has argued elsewhere, however, that the generality constraint is *not* an appropriate constraint on genuine concept possession (Carruthers 2009). What *is* essential to concepts is that they should be capable of recombining with *some* other concepts of appropriate adicity to constitute novel thoughts. For it is essential to concepts that they should be the building blocks of thought. But to insist that concepts must be capable of recombining with *all* other concepts is, in effect, to insist that genuine thinkers must be capable of *creative* thought. But this is not an appropriate constraint. Why should capacities for creative thought be made a necessary condition for capacities to think at all? Surely thinking is one thing, and creative thinking is quite another (while being much more demanding).

Moreover, even if we were to concede that animals don't possess genuine concepts, but only *proto*concepts (Dummett 1991), it is far from clear why seeing one's behavior in light of a protoconcept, and guiding it appropriately, should not be sufficient for pretense. Suppose we were to allow that cats have only a protoconcept of killing, not a real concept. Still, if a cat imagines itself as killing prey when leaping on and ripping apart a piece of string, why would this not qualify as a genuine instance of pretense? It would surely qualify as an instance of embodied imagination and that, we think, should be enough.

Since it appears to make no difference for our purposes whether animals have concepts or only protoconcepts, we propose to allow that they have the former. Whether they have the *right* concepts needed to turn instances of rough-and-tumble play into pretend play is another matter, however. For notice that lambs will butt their heads together although they have never seen adult males competing similarly. (Lambs are born in the spring, but the rut takes place in the fall.) And a kitten will pounce on a piece of string although it has been reared indoors and has never seen a hunt, and perhaps never even seen a mouse or a bird. It is possible, of course, that these animals have *innate* concepts of the relevant kinds. It may be that lambs are born with a concept of fighting for dominance. And it may be that kittens are born with the concepts *hunt* and *kill*.

It seems equally possible, however – and perhaps rather more plausible – that affordances in the environment (the presence of another lamb; a small moving object) should activate an innate motor plan, doing so in the absence of any of the concepts required to transform the activity into one of pretense. We know that this sort of thing is possible, since we know that in humans motor plans are activated by affordances in the environment. Thus the mere sight of a hammer will initiate a motor plan to grasp it, which needs to be suppressed by top-down signals if the action is not to be executed (Frith et al. 2000; Negri et al. 2007).

Can an account of animal play in terms of environmentally triggered motor plans explain why a kitten leaping on his brother does not *really* kill him (which is presumably what the motor plan in question is designed to do), but only wrestles with him? It can easily be extended to do so, provided the kitten feels some sort of bond of affection toward his brother. For we can then suppose that there is a conflicting motivation that blocks the full execution of the motor plan in question. We can say that although the behavioral program for killing is triggered by the presence of the brother, and is partially carried through, the kitten doesn't kill his brother because he doesn't want to hurt him.

Even if these suggestions are plausible, it is hard to establish definitively that the rough-and-tumble play of animals does not qualify as a form of pretense. What we *can* say with confidence, however, is that animals do not pretend *very much*. Specifically, the young of each species at best engage in one or two species-specific forms of pretense. Pretense in animals, if it occurs at all, is very narrowly circumscribed, confined to one or two activities, and presumably results from a domain-specific innate predisposition. This is in marked contrast to human children, whose pretense knows no limits. Children can (and do) pretend to perform familiar adult activities. But they also pretend to be birds or animals, as well as pretending that an object of one kind (a block of wood, say) is an object of another sort (a fire truck, for example). Even if pretend play is not unique to humans, routine engagement in domain-general forms of pretense certainly is. This is sufficient to set up the puzzle of the next section: why (for what evolutionary purpose) do children do it? The puzzle is especially pressing since many animals have the imaginative capacities required for pretense, as we noted at the outset of this section.

## 4 The distal function of pretense: creativity

We have suggested elsewhere that pretense is an adaptation that serves to enhance adult forms of creativity (Picciuto and Carruthers 2014). This idea provides a solution to the puzzle just noted, since humans are uniquely creative, and since creativity of various sorts plays such a large role in human culture and in the explanation of human adaptability.

We allow, of course, that pretense may be *multi*functional. A feature that is initially selected for one purpose can thereafter be sustained and/or shaped, in part, because it happens to have other adaptive effects. So it may be that pretense is not *just* for creativity. It may also be for mindreading (Harris 2005), for counterfactual thinking (Harris 2000), and perhaps for much else besides. However, one mark of an adaptation is a high degree of "fit" between structure and function. Pretend play seems "fitted" to enhance creativity, we suggest, in a way that it isn't especially fitted to enhance any of the other properties that have been proposed. Specifically, pretend play is domain general whereas many of the alternatives aren't. And pretend play is itself often creative in nature, whereas the others aren't. If one just needed to practice mindreading, or counterfactual thinking, or whatever, then one wouldn't need to engage in anything creative to do so.

Consider the suggestion that the function of pretense is to enhance mindreading (Harris 2005). While pretense *may* enhance mindreading, it seems unlikely that this is its primary function. First of all, while pretense behavior emerges in children when they are about 18 months old, there is increasing evidence that infants much younger than this, even those as young as 6 months old, can engage in mindreading (Baillargeon et al. 2010; Kovács et al. 2010; Carruthers 2013; Southgate and Vernetti 2014). Another reason to believe that the function of pretense is something other than enhanced mindreading is that the latter concerns just one domain. By contrast, as noted earlier, the pretend play of human children is very much a domain-general activity. One should expect that a domain-general activity would function to enhance a domain-general capacity rather than a domain-specific one.

Another alternative proposal is that pretense serves to rehearse children's social schemata, thus enhancing their understanding of social roles (Bogdan 2013). While pretense *can* be used in this way, there are several reasons why it is unlikely that this is pretense's primary function. Most importantly, much of children's pretense has nothing to do with social schemata. A child might pretend that a brick is a fire truck, that a lump of mud is a pie, that a stick is a sword, that she is a fairy sprinkling magic dust, or that she is a dead cat. None of these pretenses involve rehearsing a (useful) social schema. Moreover, children often entertain unlikely premises. And not only are the initial premises often unlikely, so are some of pretended consequences. Children might be fighting off snakes, then dragons, and are then forced to contend with an alien or a robot invasion. In addition, children's tendencies to adhere to social schemata in their pretense varies by culture. Children raised in Eastern cultures are more likely to pretend using social schemata while children raised in Western cultures are more likely to pretend fantastic events (Farver and Shin 1997; Haight et al. 1999). If the function of pretense were to enhance social schemata, then one might expect that children from all cultures would pretend social schemata for at least the majority of the time.

Our own proposal is that the function of pretense is to enhance domain-general forms of creativity. An initial puzzle for this idea, however, is to explain why *embodied* imagination (that is: pretense) should be needed. For imagination alone can be creative, and imagination alone could presumably serve to practice creative idea generation. In reply, recall that pretense off-loads most of the representational demands of imagining, which explains why children should start out their imaginative lives by pretending. We speculate that this enables children to begin practicing creative idea generation at significantly earlier ages than would otherwise be possible.

Creativity is generally taken to mean the process of creating thoughts, actions, or objects that are both novel and valuable. (See Chapter 13 of this volume.) In our view, creativity is not restricted to those thoughts, actions, and objects that are novel to *all* humans and valuable to *all* humans. Rather, creativity can involve products that are novel and valuable to the creator. This is what Boden calls *psychological creativity* as opposed to *historical creativity* (Boden 2004). For example, someone looking at a roll of duct tape and realizing for the first time that it could be used as a book binding is certainly not historically creative. She may, however, be psychologically creative if the thought is new to her and yields an outcome she values.

The most widely adopted account of creativity in the scientific literature is the so-called "Geneplore" model (Finke et al. 1992; Ward et al. 1999). On this view, creativity is a two-factor process: one generative and one exploratory (hence the name). In the first phase novel and unobvious ideas or hypotheses are produced. In the second phase, these products are explored and evaluated. Then the best or most apt idea is selected or implemented. We assume that this account is broadly correct.

Consistent with our view, pretend play – specifically imaginative pretend play at a given age – was found to correlate with creativity 4 years later (Russ et al. 1999). Moreover, when children are given play opportunities, as opposed to repetitive copying, this boosts their subsequent creativity in unrelated domains when tested a few minutes later (Howard-Jones et al. 2002). In addition, it turns out that people with autism, who show a marked absence of pretend play in infancy, are also less creative than typical people in adulthood (as well as having well-known mindreading deficits). People with autism are less generative overall, while also producing less novelty and showing less imagination (Craig and Baron-Cohen 1999). These findings are just what one might predict if the function of pretend play were (at least in part) to enhance the generative component of creativity. For pretense, as we have seen, involves producing imaginings and enacting them. The fact that it is specifically imaginative pretend play that correlates with creativity gives this idea some weight. But of course what are really needed, at this point, are longitudinal correlation studies and (perhaps unethical) longitudinal interventions to demonstrate the long-term impact of pretend play in childhood.

One problem with our proposal, however, is that not all pretense is particularly creative. Sometimes children return again and again to the same pretend scenarios. How would this enhance creativity? In reply it can be said that mundane forms of pretense are consistent with the proposed function, provided that children engage in them for other reasons: perhaps to achieve a sense of familiarity and security, or because their enjoyment of a specific imaginative episode is so great. Moreover, even if mundane pretense does not enhance the generative component of creativity, it may enhance other aspects of creativity, as we note below. For example, even mundane pretense requires the child to suppress routine, obvious, or reality-based responses.

Another problem is that, while we have argued that pretense is a form of embodied imagination, not all creativity seems to involve imagination. For example, there are instances of spontaneous musical, athletic, and other sorts of improvisation that seem clearly creative, yet don't involve generating imaginings of what the products could be like before evaluating and enacting them. On the contrary, these improvisations happen online and "in the moment." One possibility is that pretense may function to develop and enhance cognitive forms of creativity specifically, rather than creativity more generally. But in fact we think that there is still a large degree of structure–function match even with online forms of creativity. Thus pretense may exercise and develop other mental capacities required for creativity besides the generative aspect of imagining.

What pretense has in common with creativity of all kinds, including musical and athletic improvisation, is that an obvious option or response is bypassed, and instead an unobvious option or response is selected. If a child looking at a banana is to pretend that the banana is a telephone, then she must bypass the obvious response: her sensory systems will all be informing her that what she is looking at is a banana. Instead, she must suppress the obvious tendency to see the object as a banana, and select the option of seeing it as a telephone instead. Likewise a jazz improviser needs to bypass the obvious – familiar or expected – continuation of a musical phrase while selecting something more surprising.

Consistent with these ideas, it seems that creative cognition is distinguished by a kind of defocused attention combined with cognitive control (Bristol and Viskontas 2006; Christoff et al. 2007), combining together aspects of focused problem-solving (cognitive control) with unguided thinking (or "mind-wandering"). To be creative one has to allow oneself to attend more widely, permitting alternative ideas or behaviors to "bubble up" and be selected, but at the same time one has to bypass more obvious ideas and behavior, maintaining focus while alternative possibilities are explored and evaluated. We suggest that part of the function of pretense is to foster the availability and selection of unobvious representations in adulthood, thereby supporting creativity. Consistent with this suggestion, it has been found that high levels of creative achievement among adults are linked with low levels of what psychologists call "latent inhibition" (Peterson et al. 2002; Carson et al. 2003), meaning that they tend to distribute their attention more widely, and maintain a range of activated representations that aren't obviously relevant to the task in hand.

Moreover, pretense (even mundane pretense), like creativity, often involves a capacity for sustained focus while working within the scope of an initial supposition. Pretending generally takes time, as well as involving a number of intermediate stages. During that time the child needs to keep in mind the relevant pretend suppositions, and needs to maintain her focus while the pretense is acted out. In addition, she often needs to do so while new suppositions are introduced, thereby elaborating the pretend episode. It may thus be part of the function of pretense to enhance people's capacity to focus on a novel idea or activity while it is being explored, evaluated, or implemented.

## 5 Conclusion

We have suggested that pretend play is a form of embodied imagination. The embodied aspect helps children to maintain both their focus on, and the intensity of, their imaginings. Human children may be the only creatures to engage in pretend play, and they are certainly unique in the range and domain-generality of their pretense. And of course humans (both children and adults) are the only creatures to exhibit significant amounts of creativity across multiple domains. We have thus suggested that an intrinsic motivation to engage in pretense is an innately channeled disposition that is designed to enhance adult creativity. Pretense not only encourages the generation of new ideas, but also enhances other capacities that are necessary to creativity, such as suppressing obvious responses while selecting and developing unobvious ones.

## Further reading

G. Currie and I. Ravenscroft, *Recreative Minds: Imagination in Philosophy and Psychology* (New York: Oxford University Press, 2002) is an insightful and wide-ranging discussion of imagination and its role in human cognition. P. Harris, *The Work of the Imagination* (New York: Blackwell, 2000) contains innovative research on pretense in children, and an argument for its function in developing rationality. The second chapter of S. Nichols and S. Stich, *Mindreading* (New York: Oxford University Press, 2003) outlines a theory of the cognitive architecture underlying pretense. K. Walton, *Mimesis as Make-Believe: On the Foundations of the Representational Arts* (Cambridge, MA: Harvard University Press, 1990) is a wide-ranging and influential discussion connecting children's pretend play and make-believe with representational art.

## References


Baillargeon, R., R. Scott, and Z. He (2010) "False-Belief Understanding in Infants," *Trends in Cognitive Sciences* 14: 110–118.

Bermúdez, J. (2003) *Thinking without Words*, Oxford: Oxford University Press.

Boden, M. (2004) *The Creative Mind*, 2nd edn., London: Routledge.

Bogdan, R. (2013) *Mindvaults*, Cambridge, MA: MIT Press.

Brandom, R. (1994) *Making It Explicit*, Cambridge, MA: Harvard University Press.

Bristol, A., and I. Viskontas (2006) "Dynamic Processes within Associative Memory Stores: Piecing together the Neural Basis of Creative Cognition," in J. Kaufman and J. Baer (eds.) *Creativity and Reason in Cognitive Development*, New York: Cambridge University Press.

Carruthers, P. (2009) "Invertebrate Concepts Confront the Generality Constraint (and Win)," in R. Lurz (ed.) *The Philosophy of Animal Minds*, New York: Cambridge University Press.

Carruthers, P. (2013) "Mindreading in Infancy," *Mind & Language* 28: 141–172.

Carruthers, P. (2015) *The Centered Mind: What the Science of Working Memory Shows Us about the Nature of Human Thought*, Oxford: Oxford University Press.

Carson, S., J. Peterson, and D. Higgins (2003) "Decreased Latent Inhibition Is Associated with Increased Creative Achievement in High-Functioning Individuals," *Journal of Personality and Social Psychology* 85: 499–506.

Christoff, K., A. Gordon, and R. Smith (2007) "The Role of Spontaneous Thought in Human Cognition," in O. Vartanian and D. Mandel (eds.) *Neuroscience of Decision Making*, New York: Psychology Press.

Craig, J., and S. Baron-Cohen (1999) "Creativity and Imagination in Autism," *Journal of Autism and Developmental Disorders* 29: 319–326.

Currie, G., and I. Ravenscroft (2002) *Recreative Minds: Imagination in Philosophy and Psychology*, Oxford: Oxford University Press.

Damasio, A. (1994) *Descartes' Error*, London: Papermac.

Dummett, M. (1991) *Frege and Other Philosophers*, Oxford: Oxford University Press.

Evans, G. (1982) *The Varieties of Reference*, Oxford: Oxford University Press.

Farver, J., and Y. Shin (1997) "Social Pretend Play in Korean- and Anglo-American Preschoolers," *Child Development* 68: 544–556.

Finke, R., T. Ward, and S. Smith (1992) *Creative Cognition*, Cambridge, MA: MIT Press.

Friedman, O., K. Neary, C. Burstein, and A. Leslie (2010) "Is Young Children's Recognition of Pretense Metarepresentational or Merely Behavioral?" *Cognition* 115: 314–319.

Frith, C., S.-J. Blakemore, and D. Wolpert (2000) "Abnormalities in the Awareness and Control of Action," *Philosophical Transactions of the Royal Society of London B: Biological Sciences* 355: 1771–1788.

Gendler, T.S. (2000) "The Puzzle of Imaginative Resistance," *Journal of Philosophy* 97: 55–81.

Gendler, T.S., and K. Kovakovich (2005) "Genuine Rational Fictional Emotions," in M.L. Kieran (ed.) *Contemporary Debates in Aesthetics and the Philosophy of Art*, Oxford: Blackwell, 241–253.

Gilbert, D., and T. Wilson (2007) "Prospection: Experiencing the Future," *Science* 317: 1351–1354.
Haight, W., X. Wang, H. Fung, K. Williams, and J. Mintz (1999) "Universal, Developmental, and Variable Aspects of Young Children's Play: A Cross-Cultural Comparison of Pretending at Home," *Child Development* 70: 1477–1488.
Harris, P. (2000) *The Work of the Imagination*, Oxford: Blackwell Publishing.
Harris, P. (2005) "Conversation, Pretense, and Theory of Mind," in J. Astington and J. Baird (eds.) *Why Language Matters for Theory of Mind*, New York: Oxford University Press.
Howard-Jones, P., J. Taylor, and L. Sutton (2002) "The Effect of Play on the Creativity of Young Children during Subsequent Activity," *Early Child Development* 172: 323–332.
Hurley, S. (2006) "Making Sense of Animals," in S. Hurley and M. Nudds (eds.) *Rational Animals?* Oxford: Oxford University Press.
Kovács, Á., E. Téglás, and A. Endress (2010) "The Social Sense: Susceptibility to Others' Beliefs in Human Infants and Adults," *Science* 330: 1830–1834.
Leslie, A. (1987) "Pretense and Representation," *Psychological Review* 94: 412–426.
McDowell, J. (1994) *Mind and World*, Cambridge, MA: Harvard University Press.
Negri, G., R. Rumiati, A. Zadini, M. Ukmar, B. Mahon, and A. Caramazza (2007) "What Is the Role of Motor Simulation in Action and Object Recognition? Evidence from Apraxia," *Cognitive Neuropsychology* 24: 795–816.
Nichols, S., and S. Stich (2003) *Mindreading: An Integrated Account of Pretence, Self-Awareness, and Understanding Other Minds*, Oxford: Oxford University Press.
Onishi, K., R. Baillargeon, and A. Leslie (2007) "15-Month-Old Infants Detect Violations in Pretend Scenarios," *Acta Psychologica* 124: 106–128.
Peterson, J., K. Smith, and S. Carson (2002) "Openness and Extraversion are Associated with Reduced Latent Inhibition: Replication and Commentary," *Personality and Individual Differences* 33: 1137–1147.
Picciuto, E. (2009) "The Pleasures of Suppositions," *Philosophical Psychology* 22: 487–503.
Picciuto, E., and P. Carruthers (2014) "The Origins of Creativity," in E. Paul and S. Kaufman (eds.) *The Philosophy of Creativity*, Oxford: Oxford University Press.
Russ, S., A. Robins, and B. Christiano (1999) "Pretend Play: Longitudinal Prediction of Creativity and Affect in Fantasy in Children," *Creativity Research Journal* 12: 129–139.
Southgate, V., and A. Vernetti (2014) "Belief-Based Action Prediction in Preverbal Infants," *Cognition* 130: 1–10.
Tomasello, M., M. Carpenter, J. Call, T. Behne, and H. Moll (2005) "Understanding and Sharing Intentions: The Origins of Cultural Cognition," *Behavioral and Brain Sciences* 28: 675–691.
Ward, T., S. Smith, and R. Finke (1999) "Creative Cognition," in R. Sternberg (ed.) *Handbook of Creativity*, Cambridge: Cambridge University Press.
Weinberg, J.M., and A. Meskin (2006) "Puzzling over the Imagination: Philosophical Problems, Architectural Solutions," in S. Nichols (ed.) *Architecture of the Imagination: New Essays on Pretence, Possibility, and Fiction*, New York: Oxford University Press.

# 24
# CAN ANIMALS IMAGINE?

*Robert W. Mitchell*

Can humans imagine? Here the answer seems obviously "yes." Can nonhuman animals imagine? Here the answer seems considerably less obvious. It matters not only which nonhuman animals (hereafter, 'animals') we're talking about, but also what we mean by imagination. This essay addresses this question by exploring psychological studies within a philosophical context.

In this essay, "imagination requires that an organism has an idea which it seeks to examine in its actions or mind" (Mitchell 2002, 4; see also Strawson 1970, 54; Bogdan 2005). Imagination is thus an exploration of mental states or action; this exploration can occur as mental states happen (e.g., daydreaming) or while engaging in actions (e.g., pretending, thinking). In this essay, I explore animals' capacity for imagination along three dimensions: having mental images, seeing (or otherwise perceiving) something *as* something else or otherwise pretending, and being creative (see, e.g., Strawson 1970).

## Mental imagery

Mental images are quasi-perceptual experiences. In quality they are similar to, but are not, perceptions. Such images seem to occur as part of conscious experiences, and the experiencer is typically aware of the image as nonperceptual, i.e., as not providing information about the current state of affairs. Mental images can be outside our control, as in dreams, or they can be manipulable, as suggested for problem-solving (see Thomas 2014). Visual images, e.g., can range from mechanical responses in perception, like afterimages, to static phenomena like simple photograph-like images, to active phenomena like dreams, to even more active ones, in the sense of intentionally created images (see Thomas 2014). Although generally my concern here is with active imagery, in a few cases (insects) I discuss more static imagery.

Images can be from a first- or third-person perspective (Libby et al. 2009). Casey (1976/2000) posits that imagination is either imagining *that* something is the case (third person) or imagining *how* to do something (first person), and that either type can proceed with or without perception-like mental images ("sensuous" experiences). When imagination occurs without mental images, what is imagined is simply postulated to be so (e.g., I may imagine that I am traveling in a car without visualizing the car). In the sensuous variants, third-person imagining that something is the case usually entails examining or employing a visual image or listening to auditory images, whereas first-person imagining how to do something usually entails a mix of kinesthetic and visual imagery experiences (e.g., imagining tying one's shoelaces) or auditory imagery in self-talk (e.g., "I am looping the left lace around the right lace"). Third-person imagining might be helpful in thinking about how someone else might have done something, or translating that visually imagined action into kinesthetically experienced bodily action (Mitchell 2012). In both first- and third-person sensuous images, imaginers engage in *perceiving* or *experiencing* something *as* something else. In nonsensuous variants of imagining that or imagining how, organisms simply accept something as true or explore it without imagery at all. This type of imagining can also be the background for imagistic thoughts; as Reisberg and Heuer (2005, 53) state, images can serve as "hybrid representations" that have both "depictive and descriptive aspects."

In humans, visual mental images usually do not exactly replicate perceptual experiences. In contrast, auditory images are more likely to be exact replications – we sometimes have trouble distinguishing actual words from inner speech, sometimes wonder if we said aloud what (we hoped) we said only to ourselves (Strawson 1954, 53). Musicians can have quite extensive and accurate auditory imagery for music (Sills 2005).

Often, when used in animal problem-solving contexts, 'imagination' is shorthand for some process presumed to either involve or do the work of mental images (Hobhouse 1901). Honeybees, e.g., designate to other bees in their hive, by moving their bodies in a "waggle dance," the location of food they have discovered so that the other bees can get to the food. Gould (1990, 100) placed food in an unlikely place – the middle of a lake – and posited that hive bees told by the dancing bees that food is available there may "imagine" (in quotes in the original) the location of the food. If what they've imagined is judged to be implausible when compared to their "cognitive map" of the locations, as would the middle of a lake, they will reject the location. (Cognitive maps are mental images of significant landmarks in relation to a goal that organisms use to guide their actions.) In support of this hypothesis about the bees' use of imagination, researchers noted that no bees arrived at the lake-center location but many bees arrived at an equidistant (plausible) location in the forest. Upon replication (Wray et al. 2008), however, bees informed about an implausible, lake-center location were just as likely to go there as bees informed about an equally distant, plausible, land-based location, suggesting that the bees did not assess their imagined cognitive map of their surrounding, if they had one.

Some background is necessary to discuss imagery further. First, imagery depends on and derives from perception. Second, images come with their interpretation attached, such that they are difficult to reinterpret, whereas perceptions are more easily reinterpreted. A consequence is that it is easier to solve novel problems by transforming one's perception of the situation than by reenvisioning one's imagery of the situation; another consequence is that when all the perceptual aspects of a novel problem are available, conscious manipulation of mental images is not likely to be used to solve the problem. Third, active imagery is often a part of the initial development of complicated actions, but as skills develop, imagery diminishes (James 1890). Similarly, actions repeated daily (e.g.) can be done without consciousness. Fourth, mental imagery is typically experienced at some level of consciousness, even if only by being attended to. (There may be scope for "unconscious" imagery in the form of activated schemas.)

### Mental imagery and perception

Mental images depend on our perceptual modalities. Our inner experiences are easily described by comparison with our perceptions (Strawson 1954, 53) precisely because of this dependence. We can have visual, auditory, tactile, kinesthetic, olfactory and gustatory images, if we have experienced the congruent perceptions (see Lacey and Lawson 2013). Images in humans occur with activation of perceptual (or perception-related) areas of the brain, with visual areas activated by visual images, etc. (Finke 1986; see also Markman et al. 2009). Thus, it seems plausible that the same is true for nonhuman animals: if they have mental images, then these are similar, at least in some aspects, to their perceptions (Mitchell 2013).

Humans can have spatial imagery devoid of vision-like content, as discovered in blind people and people whose visual brain areas have been destroyed, though such imagery likely derives from perceptual experience of space (Reisberg and Heuer 2005, 58–59). For normal, sighted people, there is extensive, but not complete, overlap between areas of the brain involved in vision and imagery. In some cases, the nonoverlapping brain areas may produce spatial imagery that is not visual. For animals, we are as yet unaware as to whether images must necessarily be formed when these activations occur, though it seems likely that they are. We also do not know which perceptual aspects are experienced in animal imagery: e.g., we cannot tell if animals experience visual imagery, or spatial imagery without visual imagery, or both together or in sequence.

Almost no one doubts that mammals and birds have imagery of some sort, as in dreams (McNamara et al. 2007), and scientists posit the existence of imagery to explain these and other animals' behavior. For example, when leaving their nest, ants, bees and wasps stop to look at it, then move on, then stop to look, then move on, in an iterative process. Current theory is that they are doing something comparable to taking snapshots which they then use, as they return to their environment, to find their way back (Gould 1990; Wehner and Menzel 1990; Durier et al. 2003). This form of imagery seems mechanistic, but other forms attributed to animals are less automatic.

## *Insight*

Insight is a form of planning originally defined by Köhler (1925/1976, 190; italics removed) in his studies of great ape tool use as "the appearance of a complete solution with reference to the whole lay-out of the field." In insight tasks, subjects are "brought … into situations in which all essential conditions were actually visible, and the solution could be achieved immediately" (Köhler 1925/1976, 266), though it can take some time for subjects to figure out the solution. In Köhler's view, insight occurs through a reinterpretation of perceptual information, likely without conscious manipulation of mental imagery. Köhler likens insight to seeing something as something else, though other researchers present insight as evidence of mental imagery.

Insight was present when ravens solved a novel problem, obtaining a piece of frozen meat. The meat was attached to a string, and was only attainable by pulling up the string. After trying other methods, they succeeded by pulling up and holding the string iteratively. According to Heinrich and Bugnyar (2007, 66, 67), the ravens' insight required manipulation of mental images: these ravens "have the ability to test actions in their minds and project outcomes of these actions"; to solve the problem, they "imagined possibilities and figured out what steps to take." Heinrich and Bugnyar hypothesize that the ravens imagined themselves performing actions, via mental images, and then performed the actions that worked in their imagined scenarios.

It's here worth noting that the evidence provided to support this conclusion – that the ravens' actions are not instinctual, that they occurred soon after elaborate observation and inadequate responses, and that they resulted from neither prior experience with the problem nor trial and error – is rather limited. (Other excellent problem-solvers, chimpanzees and orangutans, also engage in extensive observation: Köhler 1925/1976; Russon and Galdikas 1995.) In fact, the postulation of mental imagery seems unnecessary as the solution was entirely observable to the ravens as it ensued: they pulled up the string, held it down and did this repeatedly until the food was available; they could see what they were doing as they were doing it. The ravens showed insight, but the perceptual availability of the problem domain means that they could have achieved this insight without mental imagery. Köhler's emphasis that insight occurs with the perceptual availability of everything needed to solve a problem suggests that seeing the consequence of their actions, rather than mental imagery, explains the results. Insight is a form of "seeing as," much as Köhler (1925/1976) envisioned (see discussion in the section on "Perceiving as and pretending," pp. 332–334).

### *Using mental images to solve novel problems*

To think about mental images as a problem-solving method, we need to keep two things in mind. First, we humans often solve problems without any form of imagery. This was important in the latter part of the nineteenth century when scientific psychology began, because many psychologists (based on a long philosophical tradition – see Manser 1967, Mitchell 2013, and Fabian Dorsch, "Hume," Chapter 3 of this volume) had previously presumed that all thoughts have an imagistic base in consciousness (see Mandler's 2007 history of the issue). Some of these early psychologists found that people have imageless thoughts – they simply know the answer to a problem without any apparent preceding imagery (in the form of visual images, inner speech or other mental imagery).[1] So to presume that animals *must* have mental images to solve problems, or *must* use a series of images to solve problems, would be problematic.

Second, when humans keep an image in mind, it is almost always already catalogued as an image of one thing and not another (it has an "attitude" attached to it or a perspective taken toward it: Rollin 1989; Mitchell 2013). Intentionally reenvisioning an *image* as something other than what it is already catalogued as (coming up with a new attitude toward it) is difficult for most people, even though intentionally reenvisioning an already catalogued but currently experienced *perception* is relatively easy (Reisberg 1996; Reisberg and Heuer 2005). For example, a line drawing of Texas that is upside-down is much easier to recognize as Texas than a mental image of the line drawing. Thus, when problem-solving solutions come to people via imagery, they are usually already solved; it's not that people consciously imagine moving images to solve problems by creating a new attitude toward those images, but rather that the image comes with the problem solved. What occurs in consciousness is *already* the solution (Maier 1931).

Solving a problem via talking to oneself can often show evidence of reasoning and, thus, of manipulating auditory imagery to solve the problem, but this solution is not available to most animals, as they are apparently without language. However, if some animals have communications systems like language (e.g., Slobodchikoff 2012), it may be that they can experience meaningful auditory images that are useful for problem-solving (contra Carruthers 1996, 228–229).

### *Self-images and kinesthetic-visual matching*

What behavioral options would the ravens have envisioned to solve the problem, and how would they have envisioned them? When the image-based solution is elaborated, it becomes problematic. Let's suppose that a raven had visual images of itself solving the problem. To have the image function as a solution, the raven had to have several attitudes toward it, including recognizing that the image applies to reality (and is not hallucinatory), the image is a solution to the problem, and the imagined action is doable by itself. (Droege's 2012 discusses complications about animal consciousness.) In particular, the raven would need a way to translate the visual image into action; indeed, it would need a way to know that the image is of itself.

The same skill works for both translation and self-identification: kinesthetic-visual matching (Mitchell 2012). Only if the raven were able to match between a visual image and its own bodily movements, felt kinesthetically, that were similar to those in the visual image, could the raven use the image to come up with an action to perform. But there is no evidence that ravens have kinesthetic-visual matching, usually evinced by mirror self-recognition, bodily imitation or recognition of being imitated (Mitchell 1993). Evidence that these activities require kinesthetic-visual matching is convincing (see reviews in Mitchell 2012, recent evidence in Zmyj et al. 2013), so much so that diverse scientists have "independently" promoted it as "their" explanation (see Dolins and Mitchell 2010, 341–342)! So far, only some apes and cetaceans show all of these skills, while some elephants, magpies (though see Soler et al. 2014), and, perhaps, some monkeys show mirror self-recognition (see Mitchell 2012), and thus only such creatures could use visual images to solve problems requiring use of their own body.[2]

Ideas similar to those posited for imagination in the ravens have been common in comparative psychology. Romanes (1883/1900, 151) described imagination as present when "animals show … by their actions that they have in their 'mind's eye' a picture or representation of absent objects." Carruthers (1996) presented the idea that imagery in animals can be used to solve problems, but does not exhibit conscious thinking, as conscious thoughts require conceptualization, which he believes animals may not possess. In attempting to discount conceptual and thus conscious understanding in Köhler's chimpanzees, he posits a puzzling kind of unconscious imagining:

> what the chimp has to be able to do, to arrive at a sudden solution to such a problem, is *imagine* the boxes piled one on top of the other, and to visualise, and then act on, the result. Although this is intelligent and sophisticated, there is no reason to believe that the chimp must also be capable of thinking about its own sequence of images, and so no reason to believe that the chimp's own thoughts are conscious ones.
>
> *(Carruthers 1996, 221)*

Yet it is hard to understand how imagining the solution would be useful if the chimpanzee could not recognize it *as* a solution (i.e., conceptualize). Not surprisingly, Carruthers (2006, 140–146) now believes that chimpanzees can consciously engage in mental rehearsal: consciously imagining actions and outcomes, and then selecting the most advantageous sequences.[3]

Osvath and Karvonen (2012, 1) posit similar imagery in proposing that a chimpanzee "recombined episodic memories in perceptual simulation" to engage in innovative deception. (Episodic memory is the conscious experience of one's own past events recognized as past events, and perceptual simulation is mental imagery.) The chimpanzee liked to break off pieces of rock, store them and get them later to throw things at visitors. Although initially (in 1997) he placed projectiles together in front of rock walls (visible to outsiders), he later (in

2010) hid projectiles he planned to throw at people behind different types of natural coverings (rocks, logs) and covering he moved (hay) (Osvath and Karvonen 2012). The chimpanzee had to hide the projectiles because zoo guides warned visitors when they saw him with rocks. Consistent with other great apes' concealments and deceptions, the chimpanzee's concealments appear to be variations on well-scripted actions (Mitchell 1999), though, as the authors note, little is known about the initial development of the chimpanzee's concealings. The chimpanzee was, however, likely to be knowledgeable about the scripts[4] behind his actions and their consequences in particular contexts, and to have strategically used his knowledge of these scripts to achieve his own ends. Though it seems obvious that the chimpanzee planned to use the rocks later, it is not clear that either episodic memory or mental imagery was required to do so.

## *Cognitive mapping and episodic memory*

While it seems likely that animals derive images from their perceptual experience, their *manipulation* of these mental images for *novel* problem-solving remains tantalizing but unsupported. However, animals might use images for solving problems more generally in planning. Just as humans do (e.g., James 1890, 147, 275), animals might use images from past experiences to guide them to return somewhere they have been before. They may desire to go to a particular place, and experience images that are encoded as showing them the way to this place (imagining that this is the way to go). How exactly these images are experienced is up for grabs, and whether or not they are required for the remarkable feats of memory shown by some animals (as suggested for caching birds: Emery and Clayton 2004) remains open. Another open question concerns the representative nature of these images, especially how much (if at all) they are like maps (Bennett 1996; Gibson 2001; chapters in Dolins and Mitchell 2010). Perhaps representations begin as episodic (perception-like) memories of experiences with attached complex attitudes, and eventually morph into concepts that are more flexible than imagery (Piaget 1945/1962), though the possibility of experiencing the episodic memories remains.

Comparative psychologists wonder if scrub jays who cache food engage in episodic (conscious) memory – in particular, cognitive maps – to find food in hundreds of cached locations. The evidence suggests that scrub jays know what food is in the cache, where it is and how long the food can remain fresh – that is, they have consciousness of what, where and when – features known as the "www" criteria for episodic memory. Scrub jays, e.g., will look in locations (*w*here) containing more perishable food items (*w*hat) soon after they have cached them (*w*hen), but not much later. This issue has now generalized to questions of mental time travel, questions which concern whether animals can "project" themselves into the past and future. More specifically, we might question whether animals can use "episodic-like" memory to make predictions about future events based on knowledge of past events (see Droege 2012; Feeney and Roberts 2012; Raby and Clayton 2012; Dorothea Debus, "Imagination and memory," Chapter 10 of this volume). As these authors note, many animals engage in behavior that appears to take into account future action, but the path to knowing whether reimagining the past and/or imagining the future account for these behaviors has multiple roadblocks, both conceptual and empirical: Do scrub jays experience themselves autobiographically, able to place memories in a coherent organization of past, present and future? Do they have a sense of absolute time? Can neuropsychological measures allow us to know whether similar brain areas are used when engaging in future-directed behaviors? While proponents (Raby and Clayton 2012) acknowledge supportive evidence for short-term planning in corvids and apes, they agree with the skeptics (Feeney and Roberts 2012) that it is uncertain whether animals engage in mental time travel for long periods of time.

Scrub jays are also presumed to engage in a form of imagination called "experience projection." In experience projection (Emery and Clayton 2004, pp. 1906–1907), organisms engage in role-playing by mentally simulating actions, experiences or perspectives of others, or by extrapolating their own actions, experiences or perspectives onto others and making predictions about others from such simulation or extrapolation. Experience projection is not assumed present for ordinary scrub jays, who avoid caching when being observed by potential competitors and, when they have been observed while caching, recache upon the observer leaving (Clayton et al. 2007, 516, fig. 12). The interpretation of these actions of recaching and avoiding caching is that the jays are aware that the observer may take their cached food (514–516). Thus, the authors state that ordinary jays know already (prior to their own pilfering of others' caches) that an observer is a potential pilferer and thus recache as a result (516, fig. 12). Clayton et al. (2007, 519) posit experience projection specifically in scrub jays who have pilfered from others' caches, providing evidence that jays who have pilfered recache more than jays who have not upon being observed (519, fig. 19). In their view, jays who are pilferers recache more of their own food following the presence of an observer than in private, in comparison with jays who had not pilfered, because the former "have transferred their previous experience of being a pilferer to a current situation in which their own caches might be stolen" (Emery and Clayton 2001, 445). In this study, contrary to what had been observed earlier, jays who had not pilfered who were observed while caching did *not* recache more when given the chance than when they had cached in private. Note also that it is not jays who have experienced their own cache being pilfered who recache more, but rather those who have pilfered from others. But matters here need further study, since it cannot be both that jays ordinarily recache following the departure of an observer of their caching, and that only jays who have themselves pilfered do so. Thus, the evidence of experience projection in jays is unconvincing.

## Perceiving as and pretending

Perception and images are similar in that when we perceive or imagine, we experience something as a particular thing: that is a dog, that line is longer than this line, that smells like chocolate. As with images, we can be wrong in our perceptions, as when the "dog" was a cat, the line being longer was an illusion, or the "chocolate" was carob; and we can be uncertain, as when we perceived something was spinach but it didn't taste right. Perception-action theory (Thomas 1999; O'Regan and Noë 2001) proposes that perception is not a fixed process, but depends on "continual updating and refining of procedures (or 'schemata,' …) that specify how to direct our attention most effectively in particular situations: how to efficiently examine and explore, and thus interpret, a scene or object of a certain type" (Thomas 1999, 218). Mental imagery is, then, just a continuation of exploratory aspects of perceptual processes. Both perception and imagery occur through

> the ongoing activity of schema-guided perceptual exploration of the environment. Imagery is experienced when a schema that is not directly relevant to the exploration of the current environment is allowed at least partial control of the exploratory apparatus. We imagine, say, a cat, by going through (some of) the motions of examining something and finding that it is a cat, even though there is no cat (and

> perhaps nothing relevant at all) there to be examined. Imagining a cat is seeing nothing-in-particular *as* a cat ...
>
> (*Thomas 1999, 218*)

Perception-action theory is useful in understanding imagination, because it ties mental imagery to other imaginative processes of perceiving as and pretending.

The Gestalt psychologist and philosopher Wolfgang Köhler (1925/1976, 106) introduced the idea of "seeing as" in his problem-solving work with chimpanzees. Köhler writes that, in their uses of several objects (a wire, a rock, a box and a branch) to function as a stick, chimpanzees "*see* [each object] *as a stick*." Such seeing as may not require extensive imaginative skills: sometimes we use the construction "seeing *x* as *y*" to emphasize a new way of seeing something, as compared with an earlier visual experience of that same thing (Wittgenstein 1953; Dunlop 1984). For Köhler in his study of chimpanzee problem-solving, perception incorporates "seeing as," which occurs as a result of the chimpanzees wanting to solve a problem, and may not require imaginative visualization outside of perception itself. His view that animals reconfigure their perceptual rather than imaginal experiences fits nicely with Reisberg's (1996) view that it is easier to do so with perception than with imagination.

What is interesting about some instances of seeing as is that organisms can experience something as something else that they know it is not, or something as nothing. An example of seeing nothing as something is the sign-using orangutan Chantek signing that there was a "cat" when there wasn't (a frequent game), and then if a cat appeared, he was surprised and acted differently from when he simply saw a cat (Miles 1986, and pers. commun., during the author's 1987–88 postdoctoral fellowship with H. Lyn Miles, Yerkes Regional Primate Research Center, Atlanta, GA). When "seeing as" occurs as an awareness of possible perceptions of something (as in exploring it in relation to an idea), it may express, or lead to the development of, representational skills and make-believe (Dunlop 1984; Walton 1990; Mitchell 1994).

Walton (1990) introduced the idea of "ad hoc props" in make-believe games of children, where children decide that an object (or nothing) is something: a stick is a hammer, their finger is a screwdriver, and nothing is a fork or an imaginary companion. The comparison is to "props" per se; Walton uses 'props' to refer to art objects, which "mandate imaginings." *Ad hoc* props do not mandate any particular imagining. (See Kathleen Stock, "Imagination and fiction," Chapter 15 of this volume.) Children, in fact, prefer to pretend with objects that are as much like the objects they imagine them to be, and which thus "mandate imaginings," but they can pretend with unlike objects especially when realistic objects are not available (see Mitchell 2002, 310–311). Pretending with objects is a form of seeing as (I'm seeing this stick as a sword), just as bodily pretending is a form of acting as if you were someone else (I'm a dragon!). (See Elizabeth Picciuto and Peter Carruthers, "Imagination and pretense," Chapter 23 of this volume.) Children's pretending is often easy to detect, because it so often looks like activities or events the children experienced or because children describe their pretenses, but it is not always evident what they are imagining. We might think, e.g., that young children playing with dolls are imagining that they are animating babies, but in fact young children have difficulty recognizing that dolls represent people (Smith 1999). In addition, children's verbal descriptions can be at odds with the behavior they are enacting (see Mitchell 2002). Detecting animal pretending introduces additional difficulties, as animals (other than sign-using apes) do not describe their activities. Researchers who know their animals well through extensive observation can often detect similarities between normal activities and what they take to be pretend activities. Yet scientists are often hesitant to describe animal activities as pretense, for fear of being accused of anthropomorphism. As a backlash against the psychological overinterpretation of animals' activities following Darwin, psychological behaviorism directed scientists to focus on "behavior," which referred to animals' movements relatively denuded of psychological interpretation (see, e.g., Mackenzie 1977). Although many psychologists have moved away from strict behaviorism, they are still expected to be skeptical toward any implication of complex psychology in animals (Mitchell et al. 1997). When Alex the talking parrot, who understood word meanings and used words appropriately, was left alone at night, he reproduced a variety of conversations he had engaged in, playing both parts, but researchers left the description of this as play, not pretense (Pepperberg et al. 1991); yet if a child did this, it would be considered pretense. If your cat seems to be chasing after nothing, is this an imaginative seeing nothing as something (an exploration of an idea via its actions), or can this be denigrated to acting out some "instinctive" reaction? Most scientists assume nonpretense options, or express ambivalence (see Mitchell 2002), likely as a result of the aforementioned fear of accusations of overinterpretation. The same occurs in philosophy (see Gennaro 2006, 11).

Only with great apes are scientists comfortable attributing pretense. This is in part because we expect great apes to be quite smart for phylogenetic reasons: they are our closest living relatives and are so much like us. Pretending requires intelligence because it is assumed to be a symbolic enactment, indicating representational knowledge. Great apes pretend, though all but a few instances of the more complicated pretenses occur only in human-reared apes who enact imitations of their own and others' actions; there is not a lot of complicated pretense in the wild (see Mitchell 2002).

In discussions of captive apes, the chimpanzee Viki acting as if pulling a nonexistent pull toy, a rather elaborate pretense, is almost always mentioned, or her imitation of her human father's reading a newspaper. But other apes engage in pretense as well: a gorilla enjoyed hiding an item in her mouth and acting toward her owner as if searching everywhere for it; a chimpanzee, soliciting another chimpanzee's help, reenacted the rope-pulling needed to solve a problem and then looked at the other chimpanzee; an orangutan reenacted part of his caregivers' cooking techniques. Still, based on the available evidence, pretending doesn't seem to be as much a part of apes' everyday life as it is for many children.

Animals do engage in deception, which some researchers regard as a form of pretense. A captive gorilla repeatedly acted as if about to bang on a window in her enclosure, but stopped herself before hitting the glass, apparently to see visitors' reactions; a captive chimpanzee appeared to be interested in his toes until people got close to him, at which time he sprayed them with water held in his mouth (see Mitchell 1999). But whether or not to include evidence of deception as evidence of pretense is unclear, in part because most deceptions are relatively unelaborated re-creations; in addition, the fact that deceptions serve specific functions suggests that, at least potentially, the deceiver is not acting out an idea to see what will happen in that s/he already knows (see Mitchell 2013). Still, if deception requires planning, then how much imagination is needed is an open question that requires philosophical insight *and* psychological experimentation (Lurz 2011).

## Creativity

Creativity seems inherent in many pretenses and problem solutions, but is also suggested in novel behaviors across a variety of domains, including social manipulation and tool use (Kaufman and Kaufman 2015; Reader and Laland 2003). A common definition of creativity is "the ability to produce work that is both novel (i.e., original, unexpected) and appropriate (i.e., useful)" (Sternberg and Lubert 1999, 3); see also Dustin Stokes, "Imagination and creativity," Chapter 18 of this volume). Imaginativeness in relation to creativity may concern how innovative the product is, or how uniquely beautiful, rather than referring necessarily to the psychological processes that led to the creative act or product. Imagination in this sense of creativity is relatively objective, in that one can evaluate the novelty, uniqueness or beauty of the product. Thus, the elaborate bowers of male bowerbirds, which incorporate colorful items into the nest to entice females, are each unique and show creativity in individualized aesthetic placement of objects to entice mates (see Layman 2010). If every, or almost every, species member engages in an activity or produces a product in similar ways, then we are unlikely to believe that creative imagination is present in the activity or product. Thus, although all male bowerbirds of a species create similar bowers, they decorate them differently, and the innovation is in the decoration, not in the bower building per se.

Boden (1994, 77) critiques the idea of creativity as something merely novel and appropriate, arguing instead that creativity requires transformation of conceptual spaces, specifically, new ways of producing something, not simply novel productions. Creativity, for Boden, requires violating already organized structures or conceptual rules, to put in place a new understanding. Thus, bowerbirds are not, under this view, creative, as the rules of creating bowers *could* have resulted in this or that particular bower. Creativity consistent with Boden's idea is present in captive dolphins rewarded to produce completely novel actions (Pryor et al. 1969). One dolphin so rewarded enacted several, including a backward flip, and swimming while twisting her body around her body center, actions not observed to have occurred spontaneously in any species of dolphin and are thus outside the "rules" of actions.

## Conclusions

Research on imagination in animals has focused on three forms: mental imagery, pretending and other forms of "perceiving as," and creativity. All three forms seem present in at least some animals and might be coordinated under perception-action theory (Thomas 1999) as elaborations of perceptual (or perceptual-motor) activities. The evidence for animals (and humans) manipulating mental images to solve novel problems remains problematic; rather, "seeing as" appears to be prominent. Pretending and creativity appear rare in animals outside captive situations, and the evidence for elaborate pretend skills rests on members of a few species: great apes, parrots and cetaceans. Philosophical assessment and experimental research will have to continue in tandem to produce a coherent understanding of the imagination of animals.

## Acknowledgments

I greatly appreciate thoughtful appraisals and suggestions from Amy Kind and an anonymous referee that helped to improve the chapter.

## Notes

1 Although one might want to argue here that introspection is not reliable – and hence imageless thought is problematic, as it requires introspection – the same is true for mental imagery: we only know of its existence because of introspection. See Strawson's (1954) discussion of introspection.

2 To argue that ravens might use the kinesthetic-visual matching necessary to understand mental images of themselves and put them into action, but be incapable of using those same self-images to recognize themselves in a mirror, strains credulity. Indeed, kinesthetic-visual matching is expected to be present if visual self-images are to be used in planning (see Mitchell 1994).

3 Carruthers (2006) also posits an unconscious "mental rehearsal" that happens as one engages in and adjusts one's actions to satisfy one's goals in a changing environment (e.g., in catching a ball), but this use of "mental rehearsal" seems incoherent, as nothing is rehearsed. In addition, Carruthers (2006) clearly indicates that such instantaneous "rehearsal" is unrelated to the conscious mental rehearsal he posits in chimpanzees.
4 Scripts are schemas codifying the sequence of actions in an event.

## References


Bennett, A.T.D. (1996) "Do Animals Have Cognitive Maps?" *Journal of Experimental Biology* 199: 219–224.

Boden, M. (1994) *Dimensions of Creativity*, Cambridge, MA: MIT Press.

Bogdan, R.J. (2005) "Pretending as Imaginative Rehearsal for Cultural Conformity," *Journal of Cognition and Culture* 5: 191–213.

Carruthers, P. (1996) *Language, Thought and Consciousness: An Essay in Philosophical Psychology*, Cambridge: Cambridge University Press.

Carruthers, P. (2006) *The Architecture of the Mind*, Oxford: Oxford University Press.

Casey, E.S. (1976/2000) *Imagining: A Phenomenological Study*, 2nd edn., Bloomington: Indiana University Press.

Clayton, N.S., J.M. Dally, and N.J. Emery (2007) "Social Cognition by Food-Caching Corvids: The Western Scrub-Jay as a Natural Psychologist," *Philosophical Transactions of the Royal Society B: Biological Sciences* 362: 507–522.

Dolins, F.L., and R.W. Mitchell (eds.) (2010) *Spatial Perception, Spatial Cognition: Mapping the Self and Space*, Cambridge: Cambridge University Press.

Droege, P. (2012) "Assessing Evidence for Animal Consciousness: The Question of Episodic Memory," in J.A. Smith and R.W. Mitchell (eds.) *Experiencing Animal Minds: An Anthology of Human–Animal Encounters*, New York: Columbia University Press.

Dunlop, C.E.M. (1984) "Wittgenstein on Seeing and 'Seeing-as,'" *Synthese* 60: 349–367.

Durier, V., P. Graham, and T.S. Collett (2003) "Snapshot Memories and Landmark Guidance in Wood Ants," *Current Biology* 13: 1614–1618.

Emery, N.J., and N.S. Clayton (2001) "Effects of Experience and Social Context on Prospective Caching Strategies by Scrub Jays," *Nature* 414: 443–446.

Emery, N.J., and N.S. Clayton (2004) "The Mentality of Crows: Convergent Evolution of Intelligence in Corvids and Apes," *Science* 306(5703): 1903–1907.

Feeney, M.C., and W.A. Roberts (2012) "Comparative Mental Time Travel: Is There a Cognitive Divide between Humans and Animals in Episodic Memory and Planning?" in J. Vonk and T.K. Shackelford (eds.) *The Oxford Handbook of Comparative Evolutionary Psychology*, New York: Oxford University Press.

Finke, R.A. (1986) "Mental Imagery and the Visual System," *Scientific American* 254: 88–95.

Gennaro, R.J. (2006) Review of *Consciousness: Essays from a Higher-Order Perspective*, by Peter Carruthers, *Psyche* 12(4): 1–13, <http://www.theassc.org/files/assc/2645.pdf>.

Gibson, B.T. (2001) "Cognitive Maps Not Used By Humans (*Homo sapiens*) during a Dynamic Navigational Task," *Journal of Comparative Psychology* 115: 397–402.

Gould, J.L. (1990) "Honey Bee Cognition," *Cognition* 37: 83–103.

Heinrich, B., and T. Bugnyar (2007) "Just How Smart Are Ravens?" *Scientific American* 296: 64–71.

Hobhouse, L. (1901) *Mind in Evolution*, London: Macmillan & Co.

James, W. (1890) *The Principles of Psychology*, New York: Henry Holt.

Kaufman, A.B., and J.C. Kaufman (eds.) (2015) *Animal Creativity and Innovation*, Amsterdam: Elsevier.

Köhler, W. (1925/1976) *The Mentality of Apes*, 2nd edn., New York: Liveright.

Lacey, S., and R. Lawson (eds.) (2013) *Multisensory Imagery*, New York: Springer.

Layman, T. (2010) "Build It – and They Will Come," photo essay, *National Geographic* website, <http://ngm.nationalgeographic.com/2010/07/bowerbirds/laman-photography>.

Libby, L.K., E.M. Shaeffer, and R.P. Eibach (2009) "Seeing Meaning in Action: A Bidirectional Link between Visual Perspective and Action Identification Level," *Journal of Experimental Psychology: General* 138: 503–516.

Lurz, R. (2011) *Mindreading Animals: The Debate over What Animals Know about Other Minds*, Cambridge, MA: MIT Press.

Mackenzie, B.D. (1977) *Behaviourism and the Limits of Scientific Method*, Atlantic Highlands: Humanities Press.

Maier, N.R.F. (1931) "Reasoning in Humans II: The Solution of a Problem and Its Appearance in Consciousness," *Journal of Comparative Psychology* 12: 181–194.
Mandler, G. (2007) *A History of Modern Experimental Psychology*, Cambridge, MA: Bradford Books.
Manser, A.R. (1967) "Images" and "Imagination," in P. Edwards (ed.) *The Encyclopedia of Philosophy*, vol. 4, New York: Macmillan Publishing and Free Press.
Markman, K.D., W.M.P. Klein, and J.A. Suhr (eds.) (2009) *Handbook of Imagination and Mental Simulation*, New York: Psychology Press.
McNamara, P., C. Nunn, R. Barton, E. Harris, and I. Capellini (2007) "Phylogeny of Sleep and Dreams," in D. Barrett and P. McNamara (eds.) *The New Science of Dreaming*, vol. 1, Westport, CT: Praeger.
Miles, H.L. (1986) "How Can I Tell a Lie? Apes, Language, and the Problem of Deception," in R.W. Mitchell and N.S. Thompson (eds.) *Deception: Perspectives on Human and Nonhuman Deceit*, Albany: SUNY Press.
Mitchell, R.W. (1993) "Mental Models of Mirror-Self-Recognition: Two Theories," *New Ideas in Psychology* 11: 295–325.
Mitchell, R.W. (1994) "The Evolution of Primate Cognition: Simulation, Self-Knowledge, and Knowledge of Other Minds," in D. Quiatt and J. Itani (eds.) *Hominid Culture in Primate Perspective*, Boulder: University Press of Colorado.
Mitchell, R.W. (1999) "Deception and Concealment as Strategic Script Violation in Great Apes and Humans," in S.T. Parker, R.W. Mitchell, and H.L. Miles (eds.) *The Mentalities of Gorillas and Orangutans*, Cambridge: Cambridge University Press.
Mitchell, R.W. (ed.) (2002) *Pretending and Imagination in Animals and Children*, Cambridge: Cambridge University Press.
Mitchell, R.W. (2012) "Self-Recognition in Animals," in M.R. Leary and J. Tangney (eds.) *Handbook of Self and Identity*, 2nd edn., New York: Guilford Press.
Mitchell, R.W. (2013) "Comparative Issues in the Study of Imagination," in M. Taylor (ed.) *The Oxford Handbook of the Development of Imagination*, Oxford: Oxford University Press.
Mitchell, R.W., N.S. Thompson, and L.H. Miles (eds.) (1997) *Anthropomorphism, Anecdotes, and Animals*, Albany: SUNY Press.
O'Regan, J.K., and A. Noë (2001) "A Sensorimotor Account of Vision and Visual Consciousness," *Behavioral and Brain Sciences* 24: 939–1031.
Osvath, M., and E. Karvonen (2012) "Spontaneous Innnovation for Future Deception in a Male Chimpanzee," *PLoS One* 7(5): e36782.
Pepperberg, I.M., K.J. Brese, and B.J. Harris (1991) "Solitary Sound Play during Acquisition of English Vocalizations by an African Grey Parrot (*Psittacus erithacus*): Possible Parallels with Children's Monologue Speech," *Applied Psycholinguistics* 12: 151–178.
Piaget, J. (1945/1962) *Play, Dreams, and Imitation in Childhood*, New York: W.W. Norton.
Pryor, K.W., R. Haag, and J. O'Reilly (1969) "The Creative Porpoise: Training for Novel Behavior," *Journal of the Experimental Analysis of Behavior* 12: 653–661.
Raby, C.R., and N.S. Clayton (2012) "Episodic Memory and Planning," in J. Vonk and T.K. Shackelford (eds.) *The Oxford Handbook of Comparative Evolutionary Psychology*, New York: Oxford University Press.
Reader, S.M., and K.N. Laland (eds.) (2003) *Animal Innovation*, Oxford: Oxford University Press.
Reisberg, D. (1996) "The Nonambiguity of Mental Images," in C. Cornoldi, R.H. Logie, M.A. Brandimonte, G. Kaufmann, and D. Reisberg (eds.) *Stretching the Imagination: Representation and Transformation in Mental Imagery*, New York: Oxford University Press.
Reisberg, D., and F. Heuer (2005) "Visuospatial Images," in P. Shah and A. Miyake (eds.) *The Cambridge Handbook of Visuospatial Thinking*, New York: Cambridge University Press.
Rollin, M. (1989) *Mental Imagery*, New Haven: Yale University Press.
Romanes, G.J. (1883/1900) *Mental Evolution in Animals*, London: Kegan Paul, Trench, & Co.
Russon, A.E., and B.M.F. Galdikas (1995) "Constraints on Great Apes' Imitation: Model and Action Selectivity in Rehabilitant Orangutan (*Pongo pygmaeus*) Imitation," *Journal of Comparative Psychology* 109: 5–17.
Sills, H. (2005) "Time Remembered," *KronoScope* 5: 59–72.
Slobodchikoff, C.N. (2012) *Chasing Doctor Dolittle: Learning the Language of Animals*, New York: St. Martin's Press.
Smith, C.M. (1999) "Young Children's Use of Dolls to Represent Themselves," PhD diss., University of Illinois at Urbana-Champaign, IL.

Soler, M., T. Pérez-Contreras, and J.M. Peralta-Sánchez (2014) "Mirror-Mark Tests Performed on Jackdaws Reveal Potential Methodological Problems in the Use of Stickers in Avian Mark-Test Studies," *PLoS One* 9(1): e86193.

Sternberg, R.J., and T.I. Lubart (1999) "The Concept of Creativity: Prospects and Paradigms," in R.J. Sternberg (ed.) *Handbook of Creativity*, New York: Cambridge University Press.

Strawson, P.F. (1954) Critical notice of *Philosophical Investigations*, by L. Wittgenstein, *Mind* 63: 70–99.

Strawson, P.F. (1970) "Imagination and Perception," in L. Foster and J.W. Swanson (eds.) *Experience and Theory*, Amherst: University of Massachusetts Press.

Thomas, N.J.T. (1999) "Are Theories of Imagery Theories of Imagination? An Active Perception Approach to Conscious Mental Content," *Cognitive Science* 23: 207–245.

Thomas, N.J.T. (2014) "Mental Imagery," E.N. Zalta (ed.) *Stanford Encyclopedia of Philosophy*, <http://plato.stanford.edu/entries/mental-imagery/index.html#EnaThePerIma>.

Walton, K. (1990) *Mimesis as Make-Believe: On the Foundations of the Representational Arts*, Cambridge, MA: Harvard University Press.

Wehner, R., and Menzel, R. (1990) "Do Insects have Cognitive Maps?" *Annual Review of Neuroscience* 13: 403–414.

Wittgenstein, L. (1953) *Philosophical Investigations*, trans. G.E.M. Anscombe, Oxford: Blackwell.

Wray, M.K., B.A. Klein, H.R. Mattila, and T.D. Seeley (2008) "Honeybees Do Not Reject Dances for 'Implausible' Locations: Reconsidering the Evidence for Cognitive Maps in Insects," *Animal Behaviour* 76: 261–269.

Zmyj, N., W. Prinz, and M.M. Daum (2013) "The Relation Between Mirror Self-Image Reactions and Imitation in 14- and 18-Month-Old Infants," *Infant Behavior and Development* 36: 809–816.

# 25
# IMAGINATION AND RATIONALITY

*Ruth M.J. Byrne*

People often create alternatives to reality and imagine "what if …" and "if only …" These counterfactual thoughts are alluring in everyday thinking, e.g., "if only there had been fruit in the fruit bowl, I wouldn't have eaten all that chocolate." Counterfactuals implicate both imagination and reason. People rely on their imaginative skills to create many different sorts of counterfactual alternatives to reality. They rely on their reasoning skills to make many different sorts of inferences from these imagined counterfactuals.

In this chapter I first consider imaginative skills. I sketch the key role of the counterfactual imagination in human thinking. People rely on counterfactuals to explain the past, prepare for the future, modulate emotions, and support moral judgments (see Byrne 2015 for a review). I describe the influence of knowledge on the plausibility of the counterfactuals that people create and outline several alternative explanations of the cognitive processes that underlie the imagination of counterfactual alternatives. In the second part of the chapter, I consider reasoning skills. I consider several alternative explanations of how people reason with counterfactuals. I assess the psychological evidence that people envisage dual possibilities to understand and reason with counterfactuals. I conclude with the suggestion that counterfactuals provide an important bridge between reasoning and imagination (e.g., Byrne 2005). Imagination and reasoning depend on the same sorts of underlying computational processes: reasoning depends on cognitive processes that support the imagination of alternatives, and imagination depends on cognitive processes that are based on the same core processes.

## Counterfactuals and the imagination

The counterfactual imagination plays a key role in human thinking, to explain the past, prepare for the future, modulate emotions, and support moral judgments (e.g., Byrne 2015). The tendency to think "what if …" and "if only …" may underlie creative cognition in fiction, daydreaming, fantasy, and pretense (e.g., Kahneman and Tversky 1982a).

Counterfactuals serve several important psychological functions (e.g., Epstude and Roese 2008). For example, they help people to explain the past, by excusing and defending past behavior (e.g., Markman, Mizoguchi et al. 2008; McCrea 2008). Their explanatory impact often depends on their identification of various sorts of relations between past events, such as causal relations (e.g., Spellman and Mandel 1999; McEleney and Byrne 2006; see also Frosch and Byrne 2012). Philosophers since Hume and Mill have suggested that a causal relation, e.g., "striking the match caused it to light," contrasts reality to a counterfactual alternative, e.g., "if the match had not been struck it would not have lit" (e.g., Nickerson 2015). As a result, counterfactuals often play a role in analyses of historical and political events to establish the potential causes of events, e.g., "if Hitler had not invaded Poland when he did, would the course of World War II have been different?" (e.g., Tetlock and Belkin 1996).

Counterfactuals also help people to prepare for the future, by assisting in the formation of intentions and in decision-making. For example, when people imagine how a bad event could have been prevented and how the event could have turned out better, they form intentions to carry out actions that will lead to a better outcome in the future (e.g., Markman, McMullen et al. 2008; Epstude and Roese 2011). Counterfactuals help people to learn from mistakes and provide a road map to transition from a bad situation in the past to a better situation in the future (e.g., Epstude and Roese 2008). They also help people to make decisions. For example, even young children switch to a different choice on a subsequent task when they feel regret about their selection, once they discover that a better outcome would have resulted from the nonchosen alternative (e.g., O'Connor et al. 2014).

Counterfactuals amplify emotions such as regret and guilt, and relief and satisfaction (e.g., Kahneman and Miller 1986). An emotion such as regret depends on the comparison of the way a situation turned out, and how it could have turned out differently (e.g., Epstude and Roese 2008; Zeelenberg and Peters 2007). Similarly, guilt is amplified when people imagine how an outcome could have turned out differently as a result of a change to their actions, whereas shame is amplified when they imagine instead a change to their personality (e.g., Niedenthal et al. 1994). Well-being can be affected by the emotions amplified by counterfactual thoughts, for example, most people imagine how things might have turned out differently after traumatic life events such as bereavements or accidents and these counterfactual thoughts can contribute to their distress (e.g., Davis et al. 1995).

Counterfactuals support legal and moral judgments about fault, responsibility, and blame, e.g., "if the defendant hadn't been provoked, the assault wouldn't have occurred" (e.g., Branscombe et al. 1996). Judgments of sympathy and punishment are affected by how readily a counterfactual can be imagined (e.g., Macrae et al. 1993). Counterfactuals affect judgments of blame, and influence assessments of whether the protagonist could have done something differently to prevent the event, and whether the protagonist *should* have done something differently to prevent it (e.g., Alicke et al. 2008; Malle et al. 2014; see also McCloy and Byrne 2000; Walsh and Byrne 2007).

Given its many functions, the loss of the ability to imagine counterfactual alternatives to reality has devastating consequences. Individuals can become impaired in spontaneous counterfactual thoughts when they have sustained damage to the prefrontal cortex (e.g., Gomez Beldarrain et al. 2005; see also Knight and Grabowecky 1995). Likewise, individuals with advanced Parkinson's disease, and individuals with schizophrenia exhibiting prefrontal dysfunction, are also impaired in the spontaneous creation of alternatives to reality (e.g., McNamara et al. 2003; Roese et al. 2008; see also Hooker et al. 2000). Children with high-functioning autism spectrum disorders also construct different sorts of counterfactuals compared with typically developing children (e.g., Begeer et al. 2009). The difficulties such individuals experience in imagining alternatives to reality has widespread consequences, not only for their ability to understand intentions and make decisions, but also for their experience of emotions such as regret, and the accuracy of their social attributions such as blame and responsibility (e.g., Gomez Beldarrain et al. 2005; Roese et al. 2008). Perhaps unsurprisingly, the counterfactual imagination has attracted considerable attention from scholars in the cognitive sciences, including psychology, philosophy, neuroscience, anthropology, and linguistics (e.g., Byrne 2002).

### The creation of counterfactual alternatives

People construct a mental representation of reality, and some aspects of their mental representation of reality appear to be more mutable than others. For example, they tend to change their mental representation of the facts of an event, such as a bad examination performance, by adding something extra to the event, e.g., "if only she had studied for longer ...," rather than by deleting something about the event, e.g., "if only she had not focused on just one topic ..." (e.g., Epstude and Roese 2008; Kahneman and Tversky 1982a). Remarkably, most people tend to change the same sorts of things in their representation of reality when they imagine an alternative to it, almost as if there were "fault lines" in their representation of reality, junctures or joints that most people zoom in on to imagine how things could have taken a different turn (e.g., Kahneman and Tversky 1982a). Their knowledge of reality influences the plausibility of the counterfactual alternatives to reality that they create.

One illustration of these remarkable regularities in the counterfactual imagination is that people tend to change exceptional events to be normal (e.g., Kahneman and Tversky 1982a; Dixon and Byrne 2011). For example, when an individual is in a car accident on his way home by an unusual route, most participants imagine "if only he had driven home by his usual route ..." When he is in a car accident on his way home after he left work early, they imagine, "if only he had left work at his usual time..." (e.g., Kahneman and Tversky 1982a).

Another illustration of the remarkable regularities in the imagination of counterfactual alternatives is that people tend to change events within their control rather than events outside their control (e.g., Girotto et al. 1991; McCloy and Byrne 2000). For example, when an individual is delayed on his way home to take care of his sick wife, by various events such as a traffic jam, an asthma attack, calling into a bar for a beer, most participants imagine "if only he hadn't called into the bar for a beer" rather than, "if only he hadn't been caught in a traffic jam" (e.g., Girotto et al. 1991; Markman et al. 1993).

There are many other examples of fault lines that most people tend to zoom in on, such as the most recent event in an independent sequence of events (e.g., Miller and Gunasegaram 1990; Byrne et al. 2000, Walsh and Byrne 2004), or actions rather than inactions (Kahneman and Tverksy 1982b; Byrne and McEleney 2000). These fault lines demonstrate the role of knowledge in the creation of plausible counterfactual alternatives. Several different explanations of the cognitive processes that underlie the imagination of counterfactuals have been provided to account for them.

### Alternative explanations

One view is that most people zoom in on fault lines in their representation of reality, such as exceptions or controllable events, because these events are the most probable events that could change the outcome (e.g., Petrocelli et al. 2011). For example, people consider the impact of a counterfactual such as "if he had chosen door 2 then he would have won" to be greater when it has a high conditional probability, i.e., when the contestant nearly chose door 2, and when he knew a lot about the questions that he would have been asked had he chosen it (e.g., Petrocelli et al. 2011). Against this view is the observation that the counterfactuals people create do not appear to be guided by likelihood. For example, when an individual's car is hit by another car at an intersection on an unusual route home, people tend to zoom in on the unusual route home and say "if only he had gone home by his usual route…" They do not tend to imagine an alternative to the most improbable event – two cars being in exactly the same place at exactly the same time (e.g., Kahneman and Tversky 1982a).

Another view is that most people zoom in on the fault lines because they provide readily available alternatives (e.g., Kahneman and Tversky 1982a). The availability of alternatives is determined by factors such as norms (e.g., Kahneman and Miller 1986). A test of this account is that the fault lines can be eliminated when the initial representation of reality explicitly includes different alternative possibilities (e.g., Byrne 2005). One illustration is that people do not change events within their control when they experience the event rather than read about it. For example, when people read about someone who has to chose between envelopes that contain an easy or difficult sum, and who subsequently fails to solve the sum within the given time, they imagine "if only she had chosen the other envelope," that is, they focus on the event within the protagonist's control. But when a participant him- or herself is placed in the situation and has to choose between two envelopes, and attempt to solve the sum, and subsequently fails, most participants do not focus on their choice of envelope, instead they focus on aspects of the situation outside their control, such as "if only I had been able to use pen-and-paper …" or "if only I had had more time …" (e.g., Girotto et al. 2007; see also Pighin et al. 2011). Similarly, the tendencies to zoom in on exceptions, actions, recent events, and so on, can also be eliminated by the provision of different alternatives in the initial representation of reality (e.g., Byrne 2015). The elimination of the tendency to zoom in on the fault lines when the initial representation of reality explicitly includes different alternatives provides some support for the idea that people focus on the fault lines because they are junctures that provide readily available alternative possibilities. The counterfactual imagination depends on various cognitive processes, including working-memory skills to simulate alternative possibilities simultaneously, and inhibitory-control skills to suppress attention to the mental representation of reality so that an alternative to reality can receive attention (e.g., Beck et al. 2011; Drayton et al. 2011).

In summary, people rely on counterfactuals for many diverse purposes, for example, to explain the past, prepare for the future, modulate emotions, and support moral judgments. Their knowledge influences the plausibility of the counterfactual alternatives that they create. A key explanation of the cognitive processes that underlie the imagination of counterfactual alternatives emphasizes the simulation of alternative possibilities. In the next section, I outline how people reason with counterfactuals and consider alternative explanations of the cognitive processes underlying reasoning.

## Counterfactuals and reasoning

There is no current consensus about the cognitive processes that underlie counterfactual reasoning; for example, people may imagine alternative possibilities or "mental models" (e.g., Byrne and Johnson-Laird 2009; Johnson-Laird and Byrne 1991, 2002; see also Johnson-Laird et al. 2015); or they may calculate the probability of outcomes based on their beliefs (e.g., Evans and Over 2004; Oaksford and Chater 2007). A key distinguishing feature between these alternative accounts is whether people consider multiple possibilities or just a single model when they understand a counterfactual conditional.

One view is that people understand and create counterfactuals by mentally simulating multiple possibilities (e.g., Kahneman and Tversky 1982a). They may construct mental models that are "iconic" in capturing structural aspects of the elements simulated (e.g.,

Johnson-Laird 1983, 2006). When people understand an ordinary conditional, e.g., "if there was an apple then there was an orange," they initially think about just one possibility corresponding to the way the world would be if the assertion were true,

There was an apple and there was an orange

(e.g., Johnson-Laird and Byrne 2002). The representation differs from a simple conjunction because people make a "mental note" that there may be alternative possibilities, which they have yet to think about (e.g., Johnson-Laird et al. 1992; see also Khemlani et al. 2012). The limitations of human working memory lead to parsimonious mental representations (e.g., Barrouillet et al. 2008; Johnson-Laird et al. 1992). People tend to think only about true possibilities and so they do not usually imagine the false possibilities ruled out by the conditional, such as

There was an apple and there was no orange

(e.g., Espino et al. 2009; Johnson-Laird and Byrne 2002). Their mental models can be "fleshed out" if need be, and they can think about several alternative true possibilities (e.g., Johnson-Laird and Byrne 2002). Hence people can reach different interpretations of a conditional. For example, they may understand the conditional by envisaging just two possibilities,

There was an apple and there was an orange
There was no apple and there was no orange

corresponding to a "biconditional" interpretation, or they may also think about a third possibility,

There was an apple and there was an orange
There was no apple and there was no orange
There was no apple and there was an orange

corresponding to a "conditional" interpretation. An important step in the development of reasoning is the ability to think about alternative possibilities (e.g., Gauffroy and Barrouillet 2011). On the mental model account, people understand a counterfactual by simulating reality and its alternatives. Strikingly, for a counterfactual conditional such as "if there had been an apple there would have been an orange," people construct multiple possibilities from the outset, to mentally represent both reality and an alternative to it (e.g., Byrne 2005, 2007). They imagine the conjecture,

There was an apple and there was an orange

and they also imagine the presupposed reality,

There was no apple and there was no orange.

They may tag each possibility to capture its epistemic status, that is, the model, "there was an apple and there was an orange," may be tagged to indicate that it corresponds to the counterfactual conjecture, and the model, "there was no apple and there was no orange," may be tagged to indicate it corresponds to the known or presupposed facts.

An alternative view is that people understand counterfactuals by mentally simulating just a single possibility. On this view, people understand a conditional "if *A* then *B*" by adding the "if" part, *A*, to their beliefs and calculating the probability of the "then" part, *B* (e.g., Evans and Over 2004). They think about true antecedents only (*A*), and they do not think about their belief in the negated "if" clause (not-*A*) or whether or not the "then" clause follows in such circumstances (e.g., Over et al. 2007). A conditional such as "if there was an apple then there was an orange" directs attention to the situation in which there are apples (e.g., Evans and Over 2004). People compare the situation,

There was an apple and there was an orange

to the situation,

There was an apple and there was no orange

to assess their belief in the likelihood of each situation. On this account, people understand a counterfactual by simulating only a single model (e.g., Evans and Over 2004). The counterfactual, "if there had been an apple then there would have been an orange," is evaluated with reference to the likelihood of the counterfactual situation,

There was an apple and there was an orange

(e.g., Evans 2007, p. 74). The model combines numerical values to represent both the strength of belief in the counterfactual consequent given the counterfactual antecedent, and strengths of belief in each of the implied facts – that there is no apple, and that there is no orange, and so only one model is constructed (e.g., Evans et al. 2005, p. 1049). The probability of a conditional "if *A* then *B*" is the conditional probability, that is, the probability of *B* given *A*: *Probability* $(B|A)$.

In the next sections, I first consider evidence that people construct multiple possibilities to understand a counterfactual, and then evidence that the inferences people draw from counterfactuals differ from the inferences they draw from ordinary conditionals.

## *Dual possibilities*

Counterfactuals typically use the subjunctive mood, e.g., "if he *had* caught the plane he *would have* arrived on time" unlike regular conditionals in the indicative mood, e.g., "if he caught the plane he arrived on time." But the subjunctive mood, e.g., the use of "would have" is not necessary to convey a counterfactual (e.g., Dudman 1988). A counterfactual can be expressed even in languages such as Chinese that do not usually rely on linguistic markers for it (e.g., Au 1983). The counterfactual "if he had caught the plane he would have arrived on time" conveys the presupposition that its "if" part is false (he didn't catch the plane) and its "then" part is false (he didn't arrive on time). The meaning of a counterfactual cannot be a function of the truth of its components, contrary to truth-functional accounts of conditionals (for a review see Nickerson 2015). Philosophical analyses of counterfactual conditionals led to the milestone development in logic of "possible world" semantics (e.g., Stalnaker 1968; Lewis 1973). Their meaning is their truth in the closest possible world, one that is the same as this world except that the conditional is true in it. However, the proposal has led to considerations of the difficulties of assessing the similarity of possible worlds (e.g., Williamson 2007; Kratzer 2012). Moreover people do not have the cognitive capacity to consider all of the potentially infinite set of possible worlds (e.g., Byrne 2005).

Nonetheless an enduring truth about counterfactual reasoning is that when people understand a counterfactual, they recover and represent the presupposed reality for comparison (e.g., Byrne 1997). The first psychological experiments on counterfactual conditionals carried out forty years ago revealed this intriguing observation (e.g., Fillenbaum 1974). Participants were given various sentences to read, including conditionals, e.g., "if he ate the fish he got sick," counterfactuals, e.g., "if he had caught the plane he would have arrived on time," and categorical statements, e.g., "he didn't get a raise." After reading the sentences, participants were given a surprise memory test. They were shown a set of sentences, containing some of the sentences they'd seen before and some sentences that were new. Their task was to identify for each sentence whether they had been given it in the earlier part of the experiment, or not. The results showed that participants made mistakes related to the counterfactual conditionals they had seen. They mistakenly believed that they had been given sentences such as "he did not catch the plane" and "he did not arrive on time" (e.g., Fillenbaum 1974). Similarly, people believe that someone who utters a counterfactual conjecture about an alternative to reality is attempting to communicate something about reality itself. For example, in an experiment people were told "Molly says: if the car had run out of petrol it would have stopped" and they were asked "what did Molly mean to imply?" They were given the set of options, (a) the car ran out of petrol, (b) the car did not run out of petrol, (c) the car stopped, (d) the car did not stop, (e) nothing is implied (e.g., Thompson and Byrne 2002). Most people judged that Molly meant to imply that the car did not run out of petrol, and the car did not stop. When they were given the ordinary conditional "Molly says: if the car ran out of petrol it stopped," they tended to say that none of the categorical statements were implied. These results indicate that counterfactual conditionals convey not only an imagined conjecture similar to the hypotheticality of an ordinary conditional, but also something about the known or presupposed facts. The evidence supports the idea that people understand counterfactual conditionals by envisaging two possibilities: reality and the imagined alternative to it.

A further line of evidence that people keep in mind both possibilities comes from experiments that examine whether people expect a story that contains a counterfactual to continue by referring to reality, or to continue by referring to the imagined alternative to reality. In an experiment participants were given short stories such as one about Miguel who goes to a fruit market with his sister, and she tells him, "if there had been apples, there would have been oranges." When they get to the market, the seller tells them, in fact, "there are no apples and there are no oranges" (Santamaria et al. 2005). Participants read many different short stories about many different situations, such as fruit markets, flower gardens, stationery stores, and so on. Each story contained a counterfactual, such as "if there had been apples, there would have been oranges" and some sentences later, it contained a conjunction, which either referred to what was mentioned in the counterfactual, "there are apples and there are oranges," or referred to the opposite of what was mentioned, "there are no apples and there are no oranges," or to some other contingency, e.g., "there are apples and there are no oranges." Participants read the stories presented on a computer screen one sentence at a time, and they pressed a key to see each new sentence in the story. The length of time they took to read each sentence was recorded. The key measure was how long participants took to read a target conjunction, e.g., "there are no apples and there are no oranges," when it was "primed" by the counterfactual. For comparison, participants also read stories that contained ordinary conditionals, such as "if there are apples, there are oranges" also followed by a conjunction referring to what was mentioned, "there are apples and there are oranges," or a conjunction that referred to the opposite of what was mentioned, "there are no apples and there are no oranges," or some other contingency. The results showed that when participants were primed by a counterfactual, "if there had been apples, there would have been oranges," they read the conjunction that referred to the *opposite* of what was mentioned, "there are no apples and there are no oranges," much more quickly compared with when they were primed by the ordinary conditional "if there are apples there are oranges." Importantly, when they were primed by the counterfactual, they also read the conjunction that referred to what was mentioned, "there are apples and there are oranges," just as quickly as when they were primed by the regular conditional. The findings suggest that participants envisage both possibilities for the counterfactual. They are primed to expect the story to continue with reference *either* to the conjecture (what was mentioned in the counterfactual) *or* with reference to the presupposed reality (the opposite of what was mentioned). In contrast, when they are primed by an ordinary conditional, they expect the story to continue with reference to what was mentioned in the conditional (e.g., Santamaria et al. 2005; see also De Vega et al. 2007). People also keep in mind two possibilities when they understand "even if" semifactuals, such as "even if there had been apples there would have been oranges" (Santamaria et al. 2005; see also Moreno-Rios et al. 2008; McCloy and Byrne 2002).

When people understand a counterfactual conditional, they must also resolve the conflict between the real world and the imagined counterfactual alternative. Whether an individual pays attention to the factual reality or to the counterfactual alternative can have many consequences, including for emotional experiences. For example, an individual who had a ticket but did not board an airplane that crashed may experience relief when he or she focuses on the reality, but anxiety when he or she focuses on the counterfactual alternative of what could have happened (e.g., McMullen and Markman 2000). Resolving the conflict between the counterfactual alternative and reality can lead to an initial brief disruption in the immediate comprehension of a counterfactual conditional (e.g., Ferguson and Sanford 2008). For example, participants in an experiment were given conditionals such as "if cats are hungry they usually pester their owners until they get fed" and they were given additional information that was either consistent with the real world such as "families could feed their cat a bowl of fish and it would gobble it down happily" or inconsistent with the real world, such as "families could feed their cat a bowl of carrots and it would gobble it down happily" (e.g., Ferguson and Sanford 2008). In another condition they were given counterfactual conditionals such as "if cats were vegetarians they would be cheaper for owners to look after" and they were given the additional information inconsistent with the real world "families could feed their cat a bowl of carrots and it would gobble it down happily." The experiment measured where participants' eyes focused as they read the sentences, using eye-tracking technology. The key measure was the duration of eye fixations made on first entering a region of text until an eye movement exited the region (e.g., carrots, fish), which provides an indication of the difficulty experienced when participants initially processed the region of text. The results showed that participants' eyes moved through the region of text fastest when they read the information consistent with the real world (e.g., fish). But crucially, they took as long to read the information inconsistent with the real world (e.g., carrots) whether they had first read the counterfactual conditional, or the ordinary conditional (e.g., Ferguson and Sanford 2008). The results showed that real-world violations were not neutralized by the counterfactual context, indicating that participants continued to process the counterfactual conjecture in terms of their real-world knowledge. The initial disruption by reality is rapidly resolved. Overall, the findings show that people think about the real world as well as the imagined alternative.

When participants read or hear counterfactuals, activation in the brain, measured by functional magnetic resonance imaging (fMRI), occurs in areas associated with mental imagery, also suggesting that people imagine the counterfactual alternative as well as envisage reality (e.g., Kulakova et al. 2013; see also Barbey et al. 2011). When people create a counterfactual alternative that is better than a bad past outcome, similar brain regions are activated as when they remember bad past outcomes, or imagine good future outcomes – areas associated with memory as well as areas associated with mentalizing about intentions and goals. And there is increased activation in areas related to conflict detection, because of the need to consider both the factual and counterfactual alternative (e.g., Van Hoeck et al. 2013).

## *Reasoning with counterfactuals*

Psychological experiments suggest that to be able to reason well, people need to be able to imagine alternative possibilities (e.g., Johnson-Laird and Byrne 2002). Consider the simplest conditional inference – given the ordinary conditional,

If Linda was in Dublin then Cathy was in Galway,

and the information,

Linda was in Dublin,

almost all participants in experiments will accept the *modus ponens* conclusion:

Therefore Cathy was in Galway.

Given the conditional above and the information,

Linda was not in Dublin,

many participants in experiments tend to accept the *denial of the antecedent* conclusion:

Therefore Cathy was not in Galway

(for a review see Manktelow 2012). Their acceptance of the *denial of the antecedent* inference may indicate that they have interpreted the conditional premise as consistent with only the two contingencies for the biconditional interpretation:

Linda was in Dublin and Cathy was in Galway
Linda was not in Dublin and Cathy was not in Galway.

To refrain from the *denial of the antecedent* inference requires people to think about a counterexample – a possibility in which the premises hold but the conclusion does not (e.g., De Neys et al. 2005; Markovits et al. 2010). They must consider the further contingency:

Linda was not in Dublin and Cathy was in Galway.

Many experiments have shown that people make more mistakes, and they take longer to reach conclusions, when an inference requires them to consider multiple possibilities, compared with when it requires them to consider just a single possibility (e.g., Johnson-Laird et al. 1992; De Neys et al. 2005; Markovits et al. 2010; Juhos et al. 2015). Inferences that depend on counterexamples create activation in specific areas of the brain: when brain activity is measured using fMRI, inferences that require participants to consider counter-examples activate the right frontal pole in the prefrontal cortex more than inferences that do not require them to think about such possibilities (e.g., Kroger, et al. 2008; see also Fangmeier et al. 2006).

People make inferences by constructing and combining mental models. The *modus ponens* inference can be made by an immediate inspection of an initial possibility (e.g., Reverberi et al. 2012). Other inferences such as the *denial of the antecedent* inference require more effort, including the systematic construction and combination of alternative possibilities. The more models that reasoners must entertain, the more difficult it is to reason correctly (e.g., Johnson-Laird et al. 1992).

Participants make different inferences from counterfactual conditionals compared with ordinary conditionals: they reason readily about both reality and its counterfactual alternative. For example, given an ordinary conditional such as

> If Linda was in Dublin then Cathy was in Galway

and the information,

> Cathy was not in Galway,

only about half of participants in experiments tend to make the *modus tollens* inference:

> Therefore Linda was not in Dublin.

But when participants are given the counterfactual conditional,

> If Linda had been in Dublin then Cathy would have been in Galway,

and the information,

> Cathy was not in Galway,

most participants make the *modus tollens* inference to,

> Therefore, Linda was not in Dublin

(e.g., Byrne and Tasso 1999). And they also make the *modus ponens* inference from the counterfactual conditional, and the information "Linda was in Dublin," just as readily as they do from the ordinary conditional (see also Moreno-Rios et al. 2008; Egan et al. 2009; Egan and Byrne 2012). In other words, they can readily make inferences about either the imagined possibility or the real-world presupposed facts for the counterfactual conditional.

In summary, current alternative explanations of how people reason with counterfactuals differ in their proposals about whether people simulate a single possibility or multiple possibilities. Evidence from studies that examine the comprehension of counterfactuals supports the idea that people envisage dual possibilities: they mentally represent the possibility corresponding to the counterfactual conjecture, and they also mentally represent the possibility corresponding to the known or presupposed facts. Evidence from studies that compare the inferences people make from counterfactuals and ordinary conditionals also supports the idea that people envisage more possibilities for counterfactuals.

## Conclusions

Counterfactuals provide an important bridge between reasoning and imagination (e.g., Byrne 2005). People often imagine "what if …" and "if only …" and they create counterfactual alternatives to reality. Most people tend to change the same sorts of things about reality when they imagine an alternative to it, almost as if there were "fault lines" in their mental representation of reality. The tendency to zoom in on fault lines arises because people rely on the availability of alternative possibilities in their initial mental representation of reality. The counterfactual imagination relies on cognitive processes that maintain a mental representation of reality, modify the mental representation of reality in systematic ways to create an alternative to it, and switch attention from one representation to the other, updating and inhibiting each representation as required.

The core cognitive processes that support the counterfactual imagination also support reasoning with counterfactuals. When people reason, they imagine alternative possibilities and entertain counterexamples to conclusions. They usually make more mistakes when an inference requires them to consider multiple possibilities. But when people understand a counterfactual conditional, they mentally represent the conjecture and they recover and represent the presupposed reality for comparison. They readily simulate multiple possibilities from the outset, which affects their comprehension of counterfactuals, and the inferences they make from them.

The psychological study of counterfactual conditionals suggests that reasoning and imagination may depend on the same sorts of underlying computational processes: reasoning depends on cognitive processes that support the imagination of alternatives, and imagination depends on cognitive processes that are based on the same core processes. The bridge between reasoning and imagination provided by counterfactuals illustrates some of the common cognitive processes that underlie both.

## References

Alicke, M.D., J. Buckingham, E. Zell, and T. Davis (2008) "Culpable Control and Counterfactual Reasoning in the Psychology of Blame," *Personality and Social Psychology Bulletin* 34: 1371–1381.

Au, T.K. (1983) "Chinese and English Counterfactuals: The Sapir–Whorf Hypothesis Revisited," *Cognition* 15: 155–187.

Barbey, A.K., F. Krueger, and J. Grafman (2011) "Architecture of Counterfactual Thought in the Prefrontal Cortex," in M. Bar (ed.) *Predictions in the Brain: Using Our Past to Generate a Future*, New York: Oxford University Press, 40–57.

Barrouillet, P., C. Gauffroy, and J.F. Lecas (2008) "Mental Models and the Suppositional Account of Conditionals," *Psychological Review* 115(3): 760–771.

Beck, S.R., D.J. Carroll, V.E.A. Brunsdon, and C.K. Gryg (2011) "Supporting Children's Counterfactual Thinking with Alternative Modes of Responding," *Journal of Experimental Child Psychology* 108: 190–202.

Begeer, S., M.M. Terwogt, P. Lunenburg, and H. Stegge (2009) "Brief Report: Additive and Subtractive Counterfactual Reasoning of Children with High-Functioning Autism Spectrum Disorders," *Journal of Autism and Developmental Disorders* 39(11): 1593–1597.

Branscombe, N.R., S. Owen, T.A. Garstka, and J. Coleman (1996) "Rape and Accident Counterfactuals: Who Might Have Done Otherwise and Would It Have Changed the Outcome?" *Journal of Applied Social Psychology* 26(12): 1042–1067.

Byrne, R.M.J. (1997) "Cognitive Processes in Counterfactual Thinking about What Might Have Been," *Psychology of Learning and Motivation* 37: 105–154.

Byrne, R.M.J. (2002) "Mental Models and Counterfactual Thinking," *Trends in Cognitive Sciences* 6: 405–445.

Byrne, R.M.J. (2005) *The Rational Imagination: How People Create Alternatives to Reality*, Cambridge, MA: MIT Press.

Byrne, R.M.J. (2007) "Précis of *The Rational Imagination: How People Create Alternatives to Reality*," *Behavioral and Brain Sciences* 30: 439–453.

Byrne, R.M.J. (2015) "Counterfactual Thought," *Annual Review of Psychology*.

Byrne, R.M.J., and A. Tasso (1999) "Deductive Reasoning with Factual, Possible, and Counterfactual Conditionals," *Memory & Cognition* 27(4): 726–740.

Byrne, R.M.J., and A. McEleney (2000) "Counterfactual Thinking about Actions and Failures to Act," *Journal of Experimental Psychology: Learning, Memory, and Cognition* 26: 1318–1331.

Byrne, R.M.J., and P.N. Johnson-Laird (2009) "'If' and the Problems of Conditional Reasoning," *Trends in Cognitive Sciences* 13: 282–287.

Byrne, R.M.J., S. Segura, R. Culhane, A. Tasso, and P. Berrocal (2000) "The Temporality Effect in Counterfactual Thinking about What Might Have Been," *Memory & Cognition* 28: 264–281.

Davis, C.G., D.R. Lehman, C.B. Wortman, R.C. Silver, and S.C. Thompson (1995) "The Undoing of Traumatic Life Events," *Personality and Social Psychology Bulletin* 21: 109–124.

De Neys, W., W. Schaeken, and G. d'Ydewalle (2005) "Working Memory and Everyday Conditional Reasoning: Retrieval and Inhibition of Stored Counterexamples," *Thinking and Reasoning* 11: 349–381.

De Vega, M., M. Urrutia, and B. Riffo (2007) "Canceling Updating in the Comprehension of Counterfactuals Embedded in Narratives," *Memory & Cognition* 35(6): 1410–1421.

Dixon, J., and R.M.J. Byrne (2011) "Counterfactual Thinking about Exceptional Actions," *Memory & Cognition* 39(7): 1317–1331.

Drayton, S., K.J. Turley-Ames, and N.R. Guajardo (2011) "Counterfactual Thinking and False Belief: The Role of Executive Function," *Journal of Experimental Child Psychology* 108(3): 532–548.

Dudman, V.H. (1988) "Indicative and Subjunctive," *Analysis* 48: 113–122.

Egan, S., and R.M.J. Byrne (2012) "Inferences from Counterfactual Threats and Promises," *Experimental Psychology* 59(4): 227–235.

Egan, S., J. Garcia-Madruga, and R.M.J. Byrne (2009) "Indicative and Counterfactual 'Only If' Conditionals," *Acta Psychologica* 132(3): 240–249.

Epstude, K., and N.J. Roese (2008) "The Functional Theory of Counterfactual Thinking," *Personality and Social Psychology Review* 12(2): 168–192.

Epstude, K., and N.J. Roese (2011) "When Goal Pursuit Fails: The Functions of Counterfactual Thought in Intention Formation,"*Social Psychology* 42(1): 19–27.

Espino, O., C. Santamaria, and R.M.J. Byrne (2009) "People Think about What Is True for Conditionals, Not What Is False: Only True Possibilities Prime the Comprehension of 'If,'" *Quarterly Journal of Experimental Psychology* 62(6): 1072–1078.

Evans, J.S.B.T. (2007) *Hypothetical Thinking*, Hove: Psychology Press.

Evans, J.S.B.T., and D.E. Over (2004) *If*, Oxford: Oxford University Press.

Evans, J.S.B.T., D.E. Over, and S.J. Handley (2005) "Suppositions, Extensionality, and Conditionals: A Critique of the Mental Model Theory of Johnson-Laird and Byrne (2002)," *Psychological Review* 112(4): 1040–1052.

Fangmeier, T., M. Knauff, C.C. Ruff, and V. Sloutsky (2006) "The Neural Correlates of Logical Thinking: An Event-Related fMRI Study," *Journal of Cognitive Neuroscience* 18: 320–334.

Ferguson, H., and A. Sanford (2008) "Anomalies in Real and Counterfactual Worlds: An Eye-Movement Investigation," *Journal of Memory and Language* 58: 609–626.

Fillenbaum, S. (1974) "Information Amplified: Memory for Counterfactual Conditionals," *Journal of Experimental Psychology* 102(1): 44–49.

Frosch, C., and R.M.J. Byrne (2012) "Causal Conditionals and Counterfactuals," *Acta Psychologica* 141(1): 54–66.

Gauffroy, C., and P. Barrouillet (2011) "The Primacy of Thinking about Possibilities in the Development of Reasoning," *Developmental Psychology* 47: 1000–1011.

Girotto, V., P. Legrenzi, and A. Rizzo (1991) "Event Controllability in Counterfactual Thinking," *Acta Psychologica* 78: 111–133.

Girotto, V., D. Ferrante, S. Pighin, and M. Gonzalez (2007) "Postdecisional Counterfactual Thinking by Actors and Readers," *Psychological Science* 18: 510–515.

Gomez Beldarrain, M., J.C. Garcia-Monco, E. Astigarraga, A. Gonzalez, and J. Grafman (2005) "Only Spontaneous Counterfactual Thinking Is Impaired in Patients with Prefrontal Cortex Lesions," *Cognitive Brain Research* 24(3): 723–726.

Hooker, C., N.J. Roese, and S. Park (2000) "Impoverished Counterfactual Thinking Is Associated with Schizophrenia," *Psychiatry* 63(4): 326–335.

Johnson-Laird, P.N. (1983) *Mental Models*, Cambridge: Cambridge University Press.

Johnson-Laird, P.N. (2006) *How We Reason*, Oxford: Oxford University Press.

Johnson-Laird, P.N., and R.M.J. Byrne (1991) *Deduction*, Hillsdale: Erlbaum.

Johnson-Laird, P.N., and R.M.J. Byrne (2002) "Conditionals: A Theory of Meaning, Pragmatics, and Inference," *Psychological Review* 109: 646–678.

Johnson-Laird, P.N., R.M.J. Byrne, and W. Schaeken (1992) "Propositional Reasoning by Model," *Psychological Review* 99: 418–439.

Johnson-Laird, P.N., S.S. Khemlani, and G.P. Goodwin (2015) "Logic, Probability, and Human Reasoning," *Trends in Cognitive Sciences*, 19(4): 201–214.

Juhos, C., A.C. Quelhas, and R.M.J. Byrne (2015) "Reasoning about Intentions: Counterexamples to Reasons for Actions," *Journal of Experimental Psychology: Learning, Memory & Cognition* 41(1): 55–76.

Kahneman, D., and A. Tversky (1982a) "The Simulation Heuristic," in D. Kahneman, P. Slovic, and A. Tversky (eds.) *Judgment under Uncertainty: Heuristics and Biases*, New York: Cambridge University Press, 201–208.

Kahneman, D., and A. Tversky (1982b) "The Psychology of Preferences," *Scientific American* 246(1): 160–173.

Kahneman, D., and D.T. Miller (1986) "Norm Theory: Comparing Reality to Its Alternatives," *Psychological Review* 93(2): 136–153.

Khemlani, S., I. Orenes, and P.N. Johnson-Laird (2012) "Negation: A Theory of Its Meaning, Representation and Use," *Journal of Cognitive Psychology* 24: 241–259.

Knight, R.T., and M. Grabowecky (1995) "Escape from Linear Time: Prefrontal Cortex and Conscious Experience," in M.S. Gazzaniga (ed.) *The Cognitive Neurosciences*, Cambridge, MA: MIT Press, 1357–1371.

Kratzer, A. (2012) "Modals and Conditionals: New and Revised Perspectives," Oxford: Oxford University Press.

Kroger, J.K., L.E. Nystrom, J.D. Cohen, and P.N. Johnson-Laird (2008) "Distinct Neural Substrates for Deductive and Mathematical Processing," *Brain Research* 1243: 86–103.

Kulakova, E., M. Aichhorn, M. Schurz, M. Kronbichler, and J. Perner (2013) "Processing Counterfactual and Hypothetical Conditionals: An fMRI Investigation," *NeuroImage* 72: 265–271.

Lewis, D. (1973) *Counterfactuals*, Cambridge, MA: Harvard University Press.

Macrae, C.N., A.B. Milne, and R.J. Griffiths (1993) "Counterfactual Thinking and the Perception of Criminal Behaviour," *British Journal of Psychology* 84(2): 221–226.

Malle, B.F., A.E. Monroe, and S. Guglielmo (2014) "A Theory of Blame," *Psychological Inquiry* 25(2): 147–186.

Manktelow, K. (2012) *Thinking and Reasoning: An Introduction to the Psychology of Reason, Judgment and Decision Making*, Hove: Psychology Press.

Markman, K.D., I. Gavanski, S.J. Sherman, and M.N. McMullen (1993) "The Mental Simulation of Better and Worse Possible Worlds," *Journal of Experimental Social Psychology* 29(1): 87–109.

Markman, K.D., M.N. McMullen, and R.A. Elizaga (2008) "Counterfactual Thinking, Persistence, and Performance: A Test of the Reflection and Evaluation Model," *Journal of Experimental Social Psychology* 44(2): 421–428.

Markman, K.D., N. Mizoguchi, and M.N. McMullen (2008) "'It Would Have Been Worse under Saddam': Implications of Counterfactual Thinking for Beliefs Regarding the Ethical Treatment of Prisoners of War," *Journal of Experimental Social Psychology* 44(3): 650–654.

Markovits, H., H. Lortie Forgues, and M.-L. Brunet (2010) "Conditional Reasoning, Frequency of Counterexamples, and the Effect of Response Modality," *Memory & Cognition* 38: 485–492.

McCloy, R., and R.M.J. Byrne (2000) "Counterfactual Thinking about Controllable Actions," *Memory & Cognition* 28: 1071–1078.

McCloy, R., and R.M.J. Byrne (2002) "Semifactual 'Even If' Thinking," *Thinking and Reasoning* 8: 41–67.

McCrea, S.M. (2008) "Self-Handicapping, Excuse Making, and Counterfactual Thinking: Consequences for Self-Esteem and Future Motivation," *Journal of Personality and Social Psychology* 95: 274–292.

McEleney, A., and R.M.J. Byrne (2006) "Spontaneous Causal and Counterfactual Thoughts," *Thinking and Reasoning* 12: 235–255.

McMullen, M.N., and K.D. Markman (2000) "Downward Counterfactuals and Motivation: The Wake-Up Call and the Pangloss Effect," *Personality and Social Psychology Bulletin* 26: 575–584.

McNamara, P., R. Durso, A. Brown, and A. Lynch (2003) "Counterfactual Cognitive Deficit in Persons with Parkinson's Disease," *Journal of Neurology, Neurosurgery and Psychiatry* 74(8): 1065–1070.

Miller, D.T., and S. Gunasegaram (1990) "Temporal Order and the Perceived Mutability of Events: Implications for Blame Assignment," *Journal of Personality and Social Psychology* 59(6): 1111–1118.

Moreno-Rios, S., J. Garcia-Madruga, and R.M.J. Byrne (2008) "Semifactual 'Even If' Reasoning," *Acta Psychologica* 128: 197–209.

Nickerson, R. (2015) *Conditional Reasoning*, Oxford: Oxford University Press.

Niedenthal, P.M., J.P. Tangney, and I. Gavanski (1994) "'If Only I Weren't' versus 'If Only I Hadn't': Distinguishing Shame and Guilt in Counterfactual Thinking," *Journal of Personality and Social Psychology* 67(4): 585–595.

Oaksford, M., and N. Chater (2007) *Bayesian Rationality: The Probabilistic Approach to Human Reasoning*, Oxford: Oxford University Press.

O'Connor, E., T. McCormack, and A. Feeney (2014) "Do Children Who Experience Regret Make Better Decisions? A Developmental Study of the Behavioral Consequences of Regret," *Child Development* 85(5), 1995–2010.

Over, D.E., C. Hadjichristidis, J.S.B. Evans, S.J. Handley, and S.A. Sloman (2007) "The Probability of Causal Conditionals," *Cognitive Psychology* 54(1): 62–97.

Petrocelli, J.V., E.J. Percy, S.J. Sherman, and Z.L. Tormala (2011) "Counterfactual Potency," *Journal of Personality and Social Psychology* 100(1): 30.

Pighin, S., R.M.J. Byrne, D. Ferrante, M. Gonzalez, and V. Girotto (2011) "Counterfactual Thoughts about Experienced, Observed, and Narrated Events," *Thinking and Reasoning* 17(2): 197–211.

Reverberi, C., D. Pischedda, M. Burigo, and P. Cherubini (2012) "Deduction without Awareness," *Acta Psychologica* 139: 244–256.

Roese, N.J., S. Park, R. Smallman, and C. Gibson (2008) "Schizophrenia Involves Impairment in the Activation of Intentions by Counterfactual Thinking," *Schizophrenia Research* 103(1–3): 343–344.

Santamaria, C., O. Espino, and R.M.J. Byrne (2005) "Counterfactual and Semifactual Conditionals Prime Alternative Possibilities," *Journal of Experimental Psychology: Learning, Memory, and Cognition* 31: 1149–1154.

Spellman, B.A., and D.R. Mandel (1999) "When Possibility Informs Reality: Counterfactual Thinking as a Cue to Causality," *Current Directions in Psychological Science* 8(4): 120–123.

Stalnaker, R. (1968) "A Theory of Conditionals," *Studies in Logical Theory* 2: 98–112.

Tetlock, P.E., and A. Belkin (eds.) (1996) *Counterfactual Thought Experiments in World Politics: Logical, Methodological and Psychological Perspectives*, Princeton: Princeton University Press.

Thompson, V.A., and Byrne, R.M. (2002) "Reasoning Counterfactually: Making Inferences about Things That Didn't Happen," *Journal of Experimental Psychology: Learning, Memory, and Cognition* 28(6): 1154–1170.

Van Hoeck, N., N. Ma, L. Ampe, K. Baetens, M. Vandekerckhove, and F. Van Overwalle (2013) "Counterfactual Thinking: An fMRI Study on Changing the Past for a Better Future,"*Social Cognitive and Affective Neuroscience* 8: 556–564.

Walsh, C.R., and R.M.J. Byrne (2004) "Counterfactual Thinking: The Temporal Order Effect," *Memory & Cognition* 32: 369–378.

Walsh, C.R., and R.M.J. Byrne (2007) "How People Think 'If Only …' about Reasons for Actions," *Thinking and Reasoning* 13(4): 461–483.

Williamson, T. (2007) "Philosophical Knowledge and Knowledge of Counterfactuals," *Grazer Philosophische Studien* 74(1): 89–124.

Zeelenberg, M., and R. Pieters (2007) "A Theory of Regret Regulation 1.0," *Journal of Consumer Psychology* 17(1): 3–18.

# PART V

# Imagination in ethics, moral psychology, and political philosophy

# 26
# MORAL IMAGINATION

*Mark Johnson*

For hundreds of years in mainstream Western philosophy it has been a commonplace to regard "moral imagination" as an oxymoron. The terms "moral" and "imagination" are often thought to be incompatible by those who conceive of morality as a system of *rational* moral principles and who regard imagination as a free play of images and ideas unconstrained by reason. The result of this mistaken bifurcation between reason and imagination is that imagination is not seen as having any constitutive role in determining what is right and wrong, lest we risk arbitrariness, idiosyncrasy, subjectivism, and rampant relativism.

This widespread misconception that imagination is unsuited to the lofty office of moral appraisal has led, for most of history and with only rare, though very important, exceptions, to a profound neglect of moral imagination by philosophers and psychologists. Over the past three decades, however, an increasing number of philosophers have begun to use the term unapologetically to name a crucial process of imaginative moral deliberation by which we are able to explore how experience would play out under the influence of various values and commitments. From this perspective, moral imagination is regarded as the chief means we have for reducing moral indeterminacy, resolving conflicts among competing ends, and addressing clashes of values. In short, imagination is viewed as *constitutive* of our moral reasoning and not merely subservient to the alleged application of preestablished, rationally derived moral principles.

## Imagination as a key component of moral sentiment theories

This widespread neglect of imagination is mostly the result of rationalistic theories of moral cognition that arose at the end of the eighteenth century, most notably Kant's theory of pure practical reason. This rationalism was partly a reaction against the moral sentiments theories, which held that moral judgments are based on shared feelings or sentiments, rather than on rationally derived moral laws. Moral sentiment theories recognized a significant role for imagination in moral deliberation. Francis Hutcheson, David Hume, and Adam Smith famously argued that moral judgments were not acts of reason, but were instead based on the shared human sentiments of approbation and disapprobation that we feel as we contemplate various actions and states of character. In his *Treatise of Human Nature* (Hume 1739–40) and *An Enquiry Concerning the Principles of Morals* (Hume 1751), Hume argued that only emotions and passions can move us to action, and therefore any morally effective motive must be based on our capacity to experience moral sentiments, combined with the general sympathy most people have for the well-being of others. In other words, our moral appraisals require that we put ourselves imaginatively in the place of others, and feel appropriate moral sentiments of approval or disapproval toward those contemplated acts and character traits.

A more elaborate and nuanced account of moral imagination was developed by Adam Smith in his *The Theory of Moral Sentiments* (1790). Like Hume, Smith begins with the claim that, no matter how selfish and egocentric humans may be, they are also born with a natural disposition to care for the welfare of others. We judge an action right, or a character trait virtuous, to the degree that we feel a sentiment of approval when we perform that action, or exercise that disposition in ourselves.

But how are we able to participate in the way others feel, think, and act? Smith's answer is that we can imagine how they are feeling in a given situation:

> As we have no immediate experience of what other men feel, we can form no idea of the manner in which they are affected, but by conceiving what we ourselves should feel in the like situation … By the imagination we place ourselves in his situation, we conceive ourselves enduring all the same torments, we enter as it were into his body, and become in some measure the same person with him …
>
> *(Smith 1790, I.i.1)*

This empathic capacity is "the source of fellow-feeling for the misery of others" and "it is by changing places in fancy with the sufferer, that we come either to conceive or to be affected by what he feels" (Smith 1790, I.i.1). The goal of our moral self-cultivation should therefore be to nurture our sympathetic feelings and to expand our capacity for imaginative grasp of other people's experience and situation. Smith concludes:

> that there may be some correspondence of sentiments between the spectator and the person principally concerned, the spectator must, first of all, endeavour, as much as he can, to put himself in the situation of the other, and to bring home to himself every little circumstance of distress which can possibly occur to the sufferer; He must adopt the whole case of his companion with all the minutest incidents; and strive to render as perfect as possible, that imaginary change of situation upon which his sympathy is founded.
>
> *(Smith 1790, I.i.4).*

As we will see below, Smith's subtle and sensitive understanding of the nature of, and need for, an imaginative grasp of other people's experience is very much in line with late twentieth- and early twenty-first-century treatments of moral imagination. He even recognizes the importance of our capacity to mirror the feelings and bodily states of others that neuroscientists over two centuries later will attribute to our mirror-neuron systems.

Unfortunately, the heyday of moral sentiment theories was brief. When they were eclipsed by Kantian rationalist moral philosophy, this led to a profound neglect of moral imagination for the next 120 years.

## The marginalization of imagination in moral philosophy

It is not too much of an oversimplification to assert that Kant's celebrated attack on moral feeling led to the subsequent dismissal of imagination as a source of moral insight and appraisal. This suspicion of imagination stemmed primarily from the hegemony of what I (Johnson 1993) have called the Moral Law folk theory, which can be summarized as follows:

1 Humans are distinguished from brute animals by their capacity to reason and to act under the guidance of universally binding rational principles.
2 Moral principles are rules that categorically determine which actions are morally acceptable, which are morally impermissible, and which are obligatory.
3 Acting morally requires (a) determining rationally which principle applies to a present situation, and (b) having the willpower to act on that principle in order to "do what is right."
4 To avoid moral relativism, moral laws or commands must be defined in terms of determinate literal concepts capable of fitting the concrete situations we find ourselves in.

There are two popular versions of the Moral Law folk theory. Theological versions posit absolute moral commandments issued by God (or gods), while rationalist versions regard ethical guidance and constraint as products of universal human reason. Both versions agree in denying imagination any constitutive role in moral judgment, on the grounds that imagination and reason are fundamentally different and nonoverlapping cognitive faculties. In the rationalist camp, Kant famously argued that moral laws must be universally and necessarily binding on all rational creatures, and he insisted that such universality and necessity could only be the product of a "pure" practical reason, independent of any reliance on experience or empirical considerations. Kant summarizes: "It is clear from the foregoing that all moral concepts have their seat and origin completely a priori in reason … In this purity of their origin lies their very worthiness to serve us as supreme practical principles; and to the extent that something empirical is added to them, just so much is taken away from their genuine influence and from the absolute worth of the corresponding actions" (Kant [1785], *Grounding*, 411).

By "empirical" here, Kant meant anything grounded in human experience, including anything tied to our bodily and affective selves. Although Kant did not think of our rational and bodily natures as two different substances, there is, nevertheless, a lingering dualism in his metaphysics, insofar as he regarded reason as an activity of the transcendent self or ego (as noumenal) in contrast with imagination, which he thought of as tied to our bodily (hence, phenomenal) nature. On this view, moral judgment requires a rational act of seeing how a concrete case falls under a specific moral imperative. Kant saw that this process of bringing a particular case under a universal rule cannot itself be governed by rules, for that would lead to an infinite regress of rules for correctly applying rules. However, he steadfastly insists that the moral judgment cannot be based on imagination: "Thus the moral law has no other cognitive faculty to mediate its application to objects of nature than the understanding (not the imagination)" (Kant [1781–87], *Critique of Practical Reason*, 69). In his *Lectures on Ethics* he therefore warns against subordinating rational authority to the seductive power of imagination: "If he surrenders authority over himself, his imagination has free play; he cannot discipline himself, but his imagination carries him away by the laws of association; he yields willingly to his senses, and, unable to curb them, he becomes their toy" (Kant 1775–80, *Lectures* 140).

It is this Kantian logic that most fatefully and erroneously regards moral imagination as an oxymoron – a dissonant yoking together of two allegedly incompatible ideas, namely, morality as a system of rationally derived moral laws and moral deliberation as a process of imaginative projection. Kant's influence on subsequent moral philosophy was so profound that, with perhaps the exception of philosophers such as Nietzsche, James, and Dewey, the idea that imagination might play a central role in moral appraisal and judgment is almost unheard of in mainstream Western philosophy until the late twentieth century. Delaying until later an account of Dewey's seminal contribution to the view that moral imagination is the crux of our ethical problem-solving, let us briefly consider how imagination has slowly gained a foothold in accounts of moral cognition over the past three or four decades.

## The movement toward a more constitutive view of imagination in moral cognition

In the latter half of the twentieth century, the term "imagination" begins to appear ever more frequently in discussions of ethical reasoning. One finds a number of views that promisingly acknowledge a place for imagination in our moral life. Unfortunately, most of them remain unwilling to allow imagination a fully constitutive role as performing the principal work of moral thinking. Too often, they gesture toward imagination without providing any detailed account of its operations. For example, in *Freedom and Reason* (1963), R.M. Hare acknowledges that in order to correctly apply his rationally derived Universalizability Principle to a concrete situation, we must be able to imagine that situation from various perspectives to see how it would affect others. However, Hare insists that imagination does not generate our moral obligations, but only helps us see what is required concretely in a particular situation of moral judgment. This function is carried out more by artists than philosophers, because "to cause people to exercise their imaginations is above all the task of the artist – especially the novelist and the dramatist" (Hare 1963, 181). It is through literary fictions, he suggests, that we often cultivate a sympathetic imagination that helps us understand the situation of others and empathize with them. Nevertheless, the normative dimension of the Universalizability Principle comes from reason alone.

Steven Fesmire (2003) surveys other philosophers who find a limited role for moral imagination, but who still insist that reason alone is the source of moral principles and guidance for our lives. He cites as an example Oliver Williams (1997), who treats imagination as part of Aristotelian practical wisdom, but argues that the moral constraint must issue from independently defined standards of right action. Williams claims that "while moral images and the stories they compose shape reason 'to see rightly,' they do not replace reason … The stories and images of the Christian community help one to discover God's will but, in principle, human insight and reasoning can discover this same will in the form of moral obligations" (Williams 1997, 5). Patricia Werhane (1999) also recognizes the indispensability of moral imagination for exploring different possible framings of a moral situation or problem. She investigates the crucial role of imagination – or lack thereof – in certain landmark business ethics cases. However, she nevertheless ends up stressing the necessity of rational constraints on the workings of imagination: "Moral imagination enables one to assess one's situation, to evaluate present and new possibilities, and to create decisions that are not parochially embedded in a restricted context or confined by a certain point of view … However, one should not confuse moral imagination with practical moral reasoning … imagination alone can create fantasies that, too, become dominating and falsifying narratives" (Werhane 1999, 13). What both Williams and Werhane stress is that without proper guidance from moral reason, imagination is liable to lead us astray.

John Kekes' *The Enlargement of Life: Moral Imagination at Work* (2006) at first appears to grant imagination a very substantial role in our moral understanding, but he soon qualifies this with a requirement of rational moral constraint. In a view that seems to echo some of John Dewey's key ideas (although without any serious acknowledgement of Dewey), Kekes says "[m]oral imagination, self-transformation, and reflective self-evaluation together enlarge life by enlarging its possibilities and overcoming obstacles to their realization … Moral imagination is one chief means by which this reflective self-evaluation proceeds. Its moral component is concerned with living a good life, understood as combining responsibility and fulfillment" (Kekes 2006, xiv). Kekes describes three kinds of imaginative process that he regards as crucial to human ethical behavior and fulfillment. *Corrective imagination* is a backward-looking act through which we attempt to grasp the full range of possibilities that might have been available in a past situation, but which we may have overlooked at the time. *Exploratory imagination* then permits us to investigate the range of morally appropriate actions currently available to us as we struggle with a moral problem. This capacity allows us to engage complex cognitive, emotional, and volitional processes relevant to living moral lives. *Disciplined imagination* mediates between corrective imagination's discovery of what about ourselves and the situation needs to be corrected or reconstructed, on the one hand, and exploratory imagination's survey of the moral options available to an individual, on the other. This promising assessment of the importance of imagination is, however, limited by Kekes' refusal to grant imagination a fully constitutive role. Clinging to an outdated faculty psychology, Kekes ultimately concludes that imagination must always be subject to the constraints of moral reason. This limitation is evident when Kekes criticizes Martha Nussbaum's celebration of the novelist's creative imagination as key to our moral enlightenment. Kekes responds that "the idea that living a good life is like creating a work of art, that moral imagination is a species of creative imagination in which the artists work in the medium of their own lives, is pernicious because it leads to the rejection of moral limits" (113). In the final analysis, then, Kekes does not trust imagination to do the work of moral thinking.

There is a pattern emerging in these views, in which initial enthusiasm for moral imagination comes to be tempered by a deep concern that, left unchecked by reason, imagination might lead to an uncontrolled moral relativism. In light of centuries of neglect of imagination, these and other theories do at least recognize some role for imagination in moral deliberation, and so they are definitely steps forward in moving beyond a strictly principle-governed perspective. Nonetheless, they never fully extricate themselves from the mainstream view that all or most moral constraint, as well as the definition of right action, must come from some cognitive faculty or source besides imagination. In short, the key issue is whether imagination is to be granted a *constitutive* role in moral appraisal, or whether it remains but a subsidiary function that only helps us grasp how our ultimate moral laws and values apply in a concrete situation.

In *The Many Faces of Realism* (1987), Hilary Putnam argues that moral theories are not, as many of their progenitors conceive them, issuances of some universal reason that supposedly specifies absolute constraints. Instead, every moral perspective or theory presupposes and articulates some particular *moral image of the world:*

> A moral image, in the sense in which I am using the term, is not a declaration that this or that is a virtue, or that this or that is what one ought to do; it is rather a picture of how our virtues and ideals hang together with one another and of what they have to do with the position we are in. It may be as vague as the notions of "sisterhood and brotherhood"; indeed, millions of human beings have found in those metaphors moral images that could organize their moral lives …
>
> *(Putnam 1987, 51–52)*

This embrace of a complex imaginative framework as our horizon of moral values and practices is tantalizing insofar as it suggests that moral appraisal is more about imagining how the world might be made better, than it is about applying unconditionally and eternally valid principles to a particular situation. Putnam's pluralistic moral vision is also admirable, insofar as he recognizes our need to blend a number of inherited moral images – such as liberty, equality, and brotherhood and sisterhood – into a more or less coherent view of character, right action, and flourishing. In other words, we need imaginative pictures of how our world might look under the influence of complex virtues, principles, and values. Unfortunately, Putnam has not given any detailed account of what this alleged process of constructing a moral image involves, nor has he explained how it is supposed to work in our lives.

At first glance, Richard Rorty (1989) appears to advance beyond Putnam when he embraces imagination as key to change of moral perspective. Rorty focuses almost exclusively on what he calls metaphoric "moral vocabularies" that supposedly define a culture's shared values, perspectives, and practices. He then suggests that changes from one moral vocabulary to another (such as a change from a utilitarian to a Christian, Kantian, or existentialist vocabulary) do not occur through rational analysis and argument, but rather by the imaginative supplanting of one metaphorically structured moral vocabulary by another. The proposing of a new metaphoric vocabulary is alleged to be a product of the imagination of a "strong poet" – a moral innovator who articulates a new metaphoric vocabulary that takes hold in a culture.

What Rorty gets right is that our moral systems are, indeed, structured by systematic metaphors (Johnson 1993; Lakoff and Johnson 1999; Lakoff 1996, 2008) and that novel metaphors can play a crucial role in the transformation of our moral perspective. However, Rorty offers absolutely no explanation of how imagination supposedly operates in this process of change. How do these metaphors work their magic in creating new moral vocabularies? New metaphors, according to Rorty, are simply nonrational irruptions of a new vocabulary for thinking and talking about moral values, practices, and principles. Because he insists that they are not semantic phenomena, he cannot provide any account of how they might induce meaning change. He is reduced to simply asserting that sometimes we do actually come up with new metaphors, and that is all that can be said. He espouses a view of metaphor change that he attributes to Donald Davidson, namely,

> that one should not think of metaphorical expressions as having meaning distinct from their literal ones. To have a meaning is to have a place in a language game. Metaphors, by definition, do not ... In his view, tossing a metaphor into a conversation is like suddenly breaking off the conversation long enough to make a face, or pulling a photograph out of your pocket and displaying it, or pointing at a feature of the surroundings, or slapping your interlocutor's face, or kissing him.
>
> *(Rorty 1989, 17–18)*

Because Rorty, following Davidson, denies that metaphor is a semantic phenomenon, he ignores any serious linguistic or cognitive science research on semantic change or on the workings of imagination and simply asserts that somehow a new moral vocabulary, complete and total, springs up to replace the reigning moral vocabulary. He famously describes this process as blind, contingent, and mechanical:

> Think of novelty as the sort of thing which happens when, for example, a cosmic ray scrambles the atoms in a DNA molecule, thus sending things off in the direction of the orchids or the anthropoids ... Analogously, for all we know, or should care, Aristotle's metaphorical use of *ousia*, Saint Paul's metaphorical use of *agapê*, and Newton's metaphorical use of *gravitas*, were the results of cosmic rays scrambling the

> fine structure of some crucial neurons in their respective brains. It hardly matters how the trick was done. The results were marvelous.
>
> *(Rorty 1989, 17)*

But it *does* matter how the trick was done! It matters a great deal, because our ability to explain how moral imagination actually works makes all the difference for our ability to show whether moral imagination is *constitutive* of our moral understanding, rather than merely an act of irrational rupture. It makes all the difference whether it is possible to speak of "better" and "worse" moral deliberation. Rorty had a notoriously difficult time explaining how or why one moral perspective (or vocabulary) was any better or worse than any other. He couldn't do this, because he held that there is nothing beyond or beneath vocabularies against which they can be assessed as more or less accurate: "attempts to get back behind language to something which 'grounds' it, or which it 'expresses,' or to which it might hope to be 'adequate,' have not worked" (Rorty 1982, xx).

Consequently, when it came to normative ethical claims, Rorty thought that arguments were of little practical value, and he instead praised the role of literary narratives in helping us appreciate the experience and suffering of others. This is an important insight, but it is not self-explanatory or self-justifying. Rorty observed that people of a liberal persuasion, for example, tend to value the metaphor of brother-/sisterhood and therefore set a high value on relief from cruelty as crucial for the improvement of the human condition. They are therefore attracted to fictional narratives that help us empathize with others and see them as like ourselves, as a basis for treating them with respect and minimizing their suffering. As Rorty says, with respect to one particular moral ideal, "in my utopia, human solidarity would be seen not as a fact to be recognized by clearing away 'prejudice' or burrowing down to previously hidden depths but, rather, as a goal to be achieved. It is to be achieved not by inquiry but by imagination, the imaginative ability to see strange people as fellow sufferers" (Rorty 1989, xvi). Rorty is right about the power of empathic imagination to help us enlarge the circle of people and animals that deserve our respect and care. He sees that imaginative fictions enact a narrative understanding of others' lives, struggles, and hopes, and can often engender empathy for their plight. Unfortunately, Rorty offers no account of how moral imagination works, nor has he provided any explanation of how moral vocabularies become meaningful, how they can reconfigure our experience, and how they are able to enrich our imaginative moral exploration of ethically problematic situations. For that, we are well advised to turn back to the parts of John Dewey's philosophy that Rorty dismisses as a misguided metaphysics of experience.

## Dewey's conception of moral imagination

It was the American pragmatist philosopher John Dewey who provided the most nuanced account of moral imagination as *constitutive* of moral inquiry and deliberation. In the early twentieth century, the philosophical orientation that came to be known as pragmatism provided an incisive criticism of the traditional Moral Law view of moral cognition, and it proposed a radical alternative picture of moral reasoning as imaginative deliberative problem-solving. Dewey recognized that moral imagination was constitutive of, and not just supplementary to, moral reasoning.

Dewey argued that what I have called the Moral Law theory is a misguided attempt to freeze conceptions of right and wrong for all time, based on the erroneous assumption that we inhabit a closed and completed moral universe that operates under the constraint of absolute moral laws adequate for appraising any possible ethical situation. From a broadly evolutionary perspective, Dewey emphasized the reality of change and novelty in nature and human affairs. With respect to morality, this meant that new moral problems are bound to arise from time to time. Human beings are mostly creatures of habits they have unthinkingly developed in response to regular features of their environment, and these habits more or less automatically and unconsciously determine their behaviors. Much of the time our habits may serve us reasonably well, but they can become dysfunctional in situations where novel conditions arise that were not anticipated in the formation of the original habits. Then problems typically emerge when our taken-for-granted habits are not adequate for dealing with changing conditions of experience, such as when two or more agents espouse incompatible values or conceptions of the good, or when an individual experiences conflicting values or goals in his or her life. What we need most in such cases of moral conflict is not reversion to alleged absolute, pregiven principles, virtues, or goods, because it is precisely these that may be called into question by novel conditions and events. Rather, what we need is an intelligent process of moral inquiry that helps us resolve conflicts, harmonize competing values, and expand possibilities for growth of meaning. For this reason, Dewey conceived of moral reasoning as a form of problem-solving inquiry by which we transform situations to resolve conflicts, disharmonies, and tensions, typically without knowing in advance what our end or good is or ought to be.

It is within this context of ongoing problem-solving that Dewey introduces his notion of imaginative reasoning. Recall that the reason we encounter a problematic situation in the first place is that our ordinary habits of thought, feeling, and action have ceased to let us deal adequately with the changed experiential conditions that we are encountering. What is needed in such cases is a nuanced understanding of the historical context in which our received moral values and practices arose, a deep appreciation of the sources and nature of our current moral problems, and an imaginative grasp of the possible ways experience might be transformed and carried forward for the better. Thomas Alexander has eloquently summarized Dewey's conception of imaginative intelligence in the service of moral betterment:

> We act in order to realize on a deeper, aesthetic level a sense of meaning and value in our very existence. Knowledge may play a crucial role in this, but in the last analysis, for Dewey, we are creatures seeking a kind of dynamic, embodied fulfillment that goes far beyond generating mere propositional attitudes and other abstractive cognitive needs. As active beings, we are in constant touch with the *possibilities* of our situations. Indeed, this is Dewey's definition of intelligence: to see the actual in light of the possible. This is also his definition of imagination. Imagination is rooted in organic embodiment of our existence and flowers in our highest consciously articulate moments.
>
> *(Alexander 2013, 194)*

Moral imagination is thus not a distinct *faculty;* instead, it is the expansive dimension of intelligence at work in the ongoing remaking of experience. It is a *process* of experiential transformation and growth – the embodied, situated, aesthetically sensitive manner by which experience expands and gains enriched depth, breadth, and meaning. Alexander observes that "the role of imagination becomes pivotal, for it is a phase of activity – that phase in which possible activities are envisaged in relation to our own situations, thereby amplifying the meaning of the present and creating the context from which present values may be criticized, thus liberating the course of action in itself" (Alexander 2013, 194).

Dewey famously described this exploratory phase of the moral problem-solving process as a dramatic rehearsal of possibilities for developing various courses of action, in order to see which projected course best resolves the indeterminacy of our present situation:

> Deliberation is a dramatic rehearsal (in imagination) of various competing possible lines of action. It starts from the blocking of efficient overt action, due to that conflict of prior habit and newly released impulse to which reference has been made. Then each habit, each impulse, involved in the temporary suspense of overt action takes its turn in being tried out. Deliberation is an experiment in finding out what the various lines of possible action are really like. It is an experiment in making various combinations of selected elements of habits and impulses, to see what the resultant action would be like if it were entered upon. But the trial is in imagination, not in overt fact.
>
> *(Dewey 1922/1983, 132–133)*

Moral imagination is our fundamental capacity to imagine how certain values and commitments are likely to play out in future experience, without actually performing those actions and having to deal with their lived consequences. The quality of our moral thinking therefore depends on (1) the depth and breadth of one's knowledge of the physical and social worlds he or she inhabits, (2) one's understanding of human motivation and cognitive/affective development, (3) one's perceptiveness of which factors are most relevant in a particular situation, and (4) one's ability to simulate the experiences and responses of other people with whom you are interacting. It is thus as much an affair of imagination as it is an appropriation of prior knowledge.

## Moral imagination as simulation

This fourth dimension – simulating the experience and feelings of others – is particularly important. In addition to, and integral to, our ability to imagine how various situations might play out based on different values, states of character, motivations, virtues, and principles, we also need a deep sense of how others might experience a situation. That is, we need empathy, which Franz de Waal defines as "the capacity to (a) be affected by and share the emotional state of another, (b) assess the reasons for the other's state, and (c) identify with the other, adopting his or her perspective. This definition extends beyond what exists in many animals, but the term 'empathy' … applies even if only criterion (a) is met" (de Waal 2008). In *Moral Imagination: Implications of Cognitive Science for Ethics* (Johnson 1993), I called this "empathetic imagination," which makes it possible for us to appreciate and take up the part of others: "Unless we can put ourselves in the place of another, unless we can enlarge our own perspective through an imaginative encounter with the experience of others, unless we can let our own values and ideals be called into question from various points of view, we cannot be morally sensitive" (Johnson 1993, 199). As Steven Fesmire says, "Taking the attitudes of others stirs us beyond numbness so we pause to sort through others' aspirations, interests, and worries as our own" (Fesmire 2003, 65). Empathetic imagination thus requires not just an ability to *intellectually conceive* how others see and think about their world, but also requires an ability to *feel* their moods and emotional responses to their situation. After decades and even centuries of neglect in moral philosophy and psychology, empathy has now come to be regarded in many circles as *the* basis of our ability to properly care for and nurture others, and to act morally toward them (Hoffman 2000; Gilligan 1982; Noddings 1984).

Moral imagination, both as our capacity to empathically understand and feel with others and our ability to imagine how experience would play out under the shaping influence of various values and choices, is thus dependent on our ability to simulate experiences. The new approach known as *simulation semantics* has begun to explore experimentally how people understand experiences, visual scenes, and linguistic expressions by simulating, in their own embodied neural systems, the perceptual experiences, motor programs, and affective valences that are involved in someone's having of those experiences. According to this perspective, conceptualization and reasoning are experiential simulations. Lawrence Barsalou argues that "a concept is not a single abstracted representation for a category, but is instead a skill for constructing idiosyncratic representations tailored to the current needs of the situated action" (Barsalou 2003, 521). Problem-solving and decision-making are processes of "specializing a simulated plan in different ways to see which specialization produces the best outcome … Skill results from compiling simulations for most of the plans in a domain through extensive experience" (Barsalou 1999, 605). Another simulation semantics account is provided by Ben Bergen (2012), who surveys scores of experiments showing how our processing of sentences involves successive sensory-motor-affective simulations of the scenes being described. Although Bergen's experimental focus is primarily language processing, simulation processes are operative also when we *imagine* how situations might play out under various conditions, and they are thus not limited only to reading or hearing language describing scenes and events.

Research on the human "mirror-neuron" system suggests that not only do some of the same sensory and motor neuronal groups fire when we perform certain actions as when we see another person performing those same actions, but they also fire when we *imagine* those actions happening (Decety and Grèzes 2006; Aziz-Zadeh et al. 2006; Gallese 2001). It thus appears that our mirror-neuron system is an important basis for our ability to imaginatively explore various complex courses of action. It helps us put ourselves in the place of another, that is, to appreciate, to a certain limited extent, their experience of a situation or event and to feel how they feel.

It is worth noting that, over two centuries ago, Adam Smith had already emphasized the importance of embodied simulations in our ability to sympathize with others. Although he had no explanation of embodied mirroring activity, he gave several examples of it in various places in *The Theory of Moral Sentiments*, for example:

> When we see a stroke aimed and just ready to fall upon the leg or arm of another person, we naturally shrink and draw back our own leg or our own arm; and when it does fall, we feel it in some measure, and are hurt by it as well as the sufferer. The mob, when they are gazing at a dancer on the slack rope, naturally writhe and twist and balance their own bodies, as they see him do, and as they feel that they themselves must do if in his situation.
>
> *(Smith 1790, I.i.1)*

Smith famously places this capacity to feel with and for others at the heart of our sympathetic moral understanding and appraisal. I (Johnson 2014) have summarized the key role of simulation in acts of moral imagination as follows: "*moral deliberation is a process of cognitive-conative-affective simulation. Simulation allows us to try out, via imaginative projection, various courses of action that appear to be available in a given problematic situation, and the simulation also activates emotional responses to the projected situations.* The simulations thereby permit us to give voice to various impulses, interests, and values that may be in conflict or tension and then to experience (through feeling) the extent to which a given simulation reduces, or even eliminates, the tension" (Johnson 2014, 110; italics in original). This passage emphasizes mostly our ability to imaginatively run out a possible situation without taking overt action, in order to explore how things would be under the influence of various perspectives and values. In addition, as mentioned above, the simulation process also allows us to experience something of the feelings and emotional responses of other people, both in the present problematic situation (i.e., how others see and feel about something) and also within those simulated scenarios (i.e., how others and ourselves might feel in the imagined conditions we are exploring).

## The scope of moral imagination

I have indicated above what it would mean to see moral imagination as not merely a handmaiden to the proper work of a morally practical reason, but, instead, as constituting our primary means for assessing a moral problem, projecting possible solutions, and experiencing how a situation would play out according to certain values. Taking moral imagination seriously requires us to grant it the broadest possible scope of operation in moral inquiry. Once we acknowledge that moral imagination does the primary work of moral deliberation, we will have already abandoned the fundamental tenet of the Moral Law folk theory, according to which we inhabit a closed and completed moral universe, in which principles of right, as well as conceptions of the good, are supposedly imposed on experience from some transcendent source. Instead, we will see moral deliberation as an imaginative problem-solving activity that depends on our perception of and sensitivity toward what matters in any given situation of moral conflict. It also requires an openness to move beyond our present moral habits when the need arises.

The importance of moral imagination helps account for the large number of philosophers, literary theorists, and psychologists who argue that moral cultivation comes more properly from our engagement with historical and fictional narratives than from treatises of moral philosophy that seek to articulate either absolute moral principles, catalogues of the virtues, or ultimate conceptions of the good. It is the narrative depth, complexity, and existential validity of literary fictions that situates our moral perception and appraisal in contexts that are psychologically more valid than those we typically encounter in most moral philosophy. Reading fictional narratives can be morally transformative, insofar as we come to imaginatively inhabit the world and lives of characters that are both like and unlike ourselves and the people we encounter in our lives (Gardner 1978; Eldridge 1989; Nussbaum 1990; Gregory 2009).

Our involvement with morally significant narratives can change the way we understand situations, feel toward others, and see them as vulnerable creatures worthy of our care and respect. Taking moral imagination seriously may therefore require us to abandon certain assumptions about morality that may be deeply rooted in our moral traditions. We have to give up the idea that the right moral decision is given in advance, just waiting for us to discover it and apply it correctly to our present situation. We have to move beyond the view that morality is a system of rationally derived principles that conjointly define our moral responsibilities. We have to recognize that moral deliberation is a trying out, via imaginative projection, of ways our world might be. Moral imagination is our chief resource for enhancing the quality of life for ourselves, others, and our world in general. Thomas Alexander summarizes Dewey's revolutionary view of imaginative moral deliberation as follows:

> *Morality is concerned with the growth of meaning through action.* It aims for a continuous process of integration in which new values can be discovered. This process cannot

> be guided merely by duty, pleasure, freedom, the universalizability criterion, self-interest, or any other single end. A plurality of values, however incommensurate, must be integrated. The dynamic integration is character. To acquire sensitivity to the developmental meanings of events, which define the significance of the situations in which we find ourselves and the values they possess, is what I have called here "the moral imagination." A moral imagination requires experience, a body of developing habits, education, an ability to understand the way other people think and live, and the ideal of discovering through cooperative action solutions to conflicts. It is the ability to see the meanings at issue in a given situation. It is the moral imagination which thus continually strives to create those ideals that offer the possibility of directing situations toward ends that are most fulfilling. This is what it is to have a moral character.
>
> *(Alexander 2013, 199–200)*

Moral imagination is thus not merely a single faculty for applying ethical principles to concrete situations. It is, rather, a person's way of being in and transforming their world by means of their ability to imagine how situations might develop toward greater harmony, cooperation, freedom, growth of meaning, and envisioning of moral ideals. As such, it is not a deductive process of bringing cases under rules or principles, but more like an artistic process for creatively remaking our world in search of enriched meaning and fulfillment for all concerned. It should be judged by a person's sensitivity, care, and wisdom in envisioning new ways of being in the world that harmonize competing values and open up new relations and possibilities for enhanced meaning and well-being.

## References


Alexander, T. (2013) *The Human Eros: Eco-ontology and the Aesthetics of Existence*, New York: Fordham University Press.

Aziz-Zadeh, L., S.M. Wilson, G. Rizzolatti, and M. Iacobini (2006) "Congruent Embodied Representations for Visually Presented Actions and Linguistic Phrases Describing Actions," *Current Biology* 16(18): 1818–1823.

Barsalou, L. (1999) "Perceptual Symbol Systems," *Behavioral and Brain Science* 22: 577–660.

Barsalou, L. (2003) "Situated Simulation in the Human Conceptual System," *Language and Cognitive Processes* 18(5–6): 513–562.

Bergen, B. (2012) *Louder Than Words: The New Science of How the Mind Makes Meaning*, New York: Basic Books.

Decety, J., and J. Grèzes (2006) "The Power of Simulation: Imagining One's Own and Other's Behavior," *Brain Research* 1079: 4–14.

de Waal, F. (2008) "Putting the Altruism Back in Altruism: The Evolution of Empathy," *Annual Review of Psychology* 59: 279–300.

Dewey, J. (1922/1983) *Human Nature and Conduct*, vol. 14 of *The Middle Works, 1899–1924*, ed. J.A. Boydston, Carbondale: Southern Illinois University Press.

Eldridge, R. (1989) *On Moral Personhood: Philosophy, Literature, Criticism, and Self-Understanding*, Chicago: University of Chicago Press.

Fesmire, S. (2003) *John Dewey and Moral Imagination*, Bloomington: Indiana University Press.

Gallese, V. (2001) "The 'Shared Manifold' Hypothesis: From Mirror Neurons to Empathy," *Journal of Consciousness Studies* 8(5–7): 33–50.

Gardner, J. (1978) "Moral Fiction," in *Moral Fiction*, New York: Basic Books.

Gilligan, C. (1982) *In a Different Voice: Psychological Theory and Women's Development*, Cambridge, MA: Harvard University Press.

Gregory, M. (2009) *Shaped by Stories: The Ethical Power of Narratives*, Notre Dame, IN: University of Notre Dame Press.

Hare, R.M. (1963) *Freedom and Reason*, Oxford: Oxford University Press.
Hoffman, R. (2000) *Empathy and Moral Development: Implications for Caring and Justice*, Cambridge: Cambridge University Press.
Hume, D. (1739–40/2000) *A Treatise of Human Nature*, Oxford: Clarendon Press.
Hume, D. (1751/1998) *An Enquiry concerning the Principles of Morals*, ed. T. Beauchamp, Clarendon Edition of the Works of David Hume, Oxford: Oxford University Press.
Johnson, M. (1993) *Moral Imagination: Implications of Cognitive Science for Ethics*, Chicago: University of Chicago Press.
Johnson, M. (2014) *Morality for Humans: Ethical Understanding from the Perspective of Cognitive Science*, Chicago: University of Chicago Press.
Kant, I. (1775–80/1963) *Lectures on Ethics*, trans. L. Infield, Indianapolis: Hackett Publishing Co.
Kant, I. (1781–87/1958) *Critique of Practical Reason*, trans. L.W. Beck, New York: Bobbs-Merrill. (Page reference is to the header pagination from the critical edition of Kant's works.)
Kant, I. (1785/1983) *Grounding for the Metaphysics of Morals*, trans. J. Ellington, in *Immanuel Kant: Ethical Philosophy*, Indianapolis: Hackett Publishing Co. (Page reference is to the marginal pagination from the critical edition of Kant's works.)
Kekes, J. (2006) *The Enlargement of Life: Moral Imagination at Work*, Ithaca: Cornell University Press.
Lakoff, G. (1996) *Moral Politics: What Conservatives Know that Liberals Don't*, Chicago: University of Chicago Press.
Lakoff, G. (2008) *The Political Mind: Why You Can't Understand 21st-Century American Politics with an 18th-Century Brain*, New York: Viking.
Lakoff, G., and M. Johnson (1999) *Philosophy in the Flesh: The Embodied Mind and Its Challenge to Western Thought*, New York: Basic Books.
Noddings, N. (1984) *Caring: A Feminist Approach to Ethics and Moral Education*, Berkeley: University of California Press.
Nussbaum, M. (1990) *Love's Knowledge: Essays on Philosophy and Literature*, Oxford: Oxford University Press.
Putnam, H. (1987) "Equality and Our Moral Image of the World," in *The Many Faces of Realism*, LaSalle, IL: Open Court, 40–62.
Rorty, R. (1982) *Consequences of Pragmatism*, Minneapolis, MN: University of Minnesota Press
Rorty, R. (1989) *Contingency, Irony, and Solidarity*, Cambridge: Cambridge University Press.
Smith, A. (1790) *The Theory of Moral Sentiments*, Sao Paulo, Brazil: Salvio Marcelo Soares; repr. MetaLibri Digital Library.
Werhane, P. (1999) *Moral Imagination and Management Decision-Making*, Oxford: Oxford University Press.
Williams, O. (1997) *The Moral Imagination: How Literature and Films Can Stimulate Ethical Reflection in the Business World*, Notre Dame, IN: University of Notre Dame Press.

# 27

# EMPATHY AND THE IMAGINATION

*Karsten R. Stueber*

In ordinary parlance, empathy refers to our ability to feel with and be concerned about another person and her states of mind. Accordingly, empathy and related phenomena are of interest to philosophers and other researchers in a variety of different fields studying the human propensity to enter into and maintain interpersonal and social relationships. More specifically, in investigating how humans establish and maintain those relations, researchers have been focusing on empathy's contribution to our capacity to know other persons' states of mind, our tendency to normatively and morally evaluate and judge their character and actions, and our admittedly limited ability and willingness to help others in distress. Generally it is assumed that our ability to empathize with another person is based on or activated through our ability to imaginatively take up that person's perspective. This assumption is also reflected in Mark Davis's widely used questionnaire to measure a person's disposition for empathy, where two of his subscales measure our disposition for "perspective taking" and for "fantasy" understood as "the tendency to imaginatively transpose oneself into fictional situations" (Davis 1994, 57). In the following three sections we will more closely analyze the concept of empathy, empathy's contribution to social cognition and moral agency, and the question of how our empathic abilities are related to our imaginative capacities.

## The concept of empathy

The range of psychological phenomena associated with empathy has been the focus of philosophical attention for quite some time, particularly in the moral sentimentalist tradition most prominently articulated by David Hume and Adam Smith in the eighteenth century. In that context the preferred term was, however, "sympathy," at least in works written in the English language. The term "empathy" only started to replace the term "sympathy" from the beginning of the twentieth century onward when the American psychologist Edward Titchener (1867–1927) coined it as the translation of the German term *Einfühlung* (feeling into) in 1909. The usage of this term throughout the twentieth century has been anything but well-defined, and psychological research on empathy has been hampered for a long time by a certain amount of conceptual confusion. Nevertheless, more broadly understood, all of these at times very different conceptions of empathy are united in that they all refer to various psychological mechanisms that in one way or another validate Hume's dictum that "the minds of men are mirrors to one another" (Hume 1739/1978, 365). They refer to psychological phenomena having to do with the fact that in encountering other persons our mind tends to resonate with their mental states (particularly their affective states). We often become happy in a room full of happy people and in general we tend to adopt the beliefs and attitudes of the people around us. Yet, as Smith already recognized (Smith 1759/1982, 109) – an insight that is not always sufficiently appreciated in the contemporary context – our reactions toward others do not merely resonate with and mirror their states of mind. Our reactions also constitute a mirror for others to recognize themselves and to be challenged or validated in their own reactions to a particular situation. In that sense we serve as mirrors not merely by mirroring another person's mental states and reactions but also by taking a particular stance, emotional or otherwise, toward the other person and her sentiments. In feeling sorry or in feeling compassion for the other person we seem to validate her own distress, while in being unconcerned we seem to indicate that her distress does not have to be taken seriously. Think in this context, for example, about our reactions toward children and how children learn to understand the severity of their own injuries and the conditions under which their "feelings" are legitimate in light of our different reactions toward their distress.

Yet conceiving broadly of "men's minds" as mirrors of each other does not sufficiently differentiate, from a conceptual point of view, between the various psychological attitudes that might be involved. Nowadays one commonly distinguishes more precisely between emotional *contagion, empathy, sympathy*, and *personal distress*. While the latter two reactions or feelings are certainly caused by the encounter with the other and her states of mind, they are not specifically resonance phenomena that replicate another person's mental states in one's own mind. Rather sympathy refers to a *sui generis* emotion in which I am oriented toward the other and feel concerned about her welfare (Darwall 1998). Personal distress on the other hand refers to the distress I feel that is caused by another person and her "distressed" state of mind. But in personal distress I am wholly self-focused. I am distressed about her distress in a way that I might be annoyed about something that constitutes an obstacle to my plans, like having to deal with a car that refuses to start on a very cold winter day. In being personally distressed about another person I therefore do not share the other person's distress, which has a completely different intentional object. Rather I am distressed about the other person and her states of mind.

Emotional contagion is on the other hand a paradigmatic resonance phenomenon. As the name suggests, emotional contagion occurs when we are infected or catch the same affective or emotional states as the people with whom we are in causal contact. In being affected by others in this manner we do not have to be aware of the fact that we feel a certain way because we are in the company of others. It is exactly in this respect that empathy tends to be distinguished from emotional contagion and is most often understood as a resonance phenomenon involving different levels of cognitive complexity. At its core, empathy is understood as the vicarious sharing of an affective state whereby we are clearly aware of the fact that the other person is the source of our feeling a certain way. Empathy is thus possible only if there is sufficient awareness of the self-other distinction. In this respect, most researchers from different fields tend to agree. They, however, differ in how strictly they define these and additional conditions for proper empathy. For some, empathy requires that both the empathizer and the empathized be in the same or at least a similar affective state (Coplan 2011; Jacob 2011). Others such as Hoffman (2000) define empathy such that we also empathize with a person when, without sharing their affective state, we have feelings that are "more congruent with another person's situation" than our own. According to this understanding we empathize with happy children (who do not know about their serious medical conditions) in feeling sad since this seems to be the emotion they would appropriately feel if they knew about their condition (Hoffman 2000). Even more liberally, researchers concerned with investigating social cognition are inclined to view empathy as not only the vicarious sharing of affective states but also as involving a whole range of mental states (such as beliefs and desires) that are recreated or simulated in one's mind when taking up the perspective of another person (Goldman 2006; Stueber 2006). In contrast, some philosophers in the phenomenological tradition argue against the similarity requirement since for them it insufficiently takes into account the intentional structure of our experience of the other as a minded creature. According to this line of thought, I can directly see the sadness expressed in the face of another person without having to feel like her. Indeed I could be feeling happy and yet recognize her grief (Zahavi 2010; Overgaard and Zahavi 2012).

The motivations for these different conceptions will become clearer in the following two sections that will discuss empathy more extensively, particularly insofar as it involves our imaginative capacities, and its contribution to social cognition and moral agency. Still, it needs to be acknowledged that as important as it is to distinguish proper empathy from other empathy-like phenomena, in real life our reactions do not come that neatly separated. In attending a funeral of a friend's child, for example, our own emotions are an amalgam of emotional contagion (in a room full of sadness), genuine empathy (thinking of how our friend must feel), sympathy, and personal distress (thinking about oneself and one's own children in this context). In such encounters, human beings are motivated simultaneously to take care of their broader social responsibilities (caring for the more remote other) and to take care of their responsibilities closer to home (in this case, their own children). For that very reason, various researchers are less concerned in their use of the empathy concept to distinguish neatly between emotional contagion and empathy, or between empathy and sympathy since from a phylogenetic and ontogenetic perspective these psychological phenomena are closely related. Ultimately it seems only creatures that are capable of emotional contagion are also empathetic in a more cognitively developed sense, and sympathy normally emerges in the context of empathizing with other people (see de Waal 2006; Hoffman 2000). Dependent on the discipline, researchers are therefore more likely to count emotional contagion or sympathy as a form of empathy. Pragmatically, in doing empathy research and in reading the empathy literature one is therefore not only well advised to keep the conceptual distinctions discussed above in mind but also to be aware that each research tradition might have its own unique preferences in sorting various empathy-related phenomena (Batson 2009).

## Empathy, knowledge of other minds, and the recreative imagination

While the moral sentimentalist tradition of the seventeenth and eighteenth centuries acknowledged that empathy (what was then called sympathy) contributes epistemically to knowing what might be going on in the minds of others, its focus has always been on empathy's contribution to moral judgment and moral agency. The discussion of empathy as a central epistemic means for knowledge of other minds developed only in the second half of the nineteenth century and the turn of the twentieth century when knowledge of other minds became a topic of sustained philosophical attention in the context of methodological considerations about the foundations of history and the social sciences (sciences investigating the social domain where human agency takes place). More specifically, it was Theodor Lipps who transferred the concept of *Einfühlung* from the realm of philosophical aesthetics to the philosophy of mind by declaring empathy conceived of as a resonance phenomenon to be the primary means for knowledge of other minds. In the context of this issue, Lipps was particularly interested in analyzing perceptual face-to-face encounters with others. Rejecting the inference of analogy – for reasons similar to Wittgenstein's critique later on – he suggests that such encounters lead us to automatically resonate with the sentiments and thoughts of others (Stueber 2006). Moreover, since we are in some sense aware of the fact that it is not we who are really angry or afraid, we reflexively project those feelings caused by resonance onto the other and gain some understanding of what is going on in another person's mind.

Here is not the place to discuss in great detail the merits of Lipps' conception of empathy as the central means to knowledge of other minds. Suffice it to say that even though his critique of the inference of analogy was highly influential among philosophers in the phenomenological tradition, such as Husserl, Stein, and Scheler, they generally rejected the claim that knowledge of other minds can be regarded as a form of projected resonance. Resonating in this manner I am only duplicating my own experience without being sufficiently attentive to the fact that I am trying to understand the experiences of another person. For phenomenologists, empathy is better understood as a *sui generis* perceptual act that allows me to grasp the other person's experience while respecting the fact that it is the other person's experience (Zahavi 2010). Similarly, empathy conceived of as a form of almost automatic resonance and projection does not seem to account philosophically for the epistemic difficulties that we encounter in the interpretive human sciences, trying to make sense of the states of mind of agents and authors from more distant cultures and time periods. Mere resonance and projection seems to be a rather epistemically naive manner of thinking about our capacity to make sense of distant and complex forms of life (Stueber 2006).

Nevertheless, so-called simulation theorists have revived the claim that empathy is a central means for knowing other minds in the context of the "theory of mind" debate starting at the end of the twentieth century (Goldman 2006; Gordon 1995; Heal 2003). This highly interdisciplinary debate is concerned with analyzing the underlying psychological mechanisms (and the information utilized by them) that enable us to make sense of other agents in terms of our ordinary folk psychological concepts such as beliefs, desires, and emotions. While theory theorists (Nichols and Stich 2003) claim that our understanding of other people depends on the use of a folk psychological theory, simulation theorists maintain that in understanding other minds we use ourselves as a model and simulate their mental processes in our own mind (see Shannon Spaulding, "Simulation theory," Chapter 19 of this volume).

Accordingly, like the earlier empathy theorists, simulation theorists view knowledge of other minds as a resonance phenomenon, but they view it more distinctly as a resonance phenomenon that occurs on different levels of cognitive and psychological complexity. Such theorists commonly distinguish between two empathic capacities each contributing to our mature abilities to make sense of other minds. First, one generally acknowledges a developmentally early capacity for making sense of the social world and the behavior of other people – a capacity that does not necessarily presuppose the possession of folk psychological concepts – that some authors also refer to as *basic* or *mirroring empathy* (Stueber 2006; Goldman 2011). Talk of such basic empathy has been tied to the neurobiological discovery of mirror neurons (originally in macaque monkeys but subsequently also in human), that is, the discovery that there is a significant overlap in the excitation of neurons involved in the execution and observation of certain bodily movements and goal-directed behavior (Rizzolatti and Sinigaglia 2008). It also refers to broader mirroring phenomena or "shared neural substrates" (Decety 2010; Singer and Lamm 2009) when perceiving another person's pain or emotional states. Mechanisms of basic empathy understood as neurobiological resonance or mirroring phenomena in the broad sense can thus in all likelihood be understood as contributing to a perceptually immediate and nonconceptual grasp of the goal-directedness (or *de re* intentionality) of another person's behavior (that the action is directed for example toward an object in her environment) and of the fact that her external bodily appearance is expressive of inner emotional states.

How such basic understanding of the social realm has to be further characterized is a matter of considerable controversy within the literature. Some researchers have raised serious doubts about interpreting the primary function of mirror neurons as being concerned with action understanding rather than being associated with functions that presuppose such understanding.[1] Regardless of this controversy about the primary evolutionary purpose of the mechanisms underlying basic empathy, it has been established beyond reasonable doubt that infants do understand the behavior of others as being goal-directed and as expressive of emotion. Infants have a more direct grasp of the mindedness of others than traditionally assumed. However, on its more basic level, empathy's cognitive grasp is not very far-reaching. At most it allows us to grasp that the other person feels fear, is angry, or that she moves her arm in order to grasp a glass of water. On this level empathy does not allow us to understand why and for what reasons agents feel the way they feel or act the way they do. Moreover, even if one conceives of basic empathy as a resonance phenomenon, the almost automatic nature of this process suggests that it could hardly be understood as the work of the imagination (see, however, Jacob and de Vignemont 2012).

It is the cognitively more complex form of empathy, referred to by simulation theorists either as reenactive or reconstructive empathy (Stueber 2006; Goldman 2011) that allows us to understand agents' behavior in terms of their propositional attitudes and their reasons for acting by reenacting their sentiments and thoughts.[2] Such reenactive empathy has been appropriately characterized as involving the work of the imagination, whereby the imagination is understood as the ability to entertain and even play with alternative conceptions of reality and what we take to be objectively true (see also Harris 2000). Children normally display this capacity from about two years of age onward by playing with a banana pretending that it is a telephone and in role-play pretending to be Mommy or Daddy and so on.[3] Reenactive empathy involves such imaginative capacity in that it requires us to adopt an alternative to the reality of our perspective by transporting ourselves imaginatively into the shoes of another person.

Accordingly, the imagination at work in reenactive empathy is not completely free but is constrained or guided by the purpose of making sense of another person's sentiments, feelings, or action. Gregory Currie and Ian Ravenscroft (Currie and Ravenscroft 2002) refer to the kind of imagination involved as "recreative." They define it specifically as the capacity to recreate mental states and distinguish it from the creative imagination involved in the construction of a fictional world. In utilizing the capacity of recreative imagination for the purpose of mindreading we are able to "experience" the perspective of another person but so that the empathizer is still able to recognize a difference between his attitudes and the recreated propositional attitudes. At the same time, if such recreation is intended to make sense of another person, such recreated attitudes have to be sufficiently like our normal mental attitudes, a fact that Currie and Ravenscroft acknowledge by referring to them as belief-like or desire-like imagining and so on (see also Amy Kind, "Desire-like imagination," Chapter 12 of this volume). Similarly, Goldman (2006) talks of the *enactment-* or *E-imagination*, which generates the necessary pretend states required for simulating the perspective of another. It allows us to take up or get inside the perspective of the other person rather than merely thinking about her attitudes in a more detached manner. For Goldman e-imagining feeling elated or embarrassed is therefore to be distinguished from merely supposing (or s-imagining) that one has such feelings, that is, supposing that one feels elated. Only in the first case does one recreate a state that is also sufficiently like the target state in its phenomenal quality.[4]

If the use of the recreative imagination in reenactive empathy is aimed at providing us with epistemic access to other minds, we need further assurances that imaginatively adopting the perspective of another in my own mind can provide me with knowledge of other minds. Normally we would not assume that imagining that *p* is a very reliable way of finding out whether or not *p* is true (for further discussion see Kind and Kung forthcoming). As a first step to addressing these concerns, simulation theorists argue that the pretend states produced by the e-imagination are sufficiently similar in causal powers to ordinary mental states that processing such pretend states in our own cognitive system can provide us with epistemically reliable information for predicting and explaining the behavior of another person. In this context, simulation theorists like Goldman point to neurobiological evidence showing that visual and motor imagery use neurobiological mechanisms (Goldman 2006) similar to those of vision and motor execution, or other psychological research that has shown, for instance, that imagining eating a cookie and actually eating a cookie have similar effects on subsequent choices about whether to eat more cookies (Goldman and Jordan 2013).

Yet such evidence does not seem to be sufficient for justifying the reliability of empathic imagination for the whole range of states referred to in our folk psychological vocabulary. Moreover one might wonder whether evidence for reenactive empathy can be primarily found on the neurobiological level given the familiar arguments for the nonreducibility of folk psychological states to internal properties of the brain. Accordingly, some simulation theorists argue for the central epistemic involvement of reenactive empathy and empathic imagination in an a priori manner (Heal 2003; Stueber 2006 and 2008). They suggest that understanding thought processes involving propositional content requires seeing those thoughts and sentiments as a person's reasons, since within folk psychology mental states are not merely understood as inner causes. Attributing beliefs and desires can serve explanatory or predictive purposes only if they can also be understood as a person's reasons for acting, as considerations that speak from her perspective for the action and that make her action intelligible. Such intelligibility, however, depends, for example, on grasping how a particular belief is relevant for consideration in a particular context and in light of an agent's other beliefs, desires, values, commitments, and so on. Accordingly, it requires us to be able to distinguish for each context those aspects of our mental perspective that are relevant for consideration in the specific context from those that are irrelevant. To grasp such relevance, or so it is argued, requires the imaginative use of our own cognitive resources in reenacting the thoughts of other people since it is doubtful that such capacity can be solely based on a general theory of relevance.[5] Understanding how thoughts can be reasons is possible only if in taking up the perspective of another we ourselves would regard them as considerations for doing *x* or adopting a certain attitude and so on. From that perspective, the question of whether our empathic imagination recreates states that are sufficiently similar to "normal" mental states is answered by pointing out that this is the only manner in which we understand how thoughts can cause as reasons.

In addition, we need to have truthfully recreated the other person's perspective in sufficient complexity for reenactive empathy to provide us with knowledge of specific persons and their minds. We have to have some assurance that the mental states reenacted by our empathic imagination correspond to the states that she actually has. Minimally that requires that we have imaginatively adopted the relevant pretend beliefs and desires and that we have sufficiently quarantined our own mental states from inappropriately influencing our recreation of another person's perspective and thought processes. For example, if the other person is a creationist or believes in the flat earth theory we should make sure that we have truthfully recreated the other person's perspective in sufficient detail and that we have quarantined our scientific beliefs in trying to understand the other person's thought processes and find out of how she would feel about and vote on a school curriculum that mandated the teaching of evolutionary theory. Otherwise we would just be imagining how we ourselves would feel in her situation rather than how the other person would feel.

Psychologists distinguish in this context between self-oriented perspective taking (imagining yourself in their perspective) and other-oriented perspective taking (imagining how she would feel in that situation) (see Coplan 2011). It would be an oversimplification, however, to conclude that the empathic imagination is epistemically reliable only if it is a manifestation of other-oriented perspective taking. Just imagining how we would feel were something to happen to our children is under normal circumstances sufficient for knowing how other people would feel were something to happen to their children, even if we differ in our beliefs regarding the shape of the earth. What is important for the epistemic reliability of the use of our imagination in empathy is not whether it has been self- or other-oriented perspective taking but whether its use has been sufficiently sensitive to the relevant differences between the empathizer and his target. Self-oriented perspective taking provides us with knowledge of other minds only if the empathizer and imagined target are not different in relevant respects.

Accordingly, the recreative imagination at work in reenactive empathy can provide us with epistemically reliable access to other minds only if it is guided by mechanisms that allow us to be sufficiently sensitive to relevant differences between individuals. Only in this manner are we able to recreate another person's perspective appropriately. While indeed paying some lip service to this idea, simulation theorists within the contemporary theory of mind debate have insufficiently acknowledged that such sensitivity at times requires quite a bit of knowledge about an individual's biography and her social, cultural, and historical context. In this respect, so-called narrativists – those who argue that both theory theorists and simulation theorists provide an incomplete picture of our ability for social cognition – have rightly criticized them (Gallagher and Hutto 2008). In light of the fact that the information on such differences is very often presented in narrative form, one could say that the empathic imagination is an epistemically reliable means as long as it is guided by sufficient and objectively adequate narrative information about relevant differences. Acknowledging the use of such information, however, does not mean that our understanding of others is guided solely by a psychological theory as theory theorists assert or that simulating and reenacting the other's thought processes is utterly superfluous for understanding another person's thoughts and feelings, and grasping them as her reasons for acting. The narrative information serves merely to orient us appropriately for imaginatively recreating and reenacting another person's perspective and state of mind (Stueber 2008).

Yet, we have to be careful how exactly we understand the notion of imaginatively taking up another person's point of view. Importantly, it should not be conceived of as requiring that we imagine being the other person (see Dilip Ninan, "Imagination and the self," Chapter 20 of this volume). As Peter Goldie (2011) has argued, such complete identification with another person even in the imagination is a conceptual impossibility, since our attempt to recreate the psychological point of view of another person requires that we are more aware of some of the psychological properties and dispositions of another person's mind than the person himself. In recreating another person's perspective through imaginative empathy (feeding my own cognitive system with pretend beliefs and quarantining my own relevant beliefs from such recreation), I am at the same time aware that it is not my perspective.

Acknowledging this point is not to deny the possibility of empathic understanding but rather to recognize one of the central features of the nature of interpersonal understanding, namely, that it always presupposes a certain distance between self and other. It should make us realize that there is a difference between having a certain experience or being a certain person and understanding these facts.

Having said that, we need to recognize that the scope of the empathetic imagination and understanding is limited. The greater the difference between individuals and the greater the cultural gap between them, particularly regarding well-entrenched cognitive habits and value commitments, the harder it becomes to reenact them and to appropriately quarantine our attitudes from the imaginative engagement with another person's perspective. In those cases we experience imaginative resistance, a phenomenon that has been extensively discussed in the literature in regard to our encounter with "morally deviant" fictional worlds (for its relation to the theory of mind debate see particularly Currie 2002 and Stueber 2011). At times such resistance might be overcome through greater effort and sensitivity to such differences in light of further historical, sociological, and anthropological research or through an ongoing dialogue with the relevant individuals and maybe some other more theoretical compensatory strategies. Yet even those strategies might have their limits and in those cases empathic understanding breaks down. It also needs to be acknowledged that the empathic imagination is particularly bad in allowing us to understand and predict actions (our own or those of others) that do not seem to be sanctioned by reasons in even the most minimally normative sense. Putting ourselves in another person's shoes or imagining ourselves to be in such a position does not allow us, for example, to predict the bystander effect, a well-confirmed phenomenon in social psychology, according to which individuals refuse to offer help to a person in need merely because other people are present. Similarly, imaginative perspective taking does not allow us to make sense of the fact that when provided with a choice between equally good pairs of stockings we will always choose the one on the right (see Maibom forthcoming).[6] In these cases we have to fall back on more detached strategies for making sense of the observed action, by pointing out that this is just how things are done in a particular culture or this is how humans in general react in such situations. Yet none of this should be taken to imply that imaginative empathy does not have a significant role to play in understanding other persons, particularly insofar as they are rational agents acting for reasons. It just means that there are aspects of human behavior outside the domain of rational agency within which we can appropriately use our empathic imagination to gain knowledge of other minds.

## The importance of the empathic imagination for our moral and social identity

As already noted, empathy's contribution to knowledge of other minds has not always been the predominant focus of attention. Empathy has also been conceived of as the central psychological mechanism underlying our capacity for moral judgment and moral motivations (or more broadly understood, prosocial and altruistic motivations). Moral sentimentalists such as Hume and Smith have even argued that empathy is psychologically constitutive for our capacity for moral judgment (see also Mark Johnson, "Moral imagination," Chapter 26 of this volume, and Slote 2010). In their account of moral judgment they argued both against moral rationalists like Cudworth and Clark, who viewed moral truths on analogy to mathematical truths and claimed that reason recognizes them a priori, and philosophers of "self-love" like Hobbes and Mandeville, for whom human "morality" is ultimately derived from egoistic self-interests. Moral sentimentalists argued that rationalists cannot account for the motivational aspect that we normally associate with moral judgments since reason is motivationally inert. They also objected fiercely to the claim that human beings are merely egoistically motivated. On the other hand, if moral judgment is based on empathy and related phenomena then we can more easily understand how moral judgments could also motivate us to act and do so based on a genuine altruistic desire for the welfare of the other person, which seems to be more appropriate to the moral point of view than mere self-interest.

Since the second half of the twentieth century, social psychologists have carefully studied the question of how exactly one has to conceive of the motivational force of empathy and the relation between empathic phenomena and prosocial behavior (see articles in Maibom 2014). Most significantly, Daniel Batson's experimental work (summarized in Batson 2011) is generally seen as making plausible the claim that empathy understood as sympathetic concern (experimentally induced mainly through other-oriented perspective taking) causes us to be genuinely altruistically motivated toward another person's welfare as our ultimate goal. Yet Batson distinguishes strictly between altruistic and the kind of moral motivation that is concerned with implementing a moral principle like justice. Empathy-induced altruistic motivation is ultimately about the welfare of a specific person and could cause us to violate principles of justice and fairness in order to help the person we empathize with. Similarly, Martin Hoffman (2000) sees empathy as central for the development of prosocial and moral behavior. But he does not see empathy as being constitutive for our conception of universal moral principles, given that empathy's scope tends to be restricted by well-known "here-and-now" biases that make us more empathic toward people we perceive, on a variety of dimensions, to be closer to us.

These results certainly raise some doubts about the foundational role that empathy could play in regard to our moral judgment and moral agency. Already Hume and Smith thought that empathy, given its well-known biases, could be regarded as a source of our moral judgments if and only if it is constrained by "some steady and general points of view" or the "impartial spectator" perspective. The question of whether moral sentimentalism has the resources to validate the impartial perspective from a normative point of view or whether one needs in this context to appeal to principles grounded not in sentiments but in practical reason (as philosophers of a more Kantian bent ascertain) is indeed an interesting one. Yet as it does not directly concern the issue of how the imagination is involved in our empathic capacities, it is not the place here to fully adjudicate this philosophical debate, one that is ongoing due to the recent revival of interest in moral sentimentalism (see articles in Coplan and Goldie 2011; Maibom 2014; Debes and Stueber forthcoming).

Regardless of whether empathy has a foundational role in constituting morality, it certainly can be thought of as contributing helpfully to understanding the perspective of another person. It also allows us to be more sensitive to her needs, enables us to more appropriately judge the moral character of her actions, and enhances our understanding of our obligations toward her (Sherman 1998 and Darwall 2006). The empathic imagination thus helps us to appropriately enlarge or at least maintain the domain within which we encounter each other as moral agents who owe something to each other (Scanlon 1999). Moreover, Hume and Smith might also be right in emphasizing that our empathic capacities contribute importantly to constituting us as social animals, since we are tremendously concerned about the opinions of others and are, through our empathic capacities, able to recognize how others think or might think about us. In this respect one might, for example, consider the important social emotion of shame that is dependent on our imagined or real appreciation of how others view or would view our behavior.

Insofar as empathy plays mainly an epistemic role in these contexts, the considerations in the previous section of this essay about empathy as a means to knowledge of other minds apply here as well. That empathy plays an epistemic role also allows us to understand why a number of researchers think that proper empathy requires the empathizer to share a similar affective or mental state as his target. Only if we instantiate a feeling similar to that of the other person does empathy allow us to know what or how the other person feels. And yet, the role of empathic imagination within the moral and social context is not limited to knowledge of other people. Perspective taking in this context is not only required for understanding another person but also to better grasp what we value and what aspect of our lives we think is central to our identity, moral or otherwise. For this reason, Hoffman's more liberal conception of empathy as resonating with a person in a manner that is "more congruent with another person's situation" (even if the person does not necessarily feel that way) is more adequate to the full range of functions of the empathic imagination in the social context.

Smith's considerations about what he calls illusory sympathy – or empathizing, for example, with somebody who lost his mind or empathizing with the dead – are also quite illuminating in this respect. As he points out, in regard to imagining ourselves in a situation in which we are devoid of all reason (think about a person suffering from Alzheimer's disease) or are dead, the fact that we at the same time still have reason and life makes it impossible to share such an alien perspective. And yet through these illusory forms of empathy – they do not in fact lead to knowledge of other minds – we start to appreciate more fully our normal functioning capacities and realize how much we dread death, "one of the most important principles in human nature" as Smith calls it (Smith 1759/1982, 12–13).

The use of such illusory empathy is without doubt culturally mediated and can contribute both to the maintenance and to the critique of various cultural practices, regardless of their moral character. The anthropologist Douglas Hollan, who emphasizes the culturally malleable nature and the moral fragility of our empathic capacities, links such illusory empathy for instance to practices of ancestor worship on the islands of the South Pacific (Hollan 2014). For a more contemporary example one could think of how our empathic imagination enters into debates about American football. If one is not very familiar with American football and not a fan, in seeing a hard tackle one probably tends to imaginatively identify with the person who has been tackled and feel one's own bones crushed. It is in this context indeed irrelevant whether the tackled player feels that way. Since he is well conditioned, it is indeed unlikely that he does. Such illusory empathy, however, does support our skeptical attitudes about football and our decision not to let our sons play football. Yet an avid fan of American football will most likely identify with the tackler, particularly if that tackler is from his favorite team, and strengthen in this way his enthusiasm for the sport. Interestingly though, given the recent conversations about the dangers of American football and the revelations about the detrimental effects of playing football professionally for a long time, with whom we identify in those situations might change.

To conclude, as the essay has shown, proper empathy is central for gaining access to other minds but such knowledge is only possible if the empathic imagination is guided by information that allows us to be sensitive to relevant differences between ourselves and the people we empathize with. However, as the last section suggests, the empathic imagination is more than a means to gain knowledge of other minds since its use, regardless of its epistemic adequacy, contributes importantly to constituting us as members of a social community and to our recognition of what we value as members of such a community. Whether or not empathy has a more foundational role to play in constituting moral normativity is a topic of further philosophical reflection and empirical investigation that must pay close attention to empathy's use and misuse in its broader cultural context.

## Notes

1 One needs to recognize that these critics interpret the term "mirror neurons" in a narrow sense. It has to do only with the activation of neurons in areas that are homologous to those of the monkey's brain where mirror neurons were first discovered. Not all resonance phenomena on the neurobiological level therefore count as activation of mirror neurons. It is in this sense that Decety (2010), for example, rejects the involvement of mirror neurons in affective empathy while asserting that it centrally involves "shared neural substrates." See also Csibra 2007, Hickok 2014, and Stueber 2012.
2 It has also been shown that different neurobiological mechanisms subserve this more complex empathic capacity (Goldman 2006 and 2011).
3 More concretely, in arguing for simulation theory Harris (2000) links such imaginative capacities and their display in infants to our capacities to understand other minds.
4 Goldman is doubtful whether the distinction between e-imagination and mere supposition applies across the board to all mental states. Supposing that *p*, for example, might be equivalent to "E-imagining *believing* that p" (Goldman 2006, 48).
5 In AI research this problem is commonly referred to as the frame problem. To use Fodor's terminology, to identify the relevant aspects of our belief set means to be able to put a frame around them. Yet where to put the "frame" seems to be an irreducibly open-ended and contextual affair (see Fodor 1983 and 2000).
6 Within the context of the original theory of mind debate this issue has also been discussed under the heading of "cognitive penetrability." For an extensive and fair analysis of this debate see particularly Ravenscroft 1999.

## References


Batson, C.D. (2009) "These Things Called Empathy: Eight Related But Distinct Phenomena," in J. Decety and W. Ickes (eds.) *The Social Neuroscience of Empathy*, Cambridge, MA: MIT Press, 3–15.

Batson, C.D. (2011) *Altruism in Humans*, Oxford: Oxford University Press.

Coplan, A. (2011) "Understanding Empathy: Its Features and Effects," in A. Coplan and P. Goldie (eds.) *Empathy: Philosophical and Psychological Perspectives*, Oxford: Oxford University Press, 3–18.

Coplan, A., and P. Goldie (eds.) (2011) *Empathy: Philosophical and Psychological Perspectives*, Oxford: Oxford University Press.

Csibra, G. (2007) "Action Mirroring and Action Interpretation: An Alternative Account," in P. Haggard, Y. Rosetti, and M. Kawato (eds.) *Sensorimotor Foundations of Higher Cognition: Attention and Performance XXII*, Oxford: Oxford University Press, 435–459.

Currie, G. (2002) "Desire in Imagination," in T.S. Gendler and J. Hawthorne (eds.) *Conceivability and Possibility*, Oxford: Oxford University Press, 201–221.

Currie, G., and I. Ravenscroft (2002) *Recreative Minds: Imagination in Philosophy and Psychology*, Oxford: Clarendon Press.

Darwall, S. (1998) "Empathy, Sympathy, and Care," *Philosophical Studies* 89: 261–282.

Darwall, S. (2006) *The Second-Person Standpoint: Morality, Respect, and Accountability*, Cambridge, MA: Harvard University Press.

Davis, M. (1994) *Empathy: A Social Psychological Approach*, Boulder: Westview Press.

Debes, R., and K. Stueber (eds.) (Forthcoming) *Moral Sentimentalism*, Cambridge: Cambridge University Press.

Decety, J. (2010) "To What Extent Is the Experience of Empathy Mediated by Shared Neural Circuits?" *Emotion Review* 2: 204–207.

de Waal, F. (2006) *Primates and Philosophers: How Morality Evolved*, Princeton: Princeton University Press.

Fodor, J. (1983) *The Modularity of the Mind: An Essay on Faculty Psychology*, Cambridge, MA: MIT Press.

Fodor, J. (2000) *The Mind Doesn't Work That Way: The Scope and Limit of Computational Psychology*, Cambridge, MA: MIT Press.

Gallagher, S., and D. Hutto (2008) "Understanding Others through Primary Interaction and Narrative Practice," in J. Zlatev, T. Racine, C. Sinha, and E. Itkonen (eds.) *The Shared Mind: Perspectives on Intersubjectivity*, Amsterdam and Philadelphia: John Benjamins Publishing Co., 17–38.

Goldie, P. (2011) "Anti-empathy," in A. Coplan and P. Goldie (eds.) *Empathy: Philosophical and Psychological Perspectives*, Oxford: Oxford University Press, 302–317.
Goldman, A. (2006) *Simulating Minds: The Philosophy, Psychology, and Neuroscience of Mindreading*, Oxford: Oxford University Press.
Goldman, A. (2011) "Two Routes to Empathy," in A. Coplan and P. Goldie (eds.) *Empathy: Philosophical and Psychological Perspectives*, Oxford: Oxford University Press, 31–44.
Goldman, A., and L.C. Jordan (2013) "Mindreading by Simulation," in S. Baron-Cohen, H. Tager-Flusberg, and M.V. Lombardo (eds.) *Understanding Other Minds: Perspectives from Developmental Social Neuroscience*, Oxford: Oxford University Press, 448–446.
Gordon, R.M. (1995) "Folk Psychology as Simulation," in M. Davies and T. Stone (eds.) *Folk Psychology*, Oxford: Blackwell, 60–73.
Harris, P. (2000) *The Work of the Imagination*, Oxford: Blackwell.
Heal, J. (2003) *Mind, Reason and Imagination*, Cambridge: Cambridge University Press.
Hickok, G. (2014) *The Myth of Mirror Neurons: The Real Neuroscience of Cognition and Communication*, New York: W.W. Norton & Co.
Hoffman, M. (2000) *Empathy and Moral Development*, Cambridge: Cambridge University Press.
Hollan, D. (2014) "Empathy and Morality in Ethnographic Perspective," in H. Maibom (ed.) *Empathy and Morality*, Oxford: Oxford University Press, 230–250.
Hume, D. (1739/1978) *A Treatise of Human Nature*, Oxford: Clarendon Press.
Jacob, P. (2011) "The Direct-Perception Model of Empathy: A Critique," *Review of Philosophy and Psychology* 2: 519–540.
Jacob, P., and F. de Vignemont (2012) "What Is It Like to Feel Another's Pain?" *Philosophy of Science* 79: 295–316.
Kind, A., and P. Kung (Forthcoming) *Knowledge through Imagination*, Oxford: Oxford University Press.
Maibom, H. (ed.) (2014) *Empathy and Morality*, Oxford: Oxford University Press.
Maibom, H. (Forthcoming) "Knowing Me, Knowing You: Failure to Forecast and the Empathic Imagination," in A. Kind and P. Kung (eds.) *Knowledge through Imagination*, New York: Oxford University Press.
Nichols, S., and S. Stich (2003) *Mindreading: An Integrated Account of Pretence, Self-Awareness, and Understanding Other Minds*, Oxford: Clarendon Press.
Overgaard, S., and D. Zahavi (2012) "Empathy without Isomorphism: A Phenomenological Account," in J. Decety (ed.) *Empathy: From Bench to Bedside*, Cambridge, MA: MIT Press, 3–20.
Ravenscroft, I. (1999) "Predictive Failure," *Philosophical Papers* 28: 143–168.
Rizzolatti, G., and C. Sinigaglia (2008) *Mirrors in the Brain – How Our Minds Share Actions and Emotions*, Oxford: Oxford University Press.
Scanlon, T. (1999) *What We Owe to Each Other*, Cambridge, MA: Harvard University Press.
Sherman, N. (1998) "Empathy and Imagination," *Midwest Studies in Philosophy* 22: 82 119.
Singer, T., and C. Lamm (2009) "The Social Neuroscience of Empathy," *Annals of the New York Academy of Science* 1156: 81–96.
Slote, M. (2010) *Moral Sentimentalism*, Oxford: Oxford University Press.
Smith, A. (1759/1982) *The Theory of Moral Sentiments*, Indianapolis: Liberty Classics.
Stueber, K. (2006) *Rediscovering Empathy: Agency, Folk Psychology, and the Human Sciences*, Cambridge, MA: MIT Press.
Stueber, K. (2008) "Reasons, Generalizations, Empathy, and Narratives: The Epistemic Structure of Action Explanation," *History and Theory* 47: 31–43.
Stueber, K. (2011) "Imagination, Empathy, and Moral Deliberation: The Case of Imaginative Resistance," *Southern Journal of Philosophy* 49 (Spindel Suppl.): 156–180.
Stueber, K. (2012) "Varieties of Empathy, Neuroscience and the Narrativist Challenge to the Contemporary Theory of Mind Debate," *Emotion Review* 4: 55–63.
Zahavi, D. (2010) "Empathy, Embodiment and Interpersonal Understanding: From Lipps to Schutz," *Inquiry* 53: 285–306.

# 28
# THE ETHICS OF IMAGINATION AND FANTASY

*Aaron Smuts*

## Introduction

The "ethics of imagination" or the "ethics of fantasy" encompasses the various ways in which we can morally evaluate the imagination. For instance, many people think that it is wrong to fantasize about torturing and raping children. Others have found far less disturbing fantasies problematic. Augustine, for instance, felt guilty for merely having sexual dreams (*Confessions* 10.xxx). And many critics have complained about artworks that ask audiences to pleasurably imagine violent and prurient narratives.

As these examples make clear, this topic covers a range of different kinds of imagination: (1) fantasizing, (2) engaging with fictions, and (3) dreaming. Some clarification: By "fantasizing" I have in mind conscious, pleasurable imagining. This kind of imaginative activity can be willful or spontaneous. As with dreaming, typically fantasizing involves imagining doing something. The second kind of imaginative activity, engaging with fictions, is a kind of guided suppositional imagination via representations. In contrast to fantasy and dreams, it seldom involves imagining doing something.

Here I adopt a common, unrefined notion of the imagination. Theoretical considerations may give us good reason to select different labels; the hallucinatory character of dreaming makes it a peculiar inclusion.[1] But dreams are commonly thought to be the product of the imagination, even though we are typically unaware of this fact while dreaming. Putting aside these controversies, for present purposes all three fall under the everyday notion imaginative activity.

For each of these kinds of imaginings, we can ask questions involving at least three interrelated, but different kinds of moral evaluation: (1) the right, (2) the good, and (3) the attribution of moral responsibility. We can ask if it is right or wrong to engage in certain kinds of imagining. Alternatively, we can ask if it is good or bad. Plausibly, it is morally undesirable to dream about raping and torturing children. But it might not be wrong to do so. Right and wrong pertain to actions; goodness and badness pertain to states of affairs. We can also ask whether we can be blameworthy for our fantasies, reactions to fiction, and dreams. I will elaborate in the following sections.

As will become clear, most of the live ethical questions do not concern the mere content of imaginings. Imagining terrible things is not morally problematic in itself. It's not content that concerns us; instead, we are mainly concerned with our reactions to imagined content. When I talk of imagining something I mean to include our responses to the imagined content, not the mere content. I'm referring to the imaginative experience. The clearest, live ethical question concerns the moral value of taking pleasure in undeserved suffering, whether willfully imagined, represented, or dreamed. Fantasizing about raping and torturing innocent children is a striking example of morally dubious imaginative experience.

Much of this entry concerns general theoretical considerations and how they relate to the ethics of fantasy. In the final sections I walk through the three types of imagination and point out some of the open questions concerning each type.

## Deontic vs. evaluative questions

Typically when people hear "ethics" or "morality" they think of prohibitions and, less so, prescriptions: "Thou shall not lie." "Honor thy father and mother." Statements such as these concern what is right and wrong. They tell us what we should and shouldn't do. This is the deontic sense of "ethics" – the sense concerned with obligations. This is the familiar Ten Commandments–style of moral discourse.

If we were only concerned with deontic questions, questions about right and wrong, the task here would be to see when it might be wrong to engage in certain kinds of imaginings. We might ask questions such as: Is it wrong to fantasize about hurting someone? Is it wrong to enjoy rape porn? Conversely, we might ask if we are ever morally required to imagine something or another. Some might think that we are occasionally morally required to imagine ourselves in another's shoes, so to speak. But this kind of prescription is unusual. Prohibitions on imagining are far more familiar, though still rare.

There are probably few cases where it is unambiguously wrong to imagine something or another. The reason is fairly obvious: we typically lack the kind of control over our imagination that would be necessary to rightfully say that we ought not to imagine something or another. Plausibly, ought implies can. But we can't control, or it's unclear how to control, some kinds of imagination. The problem is most perspicuous when it comes to dreams: How, for instance, can one control whether one has sexual dreams? If one lacks control over one's dreams, it would be absurd to issue prescriptions about dream content, such as: "Thou shall not have dreams involving hot sex." That would be at least as absurd as a proscription against getting tired. Caffeine and Modafinil might help ward off sleepiness, but what in the world could we take to avoid dreams involving hot sex? If deontic issues exhaust our subject, there probably wouldn't be much to say.

We will return to deontic issues later, but for now it is important to note that there are other kinds of issues that fall under the label "ethics." These questions concern the good and the bad, rather than the right and the wrong. Questions about the good and the bad are evaluative questions. They ask about the moral value of some state of affairs. Here we might ask whether some imaginative activity is good or bad. It might be that we lack the kind of control over our dreams we need in order to say that they are right or wrong; nevertheless, it still might be bad to have dreams where we ecstatically rape and torture children. Plausibly, dreams like this are morally undesirable. I sure wouldn't want to have these kinds of dreams. And if I did, I don't think I'd tell anyone. I doubt I'm alone here. Accordingly, we might say that such dreams are bad. Unlike a proscription on some kind of dreams, it is not at all absurd to say that it would be better not to have these kinds of dreams. Whether it is wrong to dream of raping and torturing children is one thing; whether it is good or bad is another.

## Blame vs. disesteem

It is important to note a related distinction between two different ways of morally evaluating persons. The distinction I have in mind does not have a settled nomenclature in the literature. Sometimes it is mentioned as the distinction between responsibility and attributability (Shoemaker 2011). The nomenclature is unimportant, but the distinction is crucial. Blame requires robust moral responsibility; disesteem requires something much weaker.

Consider someone who knowingly and willfully causes gratuitous suffering: They torture a child for sport. Surely the torturer is blameworthy for doing something wrong. They satisfy the principal condition for the appropriateness of retributive punishment. In contrast, someone who is unmoved by a child's suffering is not a good candidate for blame. They haven't done anything wrong. But their lack of concern is plausibly bad. Accordingly, they are worthy of disesteem.

This is a common form of moral evaluation. Think of cases where you found someone's attitude, emotional response, or lack of concern off-putting, such as when someone was callously indifferent to the suffering of a small child. When we have these kinds of reactions we are engaged in a different kind of evaluation from that of blame. Most plausibly we are holding the off-putting person in disesteem.[2] We attribute some kind of undesirable attitude to the person. Typically, we don't think that people should be punished for their lack of concern. Few are fully culpable for their character. But many think that it is a flaw to be cold-hearted. It's a kind of ugliness. This is not to say that we are ever warranted in expressing our disesteem, tsk-tsk'ing with a scowl, just that disesteem is appropriate. Plausibly, if a person is a fitting object of disesteem, then it would be appropriate for her to feel shame.

Regardless of how we label the distinction, it is important. Robust moral responsibility is required in order for praise and blame to be appropriate. In contrast, something much weaker is required for disesteem and esteem. We merely need to think that an undesirable attitude is in some way representative of the person, that they lack an excuse, such as: "I was drunk" (Smith 2005). As should become clear, the ethics of the imagination will largely be concerned with attributability and not robust responsibility. In many cases we lack the kind of control over our imagination that would be required for robust responsibility; nevertheless, it is plausible that our imagination might sometimes make us worthy of disesteem.

## The intrinsic value of imagined content

Routinely fantasizing about evil is likely bad for one's moral character. One might even be led to do evil as a result of the corruption. Taking pleasure in suffering might be instrumentally bad. But since this is largely an empirical question, we must put this issue aside.

In order to keep the philosophical issues live, for the sake of inquiry we should assume that there is no reliable and systematic impact of fantasy on behavior. Accordingly, the question here is whether it is intrinsically bad to enjoy imagined evil. As my initial examples indicate, some kinds of imagining do seem very objectionable, such as fantasizing about raping and torturing children.

There is clear philosophical precedent for this view. G.E. Moore defends a similar position. He argues that there are three principal kinds of evil: (1) enjoying or admiringly contemplating things which are themselves evil, (2) hatred of the good, and (3) pain (Moore 2004, 207–214; §§124–128).[3] Here are a few cases that support Moore's claim.

### *Case (i) The banana peel*

Imagine slipping on a banana peel at the local supermarket. You spin to brace your fall, but on the way down the corner of your mouth catches on the sharp lip of a shelf. It rips your mouth wide open. Through the gaping flesh of your torn cheek, most of your teeth are visible. You scream in agony. The blood fills your mouth, pours down your face, and pools on the floor. The paramedics arrive quickly. As they tend to your wound, a crowd gathers. Some softly snicker; others just watch; many take pictures and post them on Twitter. Unbeknownst to you, most of the crowd quietly admires the scene, taking pleasure in your sobs of pain and the sight of the red oozing out of your wound.

Even if you didn't notice the snickering, even if you falsely believed that the crowd was thoughtfully concerned, their pleasurable reactions would be morally bad. They should likely feel ashamed for having such reactions. We would frown on them for feeling this way. Most plausibly, the crowd is worthy of disesteem.

I see no reason to think their reactions would be bad for you. It is hard to see how unnoticed pleasure in your suffering could impact your welfare. We need not settle the issue here. Even if it does, even if the undiscovered pleasure can be said to have some negative impact on you, the harm is most plausibly slight. It cannot account for the badness of the enjoyment. Most plausibly, the crowd's enjoyment is morally far worse than it is prudentially bad for you. Hence, the badness cannot be accounted for in terms of its welfare impact, unless we think that the crowd is also harmed.[4]

However, the putative welfare impact on the members of the crowd cannot account for the badness of their pleasure. Even if we think that the moral value of our reactions has an impact on our welfare, this would not show that it is not intrinsically bad to delight in evil. Quite the opposite: the putative welfare impact on the crowd requires that it be independently bad to enjoy evil. It is hard to see how it could be prudentially bad for them otherwise.

Either way, the welfare of the crowd is not the source of our concern. We are not worried about the poor crowd's loss in welfare, or even the negative impact this may have on their character. We do not feel pity for the malicious crowd; we feel disgust. If anyone is harmed, it is you! And it is bad to take pleasure in your suffering.[5]

### *Case (ii) Charlie the lover of bestial suffering*

If the possibility of a welfare impact on the object of suffering muddies the intuitions about the previous example, consider another example, this time with a nonhuman object. Eugene Schlossberger asks us to imagine Charlie: "Charlie derives great pleasure from the sight of animals in pain. Mind you, he never causes animals to suffer. But when he chances upon a wounded animal, the sight affords him much delight" (Schlossberger 1986, 40). We can elaborate: Charlie's favorite pastime is touring slaughter houses. Although a vegetarian for health reasons, he was overjoyed to learn that the employees of large poultry farms occasionally torture chickens for sport. Recently, he joined an animal rights group so he would have easy access to pictures of suffering beasts.

The implications are clear. Even though Charlie never causes an animal to suffer, his enjoyment of suffering beasts is troubling. His enjoyment is morally bad, but not because it is bad for the animals. Although it might be plausible that malicious pleasure harms humans, few defend a similar claim about nonhuman animals. It is implausible that wishing a dog ill harms the dog.

### *Case (iii) Moore's universe of cruel thought*

Someone might complain that the example of Charlie does not pump the right intuitions. It is hard not to worry that Charlie will someday torture a helpless animal. A cleaner example will help. Consider Moore's thought experiment: to see the badness of enjoying cruelty, he asks us to imagine a world of people solely occupied with cruel thoughts:

> If we then consider what judgment we should pass upon a universe which consisted *solely* of minds thus occupied [with thoughts of cruelty], without the smallest hope that there would ever exist in it the smallest consciousness of any object other than those proper to these passions, or any feeling directed to any such object, I think that we cannot avoid the conclusion that the existence of such a universe would be a far worse evil than the existence of none at all.
>
> *(Moore 2004, 209; §125)*

Admittedly, it is difficult to imagine a universe composed only of minds occupied with cruel thoughts, but it is even more difficult to imagine a good reason to think that such universe would be better than an empty one. Just as it seems clear that a universe occupied only by a single suffering creature is worse than an empty universe, it likewise seems bad if the universe were occupied solely by someone thinking cruel thoughts. This suggests that enjoying the bad is intrinsically bad. It is not bad merely for what it leads to. No, it is bad in itself.

### *Case (iv) Two-worlds*

If the immaterial nature of the previous example confounds things, here is a Rossian argument: Imagine two worlds, each having just one inhabitant, a sole survivor of a nuclear holocaust (Ross 1930, 140). In world A, the survivor spends her free time thinking nice thoughts. She often imagines cats playing with rubber bands on sunny window sills. In world B, the survivor lives a similar life, but rather than imagine cats, he imagines raping and torturing children. Is either world preferable?

The cat fancier in world A is a bit precious, but she is not hideously repulsive. In contrast, the survivor in world B is repugnant. I doubt that the repulsion stems from worries about the consequences of his fantasizing. Yes, compulsive fantasies of child torture are probably indicative of inclinations that we would rather not see realized. But we can put this aside. We do not have to live in either world. We are merely asked to decide which one is better. If we were given a choice to bring one or the other into existence, we should choose A. Most plausibly world B is worse. Not because we worry that a child might be tortured, or that we might be injured by this freak, but because the child-torturing fantasist enjoys evil. That's bad enough.

Once again, this scenario suggests that it is intrinsically bad to enjoy evil. In fact, the universe of cruel thought and the two-worlds examples give us reason to think that enjoying merely imagined evil is bad. Plausibly, engaging with fiction is a kind of guided imagination. Hence, it appears that in the process of making a case for the intrinsic badness of enjoying evil, we found a reason to believe the same about enjoying fictional evil (Smuts forthcoming). The implications for dreams are less clear.

## Three kinds of imagining

As noted above, there are important differences between the three types of imagination: (1) fantasizing, (2) guided imagination via representations, and (3) dreams. It is best to consider these in the order presented, as they appear to be in descending order of moral significance.[6] This is likely a result of our corresponding diminished control.

### *Imagining (1) Willful imagination or fantasy*

The focus of the ethics of imagination is not so much a matter of imagined content, as it is a matter of imaginative experiences. There is nothing morally problematic about imagining the horror faced by those working in child brothels. The best candidates for morally questionable imaginative experiences are those where someone pleasurably imagines some kind of evil. The term "fantasy" makes this clear. The notion of a sad fantasy is incoherent. If we say that someone fantasizes about raping and torturing children, we mean that he pleasurably imagines doing so. The arguments in the previous section give us good reason to think that this kind of imaginative experience is bad.

Unlike dreams, many fantasies appear to be under our control. And in so far as fantasies are under our control, it is plausible to say that we can be morally responsible for fantasizing about evil. Although a proscription on having certain kinds of dreams might be absurd, it is not the least bit absurd to say that one ought not to willfully fantasize about raping and torturing children.

Given our control over some kinds of fantasizing, it appears that the key preconditions for the appropriateness of blame can be satisfied. Some people might indeed be blameworthy for fantasizing about things they shouldn't when they could have done otherwise.

However, it isn't clear that all or even most fantasizing is under our conscious control. Fantasizing, much like daydreaming, can slip over us. People often fall into fantasies, so to speak. Call these "spontaneous fantasies." Plausibly, these instances of fantasizing are only under limited control. Accordingly, in cases of spontaneous fantasy, it's hard to see how the fantasizer could be robustly morally responsible. And if they aren't morally responsible, they are not blameworthy.

Nevertheless, spontaneous fantasies can be morally significant. Consider the case of someone who routinely spontaneously fantasizes about violently raping anyone they meet, man, woman, child, or beast. They aren't a rapist; they just pleasurably imagine raping, and they do it a lot. Similarly, we can imagine someone who spontaneously imagines raping children whenever he masturbates. There is something deeply troubling about these cases. Again, we might worry that these people will someday act on their fantasies. But, presumably, most don't. And this is beside the point. The fantasies themselves are disturbing. Although the person isn't blameworthy, the chronic rape fantasist is plausibly worthy of disesteem. If shame isn't appropriate in these cases, I'm not sure it ever is.

### *What makes fantasizing wrong when it is wrong?*

So far, I've repeatedly appealed to the example of someone fantasizing about raping and torturing children. I'm sorry about the unpleasant example, but this is the clearest case of morally problematic fantasy that I can think of. The example works for most of our purposes, but it would be nice if we had a general explanation for what makes fantasizing wrong when it is wrong, or bad when it is bad. One suggestion is as follows:

> It is wrong to fantasize about doing something that would be wrong to do *in real life*. Alternatively stated in terms of badness: It is morally bad to pleasurable imagine states of affairs that would be bad to respond to pleasurably *in real life*.

Call this the IRL theory (IRL).

Although the IRL theory may seem plausible, it is far too severe. Consider the case of a married woman who occasionally fantasizes about having sex with her personal trainer. She wouldn't do so, but she likes to imagine gripping his firm buttocks as he rhythmically thrusts against her loins. Most plausibly, it would be wrong for her to cheat on her husband. Although it probably wouldn't make her husband very happy, it seems ridiculously puritanical to say that it is wrong for her to fantasize about having sex with her trainer. Since the IRL theory suggests otherwise, we should reject the theory.

A more plausible theory holds that it is wrong (or morally bad) to fantasize about doing something that is bad *in itself*. Call this the Moorean theory (MT). It is not intrinsically bad to have hot sex with one's personal trainer. In the case at hand, the badness lies in breaking a promise to be faithful to her husband. But that's not part of the fantasy (though, of course, it could be of a different fantasy). Contrast this with fantasizing about raping and torturing children: The stuff that makes raping and torturing children bad, namely the gratuitous suffering of the children, is part of the fantasy. That's why it is bad. This is only a rough suggestion, but MT does a much better job than IRL.

### *Imagining (2) Guided imagination via representations: fiction, narratives, and pornography*

The second main form of imagination that I want to consider is what we can call guided imagination. This is the kind of imaginative activity we engage in when we respond to representations, whether they be written, aural, or visual. Think of watching a movie. One plausible account holds that we entertain the content of the movie. We imagine that what we see is taking place elsewhere. We don't believe that it's real, that we are somehow magically transported into another world. That would take mushrooms or LSD. For the sober viewer, it's as if the fiction is premised with the instruction: "Imagine this: ..." Along the way we fill in details, sympathize with characters, form questions about what will happen next, and imagine different kinds of outcomes.

All of this is controversial, but the general contours are likely correct. It seems fair to think that our engagement with fiction is a kind of imaginative activity. And just as willful imagining can provoke emotional and physiological reactions, so too can guided imagination. The question at hand is whether imaginative experiences had in response to representations, whether they be of actual of fictional objects, are ever wrong or bad.

In the previous section, we saw that there is a plausible moral difference between willful imagining and spontaneous fantasizing. The difference stems from the amount of control we have over the experiences. One might think that a similar difference applied to guided imagination. The viewer of a movie does not create, much less control, the content. This difference is important. In the case of fiction, it's plausible that content producers are sometimes to blame for producing works designed to elicit reactions that would be bad to have.

But what about the viewer? Although the viewer does not control the content, they do have some kinds of control. For starters, they can decide which kinds of representations to pursue. If someone searches on Google for "child rape porn snuff film," they are at least partially complicit in what follows. Similarly, people can close their eyes and cover their ears, leave theaters, close books, and turn off TVs. But these kinds of control are minimal. They do not constitute control over the content, but of merely of whether one is exposed to certain kinds of content.

Although we might have minimal control over exposure, our powers are far more attenuated when it comes to our reactions. The kinds of reactions we are concerned with are mostly involuntary: arousal, fear, anger, delight. And since they are largely involuntary, we lack the kind of control needed for robust responsibility. Hence, it is hard to see how anyone could ever be blameworthy for their guided imaginative experiences.

Further, someone might argue that there is another important difference between willful fantasizing and engaging with fictional works, a difference suggesting that typical engagement with fiction isn't morally problematic at all. Much everyday imagining involves what Christopher Cherry calls "surrogate fantasy." Surrogate fantasies are those that the fantasist would like to take place. They are surrogates for reality. But not all fantasies are like this. Some fantasies are "autonomous."

Cherry argues that autonomous fantasies are unlike surrogate fantasies in that the fantasist does not desire the fantasy to be actualized. It is perfectly conceivable that someone could enjoy rape fantasies, but not want to rape. Nor would he want to witness a rape. He would be horrified by the violence. But he is not horrified by merely imagined violence. On Cherry's taxonomy, his fantasies are autonomous, not surrogate. Autonomous fantasies appear to be far less morally problematic; perhaps they are morally innocuous.

Plausibly, most of our encounters with fiction are more like autonomous fantasies than surrogate fantasies. There may be many cases where the audience uses the fiction as a surrogate. But this is not typical. If we consider the kind of imagining involved in most types of fiction, it is clear that fictional engagement is typically akin to autonomous fantasizing.

To see why, it will help to make some distinctions between a few kinds of imagining. Bernard Williams's taxonomy is most useful for present purposes. He distinguishes between four different kinds of imagining: (1) as a mere spectator not in the visualized world, (2) as an actor in the imagined world doing things, (3) as an outside observer strangely watching oneself do things, and (4) as inhabiting the sphere of action, but merely observing (Williams 1973, 38–39). The first and third kinds are from the outside: One imagines oneself outside of the fictional world. The second and fourth are from a perspective inside the imagined world.

Most dreams are like the second type of imagining. Dreams are typically experienced in the first-person; we are not mere observers in our dreams. In contrast, the experience of watching films and plays, and reading novels is more like the first kind of imagining, as an external spectator. We merely observe the action occurring on the page, stage, or screen, even when the fourth wall is traversed. Contrary to some phenomenologically implausible theories of fictional engagement, we do not typically imagine ourselves as actors in, or even as impotent occupants of, the fictional world (Walton 1978, 23–24, and 1990). That would be very strange. Indeed this is the stuff of science fiction. Instead, we merely observe from the outside (Carroll 2001, 311–313). We may be startled, we may fear for the safety of a character, but we seldom, if ever, fear for ourselves.[7] And even if we do occasionally imagine what it would be like to be in a work of fiction, this would not show that we wish the fiction were real.[8] It would not show that we are engaged in a surrogate fantasy.[9]

When we imagine things in the second sense, from a first-person perspective, it is unlikely that our fantasies are autonomous. More likely than not, first-person imaginings are surrogate fantasies. We fantasize about doing things, not merely watching them done. In contrast, third-person imaginings are more often than not autonomous fantasies. Given that most fictional experiences are akin to third-person imaginings, they are likely autonomous. When we reflect on our experiences with fiction, this seems to be the case. I certainly do not wish it were the case that an ancient demon such as Bughuul (*Sinister*, dir. Derrickson, 2012) induct children into his murderous cult. Hence, if autonomous fantasizing is not morally problematic, then neither is most fictional imagining. How could it be morally bad to take pleasure in the observation of something in a fictional world that we do not want to be manifest in reality?

As the objection suggests, perhaps there is indeed an important moral difference between surrogate and autonomous fantasies. Nevertheless, it is doubtful that the autonomous nature of much guided imagination renders it morally insignificant. Earlier I considered four arguments concerning the badness of enjoying imagined suffering. The common conclusion of these arguments was that it is intrinsically bad to enjoy evil. The universe of cruel thought and the two-worlds examples show as much. I see little reason to think that our reactions to fiction are always morally neutral when autonomous.

On a plausible account of fictional engagement, when we engage with fictions we take it to be the case that a variety of things are true of a fictional world (Neill 1993). When we take pleasure in the suffering of a fictional character, we imagine it to be true in the fictional world that a character suffers. Although we believe that Anna Karenina suffers, we need not believe that she exists in the real world. She suffers in the world of the story. In most realistic fictions, we assume that the characters suffer as do people in the real world. Accordingly, enjoying their suffering is akin to enjoying guided cruel thoughts. If malicious pleasure in cruel thoughts is bad, it seems that it would be bad regardless of whether it is accompanied by a belief that the object exists in the real world.

The universe of cruel thought and the two-worlds examples appear to be morally bad even though the imagining was not accompanied by a belief in the reality of the object. Absent an explanation, I see no reason to think it unobjectionable to enjoy the evil in a fictional world. The badness is not, at least not primarily, in wanting to do bad things. It is in enjoying the bad. And the bad is enjoyed in both cases. It might be worse to have an additional desire to do bad things. But it is still bad to enjoy imagined evil without such a desire.

Although we have good reason to think that autonomous fantasies involving fictional content can sometimes be bad, we lack the full story. There remains an important open question: why does it seem worse to enjoy documentaries of real suffering than fictional suffering? This question presents a challenge. The challenge is to explain why it is worse to enjoy real suffering than fictional suffering in such a way that doesn't undermine the claim that the fictional cases can be bad.

The worries do not end here. Although it seems bad to enjoy some representations of suffering, many simply leave us flat. But we don't think that this makes someone cold-hearted. It's not as if they were left unmoved by actual, suffering. Similarly, there are many movies that feature over-the-top violence. The Crazy 88's fight scene in *Kill Bill* (dir. Tarantino, 2003) is a good example. The violence is so comically overblown, it would be very odd to think that someone should respond even remotely similarly to how they might if they witnessed the events firsthand. The difference is surely due to the fictionality of the killing. But why doesn't this make all the difference? Why doesn't it render all responses to fictional suffering morally innocuous? There is much more to be said about these issues.

### *Imagining (3) Dreaming*

We have limited, indirect control when it comes to representations: we can leave the theater, reliably avoid rape porn, and close books. But we can't just stop a dream. Nor can we start dreams or regularly willfully control their content. When it comes to dreams, we are closer to Alex strapped to a chair in *A Clockwork Orange* (dir. Kubrick, 1971), than we are to average movie viewers who can close their eyes and turn their heads. Hence, the idea that we could somehow be robustly morally responsible for our dreams seems preposterous (Sosa 2005, 9).

Contrary to the considerations above, there are reasons to think that dreams are more not less morally significant than our reactions to fiction. Despite our lack of control, some might saddle us with greater responsibilities for our dreams. On some theories, dreams appear to be surrogate fantasies. And unlike most representations, some may argue that we are the authors, in some sense, of our dreams. As a result, we might think that dreams are closer to willful imagining, morally speaking, than our reactions to fiction. Call this the Augustinian view, since he feared that sexual dreams were sinful (*Confessions* 10.xxx).[10]

It is not entirely clear which of these two contrary positions on the morality of dreams is right. Consider some of the underlying assumptions of the Augustinian view. First, is it correct to think that dreams are surrogate fantasies? Freud surely thought so (Freud 1989, pt. 2). He held that dreams are disguised fulfillments of a repressed or suppressed wish (see Wollheim 1991, ch. 3). If dreams are, as Freud thought, disguised fulfillments of repressed or suppressed wishes, then rape dreams would be particularly problematic surrogate fantasies.

Although most dreams are indeed typically first-person imaginings, those where we imagine doing things, I don't see any compelling reason to think that all dreams are surrogate fantasies. Surely many sex dreams are surrogate fantasies. But what about anxiety dreams and nightmares? The Freudian theory of dreams has only *ad hoc*, implausible things to say about nightmares. Given these glaring counterexamples to the Freudian theory, we have good reason to doubt that most dreams are surrogate fantasies.

Nevertheless, even if we reject the claim that all or even most dreams are surrogate fantasies, there are other considerations in favor of the Augustinian view. Although we do not willfully design our dreams, we appear to be their authors. (If the notion of authorship doesn't apply, since we don't aim to communicate any ideas through our dreams, we are at least their makers.[11]) Who else could be responsible? Accordingly, some might think that we can be worthy of disesteem for our dream life.

This charge isn't easy to dismiss. Although all dreams might not be surrogate fantasies and they are almost never willfully constructed, there is certainly something unsettling about someone who dreams of raping and torturing children. No one would suggest that we should feel ashamed for having nightmares or anxiety dreams. But if one regularly dreams of doing evil, we might have cause for concern. It appears that a serial dream rapist is almost as worthy of disesteem as a serial rape fantasist.

The most compelling objection to the above line of reasoning is what we might call the "idiot's excuse." Contemporary neuroscience gives us reason to think that we are essentially idiots when we dream. We aren't just idiots, we are likely as irrational as ponies due to our brain chemistry during sleep.[12] However, the idiot's excuse is only so compelling. When we consider someone with an extremely violent, or downright evil, dream life, it's hard to think that this doesn't reflect on their character, however irrational they might be while asleep.

More controversially, there might be some forms of dreaming that are closer to waking life than typical imaginings. A lucid dream is one where the dreamer knows that she is dreaming. Lucidity comes in degrees and can be fleeting. In some extreme cases, a lucid dreamer may be able to take partial control of the dream and their actions in the dream. If a lucid dreamer has this kind of control and uses it to do evil, it's plausible that they could be robustly morally responsible for their dreams, or at least what they do in their dreams. Of course, much of this rests on a host of poorly understood empirical phenomena. Once again, there is much more to say about the issue.

## Notes

1 See Jonathan Jenkins Ichikawa's entry (Chapter 11) in this volume for a discussion of the nature of dreams.

2 For a defense of this and related distinctions, see: Beardsley 1960, Oakley 1992, chs. 4–5, Blum 1980, Adams 1985, and Shoemaker 2011.
3 Hurka (2001) defends a similar account, but with a larger list in the third category. He also includes false belief and failure (15).
4 Oakley (1992, 71 and 80–83) defends a virtue theory of the badness of enjoying evil. He suggests that badness is ultimately, although indirectly, a matter of welfare.
5 Shaver (2004, 143) notes and replies to similar anti-welfarist arguments.
6 Mann (1983, 382–384) concurs. He thinks that dreams are less bad than daydreams which are less bad than lucid fantasizing.
7 Carroll (1990, 76) and Neill (1993) mark the important distinction between fearing for oneself and fearing for others. Ichikawa's entry in this volume (Chapter 11) fails to note this important distinction when considering the emotional engagement argument for the hallucination model of dreams. Davies (2006, 156), Gaut (2010, 278–281), and Tavinor (2009, 143) suggest that the phenomenology of videogame play may be an exception. Corvino (2002, 218) thinks that the participatory nature of videogames makes the possible moral problems more perspicuous.
8 Stock (2009, 367–369) argues that people often imagine themselves inside movies, where the characters stand proxy for the audience in a fiction-guided fantasy.
9 Defenders of the view that we imaginatively identify engage with fictional characters might disagree. See, for instance: Gaut 1999, 200–216, and Thomson-Jones 2008, 113–123.
10 Matthews (1981) sees no clear way for Augustine to avoid the implication. In book IX of the *Republic*, Plato advises us to tame the lower self before sleep. Apparently, he is also concerned about dream content.
11 Mann (1983) argues that it is bad to construct an immoral dream.
12 Clark (2005) summarizes many of the differences. Blackmore (2004, ch. 23) explains the known differences between the sleeping and the awake brain.

## Further reading

I'm unaware of any systematic treatment of the ethics of fantasy. The literature on fiction is the largest, but it typically only indirectly addresses the issues discussed here.

Cherry (1985 and 1988), Corvino (2002), Kershnar (2004 and 2005), and Neu (2002) discuss the morality of fantasy.

Livingston and Mele (1997, 166–171), Hurka (1992, 158–160; and 2001, 162–171), Gaut (1998a, 186; 1998b, 231, 233, 236; and 2007, 231, 233, 236), Hazlett (2009), Moran (1994, 105), Walton (1994), and Smuts (2013) are the only recent discussions that I am aware of that explicitly deal with the morality of enjoying fiction. Tavinor (2009, ch. 8) discusses videogames. Mann (1983) and Matthews (1981) are two rare treatments of the ethics of dreaming.

## References

Adams, R. (1985) "Involuntary Sins," *Philosophical Review* 94(1): 3–31.
Beardsley, E. (1960) "Determinism and Moral Perspectives," *Philosophy and Phenomenological Research* 21(1): 1–20.
Blackmore, S. (2004) *Consciousness*, New York: Oxford University Press.
Blum, L. (1980) *Friendship, Altruism, and Morality*, New York: Routledge & Kegan Paul.
Carroll, N. (1990) *The Philosophy of Horror or Paradoxes of the Heart*, New York: Routledge.
Carroll, N. (2001) "Simulation, Emotions, and Morality," in *Beyond Aesthetics*, Cambridge: Cambridge University Press.
Cherry, C. (1985) "The Inward and the Outward: Fantasy, Reality and Satisfaction," *Canadian Journal of Philosophy* 11(suppl.): 175–193.
Cherry, C. (1988) "When Is Fantasising Morally Bad?" *Philosophical Investigations* 11(2): 112–132.
Clark, A. (2005) "The Twisted Matrix: Dream, Simulation, or Hybrid?" in C. Grau (ed.) *Philosophers Explore the Matrix*, New York: Oxford University Press.
Corvino, J. (2002) "Naughty Fantasies," *Southwest Philosophy Review* 18(1): 213–220.
Davies, S. (2006) *The Philosophy of Art*, Malden: Blackwell.
Freud, S. (1989) *Introductory Lectures on Psycho-Analysis*, trans. J. Strachey, New York: W.W. Norton & Co.

Gaut, B. (1998a) "Just Joking: The Ethics and Aesthetics of Humor," *Philosophy and Literature* 22(1): 51–68.
Gaut, B. (1998b) "The Ethical Criticism of Art," in J. Levinson (ed.) *Aesthetics and Ethics: Essays at the Intersection*, Cambridge: Cambridge University Press.
Gaut, B. (1999) "Identification and Emotion in Narrative Film," in C. Plantinga and G.M. Smith (eds.) *Passionate Views: Film, Cognition, and Emotion*, Baltimore: Johns Hopkins University Press, 200–216.
Gaut, B. (2007) *Art, Emotion, and Ethics*, New York: Oxford University Press.
Gaut, B. (2010) *A Philosophy of Cinematic Art*, Cambridge: Cambridge University Press.
Hazlett, A. (2009) "How to Defend Response Moralism," *British Journal of Aesthetics* 49(3): 241–255.
Hurka, T. (1992) "Virtue as Loving the Good," in E.F. Paul, F. Miller, and J. Paul (eds.) *The Good Life and the Human Good*, Cambridge: Cambridge University Press.
Hurka, T. (2001) *Virtue, Vice, and Value*, Oxford: Oxford University Press.
Kershnar, S. (2004) "Is Violation Pornography Bad for Your Soul?" *Journal of Social Philosophy* 35(3): 349–366.
Kershnar, S. (2005) "The Moral Status of Sexual Fantasies," *Public Affairs Quarterly* 19(4): 301–315.
Livingston, P., and A. Mele (1997) "Evaluating Emotional Responses to Fiction," in M. Hjort and S. Laver (eds.) *Emotion and the Arts*, New York: Oxford University Press.
Mann, W. (1983) "Dreams of Immorality," *Philosophy* 58(225): 378–385.
Matthews, G. (1981) "On Being Immoral in a Dream," *Philosophy* 56(215): 47–54.
Moore, G.E. (2004) *Principia Ethica*, New York: Dover.
Moran, R. (1994) "The Expression of Feeling in Imagination," *Philosophical Review* 103(1): 75–106.
Neill, A. (1993) "Fiction and the Emotions," *American Philosophical Quarterly* 30(1): 1–13.
Neu, J. (2002) "An Ethics of Fantasy?" *Journal of Theoretical and Philosophical Psychology* 22(2): 133–157.
Oakley, J. (1992) *Morality and the Emotions*, New York: Routledge.
Ross, W.D. (1930) *The Right and the Good*, Indianapolis: Hackett.
Schlossberger, E. (1986) "Why We Are Responsible for Our Emotions," *Mind* 95(377): 37–56.
Shaver, R. (2004) "The Appeal of Utilitarianism," *Utilitas* 16(3): 235–250.
Shoemaker, D. (2011) "Attributability, Answerability, and Accountability: Toward a Wider Theory of Moral Responsibility," *Ethics* 121: 602–632.
Smith, A. (2005) "Responsibility for Attitudes: Activity and Passivity in Mental Life," *Ethics* 115: 236–271.
Smuts, A. (2013) "The Ethics of Singing Along: The Case of 'Mind of a Lunatic,'" *Journal of Aesthetics and Art Criticism* 71(1): 121–129.
Smuts, A. (Forthcoming) "How Not to Defend Response Moralism," *Journal of Aesthetic Education*.
Sosa, E. (2005) "Dreams and Philosophy," *Proceedings and Addresses of the American Philosophical Association* 79(2): 7–18.
Stock, K. (2009) "Fantasy, Imagination, and Film," *British Journal of Aesthetics* 49(4): 357–369.
Tavinor, G. (2009) *The Art of Videogames*, Malden: Wiley-Blackwell.
Thomson-Jones, K. (2008) *Aesthetics and Film*, New York: Continuum.
Walton, K. (1978) "Fearing Fictions," *Journal of Philosophy* 75(1): 5–27.
Walton, K. (1990) *Mimesis as Make-Believe: On the Foundations of the Representational Arts*, Cambridge, MA: Harvard University Press.
Walton, K. (1994) "Morals in Fiction and Fictional Morality," *Proceedings of the Aristotelian Society*, Supplementary Volume 68: 27–66.
Williams, B. (1973) "Imagination and the Self," in *Problems of the Self*, Cambridge: Cambridge University Press.
Wollheim, R. (1991) *Freud*, 2nd edn, London: Fontana Press.

# 29

# IMAGINATION AND THE CAPABILITIES APPROACH

*Natalie M. Fletcher*

Does imagination have a political dimension? If a significant aim of contemporary democracies is to promote the self-determination of citizens by ensuring certain crucial freedoms, imagination can be deemed as an important avenue for expanding the scope of agency. After all, it is through our imaginative faculties that we can envision our current and future contexts from more diverse frames of reference, and develop a broadened lens with which to approach and assess our lived experience. Without imagination, we run the risk of limiting our agency through a narrow, impoverished outlook that restricts our sense of opportunity and our potential to lead meaningful, fulfilling lives. In turn, we may lack the imaginative resources to see ourselves as capable agents who can contribute to enhancing the political landscapes in which we find ourselves, simply by living out and embodying the freedoms we have envisaged as most valuable.

To illuminate this political dimension of imagination, the Capabilities Approach (CA) has a lot to offer as a highly influential theoretical paradigm of human development. Since the 1980s, leading advocates of CA like Amartya Sen and Martha Nussbaum have striven to redefine how we assess the wealth of communities based on what people are actually able to achieve within their set of circumstances, focusing on the opportunities to enact desired freedoms in ways that honor agency and dignity. In light of its major political influence, notably toward the formation of the United Nations' Human Development Index, a summary measure of average achievement across areas like health, knowledge and standard of living, CA and its distinctive methods of assessing human welfare can give insight into what it might mean to conceive imagination politically as a capability.

Of course, many proponents of CA have understandably focused on the protection and promotion of basic capabilities, notably in relation to serious issues of global justice such as the alleviation of poverty and the eradication of health inequalities. Ultimately, basic capabilities are what translate into the capacity for survival; for Sen, they represent "the ability to satisfy certain elementary and crucially important functionings up to certain levels" (Sen 1992, 45). Less conceptual attention has extended to the complex capabilities that contribute to agency development or, as John Davis phrases it, on "what it means to be and develop as an individual" once survival needs are met (Davis 2009, 427). This chapter is dedicated to one such complex capability – the capability of imagination – and the ways it can contribute to our agency by expanding and enriching our envisioned options for the lives we have reason to value. The chapter begins with an overview of CA in the context of agency development, then considers imagination as a complex essential capability with a particular focus on Nussbaum's work, and ends with a look at the educational potential of imagination for children.

## The Capabilities Approach in context

The Capabilities Approach has grown out of a profound and widely held concern that current utilitarian-based economic models are inadequate – and we might even say unimaginative – because their assessment strategies do not account for all the particulars that make a human life meaningful and worthwhile (Nussbaum and Sen 1993). By focusing on the overall economic wealth of nations through indicators like a country's gross domestic product, such approaches capture only fragments or generalities about human welfare, thereby overshadowing serious inequalities and limitations in what citizens are actually able to do and be, notably with respect to their access to health care and education. What results is an inaccurate picture of a country's development: if increased wealth is evident, then key factors affecting welfare go unnoticed, like uneven distribution of resources, discrepancies between rich and poor, and unequal access to opportunities.

In contrast, CA seeks to inquire into the real opportunities people have within their socioeconomic contexts to achieve the "lives they have reason to value" (Sen 1997, p. 1959). This key phrase coined by Sen highlights a crucial distinction between CA and other economic assessments of well-being: as individuals, while we may value the human capital that we can cultivate to contribute to our community's growth, we also treasure many other dimensions of our lives that transcend the instrumentally valuable – the educational experiences that enhance our knowledge of world histories and cultures, the political engagements that enable us to express our ideas and be taken seriously, the aesthetic encounters that inspire us to imagine possible futures for ourselves and endeavor to realize them. In short, to use Kantian terms, we value ourselves as ends not merely as means.

By proposing a more holistic way of assessing and comparing quality of life across communities, CA offers a flexible, interdisciplinary and context-sensitive framework that stresses this valuation process and reflects the actual struggles we face in our efforts to design meaningful lives for ourselves. Through its emphasis on social justice and its careful study of cultural and regional differences, CA recognizes and ardently defends the plurality of freedoms that make a human life worth living, demonstrating that what might be valuable in one community might have no relevance in another (Comim et al. 2008). The term "capabilities" designates these varied and substantial freedoms: the opportunities we actually have in our specific set of circumstances to choose certain "functionings" – or beings and doings as forms of engagement – that we deem relevant and feasible for ourselves. The extent to which we can be free in these ways depends on the possibilities that our contexts afford us: our families, our socioeconomic statuses, our educational conditions and our political environments can help or hinder the development of our internal abilities and thereby affect whether we can fulfill our desired lifestyles. For instance, if we live in a repressive society that silences our speech, then even if we have learnt to express ourselves at school through public speaking classes, we will have no forum in which to exercise this ability; conversely, if our society encourages freedom of expression but we have no capacity to communicate, we will not be able to take advantage of this opportunity – in each case, our freedom is inhibited. Yet if both the internal and external factors are satisfied, we can be said to have the capability and it becomes our choice whether to use it: we can decide not to exercise our free speech despite having the capacity and opportunity to do so. The classic example of fasting versus starving in

CA literature also illustrates this dynamic: if we choose to fast out of political convictions but have the opportunity to eat and access nourishment, our capability is drastically different from that of the person who is starving because no food is available, even though our functionings appear similar (Sen 1992, 52).

And so, as Nussbaum emphasizes, CA is interested in securing capabilities and leaving functionings to individual choice:

> To promote capabilities is to promote areas of freedom, and this is not the same as making people function in a certain way … capabilities, not functionings, are the appropriate political goals, because room is thereby left for the exercise of human freedom. There is a huge moral difference between a policy that promotes health and one that promotes health capabilities – the latter, not the former, honors the person's lifestyle choices.
>
> *(Nussbaum 2011, 25–26)*

Yet what would it mean for a policy to promote imagination as a capability in a way that honors people's lifestyle choices? Proponents of CA have not devoted much time to this question, likely for two main reasons. First, although imagination can be deemed an important complex capability, the understandable concern over the stark reality of people throughout the world lacking the most basic capabilities – such as being able to access adequate nourishment, shelter and security – makes imagination a lesser priority (Sen 1992, 151). Presumably if basic capabilities could be met on a global scale, more complex capabilities like imagination would be given greater consideration. Yet a second reason may challenge this assumption: within CA, there has been much debate over whether specific capabilities should be identified at all, or whether they should emerge from communities themselves, based on their distinctive needs and customs. Sen has cautioned against advocating for a universal set of capabilities since such a selection risks becoming overly prescriptive and undermining the valuation process enabled by a community's public discourse channels (Sen 2005, 158). Nussbaum disagrees, however, offering a now widely known list of ten central capabilities – a list on which imagination figures, as we will soon see. From her perspective, this list constitutes a necessary building block for a normative theory of social justice since it offers a point of convergence for sparking an international conversation about what makes a life worth living (Nussbaum 2011, 29). In her view, provided we see the list as a proposal that is sensitive to cultural differences and open to revision, we can gain a lot from considering these abstract universal capabilities and encouraging communities to determine for themselves how such abstractions should be concretized and actualized within their particular contexts.

In this sense, CA is a highly imaginative model since it asks us to envisage the kinds of freedoms to which we should all be entitled in order to preserve and promote our agency, which Nussbaum sees as crucial to our human dignity. As she writes, "the Capabilities Approach tells us what to consider salient, but it does not dictate a final assignment of weights and a sharp-edged decision" – we must make those ultimate judgements ourselves based on what we have imagined as meaningful lives worthy of our pursuit (Nussbaum 2011, 41). Given the importance of agency in CA, imagination becomes a very significant capability as it broadens the scope of what can be envisioned as valuable. For instance, it can support the capacity for deliberation, a trait that CA theorist Geoffrey Hinchcliffe argues is crucial to agency and to developing a "self" of capability. Borrowing from Charles Taylor's notion of a "strong evaluator" making qualitative, nonutilitarian distinctions that prioritize certain life pursuits as more valuable than others, Hinchliffe argues that the self of capability is an agent who "thinks about her life in terms of ends," perceiving herself as "living out [her] valued activities through [her] own agency" whenever possible, notably in the contexts of her education and of her community life (Hinchliffe 2009, 405). For Hinchliffe, capability development involves both "the creation of opportunities" – which is largely determined by our sociopolitical framework and thus beyond our control – and "the ability to make the best of those opportunities" (406), which we can directly affect by deliberating over our existing functionings and imagining those we want and need with reference to the capabilities we may be lacking.

Through this reasoned, imaginative deliberation as agents, we are able to harness our capabilities to achieve the kind of well-being we find valuable at different phases of our lives and become responsible for our choices. In their phenomenological account of CA, Jérôme Ballet et al. emphasize the largely neglected dimension of personal responsibility in the conception of agency and freedom, "particularly with regard to the capability for a person to feel and be responsible; that is, voluntary self-constraint in order to satisfy obligations towards others" (Ballet et al. 2007, 198). Whereas Sen describes responsibility as the consequence of freedom, Ballet et al. draw from the philosophies of Martin Heidegger, Jean-Paul Sartre and Hannah Arendt in characterizing responsibility as a "constitutive characteristic of the person" and of the "richness of her nature" (187). In their view, this prioritization of responsibility expands Sen's notion of agency by suggesting that "fulfilling a set of obligations often constitutes a pre-condition for well-being" and can thus override certain claims to freedom of choice (195). On this account, since we exist in an embedded social network that we affect through our various commitments, responsibility enriches our sense of agency as "a precondition for action, whereas rights and freedom act only as 'facilitators'" (197).

What remains unclear or at least insufficiently discussed in the CA literature is what can actually fuel this evolving self-determination process – what can give our agency content and expand what we have reason to value. After all, if we have reason to value *X*, it is likely because we have weighed the worth of *X* in relation to a host of other possible considerations through careful deliberation, making our choice of *X* not only a symbol of our individuality – a contributing element to our distinctive set of capabilities – but also evidence of our responsibility as individuals who take seriously their obligations to others and their impact on them. But what can feed, supply and boost this host of possible considerations to make it sufficiently expansive? What can guard against a narrow, impoverished outlook that restricts the scope of deliberation and responsibility needed for agency? As a capability, imagination can make a significant contribution and thus deserves conceptual attention.

## Imagination as an essential complex capability

Though imagination is explored in many accounts of CA, it is often subsumed under broader categories like education, knowledge and citizenship. Nussbaum's list of central capabilities aligns imagination primarily with senses and thought but also refers to it under the capability of affiliation:

> 4 *Senses, imagination, and thought.* Being able to use the senses, to imagine, think, and reason – and to do these things in a "truly human" way, a way informed and cultivated by an adequate education, including, but by no means limited to, literacy and basic mathematical and scientific training. Being able to use imagination and thought in connection with experiencing and producing works and events of one's own choice, religious, literary, musical, and so forth. Being able to use

> one's mind in ways protected by guarantees of freedom of expression with respect to both political and artistic speech, and freedom of religious exercise. Being able to have pleasurable experiences and to avoid nonbeneficial pain. ...
>
> 7 *Affiliation*. ... To be able to imagine the situation of another.
>
> (Nussbaum 2011, 33–34)

Within this list, imagination is characterized simultaneously as a mental faculty refined through education, a creative force that allows for various kinds of self-expression, and a disposition for empathy that heightens concern for others and forms the basis of social relationships (see also Karsten R. Stueber, "Empathy and the imagination," Chapter 27 of this volume, for more on the connection between our empathetic and imaginative faculties). Elsewhere, in her many defenses of the importance of arts and humanities in education and moral development, Nussbaum presents imagination as one of three crucial democratic abilities alongside critical reasoning and global citizenship (Nussbaum 2010). In *Cultivating Humanity*, she describes it as a "quality of vision" and an "art of interpretation" best strengthened through exposure to various artistic forms (literature chief among them), adding that we are short-changed as agents if we miss out on opportunities to become more imaginative. She credits the imagination with "enabl[ing] us to comprehend the motives and choices of people different from ourselves, seeing them not as forbiddingly alien and other, but as sharing many problems and possibilities with us" (Nussbaum 1997, 85–88). Through references to multiple writers and works of fiction, she makes a case for imagination as a special kind of orientation that is rich with insight and allows us to "be an intelligent reader of [another] person's story" (Nussbaum 2006, 390).

While the features of imagination highlighted by Nussbaum are illuminating, their implications in terms of viewing imagination as a capability have not been spelled out. They seem to indicate that imagination makes possible certain complex functionings that are morally oriented – such as empathizing with a stranger, expressing compassion for a crime victim, appreciating the plight of displaced persons, or fairly interpreting unfamiliar circumstances – as well as complex functionings that are creatively oriented, such as producing a work of art, inventing a scientific device, voicing an original scholarly argument, or innovating a spiritual practice. Moreover, it would seem that imagination is required even to envisage these kinds of morally and creatively oriented "beings and doings" as options to value. Indeed, in order to imagine what we have reason to value, we must have in our mental landscape a wide range of options to consider – options gathered from our exposure to many rich and diverse sources, from our meaningful exchanges with a variety of people and environments, and from our own multifaceted experiments with creative activities and reflective practices. Presumably, only then could we confidently state that the life we have reason to value was selected against other worthwhile and noteworthy options, and begin to articulate our grounds for choosing these functionings to achieve well-being, using practical reason to "form a conception of the good life and to engage in critical reflection about the planning of one's life" (Nussbaum 2011, 34). As a capability, imagination can supply and fuel the content of our agency by expanding our range of considerations, which we can subsequently evaluate based on our capability of practical reason.

Using the language of CA, then, imagination can be defined as a capability that enables us to envision a given context from multiple, even incompatible frames of reference to ensure a broadened lens with which to approach and assess lived experience. The given context can be our own lives or the lives of other people or living beings – this flexibility captures the political orientation of imagination and the importance of portraying agents as aware of their obligations and impact. These imaginative efforts support agency by facilitating a kind of dress rehearsal with potential options for lives of value: Mark Johnson describes this simulation process as "our ability to imaginatively run out a possible situation without taking overt action, in order to explore how things would be under the influence of various perspectives and values" ("Moral imagination," Chapter 26 this volume).

To specify the capability further, this imaginative envisioning of a given context could make possible a range of complex functionings that fall under the following three categories. First, the capability of imagination could enable our acknowledgement of limited perspectives. The functionings in this category might include: being aware of the ways in which current conceptual frameworks may be excluding relevant viewpoints; calling to mind a different set of possible vantage points to diversify and problematize our existing perspectives; transcending the familiar by considering unusual or foreign possibilities and consequences; and seeking out alternative readings and interpretations of history, religion, culture and science. As Nussbaum notes, quoting Aristotle, since "we have never lived enough," by feeding imagination through narratives and deliberations about unfamiliar life experiences, we can see in our own conceptual shortcomings the need for ethical flexibility so we do not simply approach "each situation prepared to see only those items about which we already know how to deliberate" (Nussbaum 1990, 47, 67).

Second, the capability of imagination could foster our recognition of commonality. The functionings in this category might include: identifying overlaps in lived experiences between self and others; being attuned to common weaknesses and vulnerabilities among humans and other life forms; striving toward a more complete view of another's needs, goals, motivations and obstacles; refraining from dismissing as "other" what is simply foreign or misunderstood; and creating art and narratives that depict shared struggles and joys. According to Nussbaum, imagination highlights humanity's shared aims and needs in the struggle for existence, dismantling the idea of the "other" as a foreign or lesser being. Specifically, by being more imaginative, we "learn to appreciate vividly the ways in which common human weaknesses are experienced in a wide range of social circumstances, understanding how social and political arrangements of different kinds affect the vulnerabilities that all human beings share" (Nussbaum 2010, 39–20).

Third, the capability of imagination could encourage our management of competing considerations. The functionings in this category might include: being receptive to different world views; noticing the complexity of a situation rather than imposing a clear-cut black-and-white reading of it; being sensitive to a plurality of values and to conflicts arising between them; detecting tensions between personal priorities and the interests of others; and anticipating the varying effects of a new theory, invention or service on individuals and communities. Imagination can facilitate receptivity to considerations in this way by heightening respect for what Nussbaum calls the noncommensurability of the valuable things. In CA, values are seen as neither interchangeable nor replaceable, "each generating its own claims, but each having, as well, its own general definition and being instantiable in any number of particular situations and actions" (Nussbaum 1990, 68). By extension, imagination can help us to recognize and appreciate the difficulties that arise when equally important capabilities collide, seeing such clashes as tragic rather than narrowly upholding one of them at the expense of another. As Nussbaum writes, "a nation cannot satisfy the need for one capability by giving people a large amount of another … all are distinctive, and all need to be secured and protected in distinctive ways" (Nussbaum 2011, 35).

Further still, it seems that we would require the capability of imagination so conceived to even consider CA as a viable model and to perceive the capability development of others as a worthwhile investment. Indeed, the task that Nussbaum herself undertakes in the opening chapter of *Creating Capabilities* (Nussbaum 2011) – in which she strives to identify the salient features of one woman's complex life circumstances in Gujarat, India – expresses her highly attuned capability of imagination. Through encounters with women like Vasanti, Nussbaum immerses herself in life circumstances different from her own so she can fuel her imagination and begin to recognize the significant aspects that define (and, in these cases, aggravate) their quality of life: how seemingly unrelated elements like poor nutrition and physical frailty intersect with issues of gender imbalance, how domestic violence is perpetuated by a lack of financial independence due to illiteracy and unemployability, how the structure of traditional families and local policies shape self-esteem, aspirations and civic involvement, etc. Moreover, Nussbaum's extension of CA to include nonhuman animals as worthy of our moral and political concern is further evidence of her imaginative skills at work. A similar case of imagination in the service of animals can be seen in the work of animal scientist Temple Grandin, who has described her particular imaginative faculties resulting from autism as enabling a "cow's eye view" that has helped her to design systems to improve the lives of cattle, including more ethical slaughtering techniques (Grandin 2006). These are fitting examples of the capability of imagination transformed into a highly valued set of functionings aimed at envisioning and creatively implementing a new paradigm for development analysis and assessment. To put it plainly, CA itself would likely not have emerged without a well-honed capability of imagination to give it substance and scope.

## Opportunities that can fuel imagination

If imagination as a capability can help us to envisage more possibilities for lives we have reason to value, it is worth exploring the kind of opportunities it would require to foster the range of complex moral and creative functionings that expand the breadth of our agency. For illustrative purposes, let us consider three opportunities that can fuel imagination – access to conceptual resources, access to dialogical space and access to creative expression – with the understanding that these might take very different forms depending on their given context. Initially, to foster the kind of complex functionings that support agency, the capability of imagination would require access to conceptual resources, or resources that can contribute to broadening the mental concepts that make up our imaginative repertoire. Many resources can fit this specification – from art works to cultural histories to scientific innovations – and the aim would be the opportunity to access a diversity and abundance of these. Though this kind of repertoire could be interpreted as a simple reserve of accumulated facts, its purpose would be to challenge the boundaries of imaginative thinking and imaginative understanding so that we are able to envision more than we could previously, with regard to both our own context and the context of others. For instance, even if as children we do not have access to conceptual resources at home – in the form of, say, picture books – we may nonetheless have the opportunity to develop the capability of imagination through the variety of children's literature available in our school library, thus increasing the likelihood of our envisioning given contexts from more varied frames of reference at an early age. These resources would include those in the accepted canons as well as those that are lesser known: artistic masterpieces alongside local or marginalized works; orthodox views of the humanities and social sciences alongside revisionist interpretations; prevalent scientific theories and discoveries alongside contested or peripheral ones; ancient languages versus new dialects with their ever-changing connotations. Access to such divergent narratives can help us to acknowledge the dangers of limited perspectives and adopt a broader imaginative lens when exposed to similar variances in the future. As Johnson argues in *Moral Imagination: Implications of Cognitive Science for Ethics*, this kind of opportunity can initiate us into appreciating how our understanding of situations depends on the way they are framed: "knowing about the precise nature of the particular frames we inherit from our moral tradition and apply to situations is absolutely essential, if we are to be at all aware of the prejudgments we bring to situations" (Johnson 1993, 192). Exposure to what others have historically had reason to value can help to enrich our options for what we ourselves might value in our current circumstances.

A second and related opportunity that the capability of imagination would need to flourish is access to dialogical space, or occasions for us to examine, interrogate and problematize the aforementioned kinds of conceptual resources through discussions with others. Since conceptual resources in their diversity and abundance do not present a unified picture of a given context but rather reveal its inherent tensions, clashes and inconsistencies, we could benefit from opportunities to collaboratively grapple with these so as to further enrich our imaginative thinking and understanding about the multiple frames of reference that inform our envisioning. For instance, adults with low education levels may have access to wide-ranging conceptual resources through the Internet but have no opportunity to question and examine the medium's conflicting messages, making dialogical space all the more important to enlarge their imaginative repertoire, develop their critical literacy and allow them to explore with others how these resources may contribute to what they have reason to value. Although conceptual resources can offer rich and varying perspectives, the communication is one-sided, whereas dialogue about these resources can create live interactions with others and with their interests, concerns, beliefs, ideals, wonders and trepidations, thereby uncovering our hidden biases and assumptions. By exploring another person's perspective or experience through imagination, we may for the first time come to see certain issues as problems because we have had a chance to view them through the eyes of others, thus realizing the possible consequences of our own ideas and broadening the scope of what matters to us. Returning to Taylor's notion of strong evaluations, this dialogical space can enable collective deliberation about values, meaning we can contribute to each other's value assessments by strengthening the reasons for prioritizing certain life pursuits over others: "The strong evaluator can articulate the reasons why A is more attractive than B, because he has a vocabulary of worth – a language of qualitative contrast that is predicated upon a vision of what constitutes a meaningful life" (Redhead 2002, 160).

Finally, in addition to benefiting from access to conceptual resources and dialogical space, the capability of imagination requires access to creative expression that fosters complex functionings relating to agency development. Creative expression could encompass many activities, from community art projects to local activism initiatives to the design of more ecologically sustainable lifestyles. While exposure to diverse frames of reference through conceptual resources and dialogical exchanges can significantly broaden the capacity for envisioning given contexts, we can also gain from occasions to internalize, individualize and even concretize our new perspectives through our own creative work. By taking ownership of our imaginative repertoire in this way, we can begin to embody and act out our own distinctive valued commitments. For instance, if we have access to highly motivating conceptual resources and dialogue about environmental issues at work but have had no occasions at home to transform these opportunities into valued functionings for greener living, our work context can provide the space to imagine and implement sustainable lifestyle changes that heighten our agency within our domestic setting. And so, beyond its intrinsic worth as a fulfilling experience, access to creative expression may also play an important instrumental role in contributing to our sense of agency. If through our concretized imaginative efforts we are able to self-identify as agents capable of effecting change, we may be likelier to want to engage in similar pursuits again and believe in our ability to transform resources into the functionings we value – our imaginative repertoire will include more vivid pictures of our possibilities for agency.

Of course, these descriptions and examples serve only illustrative purposes – the capability of imagination can be supported in myriad ways, depending on the political context in question and the society's particular conversion factors. That said, are the effects of imagination so conceived necessarily beneficial to our agency or can they also be detrimental, as some key research outside CA suggests? Conceivably, imagination might distort our choice of functionings by exposing us to types of thinking and acting that are morally questionable, introducing dubious alternatives that we would not have otherwise considered worthwhile. In her analysis of moral and aesthetic defects, Amy Mullin cautions against the possible moral corruption that can arise from habitual exposure to works of art that present an unethical position: "Certainly even a single instance of such an imaginative experience can destroy a kind of moral innocence, in which, for example, some kinds of cruelty had simply never occurred to one" (Mullin 2004, 252). Similarly, as Gregory Currie observes in his account of imagining as simulation, since some circumstances can be tough to envision due to our particular lived experiences, when we try to determine what is worth pursuing, imagination can also lead us astray and produce an unreliable mental picture of the potential merits and outcomes of a situation: "we sometimes think we have acquired knowledge through imagining when all we have really acquired is erroneous belief" (Currie 1995, 254). As a capability, could imagination not lead to functionings that impede the deliberation and responsibility needed for agency, say by making us more susceptible to advertising techniques which lure us into envisioning lifestyles that risk transforming us into rampant, thoughtless consumers? In terms of our interpersonal and political commitments, could we become so adept at imagining the plight of others that we become less able to actually listen to their own interpretations of their circumstances? More generally, could imagination make so many options valuable that we become disoriented and overwhelmed by the sheer amount of possibilities for agency?

Clearly, imagination needs guidance to enable functionings that support deliberative, responsible agency. Other complex capabilities can help in this process, like practical reasoning and affiliation, which Nussbaum entrusts with the "architectonic role" of organizing and powering all other capability freedoms toward the formation of a socially sensitive and dignified conception of the good life (Nussbaum 2011, 39). Additionally, it would be useful to specify within our particular contexts some minimum thresholds of the capability of imagination to help determine its purview. As Nussbaum warns, without basic thresholds, we risk developing adaptive preferences: we may simply adjust to what we believe is realistic to expect from our lives and content ourselves with conditions that might otherwise be perceived as inadequate, even unjust (82–84). If the capability of imagination is fostered to specific degrees, however, we may more readily see such narrow pictures as insufficient and as threatening to the scope of our agency, given what we have had the chance to envision as possible and potentially valuable in our lives. For instance, to defuse threats to imagination as a capability, we may question and want to protect against unwarranted censorship, such as questionable bans on library books or whitewashing strategies. We may also want to prevent commercial and political propaganda – like bandwagon and card-stacking techniques – unless the materials are being used transparently to spark discussion on controversial topics. Through our imaginative play, we may become suspicious of indoctrinating policies, such as state-sponsored content or one-sided curricula: for example, we might wonder whether schools that serve a specific mission to transmit particular religious or moral beliefs pose a threat to imagination because they might be restricting children's access to diverse conceptual resources, limiting dialogue to a homogeneous group of like-minded students or focusing on creative expression that aligns with the ideologies they promote.

Further, we may be concerned with issues of marginalization, wanting our minimum thresholds to reflect a more inclusive conception of how individuals with exceptionalities and special needs might function in accordance to the capability of imagination. For instance, in an article on disability and CA, Michael Watts and Barbara Ridley present the heartening approach used by the Drake Music Project, a nonprofit organization that supplies technical equipment to individuals with disabilities to enable their agency as musicians – a capability previously denied to them. They write: "In giving them these opportunities to achieve outcomes that they valued and had reason to value the Drake Music Project greatly increased their well-being" (Watts and Ridley 2007, 159). As these kinds of initiatives demonstrate, within the capability of imagination lies not only the opportunity for the transformative experience of enabling certain desired functionings, but also of visualizing a more expanded sense of self and a more valued way of life. In Nussbaum's words, "the imagination is a hardy plant. When it is not killed, it can thrive in many places" (Nussbaum 2006, 394). At worst, in oppressive circumstances that greatly restrict agency, if available, the Internet can ensure at least a bare minimum threshold of imagination since it grants access to varied sources, online networking tools and self-publishing avenues. At best, the capability of imagination can flourish within educational contexts that support access to conceptual resources, dialogical space and creative expression from an early age – something CA is uniquely positioned to promote.

## The capability of imagination in education

As a political framework, CA is distinctive in its concern for the agency and capability development of children. This consideration adds another political dimension to the capability of imagination since it boldly proposes a more imaginative understanding of children as emerging agents who need opportunities in their educational contexts to envision the lives they will have reason to value as they grow up. Recent work on children and capabilities suggests that while total self determination may not be possible or advisable in childhood, children in their various stages of development already exercise agency in meaningful ways. Mario Biggeri et al. contend that the evolving capabilities of children should be acknowledged despite their seeming unimportance, claiming it is a mistake to treat them merely as "future adults" or "recipients of freedoms" rather than as agents in their own right, "able to express their points of view, values and priorities" (Biggeri et al. 2011, 22). They note, for instance, that "the capacity to demand specific objects, toys, food or to move around the house may appear trivial from an adult's perspective, but may constitute big decisions and progress in the eyes of the child" (18). Of course, the issue of conversion factors specifically affects children's ability to transform resources into functionings since they are all the more limited by internal factors such as age and skill level, and by external factors like their family environment, their school, and their society's public policies. Given children represent a highly heterogeneous group, their capacity for agency must be nurtured in terms of their evolving, complex capabilities, some of which will lose relevance or change considerably as they grow up.

Research on education within CA has contributed immensely to clarifying the meaning of capabilities and functionings with respect to children. In a school setting, children's functionings are understood as their achieved learning outcomes – "beings and doings" that range from reading a book and writing a story, to discussing with classmates and listening attentively – while their capabilities are described as their opportunities to fulfill these outcomes, the potential they exhibit for various achievements in relation to the possibilities their educational contexts afford them. In this way, education acts as one of many conversion factors in their lives: they are either limited or empowered by their school experience (the curriculum, the teacher, the facilities, the learning atmosphere, etc.) to transform their resources into valuable functionings and prepare them for meaningful agency later in life. As a capability, imagination thus becomes an important way to achieve certain key functionings like "being able to visualize life plans" (Walker and Unterhalter 2007, 51). As such, educational accounts in CA tend not to be value-neutral: They reflect a commitment to what have been called "autonomy-facilitating" pedagogies, which treat children as budding agents whose ongoing process of agency development should be protected from "capability-destruction," a term that Nussbaum uses to denote actions like drug abuse that "appear to destroy some or all capabilities" (Nussbaum 2011, 26–27). She argues that while adults should be free to destroy capabilities if they so choose, "children, of course, are different; requiring certain sorts of functioning of them (as in compulsory education) is defensible as a necessary prelude to adult capability" (26). Melanie Walker and Elaine Unterhalter make similar claims about protecting children's freedoms, drawing on the ideas of Harry Brighouse:

> Education that contributes to unfreedoms would be deeply incompatible with the capability approach. We need to be clear that respecting a plurality of conceptions of the good life (and hence of how education is arranged) is not the same as endorsing all versions of the good life, and this has clear educational implications. The key issue here is that to count as education, processes and outcomes ought to enhance freedom, agency, and well-being.
>
> *(Walker and Unterhalter 2007, 15)*

But what would this kind of autonomy-facilitating pedagogy look like, notably with respect to the capability of imagination? In her book *Not for Profit: Why Democracy Needs the Humanities*, Nussbaum bemoans the current silent crisis in education caused by an overemphasis on profit-oriented pursuits and resulting in "flaws in reasoning, parochialism, haste, sloppiness, selfishness [and] narrowness of the spirit" (Nussbaum 2010, 142). She argues instead for an education model rooted in the arts and humanities that promotes democracy by nurturing the critical reasoning, global consciousness and imagination required for individuals to "see other human beings as full people, with thoughts and feelings of their own that deserve respect and empathy" (143). Toward this end, she advocates a particularly promising pedagogical model – the Philosophy for Children program founded by educational philosopher Matthew Lipman. Weighed by similar concerns about small-mindedness, Lipman adapted the pragmatist ideas of Charles Sanders Peirce and John Dewey in his design of the Community of Philosophical Inquiry (CPI), a dialogical method intended to foster multidimensional thought (or combined critical, creative and caring thinking), which he viewed as "a balance between the cognitive and the affective, between the perceptual and the conceptual, between the physical and the mental" (Lipman 2003, 200–201). A CPI can equip children – and, for that matter, adults – with the means to tackle contestable questions they deem central to their lives and formulate reasonable, revisable judgements through structured group discussion.

Since a community of inquirers is co-responsible for intertwining their individual perspectives and locating shared aims, a CPI is most successful when it emphasizes imagination – it is precisely the multiplicity of voices that deepens and authenticates the process of envisioning contexts from multiple frames of reference. Community members are asked to deliberate about what they value, share ideas from their own distinct lived experiences, and fulfill their obligations to fellow inquirers by taking responsibility for their involvement in the dialogical process. These dialogues cultivate a host of functionings that reflect an attuned imagination, from listening attentively, resisting bias and detecting assumptions to seeking missing perspectives and taking alternative views seriously. In turn, these functionings help create a more inclusive environment: Walker and Unterhalter offer the example of a learner who "might value the capability for voice, but finds herself silenced in a classroom through particular social arrangements of power and privilege" and thus "needs social arrangements that are sensitive to her ways of expressing herself" in order to benefit from dialogical space (Walker and Unterhalter 2007, 10). Since a CPI offers supportive, age-appropriate parameters to facilitate children's experimentation with agency in their collective imagination, "the shared experience of being part of a [CPI] increases and enriches the process of building an identity in an interpersonal context in which each and every agent is recognized as a valuable thinker" (Biggeri and Santi 2012, 387).

## Enlarging imagination's prospects

This chapter has sought to show why the capability of imagination is valuable in its own right, not merely as a competency subsumed under broader categories like education or citizenship, but as a promising complex capability with political dimensions that can support agency development. When fueled by opportunities for rich resource discovery, meaningful exchanges and creative experimentation, the capability of imagination can offer us significant sources of fulfillment by expanding the range of options to consider as we visualize and create lives we have reason to value – something seemingly simple takes on complexity, something formerly dismissed takes on importance, and something once unknown becomes most valuable. As we have seen, CA's distinctive framework and literature offer interesting insights into what it might mean to conceive imagination politically as a capability and to explore the kind of fruitful functionings it can enable. Still, the concept deserves more attention from both theoretical and empirical researchers to help enlarge its prospects and determine its limitations. It is only with a rich and diverse mental landscape that we can confidently affirm the life we have reason to value was selected against other worthwhile options, and begin to articulate our grounds for choosing the functionings we envision for our well-being and meaning-making. As a capability, imagination seems primed to help us in this endeavor – and it is worth discovering precisely how.

## References

Ballet, J., J.-L. Dubois, and F.R. Mahieu (2007) "Responsibility for Each Other's Freedom: Agency as the Source of Collective Capability," *Journal of Human Development* 8(2): 185–201.

Biggeri, M., and M. Santi (2012) "The Missing Dimensions of Children's Well-Being and Well-Becoming in Education Systems: Capabilities and Philosophy for Children," *Journal of Human Development and Capabilities* 13(3): 373–395.

Biggeri, M., J. Ballet, and F. Comim (eds.) (2011) *Children and the Capability Approach*, London: Palgrave Macmillan.

Brighouse, H., and I. Robeyns (eds.) (2010) *Measuring Justice: Primary Goods and Capabilities*, Cambridge: Cambridge University Press.

Comim, F., M. Qizilbash, and S. Alkire (eds.) (2008) *The Capability Approach: Concepts, Measures and Applications*, Cambridge: Cambridge University Press.

Currie, G. (1995) "The Moral Psychology of Fiction," *Australasian Journal of Philosophy* 73(2): 250–259.

Davis, J.B. (2009) "The Capabilities Conception of the Individual," *Review of Social Economy* 67(4): 413–429.

Grandin, T. (2006) *Thinking in Pictures: My Life with Autism*, London: Vintage.

Hinchliffe, G. (2009) "Capability and Deliberation," *Studies in Philosophy and Education* 28: 403–413.

Johnson, M. (1993) *Moral Imagination: Implications of Cognitive Science for Ethics*, Chicago: University of Chicago Press.

Lipman, M. (2003) *Thinking in Education*, Cambridge: Cambridge University Press.

Mullin, A. (2004) "Moral Defects, Aesthetic Defects, and the Imagination," *Journal of Aesthetics and Art Criticism* 62(3): 249–261.

Nussbaum, M. (1990) *Love's Knowledge*, Oxford: Oxford University Press.

Nussbaum, M. (1997) *Cultivating Humanity: A Classical Defense of Reform in Liberal Education*, Cambridge, MA: Harvard University Press.

Nussbaum, M. (2006) "Education and Democratic Citizenship: Capabilities and Quality Education," *Journal of Human Development* 7(3): 385–395.

Nussbaum, M. (2010) *Not for Profit: Why Democracy Needs the Humanities*, Princeton, NJ: Princeton University Press.

Nussbaum, M. (2011) *Creating Capabilities: The Human Development Approach*, Cambridge, MA: Harvard University Press.

Nussbaum, M., and A. Sen (eds.) (1993) *The Quality of Life*, Oxford: Oxford University Press.

Redhead, M. (2002) *Charles Taylor: Thinking and Living Deep Diversity*, Lanham: Rowman & Littlefield.

Sen, A. (1992) *Inequality Re-examined*, Oxford: Clarendon Press.

Sen, A. (1997) "Human Capital and Human Capability," *World Development* 25(12): 1959–1961.

Sen, A. (2005) "Human Rights and Capabilities," *Journal of Human Development* 6(2): 151–166.

Walker, M., and E. Unterhalter (eds.) (2007) *Amartya Sen's Capability Approach and Social Justice in Education*, New York: Palgrave Macmillan.

Watts, M., and B. Ridley (2007) "Evaluating Musical Dis/abilities: Operationalizing the Capability Approach," *International Journal of Research & Method in Education* 30(2): 149–162.

# PART VI

# Imagination in epistemology, philosophy of science, and philosophy of mathematics

# 30
# IMAGINATION AND LEARNING

*Greg Currie*

To imagine that I am rich is not to learn that I am rich, and to imagine riding a bike is not to know how to ride one. How can indulgent imagination lead to anything as serious as learning? Despite the unpromising contrast, some pathways to learning pass through the imagination; some even start with it. And imagination is not merely a cause of our learning; sometimes it helps justify our claim to have learned.[1] Imagination can also be a source of ignorance and error, as we shall see.

There are distinct pathways to imagining itself. There are internally generated or *autonomous* imaginings, as when I decide to imagine being rich, or find myself imagining it; there are externally *guided* imaginings, where I imagine the life of a millionaire as described in a novel, movie or play. Both kinds of imagining are constrained: all imaginings are constrained internally by the dependence of imagination on other mental and bodily systems, while guided imaginings are constrained by the material, often a narrative, which is their source. These constraints are crucial to understanding how learning from imagination is possible.

## Learning

We will take "learning" in a broad sense. Learning does not consist only of coming to know the sorts of things one could report on an exam paper; knowledge of this kind – that the Battle of Hastings occurred in 1066, for example – we will call sentential knowledge. I may know that Jane's dress is *this* color (said with a pointing gesture at a color sample) without having a name, description or perhaps even any concept to apply to the color; what I have is propositional knowledge not fully articulable, at least by me. Then there is learning which is propositional without representing knowledge acquisition. Converts from the Aristotelian-Ptolemaic view to Newtonian mechanics and gravitation learned something, though it was not a transition from falsehood to truth. Their learning consisted in epistemic improvement, but not in knowledge.[2]

What about knowing-how, often said not to be a matter of knowing any proposition? In some cases knowing how to do things really is just a matter of knowing some proposition; I know how to checkmate you when I know that checkmate will result if I move my knight to a certain square (Snowdon 2004). Many cases of knowing how to do things are not, or do not seem, amenable to this reductive treatment. You may know how to ride a bike without, apparently, knowing any propositions about bike riding, and knowing them would anyway not guarantee that you could ride a bike; for that you need bike-riding practice.[3]

Imagination is often said to lead to knowing-what-it-is-like (acquaintance, as I shall say). Imaginative projection into another's situation is said to acquaint us, sometimes, with what it is like to be in that situation, and literary, dramatic and cinematic fictions scaffold such projections, giving us a sense of what it is like to take part in a battle or to live under Stalin's tyranny (these are cases of guided imagination, explored more fully later on). What sort of knowing is acquaintance? Propositional knowing according to some. Jackson claims that knowing what it is like to see the blue of the sky is knowing some fact or proposition, and that physicalism is therefore false; one can know all the physical facts about color and still not know this fact.[4] But if knowing-how is not always propositional, then acquaintance might not be propositional either. Some have argued that acquaintance is just a form of knowing-how; when I learn what it is like to see the blue of the sky I come to have certain abilities: the ability to remember what seeing the sky is like, to imagine the color of the sky, and more generally "abilities to predict one's behaviour by imaginative experiments."[5] But we are not obliged to say that acquaintance is propositional knowledge or it is knowing-how. We may hold instead that acquaintance is a third, distinct kind of knowing (Conee 1994; Tye 2009).

I will treat sentential knowledge as a subspecies of propositional knowledge. And to show that imagination aids propositional learning I will take it as sufficient to show that it aids the transition from less reasonable to more reasonable belief. For present purposes I will treat the categories propositional knowledge, knowing-how and acquaintance separately but without inquiring further into their natures and relations; such inquiries would be arduous, and we can afford to operate with an intuitive understanding of these notions. So our focus here will not be exclusively on propositional *knowledge*, since there are cases of change to propositional belief which constitute learning without constituting the acquisition of knowledge, nor on *propositional* knowledge, since there are other kinds of knowing.

There is another reason for not putting knowledge at the center of this inquiry. For knowing-how and acquaintance there is nothing comparable to the belief/knowledge distinction. There is not, in addition to the set of things I know how to do, a set of things I merely believe how to do. I may falsely believe that I know how to ride a bike but in that case I just have a false propositional belief; I can't falsely or unreasonably believe how to ride a bike. What I have is a range of skills possessed with different competencies; I may be better at riding a bike than at driving a car. Similarly, I might have a merely crude, coarse-grained understanding of what it is like to live in a tyranny. Knowing-how and acquaintance seem to run parallel to reasonable belief rather than to propositional knowledge: categories with variation from the tolerable to the perfect.[6] And if imagination is capable of helping us improve our knowing-how and acquaintance at any level that will count, in my book, as a win for the learning-from-imagination thesis. Given this very inclusive account of learning, it would be difficult to claim that this essay stacks the cards against the learning-from-imagination thesis.

## Imagining

Whether we think imagination leads to learning will depend partly on what we count as imagination. It is standard to divide the imagination into a propositional kind, as when I imagine that there is a tree in front of me, and an experiential kind: I visualize, or visually imagine a tree, have a tactile image of the rough bark or a motor image of moving my hand over it. Propositional imagining can be thought of as an imaginative counterpart of belief, while experiential imaginings in the various modalities are counterparts to corresponding forms of sensory experience: sight, touch, our internal awareness of the disposition and movement of our bodies (Budd 1989; Currie and Ravenscroft 2002).

What of assuming or supposing that *P*? Are these ways of propositionally imagining that *P*? If they are, it is clear that we can learn, and indeed gain knowledge from imagination. Proof by *reductio* works by having us assume *P* and derive a contradiction, which allows us to conclude that not-*P*; simple proofs that root 2 is irrational take this form. This technique is not confined to mathematics and logic. I come to know that Jack is not the murderer (a contingent proposition if ever there was one) by combining the assumption of his guilt with something I know to be true – that the murderer must have been at the Cathedral by 9 p.m. – and deriving something I know to be false: that Jack was there at 9 p.m. Some have said that assuming is not imagining, on the grounds that imagining is susceptible to what is called imaginative resistance and assuming is not, or that imagining is affect-involving while assuming is not.[7] I resist the imagining offered to me by a novel in which it is part of the story that slavery is good; I don't resist the invitation to suppose it good as part of a philosophical argument about the nature of goodness (Walton 1994). And talk of imagining suggests the affectively engaged state we experience when engrossed in a novel, while assuming seems more appropriate to the careful, affectively neutral construction of an argument.

For what it's worth, I think of assumption as a kind of imagining. It does not seem wrong to say, in the philosophy seminar, "imagine slavery is moral justified," when your purpose is to develop a metaethical argument. And suppose (or imagine) that while engaged in a philosophical thought experiment about moral responsibility I take on the assumption that I'm the only person left alive after a nuclear war; at first this has little or no emotional effect on me and I dispassionately explore my moral situation. Gradually I start to imagine details of the case which make vivid its horror and loneliness; distressing emotions start to be felt. Did I, at some point in this process, go from one state, assuming, to another, imagining? If I felt a twinge of emotion but kept my mind on the argument would I be assuming or imagining? I'd rather say there was no change in my propositional attitude; what changed were its effects, as other imaginings concerning the details of the situation were brought into play. As I imagined in more detail, making causal connections between events as I imagine them and introducing some vivid sensory imaginings, unpleasant affects became noticeable, at which point I might experience imaginative resistance. "Assume" and "suppose" are good words to use when we want to emphasize the nonaffective nature of our imaginative projects; we need not think that they denote a state-type distinct from imagining.

Still, this debate is not crucial to our inquiries. If supposing is imagining then we can all agree that there is a kind of imagining capable of generating learning. An interesting question then remains: does nonsuppositional imagining – the kind of affectively engaged imagining that comes with daydreams, novel reading and the empathic attempts to understand the life of another or your own future self – have the same capacity? We may all apply ourselves to that question, regardless of what we think about the relation between imagining and supposing. To that question I turn in the next section. But it is important to note that any act of imagining, especially when sustained, is likely to involve imaginings of various kinds. While reading *War and Peace* one propositionally imagines that Pierre and Prince Andrei are talking together; one is also likely to have visual and perhaps auditory imaginings of the scene; one may have proprioceptive and motor imaginings when Prince Andrei is wounded at Austerlitz.

## Reliable and unreliable imaginings

If you found that your colleagues at the same level as you were all earning more than you, would you be distressed? Let's say you answer yes (most people do), so you come to believe the conditional

1 If my co-workers all earned more than me I would be distressed.

How did you come to believe that? Very likely, your belief was brought about (partly) by your imagining; you imagined hearing the news about your co-workers' superior pay, and you found this a distressing thing to imagine. We think that, by and large, if imagining *P* makes us unhappy, *P* will make us unhappy.

Suppose (1) is true. Then affectively engaged imagining gave you a true belief, and did so because it was a case of affectively engaged imagining. Does that make such imaginings a pathway to learning? Not every source of a true belief is happily described as something from which we can learn, even on our generous construal of learning; if a drunk in a bar tells you – truly, as it happens – that the economy is going downhill and you believe her, we would not rate her a source of learning. Drunks in bars are unreliable on the economy and so, perhaps, is imagination as a guide to how we would feel in various situations.[8] Is it? This is an important question because many life-changing decisions are made partly on the basis of comparing how we feel when we imagine the various outcomes. The imagination-based approach to deciding whether or not to become a parent is notably unreliable given the radical and unpredictable personal changes, including changes of basic preference, that becoming a parent brings with it (Paul 2015). Research into what is called "affective forecasting" has thrown up other, less dramatic examples of unreliability (Gilbert et al. 1998). People tend to expect that both they and their partners will be more upset by their own and the other's transgressions in a relationship than they actually are; these people may imagine the transgression, generating an emotional response which suggests to them greater unhappiness in the actual situation than actually occurs. In one study of this phenomenon participants correctly predicted that they would be more distressed in the role of offender than in the role of victim, but incorrectly predicted that their partner would be more distressed as victim than as perpetrator, suggesting difficulties with imaginative projection into another's situation (Green et al. 2013).

One reason for a general tendency to overestimate emotional responses to events is *immune neglect*: the neglect in one's imagining about the future of the coping strategies we adopt to insulate ourselves from negative emotion; this is of significance for understanding the widely observed reluctance to disengage from abusive relationships. But people also overestimate positive emotional responses; those asked to estimate the positive affect associated with being on a date on St. Valentine's day neglected the anxiety that often attends such encounters (Green et al. 2013). There is also evidence that the affect we feel (positive or negative) when we experience a situation (and presumably, when we imagine it) "isn't tied to the representations that produce it" (Carruthers 2011, 136). People rate their satisfaction with their lives more positively on sunny days than on dull ones, failing to segregate the affect associated with life satisfaction from that due to the weather.[9] In imagining a situation, the intrusion of inessential or unlikely details may tip the scales of affect in a misleading direction.

Perhaps the lesson here is that there is no general answer to the question "can we learn through imagination how we would feel in situations we have not encountered?" and that it should be replaced with a series of narrower questions of the form "can we learn through imagination about the valance (duration, intensity) of our feelings in a situation of kind *S*?" To some (but only some) questions with this form the answer will most likely be yes.

Where imagination is a poor guide to how you will feel in a situation it may still be useful for predicting and explaining the behavior of other people. One party in the so-called "Theory vs. Simulation Debate" holds that we predict some (perhaps a good deal) of other people's behavior by simulating their mental states; in these situations what we imagine plays, if things go well, a similar inferential and affective role to the beliefs those people actually have. If our imaginings then make a certain option *C* seem more attractive than other salient ones, that is supposed to be evidence that the person in question will actually choose *C*. It has been argued that this is a better and more economical way to predict the behavior of others than to appeal to a "folk psychological theory." A substantial and, in part, empirical debate has gone on concerning whether this is so.[10]

We will not try to settle that debate here. However, the following thought is attractive. Whether or not imaginings (sometimes, often, usually) track the inferential and affective path of another's beliefs, they have a very good chance of tracking the inferential and affective path of that other's *imaginings*, and that will help me to predict your decision when it is based on what you imagine about the future. If both you and I decide whether to choose option *C* by imagining how we would feel if *C* were realized, and if you and I have relevantly similar preferences and make relevantly similar errors, then I can predict that you will choose *C* by noting that my own imagining picks out *C* as best. Both your imaginings and mine may be hopelessly unreliable when it comes to predicting how we really would feel, but my imaginings may still do very well at predicting your future choice.

Common experience suggests that imagination helps us to predict not merely our own affective responses to future outcomes but the causal development of those outcomes themselves. There are, of course, limits to this: we should not try to estimate the time by imagining looking at our watches. Where imagination does better is in relation to processes involving our own bodily interventions. We have some capacity to estimate whether we will be able to climb from that branch of a tree to the one above, without actually having to try it out. Perhaps we do this by imagining the act of climbing.[11] How this might be done in such a way as to provide reliable information is not well understood, but it could hardly be done at all if imagining moving failed to respect the constraints on actual movement. A puzzle then arises: no one other than a few experts knows what those constraints are, since they depend on very unobvious facts about the construction of our bodies. But the obvious answer is that we do not *need* to know, as we do not need to know how cognition and emotion interact in order (sometimes) to predict our emotional responses to situations. As long as imagining *P* has emotional effects very like those of belief, I can simply read off the emotional effect of imagining I am paid less than my peers and conclude that I would dislike being paid less.

We may wonder why imagination parallels belief in this way. One plausible answer is that it simply uses the same causal pathways as belief; there is one system for connecting propositional attitudes with affect, and it works in the same way regardless of whether the inputs are beliefs or imaginings. And we can apply this idea to the case of imagined movement, assuming that imagining movement and really moving activate the same system dedicated to initiating and controlling action. This would ensure that imagined movements are constrained by the factors that constrain real movement, as is required if the former is to be predictive of the latter. There is a good deal of evidence now available both for the idea that imagined movement is constrained in the way that real movement is, and for the idea that the two depend on common systems in the brain. For example, it is possible to study the time it takes people to imagine moving their hands into certain orientations, and these times turn out to be functions of the factors that constrain actual hand movement, such as awkwardness of the target position (Parsons 1994). And deficits in actual performance due to brain damage (Parkinson's disease in this case) are sometimes predictable from imagined performance; patients impaired on performance of a certain sequence of finger movements were equally impaired in imagining performing the action (Dominey et al. 1995). However, the correspondence between real and imagined actions is relatively fragile. While real and imagined walks over a certain distance took very similar times for subjects instructed to form careful mental images of the target location, the correspondence was significantly worse for uninstructed subjects, and for subjects asked to carry heavy packs (Decety et al. 1989).

What, then, should we say about the reliability of the various forms of imagining when it comes to predicting outcomes and our responses to them? We may think about reliability in different ways. First, we may ask how reliable something is at performing a specific task; imagination is reliable (perhaps) when used to estimate walking time over a short distance on the flat and without heavy equipment; it is not good at estimating the time taken to walk with a heavy pack. Secondly, we may ask how generally reliable something is. Considered in a wholly unrestricted form, this is not usually a useful measure. Though my car is hopelessly unreliable when driven through water, vertically up cliffs or in space, I would not complain that it is unreliable. What matters is that it does well in the environments it was designed for. Perhaps the most useful generality we could get about the reliability of some form of imaginative activity is its reliability in situations Darwinian forces designed it for. Climbing trees, crossing streams and walking in open country are plausible cases of actions within that domain.

## Imaginings guided by fiction

We have seen how imagining is internally constrained; constrained by the architecture of the mind. We turn now to situations in which the imagination is constrained externally. Both kinds of constraints contribute positively to the imagination's capacity to generate knowledge. Internal constraint helps to ensure a degree of correspondence between what we imagine doing and feeling and how we really would act and feel in a given situation. External constraint provides us with opportunities for the sustained imaginative exploration of scenarios which would otherwise be opaque to us.

Imagining ourselves in the shoes of others is often difficult; we may know very little about how they conceive their situations, or about their preferences. One of the attractions of a work of fiction is that it guides us in our imaginings, providing detail about a character's psychology that we could not expect to get in real life. Not all the guided imaginings of fiction are imaginings about the inner states of characters: we also imagine that Pierre inherits a great deal of wealth, that Natasha nearly elopes with Anatole, that Prince Andrei is wounded. But these objective imaginings also help us understand the inner lives of characters; a person's mental states can often be inferred with some probability from detailed knowledge of their situations.

In one sense we learn nothing by imagining Natasha's mental life, no matter what the complexity and vividness of our imaginings; she, after all, does not exist. But an attractive thought is that in doing this kind of imagining we exercise, refine and extend our sensitivities to the mental lives of real others, becoming in the process more insightful and empathic.[12] We acquire or improve a skill.

Are there reasons to be confident that our imagined interactions with fictional characters will be relevantly similar to those we would or might have with real people? If the answer is no then we may be concerned that the effect of the fiction-as-simulation will be to distort our capacities and not to enhance them. On one side of this question is the widespread conviction that authors of quality fictions have a subtle understanding of human psychology which they are able to embody in their characters. We should ask how we might assess a claim which seems to require that we have some standard, available to at least discerning readers, of truthfulness in human psychology against which the efforts of authors can be assessed. One answer is that readers have a sound though certainly incomplete and imprecise intuitive understanding of psychology and can make the relevant judgements themselves. Most readers probably think of themselves in this way: we make rapid judgements of plausibility in the doings of fictional characters without stopping to check against psychology textbooks.

A significant question is then whether our intuitive understanding is reliable. We can say with confidence that it is less than fully reliable. For fifty years social psychology has been finding good reasons to think that people regularly and systematically misunderstand their own motives and those of other people and are ignorant of the situational factors and unconscious biases that regularly influence our decisions.[13] Our judgements about what, in fiction, constitutes realistic motivation or behavior will reflect these errors.

One response to this pessimism is to argue that the errors exposed by social psychology are in fact marginal and don't much compromise the psychological competence of authors and readers (or anyone else). Another does not seek to quantify the extent of our error but insists that, however wrong our ordinary, prescientific understanding of ourselves is, it is unlikely to be replaced by scientific theorizing which to most of us does not come easily and which is cumbersome to apply in our real-time interactions with other people. Further, we manifestly have considerable success in understanding and engaging with others, so this prescientific understanding, however far it may be from the truth about human motivation, has a good deal of instrumental value, just as Ptolemaic astronomy, though wildly false, does a reasonable job of tracking planetary positions. If engagement with imaginative literature sharpens the capacities which go with this certainly useful prescientific understanding, that is all the justification we need to call it an aid to learning.

True, the response continues, many characters and situations in the most highly regarded and enduring fictions are unrealistic, even by the standards of our common conception of human motivation. But empathizing with rather unrealistic characters such as Little Nell may aid the development of empathic skills, exercising the empathy system more effectively than responding to boringly real people does.

Let us look more closely at the idea that guided imagination is a provider of empathic skills

## Learning to empathize

How we learn skills is surely an empirical question. Is there some body of data against which we can assess this idea? Recent psychological experiments have, it is claimed, found improvements in empathic skills as a result of exposure to brief fictional stories. In one study empathy was measured immediately after the reading through the application of the "reading for the eyes" test which measures people's ability to infer mental states from direction of gaze and which is said to be predictive of empathy (Kidd and Castano 2013). It is not clear whether there were any lasting effects and the choice of reading materials and other aspects of the study have been criticized.[14] Another concern is that fiction's supposed capacity to enlarge empathy would be a good thing only if it led to prosocial behavior; empathy has little value if it makes no difference to our actions. But the test of empathy used in this experiment and in some others did not demonstrate any change of behavioral disposition. Another experiment (Johnson 2012) did probe for helping behavior by having the experimenter drop some pencils after the reading; a correlation was observed between those who helped and those who reported high levels of "transportation" or imaginative engagement with the story. Since helping behavior was manifested immediately after the reading it is unclear how long the effect lasted; we know that trivial events like finding a dime in a phone booth can lead to exactly the same immediate helping behavior, without, presumably, leading to shifts in a person's outlook or dispositions.

We need, it seems, to make some distinctions between ways that guided imaginings might affect behavior. We should first of all distinguish between the development of capacities and what psychologists call "priming," wherein exposure to one stimulus affects response to another via an automatic and temporary spreading of activation in a cognitive network. Experiments by Bargh and colleagues suggest that mere exposure to words like "strive" caused enhanced performance on a demanding cognitive task; exposure to such words is probably just a temporary disruption to normal patterns of behavior. Similarly, it is plausible that exposure to the fictional texts of the experiment simply primed subjects for an atypically empathetic response.[15] It will be said that temporary and automatically induced changes are better than nothing. That may be true, but the friends of learning from literature have expected something more like thoughtful and reflective learning. With that in mind, we should now make a further distinction.

Our skills and capacities may serve different kinds of purposes. Some skills quickly arrive at an undemanding and unreflective steady state, as with my bicycle riding which is designed only for the village shops. But another kind of skill requires maintenance of higher-level control even though individual components of the action are performed so quickly as to defy rational oversight, as with the kind of piano playing exemplified by an aspirant performer. The pianist's behavior never becomes automated in the way that my bicycle riding does; the pianist is not able to let her mind wander; she must be constantly assessing and modulating her performance (Annas 2011). This is an important distinction for us because, as is often noted, unconstrained and unreflective empathy often does not lead to morally desirable results. Helping behavior produced by empathy tends to be arbitrarily disposed, favors those close to us with whom we empathize easily, and proceeds without regard to justice or economy of means; it makes us sensitive to the individual victim of a policy and indifferent to the many whose lives the policy saved. As psychologist Paul Bloom says,

> if a planet of billions is to survive, however, we'll need to take into consideration the welfare of people not yet harmed – and, even more, of people not yet born. They have no names, faces, or stories to grip our conscience or stir our fellow-feeling. Their prospects call, rather, for deliberation and calculation. Our hearts will always go out to the baby in the well; it's a measure of our humanity. But empathy will have to yield to reason if humanity is to have a future.[16]

If reading literature simply enlarges our empathic responses without giving us the power to modulate and direct them it will arguably do little good. And some of the greatest literature seems vulnerable to the worry that empathy distorts moral judgement: Tzachi Zamir points out that we care deeply about Cleopatra's death but give no thought to the deaths of Charmian and Iras whose poetry is less memorable.[17] What we would like, and what serious advocates of learning from literature surely hope for, is that literature will help us to be more thoughtful and discriminating empathizers, capable of putting our empathic capacities to good use by having moral reasoning in an oversight role. The currently available evidence, even on the most optimistic construal, does not support the theory that literature does this.

Finally, there is some reason, far from conclusive, to think that empathizing with fictional characters will actually depress people's tendency to behave well toward others.[18] Recent literature on the topic of "moral self-licensing" claims to identify a homeostatic system governing conscientious behavior, mediated by subjects' perception of their own status as just and rational beings. In one experiment subjects offered a vitamin supplement subsequently smoked more than controls did (Chiou et al. 2011). In another, subjects given an opportunity to establish nonracist credentials were then more likely than controls to endorse a view which might be seen as racially problematic (Monin and Miller 2001). The hypothesis is that the prior behavior enhances a sense of self-worth which in turn gives people the feeling of being licensed to behave less well subsequently. (The converse pattern is also observed, of prior irresponsible behavior being compensated for by subsequent conscientiousness.)

Might the person who has spent the day being deeply empathic while reading *Anna Karenina* then feel licensed to pay less attention to the troubles of those real people around them? The time and effort empathizing with Anna Karenina did Anna no good – she, after all, does not exist – and the reader well knows that; the reader could not reasonably claim to have done enough good for the day to be able to pay less attention to her friend's distress. But self-licensing is not to be understood as a process mediated by rational inference. It is better seen by analogy with the processes that make us unwilling to walk home down a dark alley after the horror movie. We know all the arguments to the effect that there is no more danger there than there was the previous evening, but the prospect feels unpleasant enough to make us choose another route. Imagined dangers can affect our subsequent decision-making in ways that are like those of real dangers. It is not hard to believe that imagined good deeds can have the same effects on our self-worth as real ones. Indeed, we know that self-licensing can be produced by merely imagined activity; subjects in another experiment designed to induce self-licensing were more prone to frivolous purchases (luxury jeans vs. dull vacuum cleaner) after they had imagined volunteering for community service (Khan and Dhar 2007).

## Imagination and the messages in fiction

The guided imaginings provided by fiction involve a communicative element.[19] The author communicates her story to the reader by producing a certain text, but that text has to be understood as a guide to what imaginings are intended; we are expected to imagine many things not explicitly stated but merely implicated, and much that's written in the text has to be understood metaphorically or as the product of an ironic or unreliable narrator. This communicative element introduces the possibility of learning by testimony or other means which depend on assumptions about the reliability of an agent whose opinions are in some way made manifest by the text.

One way for the belief that *P* to spread from agent to agent is for someone to openly and explicitly assert *P* and for the hearer to believe *P* in consequence. This is by no means the only way. Much that is communicated is implicated rather than said, as my saying "It's gone seven" implicates, given the right context, that we are late. I can also communicate this by deliberately looking at my watch and frowning rather than saying anything. And if I simply happen to look at my watch and frown this may indicate to you that we are late without my intending to communicate anything. Doing all sorts of things other than making assertions can spread belief, and writing fiction may be one of them. According to Mark, Jesus told the story of the Good Samaritan (something we are intended to imagine rather than to believe) in response to the question "Who is my neighbor?" Understood literally and as seriously meant, the story would be a change of subject and hence a deviation from conversational cooperativeness. Hearers try, therefore, to understand the story as providing an answer to the question; they take it that Jesus wishes to convey that our duties to neighbors extend well beyond our own cultural group, and they have some confidence in that opinion because the story seems well suited to get that unstated message across. Perhaps in less obvious ways Proust's telling of his novel cycle is evidence that he believes, and wants us to believe, various things about love, time and memory.[20]

In cases like these we have a story to be imagined and, we assume, a seriously meant message put forward as a candidate for belief. If Jesus had told a story in which the Samaritan robbed the victim, the implied message would be very different. But we should not suppose that it is only the general outline of the story which matters for the identification of the proposition communicated; details matter a great deal. Jesus' parable of the prodigal son is meant to indicate something important about God's relation to us. Knowing what depends on a finely tuned sense of the affective bonds between the father and the son. That way Jesus gives us an emotionally rich understanding of what it is to value human freedom even at the cost of God's suffering: God's relation to us is like the one we imagine between the father and the son of the story. Similarly, Proust may be understood as communicating, not merely the thought that love is irrational (something we probably know already), but that it is irrational in *these* ways – the ways exemplified in the details of relations between Marcel, Albertine and the rest of them.

Advocacy of this communicative model of learning from fiction again raises questions about the extent to which readers would be acting rationally in treating the authors of fictions as reliable. The rationality of trust in Jesus depends, presumably, on difficult questions about faith and revelation that we cannot settle here, if at all. But the same question asked about Proust is not easy either. We might happen to know from personal acquaintance that Proust is extremely wise, but this is not the situation of most readers. We might argue that Proust's wisdom is manifested in his skill in composition, character construction and the other hard tasks of sustaining a narrative. But it is not clear that there is a significant correlation between the personal qualities thus manifested and reliability on matters to do with love, time and memory. Nonetheless the manifestation of these sorts of qualities does seem to influence the credence we give to the opinions of people with those qualities; we are more likely to believe someone if we admire her than if we don't, irrespective of whether the qualities we admire are indicators of reliability of this subject (Harris and Corriveau 2011). Seen in this way we might think of great literature as epistemic traps rather than as fonts of learning.

## Conclusion

Sometimes a very broadly phrased question about learning can be framed and answered in the affirmative. Is testimony a source of learning? Certainly. Lying and other forms of epistemic irresponsibility are not so common that they cast doubt on the general proposition that testimony does more epistemic good than harm – imagine our predicament as learners without it. A comparably general question about imagination as a source of learning is harder to answer and at this stage of the debate seems rather a distraction. We need to focus on the small-scale structure of particular scenarios in which imagining brings about cognitive change. That focus requires serious experimental work together with a philosophically structured understanding of the options for describing and explaining those cognitive changes.

## Notes

1 This claim sounds less controversial now than it would have thirty years ago. Significant for the change has been the idea that imagination, by structurally mimicking belief, gives us insight into the beliefs, and the decisions, of others (for somewhat different formulations, on which there have been subsequent commentary, see Gordon 1986 and Heal 1984). For other and more recent optimistic perspectives on imagination's epistemic role see Williamson forthcoming and Kind forthcoming.
2 Intuitively, the idea that the earth is spherical is truer – closer to the truth, more verisimilar – than the idea that it is flat, though no one seems to have come up with a satisfactory account of what it takes for one proposition to be closer to the truth than another. See Oddie 2014.
3 Some have argued recently that knowing-how really is a kind of propositional knowledge; you know how to ride a bike when, for some way *w* to ride a bike, you know under a practical mode of presentation that *w* is a way for you to ride a bike. See Stanley and Williamson 2001.
4 Jackson 1982.
5 Lewis 1983, 1988. The abilities account of Mary's knowledge was first proposed in Nemirow 1980.
6 An objection to the propositional account of knowing-how is that one may have knowledge of how to do *F* based on a source which is correct but so improbably correct that one could not claim to know the propositions in question even though one believes them; nonetheless, you are very well equipped to *F*. See Cath 2011.
7 Gendler 2000. See also Kind 2013; Spalding 2014.
8 So it is not simply moving closer to truth that makes for learning; the process that gets you closer should be reliable, to a degree. How reliable may depend on the stakes.
9 See Schwarz and Clore 1983. People do make the segregation if the state of the weather is drawn to their attention.
10 See, e.g., Heal 1996; Stich and Nichols 1997; Mitchell et al. 2009.
11 Tim Williamson (forthcoming) emphasizes this aspect of imagination's power.
12 Nussbaum argues that readers of fiction are placed, with respect to characters, in a position parallel to that of the sympathetic judge (Nussbaum 1997). For criticism see Posner 1997.
13 A classic of this sort of investigation is Nisbett and Wilson 1977. On situational factors see the review of evidence in Currie 2010, ch. 11; on unconscious bias one might start with Greenwald and Banaji 1995.
14 See Mark Liberman, "Annals of Overgeneralization," Language Log [blog], October 8, 2013, <http://languagelog.ldc.upenn.edu/nll/?p=7715>.
15 See Bargh et al. 2001. But the existence of priming effects in the domain of social psychology has recently been questioned; see Shanks et al. 2013.
16 Bloom 2013; see also Pappas 1997.
17 Paper delivered at Shakespeare and Philosophy conference, University of Hertfordshire, August 2014.
18 I owe this suggestion to Catarina Dutilh Novaes.
19 This section draws on material from Ichino and Currie in prep. See also Friend 2014.
20 I leave aside here the possibility of understanding the text as containing many explicit assertions about these things, though the decision between this and regarding such statements as emerging from a fictional and possibly unreliable narrator is not easy to make.

## References

Annas, J. (2011) "Practical Expertise," in J. Bengson and M. Moffett (eds.) *Knowing How*, Oxford: Oxford University Press.
Bargh, J.A., P.M. Gollwitzer, A. Lee-Chai, K. Barndollar, and R. Trötschel (2001) "The Automated Will: Nonconscious Activation and Pursuit of Behavioral Goals," *Journal of Personality and Social Psychology* 81: 1014–1027.
Bloom, P. (2013) "The Baby in the Well," *New Yorker*, May 20, <http://www.newyorker.com/magazine/2013/05/20/the-baby-in-the-well>.
Budd, M. (1989) *Wittgenstein's Philosophy of Psychology*, London: Routledge.
Carruthers, P. (2011) *The Opacity of Mind*, Oxford: Oxford University Press.
Cath, U. (2011) "Knowing How without Knowing That," in J. Bengson and M. Moffett (eds.) *Knowing How*, Oxford: Oxford University Press.

Chiou, W.B., C.C. Yang, and C.S. Wan (2011) "Ironic Effects of Dietary Supplementation: Illusory Invulnerability Created by Taking Dietary Supplements Licenses Health-Risk Behaviors," *Psychological Science* 22(8): 1081–1086.

Conee, L. (1994) "Phenomenal Knowledge," *Australasian Journal of Philosophy* 72: 136–150.

Currie, G. (2010) *Narratives and Narrators: A Philosophy of Stories*, Oxford: Oxford University Press.

Currie, G., and I. Ravenscroft (2002) *Recreative Minds: Imagination in Philosophy and Psychology*, Oxford: Oxford University Press.

Decety, J., M. Jeannerod, and C. Preblanc (1989) "The Timing of Mentally Represented Actions," *Behavioral and Brain Research* 34: 35–42.

Dominey, P., J. Decety, E. Brouselle, G. Chazot, and M. Jeannerod (1995) "Motor Imagery of a Lateralized Sequential Task Is Asymmetrically Slowed in Hemi-Parkinson's Patients," *Neuropsychologia* 33: 727–741.

Friend, S. (2014) "Believing in Stories," in G. Currie, M. Kieran, A. Meskin, and J. Robson (eds.) *Aesthetics and the Sciences of Mind*, Oxford: Oxford University Press.

Gendler, T.S. (2000) "The Puzzle of Imaginative Resistance," *Journal of Philosophy* 97(2): 55–81.

Gilbert, D.T., E.C. Pinel, T.D. Wilson, S.J. Blumberg, and T.P. Wheatley (1998) "Immune Neglect: A Source of Durability Bias in Affective Forecasting," *Journal of Personality and Social Psychology* 75: 617–638.

Gordon, R. (1986) "Folk Psychology as Simulation," *Mind & Language* 1: 158–171.

Green, J.D., J.L. Davis, L.B. Luchies, A.E. Coy, D.R. Van Tongeren, C.A. Reid, and E.J. Finkel (2013) "Victims versus Perpetrators: Affective and Empathic Forecasting Regarding Transgressions in Romantic Relationships," *Journal of Experimental Social Psychology* 49: 329–333.

Greenwald, A.G., and M.R. Banaji (1995) "Implicit Social Cognition: Attitudes, Self-Esteem, and Stereotypes," *Psychological Review* 102: 4–27.

Harris, P.L., and K.H. Corriveau (2011) "Young Children's Selective Trust in Informants," *Philosophical Transactions of the Royal Society B: Biological Sciences* 366(1567): 1179–1187.

Heal, J. (1984) "Replication and Functionalism," in J. Butterfield (ed.) *Language, Mind and Logic*, Cambridge: Cambridge University Press.

Heal, J. (1996) "Simulation and Cognitive Penetrability," *Mind & Language* 11: 44–67.

Heal, J. (1997) "Indexical Predicates and Their Uses," *Mind* 107: 619–640.

Ichino, A., and G. Currie (In prep.) "Truth and Trust in Fiction," in H. Bradley, P. Noordhof, and E. Sullivan-Bissett (eds.) *Art and the Nature of Belief.*

Jackson, F. (1982) "Epiphenomenal Qualia," *Philosophical Quarterly* 32: 127–136.

Johnson, D. (2012) "Transportation into a Story Increases Empathy, Prosocial Behavior, and Perceptual Bias toward Fearful Expressions," *Personality and Individual Differences* 52: 150–155.

Khan, U., and R. Dhar (2007) "'Where There Is a Way There Is a Will?' Effects of Future Choices on Self-Control," *Journal of Experimental Psychology: General* 136(2): 277–288.

Kidd, D.C., and E. Castano (2013) "Reading Literary Fiction Improves Theory of Mind," *Science* 342: 377–380.

Kind, A. (2013) "The Heterogeneity of the Imagination," *Erkenntnis* 78: 141–159.

Kind, A. (Forthcoming) "Imagining under constraints," in A. Kind and P. Kung (eds.) *Knowledge through Imagination*, Oxford: Oxford University Press.

Lewis, D. (1983) "Postscript to 'Mad Pain and Martian Pain,'" in *Philosophical Papers*, vol.1, Oxford: Oxford University Press.

Lewis, D. (1986) "What Experience Teaches," in W.G. Lycan (ed.) *Mind and Cognition*, Oxford: Basil Blackwell.

Mitchell, P., F. Zeigler, and G. Currie (2009) "Two Routes to Perspective: Simulation and Rule-Use as Approaches to Mentalizing," *British Journal of Developmental Psychology* 27: 513–543.

Monin, B., and D.T. Miller (2001) "Moral Credentials and the Expression of Prejudice," *Journal of Personality and Social Psychology* 81: 33–43.

Nemirow, L. (1980) Review of *Mortal Questions*, by Thomas Nagel, *Philosophical Review* 89: 473–477.

Nisbett, R., and T. Wilson (1977) "Telling More Than We Can Know: Verbal Reports on Mental Processes," *Psychological Review* 84: 231–259.

Nussbaum, M. (1997) *Poetic Justice*, Boston: Beacon Press.

Oddie, G. (2014) "Truthlikeness," in E.N. Zalta (ed.) *The Stanford Encyclopedia of Philosophy* (Summer 2014 edition), <http://plato.stanford.edu/archives/sum2014/entries/truthlikeness/>.

Pappas, N. (1997) "Fancy Justice: Martha Nussbaum on the Political Value of the Novel," *Pacific Philosophical Quarterly* 78: 278–296.

Parsons, L. (1994) "Temporal and Kinematic Properties of Motor Behaviour Reflected in Mentally Simulated Action," *Journal of Experimental Psychology: Human Perception and Performance* 20: 709–730.
Paul, L.A. (2015) "What You Can't Expect When You're Expecting," *Res Philosophica* 92(2): 1–22.
Posner, R. (1997) "Against Ethical Criticism," *Philosophy and Literature* 21: 1–27.
Schwarz, N., and G. Clore (1983) "Mood, Misattribution, and Judgments of Well-Being: Informative and Directive Functions of Affective States," *Journal of Personality and Social Psychology* 45: 513–523.
Shanks, D., B. Newel, E. Lee, D. Balakrishnan, L. Ekelund, Z. Cenac, F. Kavvadia, and C. Moore (2013) "Priming Intelligent Behavior: An Elusive Phenomenon," *Plos One* 8: e56515, doi:10.1371/journal.pone.0056515.
Snowdon, P. (2004) "Knowing How and Knowing That: A Distinction Reconsidered," *Proceedings of the Aristotelian Society* 104: 1–29.
Spalding, S. (Forthcoming) "Imagination through Knowledge," in A. Kind and P. Kung (eds.) *Knowledge through Imagination*, Oxford: Oxford University Press.
Stanley, J., and T. Williamson (2001) "Knowing How," *Journal of Philosophy* 98(8): 411–444.
Stich, S., and S. Nichols (1997) "Cognitive Penetrability, Rationality and Restricted Simulation," *Mind & Language* 12: 297–326.
Tye, M. (2009) *Consciousness Revisited*, Cambridge, MA: MIT Press.
Walton, K. (1994) "Morality in Fiction and Fictional Morality," *Proceedings of the Aristotelian Society*, Supplementary Volume 68: 27–50.
Williamson, T. (Forthcoming) "Knowledge from Imagination," in A. Kind and P. Kung (eds.) *Knowledge through Imagination*, Oxford: Oxford University Press.

# 31
# THOUGHT EXPERIMENT AND IMAGINATION

*Roy Sorensen*

A thought experiment is a limiting case of experiment in which the question is to be answered by reflection on the experimental design rather than by execution. Imagination substitutes for perception. The reliability of the thought experiment's answer depends on how well imagination can fill a role originally intended for perception.

## Advertised advantages of imagination

To articulate (and perhaps caricature) the hopes of thought experimenters, I begin with cases in which the imagination outperforms perception.

Picture a square whose corners are midpoints of a larger square (Figure 31.1).

How much bigger is the big square?

You answer by mentally bending the corner triangles along the "crease" and tucking these triangles into the inner square. The match is perfect. You conclude that the big square is twice as big as the little square.

Imagination is doing the work rather than memory. Your mental folding of a big square into a little square was done without any square folding in the past.

The tuck work was accomplished without relying on perception. Suppose you are a disembodied mind who has never had sense organs. Your mental demonstration survives this empirical catastrophe.

Imagination is hardier than perception. Under adverse circumstances, such as those envisaged by a skeptic, perception fails to be informative. In contrast, the warrant furnished by imagination is not undercut or overridden.

This is not because imagination merely makes claims about what is possible. From what is possible, we can often infer what is necessary (as in the big square being *necessarily* double the area of the small square).

You can leverage your imagination by imagining the performance of a more powerful imaginer (Sorensen 2006). Consider two-move chess in which each side makes *two* moves each turn. Is two-move chess at least a draw for White? You know little of chess beyond its rules. Yet you can imagine perfect grandmasters competing under the amended rule. You explore the possibility that Black has a strategy that is guaranteed to win. An ideal White opponent would realize that Black has such a strategy. White would just make himself

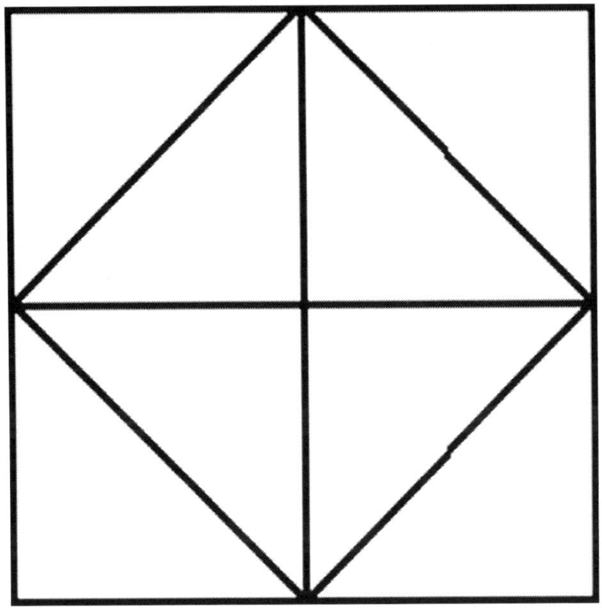

*Figure 31.1* A thought experiment in geometry

equivalent to Black by moving his knight forward and then back to its original position. Both sides would have sure wins. But that is a contradiction. You conclude that White can at least draw.

There are also advantages to imagining a weaker imaginer. Synthetic a priori truths may be mistaken as analytic because *healthy* people do the imaginative testing. Accordingly, C.H. Langford (1949) "dumbs down" to refute the analyticity of "Orange is intermediate in color between red and yellow." He imagines a man who can see orange but sees all other objects in shades of gray. The disabled perceiver has the concept of orange because he can reliably identify orange objects. However, he is not able to identify red and yellow ones, so he lacks those color concepts. Accordingly, the man who is blind to red and yellow does not know that "Orange is intermediate in color between red and yellow." Therefore, the statement is not analytic.

In René Descartes' quest for certainty, the great geometer naturally turns to thought experiment to sidestep the frailties of perception. In the *Meditations*, Descartes (1641/2008) argues that since he can imagine himself without a body, it is possible that he could exist without a body. But if he were identical to his body, this hypothetical separation would be as impossible as imagining a square without four sides. So Descartes is an immaterial being only contingently connected to his body, perhaps in the way a melody is connected to a flute. But what kind of immaterial thing is he? A key clue is his *inability* to imagine himself not thinking. After all, any act of imagination is itself an instance of thinking. Hence, Descartes is essentially a thinking being.

Is Descartes alone? No, for he has the idea of a being that has all the perfections. Since an existing being with perfections is superior to a nonexistent being, the only way to conceive of a perfect being is as existing. This perfect being would be a deceiver if He did not give a conscientious inquirer an opportunity to learn about the world. So if the inquirer steels himself against fallacies and retrains wishful thinking, he can learn about the world through his senses.

René Descartes' *Meditations* is written in the first person. But the exercise is intended for anyone who can wield the I-concept. The reader is to replicate Descartes' thought experiments. The reader will see for himself that he is, in essence, a thinking being, distinct from his body, fashioned by God to gain as much knowledge about the world as hoped by scientists.

Thought experiments make the world safe for ordinary experiments. Imagination, when mathematically disciplined, demonstrates that science is a reliable collective enterprise, crucially different from the scholastic institutions that intimidated Bruno, Galileo, and Descartes himself.

In addition to exposing a wide vista for theorists, thought experiments present practical opportunities. Consider the "triple contract" invented to circumvent usury laws (Jonsen and Toulmin 1988, 188–189). Borrower is willing to pay 5 percent interest for a loan from Lender and Lender is willing to loan the money at that rate. But usury laws forbid the transaction. Is there a legal substitute for borrowing money with an interest payment?

The Dominican theologian John Eck, who debated Martin Luther in Leipzig in 1519, suggested a way to contract around the usury prohibition. The first contract makes Lender and Borrower partners in a business venture. The second contract insures Lender against loss of his capital in exchange for taking a lesser percentage of the profits – perhaps 0 percent. A third contract guarantees that Lender receives a set rate of interest, usually 5 percent. Each contract is legal so the conjunction of contracts is legal. They yield the same result as the illegal 5-percent loan. Ulrich Kuehne characterizes the triple contract as the most lucrative thought experiment in history.

Savor the safety and economy of thought experiments! You answered "How much bigger is the big square?" without any paper – or paper cuts. You are justified in your conclusion even if the *diagram* is not a perfect square. Your imagination transcends what you can perceive. For you are warranted in concluding that the big square is *exactly* twice as big as the little square. With perception, there is always measurement error. The imaginary square, as opposed to the diagram, has sides that are perfectly straight and at perfect right angles.

Regular experiments need to be replicated, reviewed, and revisited. The mental folding need not be repeated. Imagination gets the job done on the first try.

There is no need to check for leaks, contamination, or procedural errors. The thought experimenter harnesses the clean, renewable power of stipulation. Imagination achieves the experimentalist's ideal of control.

Perception ends inquiry with a brute "Like it or lump it" contingent fact. Imagination serves up the "Aha!" of explanatory necessity. You *understand* why the big square doubles the size of the little square.

## Scientific thought experiments

Scientists covet the certainty and precision of geometry. Galileo was convinced that "the book of nature is written in the language of mathematics, and its characters are triangles, circles, and other geometric figures, without which it is humanly impossible to understand a single word of it" (*The Assayer*, 1623, in Stillman and O'Malley 1960, 183–184). Accordingly, he abandons the irregularities and imperfections of ordinary moving objects. Galileo retreats to the more controlled setting of a windless, level, laboratory. Little wonder that, in turn, Galileo makes pilgrimages from this halfway house to the temple of Platonic solids situated on a boundless, frictionless plane. Thought experiment is an ideal to which the laboratory experiment aspires.

Compare Galileo's two objections to Aristotle's principle that heavier objects fall faster than lighter objects. According to legend, Galileo ascended the leaning Tower of Pisa and simultaneously dropped a cannon ball and a musket ball. The balls landed simultaneously.

Well *nearly*. As Galileo conceded, the heavier ball actually does land first. The only embarrassment for Aristotle is that the race is surprisingly close.

To secure the tie between the heavy ball and the light ball, Galileo must *imagine* the balls falling in a vacuum. Since Aristotle has principled opposition to the possibility of a vacuum, Galileo's afterthought begs the question.

More effective is Galileo's thought experiment in which a heavy object attaches to small object during descent, say, two blobs of lava spewed by a volcano. Aristotle's physics implies conflicting predictions. On the one hand, the little blob is moving more slowly. Therefore, fusing the small blob to the big blob should retard the big blob, yielding a slower composite blob. On the other hand, the composite blob is heavier than the initial big blob. Therefore, the composite should speed up the big blob. Contradiction.

This thought experiment is an internal criticism of Aristotle's theory of motion. Galileo defeats Aristotle with Aristotle's own principles and by Aristotle's own standards. In The *Dialogue concerning the Two Chief World Systems* Galileo repeatedly contends that Aristotle's physics implies consequences that are implausible within Aristotle's system (Finocchiaro 1974).

In *The Structure of Scientific Revolutions* Thomas Kuhn (1962, 152–153) intimates that internal critique is the only rational form of scientific criticism. External criticism begs the question by imposing alien vocabulary and standards. This perspectivalism makes Kuhn (1977) receptive to the power of thought experiments. Whereas experiments compel opponents to revise theoretically uninteresting background assumptions (a leak, contamination, bias), thought experiments strike at the theory itself. All rational defeat is self-defeat.

Galileo often segues from experiments to thought experiments that attain the conditions he cannot impose in a laboratory. For instance, Galileo initially uses a U-shaped track to establish the law of equal heights (a ball will regain the same height from which it was released). Lowering and extending the right arm of the U just makes the ball roll further to recover the initial height:

Galileo then imagines the right arm lowered to a flat infinitely extended plane. Since the ball never regains its originally height, it continues to travel forever in a straight line.

The thought experiment's prediction conflicts with Aristotle's commonsense theory that objects slow after being disturbed, tending toward their natural state of rest. Galileo remained enough of an Aristotelian to believe that the "straight line" would slightly curve like the "straight path" of a ship on the vast expanse of the globe. (Descartes is the first to believe what his mental eye indicates: a simple *straight* path.) Galileo is also spooked by the prediction that the ball will continue forever. Any finite sample of experience is too small to justify an infinite prediction.

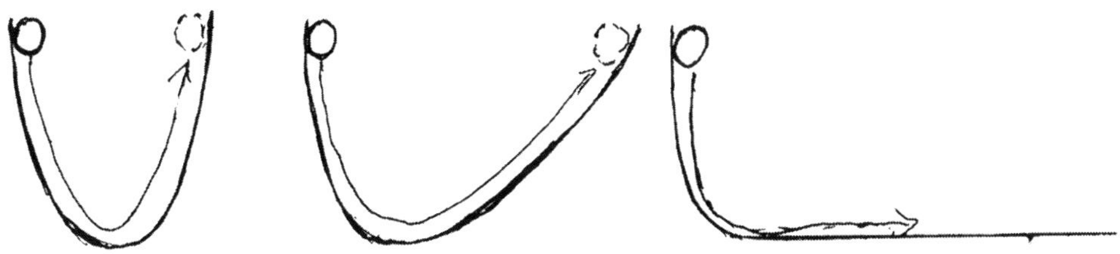

*Figure 31.2* An example of a U-shaped track.

Galileo's half-believed principle of inertia was later incorporated, more wholeheartedly, into Isaac Newton's catechism – as the first of three laws of motion. Breaking with Galileo's horror of action at a distance, Newton added a universal law of gravity. "Every body is attracted to every body" precludes fulfillment of the first law's antecedent: if *an object is not subject to other forces*, then it will either remain at rest or continue in motion in a straight line. Thus it is physically impossible to directly test the first law of motion with an experiment. The only tool left is thought experiment.

Galileo extended physical speculation to biological questions such as "Why are the largest animals found in the sea?" His basic answer was elegantly extended by W.K. Clifford to address the more general question "Why is there a size limit for organisms?" Clifford envisages cubical organisms that absorb nutrients through their surfaces. The ratio of the organism's volume to surface area grows at geometric rate. When the cube's length is $n$, its area is $6 \times n^2$ while its volume is $n^3$. Therefore, the cube organism must use more of its faces to maintain its mass. Eventually, the cube has grown so large that all faces are needed just to sustain its increased volume. The organism can no longer grow.

## A Platonic account of thought experiment

Galileo's use of thought experiments emboldened Alexandre Koyré (1978) to reinterpret the hero of empiricism as a rationalist. According to Koyré, many of the experiments Galileo appears to be reporting are actually thought experiments. We misread Galileo through empiricist spectacles, magnifying the degree to which he relies on experience. Through empiricist lenses, doubts about whether Galileo executed his experiments are charges of scientific dishonesty. Empiricists rush to Galileo's defense by replicating some of their hero's more surprising experiments. Koyré protests that no misconduct was insinuated: all Galileo aspires to in his *Dialogue concerning the Two Chief World Systems* is the verisimilitude of a Plato recounting Socrates' dialogues.

Plato viewed the world of perception as a distortion from ideal forms. All natural "squares" merely approximate the straight lines of a genuine square. Since we know this, we must have access to Squarehood.

Plato inherited many objections to perception from Parmenides and the skeptics. Here is an experiment, related by Aristotle, which seems to refute experiments. Submerge your left hand in cold water and right hand in hot water. Now submerge both in lukewarm water. The lukewarm water will feel hot to the cold hand and cold to the hot hand. If perception were reliable, then its predictions would at least be consistent – at least within the same sense modality! The testimony of the senses, even when competent, is suborned by expectation and desire.

Plato believed that our difficulty grasping the forms shows that our access to them is indirect. In the *Meno* he reduces imagination to memory and memory to a prenatal *perception* of the forms. The shock of birth has addled our memory. We amnesiacs cannot spontaneously recollect but can recognize correct answers. We resemble actors who need a cue to recall a line.

Often an actor does not realize that he has forgotten. His ignorance must be exposed. Embarrassment rouses the vain from lethargy.

Socrates adopts the role of an absent-minded prompter who has his own troubles remembering the script. Actor and prompter work together as half-wits, trying to fuse their respective fragments into a coherent whole.

In the *Meno* (84b–d), Socrates helps an uneducated slave boy discover how to double a square (by means of Figure 31.1, starting from the center square and adding triangles that each have a quarter of the area).

Plato's recollection model of thought experiment does not assign any justificatory role to imagery. The images are instead triggers, kin to the surreal images employed by Simonides of Keos (*c.*556–468 BC) in his method of loci. If I wish to present this article as a lecture, Simonides recommends I picture the key points as images distributed on the route from my office to my home. As I exit my office I confront a billboard on the lawn "Advertised Advantages of Imagination." In the parking lot there is laboratory equipment to mark the section on scientific thought experiments, at the first traffic light Plato is conversing with Socrates, ... As I travel along the familiar path home, the bizarre images pass the baton of attention to the next cue in the sequence.

Mnemonics store information without justifying it – as evident from outdated mnemonics such as the planetary "My Very Educated Mother Just Served Us Nine Pizzas" (the demotion of Pluto compels a switch to "Many Very Educated Men Just Screwed Up Nature"). A further sign that mnemonic utility is summative rather than justificatory is that we do not prefer true mnemonic sentences to false ones. I can memorize the life cycle of cells (Interphase, Prophase, Metaphase, Anaphase, Telophase, Cytokinesis) with the false "Idiotic Penguins Make Antarctica Too Cold" or with the true "I Pee More After Tea Constantly." I prefer the false mnemonic because the absurdity improves memorability. The surreal images function as quotation marks, suppressing distracting inferences. In contrast, the bizarre imagery of Clifford's hungry cube is a side effect of simplification, not an intended feature.

If imagination is only a memory aid, then Plato counts among the skeptics about thought experiment. For thought experiments purport to justify, not merely trigger answers. Merely providing a richer array of triggers than perception would yield only a quantitative advantage over perception. Plato ranks pictures of horses (which are copies of copies of Horsehood) as having even lower educational value than horses. If the mental image in a thought experiment is a *picture*, then all of Plato's complaints about art extend to thought experimenters.

The contemporary Platonist James Robert Brown (1991) abandons Plato's doctrine of recollection and renounces Plato's contempt for the empirical world. Brown thinks there is a mental eye that works analogously to the physical eye. Whereas the physical eye views particulars, the mental eye views universals. Why do you deny that the equilateral triangle is the loneliest polygon? Out of concern that there might be lonelier polyhedra? No, you mentally see that being a polygon *precludes* loneliness.

Brown's mental eye has enough resolution to reliably distinguish a square from a pentagon but not enough to distinguish an enneacontagon (90 sides) from a hectogon (100 sides). If Brown fails to take a close look he might even mistake a nonagon (9 sides) as a decagon (10 sides). In these circumstances, he sees a nonagon but fails to *see that* it is a decagon (in Fred Dretske's terminology, Brown distinguishes nonepistemic perception from belief-laden epistemic perception).

In the *Timaeus* Plato presents a version of atomism designed to preclude the void. He envisages a universe completely packed with five types of atoms based on the five regular polyhedra. Johannes Kepler portrays these "Platonic Solids" (Figure 31.3) in his *Mysterium Cosmographicum* (1596, 2nd edition 1621). Aristotle objects that these solids cannot complete space. Interstitial gaps precipitate under all packings. Plato had misconstrued an absence of seen gaps as a sighting of an absence of gaps.

Ironically, Aristotle goes on to commit a purer version of the fallacy by claiming that tetrahedra can complete space. The error persisted for 1,700 years despite the slight gaps being readily discernible by those fitting physical tetrahedra together on a tabletop. Consolation prize: tetrahedra do fill a larger percentage of a volume than any other shape when the packing is by random pouring and shaking (76 percent compared with 64 percent for spheres).

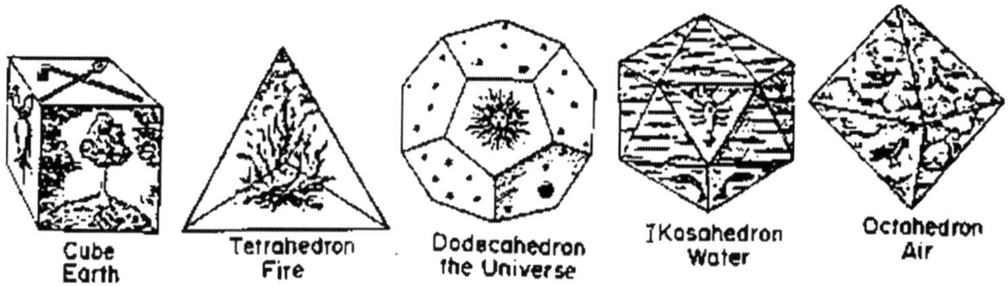


*Figure 31.3* The gaps in Platonic solids (drawing from Kepler)

Modeling improves on the mind's-eye level of resolution. Modeling also overcomes our spatial imagination's bias in favor of alignment and against tilts. Brown's methodology is binocular; we should use both the physical eye and the mental eye. The physical eye can process more detail than the mental eye. James Watson and Francis Crick used a modeling kit to produce a structure that met all the empirical constraints required for the DNA molecule.

When conditions are favorable, the mental eye can spot forms responsible for laws of nature. The thermodynamicist's discovery that every body has heat consists in seeing that body-hood necessitates heatedness. A finite list of observations would never provide sufficient grounds for inferring that all bodies have heat. The list would never yield the counterfactual: if there were a body in a certain region, it would have heat. According to Brown, a generalization's lawhood is based on the relationship it tracks between forms. Some, but not all, of these relationships are a priori.

Both the physical eye and mind's eye are partly mysterious in their mode of operation. If we needed to know how eyes work *before* being entitled to believe what they indicate, then we could not learn anything about how they operate. We rely on eyes to learn how eyes work.

In the case of the physical eye, much has been learned about the causal chain leading up to visual consciousness. The last stage, an instance of the mind-body problem, has been recalcitrant.

Scientists chiefly discuss the stage of the perceptual process that yields to their methods. Brandishing this progress report, critics compare the knowability of the physical eye with the obscurity of the mental eye. John Norton (2004) presses the objection negatively; the mental eye can explain only successful perception, never failure. All efforts to explain errors by the mental eye are parasitic analogies. The mental eye cannot be literally blocked or be out of range or be dazzled by too much light.

The phenomenology of the mental eye is evidence of its operation. Few deny having imagery. But many dismiss the imagery as nonfunctional heat from the working brain.

Experimental psychologists studying deduction challenge this general epiphenomenalism. Spatial imagery allows for modeling that makes transitive inferences faster and more accurate (Knauff 2013). Irrelevant visual imagery impedes inferences by consuming working memory. Other imagery has no discernible effect and might indeed be epiphenomenal. This mixed pattern coheres with brain scans and neurological theory.

## Describing mental imagery

Narratives of mental imagery vary much more than narratives of public scenes (though both are surprisingly variable, as notorious from studies of eyewitness testimony). The most conservative hypothesis is that people merely vary in how they describe imagery. The more anarchic alternative is that the variation reflects substantive, private variation (Faw 2009). John Locke (1689/1975, II.xxxii.15) considers the possibility of hidden variation in his discussion of the hypothesis that two people could have inverted color spectra (where you see green, I see red, where you see yellow, I see blue, and so on around the red-orange-yellow-blue-indigo-violet circle of hues). The subtlety of the link between image and behavior may have inspired John Dalton to test the hypothesis that some people, himself included, are color blind. Thought experimenters may differ in how much they rely on mental imagery – and whether they experience any imagery at all.

In blindsight, the physical eye works without visual phenomenology (though much impaired). The mind's eye may also be capable of operating without phenomenology. Bees see. Plausibly, they have no more phenomenology than the "eye" of an automatic door opener. Believers in a mental eye should welcome primitive eyesight because it provides the only response to a charge of circular explanation. If the mental eye is just as sophisticated as physical eyes, then there is no explanatory progress. If the mental eye can be reduced to simpler forms of seeing, then we assume less and less, and therefore explain more and more.

For theorists, descriptions of imagery have been colored by their roles in explaining reasoning. In the square-folding thought experiment, most people picture the square as white. But the color is incidental to the demonstration that the big square is twice as big as the little square.

Many people also ascribe a familiar size to the square. The size is irrelevant to justifying the conclusion. Indeed, for the sake of generality, the imaginary square must be of arbitrary size.

This need for generality motivated John Locke's doctrine of abstract ideas. For the thought experiment to constitute a proof, the square must be representative of all squares. To obtain this representative idea, we take a particular idea of a square and erase all of those features that vary between squares. The result of this abstraction is a square that lacks any specific size, orientation, or color. The abstract square functions as an arbitrary individual in pre-Fregean quantification theory.

Locke sees the possession of abstract ideas as a qualitative difference between people and animals. He also sees the ratio of abstract to particular ideas as a measure of education. The ideas of children and savages are dominated by richly detailed imagery. Study displaces mental imagery in favor of abstract thought.

This implication was reinforced by syllogistic accounts of deduction. Pictures play no role in Aristotle's presentation of deduction (though Venn diagrams became a standard supplement in twentieth-century presentations of syllogistic reasoning). Aristotle's premises and conclusions are *sentences*. Pictures lack truth-values. Consequently, purely pictorial "reasoning" cannot be assessed for validity.

Aristotle believed that images were essential to thinking. But this is compatible with imagery being captioned with sentences. Maps are explicitly and implicitly annotated (indicated direction, scale, and so forth). A picture tells a thousand words but only after we whisper a few words about how to interpret the picture.

Francis Galton compared the imagery of highly educated men with the imagery of students. The students could vividly picture their morning breakfast table: cups, spoons, tablecloth, silverware, and so forth. The educated men had little imagery.

> My own conclusion is, that an over-readiness to perceive clear mental pictures is antagonistic to the acquirement of habits of highly generalized and abstract thought, and that if the faculty of producing them was ever possessed by men who think

> hard, it is very apt to be lost by disuse. The highest minds are probably those in which it is not lost, but subordinated, and is ready for use on suitable occasions.
>
> *(Galton 1880, 304)*

Galton's original data do not support his conclusion (Brewer and Schommer-Aikins 2006). He appears to have acquired anecdotal evidence of scientists who reported little imagery and let this bias his statistical analysis. Galton then explained the "result" with a Lockean theory that was already in circulation (and which may have influenced the anecdotal evidence).

Nevertheless, Galton's experiment helped to dethrone mental images from the new kingdom of psychology. Despite being founded by introspectionists, the real progress seemed to come from animal psychology where introspection was unavailable. This emboldened some behaviorists to declare war on introspection. John Watson denied having any mental imagery. Yet he understood the thought experiments of others and conducted his own.

Bertrand Russell believed Watson's denial of mental imagery to be an overzealous distortion of the data to fit a theory – perhaps abetted by the learned Watson's dearth of particular imagery. If Watson's self-report is accurate, however, some thought experimenters do not rely on imagery.

## Deimagining thought experiments

Albert Einstein emphasized that he thought in pictures rather than words. He reports acquiring language late and being perceived as slow-witted. Yet he also traces his theory of relativity to a thought experiment conducted at age sixteen (in which he rides a light beam). These remarks, when combined with his later rationalism, have prompted speculation that Einstein was a savant.

Islands of genius are most salient when the savant has very low general intelligence. Do some idiot savants owe their knowledge to nonempirical sources? Some empiricists answer by reconstructing savant performance with techniques (such as calendar algorithms) that *could* yield the results of the savant. Why postulate magic when the empiricist can replicate the magician's trick?

John Norton applies the same reconstructive approach to Einstein's thought experiments. He generalizes from these paradigm cases: "Thought experiments are arguments which: (i) posit hypothetical or counterfactual states of affairs, and (ii) invoke particulars irrelevant to the generality of the conclusions" (Norton 1991, 129).

For over twenty years, Brown has tried to refute Norton with thought experiments that cannot be analyzed as arguments. Norton meets Brown's challenge by proposing arguments that could have produced knowledge of the thought experimenter's conclusion.

Norton thinks empiricism entails the further claim that the thought experimenter actually based his knowledge on the specific argument Norton reconstructs. He disagrees with bare evidentialists who think we know a proposition simply by virtue of having adequate evidence for it. (Sherlock Holmes has no more evidence than Watson but knows more – thanks to his greater ability to deduce truths from their identical premises.)

The skeptic will welcome Norton's high standard. If the premises are even slightly inaccurate they cannot be known and so there will be no knowledge to transmit to the conclusion.

When attributing priority, scientists do not require that the discoverer's reasoning be free of all falsehoods and fallacies. Slight mistakes are common at the cutting edge of research. So Norton is adopting a standard higher than scientists in their priority disputes. Even mathematicians do not transfer credit of discoveries to David Hilbert after conceding that he has corrected Euclid's slightly flawed proofs.

This tolerance of minor errors suggests that some of the shortfall is compensated by collateral sources of justification. Knowers can trip without falling because they have backup bases for their knowledge claims: perception, testimony, memory, and, arguably, the mental imagery weaving these together. There is no need to find a single perfect argument.

The mental imagery stimulated by an argument can be strong enough to compensate for the invalidity of the argument:

> Some people can correctly answer this riddle: "Picture the letter J and the letter D. Tip the D so that it sits flatly at rest. Then mount it on the top of the J. What figure does it form?"
>
> Therefore, *you* can correctly answer the riddle.

The argument can be made inductively strong by leading with "Almost all" rather than "Some" in the premise. The argument would then stand on two legs instead of one.

Although the order of premises is irrelevant to validity, it is relevant to spatial imagery that reinforces transitive inferences (Knauff 2013, 28):

> The summit of Aconcagua is above the summit of McKinley.
> The summit of McKinley is above the summit of Elbrus.
> Therefore, the summit of Aconcagua is above the summit of Elbrus.

If a thought experiment is an argument with picturesque elements, those elements could help to justify the conclusion – as demonstrated in the literature on mental modeling (Gendler 2004).

Why isn't the mountain argument a thought experiment? (Norton is silent. He concedes that he has not given a sufficient condition for thought experiment.) Adding further picturesque elements (mountaineers, snow, clouds) makes no progress toward thought experiment status.

Those who classify thought experiments as experiments, such as Roy Sorensen (1992), answer that the mountain argument lacks an experimental design. An experimenter manipulates an independent variable to answer a question about its relationship with a dependent variable. Instead of physically manipulating the variables and checking the effects by perception, the thought experimenter manipulates by supposition, stipulation, and other acts of imagination.

Sorensen (1992, ch. 6) agrees with Norton that all thought experiments can be reconstructed as arguments (given a capacious standard for attributing arguments). However, Sorensen does not intend his rational reconstructions to be psychological reports. Neither does Soren Häggqvist (1996). Their reconstructions are *regimentations* of experimental reasoning. The psychological basis of the thought experimenter's knowledge is a chaotic hive of collectively reliable mechanisms, not the distillation polished by the logician.

For the dual-process theorist, thought experiments are at home in System 1 while formal arguments are based in System 2. System 1 is automatic, unconscious, intuitive, associative, high-capacity, and fast. System 2 is voluntary, explicit, effortful, low-capacity, and slow. Just as natural selection has made us physically lazy, it has made us mentally lazy. We stick with System 1 judgments when available. System 2 steps in only when System 1 fails to nominate a candidate or has its candidate defeated. The systems have complementary strengths and weaknesses. Effective thinking combines both, with personal variations in the mix reflecting individual variation in aptitudes and tastes. Intuitive thinkers tend to view formal presentations as ritualistic excrescences, putting braces on healthy legs. Formal thinkers view intuitive presentations as fancy dress that conceals the true support structure.

But let us resist going all the way with the romantic stereotype of imagination. Logicians assign several justificatory roles to imagination in argument appraisal. They informally test validity by trying to imagine a situation in which the premises are true and the conclusion is false. Consider an argument based on biblical passages (such as Isaiah 11:12 and Revelation 7:1): "The earth has four corners, therefore, the earth is flat." The inference is invalid because we can imagine the earth as a tetrahedron.

If we succeed in imagining a countermodel, then the argument is invalid. If we fail, then *either* the argument is valid *or* we have not been sufficiently imaginative. Assessing the probability of the second disjunct takes us beyond logic into psychology. So the imagination method is less decisive and certainly less purely logical when it comes to proving validity.

In formal proof, the asymmetry of testing runs in the opposite direction. Showing that an argument instantiates a valid argument form suffices for proving validity but showing that an argument instantiates an invalid form is not sufficient for proving invalidity.

> All men equal in height to George Washington are men taller than James Madison.
> No men equal in height to George Washington are men taller than Abraham Lincoln.
> Therefore, all men taller than Abraham Lincoln are men taller than James Madison.

This argument has the invalid AEA-3 form (invalid by *mood*, according to the rule that an affirmative conclusion cannot be derived from a negative premise). Yet the argument is valid by virtue of "taller than" being asymmetric and transitive. The formal approach can prove validity but cannot prove invalidity (except for the special case in which all the premises are logical truths and the conclusion is a logical falsehood).

Since the strengths and weaknesses of the formal and informal tests run in opposite directions, logicians balance performance by using both tests.

In addition to providing this general role for imagination in testing validity (and especially disproving validity) logic provides a special role for imagination for arguments that rely on supposition. In *reductio ad absurdum* and conditional proof a premise is *supposed* rather than asserted.

Conclusion: There is an undamning resemblance between the types of imagination Norton dismisses as merely illustrative and those routinely employed in validity checks.

## Empiricist approximations to rationalism

Charles Darwin writes in his notebook: "Plato says in Phaedo that our 'imaginary ideas' arise from the preexistence of the soul, and are not derivable from experience – read monkeys for preexistence." Trial and error provides a second source of vicarious experience: "reason and not death rejects the imperfect attempts" (Darwin 1974, 160).

Although Ernst Mach (1976) did not have access to Darwin's speculations about mental trial and error, he writes as if he did (Sorensen 1992, ch. 3). Mach believes that we have "instinctive knowledge." Children have an innate fear of the dark because the dark is indeed dangerous for these highly visual creatures.

W.V. Quine later appealed to the generate-and-eliminate mechanism to explain why children acquire 'green' rather than 'grue': "Creatures inveterately wrong in their inductions have a pathetic but praiseworthy tendency to die before reproducing their kind" (Quine

1969, 126). Our sense of resemblance is shaped by a genetic endowment. This gives us a running start in refining our knowledge of natural kinds.

Evolutionary psychology provides a mechanism by which our imaginations could fit the world. Our difficulty in imagining a world in which grue inductions worked better than green inductions is evidence that the natural kinds governing the world fit more closely with green than grue.

We can run simulations that have some reliability because our imagination has been shaped by the environment. This fit can be improved by experience. Consequently, the imagination of experts is more reliable than that of novices.

Mach had proposed a poor man's rationalism. His synthetic a priori is relative to a given set of assumptions (to which we often acquiesce because of an illusion of independence from our past experience). Since the a priori is relative to a changing background, thought experimenters could get different results. Experiment improves thought experiment by improving background beliefs. A thought experiment by a physics professor is more reliable than a thought experiment by her student. But once that student becomes a professor, experience will favor the new professor over the old.

## Conflicting experiments and thought experiments

In *The Science of Mechanics*, Ernst Mach explains how a sprinkler rotates by water being pushed through its nozzles (Figure 31.4). If the sprinkler is submerged in water and water drawn *into* the nozzles will the sprinkler rotate in the opposite direction?

Most people answer yes. They are impressed by the push–pull symmetry of the two scenarios.

Is the appearance of symmetry due to the coarse grain of the imagery? To the naked eye, the moon looks as smooth as Aristotle describes. When Galileo zoomed in with a telescope,

*Figure 31.4* Reverse sprinkler (drawing from Mach)

he was intrigued by the irregularities. When Mach mentally zoomed in on the stream entering the nozzle, he noticed that liquid was being pulled in from all directions. This contrasts with the single direction in which water is pushed out. Mach's fine-grained counterimagery suggested that the reversed sprinkler might not rotate at all.

When Mach actually constructed a reverse sprinkler there was only some quivering. Mach considers the issue settled.

This absence of reverse rotation was replicated by Richard Feynman (in ignorance of Mach). However, Feynman did not report his experiment – later admitting that there had been a messy explosion. He instead presented the reverse sprinkler as a physics riddle. This led to much discussion and some experiments. Many of the experiments agreed with Mach's. But some experimenters reported reversal. To resolve the inconsistency, several commentators characterize the reversal as too weak to readily overcome friction, turbulence, and other nuisance factors. They agree that an *ideal* sprinkler would reverse.

Is this a vindication of the coarse-grained thought experiment? Since the thought experiment appealed to symmetry, it predicts the forces should be equal. At best, the coarse-grained thought experiment gets the directionality correct.

## Conflicting modes of imagination

Just as experiments can conflict with experiments, thought experiments can conflict with other thought experiments (Norton 2004, §2). If there is no more reason to accept one application of the method than the other, then the particular thought experiments cancel out. Should the method that generated them be abandoned?

The moderate replies that the method is misapplied. From a pedestrian perspective, anamorphic stop signs are illegible strips of paint. From the more distant perspective of the approaching motorist, STOP is clearly and emphatically inscribed. The near and distant perspectives do not cancel out; the distant perspective is the reliable perspective.

René Descartes gave primacy to the first-person perspective. Johann Wolfgang von Goethe was following Descartes when he professed an inability to imagine himself dead: "It is quite impossible for a thinking being to imagine nonbeing, a cessation of thought and life. In this sense everyone carries the proof of his own immortality within himself" (Eckermann, *Conversations with Goethe*, 1852, cited in Nichols 2007, 215).

Yet Goethe seems to readily imagine *other* people dead. When his sister Cornelia died in 1777, Goethe wrote to his mother: "With [the death of] my sister a strong root that held me to the earth has been cut down; the branches above, which had their nourishment from this root, must perforce die" (Goethe 1962–67, 1: 240, November 16, 1777). When Friedrich Schiller died, Goethe wrote to Zelter in 1805: "I thought myself lost and lose now a friend and with him the half of my existence" (in Goethe and Zelter 1887, 32). In 1816 he is again grief-stricken over his wife Christiane.

Goethe's imaginative obstacle emerges from the epistemological ideal of direct verification. To bypass doubts about the reliability of informants a responsible investigator will personally check. Given that the meaningfulness of a claim amounts to the conditions under which it can be known to be true, there must be a potential, first-person discovery of the fact. But nothing counts as me discovering my death.

Critics of George Berkeley's "To be is to be perceived" claimed that they could imagine an unobserved tree. Berkeley countered that they were instead imagining themselves discreetly observing the tree. Defenders of absolute space claimed to imagine a universe consisting of a single moving ball. Berkeley countered that they were really imagining a universe consisting of à ball and themselves tracking the ball path – often with a telltale sweep of the finger!

Can I imagine being Napoleon? Not from a third-person perspective says Bernard Williams (1966, 41–42). For then the differences between our properties underscore our distinctness. There is not room enough for both Napoleon and me in the identity relation.

Indeed, I seem essentially distinct from Napoleon. From the third-person perspective, I must include facts about my origin from a pair of twentieth-century Norwegians. Given the necessity of origin, I am a highly contingent being who could have only originated from the parents I actually had. When the empathic historian invites me to imagine being Napolean, and thus born from eighteenth-century Corsicans of noble Italian ancestry, he is asking the impossible.

Yet, from the first-person perspective, I succeed in imagining being Napoleon. 'I' refers without the mediumship of a description. This direct reference clarifies Immanuel Kant's claim in the *Critique of Pure Reason* that the representation of *I* is the poorest of all representations (B408). Since, there are no requirements on what *I* must be, I am a liquid that can fill any vessel!

That vessel need only be a potential agent. I can follow Étienne Bonnot de Condillac's thought experiment in which I begin as a statue and then am gradually endowed with richer and richer senses. I can date myself back to my conception (and condemn all abortion as filicide – "When would my mother have been entitled to kill *me*? Never!"). In his discussion of the paralogisms, Kant conjectures that the first-person perspective fosters the belief that the self is simple, persists over time, and is immortal.

From the third-person perspective, I have essential properties. From the first-person perspective, so favored by the existentialists, I lack an essence.

This divergence of perspectives suggests that there can be framing effects. Consider John Locke's thought experiment in which a prince awakes with the memories of a cobbler and the cobbler awakes with the memories of the prince. The prince and cobbler have switched bodies! Locke concludes that personal identity tracks psychological continuity rather than bodily continuity.

Bernard Williams (1970, 168) then asks me to suppose that *my* memories will be changed to match those of a cobbler. The cobbler's memories will be replaced by memories (or "memories") that match my old memories. From this first person perspective, I now seem to be imagining my amnesia rather than my body transfer.

Prior to Williams' redescriptions, we expect the distinction between the first- and third-person to align with the distinction between the mental and the physical. But the I-concept, driven by the logic of indexicals, seeps through categorial barriers.

Williams tentatively sides with the first-person perspective. He allies with Descartes and the Berkeleyan verificationists.

Others favor the objectivity of the third-person perspective. God views the universe *sub specie aeternitatis*. This "view from nowhere" transcends the limits of particular perspectives.

A third set of commentators (Sider 2001, 198) take the framing effect to cancel out the credibility of thought experiments based on either perspective. Shaun Nichols (2008) appeals to psychology and the logic of indexicals to overcome Williams' presumption in favor of the first-person perspective.

## Propositional confusion

René Descartes infers that his mind is distinct from his body from the fact that his mind and body have different properties. His mind has the property of being imaginable as existing without a body. His body lacks this property. Descartes concludes that his mind is not identical to his body.

This reasoning can be parodied: Georgius Ulicovius Lithuanus can be imagined existing without Gottfried Leibniz. Leibniz cannot be imagined as being distinct from Leibniz. Therefore, Georgius Ulicovius Lithuanus is distinct from Leibniz. The conclusion is false because Leibniz wrote a political essay under the pseudonym Georgius Ulicovius Lithuanus. As Gottlob Frege stressed, Leibniz's law of the substitutivity of identicals cannot be applied straightforwardly to attitudinal properties.

After Frege, mind-brain identity theorists interpreted these difficulties as showing there are *contingent* identities: Hesperus is Phosphorus, water is $H_2O$, lightning is electrical discharge. They conceded that Descartes had refuted "Necessarily, all minds are brains." So the mind-brain identity theorists retreated to: "Actually but not necessarily, all minds are brains." (To raise consciousness about the issue, Ullin Place bequeathed his brain to the University of Adelaide, to be displayed with the query: "Did This Brain Contain the Consciousness of U.T. Place?" The curious are directed to the Anatomy Museum, Medical School Building, Frome Road.)

In *Naming and Necessity*, Saul Kripke had ill-tidings for the battle-hardened mind-brain identity theorists: they had retreated to a position that was logically impossible! Any identity statement, if true, is necessarily true.

Kripke's good news was that necessary statements could be a posteriori. "Heat is molecular motion" seems contingent because we confuse the necessary proposition that heat is molecular motion with the contingent proposition that the *sensation* of heat is caused by molecular motion. The sensation of heat was used to pick out a physical phenomenon: *Call whatever is causing this hot feeling "heat."* This description was merely fixing the referent. The description is not defining 'heat' as what causes heat sensation. After all, human beings could have been built to have that sensation in response to snow (and do have the sensation in response hot peppers). The materialists were now poised to revert to their original, stronger doctrine: "Necessarily, minds are brains."

But Kripke introduces a last-minute hitch. We do not use an intermediate mental state to pick out pain in the way we use the hot feeling to pick out heat. We directly refer to pain because mental states are self-presenting.

## Attitude confusion

Ardor up, the mind-brain identity theorist, Thomas Nagel (1974, 445 n. 11) proposed an alternate source of confusion. Instead of confusing the propositions, I confuse the attitudes. What appears to be a single propositional attitude, imagination, is actually a pair of attitudes. Specifically, I confuse sympathetic imagination (putting myself in a conscious state resembling the thing itself) and perceptual imagination (putting myself in a conscious state resembling the state I would be in if I perceived it). When the neuroscientist identifies pain with C-fiber stimulation, I appear to easily refute his claim by imagining feeling, say, *pleasure* when the C-fiber fires. I am sympathetically imagining pleasure while perceptually imagining C-fiber firing. This makes the connection between pain and C-fiber firings appear contingent. For I appear able to bind my separate imaginings into a single imagining of C-fiber firing without pain.

There would certainly be a fallacy if I were assuming that imagination collects over conjunction: *p* is imagined and *q* is imagined, therefore, *p*-and-*q* is imagined. I can consistently imagine an irresistible force. I can consistently imagine an immoveable object. However, this does not entail I can consistently imagine an irresistible force coexisting with an immoveable object.

I am more charitably interpreted as imagining a painless C-fiber firing in the way I imagine nonsticky chewing gum (Doggett and Stoljar 2010). I combine a tactile imagining with a visual imagining yielding a perceptual imagining. What prevents me from combining sympathetic and perceptual imagining into a more general kind of imagining? If there is no general imagining, then how do I imagine the possible truth of the mind-brain identity thesis? To understand the thesis I need to imagine pain and C-fiber firing co-occurring.

'Imaginable' has the same generality as 'interesting.' Numbers, people, and ideas can all be interesting. Since what is interesting must be imaginable, 'imaginable' must be as capacious as 'interesting.'

Nagel's restriction is also incomplete. He fails to exclude thought experiments that make no use of sympathetic imagination (imagining everybody is mindless) or no use of perceptual imagination (imagining a world in which there is nothing but my disembodied mind). Either of these scenarios is incompatible with "Necessarily, minds are brains."

Imagination may have its internal conflicts and limits. But they parallel the internal conflicts and limits of perception. Since experimenters are committed to resolving those internal divisions for perception, they will bequeath precedents for the thought experimenter. Consequently, Descartes' thought experiments will continue to haunt mind-brain identity theorists in the twenty-first century.

## References


Brewer, W.F., and M. Schommer-Aikins (2006) "Scientists Are Not Deficient in Mental Imagery: Galton Revised," *Review of General Psychology* 10(2): 130–146.

Brown, J.R. (1991) *Laboratory of the Mind*, London: Routledge.

Darwin, C. (1974) "Essay on Theology and Natural Selection," in *Metaphysics, Materialism, and the Evolution of Mind*, ed. P.H. Barrett, Chicago: University of Chicago Press.

Descartes, R. (1641/2008) *Meditations on First Philosophy*, trans. M. Moriarty, Oxford: Oxford University Press.

Doggett, T., and D. Stoljar (2010) "Does Nagel's Footnote Eleven Solve the Mind-Body Problem?" *Philosophical Issues* 20(1): 125–143.

Drake, S., and C.D. O'Malley (1960) *The Controversy on the Comets of 1618*, Philadelphia: University of Philadelphia Press.

Faw, B. (2009) "Conflicting Intuitions May Be Based on Differing Abilities," *Journal of Consciousness Studies* 16(4): 45–68.

Finocchiaro, M.A. (1974) "The Concept of *Ad Hominem* Argument in Galileo and Locke," *Philosophical Forum* 5: 394–404.

Galton, F. (1880) "Statistics of Mental Imagery," *Mind* 5: 301–318.

Gendler, T.S. (2004) "Thought Experiments Rethought – and Reperceived," *Philosophy of Science* 71: 1152–1164.

Goethe, J.W. (1962–67) *Briefe*, 4 vols., eds. K.R. Mandelkow and B. Morawe, Hamburg: Christian Wegner.

Goethe, J.W., and C.F. Zelter (1887) *Goethe's Letters to Zelter: With Extracts from Those of Zelter to Goethe*, London: G. Bell & Sons.

Häggqvist, S. (1996) *Thought Experiments in Philosophy*, Stockholm: Almqvist & Wiksell International.

Jonsen, A.R., and S. Toulmin (1988) *The Abuse of Casuistry: A History of Moral Reasoning*, Berkeley: University of California Press.

Knauff, M. (2013) *Space to Reason*, Cambridge, MA: MIT Press.

Koyré, A. (1978) *Galileo Studies*, trans. J. Mepham, Atlantic Highlands: Humanities Press.

Kuhn, T. (1962) *The Structure of Scientific Revolutions*, Chicago: University of Chicago Press.

Kuhn, T. (1977) "A Function for Thought Experiments," in *The Essential Tension*, Chicago: University of Chicago Press.

Langford, C.H. (1949) "A Proof That Synthetic *A Priori* Propositions Exist," *Journal of Philosophy* 46: 20–24.

Locke, J. (1689/1975) *Essay concerning Human Understanding*, Oxford: Oxford University Press.
Mach, E. (1976) "On Thought Experiments," in *Knowledge and Error*, trans. J. McCormack Dordrecht: Reidel, 134–147.
Nagel, T. (1974) "What Is It Like to Be a Bat?" *Philosophical Review* 83: 435–456.
Nichols, S. (2007) "Imagination and Immortality: Thinking of Me," *Synthese* 159(2): 215–233.
Nichols, S. (2008) "Imagination and the I," *Mind & Language* 23: 518–535.
Norton, J.D. (1991) "Thought Experiments in Einstein's Work," in T. Horowitz and G. Massey (eds.) *Thought Experiments in Science and Philosophy*, Lanham: Rowman & Littlefield, 129–148.
Norton, J.D. (2004) "Why Thought Experiments Do Not Transcend Empiricism," in C. Hitchcock (ed.) *Contemporary Debates in the Philosophy of Science*, Oxford: Blackwell, 44–66.
Quine, W.V. (1969) "Natural Kinds," in *Ontological Relativity and Other Essays*, New York: Columbia University Press.
Sider, T. (2001) "Criteria of Personal Identity and the Limits of Conceptual Analysis," *Philosophical Perspectives* 15: 189–209.
Sorensen, R. (1992) *Thought Experiments*, Oxford: Oxford University Press.
Sorensen, R. (2006) "Meta-conceivability and Thought Experiments," in S. Nichols (ed.) *The Architecture of the Imagination*, Oxford: Oxford University Press, 257–272.
Williams, B. (1966/1973) "Imagination and the Self," British Academy Annual Philosophical Lecture, repr. in *Problems of the Self*, Cambridge: Cambridge University Press, 1973. (Page references to the repr. edition.)
Williams, B. (1970) "The Self and the Future," *Philosophical Review* 79: 161–180.

# 32
# IMAGINATION AND MODAL EPISTEMOLOGY

*Peter Kung*

We frequently use imagination to think about possibilities. Examples are easy to come by. When you plan, you imagine various courses of action you can take, and imagine the outcome of those actions before you settle on one.

Modal epistemology examines both how we think about possibilities and the epistemic status of those thoughts. Philosophers have developed a number of different concepts for different types of epistemic status, and most of them can be applied to the modal case. Do we have at least some *reason to believe* that the thoughts we have about possibilities are true? Are our possibility thoughts *justified*? *Warranted*? *Reliable*? Does the *evidence* support them? Are they *rational*? *Reasonable*? *Probable*? Do we *know* things about possibilities? For the sake of brevity, we will focus on justification and evidence, though the issues raised here apply to other epistemic statuses as well with suitable modification.

The issue addressed in this chapter is whether *imagination* can confer any positive epistemic status on our thoughts about possibility. Hume famously asserts that it can.

> Tis an established maxim in metaphysics, *That whatever the mind clearly conceives includes the idea of possible existence*, or in other words, *that nothing we imagine is absolutely impossible*. We can form the idea of a golden mountain, and from thence conclude that such a mountain may actually exist. We can form no idea of a mountain without a valley, and therefore regard it as impossible.
>
> *(Hume 1739,* Treatise*, I.ii.2)*

The task, then, is to explain how to establish this "established maxim," or to demonstrate that it cannot be established.[1]

What might a positive answer look like? As noted in the Introduction to this volume, there is no single, widely agreed-upon theory of imagination. Rather, there is a family of mental activities that do not seem inappropriate to label "imagination," that may or may not be united by a single theory.[2] In the modal epistemology literature, this has meant that different theorists focus on different aspects of imagination in constructing their positive imagination-based modal epistemologies.

One can also reject Hume's "established maxim." A skeptical worry about imagination as a guide to possibility can be put succinctly: imagination seems too permissive. We use imagination to devise all manner of wonderful creations. Our artworks, our mind-bending fictions, our daydreams, our escapist fantasies; there seems to be no limit to what we can imagine. Amy Kind and Peter Kung (Kind and Kung forthcoming) call this the *transcendent use* of imagination. If imagination is always as unconstrained as it is in its transcendent use, then it is hard to see how imagination could provide justification for belief in possibility. On the face of it, imagination seems powerful enough to create all manner of stories that many philosophers regard as impossible. For example, it seems easy enough to tell myself a story in which I am Bruce Lee's long-lost son, and that I am destined to be the world's next great martial arts master. The fact that there are good arguments that this story is impossible doesn't seem to diminish my ability to imagine it.[3]

The obvious response to the skeptical challenge is to locate *constraints* in imagination, constraints such that, when they are in effect, imagination hews to the metaphysically possible.[4] Skeptics charge that this challenge cannot be met. Antiskeptics offer competing theories of these constraints. This chapter will outline both the skeptical arguments and competing positive theories.

## 1 Skeptical worries and defeaters

Let us begin with some representative general skeptical worries.[5]

Peter Van Inwagen (1998) argues that substantive modal knowledge about "remote" modal matters is unattainable via imagination.[6] The problem is that we imagine scenarios; we cannot imagine anything close to an entire possible world. Say I imagine a scientist winning the Nobel Prize for discovering transparent iron. Perhaps I really am imagining my intended target, a transparent-iron world. But I also may be imagining a world in which the scientific community has been deceived into accepting the existence of transparent iron. To be confident that I am imagining the former world and not the latter world, I have to imagine more details to my scenario. Van Inwagen's point is that I can never add enough detail to rule out all the worlds except my intended target world. There are always going to be worlds consistent with the details I have managed to imagine that are not the target world I intended to imagine. I get to my target world only if I can imagine "at a level of structural detail comparable to that of the imaginings of condensed-matter physicists who are trying to explain, say, the phenomenon of superconductivity" (79). The upshot, Van Inwagen thinks, is that for any substantive philosophical issue, we lack the imaginative capacity to guide us to our target possibility.[7]

Mark Fiocco (2007) argues that the problem isn't that we cannot imagine at the requisite level of detail. Fiocco thinks that we need not imagine at such a fine-grained level to imagine our target world. We get to *stipulate* which world we imagine. If in imagining the scenario with the Nobel scientist I say that I am imagining the transparent-iron world, then that is what I am imagining.

Fiocco notes that this view of imagination generates a different skeptical worry. If I get to stipulate which world I am imagining, then "any world whatsoever is modally imaginable" (375). We can stipulate that we are imagining worlds that represent possible states of affairs. But we can also stipulate that we are imagining worlds that represent impossible states of affairs. Imagination itself gives us no way to distinguish between imagining possible versus impossible states of affairs, and hence imagination on its own is useless as a guide to possibility.

In practice, antiskeptics often do not engage with these sorts of general skeptical worries, except in passing. This lack of engagement can be explained by the fact that many antiskeptics do not offer positive arguments that imagination (or their favored aspect of imagination) counts as modal evidence. The positive modal evidential status of imagination (or a favored aspect of imagination) is assumed or defended in only a cursory way. However, it is acknowledged that this positive modal evidential status can be *defeated*. The general approach to modal epistemology in the literature is defensive, with theorists concentrating on explaining why the skeptical challenge posed by different classes of defeaters fails. Hence to get a grip on the imagination-based modal epistemology literature, it is important to understand the different classes of potential defeaters.

### *1.1 A posteriori necessities*

The most prominent class of defeaters comes from Saul Kripke's (1980) and Hilary Putnam's (1975) work on a posteriori necessities. The Kripke–Putnam view holds that certain statements involving proper names, like "Pope Saint John Paul II is Karol Wojtyła," and natural kind terms, like "Water is $H_2O$," are metaphysically necessary. In the case of natural kinds, this is frequently tied to a view about scientific essentialism, on which we discover the essences of natural kinds (and hence some of their necessary properties) only a posteriori. For example, in discovering that a diamond is a carbon lattice, we have discovered something about a diamond's essence.[8]

We seem to be able to imagine the falsity of a posteriori necessities. It seems like one can imagine, for example, Pope Saint John Paul II turning out to be Joseph Ratzinger, and not Karol Wojtyła. We can imagine opening the paper and reading about a massive cover-up in the Vatican; Karol Wojtyła died shortly after being elected, and Ratzinger disguised himself as Wojtyła and served as Pope John Paul II. If we can imagine this scenario, and we agree with Kripke and Putnam that the scenario is impossible, then it looks like there is a class of cases where imagination systematically gives the false illusion of possibility. The task for an imagination-based modal epistemology is to explain these cases.

### *1.2 Mathematics*

Here is a worry derived from Arnaud's criticism of Descartes in the *Fourth Objections* (in Descartes 1641/1984, 2: 141–142): sometimes it seems like our apparent ability to imagine is driven by *ignorance*.[9] When I first learned about prime numbers in primary school, the existence of a highest prime was, for me, at that time, imaginable. But it is not metaphysically possible for there to be a highest prime, so imagination misled me about the metaphysical possibilities. That is a problem, but perhaps not an insuperable problem, because we can accept that imagination can be a fallible guide. The real problem is that the young Peter Kung's ability to imagine seems to have been driven by *ignorance*. Young Peter didn't know enough about number theory to see that there was a proof that there could be no highest prime. And it seems like ignorance should not count as evidence for anything; a fortiori, it should not count as evidence for metaphysical possibility.

Another type of case routinely discussed in the modal epistemology literature is Goldbach's conjecture (GC), the claim that every integer greater than two is equal to the sum of two primes. Though mathematicians think it is true, this conjecture cannot be proven, so perhaps its falsity can be imagined.[10] We can consider a range of cases, from $2 + 3 = 5$ to there is no largest prime number, to the compactness theorem for predicate logic, to Fermat's last theorem, to GC. These cases differ in the quality of our evidence for the truth of the proposition and consequently on how confident our belief in each proposition is. We are certain or nearly certain of $2 + 3 = 5$. There is a simple proof that there is no largest prime, a somewhat more complicated proof for compactness, a very complex proof for Fermat's last theorem, and no proof for GC. In perhaps all but the simplest case, the falsity of the mathematical truths remains in some sense imaginable.

### 1.3 Philosophical cases

In addition to a posteriori necessities and mathematics cases, there look to be cases where imagination has misled us about philosophical truths.

Time travel has long been a staple in science fiction, and time travel storylines seem to be an increasingly popular device for movie and television writers. In many if not most of these stories, time travelers can change the past. But many philosophers are convinced by David Lewis (1976) that past-changing time travel is impossible because, on careful analysis, it proves to be incoherent. The truth of the philosophical claim does not appear to render time-travel stories unimaginable – Hollywood keeps cranking such stories out, after all. So past-changing time travel looks to be a case where imagination misleads us about possibility.

Another class of potential defeaters comes from fictional characters and fictional kinds. Kripke has argued (Kripke 1980; 2011, ch. 3) that not only do fictional characters not exist, but they *could not* exist. Take Sherlock Holmes: Kripke believes that there are many possible worlds that match (more or less) Conan Doyle's stories.[11] The problem is that in different possible worlds, distinct nonidentical individuals do an equally good job fitting Conan Doyle's description of Holmes. Since not all of these distinct individuals can be Holmes, Kripke concludes that there could not be a Sherlock Holmes. Similar arguments apply to fictional kinds: not only are there no unicorns, but unicorns are impossible. And, of course, it certainly seems like we can imagine Sherlock Holmes and unicorns. The claim that fictional characters and fictional kinds are impossible is more controversial than other claims about necessity or impossibility that we have canvassed above, but, nonetheless, this points to another potential class of cases where imagination might mislead us about possibility.

Kripke (1980) also argues for the necessity of origins, the thesis that an object created from a "parent" object or objects must come from those parent object(s). That sperm and egg that united to give rise to you? You necessarily come from that sperm and egg. A wooden table crafted from a particular cherry tree necessarily must be composed of wood from that very tree. Again, it seems we can imagine that objects have different origins than they in fact have, making for another set of cases where imagination seems to mislead about possibility.

## 2 Imagination-based modal epistemologies

Let us now turn from the potential defeaters to the strategies for explaining away those defeaters. The strategies presented below are not mutually exclusive. Where possible, we will also cover significant or surprising modal epistemological results that come from adopting that strategy.

### 2.1 The Kripkean error theory strategy

The most influential discussion of imagination and modal epistemology is due to Kripke (1980). Virtually every theorist working on the topic feels compelled to respond in some way to Kripke's arguments. Kripke develops his approach to modal epistemology in the same context that he argues for his theory of the necessary a posteriori, and in fact his remarks on modal epistemology are taken to be part of his argument for the existence of a posteriori necessities. Kripke sees it as his burden to explain why we need not jettison imagination as a guide to possibility in light of the necessary a posteriori.

Kripke's approach is to suggest that we *misconstrue* the scenarios we imagine. We take ourselves to be imagining something that Kripke's theory of the necessary a posteriori deems impossible. For example, I take myself to imagine Pope Saint John Paul II turning out to be Joseph Ratzinger. In Kripke's view, I really imagine different scenario, a possible scenario, and confuse the possible scenario for the impossible one. More precisely,

> When we seem to and take ourselves to imagine a situation *S* that falsifies some a posteriori necessity *N*,
> (Unimagined) We *do not* in fact imagine *S*.
> (Confusion) We imagine a situation *S′* that we confuse for *S*.
> (Possible) Situation *S′* is possible and consistent with *N*.[12]

According to Kripke, the general idea is that we can *redescribe* an imagining to make it clear to the imaginer that they were imagining *S′* and not *S*. In the Pope Saint John Paul II case, for example, I might be doing one of two things. I might be imagining

> (JR) Joseph Ratzinger *playing the John Saint Paul II role.*

I imagine that people call Ratzinger "John Paul II," that Ratzinger had himself surgically altered to resemble Karol Wojtyła, that Ratzinger traveled to Poland in 1979 and helped spark the Solidarity movement, and so on. According to Kripke, (JR) is a genuine possibility. The problem is that I mistake this for a scenario in which Ratzinger *is* John Paul II, rather than one in which he just has most of the characteristics by which we identify John Paul II. The person in (JR) is not really John Paul II, because he is not Karol Wojtyła, and John Paul II is Karol Wojtyła.

Alternatively, I might imagine:

> (KW) Karol Wojtyła, that is, John Paul II, *playing the Joseph Ratzinger role.*

I imagine that Karol Wojtyła, that particular individual, did not grow up in Poland and was never named "Karol Wojtyła." Instead his parents moved to Bavaria shortly before he was born, he was named "Joseph Ratzinger," was conscripted into the Hitler Youth, became a professor at the University of Bonn, and so on. Even though the person in (KW) fits most of the descriptions we associate with Ratzinger, he is not Ratzinger. He is Wojtyła.

The metaphysical point made by (JR) and (KW) is that in most cases, there is a difference between the person and the characteristics generally associated with the person. According to Kripke, many of the characteristics associated with a person, like their name, their place of birth, or their most famous deeds, are not necessary properties of the person. It isn't a necessary truth that Karol Wojtyła be named "John Paul II," or even become Pope at all; he could have had a different name, or never been elected Pope.

(JR) and (KW) are also supposed to make a point about imagination. Examples like (JR) and (KW) are supposed to *convince* you that you were previously mischaracterizing your imaginings, i.e., that (Confusion) is true. It's a credit to Kripke that his arguments and examples have convinced a great number of philosophers that they were in fact misdescribing their imaginings. The resulting view combines confidence in imagination as a guide to possibility with an error theory about what we imagine.[13] As Yablo (2006) puts it, on Kripke's view, "There are illusions of possibility, if you like, but no delusions or hallucinations" (327).

This view is supposed to cover all cases of the necessary a posteriori. We seem to be able to imagine discovering diamonds were made of something other than carbon. According to Kripke, that is an illusion; we can imagine a gemstone that *plays the diamond role* turning out not to be made of carbon. But that gemstone would not be a diamond. Kripke's view, then, offers a unified treatment of a wide range of phenomena: identity statements about persons (like "Pope Saint John Paul II is Karol Wojtyła"), natural kind categorization (whales are mammals), origins (Malia Obama is the daughter of Barack and Michelle Obama), and scientific identities (like gold = Au). In each case, we discover a truth a posteriori. We seem to be able to imagine the falsity of that truth. Kripke both explains why we should regard the truth as necessary and explains away our apparent ability to imagine its falsity, all the while preserving imagination as a guide to possibility.

The literature on the necessary a posteriori is vast.[14] One reason this framework has sparked so much debate is that Kripke provocatively suggests that the framework licenses *dualism*, roughly the view that the mind does not have a wholly physical nature. The metaphysical point from two paragraphs back noted that there is a difference between the person and the characteristics we use to identify the person, and that difference makes the redescriptions (JR) and (KW) plausible. However, with certain dualistic thought experiments, there is no gap between the phenomenon and the characteristics by which we describe the phenomenon and the redescription strategy thus fails. We will illustrate this by working through one famous case. I claim to imagine:

(Zombie) A *philosophical zombie*, a creature that is a molecule-for-molecule duplicate of me that lacks conscious experience.

This case potentially poses a problem for *physicalism*, the view that consciousness is a physical phenomenon. For brevity, we will work with a version of physicalism that takes conscious states to be identifiable a posteriori with physical states of the brain.[15] The resulting mind-brain identities are thus scientific identities akin to water = $H_2O$ or heat is mean molecular kinetic energy. According to Kripke's framework, those identities are necessarily true if true. Hence (Zombie) poses a potential counterexample to this brand of physicalism.

Suppose we try to apply the redescription strategy to (Zombie). Right now I have a toothache, involving the characteristic deadening feeling of a toothache. I take myself to imagine my zombie duplicate manifesting all the same physical behaviors as me but in fact having no conscious sensations of pain whatsoever. According to the redescription strategy, I do not really imagine a philosophical zombie, for if I imagine a molecule-for-molecule duplicate of me, then (according to physicalism) that duplicate must be conscious. I am really imagining my zombie duplicate *is* in pain; I just do so without imagining the deadening ouchy feeling by which I identify toothache pain. This redescription isn't plausible, Kripke thinks, because there is no gap between being in a particular conscious state and the signs by which I usually identify that conscious state. If my duplicate lacks the deadening ouchy feeling by which I identify toothache pain, then it does not have toothache pain. It doesn't make sense to say: it really does have toothache pain, just without the ouchy feeling by which you usually identify toothache pain.

The redescription strategy that handles other scientific identities so well does not work on dualism thought experiments. This means that, according to Kripke, these thought experiments stand as counterexamples to physicalism.

### 2.2 Model of modal error strategy

In an influential article, Stephen Yablo (1993) argues that a certain kind of imagining is a guide to possibility by qualifying Kripke's error theory. In Yablo's view, the modally relevant kind of imagining is imagining a situation of which *P* is held to be a true description (29).[16] That kind of imagining presents the "appearance of possibility"; imagining that *P* makes it seem that *P* is possible.

Yablo concedes that sometimes we can imagine the impossible, and hence imagination is not an infallible guide to possibility. So here Yablo departs from Kripke. The important point, however, is that imagination misleads about possibility in a predictable way, so we can formulate a *model of modal error*. Let *P* be some impossible proposition that you imagine. If the following three claims are true:

- a Q;
- b if Q then necessarily not-*P*;
- c that you find *P* imaginable is explained by your unawareness/denial that (a), and/or your unawareness/denial that (b),

then Q is a *modal defeater*. The idea is that modal error is explained by ignorance of a truth, either of some actual-world fact (a) or some modal fact (b). Dialectically, if an interlocutor provides a Q along with reason to believe (a) through (c), then that casts legitimate doubt on one's belief in the possibility of *P*.

Yablo contends that this model improves upon Kripke's handling of a posteriori necessities. You can imagine that Hesperus is a star distinct from Phosphorus, if, like the ancients, you are ignorant of the fact that "Hesperus" and "Phosphorus" both refer to the planet Venus. So Yablo thinks that Kripke's error theory of imagination does not apply when we are ignorant of certain important facts. Even if you learn that (a) Hesperus is Phosphorus, you might still be able to imagine that they are distinct if you do not know the conditional that (b) if Hesperus ≠ Phosphorus, then necessarily Hesperus ≠ Phosphorus.

If you know both (a) and (b), then Yablo thinks Kripke's error theory of imagination applies: you cannot imagine Hesperus distinct from Phosphorus. Your imagining should be redescribed in the manner described in Section 2.1.

### 2.3 Two-dimensional semantics solutions

Recently, Frank Jackson (1998) and David Chalmers (1996, 2002, 2009) have developed an influential modal epistemology embedded within the two-dimensional semantic framework that emphasizes the a priori aspects of meaning. Chalmers presents a well-developed and influential version of the framework. The framework is fairly technical and difficult to summarize in nontechnical terms, so here we will concentrate on sketching the intuitive picture, emphasizing the role of imagination.

Consider the statement, "Joseph Ratzinger becomes Pope John Paul II." As we have already seen, Kripke deems this statement necessarily false, and offers his error theory as a way to explain why it might seem imaginable and hence possible. But the nagging feeling remains that we really can imagine the name "John Paul II" applying to someone other than Karol Wojtyła. The two-dimensional framework offers a way both to accept Kripke's insight and to acknowledge something right about the nagging feeling. According to the two-dimensional framework, a statement has two senses, a *primary intension* and a *secondary intension*. A statement has a true primary intension if we can imagine a scenario "considered as actual" in which the statement is true. To imagine a scenario *as actual* is to imagine that this scenario is true in the actual world – and hence that some of our actual beliefs are false – while leaving as much else unchanged as possible. (This is also called *primary imagining*.) Take the scenario in which Karol Wojtyła dies in infancy from German measles. Imaginatively insert this scenario into the actual world. There is still a Pope Saint John Paul II – *someone* by that name led the Catholic Church from 1978 to 2005; that remains unchanged – but it is clear that it was not Karol Wojtyła, because Wojtyła never made it to adulthood. In that scenario imagined as actual, the name "John Paul II" refers to someone other than Karol Wojtyła. The primary intension of "Pope John Paul II" is the a priori slice of meaning that allows the term to latch onto Karol Wojtyła in the actual world and onto Joseph Ratzinger were the Wojtyła-dies-in-infancy world actual. Hence we can allay the nagging feeling that Ratzinger could become John Paul II by appealing to the primary intension of the statement, "Joseph Ratzinger becomes Pope John Paul II."

The secondary intension of a statement respects Kripke's insights about the necessary a posteriori. The statement, "Joseph Ratzinger becomes Pope John Paul II" has a necessarily false secondary intension. Secondary intensions are associated with imagining scenarios *as counterfactual* (also called *secondary imagining*), which works pretty much the way Kripke envisions. We hold fixed our actual-world beliefs, and imagine a nonactual possible world. For instance, we imagine a nonactual possible world in which Wojtyła dies in infancy while holding fixed our belief that Karol Wojtyła is Pope Saint John Paul II. Here, we are supposed to conclude with Kripke that in the imagined world, there is no Pope Saint John Paul II. There might be someone else who goes by that name, but it isn't the real Pope Saint John Paul II.

Chalmers connects these two intensions to modal epistemology by postulating a single space of worlds, the metaphysically possible worlds, over which we can define both primary and secondary intensions. A statement is *primary possible* if there is some possible world considered as actual in which it is true. A primary possible world is thus a metaphysically possible world. Pope Saint John Paul II is Joseph Ratzinger is a primary possibility because some metaphysically possible world, the world where Wojtyła dies in infancy and Ratzinger plays the John Paul II role, imagined as actual makes the primary intension of "Joseph Ratzinger becomes Pope John Paul II" true.

Primary imagining is not generally a guide to secondary possibility. The fact there is a possible world in which Ratzinger plays the John Paul II role – making "Ratzinger is John Paul II" true when imagined as actual – does not establish that there is any world imagined as counterfactual in which "Ratzinger is John Paul II" is true. But Chalmers argues at length that the zombie case is an exception. The reason is that both microphysical terms and consciousness terms are *semantically stable*: the primary and secondary intensions coincide.[17] For consciousness terms like "pain," the a priori slice of meaning acquaints us with the essential nature of pain: the subjective feel of painful sensations. As in Kripke's dualist argument, there is no gap between the essential nature of pain and pain role to mark a difference between primary and secondary intension. For microphysical terms, the story is a bit more complicated, but the rough idea is that the scientific theory in which the term is embedded specifies everything about the physical property picked out that a physicalist should care about.[18] Chalmers concludes that this means that the primary possibility of zombie duplicates entails the secondary possibility of zombie duplicates. And if zombies are secondary possible, then some form of dualism must be true.

### 2.4 Imagery-based strategies

Hume famously held that imagination is essentially *imagistic* and, as noted in the quote at the start of this chapter, that imagistic imagination is a guide to possibility. On an imagistic view of imagination, imagination is phenomenologically similar to perception; it involves "seeing in the mind's eye," or "hearing in the mind's ear."[19] We will cover three recent discussions of imagistic imagination as a guide to possibility.[20] These discussions – from Christopher Peacoke, Sydney Shoemaker, and Peter Kung – fit the dialectal model described in this chapter. The positive status of imagination as a guide to possibility is assumed or defended only cursorily; the emphasis is on explaining away defeaters.

Two overlapping ideas run through these three discussions. First, Peacocke and Shoemaker understand imagining as *imagining experiences*. When you visually imagine a tree, you are in fact imagining from the inside seeing a tree. It is assumed that these imagined experiences are metaphysically possible experiences; the project is to figure out what these possible experiences can and cannot tell us about metaphysical possibilities. Second, Peacocke and Kung draw a distinction between the imagistic and nonimagistic content of imagining. It is assumed that imagistic content can tell us about possibility; the focus is on investigating how we can be misled by nonimagistic content.

In a well-known paper, Peacocke (1985) argues that imagistic imagination should be understood as imagining an experience from the inside: "to imagine an F is always at least to imagine from the inside an experience as of an F" (23). Following Williams (1973), and unlike Hume, Peacocke doesn't think that imaginings must be individuated by the mental image. Say in one imaginative episode, you imagine a suitcase. Say in a second imaginative episode, you imagine a cat completely hidden behind a suitcase. The mental imagery of the suitcase might be the same in both imaginative episodes, and yet the content differs. Peacocke attributes the difference to what he calls *S-imagined* content. The imagistic content of imagination is a guide to possibility, perhaps because it is the content of a possible experience,[21] but we cannot say the same for the S-imagined content of experience. According to Peacocke, this theory allows us to make some sense of Berkeley's contention that it is impossible for there to be a tree that exists unperceived. When one imagines a tree, on Peacocke's view, one imagines from the inside an experience as of a tree. Add in the plausible assumption that to imagine an experience from the inside means imagining a perceiver,[22] and you have the conclusion that whenever you imagine a tree, you imagine the tree is perceived. One can remove the perceiver via S-imagined content – that is, one can S-imagine that there is no perceiver – but since S-imagined content is not a guide to possibility, that is no evidence that there could be a tree that exists unperceived. In sum, Peacocke thinks that imagination cannot vindicate the possibility of a tree that exists unperceived.[23]

Like Peacocke, Shoemaker (1993) thinks of imagining as imagining experiences. An imagining gives us a reason to believe that *P* is possible if we would be justified in believing that *P* were we to have an experience qualitatively like the one imagined. The view is best illustrated by reviewing Shoemaker's discussion of zombies.

Shoemaker notes that you can imagine something, like me shooting a free throw, in two ways, from the third-person perspective (as if you were a third party, observing me shooting the free throw) or from the first-person perspective (as if you were the shooter; you imagine *being me* shooting a free throw). So there are two ways we can try to imagine a zombie case, from the third-person perspective and the first-person perspective. Shoemaker denies that we can imagine a zombie case from the third-person perspective:

> The reason is that playing the causal role of pain … will essentially involve producing precisely the kinds of behavior that serve as our third-person basis for ascribing pain. We cannot be in a position to judge about someone *both* that she is not in pain *and* that she is in a state that influences her behavior in just the ways we think pain influences behavior.
>
> *(Shoemaker 1993, 506)*

Take the toothache case described in Section 2.1. When I imagine my zombie duplicate, the creature is imagined to be a molecule-for-molecule duplicate of me, and I really do have a toothache, so not only should we imagine the creature behaving exactly as if it had a toothache, but we should also imagine any test run from the observer's perspective (like a brain scan) concluding that the creature is feeling a toothache. There is no way an observer could reasonably conclude that the creature wasn't feeling a toothache. Hence according to Shoemaker we cannot really imagine a zombie case from the third-person perspective, and hence so far we have no reason to think there could be zombies.

What about imagining a zombie case from the first-person perspective? Shoemaker considers a slightly different case to make his point: try to imagine from the first-person perspective *becoming* a zombie; that is, imagine that you are gradually losing some of the conscious states you now enjoy. Let's call this imagining being a proto-zombie. The real you has a toothache; your proto-zombie duplicate is just like you except that she has lost any conscious states associated with the toothache. Now imagine *being* the proto-zombie, sitting in the dentist chair. The dentist asks you whether your tooth hurts, and, despite the fact that you feel no pain, you hear yourself answer, "Yes, I have a maddening dull pain in my tooth. It radiates through my whole head." When the dentist drills, though you feel no pain, you hear yourself yelp as if in severe pain. Shoemaker notes that if you were to have experiences like the ones you imagine, you would be profoundly alienated from your own body. You wouldn't know what to think. Are you becoming a zombie? Are you losing your mind? Is someone else taking over your body? Because it isn't clear what it is reasonable to think, Shoemaker concludes it is not clear we can imagine a zombie case from the first-person perspective. Since we cannot clearly imagine a zombie case from either third-person or first-person perspective, Shoemaker thinks even if we accept Kripke's framework, we have an alternative way to explain away the dualist thought experiments.

A final imagery-based modal epistemology comes from Kung (2010). Kung argues for a distinction between the basic imagistic content of imagining – roughly, what our imagery systems are designed to represent (in the visual case, this might be a three-dimensional array of objects in space) – and nonbasic content. Kung, like Peacocke, also thinks that there is nonimagistic content of imagining.[24] To take Peacocke's example of visualizing a black cat completely hidden behind a blue suitcase, the basic imagistic content might be: there is a blue rectangular object in front of me. The nonbasic imagistic content might include that the blue rectangular object is a suitcase. The nonimagistic content is that there is a black cat hidden behind the visualized suitcase. Kung calls nonbasic imagistic content and nonimagistic content *assigned content*.

Kung assumes that basic imagistic content can provide evidence for possibility. But he argues that assigned content cannot, on its own, provide evidence for possibility. For example, you have a lot of power to provide an unvisualized "backstory" to whatever you visualize. You can imagine that the blue suitcase belongs to Karol Wojtyła, who has just murdered Pope Saint John Paul II and is about to skip town. Imagining the backstory does not by itself provide evidence for possibility. The only constraint on the backstory, if any, is certainty: you can imagine anything in the backstory that you aren't absolutely certain is false. Though you justifiably believe, and even know, that Wojtyła is John Saint Paul II, you aren't absolutely certain of it, so you can imagine a way for it to be false. But because lack of certainty isn't an epistemic credential, your ability to imagine something in the backstory is not, by itself, evidence for possibility. Hence even though you can imagine as part of the backstory that Wojtyła is not John Paul II (meaning Kung rejects Kripke's error theory), that imagining is not a guide to possibility. Kung suggests that the arguments against the backstory apply equally to all assigned content. So here we have an alternative way to explain away the various defeaters described in Section 1. If those defeaters can be imagined only in virtue of assigned content, then, on Kung's view, we have a principled reason to think that imagining them does not provide evidence for possibility.

### *2.5 Rational reflection strategies*

Finally, we turn to strategies that emphasize our ability to rationally reflect on scenarios that we imagine and uncover inconsistency or incoherence. A number of otherwise quite different theories deploy this strategy; see Chalmers and Jackson (2001), Chalmers (2002) on negative conceivability, Geirsson (2005), and Levin (2011). Ichikawa and Jarvis (2012) offer a detailed account that places rational reflection at the heart of their modal epistemology, so we will focus on their account.

Ichikawa and Jarvis concentrate on the imaginative attitude that we take toward fiction, which they take to be a species of *supposing*.[25] Their strategy is to argue that *coherent imagining* is a guide to *conceptual possibility*, and that suitably constrained, conceptual possibility is a guide to metaphysical possibility.

Ichikawa and Jarvis assume there are rational commitments to draw inferences in imagining that mirror the rational commitments to draw inferences in belief. If you imagine that Harry Potter drops his wand, then (should the issue become relevant) you are thereby rationally committed to imagining that the wand falls to the floor. Rational commitments can be defeated by further imaginings (e.g., by imagining that the wand has the Wingardium Leviosa levitation spell cast upon it). A conceptual entailment is a rational commitment to infer in imagination that can be defeated only by either the subject's rational limitations or evidence concerning the subject's rational limitations.[26] Hence there is no conceptual entailment between imagining *Harry drops his wand* and imagining *Harry's wand falls to the floor* because that inference can be defeated. By contrast, if you imagine *Hermione has no brothers or sisters*, your commitment to imagine *Hermione is an only child* can be defeated only by your rational limitations or evidence of your rational limitations (e.g., evidence that you do not correctly grasp the concept of an only child). Ichikawa and Jarvis use this characterization of conceptual entailment to define conceptual possibility: a conceptually possible proposition is one that does not conceptually entail an absurdity.

On this definition, a posteriori impossible propositions, like Pope Saint John Paul II is Joseph Ratzinger, not Karol Wojtyła, remain conceptual possibilities. But Ichikawa and Jarvis note, using Kripkean reasoning, that Pope Saint John Paul II is not Karol Wojtyła conceptually entails something that is a falsehood: that in the actual world, Pope Saint John Paul II is not Karol Wojtyła. To forge the link between conceptual possibility and metaphysical possibility, they propose that we restrict attention to conceptually possible propositions that do not conceptually entail falsehoods about the actual world: *P* is metaphysically possible just in case *P* is conceptually possible and *P* does not entail anything false about the actual world.

Ichikawa and Jarvis acknowledge that their account crucially depends on our ability to know that a proposition does not conceptually entail some hidden absurdity. To be justified in thinking that a situation one has imagined is a genuine metaphysical possibility, one needs to be justifiably confident that the situation doesn't contain some hidden absurdity. Their strategy, and the strategy of others who take a similar approach, requires confidence in our ability to rationally reflect on our imaginings and uncover absurdities, and that failing to uncover an absurdity gives us justification for thinking that there are no hidden absurdities. They take this confidence to be as plausible as analogous confidence in the case of belief: "discovering that imaginings are coherent can't be any more difficult than discovering that beliefs are coherent, and most of us are pretty confident that most of the beliefs that we have, even if they are false, are not incoherent" (Ichikawa and Jarvis 2012, 153).

## 3 Conclusion

The motivating idea behind this chapter, that we learn about genuine possibilities by using our imaginations, is a plausible part of common sense. To make this general idea philosophically robust, defenders must confront a host of skeptical challenges. This chapter has surveyed prominent strategies for responding to these challenges. The discussion of skeptical challenges is well covered in the literature. There remains, however, a need for positive accounts that explain in detail why imagination should be taken as evidence for possibility in the first place.

## Acknowledgments

Thanks to Amy Kind and an anonymous referee for illuminating and constructive comments on an earlier draft.

## Notes

1 See Fabian Dorsch's Chapter 3 of this volume on Hume.
2 See Van Leeuwen 2013 and Balcerak Jackson forthcoming for different senses of "imagine" and Kind 2013 for arguments that there is no single unifying theory.
3 According to Kripke's (1980) influential views on the necessity of origins, if Bruce Lee is not my dad, then it is impossible for him to be my dad. See Section 1.3 below.
4 See Kind and Kung forthcoming.
5 See also Bealer 2002, Byrne 2007, and Tidman 1994.
6 Van Inwagen grants that we do have "ordinary" modal knowledge. I can know that the picture could be hung 2 feet to the left, or that Barack and Michelle Obama could have had a third child. The distinction between ordinary and remote matters is left imprecise.
7 See Dennett 1995 and Marcus 2004 for related concerns.
8 See, e.g., Ellis 2001.
9 Arnaud directs his criticism at Descartes' notion of clear and distinct perception; Descartes is clear that clear and distinct perception is distinct from imagination. Nonetheless Arnaud's worry can applied *mutatis mutandis* to imagination.
10 It is also problematic if GC's *truth* can be imagined. If imagining GC is true justifies believing that GC is possible, and GC's possibility entails GC's necessity, then we could establish GC's necessity just by imagining it to be true. It would be surprising if we could establish mathematical truths that way, without *doing* any mathematics.
11 "More or less" because Conan Doyle's stories probably contain some inconsistencies and hence cannot be entirely true in any possible world.
12 See Kung 2014 for this formulation.

13 Ichikawa and Jarvis (2012) and Kung (2014) argue that this error theory is implausible.
14 See Hughes 2004 for an overview.
15 The point of the zombie case and Kripke's criticisms of it apply to other forms of physicalism as well.
16 Like many authors, Yablo thinks that the relevant kind of imagining can be, but need not be, imagistic (Yablo 1993, 27 n. 55).
17 For objections to semantic stability, see Block and Stalnaker 1999 and Yablo 2000.
18 Stoljar 2001 for discussion of the complications.
19 See the entry on "Imagination and mental imagery," by Dominic Gregory, in Chapter 7 of this volume. The imagery in question encompasses all modalities, despite the visual connotations of the word "image."
20 See also Hart 1988. Other authors, such as Amy Kind (2001), embrace an imagistic view of imagination, but do not address the connection to possibility.
21 Peacocke suggests but does not defend this view.
22 Though see Dominic Gregory's Chapter 7 on "Imagination and mental imagery" for reasons to doubt this plausible assumption.
23 Peacocke is explicit that this is only a limited defense of Berkeley, because the possibility of an unperceived tree could be established by something other than imagination.
24 Unlike Peacocke, Kung does not view all imagining as imagining experiences.
25 See also Currie and Ravenscroft 2002 and Goldman 2006.
26 Strictly speaking, this is a characterization of conceptual entailment and not an analysis of it, though the difference does not matter for our purposes.

## References

Balcerak Jackson, M. (Forthcoming) "On Imagining, Supposing and Conceiving," in A. Kind and P. Kung (eds.) *Knowledge through Imagination*, Oxford: Oxford University Press.

Bealer, G. (2002) "Modal Epistemology and the Rationalist Renaissance," in T. Gendler and J. Hawthorne (eds.) *Conceivability and Possibility*, Oxford: Oxford University Press.

Block, N., and E. Stalnaker (1999) "Conceptual Analysis, Dualism, and the Explanatory Gap," *Philosophical Review* 108: 1 46.

Byrne, A. (2007) "Possibility and Imagination," *Philosophical Perspectives* 21: 125–144.

Chalmers, D. (1996) *The Conscious Mind*, Oxford: Oxford University Press.

Chalmers, D. (2002) "Does Conceivability Entail Possibility?" in T. Gendler and J. Hawthorne (eds.) *Conceivability and Possibility*, Oxford: Oxford University Press.

Chalmers, D. (2009) "The Two-Dimensional Argument against Materialism," in B. McLaughlin (ed.) *Oxford Handbook of Philosophy of Mind*, Oxford: Oxford University Press.

Chalmers, D., and F. Jackson (2001) "Conceptual Analysis and Reductive Explanation," *Philosophical Review* 110: 315–360.

Currie, G., and I. Ravenscroft (2002) *Recreative Minds: Imagination in Philosophy and Psychology*, Oxford: Oxford University Press.

Dennett, D. (1995) "The Unimagined Preposterousness of Zombies," *Journal of Consciousness Studies* 2: 322–326.

Descartes, R. (1641/1984–85) *The Philosophical Writings of Descartes*, 2 vols., trans. J. Cottingham, R. Stoothoff, and D. Murdoch, Cambridge: Cambridge University Press.

Ellis, B. (2001) *Scientific Essentialism*, Cambridge: Cambridge University Press.

Fiocco, M. (2007) "Conceivability, Imagination and Modal Knowledge," *Philosophy and Phenomenological Research* 74: 364–380.

Geirsson, H. (2005) "Conceivability and Defeasible Modal Justification," *Philosophical Studies* 122: 279–304.

Goldman, A. (2006) *Simulating Minds*, Oxford: Oxford University Press.

Hart, W.D. (1988) *The Engines of the Soul*, Cambridge: Cambridge University Press.

Hughes, C. (2004) *Kripke: Names, Necessity, and Identity*, Oxford: Clarendon.

Hume, D. (1739/1978) *A Treatise of Human Nature*, eds. L.A. Selby-Bigge and P.H. Nidditch, 2nd edn., Oxford: Clarendon Press.

Ichikawa, J., and B. Jarvis (2012) "Rational Imagination and Modal Knowledge," *Noûs* 46: 127–158.

Jackson, F. (1998) *From Metaphysics to Ethics: A Defense of Conceptual Analysis*, Oxford: Oxford University Press.

Kind, A. (2001) "Putting the Image Back in Imagination," *Philosophy and Phenomenological Research* 62: 85–109.
Kind, A. (2013) "The Heterogeneity of Imagination," *Erkenntnis* 78: 141–159.
Kind, A., and P. Kung (Forthcoming) "The Puzzle of Imaginative Use," in A. Kind and P. Kung (eds.) *Knowledge through Imagination*, Oxford: Oxford University Press.
Kripke, S. (1980) *Naming and Necessity*, Cambridge, MA: Harvard University Press.
Kripke, S. (2011) *Philosophical Troubles: Collected Papers*, vol. 1, Oxford: Oxford University Press.
Kung, P. (2010) "Imagining as a Guide to Possibility," *Philosophy and Phenomenological Research* 81 620–663.
Kung, P. (2014) "You Really Do Imagine It: Against Error Theories of Imagination," *Noûs* 49(3), early view, <http://dx.doi.org/10.1111/nous.12060>.
Levin, J. (2011) "Imagination, Possibility, and the Puzzle of Imaginative Resistance," *Canadian Journal of Philosophy* 41: 391–422.
Lewis, D. (1976) "The Paradoxes of Time Travel," *American Philosophical Quarterly* 13: 145–152.
Marcus, E. (2004) "Why Zombies Are Inconceivable," *Australasian Journal of Philosophy* 82: 477–490.
Peacocke, C. (1985) "Imagination, Experience, and Possibility: A Berkeleian View Defended," in J. Foster and H. Robinson (eds.) *Essays on Berkeley*, Oxford: Clarendon Press.
Putnam, H. (1975) "The Meaning of 'Meaning,'" in K. Gunderson (ed.) *Language, Mind and Knowledge*, Minnesota Studies in the Philosophy of Science, vol. 7, Minneapolis: University of Minnesota Press, 131–193.
Shoemaker, S. (1993) "The First-Person Perspective," *Proceedings of the American Philosophical Association* 68: 7–22; repr., N. Block, O.J. Flanagan, and G. Güzeldere (eds.) *The Nature of Consciousness* (Cambridge, MA: MIT Press, 1997), 503–515.
Stoljar, D. (2001) "The Conceivability Argument and Two Conceptions of the Physical," *Philosophical Perspectives* 15: 393–413.
Tidman, P. (1994) "Conceivability as a Test for Possibility," *American Philosophical Quarterly* 31: 297–309.
Van Inwagen, P. (1998) "Modal Epistemology," *Philosophical Studies* 92: 67–84.
Van Leeuwen, N. (2013) "The Meanings of 'Imagine' Part I: Constructive Imagination," *Philosophy Compass* 8: 220–230.
Williams, B. (1973) "Imagination and the Self," in *Problems of the Self*, Cambridge: Cambridge University Press.
Yablo, S. (1993) "Is Conceivability a Good Guide to Possibility?" *Philosophy and Phenomenological Research* 53: 1–42.
Yablo, S. (2000) "Textbook Kripkeanism and the Open Texture of Concepts," *Pacific Philosophical Quarterly* 81: 98–122.
Yablo, S. (2006) "No Fools Cold: Notes on Illusions of Possibility," in M. Garcia-Carpintero and J. Macia (eds.) *Two-Dimensional Semantics*, Oxford: Oxford University Press.

# 33
# IMAGINATION IN SCIENTIFIC MODELING

*Adam Toon*

## Introduction

Our commonsense view of science invites conflicting reactions to the idea that imagination plays an important role in scientific inquiry. On the one hand, the world of make-believe seems far removed from the slow, painstaking accumulation of facts we commonly take to be characteristic of the scientific method. On the other hand, we celebrate stories of great, creative leaps of the imagination in science, such as the famous story of August Kekulé's discovery of the ring structure of benzene after dreaming of a snake swallowing its own tail. This chapter will focus on the role of the imagination in one important part of scientific inquiry, namely scientific modeling. Modeling plays a crucial role in scientists' attempts to understand the world. And yet it is also puzzling since, in modeling, scientists appear to be able to learn about the world by first learning about things that don't exist, like perfect spheres or frictionless surfaces. As a result, modeling poses a range of questions for philosophers of science: What are models? How do they represent real systems in the world? How can learning about models help us to learn about those systems?

Scientists often talk of modeling in terms of the imagination. When we are presented with the Newtonian model of the solar system, for example, we might be told to "imagine that the sun and earth are perfect spheres, isolated from the other planets ..." In a similar manner, a biology textbook might ask us to "imagine a population of predators and prey, which interact in the following way ..." When we read such passages, it seems, we are being invited to turn our attention away from the blooming, buzzing confusion we find around us to ponder a simpler, more straightforward world before our mind's eye. Recently, a number of authors have suggested that paying closer attention to the imagination might help us to address the philosophical issues raised by scientific modeling. Some have also developed this idea by drawing on work in philosophy of art and fiction. These approaches fall into two camps: *indirect fiction views* and *direct fiction views*. According to indirect fiction views, when scientists represent the world in modeling they do so indirectly, via a *model system*. Model systems are simplified or idealized versions of the real world that the scientist asks us to imagine. Proponents of this approach often compare model systems to fictional characters, like Sherlock Holmes or Madame Bovary. By contrast, direct fiction views reject this appeal to model systems. According to direct fiction views, scientists represent the world directly, by asking us to imagine things about it. Proponents of this approach sometimes compare models to works of historical fiction, which represent real people, places or events. This chapter will examine both of these approaches to scientific modeling in detail and consider the motivation behind them, as well as some objections that have been raised against them.

## Scientific modeling

Scientific models may be divided into two categories: *physical models* and *theoretical models*. As the name suggests, physical models are actual, physical objects. If an engineer wishes to build a bridge, for example, she might first build a scale model to test her plans. Other well-known examples of physical models include wax anatomical models, "ball-and-stick" molecular models or mechanical orreries that show the movements of the planets in the solar system. In contrast, theoretical models are not actual, physical objects. Consider the standard Newtonian model of the orbit of the earth. This model makes many simplifying assumptions. For example, it assumes that the sun and earth are perfect spheres and that they are isolated from the other planets in the solar system. These assumptions are known to be false of the sun and earth. And yet by making them scientists are able to apply Newton's laws to predict the motion of the planets. This is a case of theoretical modeling. To apply Newton's laws we *model* the sun and earth as perfect spheres isolated from the other planets. Another familiar example is the billiard ball model of gases. In this model, we treat the molecules of a gas as if they were a collection of tiny billiard balls. Once again, this description is false in various respects. For example, it assumes that when the gas molecules collide, they ping off each other like billiard balls whereas, in reality, their interactions are more complicated. And yet, as with the Newtonian model of the planets, making these assumptions allows us to make sense of an extremely complicated real world system and make good predictions for its behavior.

Theoretical modeling is extremely common in science. Indeed, some authors argue that modeling is involved in all attempts to apply scientific theories to the world (Cartwright 1983; Giere 1988). For others, modeling is a more specialized activity, which should be distinguished from other forms of theorizing (Godfrey-Smith 2006; Weisberg 2007). On all accounts, however, theoretical modeling is a widespread and important part of scientific practice. And yet it can also seem a rather puzzling activity. One way to see this is to consider the contrast between physical and theoretical modeling. When the engineer models her bridge, she builds an actual, physical object from wood, metal or plastic. In theoretical modeling, as we have seen, scientists don't construct any physical object that serves as their model. Indeed, there typically are no actual, concrete objects that would satisfy the scientists' equations and assumptions. There are no perfect spheres that we could take out of the lab store cupboard and use to build a Newtonian model of the solar system, for example. And yet scientists often talk about theoretical and physical modeling in similar sorts of ways. The engineer builds her scale model so that she can investigate the properties of the model and thereby learn about the properties of the finished bridge. Similarly, it is often said that, in theoretical modeling, what scientists do is to construct a simplified or idealized system, called the *model system*. For example, the Newtonian model system consists of two perfect spheres isolated from the other planets and obeying Newton's law of gravitation. Like the engineer with her scale model, the scientist then investigates the properties of her model system to learn about the properties of the real system that she wishes to understand. For example, the scientist might discover that the orbit of the earth in the Newtonian model is elliptical and thereby conclude that the orbit of the earth itself is also elliptical (or at least almost elliptical).

Theoretical modeling therefore presents us with certain puzzles. How can we make sense of the fact that a large part of scientific practice seems to involve talking and learning about things that do not exist? There are several questions here. First, how should we interpret scientists' *model descriptions* (that is, the equations and assumptions that scientists write down when they formulate a theoretical model)? Model descriptions look like descriptions of actual, concrete objects (model systems). And yet, as we have seen, there typically are no such objects. What, then, is the function of model descriptions? Second, how should we interpret scientists' subsequent talk in theoretical modeling, which seems to assume that there *are* model systems which the scientists are investigating? Martin Thomson-Jones (2007, 2010) refers to this aspect of modeling as the *face value practice*, since it appears to take model descriptions at face value, as descriptions of actual, concrete objects. If these objects don't exist, then what makes some of the statements scientists utter when they engage in the face value practice *correct* (e.g., that the model earth moves on an ellipse) and some *incorrect* (e.g., that the model earth spirals into the sun)? Third, how can we make sense of the idea that scientists are able to *learn* about model systems? It seems that the scientist who uses the Newtonian model can *discover* things about her model system, such as the shape of the earth's orbit or its time period. But how is this possible when there is no actual, concrete object whose behavior she can investigate? Of course, as well as these questions concerning the nature of theoretical models, we must also ask how it is that these models allow us to learn about the real world. How is it that finding out about the behavior of tiny billiard balls or perfect spheres allows us to learn about real gases or the planets in the solar system? As we shall see, different accounts of the nature of theoretical models suggest different ways of addressing this question as well.

## Abstract object views

The most common way to try to make sense of theoretical modeling is to claim that, although there is no actual, concrete object that satisfies scientists' model descriptions, there is some other object that does satisfy them. To borrow another term from Thomson-Jones (2007, 2010), most accounts of modeling posit *description-fitting objects* to serve as model systems. One popular version of this approach treats model systems as *abstract objects*. According to Ronald Giere (e.g., 1988, 1999a, 1999b, 2004), for example, model systems are abstract objects that are defined by scientists' model descriptions. Giere understands theoretical modeling as a two-stage process. In the first stage, the scientists' model description defines an abstract object, which is the model system. In the second stage, scientists use this model system to represent a real system. They do so by specifying its similarity to the real system in certain respects and to certain degrees. According to this account, then, scientists represent the world *indirectly*, via an (abstract) model system (Figure 33.1). This approach suggests answers to each of the questions introduced above. First, it appears to offer a way to understand scientists' model descriptions: these are *definitions* of abstract objects. Second, this approach also seems to make sense of

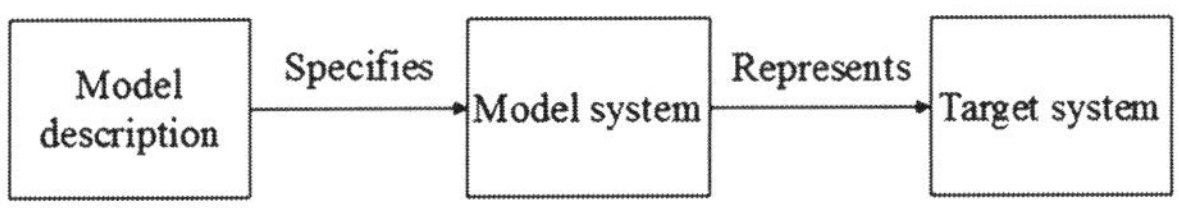


*Figure 33.1* Indirect views of modeling

scientists' subsequent talk in theoretical modeling. When scientists engage in the face value practice, it might be argued, they are simply making claims about an abstract object (their model system). Third, the abstract object view might allow us to explain how it is that we can learn about a model system. Learning about a theoretical model is a matter of finding out about the properties of an abstract object, in much the same way that learning about a physical model is finding out about the properties of an actual, concrete object.

The abstract object view of models has enjoyed considerable popularity and there are a number of different versions of this approach. Some of these understand models in more formal terms than Giere's account, as set-theoretical structures (Suppes 1960), trajectories through phase-space (Van Fraassen 1980), or mathematical structures more broadly construed (Weisberg 2013). Despite its popularity, however, the abstract object view of models also faces some challenges. First, it seems to have difficulty dealing with much of scientists' talk about models (Godfrey-Smith 2006; Thomson-Jones 2010). As we have seen, scientists often talk about model systems as if they were actual, concrete objects with spatiotemporal properties. For example, the model earth might be said to follow an elliptical orbit with a particular time period. And yet abstract objects are typically taken not to have spatiotemporal properties. The abstract object view seems to have trouble making sense of this way of talking about models. Second, critics have questioned whether the abstract object view can account for the relationship between models and the world (Hughes 1997; Thomson-Jones 2010). According to Giere (e.g., 1988, 2004), models are similar to the world in certain respects and to certain degrees. Normally, if we say two objects are similar, we mean that they share certain properties. And yet if models are abstract, it is difficult to see how they could be similar to real systems with respect to properties such as mass or time period. One response to this worry is to try to capture the relevant similarity using more formal notions, such as isomorphism (e.g., French and Ladyman 1999).

Third, some authors have argued that the abstract object view of models faces difficulties in accounting for theoretical models that are not mathematical (Downes 1992; Levy 2015). For example, descriptions of biological mechanisms are often given in concrete, nonmathematical terms, specifying the various parts of the mechanism and the way that they interact. Such descriptions are simplified and idealized in various ways, and commonly described as models by scientists themselves. And yet it is difficult to see how they can be incorporated into the abstract object view (for an attempt to do so see Weisberg 2013, 19). Finally, and perhaps most importantly, the abstract object view offers little explanation for the role that the imagination seems to play in scientific modeling. When scientists are engaged in modeling, it seems, they don't simply carry out various mathematical calculations. Instead, they imagine the concrete scenarios that the models invoke, like collections of billiard balls colliding with each other or populations of predators devouring their prey. This imaginative engagement seems to play an important role in the way that scientists develop models and explore their properties. And yet, if models are abstract objects they would seem to lack the concrete, visualizable properties that would allow them to be brought before the mind's eye in this way (Levy 2015). In response to this worry, Michael Weisberg (2013) argues that the abstract object view can still find room for the imagination to play an important role in modeling.

## Indirect fiction views

Recently, a number of philosophers of science have suggested that paying closer attention to the role of the imagination in modeling provides the key to understanding what models are and how they are used to represent the world. To develop this idea, many of these authors draw parallels between scientific modeling and other practices involving the imagination, especially our interaction with works of fiction. As discussed earlier, fiction-based accounts of modeling fall into two camps: *indirect fiction views* and *direct fiction views*. Proponents of indirect fiction views are struck by parallels between scientists' model systems and fictional characters. Peter Godfrey-Smith (2006, 734–735) introduces the idea in the following way:

> Roughly, we might say that model systems are often treated as "imagined concrete things" – things that are imaginary or hypothetical, but which would be concrete if they were real. … In making this argument, I take at face value the fact that modelers often *take* themselves to be describing imaginary biological populations, imaginary neural networks, or imaginary economies. An imaginary population is something that, if it was real, would be a flesh-and-blood population, not a mathematical object. Although these imagined entities are puzzling, I suggest that at least much of the time they might be treated as similar to something that we are all familiar with, the imagined objects of literary fiction.

According to the indirect fiction view, then, model systems should be understood in the same way as fictional characters, like Sherlock Holmes. When scientists put forward a theoretical model they ask us to imagine a fictional model system, just as Conan Doyle asks us to imagine the exploits of a fictional detective. This idea suggests a rather different approach to the various puzzles raised by theoretical modeling from that taken by the abstract object view. On the indirect fiction view, scientists' model descriptions are understood in the same manner as works of fiction that portray fictional characters. Consider the following passage from *The Hound of the Baskervilles*:

> Holmes leaned forward in his excitement and his eyes had the hard, dry glitter which shot from them when he was keenly interested.
>
> *(Conan Doyle 1902/2003, 22)*

Like scientists' model descriptions, it seems, there is no actual, concrete object that this passage describes: there is no real, flesh-and-blood detective that satisfies the description Conan Doyle gives of Holmes. And yet, just as scientists talk as if there were objects that satisfied their model descriptions, so we talk as if there were a Sherlock Holmes: we say that Holmes is highly intelligent, that he smokes a pipe and plays the violin. The indirect fiction view thus seems to offer us a way to make sense of scientists' engagement in the face value practice: it is to be understood in the same way as our talk about fictional characters. Finally, this approach suggests that there is nothing too mysterious in the idea that scientists can discover properties of model systems that go beyond those specified in their model description. After all, fictional characters have properties that go beyond those explicitly described in the text. We assume that Sherlock Holmes has a heart, and that he needs oxygen to survive, even if Conan Doyle never bothers to mention this in the story.

The indirect fiction view has a number of advantages over the abstract object view of models. First, recall that the abstract object view had difficulty accounting for the fact that scientists often talk about model systems as if they were concrete objects and ascribe spatiotemporal properties to them. We often attribute spatiotemporal properties to fictional characters, however. We say that Holmes is tall, for example, or that he lived at 221B Baker Street. Second, we saw that, if model systems are abstract, it would be difficult to see how they could be similar to real systems in any straightforward sense. But we seem to have no problem comparing fictional characters to the world. We say that Holmes is more intelligent than any real detective or compare our political situation today to that in Orwell's *1984*. The indirect fiction view also has no difficulty accounting for models that are introduced in nonmathematical terms, or even using pictures or diagrams. Fictional characters may be represented in many different ways. When they were first published in *The Strand Magazine*, the Sherlock Holmes stories featured line drawings illustrating the great detective's exploits. Finally, unlike the abstract object view, the indirect fiction view puts the imagination center stage in its account of models.

Despite its attractions, the indirect fiction view faces a number of challenges. First, critics have asked what determines the properties of model systems in this approach (Weisberg 2013, ch. 4). The indirect fiction view claims that model systems have properties that go beyond those specified in the model description, just as fictional characters have properties that go beyond those mentioned in the text. Spelling out the principles that "fill out" fictional worlds in this way has proved difficult, however. One natural proposal, sometimes called the *reality principle*, suggests that we take fictional worlds to be as much like the real world as possible, unless the text explicitly tells us otherwise (Walton 1990, ch. 4). So even if the London of *The Hound of the Baskervilles* is unlike the real Victorian London in being home to the world's greatest detective, we still assume that it is the capital of the United Kingdom, that the people who live there have blood in their veins, and so on. In the case of fiction, the reality principle faces a number of problems. For example, it seems to result in an explosion in the content of fictional worlds: if we follow the reality principle, it will be part of the content of *The Hound of the Baskervilles* that the Second World War ended in 1945 and the Berlin Wall fell in 1989, since nothing in the story contradicts this. Parallel problems arise in the case of theoretical models. Presumably, we don't wish to count it as part of the content of the Newtonian model that the earth's atmosphere contains 78 percent nitrogen and 21 percent oxygen, that the sun produces energy through nuclear fusion, and so on. Models also seem to pose their own difficulties. One issue is that some features of the mathematics in model descriptions are not carried over to model systems, because they have no physical interpretation. When we read the equations for the predator-prey model, for example, we know that we are not supposed to imagine noninteger numbers of foxes or rabbits.

One challenge for proponents of the indirect fiction view, then, is to spell out the principles that determine the properties of model systems. A second objection to the indirect fiction view concerns its starting point, namely the prevalence of the face value practice in modeling. As we saw, a major motivation behind the appeal to fiction was that scientists often talk about model systems as if they were concrete objects. But critics argue that this is not always the case: sometimes models are presented in highly abstract mathematical terms and have no obvious concrete interpretation (Weisberg 2013, ch. 4). While the indirect fiction view might be able to accommodate such cases, they would seem to undermine at least some of the initial motivation behind the approach. Perhaps more seriously, it might also be argued that such cases are beyond the reach of our imagination. Can we really imagine complex probability distributions, for example, or high-dimensional vector spaces?

Finally, the most obvious challenge for the indirect fiction view concerns the ontology of model systems. The indirect fiction view compares model systems to fictional characters. Unfortunately, the nature of fictional characters is notoriously unclear, and is itself the subject of long-standing debate. *Realists* about fictional characters argue that, even if he is not a regular, flesh-and-blood detective, we must grant Holmes *some* form of existence if we want to make sense of fictional characters. Realists therefore posit *fictional entities* and offer different accounts of the nature of these entities. For example, Alexius Meinong (1904/1960) famously draws a distinction between *being* and *existence*. On this view, Holmes possesses all the properties that we normally take him to have, like living at 221B and smoking a pipe. It is simply that, unlike a regular detective, he lacks the property of existence. Other realists argue that fictional entities are abstract entities of some kind (Van Inwagen 1977; Thomasson 1999). By contrast, *antirealists* try to make sense of fictional characters and our talk about them without positing fictional entities (e.g., Russell 1905/1956; Walton 1990). The best known antirealist theory follows Bertrand Russell (1905/1956) and analyzes a sentence like "Holmes smokes a pipe" as the claim that "there exists exactly one $x$ such that $x$ satisfies the Holmes description and $x$ smokes a pipe." The statement "Holmes smokes a pipe" is then perfectly meaningful and contains no reference to any fictional entity. The trouble is that "Holmes smokes a pipe" is now judged to be false, along with claims like "Holmes is an idiot." And yet intuitively there seems to be an important difference between these claims. (For an excellent overview of the issues raised by fictional characters, see Friend 2007.) Given the ongoing dispute between realists and antirealists, comparing model systems to fictional characters seems to offer little chance of progress.

Proponents of the indirect fiction view have responded to this challenge concerning the ontology of model systems in two main ways. First, some authors have argued that philosophers of science may simply defer problems concerning the ontology of fictional characters to philosophers of fiction. In this vein, Godfrey-Smith (2006, 735) suggests that we might accept such objects as part of the "folk ontology" of scientific modeling, even if in the end we require an account of these objects "for general philosophical reasons" (for a similar view, see Giere 2009). The difficulty with this approach is that the indirect fiction view threatens to become more of a promissory note than a fully fledged account of what is going on in scientific modeling. For example, consider the problem of explaining how model systems represent the world. Proponents of the indirect fiction view often describe the relationship between model systems and the world in terms of similarity or resemblance (Giere 2009; Godfrey-Smith 2006). And yet if, in the end, we were to adopt an antirealist account of fictional characters, then we would conclude that, strictly speaking, there are no model systems. As a result, all talk of similarity or resemblance between model systems and the world would have to be radically reinterpreted. (For a discussion of this "deferral strategy," see Thomson-Jones 2007.)

The second way in which proponents of the indirect fiction view have responded to the ontological challenge is to draw on existing theories of fiction. Thus, Roman Frigg (2010a, 2010b) has proposed a version of the indirect fiction view that draws on an influential theory of fiction due to Kendall Walton (1990). According to Walton, the text of a novel functions as a "prop" in games of make-believe: when we read the text, we are supposed to engage in certain imaginings according to the rules appropriate for works of that kind (Walton 1990, ch. 2). (See "Imagination and fiction," Chapter 15 of this volume.) Frigg offers an application of Walton's theory to scientists' model descriptions. In this account, when we read the model description for the Newtonian model of the solar system, "we imagine an entity which has all the properties that the description specifies. The result of this process is the *model-system*, the fictional scenario which is the vehicle of our reasoning: an imagined entity consisting of two spheres, etc." (Frigg 2010b, 133; emphasis in original). After imagining her model system, the scientist goes on to connect it to the real system. In this case, for example, she might specify that "the sphere with mass $m_e$ in the model-system corresponds to the earth and the sphere with mass $m_s$ to the sun" (134). Once this is done, she can "start translating facts about the model system into claims about the world" (135).

Walton's theory is antirealist concerning fictional characters. Frigg's account thus promises to preserve the structure of the indirect view of modeling while avoiding positing fictional entities to serve as model systems. The account has also been subject to criticism, however. Godfrey-Smith (2009) argues that, although it avoids positing fictional entities, Frigg's approach is committed to uninstantiated properties, which are equally mysterious (see also Levy 2015). Toon (2012, ch. 2) argues that an antirealist stance on model systems is at odds with Frigg's overall, indirect view of modeling. (For a more realist take on the comparison between model systems and fictional characters, see Contessa 2010.)

## Direct fiction views

Both the abstract object and the indirect fiction views claim that modelers represent the world indirectly, via model systems (see Figure 33.1). Direct fiction views reject this claim. According to direct fiction views, there are no model systems. Instead, scientists represent the world directly, by asking us to imagine things about it (Figure 33.2). Adam Toon (2010, 2012) develops this approach by drawing on Walton's theory of fiction, while Arnon Levy (2015) defends a similar view based on Walton's work on metaphor (Walton 1993). Recall that the indirect fiction view treats model descriptions like passages about fictional characters. By contrast, Toon (2012) introduces the direct fiction view by comparing model descriptions to works of fiction that represent real people, places and events. Consider the following passage, from Robert Graves' novel *I, Claudius*:

> Augustus assumed Antony's Eastern conquests as his own and became, as Livia had intended, the sole ruler of the Roman world.
>
> *(Graves 1934/2006, 23)*

In Walton's analysis, this passage is not about any fictional character, but about the real Emperor Augustus, as well as his wife Livia and Mark Antony. *I, Claudius* represents these people by asking us to imagine propositions about them. Some of these propositions are true, such as that Augustus defeated Mark Antony. Others appear to be entirely fabricated by Graves and so are probably false, such as that Augustus was manipulated by the scheming Livia. The direct fiction view understands model descriptions in the same way. When the scientist introduces the Newtonian model of the solar system, she does not conjure up any abstract or fictional model system. Instead, she asks us to imagine things about the solar system itself. Specifically, we are asked to imagine that the sun and earth are perfect spheres with certain masses, that they interact only with each other, and so on. Some of this is true (e.g., that the earth and sun have certain masses) while some is known to be false (e.g., that they interact only with each other).

The direct fiction view thus offers a way to interpret scientists' model descriptions: these are prescriptions to imagine the world in a certain way. Put in Walton's terms, model descriptions are "props" in games of make-believe which prescribe imaginings about real systems. Interpreting model descriptions in this way means we need not posit abstract or fictional objects to serve as model systems. This might seem to cause problems when it comes

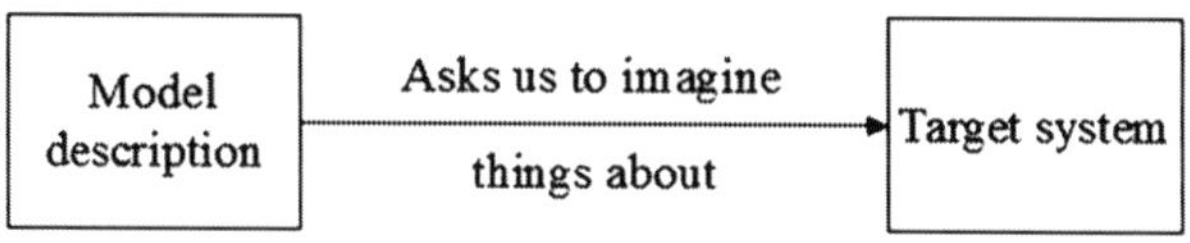


*Figure 33.2* The direct fiction view of modeling

to interpreting the face value practice, however. As we have seen, scientists talk as if there were objects that satisfied their model description. How can a direct view make sense of this? Toon (2012) offers a deflationary analysis of such talk. According to this analysis, when scientists talk about theoretical models as objects, we should not take this talk too seriously. Instead, they are engaging in pretense, "going along with" the model to tell us what it asks us to imagine. For example, if a scientist tells us that "the sun and earth are isolated from the other planets," she is not describing an abstract or fictional object; she is simply telling us that the model asks us to imagine this about the sun and earth.

The direct fiction view also aims to explain how we can learn about models without positing model systems. In this approach, learning about a model is not a matter of discovering facts about an abstract or fictional model system; it is a matter of exploring the web of imaginings prescribed by a scientist's model description. For example, the Newtonian model description asks us to imagine that various assumptions hold of the sun and earth, such as that the force between them obeys Newton's law of gravitation. If we accept these initial assumptions, however, we are also to imagine that the earth moves in an ellipse, since this follows from the equation that we write down. This is simply part of the conventions that govern our interpretation of model descriptions. That the earth moves in an ellipse is therefore part of the content of the model, even though this was not specified in the model description.

The direct fiction view has a number of advantages. Like the indirect fiction view, it acknowledges the importance of the imagination in scientific modeling and explains why modelers think and talk about models as if they were concrete objects. At the same time, it is a deflationary position that avoids the ontological problems posed by fictional characters. Critics have raised a number of objections against this approach, however. First, some have argued that the direct view fails to capture the practice of modeling. Thus, Weisberg (2007, 2013) argues that what distinguishes modeling from other forms of theorizing is precisely that it is indirect. Modelers try to understand real systems by first constructing a model system. By eliminating model systems, Weisberg argues, the direct view fails to capture this crucial aspect of modeling. In response, supporters of the direct view might agree that modelers talk as if they were constructing a model system and that this way of talking is distinctive of modeling as a theoretical practice. They simply deny that such talk should be mirrored in our metaphysical picture of what is really going on in this practice.

A second objection to the direct fiction view is that some models lack "targets," that is, they do not represent any real system (Contessa 2010; Weisberg 2007). For example, a predator-prey model might invite us to consider a population consisting of two species, predator and prey, whose numbers are governed by certain equations. And yet it might do so without claiming to represent any real population of, say, foxes and rabbits out in the world. In response, Toon (2012, ch. 3) suggests that such cases may also be understood in terms of make-believe. Taking a different line, Levy (2015) argues that many apparently "targetless" models turn out either to have targets after all, or should be regarded not as models but simply pieces of mathematics.

Finally, critics have questioned whether the direct fiction view can account for the relationship between models and the world. As we have seen, this relationship is often thought of in terms of similarities between model systems and the world. And yet the direct view denies the existence of model systems. As a result, it seems that proponents of the direct view must find a different way of thinking about the relationship between models and the world. Toon (2012, ch. 3) suggests we think of this relationship in terms of the truth or falsity of the imaginings that a model prescribes, while Levy (2015) suggests we may better understand this relationship by invoking the notion of "partial truth" (Yablo 2014).

## Physical models

So far we have focused on theoretical modeling. What about physical modeling? Does imagination play any role here? We might think that the imagination is less important in physical modeling since in these cases we have an actual, concrete object that serves as the model. Why would a scientist need to use her imagination when the model is right there in front of her on the lab bench? In fact, however, there are reasons to think that the imagination might also play an important role in physical modeling. Toon (2011) describes an empirical study examining the use of plastic "ball-and-stick" models of molecules. One finding of this study is that people who build and manipulate molecular models routinely talk as if they were building and manipulating the molecules themselves. Toon argues that we may make sense of this way of talking, as well as other aspects of the practice of molecular modeling, by understanding molecular models in a similar way to children's dolls or toy trucks. In this view, scientists imagine their plastic ball-and-stick models to be molecules, in much the same way that children imagine a doll to be a baby.

On this approach, both theoretical *and* physical models are understood as props in games of make-believe. There remain important differences between the two, however. One key difference between theoretical and physical models concerns the forms of imaginative *participation* that they allow. When we participate in a game of make-believe, we ourselves prescribe imaginings within the game. For example, if a child raises a cup to a doll, the children playing the game are to imagine that she is feeding the baby. Some games allow for more participation than others. According to Walton (1990), in the games we play with paintings, looking at a painting of Napoleon counts as looking at Napoleon. However, picking up the painting doesn't count as picking up Napoleon. On the other hand, picking up a doll *does* count as picking up a baby.

The games we play with dolls thus allow for a greater degree of participation than those we play with paintings. In a similar manner, models also differ in the degree of participation that they allow. As we saw, the direct fiction view understands the face value practice as a form of *verbal* participation in make-believe: when scientists talk about model systems, they are engaging in acts of (verbal) pretense within the game prescribed by the model. Physical models allow for a much greater degree of participation, however. For example, Toon (2011) argues that ball-and-stick molecular models allow for *visual* and *tactile* participation. In this view, scientists learn about the world using molecular models by conducting *imagined experiments*, imagining the various actions that they carry out on the models to be carried out on the molecule instead. In this way, scientists imagine themselves looking at molecules, putting them together and feeling them resist as they try to twist them or pull them apart. Focusing on the role of the imagination might thus help us to understand the way that scientists use physical models to learn about the world. (For more on physical models, see de Chadarevian and Hopwood 2004; Sterrett 2002; Weisberg 2013.)

## Conclusion

Modeling is central to scientists' attempts to understand the world. While it seems clear that modeling often involves the imagination, it is only recently that philosophers of science have begun to place the imagination at the center of their accounts of what models are and how they represent the world. Many of these accounts draw on parallels with fiction. According to indirect fiction views, scientists' model descriptions are like passages about fictional characters. By contrast, direct fiction views compare model descriptions to works of fiction that represent real people, places or events. Deciding between these approaches is likely to involve a trade-off between competing philosophical aims: while indirect views seem to remain closer to scientists' own talk about modeling, direct views appear to involve fewer troublesome metaphysical commitments. Whichever approach we follow, paying closer attention to the role of the imagination promises to provide a richer understanding of the practice of modeling and the crucial role it plays in scientific inquiry.

## Further reading

R. Giere, *Explaining Science: A Cognitive Approach* (Chicago: University of Chicago Press, 1988) offers an influential indirect account of modeling. M. Weisberg, *Simulation and Similarity: Using Models to Understand the World* (Oxford: Oxford University Press, 2013) is a recent defense of the abstract object view. P. Godfrey-Smith, "The Strategy of Model-Based Science," *Biology & Philosophy* 21 (2006) and R. Frigg, "Models and Fiction," *Synthese* 172 (2010) endorse the indirect fiction view. A. Toon, *Models as Make-Believe: Imagination, Fiction and Scientific Representation* (Basingstoke: Palgrave Macmillan, 2012) and A. Levy, "Modeling without Models," *Philosophical Studies* 172 (2015) both develop versions of the direct fiction view. S. de Chadarevian and N. Hopwood (eds.) *Models: The Third Dimension of Science* (Stanford: Stanford University Press, 2004) is an excellent collection of essays on physical models.

## References

Cartwright, N. (1983) *How the Laws of Physics Lie*, Oxford: Clarendon.
Conan Doyle, A. (1902/2003) *The Hound of the Baskervilles*, London: Penguin.
Contessa, G. (2010) "Scientific Models and Fictional Objects," *Synthese* 172(2): 215–229.
de Chadarevian, S., and N. Hopwood (eds.) (2004) *Models: The Third Dimension of Science*, Stanford: Stanford University Press.
Downes, S. (1992) "The Importance of Models in Theorizing: A Deflationary Semantic View," in D. Hull, M. Forbes, and K. Okruhlik (eds.) *PSA: Proceedings of the Biennial Meeting of the Philosophy of Science Association* 1: 142–153.
French, S., and J. Ladyman (1999) "Reinflating the Semantic Approach," *International Studies in the Philosophy of Science* 13(2): 103–121.
Friend , S. (2007) "Fictional Characters," *Philosophy Compass* 2: 141–156.
Frigg, R. (2010a) "Models and Fiction," *Synthese* 172(2): 251–268.
Frigg, R. (2010b) "Fiction and Scientific Representation," in R. Frigg and M. Hunter (eds.) *Beyond Mimesis and Convention: Representation in Art and Science*, Dordrecht: Springer.
Giere, R. (1988) *Explaining Science*, Chicago: University of Chicago Press.
Giere, R. (1999a) *Science without Laws*, Chicago: University of Chicago Press.
Giere, R. (1999b) "Using Models to Represent Reality," in L. Magnani, N.J. Nersessian, and P. Thagard (eds.) *Model-Based Reasoning and Scientific Discovery*, Dordrecht: Kluwer Academic/Plenum Publishers.
Giere, R. (2004) "How Models Are Used to Represent Reality," *Philosophy of Science* 71: 742–752.
Giere, R. (2009) "Why Scientific Models Should Not Be Regarded as Works of Fiction," in M. Suárez (ed.) *Fictions in Science: Philosophical Essays on Modeling and Idealization*, London: Routledge.
Godfrey-Smith, P. (2006) "The Strategy of Model-Based Science," *Biology & Philosophy* 21: 725–740.
Graves, R. (1934/2006) *I, Claudius*, London: Penguin.
Hughes, R.I.G. (1997) "Models and Representation," *Philosophy of Science* 64: S325–S336.
Levy, A. (2015) "Modeling without Models," *Philosophical Studies* 172(3): 781–798.
Meinong, A. (1904/1960) "The Theory of Objects," in R.M. Chisholm (ed.) *Realism and the Background of Phenomenology*, New York: Free Press.
Russell , B. (1905/1956) "On Denoting," in R.C. Marsh (ed.) *Logic and Knowledge*, London: George Allen & Unwin, 41–56. (Original work published 1905.)
Sterrett, S.G. (2002) "Physical Models and Fundamental Laws: Using One Piece of the World to Tell about Another," *Mind & Society* 5: 51–66.
Suppes, P. (1960) "A Comparison of the Meaning and Use of Models in Mathematics and the Empirical Sciences," *Synthese* 12: 287–300.
Thomasson, A. (1999) *Fiction and Metaphysics*, Cambridge: Cambridge University Press.

Thomson-Jones, M. (2007) "Missing Systems and the Face Value Practice," <http://philsci-archive.pitt.edu/archive/00003519>. (Longer manuscript version of Thomson-Jones 2010.)
Thomson-Jones, M. (2010) "Missing Systems and the Face Value Practice," *Synthese* 172(2): 283–299.
Toon, A. (2010) "The Ontology of Theoretical Modeling: Models as Make-Believe," *Synthese* 172(2): 301–315.
Toon, A. (2011) "Playing with Molecules," *Studies in History and Philosophy of Science* 42: 580–589.
Toon, A. (2012) *Models as Make-Believe: Imagination, Fiction and Scientific Representation*, Basingstoke: Palgrave Macmillan.
Van Fraassen, B. (1980) *The Scientific Image*, Oxford: Clarendon.
Van Inwagen, P. (1977) "Creatures of Fiction," *American Philosophical Quarterly* 14: 299–308.
Walton, K. (1990) *Mimesis as Make-Believe: On the Foundations of the Representational Arts*, Cambridge, MA: Harvard University Press.
Walton, K. (1993) "Metaphor and Prop Oriented Make-Believe," *European Journal of Philosophy* 1: 39–57.
Weisberg, M. (2007) "Who Is a Modeler?" *British Journal for Philosophy of Science* 58(2): 207–233.
Weisberg, M. (2013) *Simulation and Similarity: Using Models to Understand the World*, Oxford: Oxford University Press.
Yablo, S. (2014) *Aboutness*, Princeton: Princeton University Press.

# 34
# IMAGINATION IN MATHEMATICS

*Andrew Arana*

The eminent mathematician Felix Klein wrote, in his intimate history of nineteenth-century mathematics, that "mathematics is not merely a matter of understanding but quite essentially a matter of imagination" (see Klein 1979, 207). Klein was responding to the turbulent trajectory of imagination's role in mathematics during the nineteenth century, which began with Gaspard Monge teaching new ways of representing three-dimensional figures in the plane to engineers at the École Polytechnique in Paris, and ended with Moritz Pasch fulminating against visualization in geometry. In that light Klein's remark concerns imagination as representation of the visual. But there is another sense of imagination that mathematicians frequently employ: imagination as the ability to think of novel solutions to problems – in other words, ingenuity.

This twofold usage of the term "imagination" was characterized by Voltaire, in his entry on imagination in the *Encyclopédie*, as distinguishing between what he called the "passive" and "active" faculties of imagination. Both are faculties of every "sensible being" by which one is able "to represent to one's mind sensible things" (see Diderot and d'Alembert 1765, 560). The passive imagination consists in the ability "to retain a simple impression of objects," while the active imagination consists in the ability "to arrange these received objects, and combine them in a thousand ways." The active imagination is thus the faculty of invention, and is linked with genius, in particular in mathematics: "there is an astonishing imagination in mathematical practice, and Archimedes had at least as much imagination as Homer" (ibid., 561).

This distinction between imagination as faculty of representation and as faculty of reconstruction, however dubious it may be as cognitive science (on this, see Currie and Ravenscroft 2002), organizes well the two primary ways that mathematicians and philosophers have understood the nature and role of imagination in mathematics. This essay will focus on just the first of these ways, since the second would make for a study of discovery in mathematics, demanding consideration of a rather different set of issues than those called for by the first (see Hadamard 1945 for such a study for mathematics, as well as Dustin Stokes, "Imagination and creativity," Chapter 18 of this volume). It will consider imagination in mathematics in the first sense from a historical point of view, noting the key moments in its conception during the ancient, modern and contemporary eras.

## 1 Imagination in mathematics in the classical era

Aristotle (1993) characterized imagination as "that in virtue of which we say that an image occurs to us" (428a1–2), and this seems to have been the basic functional view of imagination in antiquity: a mental faculty capable of receiving and reproducing presentations of the senses. Aristotle also held that imagination can also produce images when no sense perception has taken place, as it does in dreams (428a6), and is thus capable of augmenting thought by unseen images that are presumably close to what has been seen before. This is an important accommodation since Aristotle seems to hold that all thought, even speculative thought, requires images (432a3; also see Deborah K.W. Modrak, "Aristotle on *phantasia*," Chapter 1 of this volume).

The role of imagination in ancient mathematics was most evident in the reasoning of geometric practice, in which one ordinarily reasoned with diagrams. To illustrate this role, let's briefly consider an example from Euclid. In the first proposition of *Elements* Book I, Euclid considers the problem of constructing an equilateral triangle (Figure 34.1). Given a line segment $AB$ to be a side of the triangle, Euclid produces two circles with radius $AB$, centered at $A$ and $B$, respectively. Let $C$ denote one of the points where the two circles intersect, and consider the triangle $\Delta ABC$. Since $AC$ and $BC$ are also radii of their circles, it follows that the three sides are equal, and thus $\Delta ABC$ is equilateral.

In Greek practice this argument makes essential use of its diagram, as has been cogently argued in Manders (2008). Such reasoning is characteristic of ancient geometric practice. This highlights the central role of visualization and hence imagination in ancient geometric reasoning, indicating in particular the *evidential* role of imagination in Greek geometry. This role is invoked by the Greek mathematical texts themselves. Reviel Netz (1999, 52–56; 2009) has shown that these texts refer to imagination as a cognitive exercise permitting representation of parts of diagrams that are not in the diagram as physical artifact (for instance, as drawn on paper). These texts ask the reasoner to imagine parts of diagrams that would clutter the artifact or would require trying to produce a third dimension in a two-dimensional medium, both representational difficulties that would impede the diagram's usability in reasoning. Thus these texts call on the reasoner to supplement her visual apprehension of the diagram with purely mental manipulations of her representation of the diagram, in order to permit the demanded reasoning.

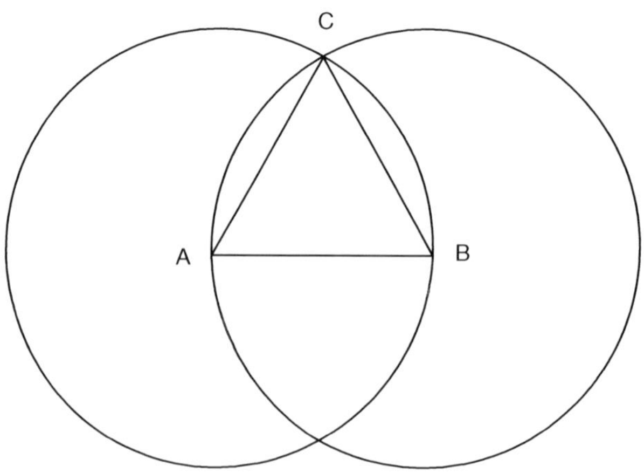


*Figure 34.1* Diagram for *Elements* Proposition I.1

In contrast, Plato famously judged geometers who described their thinking in terms of productions or constructions, physical or mental, as confused. Texts like those described by Netz are, according to Plato (2004, 527a), "ridiculous accounts" of geometry, given by geometers who "speak like practical men, and all their accounts refer to doing things." This is ridiculous, writes Plato, because in fact geometers produce arguments that "are for the sake of knowing what always is, not what comes into being and passes away … for geometry is knowledge of what always is" (527b). Indeed if geometry is to produce knowledge rather than mere opinion it must shun apprehension by construction with its apparent temporality. Thus Plato's conception of mathematical knowledge seems to leave no place for imagination.

While Plato's views were at odds with Greek geometric practice, his influence ensured that these views would continue to be engaged by ancients thinking about mathematical practice (see O'Meara 1989). Of particular importance is the Neoplatonist Proclus, since his commentary on the first book of Euclid's *Elements* would be well-known in the early modern era by being included in standard translations of the *Elements*. Writing in late antiquity with access to geometrical and philosophical texts that are now lost, Proclus sought to make sense of the constructive tradition of Greek geometry while remaining true to Plato's insistence upon the eternality of the objects of mathematical knowledge. He reconciled these by distinguishing the role of the understanding from that of the imagination in geometrical thinking: "the understanding contains the ideas but, being unable to see them when they are wrapped up, unfolds and exposes them and presents them to the imagination sitting in the vestibule" (Proclus [1992] 44). He explained this "blindness" of the understanding to the ideas of geometry as follows:

> We invoke the imagination and the intervals that it furnishes, since the form itself is without motion or genesis, indivisible and free of all underlying matter, though the elements latent in the form are produced distinctly and individually on the screen of imagination. What projects the images is the understanding; the source of what is projected is the form in the understanding; and what they are projected in is this "passive nous" that unfolds in revolution about the partlessness of genuine Nous.
> *(Proclus 1992, 45)*

Thus the geometrical knower is agent to productions of the imagination, whereby the forms contemplated by the understanding are projected onto the imagination as if onto a screen with the aid of the imagination itself.[1]

Proclus described these projections as "movement[s] of our thought," whereby the constructions of geometry would take place. As he stressed, "it is in the imagination that the constructions, sectionings, positions, comparisons, additions, and subtractions take place, whereas the contents of our understanding all stand fixed, without any generation or change" (Proclus 1992, 64). By means of this epistemological framework Proclus maintained that geometrical knowledge is both produced by construction and arrived at by contemplation of the eternal and unchanging.

According to Proclus, then, knowledge of geometrical propositions like Euclid I.1 comes about by the geometer apprehending her constructions by means of imagination, conceptualized like a writing surface on which figures can be produced. Michael Detlefsen has highlighted Proclus' view as providing a foundation for what he calls a "presentist" conception of the rigor of mathematical proofs, on which the rigor of a proof "consist[s] primarily in the keeping of an object continuously before the visual imagination or intuition of the prover during the course of a proof" (Detlefsen 2005, 237). Detlefsen identifies this presentist conception of rigor as operative in classical synthetic geometry, in which constructive, diagrammatic proofs like those of Euclid I.1 were the norm.[2]

The presentist conception of rigor would be challenged in the modern era as a competing formalist ideal of proof arose with the development of algebraic methods. Conceptions of the role of imagination in mathematical thinking shifted alongside the rise of algebraic methods. The next section traces this cluster of changes in modern mathematics.

## 2 Imagination in mathematics in the modern era

The Middle Ages saw the locus of geometric investigation move to the Arab world, where geometers continued in the classical tradition with initial excursions into algebra (see Rommevaux [2009]). In the sixteenth century the Latin translations by Francesco Barozzi and Federico Commandino of Pappus, Euclid, Proclus and other classical mathematical texts inaugurated a resurgence of interest in geometry in the Renaissance West. The Jesuit Christoph Clavius reformed the mathematics education of his order's schools (including La Flèche, where Descartes would be educated), publishing his own edition of the *Elements* as well as a text on algebra that brought together Italian and German advances in the theory of equations birthed in the Arab world (see Sasaki 2003, ch. 2).

In addition to the expected Aristotelianism, Clavius' writings evinced Neoplatonist leanings reflecting his interest in Proclus, and these leanings would influence in particular reflections on the role of imagination in mathematics in the seventeenth century. For instance, the Neoplatonist Giuseppe Biancani published in 1615 a commentary on the parts of Aristotle's work that address mathematics, and included a supplement on the nature of mathematics. Biancani differentiated reasoning and imagination following Plato's discussions of each in Book VII of the *Republic*, arguing that reasoning rather than imagination is the source of mathematical knowledge, since "anyone who considers geometrical demonstrations will clearly see that they work not by flimsy imagination, but by very complicated reasonings, for there are many in which fifty to sixty inferences are connected to one another ... but imagination lacks any inferences" (see Mancosu 1996, 199–200).

Views toward imagination in mathematics shifted in a genuinely new way with René Descartes. Until the 1630s, Descartes' mathematical accomplishments were an extension of the constructive tradition of classical geometry, furthering a program that had been started by François Viète (see Viète 1983). Classical geometers concerned themselves with the construction of figures, but they characteristically took the methods legitimate for such construction to be restricted in certain ways (e.g., to ruler and compass). The ancient consensus seems to have been that the knowledge of figures produced by construction, and of those constructions themselves, was warranted only to the extent that those constructions consisted of motions that were traceable with sufficient *exactness*. Certain constructions, like that of the spiral (sweep a ray fixed at a central point at a uniform speed while also uniformly moving a point along that ray, and trace a curve by that moving point) were judged to be "mechanical" and hence inexact by, e.g., Pappus, but the ancients never satisfactorily articulated a criterion of which constructions were adequately exact.

Pursuing this unresolved ancient issue, in *La Géométrie* Descartes posited that the legitimate curves were those that can be "imagined to be traced by a continuous motion or by several successive motions where the latter ones are entirely regulated by those which precede" (AT 6: 390; see Descartes 1902). These constructions were to be carried out using instruments, and since his early twenties Descartes had been developing new compasses that satisfied this "single motion" criterion (see Bos 2001, 237–251). By noting that these constructions could be "imagined" rather than carried out publicly, Descartes was endorsing a view of imagination's role in geometrical knowledge that he had inherited from Proclus. A more explicit endorsement of this view was given by Descartes' contemporary Johannes Molther, who wrote as follows:

> But if someone would judge that geometry at its most pure should be practiced just by action of the mind and based only on its postulates, then even he would idealize, by mathematical abstraction, the ideas of a material ruler, or a compass, and he would grasp these ideas in his mind so that rulers and compasses would do their work by an interior sense in the imagination. And thus it would be easy to imagine thinkingly the process of which we have shown how it is performed in reality.
>
> *(see Bos 2001, 200)*

As a consequence of this view, the legitimacy of a method of construction was determinable by whether that method could be carried out in the imagination with adequate clarity and distinctness. Thus Descartes held that constructions meeting his "single motion" criterion of geometric legitimacy were as legitimate in geometry as the classical constructions using just ruler and compasses, because all such constructions required the imagination to control only one motion at a time. By contrast, the usual construction of a spiral demanded the control of two independent motions.[3] While in *La Géométrie* Descartes offered no explanation of why the single motion criterion should determine which constructions are legitimate in geometry, he offered considerations that permit such an explanation in *La Dioptrique*, published alongside *La Géométrie* with the *Discours de la Méthode* in 1637. In *La Dioptrique* he wrote that "it is impossible to see more than one sole object at a time distinctly" (AT 6: 163), so that a construction demanding visual attention to more than one object, as in the case of the spiral, could not be carried out with adequate distinctness to generate knowledge of the resulting curve.[4] Thus Descartes' justification for his extension of classical geometry to new methods of construction rested on a psychological commitment concerning the limits of visual attention, and by virtue of the close connection between vision and imagination for Descartes, of the limits of imagination (see Dennis Sepper, "Descartes," Chapter 2 of this volume).

As Rabouin (2010) has argued, Descartes did not develop his method of applying algebra to geometry until the early 1630s. This work, published in *La Géométrie* in 1637, brought about a dramatic shift in views toward imagination in mathematics. Though not the first work suggesting that algebra could be applied to geometry (see Panza 2007 for details on the Arabic tradition preceding the Cartesian turn), it presented a systematic program for such application. This application of algebra to geometry permitted the solution of geometrical problems by means of calculations for which one need have no visual representation of the relevant quantities in order to carry out.

To illustrate this new method of geometric problem-solving, let us consider a particularly clear example taken from Bernard Lamy's textbook (Lamy 1692, 315–317), an important text in the diffusion of Descartes' methods in the seventeenth century. For $\Delta BAC$ an isosceles triangle, Lamy raises the problem of cutting the sides $AB$ and $AC$ by a line $DE$ parallel to the base $BC$ such that $DB = DE$. Lamy presents two solutions to this problem, to show how a purely geometrical ("synthetic") solution differs from a solution that applies algebra.

In the first solution (see the left diagram of Figure 34.2), we begin by bisecting $\angle ABC$. Let $E$ denote the point where the bisecting line cuts $AC$. Construct a line parallel to $BC$ through $E$, and call this segment $DE$. Then $\angle CBE$ and $\angle DEB$ are alternating angles and hence congruent. Since $\angle CBE$ and $\angle DBE$ are congruent by bisection, it follows that $\angle DBE$ and $\angle DEB$ are congruent. Then $\Delta DBE$ is isosceles, and so $DB = DE$, as we wanted to produce.

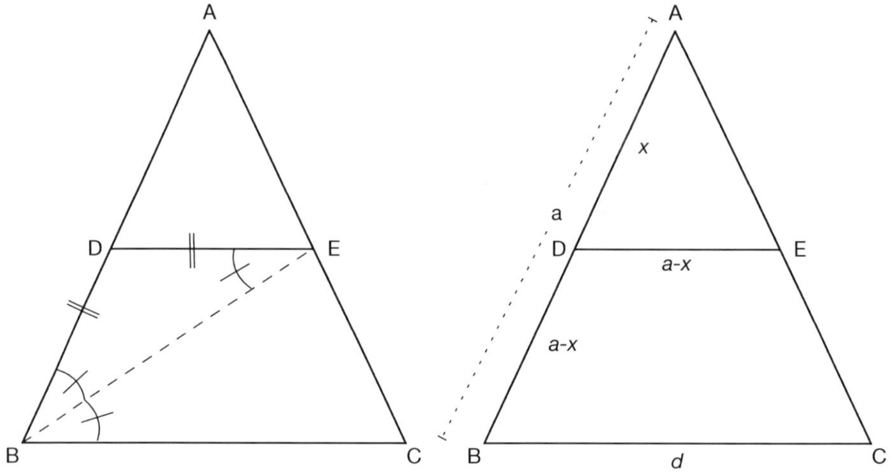


*Figure 34.2* Diagrams for Lamy's example

In the second solution (see the right diagram of Figure 34.2), let $a$ denote the given quantities $AB = AC$, and let $d$ denote $BC$. Let $D$ denote a point between $A$ and $B$, and let $x$ be $AD$, so that $DB$ has length $a - x$. We want to find $x$ such that $DE$ also has length $a - x$. Since $\Delta ADE$ and $\Delta ABC$ are similar triangles, we have that

(1)
$$\frac{a}{d} = \frac{x}{a - x}.$$

Then

$$xd = a(a - x) = a^2 - ax$$

which implies that

$$a^2 = xd + ax = x\,(d + a),$$

and thus

$$x = \frac{a^2}{d + a},$$

the quantity we wanted to find.

As noted earlier, the first solution relies on purely geometrical reasoning, while the second uses algebraic reasoning as well. Note that the algebraic reasoning in the second proof is not interpreted geometrically; after establishing the ratio (1) geometrically, the solution proceeds algebraically, with a series of computations that are not interpreted geometrically, and need not be in order for the solution to succeed.

Descartes lauded his method for providing proofs with the latter characteristic. As he put it in the *Discours*, ancient geometry was "always so attached to the consideration of figures that it cannot exercise the understanding without greatly tiring the imagination" (AT 6: 17–18). The algebraic steps of his method permitted the solver to avoid imagining the figures being considered, and thus afforded a significant economy of thought. As Descartes knew, the solutions of some geometric problems involved quite complex diagrams, with dozens of lines and circles (not to mention the chiliagon). Keeping track of the relevant pieces while reasoning about such figures was rather demanding on the imagination of problem-solvers.

Descartes' view takes a stand on what came to be a central dispute in the eighteenth and nineteenth centuries: ought one of these types of reasoning, geometric or algebraic, have priority over the other in geometric problem-solving? Not only did Descartes proclaim the value of algebraic methods in reducing demands on the imagination, he also declared it a better method for the discovery of new solutions. In taking this stand, however, Descartes offered a challenge to the presentist ideal of rigor offered by Proclus. The presentist ideal maintains that the rigor of a proof consists in a follower of that proof keeping the objects of the proof in view, employing not only visual perception but also imagination and memory. In addition to rigor, an advocate of geometric reasoning over algebraic reasoning may hold that the employment of imagination provides for mathematical understanding by enabling apprehension of visualizable content itself. Descartes' view suggests a counter-ideal to these, in which the role of imagination in geometric knowledge recedes as algebraic methods provide for more efficient and indeed more general knowledge, since algebra is not limited to quantities that are readily visualizable.

This dialectic came to blossom during the eighteenth and nineteenth centuries, but it began picking up steam already in the late seventeenth century with the further development of algebraic analysis. For instance Gottfried Wilhelm Leibniz, in letters to Christiaan Huygens in the 1690s, promoted his new infinitesimal methods in terms of the relief it provides to the imagination:

> For what I love the most about this calculus is that it gives us the same advantage over the ancients in Archimedes' geometry that Viète and Descartes gave us over the geometry of Euclid or Apollonius, by relieving us of the use of the imagination.
>
> *(Letter dated 8 January 1692; see Huygens 1888–1950, p. 227)*

In another letter to Huygens he specified that the imagination was to be avoided because it "often works as by chance" (letter dated 21 September 1691; see Huygens 1888–1950, vol 10, p. 157). Leibniz thus judged the imagination both overly laborious and unmethodical in problem-solving, compared with algebraic analysis.

This burgeoning philosophical dispute was shaped as well by purely mathematical concerns, in particular to limitations of algebraic analysis, to which practitioners became attuned as knowledge of algebraic methods spread. Descartes himself was aware of these limitations, having recounted to Princess Elisabeth a problematic algebraic solution to Apollonius' problem of the three circles (given three circles in a plane, construct a circle touching all three). In November 1643 Descartes suggested to Elisabeth that she practice her algebraic skills by finding an algebraic analysis for this problem (in the case when the given circles have a triangular arrangement), having pursued his own algebraic analysis (AT 4: 46–47; see Descartes 1901). His suggestion was presumably ironic, since he explained to her how to find an equation whose solution could be used to solve the problem, but did not actually present this equation, presumably because he knew (but did not say) that the equation has eighty-seven terms, each a product of six factors (see Henk Bos' essay in Verbeek et al. 2003 for details). Descartes was content with discovering how to solve a problem, without carrying out the details.[5] That luxury, afforded to him in virtue of being a theoretician, was not available to those who sought to employ algebraic analysis in order to solve problems in full detail (for instance, in mathematical physics or other applied work). Thus the relief to the imagination allegedly offered by algebraic analysis brought with it other intellectual costs, and the reckoning between these costs would occupy considerable attention in the future.

Descartes' views on imagination influenced many in the ensuing years, but special attention should be given to their transformation in the works of Nicolas Malebranche. This is because Malebranche's extensive criticisms of imagination were received widely by mathematicians, as a result of his followers including several writers of mathematical textbooks that would play a key role in the diffusion of Cartesian algebraic analysis. Like Descartes, Malebranche emphasized the importance of visual attention for geometrical knowledge, noting that geometers who use algebraic analysis recognize that "their minds cannot be applied to several figures at the same time" and thus apply algebra so that they can "perceive all in one glance what they would not be able to see otherwise" (Malebranche 1674, 3.1.3, p. 332).

While pursuit of geometry can improve the attentiveness of the mind by giving it occasion to exercise control over the imagination, its being "evident and very agreeable" was also a source of error for the geometer (Malebranche 1675, 6.4, p. 290). For Malebranche held that the love of pleasure prevents us from discovering the truth, since pleasure is concerned with the sensible, which points us away from God, in whom alone truth can be found. Malebranche argued that "it is necessary that the senses and the passions are silent, if one wants to hear the word of truth, distance from the world and contempt for all sensible things being necessary as much for the perfection of the mind as for the conversion of the heart" (Malebranche 1675, 4.11, p. 85). This is cause for the geometer to favor algebraic analysis over the synthetic reasoning of the ancients, Malebranche continues, not only because of its fruitfulness, certitude and its ability to direct the mind "infallibly to its goal" but more importantly because it has "nothing dazzling nor attractive for men for the sole reason that it has nothing sensible" (ibid., p. 87). The pursuit of geometrical knowledge by algebraic means thus protects the geometer from the temptations of the imagination, which lead toward pleasure and thus sin.[6]

Around the turn of the eighteenth century three mathematicians deeply influenced by Malebranche, Jean Prestet, Bernard Lamy, and Charles-René Reynaud, published mathematical textbooks that, as mentioned before, were crucial in the diffusion of Cartesian algebraic analysis, bridging the generations between Descartes and Lagrange.[7] Prestet (1689) included a brief discussion of geometry in the style of Euclid (without giving figures), turning then to an extensive discussion of the elements of algebra. Prestet justified this organizational imbalance between classical geometry and algebra in Malebranchian terms: "Because as all sciences ought to aim at enlightening the mind, one ought not highly esteem the use of these expressions by lines that speak only to the eyes and to the imagination" (Prestet 1689, p. xv). One ought to favor algebraic over classical geometric methods, he continued, because "the study of mathematics is very proper for learning to dispel the illusions of the senses, to correct the derangement of the imagination, and to moderate the proud impetuousness of our passions" (ibid., pp. xviii–xix).[8]

Lamy (1692), from whom the example of algebraic analysis given above was drawn, includes treatments of geometry by both the classical and analytical methods. He emphasized that the latter approach was general, while classical solutions were by contrast "particular and proper to the sole problem" to which they were directed (317). He seems to have meant that the analytic method, designating unknown quantities by variables, using the configurations occurring in the problem to set up equations and then solving these equations by analytic means did not demand attention to the particular geometric configurations represented by those equations or calculations. Its reasoning, once the equations were set up, could proceed without further reference to the figure. A classical solution on the other hand must employ geometric propositions involving for instance similarity and congruence in its reasoning, and these reasonings demand steady attention to the figure. Analytic reasoning thus reduces the need for visual attention by means of the imagination. He lauded this feature of such proofs, expressing again in Malebranchian terms that reducing the use of imagination had spiritual benefits:

> We can only see by the imagination that which is bodily; those therefore that make use only of their imagination cannot perceive spiritual things, they do not even believe there to be any [spiritual things], because they find no images in their imagination; just as in seeking bodies with the hands, if we find nothing that resists, we believe that there is nothing.
>
> *(Lamy 1692, p. ii; also see Dominic Gregory, "Imagination and mental imagery," Chapter 7 of this volume)*

Reyneau's was the last of these textbooks to appear (see Reyneau 1708). Malebranche praised it in later editions of *De la Recherche de la Vérité*, and it was one of the key texts in d'Alembert's mathematical education. Reyneau like Lamy stressed the Cartesian method of applying algebraic analysis to geometry, though most of the text's pages are devoted to the details of solving algebraic equations. Like Prestet and Lamy, Reyneau described the value of his methods in Malebranchian terms. Human minds are limited in that they cannot see in a single view many objects at the same time. Thus classical geometric reasoning is overly demanding on the imagination, and for its relief the geometer turns to algebraic analysis. He described this relief in the following terms:

> These new methods, reducing geometry to a simple and easy calculus, released that which had been encumbered by figures, that is to say, all that had tired the imagination, and had filled the capacity of the mind. They left it the freedom to penetrate its subject, and to discover with evidence all that had been closed.
>
> *(Reyneau 1708, p. iii)*

These texts of Prestet, Lamy and Reyneau marked a turning point in conceptions of the role of imagination in mathematics. By being published in textbooks lodged in mainstream eighteenth-century mathematics, their views had reach among practitioners that philosophical texts could not. They helped normalize a narrative of the value of algebraic analysis and its role for displacing reliance on imagination in geometry that would persist into the nineteenth century. Jean d'Alembert for instance would write of algebra in his *Encyclopédie* entry on it that "it relieves the memory and imagination in diminishing many of the efforts that it would have been obliged to make for retaining the different things necessary for the discovery of the truth for which it worked, and that one wanted to keep in mind" (see Diderot and d'Alembert 1751, 259). He expanded on this in his entry on the application of algebra to geometry:

> [W]hen I designate all the lines by algebraic characters, I will be able to carry out many operations on these characters, while thinking of neither the lines nor the figure, and this is an advantage it has. It relieves the mind, because when using analysis the mind does not have to use all its forces to solve certain problems; the use of analysis saves these forces as much as possible.
>
> *(see Diderot and d'Alembert 1751, 551)*

Thus algebraic analysis in geometry is valuable according to d'Alembert because of its "opacity": it permits geometric problem solution without imagination of the figure being investigated.

As the eighteenth century closed, Condorcet published a retrospective on the century's accomplishments in the guise of an elegy for the recently departed Leonhard Euler. In contrast to the views just recounted, he lamented the laboriousness of algebraic work, noting that "the rigor with which it separates from this idea [of magnitude] everything which, by occupying the imagination, could give some rest to the intellect" rendered it "too foreign to our nature" as agents for whom imagination plays a central role in cognition, and too "distant" from ordinary thought, for humans to use these methods with ease (Condorcet 1786, 42). The application of algebra to geometry forces geometers to forget the object they seek, and "the goal where one wants to arrive, the point from where one left, disappear equally in the eyes of the geometer" (ibid.). Condorcet's view offered a renewed defense of imagination in mathematics, against the other eighteenth-century views surveyed here. It thus presaged developments in the nineteenth century to which we now turn.

## 3 Imagination in mathematics since the nineteenth century

The debate between advocates of algebraic and classical "synthetic" methods in geometry continued with an attempt at reconciliation by the school of Gaspard Monge. Monge's teaching in descriptive geometry at the École Polytechnique, in which he taught new ways to represent three-dimensional figures in two dimensions, emphasized an intimate correspondence between analytic computations and classical-style constructions, so that "there is no construction of descriptive geometry that cannot be translated into analysis ... [and] each analytic operation can be regarded as the writing of a geometrical presentation [*spectacle*]" (Monge 1795, 16, repr. in Dhombres 1989; see Chemla 1998, 166 also). As Belhoste (1998) stresses, Monge's teaching would carry a considerable influence in the nineteenth century. Michel Chasles, a member of Monge's school, characterized the "useful influence of descriptive geometry" on geometry more generally by noting that it frees geometrical reasoning "from this complication of figures whose usage distracts the attention that one fundamentally owes to the ideas, and hinders imagination and language" (Chasles 1837, 190). The improved focus provided to the imagination described here can be illustrated by turning to projective geometry, whose development blossomed during the nineteenth century.

The idea of projective geometry is to study configurations of points and lines that are unchanged when we "project" those configurations. By "projecting" one can think for instance of projecting a globe onto a plane to make a map, representing a shift in perspective of an observer. Such projections were the means by which Renaissance artists drew realistic perspectives. A key was noting that to get such perspectives to look right, parallel lines had to meet at the horizon. Thus projective geometry includes a point at infinity, where parallel lines meet. Projective geometry is thus the study of configurations of points and lines, including a point at infinity, that are invariant under projective transformations like the globe one just described.

Though geometers before the nineteenth century had pursued projective geometry, its development took flight with the work of Jean-Victor Poncelet, a member of the school of Monge. Poncelet noted that in "ordinary geometry," one "never loses sight" of the figure and "never draws consequences that cannot be painted in the imagination or in sight by sensible objects" (Poncelet 1822, xxi). The projective geometer too attends to figures, but employs a rather different notion of figure, one which may not be accessible to imagination, at least not as traditionally conceived. Jemma Lorenat has illuminated this new notion of figure arising in nineteenth-century geometry (in Lorenat 2015). Lorenat draws on work of Dominique Tournès that identifies a type of diagram called a "virtual diagram," a diagram "that one must have in mind, but that is no longer physically drawn on the paper, or at least which is left to the reader to draw" (Tournès 2012, 272). Instead, these diagrams are described in words, either text or speech. The typical failure of such descriptions to specify fully the intended figure avails the geometer of generality: her reasoning need not refer only to a single figure, but to any figure meeting the given specifications. This sort of generality had been an important part of earlier cases for the superiority of algebraic reasoning, since algebraic variables range over classes of objects.

Additionally, virtual figures permit the geometer to work with figures containing what were called "imaginary" points, like the points at infinity described earlier. Michel Chasles characterized an imaginary point as a "*being* of reason without existence, but to which one can however suppose some properties which one uses momentarily like an auxiliary, and to which one applies the same reasonings as to a real and palpable object" (Chasles 1837, 207). While the ontology of such points remained unclear, and while such points are not visualizable in any ordinary sense, Lorenat observes that Poncelet manipulated figures with such points by projective transformations, since the relations these points have with nonimaginary points are projectively invariant. Thus imaginary points could be visualized and imagined indirectly, by attending to their relations with nonimaginary points (see Lorenat 2015, 188). This practice thus involved a new, indirect mode of visualization and imagination.

The nineteenth century also saw the rise of non-Euclidean geometries, which put further pressure on the classical conception of geometry and thus on the role of imagination in geometric thought. Until the nineteenth century Euclidean geometry was widely believed to be the geometry of human perceptual space (see Andersen 2007). Euclidean geometry includes a parallel axiom, which entails with the other Euclidean axioms that for any line and point not on that line, there exists a unique line parallel to the given line through the given point. Non-Euclidean geometries, by contrast, include a negation of this axiom. By the end of the nineteenth century geometers were largely convinced that both Euclidean and non-Euclidean geometries were legitimate mathematical theories, since they were equiconsistent (see Gray 2007, ch. 20). This left open the question of which of these geometries, if any, was the geometry of perceptual space.

Immanuel Kant's critical philosophy seemed to be committed to answering this question in favor of Euclidean geometry, and this problematized the impact of Kant's critical philosophy on mathematics. Kant's mathematical epistemology gave a central place to constructive knowledge, with the practice of classical synthetic geometry serving as a paradigm for it. Kant gave a role to imagination in the syntheses that, as he saw it, ground such knowledge; recent work, for example Domski (2010) and Friedman (2000), helps clarify some of the obscurities in his approach. But Kant's evident commitment to Euclidean geometry over its alternative blunted its applicability to mathematics as it actually stood by the end of the nineteenth century. Several philosophers attempted to reconcile Kant's views with the legitimacy of non-Euclidean geometries (see Gray 2008, in particular §§1.2.1, 6.2.3, 6.2.4); most notably Hermann von Helmholtz argued that non-Euclidean geometry is in fact imaginable, making his case on Kantian terms (see Helmholtz 1884).

Kant's views were also challenged by the acceptance of imaginary points in geometry discussed above, since it is hard to see how nonvisualizable points can be the object of synthetic judgment. Jeremy Heis has argued that Ernst Cassirer, a neo-Kantian philosopher eager to reconcile Kant's critical philosophy with contemporary geometry, judged imaginaries legitimate in geometry because of their role in "unifying and explaining facts about the so-called 'real' points" (see Heis 2011, 783). They thus play the role of "ideals" in Kantian terms, in that they help regulate cognition despite not being able to be given in experience.

David Hilbert, whose axiomatization of geometry (Hilbert 1899) permitted a newly clear conception of the metamathematics of non-Euclidean geometry, was also strongly influenced by Kant's views. Hilbert acknowledged the value of Pasch's reconceptualization of geometry, in which deduction is required to be "independent of figures" in order to be rigorous (see Pasch 1882, 43, and Schlimm 2010). Such reasoning could contain no tacit appeals to unacknowledged visual content, which might jeopardize its validity by importing an unacknowledged assumption. But this metamathematical goal of ensuring rigor did not override Hilbert's interest in the intuitive or imaginative. In his work on the foundations of arithmetic and analysis (most notably Hilbert 1926) Hilbert divided mathematics into a "real" part that is finitary and contentual, and a noncontentual "ideal" part (again echoing Kant) that concerns, for instance, imaginary numbers and infinitary propositions in analysis and set theory. The objects of real mathematics were said to be finite strings of symbols, and hence visualizable. He then outlined a project to prove the consistency of ideal mathematics by real means, a project whose feasibility is widely believed to have been undermined by the incompleteness theorems of Kurt Gödel. Hilbert's interest in imagination also carried over into his work on geometry, notably in Hilbert and Cohn-Vossen (1932) which sought to give

> a presentation of geometry, as it stands today, in its visual, intuitive aspects. With the aid of visual imagination we can illuminate the manifold facts and problems of geometry, and beyond this, it is possible in many cases to depict the geometric outline of the methods of investigation and proof, without necessarily entering into the details connected with the strict definitions of concepts and with the actual calculations.
>
> *(see Hilbert and Cohn-Vossen 1952, iii)*

Hilbert thus sought to provide for geometrical knowledge not by requiring one to follow each step of an analytic treatment or a deductive proof, but rather by enabling "intuitive understanding" by means of the imagination.

Recently philosophers of mathematics have begun considering the role of imagination in mathematics from a cognitive point of view (see Mancosu 2005 for an overview of this work). Marcus Giaquinto has given a detailed exploration of visual thinking in mathematics (in Giaquinto 2007), attending not only to diagrammatic reasoning in geometry but also to visual arithmetic reasoning. For arithmetic Giaquinto considers whether humans have an innate "number sense" for judging which of two numbers is larger in the light of contemporary work in cognitive psychology. For geometry he draws on recent psychological work on visual perception to describe what he calls "visual category specifications" for visual objects like squares; these are sets of features whose detection by our visual apparatus suffices for perceiving a figure as an object of that category. These specifications determine what he calls "perceptual concepts" of particular shapes. Possession of such perceptual concepts amounts to the disposition to judge an object of perception to have the shape specified by such a concept when that perception seems to be reliable. A perceptual concept is a geometric concept when its possession conditions also include the disposition to judge an object of perception to have the shape specified by the concept in a perfect way. He finally explains that these belief-forming dispositions can be triggered by visual experiences, and that when these dispositions are reliable, the resulting beliefs are knowledge.

## 4 Conclusions

This article has surveyed the nature and role of imagination in mathematics from antiquity through today. Particular attention has been given to the seventeenth and eighteenth centuries because they witnessed the transformation of ancient views on imagination into guises that would be approached in novel ways thereafter. Despite the challenge posed to imagination by the rise of algebraic methods in the seventeenth century, there remains today an important role for it.

## Acknowledgments

Thanks to Juliette Kennedy and Sébastien Maronne for comments on drafts of this article.

## Notes

1 Both Nikulin (2008) and Rabouin (2015) provide fuller discussions of the twofold role of the imagination as both passive and as active in Proclus' thought.
2 Rabouin (2015) shows how Proclus' view of imagination accommodates proofs by *reductio* in classical geometry as well.
3 Whether there exists a construction meeting the single motion criterion that can construct the spiral was a metatheoretic question of the kind falling beyond the scope of Descartes' conceptual framework; see Crippa 2014 for more on this question.
4 On this also see Rule 9 of the *Regulae ad Directionem Ingenii*, though as a text unfinished and unpublished during Descartes' life, one should be careful in putting hermeneutical weight on it.
5 Indeed, he seemed to think the knowledge one has when one knows how to solve a problem is much more valuable than the further knowledge gained by actually carrying out the discovered procedure in detail; see Maronne 2010.
6 Malebranche's criticisms of the imagination echo those of Pascal; see Pascal 2015. A fuller treatment of Malebranche's philosophy of mathematics can be found in Robinet 1961.
7 Both Lamy (1692) and Reyneau (1708) were lauded by Rousseau in *Les confessions*, Book VI.
8 See Schubring 2005, 52–61, 69–73, for a discussion of Prestet's orientation and relation to Malebranche.

## References

Andersen, K. (2007) *The Geometry of an Art: The History of the Mathematical Theory of Perspective from Alberti to Monge*, New York: Springer.

Aristotle (1993) *De Anima Books II and III (with Passages from Book I)*, trans. D.W. Hamlyn, Oxford: Clarendon Press.

Belhoste, B. (1998) "De l'École Polytechnique à Saratoff, les premiers travaux géométriques de Poncelet," *Bulletin de la Société des Amis de la Bibliothèque de l'École Polytechnique* 19: 9–29.

Bos, H.J.M. (2001) *Redefining Geometrical Exactness*, New York: Springer.

Chasles, M. (1837) *Aperçu historique sur l'origine et le développement des méthodes en géométrie*, Brussels: M. Hayez.

Chemla, K. (1998) "Lazare Carnot et la généralité en géométrie: Variations sur le théorème dit de Menelaus," *Revue d'Histoire des Máthematiques* 4: 168–190.

Condorcet, N. de (1786) "Eloge de Euler," *Histoire de l'Académie royale des sciences pour l'année* 783 : 37–68; repr., *Oeuvres complètes de Condorcet*, vol. 3, Brunswick: Vieweg, 1804.

Crippa, D. (2014) "Impossibility Results: From Geometry to Analysis," PhD diss., University of Paris 7–Denis Diderot.

Currie, G., and I. Ravenscroft (2002) *Recreative Minds: Imagination in Philosophy and Psychology*, Oxford: Oxford University Press.

Descartes, R. (1901) *Oeuvres*, vol. 4, eds. C. Adam and P. Tannery, Paris: Léopold Cerf. (Abbreviated AT 4.)

Descartes, R. (1902) *Oeuvres*, vol. 6, eds. C. Adam and P. Tannery, Paris: Léopold Cerf. (Abbreviated AT 6.)
Detlefsen, M. (2005) "Formalism," in S. Shapiro (ed.) *Handbook of the Philosophy of Mathematics and Logic*, New York: Oxford University Press, 236–317.
Dhombres, J. (ed.) (1989) *L'École Normale de l'An III, Leçons de mathématiques, Laplace-Lagrange-Monge*, Paris: Dunod.
Diderot, D., and J. Le Rond d'Alembert (1751) *Encyclopédie ou Dictionnaire raisonné des sciences, des arts et des métiers*, vol. 1, Paris: Briasson, David, Le Breton, Durand.
Diderot, D., and J. Le Rond d'Alembert (1765) *Encyclopédie ou Dictionnaire raisonné des sciences, des arts et des métiers*, vol. 8, Paris: Briasson, David, Le Breton, Durand.
Domski, M. (2010) "Kant on the Imagination and Geometrical Certainty," *Perspectives on Science* 18(4): 409–431.
Euclid (1956) *The Thirteen Books of Euclid's Elements Translated from the Text of Heiberg*, vol. 1: *Introduction and Books I, II*, trans. with introduction and commentary by T.L. Heath, 2nd edn., New York: Dover Publications.
Friedman, M. (2000) "Geometry, Construction and Intuition in Kant and His Successors," in G. Sher and R. Tieszen (eds.) *Between Logic and Intuition: Essays in Honor of Charles Parsons*, Cambridge: Cambridge University Press, 186–218.
Giaquinto, M. (2007) *Visual Thinking in Mathematics*, Oxford: Oxford University Press.
Gray, J. (2007) *Worlds Out of Nothing*, London: Springer.
Gray, J. (2008) *Plato's Ghost*, Princeton: Princeton University Press.
Hadamard, J. (1945) *The Psychology of Invention in the Mathematical Field*, Princeton: Princeton University Press.
Heis, J. (2011) "Ernst Cassirer's Neo-Kantian Philosophy of Geometry," *British Journal for the History of Philosophy* 19(4): 759–794.
Helmholtz, H. von (1884) "Ueber den Ursprung und die Bedeutung der geometrischen Axiome," in *Vorträge und Reden*, vol. 2, Brunswick: Vieweg, 1–31.
Hilbert, D. (1899) *Grundlagen der Geometrie*, Leipzig: B.G. Teubner.
Hilbert, D. (1926) "Über das Unendliche," *Mathematische Annalen* 95(1): 161–190.
Hilbert, D., and S. Cohn-Vossen (1932) *Anschauliche Geometrie*, Berlin: Springer.
Hilbert, D., and S. Cohn-Vossen (1952) *Geometry and the Imagination*, trans. P. Neményi, New York: Chelsea Publishing Co. (Translation of Hilbert and Cohn-Vossen 1932.)
Huygens, C. (1888–1950) *Oeuvres complètes de Christiaan Huygens*, 22 vols., The Hague: Martinus Nijhoff.
Klein, F. (1979) *Development of Mathematics in the 19th Century*, trans. M. Ackerman, Brookline, MA: Math Sci Press.
Lamy, B. (1692) *Nouveaux élemens de geometrie ou de la mesure du corps*, Paris: André Pralard.
Lorenat, J. (2015) "Figures Real, Imagined, and Missing in Poncelet, Plücker, and Gergonne," *Historia Mathematica* 42(2): 155–192.
Malebranche, N. (1674) *De la recherche de la vérité*, vol. 1. Paris: André Pralard.
Malebranche, N. (1675) *De la recherche de la vérité*, vol. 2, Paris: André Pralard.
Mancosu, P. (1996) *Philosophy of Mathematics and Mathematical Practice in the Seventeenth Century*, New York: Oxford University Press.
Mancosu, P. (2005) "Visualization in Logic and Mathematics," in P. Mancosu, K.F. Jørgensen, and S.A. Pedersen (eds.) *Visualization, Explanation and Reasoning Styles in Mathematics*, Dordrecht: Springer, 13–28.
Manders, K. (2008) "The Euclidean Diagram," in P. Mancosu (ed.) *The Philosophy of Mathematical Practice*, Oxford: Oxford University Press, 80–133.
Maronne, S. (2010) "Pascal versus Descartes on Geometrical Problem Solving and the Sluse-Pascal Correspondence," *Early Science and Medicine* 15: 537–565.
Monge, G. (1795) "Leçons à l'École Normale de l'An III," *Dhombres*, no. 989.
Netz, R. (1999) *The Shaping of Deduction in Greek Mathematics*, Cambridge: Cambridge University Press.
Netz, R. (2009) "Imagination and Layered Ontology in Greek Mathematics," *Configurations* 17(1): 19–50.
Nikulin, D. (2008) "Imagination and Mathematics in Proclus," *Ancient Philosophy* 28: 153–172.
O'Meara, D. (1989) *Pythagoras Revived: Mathematics and Philosophy in Late Antiquity*, Oxford: Oxford University Press.
Panza, M. (2007) "What Is New and What Is Old in Viète's *Analysis Restituta* and *Algebra Nova*, and Where Do They Come From? Some Reflections on the Relations between Algebra and Analysis before Viète," *Revue d'Histoire des Mathématiques* 13(1): 85–153.

Pascal, B. (2015) "L'Imagination, dans l'édition électronique des Pensées," eds. D. Descotes and G. Proust, <http://www.penseesdepascal.fr/Vanite/Vanite31-moderne.php>.

Pasch, M. (1882) *Vorlesungen über neuere Geometrie*, Leipzig: B.G. Teubner.

Plato (2004) *Republic*, trans. C.D.C. Reeve, Indianapolis: Hackett.

Poncelet, J.-V. (1822) *Traité des propriétés projectives des figures*, Paris: Bachelier.

Prestet, J. (1689) *Nouveaux élémens des mathématiques*, vol. 1, Paris: André Pralard.

Proclus (1992) *A Commentary on the First Book of Euclid's Elements*, trans. G.R. Morrow, Princeton: Princeton University Press.

Rabouin, D. (2010) "What Descartes Knew of Mathematics in 1628," *Historia Mathematica* 37: 428–459.

Rabouin, D. (2015) "Proclus' Conception of Geometric Space and Its Actuality," in V. De Risi (ed.) *Mathematizing Space: The Objects of Geometry from Antiquity to the Early Modern Age*, Heidelberg: Birkhäuser, 105–142.

Reyneau, C.-R. (1708) *Analyse demontrée ou La methode de resoudres les problemes des mathematiques*, vol. 1, Paris: Jacques Quillau.

Robinet, A. (1961) "La Philosophie Malebranchiste des Mathématiques," *Revue d'Histoire des Sciences et de Leurs Applications* 14(3–4): 205–254.

Rommevaux, S. (2009) "The Transmission of the *Elements* to the Latin West: Three Case Studies," in E. Robson and J. Stedall (eds.) *The Oxford Handbook of the History of Mathematics*, Oxford: Oxford University Press, 687–706.

Sasaki, C. (2003) *Descartes's Mathematical Thought*, Dordrecht: Springer.

Schlimm, D. (2010) "Pasch's Philosophy of Mathematics," *Review of Symbolic Logic* 3(1): 93–118.

Schubring, G. (2005) *Conflicts between Generalization, Rigor, and Intuition*, New York: Springer.

Tournès, D. (2012) "Diagrams in the Theory of Differential Equations (Eighteenth to Nineteenth Centuries)," *Synthese* 186: 257–288.

Verbeek, T., E.-J. Bos, and J. van de Ven (eds.) (with contributions from H. Bos, C.R. Palmerino, and C. Vermeulen) (2003) *The Correspondence of René Descartes*, no. 643, Department of Philosophy, Utrecht University.

Viète, F. (1983) *The Analytic Art*, trans. T. Witmer, Kent, OH: Kent State University Press.

# INDEX